CW01184254

THE ASCENT OF THE DETECTIVE

THE ASCENT OF THE DETECTIVE

*POLICE SLEUTHS IN VICTORIAN
AND EDWARDIAN ENGLAND*

HAIA SHPAYER-MAKOV

OXFORD
UNIVERSITY PRESS

OXFORD
UNIVERSITY PRESS

Great Clarendon Street, Oxford OX2 6DP

Oxford University Press is a department of the University of Oxford.
It furthers the University's objective of excellence in research, scholarship,
and education by publishing worldwide in

Oxford New York

Auckland Cape Town Dar es Salaam Hong Kong Karachi
Kuala Lumpur Madrid Melbourne Mexico City Nairobi
New Delhi Shanghai Taipei Toronto

With offices in

Argentina Austria Brazil Chile Czech Republic France Greece
Guatemala Hungary Italy Japan Poland Portugal Singapore
South Korea Switzerland Thailand Turkey Ukraine Vietnam

Oxford is a registered trade mark of Oxford University Press
in the UK and in certain other countries

Published in the United States
by Oxford University Press Inc., New York

© Haia Shpayer-Makov 2011

The moral rights of the author have been asserted
Database right Oxford University Press (maker)

First published 2011

All rights reserved. No part of this publication may be reproduced,
stored in a retrieval system, or transmitted, in any form or by any means,
without the prior permission in writing of Oxford University Press,
or as expressly permitted by law, or under terms agreed with the appropriate
reprographics rights organization. Enquiries concerning reproduction
outside the scope of the above should be sent to the Rights Department,
Oxford University Press, at the address above

You must not circulate this book in any other binding or cover
and you must impose the same condition on any acquirer

British Library Cataloguing in Publication Data

Data available

Library of Congress Cataloging in Publication Data

Data available

Typeset by SPI Publisher Services, Pondicherry, India
Printed in Great Britain
on acid-free paper by
MPG Books Group, Bodman and King's Kynn

ISBN 978–0–19–957740–8

1 3 5 7 9 10 8 6 4 2

To Udi and Yoad with much love

ACKNOWLEDGEMENTS

I owe an overwhelming debt of gratitude to Bob Morris and Joanne Klein, who took the time to read this entire manuscript and offered invaluable comments. I have also been the beneficiary of insightful critiques by John Beattie, David Cox, Helen Carr, and colleagues in the English Department at the University of Haifa, Daphna Erdinast-Vulcan, Sarah Gilead, and Ayelet Ben-Yishay. Special thanks go to Clive Emsley for his sustained support over the years, and to Jenny Emsley for her unfailing warm welcome. My deepest appreciation to Pam and David Lavis and Mazal and Jeff Cohen, who opened their hearts and homes to me during my many visits to libraries and archives in London. Lastly, no words can fully express my gratitude to my brother-in-law, Isie Kleiner, for his steadfast assistance and endless kindness. This work would not have seen the light of day without the love and encouragement of my husband and son, to whom the book is dedicated.

CONTENTS

List of Figures	xi
List of Tables	xiii
INTRODUCTION	1

PART ONE. THE DETECTIVE IN HIS WORK MILIEU

1. POLICE DETECTION IN ENGLAND: EIGHTEENTH CENTURY–FIRST WORLD WAR	13
2. FROM BOBBY TO DETECTIVE	62
3. THE DETECTIVE AS WAGE-EARNER AND OFFICIAL CRIME FIGHTER	101

PART TWO. DETECTIVES AND THE PRINT MEDIA

INTRODUCTION	147
4. THE UNIQUELY SYMBIOTIC RELATIONSHIP BETWEEN DETECTIVES AND JOURNALISTS	156
5. THE CHANGING IMAGE OF POLICE DETECTIVES IN THE PRESS	187
6. POLICE DETECTIVES IN FICTION	226
7. POLICE DETECTIVES AS AUTHORS	272
CONCLUSION	298
Notes	310
Select Bibliography	382
Index	415

LIST OF FIGURES

1. 'Trial of the Detectives at the Old Bailey', *Illustrated London News*, 3 Nov. 1877. — 39
2. 'The System of Anthropometry', *Windsor Magazine*, 6 (June 1897). — 51
3. 'Portrait of Ex-Detective Sergeant William Record, D Division, Metropolitan Force', *Police Review*, 24 Oct. 1902. — 90
4. 'How Scotland Yard Detectives Are Trained', *Punch*, 12 Mar. 1913. — 99
5. 'Uniformed and Non-Uniformed Policemen in Action', *Illustrated Police News*, 25 Jan. 1868. — 106
6. 'Detectives who Guard King Edward', *Penny Illustrated Paper*, 21 Sept. 1907. — 120
7. 'Detective Sergeant William Record in his "Scraps" Costume', *Police Review*, 24 Oct. 1902. — 141
8. 'Detective Sergeant Benjamin Leeson Disguised as a "Tough"', in Benjamin Leeson, *Lost London* (London: Stanley Paul & Co., 1934). — 142
9. 'Is Detection a Failure?', *Punch*, 20 Oct. 1888. — 184
10. 'One of the Detective Force', *Cleave's Penny Gazette of Variety and Amusement*, 15 Oct. 1842. — 190
11. 'Bull's Eye on Bobby', *Punch*, 25 Aug. 1877. — 203
12. 'Disguised—or the Undetectable Detective', *Fun*, 4 Mar. 1885. — 206
13. 'The Arrest of Hudson for the Yorkshire Murders', *Illustrated Police Budget*, 29 June 1895. — 220
14. 'The Arrest of Oscar Wilde by Two Police Detectives', *Illustrated Police Budget*, 13 Apr. 1895. — 221
15. 'Detective Inspector Trusco about to Make an Arrest in a Joint Operation with Private Detective Martin Hewitt', in Arthur Morrison, 'The Case of the Dead Skipper', in *Adventures of Martin Hewitt* (London: Ward, Lock & Co., 1896), 105. — 251
16. 'Detective Dr Thorndyke in the Midst of a Forensic Investigation', in R. Austin Freeman, *John Thorndyke's Cases* (London: Chatto & Windus, 1909). — 254

LIST OF TABLES

1. Distribution of the CID detective hierarchy and annual wages in the Metropolitan Police, by rank with annual increments, 1881 — 113
2. Distribution of ranks in the uniformed and CID branches within the Metropolitan Police, 1912 (%) — 113

INTRODUCTION

Police detection in England, practised in the eighteenth century on a rudimentary basis, coalesced during the nineteenth century into a new service branch and a new constraining force in society that was to emerge in time as a source of inspiration and imitation worldwide. The principal roles of police detectives were to capture criminals and help bring them to justice, as well as to protect the state against internal subversion. They came to constitute a pivotal factor in defining crimes and suspects, obtaining evidence that would stand up in court, punishing offenders, and, more broadly, enhancing the power structure of society. In the main, the modern police network, which spread throughout England by the mid-nineteenth century, was founded as a preventive police. However, while uniformed policemen symbolized this priority most overtly, plain-clothes detectives gradually emerged as the key instrument in the fight against crime. Their tasks were essential in a society whose elite was increasingly intolerant of crime and social disorder, yet also sensitive to public opinion and anxious to retain the legitimacy of its political authority.

The impact of this new vocation proved considerably greater than the sum of its tasks, with wider repercussions than in the domain of criminal investigation alone. In fact, detectives formed a small fraction of police manpower throughout the Victorian and Edwardian period, and most forces had no detective department at all. Only a few hundred police detectives were employed in England in the mid-Victorian era, their number doubling or even trebling by 1914.[1] Still, the figure of the detective embodied characteristics that caught the imagination of the public from the top of the social pyramid all the way down. As the nineteenth century progressed, police detectives became a topical subject in all the contemporary media. By the First World War, the English detective, whether official or private, stood out as a central figure in the gallery of English archetypes. The fame of Scotland Yard transcended national boundaries and reached the far corners of the world, maintaining this special status to this day.

This book explores the occupational life of detectives who served in English police forces during the Victorian and Edwardian era by focusing both on their work experience and on their representation in the press and in literature. Significantly, it is difficult to differentiate between their authentic life and what was written about them at the time, as their public image became an integral part of their history. The book therefore juxtaposes social reality with cultural production as a means of highlighting the interplay between them, offering a broad perspective on the perennially intriguing figure of the detective.

Official thief-takers did operate in London during the eighteenth and early nineteenth centuries, but a detective branch fully employed to serve the public was introduced into police forces only in 1842, first in the newly created Metropolitan Police of London, and thereafter in the City of London Police and in several provincial forces. Although this did not lead to a significant change in the practice of detection in the first few decades, it marked the beginning of a profound shift in the culture of law enforcement, whose implications would unfold in later years. The First World War and the period immediately following altered many of the issues discussed in this book, thereby defining 1842–1914 as the natural boundaries of the formative years of English detectives, and of this volume.

Such a book is long overdue. While the history of the uniformed police in Britain has prompted considerable research in the last three decades, enhanced by the insights of new theoretical perspectives and interdisciplinary approaches, little scholarly attention has been devoted to the lives of actual detectives in a historical context, despite the sustained interest of researchers in fictional detectives and the singular presence of the figure of the detective in today's media. Historical studies of the detective police in Britain were mostly conducted during the inter-war and post-Second World War periods and were generally limited to the institutional development of the Criminal Investigation Department (CID) of the Metropolitan Police or to the most dramatic cases tackled by its officers. Since the 1960s, research about the detective force prior to the First World War has been confined mainly to a chapter or brief mention in books dealing with the evolution of the police as a whole, and to several recent articles.[2] As a small occupational group that did not play a role in industrial struggles or the trade-union movement, British police detectives did not win the notice of labour historians. Although the serial killer Jack the Ripper has given rise to an entire industry of books and articles on the subject, few of these examine the intricate world of police detectives, and most are intended for popular consumption. Much has been written about detective fiction and the image of detectives in literature, but mostly from the perspective of literary criticism rather than police history. No attempt has been made to integrate the social and cultural histories of police detectives.

These omissions are rectified in the present volume by tracing hitherto unexplored aspects of the maturation of the occupation of detection in Victorian and Edwardian England, drawing on recent historical research and a wide variety of primary sources to cast new light both on the work culture of police detectives and on the extraordinary effect this small body of police workers had on the contemporary print culture. By relating the lives of police detectives to a whole matrix of social and cultural practices, the book adds to an understanding not only of the world of the police and the criminal justice system, but also of changing social norms and the rise of the mass media in the period under discussion.

The book is divided into two parts. The first examines the evolution of the occupation of police detection and the detectives' work milieu. Men whose duties were the capture of offenders and the search for evidence against them had long existed in English society, but most were private agents working for a fee or reward. The employment of detectives by the state (both local and central) was slow and gradual. It was only in the Victorian period, as part of the expanding involvement of government in the life of its citizens, that the state took primary responsibility for the criminal justice system, relying progressively on its own detectives. Still, the state did not monopolize crime control, and private persons and agencies continued to provide detective services to the population. In fact, some scholars suggest that the identification of the police with the modern criminal justice state 'may come to be seen as a historical blip in a more enduring schema of policing as an array of activities undertaken by multiple private and public agencies, and individual and communal endeavours'.[3] These scholars observe that, from the late twentieth century, this diversity had again become more prominent, with the growing tendency to privatize and commercialize crime control functions. Whether this tendency continues or not, the period under review was decisive in consolidating the occupation of detection and turning official detectives into the spearhead of the fight against crime and a tool to preserve the social order.

Starting in 1842, detectives were set apart from their uniformed colleagues to become fully-fledged investigators of crime in several of the newly formed police forces, creating the organizational infrastructure that essentially persists to the present day. As a collective entity, the emerging police detectives were indicative of the growing importance of the public sector, increasingly regarded by the elite as a vital service to society that should be maintained by public funds. Chapter 1 depicts the gradual replacement of traditional forms of private and community detection by official bodies specializing in crime, and the consequent expansion of state control and punitive authority. As this process started in the eighteenth century, the period before 1842 will be discussed briefly.[4] The chronological nature of the chapter serves as a backdrop for the rest of the book.

As employees of the state and of local governments, all police officers both uniformed and plain clothes—were subject to predetermined strategies of employment. Central to these strategies was the concept that preventive and detective functions were largely interwoven, so that detectives were an integral part of the police force. As such, they shared the same general occupational culture. This culture, as embodied in London's Metropolitan Police during the period studied, has been documented in detail in the author's previous work, *The Making of a Policeman: A Social History of a Labour Force in Metropolitan London, 1829–1914* (2002). That volume focused on the employment strategies of police authorities and on policemen as employees: their socio-economic background, work conditions (and their reactions to them), mobility within the ranks, off-duty activities, and personnel relations. The present book, in focusing on the specific milieu and work life of police detectives, may be regarded as a companion volume.

Intrinsic to the organizational structure of police detection was the principle of recruiting detectives almost exclusively from the uniformed ranks. Such detectives thus had first-hand experience of basic police duties. Chapter 2 explains the policy of internal recruitment of detectives as part of a wider manpower strategy adopted by police management; the selection procedures; and the route that led working-class lads to become policemen and eventually detectives. It also illuminates the detectives' socio-economic background, the attributes required for promotion to detective status, the driving force that motivated policemen to apply for this speciality, and their acquisition of professional knowledge.

'Beat-walking', considered 'the one great feature of police duty', was the responsibility of the uniformed branch, which engaged the vast majority of police employees.[5] Detectives, however, constituted the more esteemed branch. They were subject roughly to the same conditions of service as other policemen, but the authorities, keen to recruit the best men in the force to serve as detectives, offered them certain benefits denied to their uniformed colleagues. Chapter 3 briefly outlines the employment conditions common to both branches, while providing details about the special set of compensations that detectives received, other material rewards, job satisfaction, and the attractions as well as pressures of detective work that had the effect of elevating the status of detectives as 'a class apart in the police'.[6] The chapter also discusses the interaction between this particular kind of policeman and the public. The modus operandi of detectives and how it affected their relations with the policed community merits a much larger treatment, which cannot be incorporated here owing to space limitations. Nevertheless, an exploration of the significant relationships that developed provides a concise transition to the next part of the book—namely, an examination of the standing of police detectives in society.

Essentially, Part One of the volume reflects the interplay between the individualistic nature of detection and the collective framework in which it functioned. On the one hand, as aptly observed in an article in the *Edinburgh Review* as early as 1852, success in detection 'depends much upon individual qualifications, sagacity in drawing inferences from slight things, fertility of resource, a blood-hound tenacity of pursuit, intimate acquaintance with the habits of thieves, and of their probable mode of acting in particular circumstances, and in the knack (and here real genius displays itself) of making a *cast* in the right direction in search of a clue'.[7] On the other hand, the police institution supplied detectives with ongoing organizational coordination and an infrastructure to better their performance, as recognized by the author of this article: 'Though the value of this branch of police is in a great measure determined by the personal qualifications of its officers, yet the new system has the additional advantage of giving increased means of detection by the power of combining and keeping in continuous and systematic action' the efforts of its individual members.[8] The first three chapters of the book illuminate this duality by describing the experiences of individual detectives alongside the principles and procedures of the detective body as a whole.

INTRODUCTION

The detective was not only a real figure; he was also a cultural construct. He emerged at the threshold of a new era of mass communication marked by increasing numbers of people who had the leisure, ability, and resources to read the unprecedented variety of texts proliferating at the time. This in turn fed the growing public hunger for information about the world of crime and law enforcement and an affinity for crime and detective literature that has typified British society ever since. Indeed, only by analysing the mutual influence between police sleuths and printed texts can the breadth and distinctiveness of the detective's impact on English society of the time be understood. Moreover, given that the Metropolitan Police, unlike other police forces in the country, worked under the direct authority of the Home Office, and that provincial detectives, too, were seen as agents of the state, the image of the occupation was relevant to the stability of the established order generally. Accordingly, Part Two of the book traces the broad cultural developments that brought the detective to public notice and shaped the dynamic discourse about the English detective, and surveys the changing image of the modern police detective from the inception of his vocation at the beginning of the Victorian era through its decisive period in the latter nineteenth and early twentieth centuries.

Overall, police detectives underwent a dramatic transformation in their social standing from a small, unskilled, and relatively marginal cluster of men to an established body whose professional reputation would transcend national boundaries. With the passage of time, detectives came to be perceived as specialists fulfilling their tasks by means of professional knowledge, intuition, rational observation, and hard work. This recognition was not easily won. The very notion of a highly organized and all-encompassing police force had elicited fierce resistance at the start, with plain-clothes policing provoking the deepest concerns. These apprehensions were an important reason for deferring the formation of detective departments once modern police forces appeared on the scene, and why they remained small even when they were eventually organized. The traditional suspicion of plain-clothes policing cast a long shadow over the image of police detectives for many years.

The gradual shift in the perception of the detective role was the product of many factors, but was most saliently related to issues of representation and cultural formation. Most inhabitants of the British Isles learned about police detectives from the printed word. While literary texts lavished considerable attention on detectives, it was the press that had an almost obsessive interest in plain-clothes policing, reporting about its diverse aspects regularly. In effect, the press defined the terms of the cultural and political debate over police detection and was the principal source of the public image of police detectives. The interrelationship that grew between journalists and detectives played a key role in this context, as discussed in Chapter 4. Evolving as occupations side by side, journalism and police detection developed interdependencies that helped them perform their respective tasks, while also enhancing their social status. These contacts, however, also evoked tension and conflict. The chapter reveals the complex relations and the culture of exchange that unfolded between journalists and detectives during this seminal period for both occupations. This discussion is followed in Chapter 5 by an analysis of the metamorphosis of the image of the police detective from menacing figure to national celebrity, and the role played by the press in this process. Based on a review of a large array of newspapers and periodicals, this survey captures the popular perception of the system of crime control at the time.

Although detective fiction projected varied images of police detectives, certain patterns are discernible across a range of literary texts, revealing a less complimentary portrayal of police detectives than in the press. In fictional works, they are often described as mediocre and incompetent. Moreover, the mounting body of fictive texts incorporating detectives in the narrative preferred to concentrate on the private detective, whether amateur or paid practitioner, presenting him or her as the dominant crime fighter in society. Chapter 6 portrays the literary image of the police detective in both canonical and non-canonical texts and explains it in the context of contemporary sensibilities and concerns.

Around the time that Sherlock Holmes made his appearance in literature in the late nineteenth century, a number of retired police detectives entered the literary ranks and wrote memoirs that were published by the most distinguished publishing houses in the country, initiating a trend that continued for several decades. Chapter 7 traces the motivations of both the detectives and the publishers. In addressing the public directly and presenting the ins and outs of their work retrospectively, these detectives-turned-writers not only conveyed their subjective experiences in police service, but also contributed to moulding the image of police detectives.

An underlying theme running through this volume is the unique character of the occupation of the police detective, who came from a predominantly working-class origin. Unlike most workers in modest circumstances, police detectives were expected to engage in a considerable amount of reading and writing in their daily routines. For the progressively important task of information-gathering, they needed to master methods of information retrieval and sorting, and generally to function in an expanding police bureaucracy. Further, the substance of their work dictated an exceptional relationship with the print media. Arguably, no other occupation based mainly on employees from a plebeian background maintained such a dynamic relationship. Increasingly, the press reported, commented on, and explored issues relating to police detection. Local and national newspapers and journals of all political orientations, whether staid or lightweight, illustrated or not, took up this topic. The literary world, too, made detectives and detection a central focus in both fiction and non-fiction, so that by the end of the nineteenth century the detective had turned into an archetypal figure and the linchpin of a new genre: detective fiction. The theatre and the music hall gave them pride of place on stage. Towards the end of the period, police detective characters also figured in the rising film industry. In the process, some police detectives established close ties with journalists and novelists—several of whom set themselves the task of improving the image of detection in their writings—and eventually they themselves participated in the contemporary print culture by publishing their memoirs. Indeed, there were few if any occupations then whose public image and self-image evolved so singularly from its interrelationship with the media.

The book relates to police detectives throughout England, but the experiences described in it are most typically those of London detectives, and specifically of the detective branch of the Metropolitan Police. London was then one of the largest cities in the world, the site of vast wealth and prolific consumption, the seat of government and the centre of an expanding empire, which reached its height in the Victorian and Edwardian era. Its domain was intimately associated with crime and public disorder. As a close observer of the police commented at the end of the period: 'For criminals, as for experts in other trades, all roads lead to London. Your expert criminal, whatever his branch of rascality, sooner or later tries his hand in the metropolis, and so there is a continual inward and outward flow of persons.'[9] Accordingly, strategies for tackling crime were first conceived and tried there. Similarly, its crime fighters confronted a far greater number and variety of offences than their counterparts elsewhere and acquired expertise absent in other forces. They also performed certain national and imperial functions and extended assistance to provincial and colonial police forces, which elevated their status within and outside the police. In effect, the Criminal Investigation Department, as the detective branch of the Metropolitan Police became known in 1878, functioned as a hub of detective operations in the country. Forming by far the largest contingent of police detectives in Britain, and stationed precisely in the centre of the country's print industry, they attracted the bulk of media attention, their exploits—and failures—featuring routinely in discussions of crime detection in the country. When the public thought about detectives, it drew on the image of the London detective. So identified did police detectives become with the London force that Scotland Yard, the headquarters of the Metropolitan Police and its detective force, became synonymous with British undercover law enforcement as a whole.

However distinct the service in the Metropolitan Police CID and the history of each detective force were, detective departments (which existed in cities and large towns only) were governed by similar organizational principles, and detectives shared common occupational experiences throughout England. The approach adopted in this book, giving London detectives centre stage, is guided by this conception of the similarities among detectives, on the one hand, and the predominance of the London sleuths, on the other. Still, research about provincial detectives and particular forces, with reliance on local archives, is needed. After all, Britain was known for its 'local approach' to changes in society, with the Victorian state devolving much of its authority and initiative to the local level. Furthermore, histories of detectives are also called for in the Irish and Scottish police contexts; these are not dealt with in the present study, as they functioned under different criminal justice systems. Lastly, a single volume about police detectives in England cannot cover the wealth of topics associated with their existence in the period under discussion. The original manuscript was twice the size of the final version. Space considerations dictated the omission of many issues and the constriction of others. This book, therefore, may be regarded as the basis for further exploration of the life and work of police detectives in Victorian and Edwardian England, as well as of the history of detection generally. For example, much more research needs to be devoted to such topics as the detectives' relationships with the policed community; the investigative process; the impact of changes in the criminal justice system on detective work; and the detectives' interpretation of the law and legal procedures. I leave this to the many excellent scholars investigating crime and policing in Britain at present, and to future researchers who join the ranks of historians of criminal justice.

PART ONE
THE DETECTIVE IN HIS WORK MILIEU

I

POLICE DETECTION IN ENGLAND: EIGHTEENTH CENTURY–FIRST WORLD WAR

When the first modern police force in England—the Metropolitan Police of London—was founded in September 1829, its leaders stressed that its main purpose was the prevention of crime. Significantly, the first instruction book for the force declared that 'the security of person and property, the preservation of the public tranquillity, and all the other objects of a Police Establishment, will thus be better effected, than by the detection and punishment of the offender, after he has succeeded in committing the crime'.[1] While the newly created Metropolitan Police did employ some police officers in plain clothes, no detective department was established for thirteen years, and only a handful of men were appointed when such an initiative was undertaken in 1842. Similarly, all other English police forces, which by the late 1850s had gradually been formed or reformed, adopted the primacy of prevention over detection as the cornerstone of their system of law enforcement. Additional detective departments were set up from the mid-nineteenth century onwards, but solely in the large provincial cities and towns and in the City of London.[2] They were small, and they constituted a meagre percentage of each police force.

The impulse to favour a policy of prevention over detection stemmed from a widespread conviction that the uninterrupted presence of uniformed police patrols in the streets and thoroughfares would greatly reduce the incidence of crime 'by making it evident [to disorderly and suspicious persons] that they are known and strictly watched, and that certain detection will follow any attempt to commit the crime'.[3] The preventive approach aimed partly at lessening opportunities to offend by placing 'difficulties in the way of obtaining the objects of temptation'—for example, by instructing the public to avoid 'the incautious exposure of property' and to resort to expedients such as the use of cheques.[4] More importantly, the idea of patrol, as explained by Edwin Chadwick, a dedicated police reformer and a student and friend of the utilitarian philosopher Jeremy Bentham, was to decrease 'the motives to commit crime'.[5] The guiding notion was the utilitarian principle that people tend to avoid what may cause them pain. The conspicuousness of patrolmen spread over the policed territory was supposed to signal a clear message to potential violators of the law that they were under constant observation and therefore at considerable risk of being apprehended during the offending act. Donning a uniform was a pivotal component of this strategy. Effective prevention depended on publicity. The uniform distinguished the policeman from the ordinary citizen and ascertained his identity as representing legal sovereignty, power, and dominance. The warning that detection, followed by punishment, was bound to eventuate even if the offender was not caught red-handed was also intended to discourage unlawful behaviour. Both functions—prevention and detection—were at the heart of the system of policing, the hope being that the former would diminish the need for the latter.

No single factor can account for the structure and mode of operation of the emerging police forces. Significantly, however, the period before and during their inception was marked by fundamental changes in British society that transformed its landscape and fabric. The advent of the industrial economy, rapid urbanization, and a population explosion, accompanied by class conflict, gave rise to deep-seated concerns and intensive debate about the state of society and the adequacy of existing practices. Of necessity, redefinitions of deviance and a rethinking of the imposition of order were integral in this questioning. The parliamentary acts that produced organized police forces in England between 1829 and 1856 had been preceded by several decades of public controversy over the need to set up new agencies of law enforcement and the shape they should take.

Undoubtedly, evidence of crime and the growing perception of it as threatening life and property prompted a sense that more expedient means than had existed in the past should be adopted to combat lawbreaking.[6] Mounting reverence for private property, the criminalization of certain traditional rights such as poaching, and the disintegration of time-honoured control mechanisms rendered propertied people less tolerant of property transgressions. Intolerance was reinforced by official statistics of rising crime, primarily property offences (although not burglary), from the first decade of the nineteenth century until the mid-nineteenth century.[7] Transitions in the economy induced novel types of crime. With the growth of manufacture and trade, the concomitant commercialization and habits of consumption created new possibilities for petty property- and work-related offences, exploited by people of all classes. Moreover, in an economy increasingly dependent on finance and investment, white-collar crime by 'polite society' also expanded, affecting more lives and in fact the economy as a whole.[8] That the eighteenth- and early nineteenth-century press enthusiastically publicized acts of crime, particularly sensational crime (such as the brutal Radcliffe Highway murders of seven people in 1811, the assassination of Prime Minister Spencer Perceval in 1812, and an abortive attempt to assassinate members of the Cabinet in 1820) and profiles of criminals, only heightened the resolve among reformers to isolate offenders from society. Prevention was perceived as the best anti-crime measure.

Urban environments, even if the cause of adulation as symbols of the country's formidable achievements, became inextricably linked with rising crime, especially of the serious kind requiring a professional response. As cities grew, they seemed to harbour greater opportunities for crime and the evasion of justice as compared to rural regions, although there, too, crime appeared to be on the rise. In Edwin Chadwick's view: 'In thinly peopled neighbourhoods and small towns every individual is known, and his acts are subjected to the inspection of his neighbours', but 'as population advances, the opportunities for observation diminish'.[9] Supposedly nurturing depravity and idleness in the poor, cities were perceived as making the life of law-abiding citizens considerably less safe. They were also thought to be more dangerous for sheltering full-time criminals.[10] The metropolis, locus of centralized power and unprecedented prosperity existing side by side with appalling poverty, vice, and loose conduct, epitomized the defective check on criminality and deviance, and generally the long-term dire consequences of urbanization. London at the beginning of the nineteenth century contained over a million people (in a population of close to nine million in England and Wales). This was where the issue of social control appeared most urgent. Accordingly, ideas of reform focused on London, the prime site of experiments with official and unofficial law enforcement.

Implicit in the popular discourse of the time about criminality was the notion that crime jeopardized the stability of society and the political order. The transformations in the class structure in Britain seemed to augur a worsening of this predicament. The decline of the old paternalist social patterns and the emergence of an assertive and demanding working class that challenged the norms of the governing elite, sometimes by acts of violence, convinced members of the establishment that a more rigorous policing system was imperative.[11] In an atmosphere of heightened dissonance between labour and capital, and radical exhortations to modify property and political relations, the criminality of the lower reaches of the social ladder appeared all the more menacing. At certain times, improved means of internal pacification were deemed especially pressing. While the French Revolution was greeted enthusiastically by many English Whigs and other political observers, it soon evoked apprehensions of a similar occurrence in Britain. Luddite protests (mainly in the form of destroying machines) and other periodic outbursts of rural disquiet, beginning in 1811–12 and continuing on and off for two decades, were other sources of alarm. So were urban demonstrations and violent riots in the post-Napoleonic era, and periodically thereafter, and around the first reform bill in the early 1830s, which in 1832 significantly extended the vote predominantly to the middle classes. Both government and the upper economic echelons were in need of better protection.

Conceivably, therefore, the major catalyst for the foundation of the Metropolitan Police and the other organized police forces in the land was not necessarily the need to quell crime, but more likely the requirement to ensure the maintenance of order, though the two were viewed by members of the ruling strata as interrelated. Apart from Metropolitan policemen and special constables, the army and yeomanry were often called upon to put down explosive eruptions and restore peace, but this was an unpopular solution. Uniformed civil patrols were a viable alternative for those who held that 'the army was a heavy-handed instrument to use against peaceable demonstrators and a cumbersome one against fast-moving rioters'.[12] Calling up the army was also seen as incompatible with Englishmen's liberties and closely associated with state tyranny.

Notions of a minimal state were still prevalent among the governing classes during the late eighteenth and early nineteenth centuries,[13] yet, pervaded by a mounting sense of insecurity as a result of the disparate threats they faced, they sought greater surveillance over the lower classes—the majority of the population. Moreover, their goal was not only to curb lawlessness and protest. Underpinning the transformation of the police in England also lay a growing aspiration for a more disciplined and ordered society to fill the demands of industrial capitalism—namely, a reliable workforce. Such an aspiration was not explicitly defined, but rather was manifested in a general impetus to reassert hegemony over the subordinate sectors of the social hierarchy. To attain this goal, dealing with habitual offenders and disorderly behaviour on the margins of society or dissuading potential lawbreakers from engaging in criminal activity was insufficient. What was required was to monitor the social environment in its entirety and to regulate the habits and moral disposition of the 'lower levels'.[14] Essentially unconcerned with exacting retribution, the new model was primarily corrective,[15] designed to mould the conduct of the working classes with a view to turning them into a productive and compliant labour force. This also conformed with bourgeois values in private life. Organizing the police as a comprehensive mechanism of social control was meant to achieve all these aims by 'superintendence'[16] rather than overt coercion, and, more specifically, to meet the needs of expanding urbanity in managing large numbers of people. This form of control was not confined to the police but was part and parcel of a larger trend embracing governments and civil institutions, such as schools, hospitals, local charities, workhouses and scientific organizations, in attempts—by no means orchestrated or methodical—to ensure a deferential society.[17]

Yet, in prioritizing prevention over the detection of crime—both in rhetoric and in practice—the reformers of the London police were also guided by a desire to mitigate the widespread opposition to the very notion of systematic policing: an emphasis on deterrence was considered more acceptable to society.[18] Accordingly, the wording of the first instruction book of the Metropolitan Police downplayed the importance of detection, assuaging the public by giving this aspect of police work a secondary role. This policy reflected the attention given to the views of influential groups and their spokesmen in the public sphere, a feature of the modern English police from the outset.[19] Whether in London or in the provinces, the emerging police forces constituted pragmatic compromises between the aspirations of the various proponents of police reform and the demands of other opinion moulders to preserve extant policing patterns or at least not to alter them drastically.[20] The British state, reacting with a firm hand to the accumulated challenges, evinced a tendency, as the century progressed, not only to rely on force in safeguarding ruling-class domination, but also to come to terms with the sentiments of different social groupings, or in any case to appear to do so.

The police authorities were convinced that allaying public anxieties and securing the public's trust and confidence in the new force depended to a large extent on the demeanour of the law enforcers, a message inculcated in the rank and file as soon as the police forces were launched. Their instruction books contained a warning to officers to work strictly within the rules of the law, but also to look respectable, control their temper, and 'be civil and attentive to all persons, of every rank and class', on and off duty.[21] The authorities were also determined to restrain police powers by punishing officers severely if their manners were reported as unbecoming, most commonly when they were found drunk or otherwise unruly. While in practice police officers often ignored such instructions, the rhetoric set a conciliatory tone. On the one hand, the newly formed police reaffirmed the relationship of rulers to ruled in society, but, on the other, their public-service function was stressed repeatedly, reflecting a policy of public appeasement in an attempt to mould the kind of police that would not be regarded as un-English.[22]

Given the preference for preventive and uniformed policing, how did the detective police evolve and expand in England, and how was it affected by influential opinion? Clearly, the modern police did not disapprove of crime investigation, and saw it as inevitable. How, then, did the body of police detectives develop alongside the uniformed branch? In order to understand the evolution of detectives within the modern police, an exploration of the type of detection that existed prior to 1842—the precursors of the famed English detectives—is illuminating. The study of this period will also reveal the origins of the misgivings about detection.

CRIME DETECTION BEFORE THE FOUNDING OF THE REFORMED POLICE

Customarily, police functions were the preserve of the local government. They were carried out by a motley assortment of individuals and bodies who attempted to provide some protection for the population in the areas under their control. The pivotal figure in the enforcement of the law was a part-time and (often) unpaid parish constable who acted as a kind of executive agent for the local justice of the peace (also unpaid). He served for one year (or more) as part of rotating duties to the parish or, increasingly, was hired as a substitute by citizens who opted to avoid this community service.[23] In towns, another key person who guarded citizens and their property against offenders was the night—and sometimes day—watchman, who was paid low wages. While the watchman commonly guarded premises and the streets, the constable was principally assigned to keep the peace, enforce proper behaviour in public among the fringes of society—vagrants, drunks, loitering prostitutes, and suspicious persons—deal with crime and small-scale public disturbances, and carry out a variety of other responsibilities.[24] Vested with time-honoured common-law powers of arrest and prosecution, the parish constable and the watchman occasionally caught violators red-handed, traced persons suspected of wrongdoing, apprehended individuals whose transgression was self-evident, and started criminal proceedings.[25] Constables would sometimes probe offences, including homicides, and prepare evidence against the perpetrators.[26] Yet, not infrequently this was done solely for a reward, as such assignments were time-consuming for part-time officers and at times dangerous, and would not be addressed otherwise.[27] Magistrates and justices of the peace would also take up criminal investigative tasks, such as questioning suspects.[28] However, generally, official law-enforcers were not expected to take the initiative to solve crimes by pursuing clues as a routine,[29] or to carry on policing duties outside their parishes and wards. Thus, formal detection was mostly ad hoc, contingent on the good will and free time of law-enforcers who were not experts in gathering information or acting upon it. In this they were no exception in the administration of the law, which consisted largely of lay, unpaid, untrained, amateur magistrates and part-time local officials.[30]

At the heart of the official anti-crime strategy lay a brutal code of penalties, called the 'Bloody Code' by contemporaries. The English establishment, though proud of its humane traditions, enacted approximately 200 capital offences during the eighteenth century, the vast majority property crimes.[31] Evidently, punishment was not designed to fit the severity of the offence. The underlying premiss behind this oppressive policy was that stringent penalization, even for slight offences, would disincline people from violating the law. The display of hangings and the spectacle of corporal punishment inflicted in public were also assumed to be effective warnings. People continued to commit offences, of course, but, as a by-product of the patchy and uncoordinated policing arrangements, a great many perpetrators were never charged. Moreover, precisely because of the disproportional penalties, discretion was exercised at all levels of the criminal justice administration, inter alia in small communities where justices of the peace and constables were guided by their relations with the victims or the transgressors and their evaluation of the effects of punishment on the locality.[32] Capital sentences were often commuted and replaced, usually by transportation, and from the late eighteenth century increasingly by incarceration. The victims themselves, showing compassion, sometimes refrained from prosecuting and let the offenders escape a penalty altogether.[33]

Furthermore, not only did the local authorities abstain from pursuing or trying every single offender, but by and large they left these weighty functions to self-help and private enterprise.[34] While maintaining internal (and naturally external) peace was more likely to be perceived as the responsibility of the public purse, crime was treated more as a personal matter. The government did initiate and prosecute cases viewed as a direct peril to the interests of the state, such as treason, riots, and sedition;[35] profiteering in foodstuffs; assault on public officers; serious non property offences such as murder, man slaughter, and infanticide;[36] and exceptional offences against property, such as coining and forgery.[37] In addition, the government helped defray costs of prosecutions in some instances, and offered rewards as an incentive to private persons to assist officers of the law.[38] Recent studies have shown that English criminal prosecution was in fact more publicly instigated than historians had previously thought.[39] Still, as a general rule, even though the administration encouraged bringing felons to court and prosecuting them, it was the aggrieved person who normally set the legal procedure in motion, searched for incriminating clues, bore the costs, and conducted the entire court process, either alone or with the assistance of family members, neighbours, friends, or people with commercial interests, until verdict was handed down.[40] Even the prosecution of a murder case was on occasion left to the individual, although voluntary detection for the most part dealt with property crimes. The well-to-do could always rely on their own employees to protect or recover property.[41] Many incidents were resolved outside the courts, with the victims settling with the suspects. In cases of theft, in particular, the owners often preferred to negotiate the return of pilfered merchandise, a procedure that was often less costly and less strenuous. Small communities frequently refrained from resorting to the official administrators of the law, opting to use informal social sanctions against lawbreakers or deviants in their midst.

Increasingly, however, victims who were determined and financially able to catch their offenders, and may have already exhausted their own inquiries in the locality, paid others to do the job for them. Beginning in the seventeenth century, and perhaps even earlier, with the growing commercialization of services, a new occupation emerged: persons who specialized in the pursuit and arrest of lawbreakers. So much in demand were their services that by the first half of the eighteenth century these 'thief-takers', as they were known (for dealing mainly with the widespread concern with property offences), became 'familiar figures', operating mainly in London but also in several other cities and towns.[42]

The administration of criminal law in London was riddled with corruption.[43] Even magistrates—notably the so-called trading justices, who were paid fees for executing their judicial tasks and tended to be of marginal gentility—fell into disrepute, for many were known to have engaged in shady or even illicit activities.[44] The thief-takers easily accommodated themselves to such a milieu. Some had a criminal record to start with,[45] but became more deeply enmeshed in criminality by the lure of financial benefits. During the 1690s, in the wake of difficulties in the London economy that produced high levels of crime and street violence, several new parliamentary statutes offered rewards for conviction in order to encourage the prosecution of highwaymen, housebreakers, burglars, petty thieves, coiners, plotters, and other offenders.[46] Local authorities, banks, insurance offices, and other private companies did the same.[47] Private persons offered rewards for the return of stolen goods.[48] The main result of these offers, however, was the encouragement of thief-taking. In 1720, after the War of the Spanish Succession of 1702–13, the demobilization that followed, and another crime wave, a royal proclamation offered an additional and very large reward for the conviction of street robbers in London. The offer of statutory as well as private rewards for capture, conviction, or provision of corroborative testimony induced many thief-takers to adopt objectionable practices.

To augment the chances of success in such endeavours, thief-takers colluded with criminals beyond the call of duty, resorted to intimidation, perjury, and blackmail, fabricated evidence, and forced false confessions, thereby framing innocent people.[49] Some manufactured criminal cases, stage-managed trials, received stolen goods and sold them to the original owners, and released perpetrators for a fee.[50] As historian Ruth Paley observed, 'thief-takers were in business not to detect crime but to commit it'.[51] Contemporaries were aware of this culture of detection, and, although the attitude of the public to thief-takers was not invariably hostile,[52] they were widely associated with unscrupulous complicity in lawbreaking. The roots of detection thus lay in the infringement of the law. As will be seen in the second part of the book, it would be a long journey until this taint was removed.

Still, other methods of collecting information and bringing suspects before a judge existed within the bounds of the law. Prominent among them were voluntary associations for the prosecution of felons (funded by private subscription), which, though present earlier in the eighteenth century, spread throughout England from approximately the 1770s until their gradual decline in the mid-nineteenth century, numbering in the hundreds during this period.[53] Such associations took on some patrol work, but their main function was to detect, arrest, and prosecute offenders who victimized their subscribers, and to retrieve stolen goods.[54] To attain these aims, they circulated details of the cases they handled, offered fees as an incentive to provide evidence, and paid people, including parish constables, to track suspects.[55]

Another avenue available to aid victims of crime, local officials, thief-takers, and private societies in obtaining incriminating evidence and retrieving stolen property was press advertisements and handbills, which carried descriptions of offenders and of stolen goods, with offers of rewards for information over a wide geographical span.[56] There were also less costly detective techniques, such as having a bellman, or public crier, announce a quest for criminal intelligence.[57] However, money increasingly played a significant role in crime investigation. In this way, private services filled a vacuum in an underpoliced society, in which it was generally up to individuals to decide whether to take action if a crime was committed.

Nonetheless, in parallel with the development of innovative ventures for personal gain or self-help, a more resolute official effort to employ a permanent cadre of crime investigators slowly emerged, guided by the notion of the public good. Initial steps were taken in the metropolis by Colonel Thomas De Veil, justice of the peace for Westminster and Middlesex and the first chief magistrate of the Bow Street Public Office in Covent Garden (1739–49), who hired thief-takers and paid them fees for their services at government expense. The Bow Street Office thus became a centre for both judicial and policing acts.

However, the first systematic experiment in official crime investigation, albeit limited in scope, resulted from the initiative of two magistrates who were also (half-)brothers. The novelist Henry Fielding became the chief magistrate in the Bow Street Office in 1748, at the end of the War of the Austrian Succession and the beginning of another familiar post-war crime wave. He persuaded the government that the policy of large supplementary rewards did not discourage crime. Instead, he requested financial support to sustain a group of men, some of them constables of Westminster parishes, 'to seek out and arrest serious offenders', particularly 'highwaymen and street robbers whose activities caused panic in the capital from time to time', and to bring them to court for examination and commitment to trial.[58] Tasked with searching for information, these men used informants and disguise, thus familiarizing themselves with the habits of criminals. Their activities extended to the countryside as well. In time they would be known as the Bow Street Runners (although, because of the derogatory connotations, they called themselves Principal or Senior Officers, or simply Officers)[59]—considered by many scholars as Britain's first police detectives. 'Runners' was slang first for men who escorted prisoners between magistrates' courts and gaols and then for officers who pursued and apprehended suspected offenders.[60] At first the Runners numbered no more than seven, but in the next few decades a handful more were added.[61] Henry Fielding's blind brother, John, who replaced him as chief magistrate at Bow Street Office (1754–80), continued his endeavours to promote a more effective investigation of crime by using the skills of the Bow Street personnel. Having gained official sanction from the Bow Street magistrates, the Runners also worked for private people.[62] They thus combined both official and private functions.

The Fieldings' objective was to mould thief-takers who would be devoid of the negative associations with illegal means.[63] In addition to choosing their thief-catchers with care, and dismissing the unsuitable ones, they supervised their activities closely.[64] Further, while the Runners received rewards for fulfilling their duties, they also earned a small retainer, thereby attenuating the potentially corrupting temptations integral in rewards and demonstrating their professionalism and official standing to the public. It may be said that the Fieldings started the long process of detaching detection from the underworld and elevating it to the status of a public service, although by virtue of the opportunities available to them the Runners were accused of shady practices.[65]

In addition to their policing activities, the Fielding brothers also exhibited original thinking in understanding the importance of gathering and disseminating criminal intelligence as a way of bettering the justice system in both its preventive and investigative functions. With this aim in mind, they launched a number of publications calling upon the public to report offences perpetrated against them, and carrying descriptions of offences, missing property, and suspects, with requests for information.[66] Data about crime were also sent to selected newspapers published by others. In doing so they laid the foundations for the complex relations that were to develop in the nineteenth century between police detectives and the press, as will be discussed in Chapters 4 and 5. These innovative measures were initiated with the objective of making the Bow Street Office a centre of information about crimes and criminals, with the information then distributed to administrators and communities all over the country.[67]

Presumably, the Fieldings and their immediate successor, Sampson Wright, were successful in establishing the relatively good reputation of the Bow Street Runners and distinguishing them from shadowy thief-takers, for in 1792 parliament passed the Middlesex Justices Act with no serious opposition, forming seven new Public (also referred to as Police) Offices in London modelled on the Bow Street Office.[68] Each Office operated as a court, directed by three stipendiary magistrates who employed officials and police officers, including a small number of paid constables, who carried out tasks similar to those of the Bow Street Principal Officers—apprehending and prosecuting felons. The distinction between the corruptible thief-taker and the detective hero who represented the interest of society advanced a step.

That the expansion of the official detective force took place at this juncture, after nearly forty years during which the Bow Street Runners had been the only formal group tasked almost exclusively with the investigation of crime, was not coincidental. Given the fundamental changes in society, the late eighteenth century witnessed an intensified search by the social hierarchy for diverse avenues to stem and detect crime, both in theory and in practice. The proposals to accomplish this varied, but all were couched in the language of improvement—namely, making the forces of law and order more effective and the likelihood of charging offenders more certain.[69]

In the event, the establishment of the additional Public Offices constituted a landmark in the evolution of police detection in London and elsewhere. First, it multiplied the size of the detective contingent several times over, although the total number of designated crime fighters in all eight Public Offices never exceeded sixty or seventy. Secondly, it signified the government's intent to professionalize crime investigation. Salaried and permanently employed, the magistrates and the constables in the Public Offices amassed vocational experience that improved their performance. Thirdly, since the Public Offices were under the direct supervision of the newly formed Home Office, and their officers were partly funded by government, the 1792 Act stepped up the centralization of law enforcement and heightened the trend towards greater state responsibility for crime investigation. While the fledgling police officers followed in the Bow Street Runners' footsteps in combining policing with private work, their primary affiliation was to the official Public Offices. Indeed, these officers routinely investigated, arrested, and prosecuted people suspected of theft, even without the involvement of the victims.[70]

The Principal Officers had no scarcity of work, and were extensively employed until they were dismantled in 1839 (see below). During this period, some of the characteristics later to be typical of police detection were fixed. A view was formulated within the Public Offices that valued crime investigators more than ordinary police personnel, and the pattern of prudent selection of detectives became entrenched. The vast majority of Principal Officers served a long apprenticeship within Bow Street or the other Public Offices.[71] Evidently, even then detection was deemed a speciality, requiring distinct skills and a substantial period of preparation. Moreover, of the various Principal Officers, those at Bow Street enjoyed a special status, foreshadowing the unique standing subsequently held by the central detective branch at Scotland Yard. Like their successors, the Bow Street Principal Officers were perceived by many (including themselves) as a 'superior class of men', surpassing other Principal Officers.[72] Their performance was especially prized and given relatively wide exposure in the media.[73] They were also better paid, and, no less importantly, their services were sought nationwide.[74]

Although the activity of the coterie at Bow Street reached the far corners of the country, at no time did its size exceed eleven men, albeit London, with its seven other Public Offices, was better provided than the provinces.[75] Moreover, despite mounting concerns about levels of crime, and pressure to capture all offenders, the Principal Officers at the various London Public Offices remained the only formal detectives in England, apart from a few attempts in provincial England to set aside ordinary officers for detective work. Instead, other measures were adopted by criminal justice administrators to curb crime. During the second half of the eighteenth century, patrols were augmented in the capital city and its environs, and greater numbers of urban law-enforcers were remunerated.[76] Street lighting was introduced in London and some provincial towns. These trends endured into the early nineteenth century. In 1800 the government took over a private venture that had been started by several West India merchants in 1798 to stop river crime, and founded the Thames River Police, whose function was to detect and prevent pilfering from cargo ships and warehouses.[77] Five years later, a mounted patrol was re-established (a short-lived horse patrol had operated in 1763–4), whose uniformed officers patrolled the major roads around the metropolis. The patrolmen had powers of pursuit, but concentrated on the containment of prospective malefactors.[78] The early nineteenth century also saw the expansion of day and night foot patrols, especially in and around urban areas, but these were deployed only occasionally for investigative purposes. Apparently, central and local governments preferred to focus their efforts on the preservation of order and the prevention of crime, and depended on existing law-enforcers to deal with crime detection as well. The Metropolitan Police and subsequent forces were organized along the same lines, based on the premiss that deterrent action was the best answer to crime.

THE RELUCTANCE TO INSTITUTIONALIZE POLICE DETECTION

While methods aimed at controlling crime were introduced both in London and in the provincial towns in a piecemeal manner for decades prior to the formation of the Metropolitan Police in 1829, and many public figures and commentators advocated a better system of regulation,[79] others strongly objected to changes in policing arrangements and particularly to wholesale reforms.[80] The reasons for opposing stringent constabulary reforms were manifold, not least the reluctance to incur increased costs.[81] However, the common theme that ran through the rhetoric of the various critics was the apprehension that the proposed police would be intrusive and trample over the liberties of the people.[82] References to the hallowed right of the English people to personal freedom had long been commonplace in public discourse on many, sometimes contradictory, issues, voiced by radicals and members of the establishment alike.[83] The notion of liberty was often equated with Englishness itself,[84] even though the

British state manifested inconsistency concerning the values of individual freedom—undoubtedly in Ireland and in the colonies, but also in mainland Britain.[85] In the context of policing, the argument repeatedly underscored, as expressed by the 1822 parliamentary Committee on the Police of the Metropolis, was: 'It is difficult to reconcile an effective system of police, with that perfect freedom of action and exemption from interference, which are the great privileges and blessings of society in this country', and that 'the forfeiture or curtailment of such advantages would be too great a sacrifice for improvements in police, or facilities in detection of crime, however desirable in themselves if abstractedly considered'.[86]

The term 'freedom of action' had several connotations, but above all it was used to resist suggestions to centralize control over law enforcement. While opponents focused on the fear of a systematic and powerful police force, the vast majority objected more broadly to placing more power in the hands of central government. The underlying belief was that Britain had achieved its riches and superior position in the world because of the contribution of individuals rather than the state, and that individuals should therefore be free to pursue their interests as they saw fit without state interference.[87] Beyond casting doubts in the ability of government to improve society, some commentators maintained that centralized power tended to become tyrannical even if the men in authority were liberally minded.[88] Underpinning such ideas were self-serving considerations. Aside from the radical camp, which stood firm against any encroachment on political activity, opposition emanated from several interested institutions, principally magistrates and justices of the peace, local parishes, and the City of London, whose authority was liable to be curtailed by the proposed plans for a centrally controlled police force. These critics, and others who distrusted the potential expansion of state power, time and again warned that such a force might one day become 'the active tool of a despotic government'.[89] Local elites in urban and rural England preferred to tolerate a relatively high incidence of crime than to lose local autonomy and control over policing and expenditure.[90] In any case, a great proportion of crime consisted of petty larceny impelled by poverty.[91]

Notably, while opponents of the police referred in their critiques to the police generally, it was the figure of the spy specifically that appeared to personify the deepest threat to freeborn Englishmen. Central to misgivings over heightened state interference was the concern that a unified and highly regulated police force, accountable to the government, would utilize, or actually become, an espionage network, absorbed in the scrutiny of citizens of all ranks of society and meddling in their private as well as political affairs in order to advance the autocratic ambitions of central authority rather than crime control.[92] The implication was that strong states and police espionage were interdependent. The proof was the despotic states on the Continent. Moreover, the menace embodied in the figure of the spy was not only his role as a government agent. Although spies were supposed to engage primarily in undercover political policing, the label 'spy' was widened in common parlance to include invisible police agents generally, as the term 'detective' or 'detective police' did not come into use until the 1840s.[93] Thus, the negative connotations of the word 'spy' served as a convenient bogey to reinforce opposition to police reform, whether in London or in the provinces.[94] In fact, even though the real spies dealt more in prevention than in detection[95]—keeping watch over potential subversives without being seen in an attempt to identify as well as predict crime—so loaded was this term that even after mid-century it was occasionally employed to express a derogatory attitude towards detectives.

The vexing issue was not the function of detection, nor necessarily the wearing of plain-clothes attire. After all, before 1829 most law-enforcers did not dress in uniform, although watchmen used some identifying marks and patrolmen increasingly wore some type of outfit. The Principal Officers always operated in plain clothes and carried no official identification apart from a small hollow tipstaff in which a magistrate's warrant could be inserted.[96] It was the clandestine environment implied by the word 'spy' that bound the detective to this figure. The entire discourse on policing was infused with the supposition that secrecy provided temptations for police agents to exceed their legal authority and resort to all kinds of insidious practices, including, worst of all, to provoke others to commit crime. It was not as if secret agents were banned. For many years the British parliament had sanctioned their employment. Rather, the objections reflected the growing perception that secrecy, particularly if systematic, was incompatible with good government, and certainly with democracy. To Bentham, it was 'an instrument of conspiracy', and therefore 'ought never to be the system of regular government'.[97] Lord Acton claimed that 'everything secret degenerates'.[98] In as much as British society largely 'recognized itself as a free country precisely by the absence of the multiple forms of public secrecy which characterized repressive regimes abroad',[99] a covert form of policing was not embraced.

The most widespread unease with police officers whose vocation was not obvious concerned those who actually falsified their identity, as disguise not only helped conceal their police role but also connoted an a priori intention to cover up devious deeds.[100] For the liberal philosopher John Stuart Mill, disguise was 'a badge of slavery'.[101] More generally, the notion of disguise aggravated the sensibilities of a nascent modern society, especially in the expanding cities, where it was relatively easy to change one's identity. At a time when social differences between higher and lower origins were being re-encoded, the notion of concealed identity heightened anxiety about growing anonymity and alienation, particularly in the middle classes, whose status was often precarious. In such an atmosphere, the claim to be someone else was viewed as blurring these distinctions and threatening the sense of security and assurance of knowing who was who.

Doubts regarding the very nature of investigative work were also evoked by an awareness that, in order to perform their tasks adequately, crime fighters needed to be in close proximity to the underworld, and that this proximity made them susceptible to foul practices. Thief-takers were known to have been implicated in breaches of the law and to connive with criminals. The Bow Street Runners, too, were alleged to have overstepped the law.[102] There was no reason to suppose that these misdeeds would not persist with the new police. Thus, non-uniformed investigative work was bound up with an amalgam of negative associations: central and authoritarian government, excessive invasion of the political and private spheres, curtailed freedom, the anonymity of the city, spying, disguise, corruption, and unwholesome ties with wrongdoers. Beat officers, who, because of their visibility, were under almost constant public inspection, were regarded as less prone to—though not immune from—malpractice.

The model of what to avoid in the new police was the French criminal justice system, or rather what was known or assumed about it. Other continental countries were also invoked as negative examples, but France was the 'other' against which English standards and ideals were ordinarily measured. The strongly centralized French police system was regarded by many, including the outspoken Glaswegian merchant and later London magistrate and police reformer Patrick Colquhoun, as the most efficient in Europe. For most observers, however, it also symbolized the reason for their anxieties.[103]

References were made to the pervasive French intelligence network, described as invasive and aggressive and marked by censorship and the abuse of civil liberties—just the sort of behaviour expected of surreptitious police work. The appointment in 1812 of Eugène-François Vidocq, an ex-convict and informer, to head the Sûreté—the detective department of the Paris police—and the recruitment of other former convicts to the squad, further underscored the French police as a model to exclude. Belabouring the point, commentators drew attention to the fact that the very origin of the word 'espionage' was French.[104]

THE NEW POLICE FORCE IN LONDON

Aiming to attain public support for the newly formed police force in London, its architect, Home Secretary Robert Peel, tried to reconcile the diverse public pressures with his own agenda. The creation of the Metropolitan Police by parliamentary act in 1829 was a triumph for him and for reformers like Patrick Colquhoun who wanted to replace the disparate police forces in London with a single centralized administration so as to exert overall surveillance of the population.[105] The exception was the City of London Police, which managed to retain its autonomy, as Peel wanted to avoid confrontation with the local leadership.[106] The formation of the Metropolitan Police was also an achievement for supporters of state control over the police, as the new force was under the direct supervision of the Home Office. For the first time, the majority of police officers in the capital were state employees. Overall, this marked another step in the diversification of the state's functions and the augmentation of its power.

To dispel apprehensions that the police would resemble a standing army,[107] Peel was intent on identifying it as a purely civil police force. Although a uniformed patrol obviously connoted a military image, and Metropolitan policemen endured harsh discipline and drill exercises, their outfit consisted of a civilian-style blue (and not red) tailcoat and trousers, overcoat, boots, and a leather top hat (replaced later by a helmet), with an identification letter and number on the coat collar.[108] Moreover, they carried truncheons—not firearms—issued only when there was a perceived need. All employees were salaried, not dependent on rewards, and thus less prone to corruption. The force, through respectful behaviour, also aimed to assure the public that it was not an organized army of spies and informers in the service of the high and mighty.[109] To strengthen this impression, no detective unit was formed in the Metropolitan Police in 1829.

This formula, nevertheless, was far from pleasing to everyone. In fact, the appearance of uniformed policemen in the streets was widely perceived as an attack on English liberties.[110] However, while the lower socio-economic groups resented and feared the new police, 'respectable opinion' soon became more receptive to the institution, as will be seen in Chapter 5. Yet, lingering hostility towards covert policing was manifested in the early 1830s in the overwhelmingly indignant public response to the revelation that a police agent, Sergeant William Popay, had assumed a false identity for over a year (from February 1832 to March 1833), penetrated the radical National Political Union, and pretended to be a militant member who supported violent tactics.[111] This disclosure confirmed to the public what undercover policemen could do in the name of government. Even the parliamentary committee set up to look into the case criticized Popay's conduct.[112] It was one thing to obtain information to help identify perpetrators of crime, quite another to incite to crime. Presumably, the publicity surrounding the affair was a factor in delaying the formation of a detective branch in the force.

The occasional use of plain-clothes policemen in the new police force was not confined to spying on political agitators. When the need arose to observe and pursue offenders, and conduct investigations without being noticed, uniformed officers were instructed to shed their uniform temporarily and discharge their duties clandestinely, although some magistrates regarded this as 'a dangerous precedent'.[113] The tendency was to engage selected men who stood out as intelligent and energetic, had attained results in their investigative work, or were experienced in areas vital to crime detection, such as disguise or horse stealing.[114] Some were repeatedly employed in plain clothes, but no formal department was created for them. That Principal Officers, spearheaded by the Bow Street men, continued to provide expert investigative services for the entire country for a period of ten years after the initiation of the Metropolitan Police also had a delaying effect, as there was no pressing call to institute a rival corps.[115] Furthermore, disapproval of a detective department also existed within the force. Of the two commissioners of the Metropolitan Police, Colonel Charles Rowan (1829–50) and the lawyer Richard Mayne (1829–68), the former disliked the idea intensely and thwarted proposals for a detective department, even after the abolition of the Bow Street Runners in 1839.[116] Apparently, he preferred to concentrate efforts on developing the preventive side of the new police, confident that, when necessary, uniformed policemen were capable of fulfilling detection tasks.

THE RISE OF SCOTLAND YARD

Nevertheless, a growing body of opinion held that the current arrangements—the occasional use of ordinary policemen for crime investigation—should be replaced by a permanent force of detectives.[117] Pressure built up in the wake of several well-publicized failures in detection, and the absence of any detective unit in the country after 1839.[118] This is well illustrated in the press coverage of the murder of Lord William Russell (uncle of Lord John Russell, formerly home secretary and later prime minister) in May 1840. Two days after the murder, *The Times*, the leading daily paper, cynically observed that the Metropolitan Police had no clue yet that could lead to the discovery of the murderer, and that its work in the case and in other recent murder cases had 'proved utterly unavailing'.[119] The paper acknowledged that it had supported the establishment of the Metropolitan Police, but it now saw that, while the police were good at prevention 'by the constant display of power and vigilance', they had no time for investigations. Contending that the Bow Street Runners were better experienced than their counterparts in the Metropolitan Police, the paper recommended that they be called back, undoubtedly provoking chagrin within the new force, whose members regarded the Runners as their rivals.[120] For its part, the *Southern Star and London and Brighton Patriot* surmised that 'the prevailing opinion of the city aldermen', with whom its reporter had conversed, was that 'this diabolical murder will lead to the establishment of a detective police'.[121]

Gradually, it became evident to the police leadership that the chances of patrol officers interrupting a crime were slight, and that special personnel and professional knowledge were required to trace the offenders after the event. The escape in April 1842 of Daniel Good from police custody after he had brutally murdered and dismembered his wife, and his evasion of capture for fifteen days—when he was caught by chance—sparked an outcry in the press, accusing the police of negligence and lack of investigative expertise.[122]

In this the press served as a pressure group lobbying for improved detection.[123] Once again, while the preventive capacity of the new police was highly praised, their ability to detect crime was compared to that of the old Bow Street Runners and was found wanting. An attempt on the life of the young Queen Victoria in May 1842—one of several during that period—might also have added some urgency in prevailing upon decision-makers to institute a separate detective department within the Metropolitan Police in August 1842. This marked the official, if tentative,[124] start of Scotland Yard—the famous detective team stationed in the Metropolitan Police headquarters—which would become a familiar name far beyond the British borders.[125]

Still, a combination of lingering belief in the ability of beat officers to quell crime and a latent distrust of undercover policing resulted in a quite small detective force and a slow increase in detective manpower in the following years. Two inspectors and six sergeants—most of them chosen from the pool of veteran plain-clothes officers in the Metropolitan Police—were appointed to the new department, fewer than the number of Bow Street Runners.[126] Soon it became apparent that non-uniformed men were needed to carry out detective tasks, not only in the central office but also in the seventeen divisions that made up the Metropolitan Police District (each division was divided into subdivisions, sections, and beats). Given the scruples about permanent detectives, these officers were temporarily taken from the uniformed ranks, and returned to them upon the completion of their assignments or after a fixed period of time, although, increasingly, several remained in plain clothes for long periods.[127] Such auxiliaries assisted in investigating crimes and arresting offenders as well as in gathering intelligence, thus combining reactive and proactive functions. They were assigned to mingle unnoticed in mass gatherings, keep 'felons' and 'persons of bad character' under observation, visit places 'of bad repute' in order to pre-empt robberies, burglaries, and violent street crimes, and follow perpetrators once a crime was committed.[128] These tasks involved a considerable amount of patrolling, but, unlike uniformed policemen, the provisional plain-clothes officers were not confined to a beat. Although they played, and would continue to play, an important role in the divisions' fight against crime, they were not considered detectives and therefore did not acquire the detectives' special standing, higher pay, and other privileges within the police system.[129] Employing them, along with extensive reliance on informers and informants to obtain hard-to-get information about criminals, both ordinary and political, helped the force cope with the problem of the small size of the detective unit. The use of informers and informants also reduced the 'objectionable' practice of detective officers assuming a 'feigned character' to investigate crime.[130]

In the course of a quarter of a century, the number of permanent detectives at Scotland Yard grew to fifteen only, plus one clerk sergeant.[131] Nevertheless, they increasingly attracted public attention. In the late 1850s, about fifteen years after the formation of the detective branch, several books about London described them as an integral component of city life.[132] This was also reflected in the world of art. The monumental painting *The Railway Station* by William Powell Frith (1862) depicts a large number of passengers about to board a Great Western Railway train at Paddington Station (see the cover image of this volume). In a scene that captures the flux of modern life in the Victorian period—symbolized by the dynamic and diverse crowd and the new rail technology—the painter made a point of including a detail of two detectives arresting a suspect, a revealing piece of evidence of their role in society by then. The figures are modelled on two real-life detective sergeants in the City of London Police—Michael Haydon (with handcuffs in hand) and James Brett (with his hand on the suspect's shoulder), both well known in their day.[133]

Strong apprehensions about the employment of unidentified policemen nevertheless persisted both inside and outside the police (see Chapter 5). In a verbal communication to superintendents in 1845, Commissioner Charles Rowan re-emphasized that 'no man shall disguise himself without particular orders' from the commissioners, and will do so only in a 'very strong case of necessity'.[134] In evidence given to the Committee on the Sunday Liquor Trade in the late 1860s, Commissioner Richard Mayne expressed qualms about the recent practice of plain-clothes policemen putting on 'a different dress' while carrying out surveillance of publicans, calling it 'an objectionable concealment... intended to mislead persons'.[135] Even if their rhetoric was sometimes designed to appease public opinion, it revealed a conflict between the fear that plain-clothes policing 'gives occasion to a charge of Police being employed as spies and in other improper ways' and an awareness that it was indispensable in certain circumstances.[136]

Several developments during the 1860s, whose roots went back to the 1850s, coalesced to impress official circles that the existing pattern of detection in the metropolis required far-reaching modification. The almost total cessation of transportation to Australia in the 1850s (its official abolition was effected in 1867) meant that serious offenders now remained in England. While this accelerated the use of imprisonment as a common means of penalization, it also necessitated the release of thousands of former convicts into the streets. Concern about this situation peaked in 1862 in the wake of panic caused by rising incidents of garrotting—a form of violent street robbery widely attributed to discharged prisoners. The Penal Servitude Act of 1864 mandated police supervision of ticket-of-leave men (prisoners released on licence).[137] In 1867, the seizure of two Fenians from a prison van in Manchester, during which a police officer was killed, and a later attempt to free the mastermind of the operation from Clerkenwell prison (in London), which resulted in the slaying of twelve people, injury to many others, and wrecked houses,[138] had the effect of extending detectives' duties significantly outside London and abroad.[139]

The weight of these events, and warnings about further plots, led to the formation of a committee by the Home Office in 1868 to review the administration and functioning of the Metropolitan Police, with special attention to the detective branch. Among other recommendations, the committee was emphatic that neither the number of uniformed policemen nor the number of detectives was sufficient to meet the new challenges.[140] A radical increase—to 207 full-time detectives—was implemented by Colonel Edmund Henderson, who took over the post of commissioner in 1869, although he was aware that the detective concept still touched a raw nerve in the public.[141] Despite this significant expansion, however, detectives comprised no more than 2.3 per cent of a force of nearly 9,000 men that year.[142]

Henderson was also responsible for a major restructuring of the detective system in the metropolis. In the belief that temporary plainclothes policemen could not master the skills demanded by detective work, and that such skills were imperative throughout the policed territory, Henderson's innovation consisted of permanently attaching fully-fledged detectives to each of the by then twenty police divisions, thereby covering the London Police District with a detective network. However, these divisional detectives held the ranks of constables and sergeants only—an indication of their lower professional skills and status vis-à-vis the Yard men who were sergeants and above. Henderson also extended the scope of duties of the full detectives. In addition to investigating the circumstances of local crimes and familiarizing themselves with the addresses, haunts, and habits of criminals and individuals known to be ill-disposed,[143] detectives were expected to visit prisons regularly in order to identify suspects and acquaint themselves with the faces and, if possible, modes of life of the inmates and those about to be discharged.[144] The guiding idea was that crime could best be controlled by accumulating information and monitoring the previously convicted—an idea that informed the policies of other police forces. When not occupied with other duties, detectives were required to accompany uniformed policemen on patrol and back them up in their work.[145] Anticipatory action thus became a fundamental aspect of the detective role, particularly in the divisions, where the bulk of the London detectives served. Detective duties were designed not only to secure intelligence about crimes committed—whether a suspect was identified or not—but also to get a deeper understanding of the criminal community, deter criminals from involvement in crimes, control the breeding ground of criminals-to-be, and inform magistrates and judges about past convictions of suspects. Monitoring indoor as well as outdoor locations also allowed detectives to witness offences or stop them before they occurred. To a certain extent, this strategy was a sequel to that initiated by the Fieldings of gathering criminal intelligence not only for immediate purposes but with a view to storing it for future use. Aided by the new ability to record and duplicate images by means of the camera and other reproduction techniques, the acquisition of certain forms of knowledge now preoccupied crime controllers increasingly.

Significantly, the use of temporary plain-clothes constables in the divisions was not relinquished.[146] Although they were not considered sufficiently competent to engage in investigations, they served as auxiliary patrol forces for the prevention of crime and its detection after commission in areas requiring additional crime fighters or in periods, especially winter, when crime, notably theft, was likely to rise.[147] Temporary service in plain clothes was also valuable as a probationary period for enrolment in the detective police. Conditions of employment, though, continued to be those of ordinary policemen, except for certain special allowances given.

Predictably, the transition effected by Henderson strengthened the identity of detectives as performing a separate function from that of uniformed policemen, but it also strained relations between them. That they received special rates of pay, plain-clothes allowances, and travel expenses aggravated this separation (see Chapter 3). For their part, divisional detectives resented having to take orders from uniformed officers who were 'absolutely ignorant of detective work' and who often assigned the detectives to trivial or non-detective tasks.[148] The changes also introduced the distinction between the prestigious group of detectives at police headquarters—popularly known as Scotland Yard—numbering twenty-six in 1869—and the divisional detectives.[149] This was partly a consequence of the considerable amount of patrolling entailed in divisional work.[150] By contrast, detectives in the central office did little preventive work and customarily handled the 'higher classes of crime' in the metropolis and at times in the provinces, such as murder and other violent crimes, swindling, forgery, and turf fraud, extradition cases and missing persons, government and other official inquiries, and assignments for foreign governments as well. It also carried out investigations of a non-criminal nature—for example, applications of foreigners for naturalization.[151] Moreover, the central team intervened in local crime when the commissioner decided that the divisional detectives were unable to resolve it, when inquiries had to be made in several divisions simultaneously, or when the seriousness of the crime demanded special treatment. Divisional detectives viewed Scotland Yard men who were sent to help them as 'interlopers' and tended to keep back relevant information,[152] aggrieved that, while they provided the necessary local background for uncovering cases, Scotland Yard men took the credit and the rewards.[153]

The passage of the Habitual Criminals Act in 1869 and the Prevention of Crimes Act in 1871, which tightened control over criminals after their release from prison and required more systematic records of convicted persons (including the use of photography), imposed greater responsibilities on officers specializing in fighting crime.[154] Additionally, more or less from this period, as shown by Stephen Petrow in his research on the Metropolitan Police, officers both in uniform and in plain clothes were tasked with greater supervision and suppression of behaviour regarded by some pressure groups as immoral, such as prostitution, drunkenness, and betting.[155] In the light of these added duties, the new divisional detective system began to elicit considerable criticism from police officials, who felt that it did not function effectively. Apart from pinpointing the detrimental effects of the 'spirit of rivalry' and 'jealousy' on the efficacy of the force,[156] senior officers were concerned that, as an outcome of the decentralized structure and the localization of investigations, each division acted as a separate unit, with little cooperation or exchange of information between them.[157] This trend was accentuated by the practice of ceasing surveillance of a suspect beyond the bounds of the division unless the detective found that the suspect was about to commit an offence.[158] Yet, little was done to modify the newly instituted organizational format.

Then, in 1877, a shocking revelation confirmed what the public had initially feared: corrupt practices, including the collusion of the police with criminals, were endemic in the very group considered the elite of all detectives in the land. To the dismay of both police officials and the rank and file, three chief inspectors (a rank introduced in 1868)—Nathaniel Druscovich, William Palmer, and George Clarke—and Inspector John Meiklejohn, all four from the detective department at Scotland Yard, were suspected of fraud, forgery, and receipt of bribes, and of warning perpetrators of intended police action. During the trial, witnesses accused many more detectives, some from the City of London Police, of bribe-taking.[159] All were exposed as a result of disclosures by convicts about a turf swindle in which the police were deeply embroiled. The lengthy trial in the Old Bailey (24 October–20 November 1877) provoked intense public interest. The court was packed (see Figure 1) and hundreds of people assembled in the streets 'in the expectation of seeing the eminent inspectors arrive in the van in which they had so often conducted other prisoners in the course of their long career in the police service'.[160] Three of the four senior officers were sentenced to two years' hard labour; Clarke, who was second in command at Scotland Yard, was acquitted. The disclosures left a stigma on the reputation of all detectives (see Chapter 5), especially when it became known that all were veteran officers (Clarke had been in the service for thirty-seven years, Palmer for twenty-two, Druscovich for sixteen, and Meiklejohn for thirteen),[161] and that the practices had been ongoing for several years.

The trial precipitated the formation of yet another commission of inquiry by the Home Office, this time concentrating on the Metropolitan Police detective force, although detailed testimony about detective departments in several other big cities and in the City of London Police was also heard. The Departmental Commission on the State, Discipline, and Organisation of the Detective Force of the Metropolitan Police (1878) began its sessions only a few days after the end of the trial and sat for two months hearing accusations about defects in the system of detection and recommendations for amelioration. The substance of the commission's final recommendations was greater centralization of control and information in the Metropolitan detective branch, some even suggesting that the detective force at the

Figure 1. 'Trial of the Detectives at the Old Bailey', *Illustrated London News*, 3 Nov. 1877.

commissioner's office should become the detective agency of the entire country.[162]

The ensuing reorganization, which fixed the distinctive structural features of the detective system in the Metropolitan Police, was carried out by Howard Vincent, whose appointment as director of the newly formed Criminal Investigation Department (CID) on 6 March 1878 came as a surprise. The son of a baronet, Vincent was a barrister and a journalist, inexperienced in police matters and, at 29, young for the job.[163] He won the appointment after taking the initiative of going to Paris to study the French detective system and drafting a report in which he recommended it as a prototype worthy of adoption. His intimate acquaintance with persons with good connections helped as well.[164] A strong advocate of centralization, Vincent worked out plans to unify the entire detective network in the Metropolitan Police under his directorship.[165] Frederick Adolphus Williamson, in charge of the coterie at Scotland Yard, was appointed its superintendent. Notably, the title of the restructured department—CID—by which it was famously known thereafter, contained no mention of the word 'detective'.[166] Detective forces in provincial towns occasionally used the same appellation.

Vincent's scheme again illuminated the underlying tension between the uniformed and the detective branches of the Metropolitan Police. Aside from the higher remuneration received by detectives,[167] a major bone of contention was control over divisional detectives, which was taken out of the hands of the divisional superintendents. Fighting for their authority and status, the divisional superintendents presented a complaint against this decision and announced that they could not be responsible for tracking criminals in their districts.[168] Ultimately, a compromise course was adopted, which retained the decentralized system in London, but with greater control by Scotland Yard.

Some of the senior police officers who appeared before the commission in 1877, including Commissioner Henderson and Assistant Commissioner Colonel D. W. Labalmondrière, called for a reduction in the number of detectives with the aim of releasing them from patrol work and assigning them to inquiries alone.[169] Nonetheless, the size of the detective force continued to grow, albeit not significantly. In 1879, the entire CID in the Metropolitan Police comprised 267 men in a total force of about 11,000 officers.[170] Only some thirty officers made up the central force. Over the next ten years the CID reached about 300 in a force of just over 14,000.[171] Ten per cent were attached to the central office, and about ten or twelve men were employed in most divisions, each of which might extend to 70 or 80 square miles.[172] In addition, it was customary to appoint uniformed men to work in plain clothes under the direction of CID officers in what were called 'winter patrols' from 1 October to 31 March, not to investigate crime, but 'to keep...eyes open for any suspicious job—little or big—that may *need* investigating'.[173] Provisional appointees, these officers rendered the system elastic, as the detective force could be augmented, if necessary, by several hundred men.[174] Uniformed officers were asked to remove their uniform and help detectives in their work, including the odd investigation.[175]

THE GROWTH OF PUBLIC DETECTION IN PROVINCIAL ENGLAND

Meanwhile, despite substantial and prolonged opposition, organized and regularly paid police forces slowly and haphazardly spread over the landscape. The Municipal Corporations Act of 1835 required the formation of a police force in each of the incorporated boroughs. The County Police Acts of 1839 and 1840 enabled justices to establish a paid police force in rural England and Wales. Yet only the passage of the County and Borough Police Act of 1856 made police forces mandatory in every county in England and Wales. All these acts had been fiercely opposed by long-standing arguments that a changed police force would be expensive, centralized, and interventionist, it would resemble continental spy networks, and it would pose a threat to local institutions.[176] Generally, the rural gentry and magistrates were more hostile than their urban counterparts to a comprehensive police system, and modifications were more likely to be introduced first in urban districts.[177] Still, even before the acts were passed, a consensus emerged among the provincial elites in support of some form of police reorganization.[178] This endorsement strengthened during the 1830s and 1840s when, in addition to looming worries about rising crime rates, social turmoil mounted throughout the country.[179] The implementation of the Poor Law Amendment Act of 1834 (allowing relief only to inhabitants of workhouses and not as a family minimum wage, as previously) itself fomented numerous uprisings, which the newly established Metropolitan Police force was summoned to quell. The Act also increased the number of vagrants—long regarded as incipient, if not actual, criminals.[180] The late 1830s saw the advent of the Chartist movement for political reform (principally calling for the extension of the vote to all adult males), which embodied pent-up anger that exploded periodically in ways that augured the prospect of a general upheaval. There were also other large-scale public disorders that parish constables could not handle.[181] Even then, many members of the propertied classes still favoured doing no more than ameliorating the existing machinery of law enforcement. Gradually, however, resistance to a new police system abated.[182] By the late 1850s, only very small communities had no resident policemen.[183] The total number of police forces in England and Wales was 239.[184]

The formation of a national network of professional police forces, all centrally run, was part of a series of broader shifts in the criminal justice system in Britain. As far back as the later eighteenth century, some publicists argued against the use of discretion and the prevalent randomness in sentencing procedures, and criticized the 'Bloody Code' as inhumane and unlikely to deter.[185] Increasingly, preference was expressed for a more moderate criminal law and penal policy and for making punishment fit the severity of the crime. These discourses would become louder in the early nineteenth century, side by side with a reduction in capital offences, hangings, shaming punishments, and the public display of corporal penalties. In 1868 public hangings were abolished and executions were thereafter carried out inside prisons, although still carried out in front of witnesses to ensure fair play. Incarceration progressively became the principal form of punishment for serious crime and a tool for attempting to change the behaviour of offenders. Better policing was widely believed to diminish the need for severe and indiscriminate penalization. In tandem, growing pressure was exerted by some urban and rural leaders to ensure the capture of offenders, which called not only for a new police reconfiguration in all areas, but also for more crime investigation.

London pioneered many of the changes in criminal justice institutions in the country. The novel Metropolitan Police force, though not an improvement on previous police arrangements in every respect, became the paradigm of a civilian, preventive, uniformed, salaried, and systematic police force that was carried over to other parts of the country. The thrust of its responsibilities revolved around patrol and maintaining order; crime detection occupied only a small fraction of police resources.[186] In one significant respect, however, the London model was not adopted outside the capital. Although Home Secretary Robert Peel and Edwin Chadwick intended to augment national power and set up a state police system, the local authorities in the boroughs, counties, and the City of London succeeded in preserving their governance over the police in their respective areas, even if the County and Boroughs Act of 1856 entitled the Home Office to a measure of central inspection.[187] The Metropolitan Police was actually the only force accountable to the central government. This was another example of the pattern of compromise that typified police reform in England. The implication of this arrangement was that provincial detectives, unlike their counterparts in the Metropolitan Police, were not state employees, and were subject to the expectations and decisions of the local authorities.

Some provincial leaders 'thought detection the best form of protection', mainly as it was cheaper than prevention,[188] but, while the size of the uniformed contingent grew at a rapid pace alongside the expansion of the urban population (which in mid-century exceeded that of rural England for the first time), the number of designated detectives remained small. Police forces varied greatly in the amount of manpower devoted to investigative tasks, but the rural areas proved the slowest not only in adopting regulated policing mechanisms generally, but also in making provisions for more professional crime investigation. In fact, throughout the period, fully-fledged detective departments were confined to a few urban centres only.

Some villages had only a single policeman, who did all the necessary work demanded of police officers—preventive and detective. Even in larger communities there was hardly any distinction between ordinary police work and detective work, as had been the situation in London in the embryonic stages of the modern police. When required, uniformed policemen would be asked to perform plainclothes duties, such as conducting investigations or following offenders, and then revert to their uniformed duties.[189] Their general policing knowledge was deemed suitable to deal with this type of law enforcement. In any event, the anonymity of detectives was virtually an impossibility in small communities where everyone was known. In cases where a more professional approach seemed unavoidable, the policemen who stood out as particularly competent would be entrusted with investigative assignments, supervised by senior officers. In this way, even if not employed as full-time detectives, such officers would acquire some expertise in discharging detective tasks. Otherwise, the officers in charge of divisions, assisted by their immediate subordinates, did all the criminal investigative work.[190] In some small boroughs the police head himself took it on. In a number of forces an officer at the headquarters was specially employed for detective duties.

Provincial officers would thus shift between uniformed and what in some cities would be considered detective duties, depending on local circumstances. They mainly kept public order but also filled social-welfare functions, such as serving as poor-law relieving officers, inspecting weights and measures, extinguishing fires, directing strangers who lost their way, and restoring lost children to their anxious parents. These tasks were combined with monitoring thieves and their haunts, visiting public and lodging houses, tracking perpetrators of crime, and investigating burglaries, housebreaking, highway robberies, pickpocketing, petty theft, thefts from farmhouses, poaching, serious felonies committed by tramps, swindlings, forgeries, counterfeits, baby farming, holdups of mail coaches, farm fires, breaking up gangs of thieves and poachers, attending police courts, and accompanying royalty on their tours of the country.[191]

Some large urban forces, such as Manchester, Birmingham, Leeds, and Liverpool, decided that the number of criminal cases in their area justified detective specialization and formed permanent squads of detectives more or less concomitantly with the Metropolitan Police.[192] In such large communities, anonymity was more feasible and therefore conducive to catching offenders in the act and more efficient crime investigation. As in London, each squad initially had only a handful of detectives (Leeds, for example, had three),[193] located at headquarters. In the following decades, with the decline of the Chartist movement, when fears of a major upheaval receded and more stress was put on stemming ordinary crime, the idea of detection spread to other cities and large towns. Existing detective departments expanded, but the overriding reliance of the police on the prevention of crime and uniformed police, and perhaps the desire to cap costs of prosecutions, kept these units small.[194] In 1877, the police in Birmingham accorded 16 of their 520 officers the title of detective, in Liverpool 28 of 1,200, and in Leeds 11 of 355.[195] The City of London Police, operating in the financial centre of the world, had 77 detectives in a force of 796 (though the figure of 77 included plainclothes patrolmen who were not detective constables).[196]

As in the Metropolitan Police, the ultimate purpose of police detection was to capture and convict criminals.[197] Yet, here, too, no single function encompassed the essence of police detection. It was commonly accepted all over the country that 'the principal duty of a Detective Officer is the investigation of and inquiry into criminal cases',[198] but that, in order to be effective in their work, detectives (particularly of the lower ranks) had to 'make themselves well acquainted with all the criminals in their districts, their associates, habits, places of resort, and residences'.[199] Patrolling without a specific suspect or offence on hand also absorbed much of the detectives' work time.[200] Initially, the definition of who was a detective, and what 'purely detective duties' were, differed in the various forces that had detective units. In Birmingham in the late 1870s, for example, such duties referred solely to investigations of crime—that is, following up cases after they had been reported, whether by headquarter or divisional detectives.[201] Only on special occasions, such as on market days when the streets were crowded, or at races and other large gatherings when pickpockets were likely to circulate, did Birmingham detectives go out on patrol.[202] The Leeds Police differentiated between 'strict detective staff', who were always in plain clothes and mostly reserved for inquiries, and temporary 'divisional plain-clothes men', who were employed in patrolling and the supervision of places that were the resort 'of bad characters'.[203] In Liverpool in the same period detectives were bolstered by an 'auxiliary' detective staff of eight constables, most of whom did not engage in 'thief-catching', but undertook special duties, such as serving as the court usher or court messenger.[204] Increasingly, however, most detectives mixed different kinds of preventive and reactive tasks and also engaged in some patrolling. Most large forces employed fully-fledged detectives in the central office as well as in the divisions. The detective staff at headquarters was mostly recruited from the divisional detectives.[205] As in London, the central contingent was likely to inquire into serious offences and supervise detective work in the entire force. When necessary, uniformed officers would fulfil detective duties in plain clothes.

Provincial detectives gave some assistance to neighbouring forces that had no detectives.[206] Occasionally they exchanged information about criminals and their modus operandi,[207] helped detectives in other forces conduct investigations outside their jurisdiction,[208] and fought a common adversary, such as Irish terrorists. By and large, however, despite the spread of the railways, which facilitated greater mobility for police and criminals alike, cooperation between the different forces was limited. The exception was Scotland Yard. At certain times, such as during the Great Exhibition of 1851, provincial detectives would come to London to lend support,[209] but, usually, movement was in the other direction. This was where real professionalism was expected to be found. Even before 1842, Metropolitan policemen would be invited to investigate crimes outside London.[210] With the establishment of an official detective department at Scotland Yard, and the reputation it acquired as an elite force, communities with and without police detectives applied to the Yard for aid in serious and unsolved cases.[211]

People unconnected to the criminal justice system, too, thought it natural to seek its assistance. Samuel Kent, an affluent factory inspector and the father of the murdered boy in the famous Road Hill House murder case, begged that a London detective be sent to investigate the incident on the very day the body was found (30 June 1860).[212] The local superintendent, however, objected. His attitude was not uncommon. Provincial officers, although lacking the experience of officers from the metropolis, resented the aura of the Yard detectives, which belittled their own professional standing and prestige, especially when in certain well-publicized cases the London investigators attained results where they had failed.[213] Indeed, by the time Detective Inspector Jonathan Whicher of Scotland Yard arrived to investigate the murder at the Road Hill House—two weeks later—some of the clues had been destroyed. Yet, he was the one to discover the culprit.[214] Provincial detectives themselves testified that their colleagues could be unprofessional—for example, in removing a knife from the fingers of a dead woman rather than leaving it for examination by an expert.[215] They, therefore, continued to call upon the Yard, even if at times belatedly and grudgingly. Howard Vincent pointed out in 1879 that about a quarter of the work of the Metropolitan Police in the detection of crime related to 'provincial business'.[216] In time, however, the large provincial forces developed greater investigative skills.

THE CONSOLIDATION OF THE POLICE DETECTIVE'S ROLE

The emergence of detective squads in London and in provincial England, however constrained, and the extension of professional aid by designated police detectives to areas devoid of such skills, gradually established police detection as a distinct and recognized vocation. Organizationally, detectives were not set apart from other policemen. Further, detectives could not necessarily be equated with plain-clothes attire or with crime investigations alone, for there were plain-clothes policemen who were not detectives, and most detectives undertook preventive tasks alongside uniformed officers. Nevertheless, concomitant with the growing sense of corporate identity among policemen during the 1870s, detectives came to be seen as forming an occupational entity on its own.[217] The 1878 commission, convened in late 1877 (see above), had certainly looked 'at the detection of crime as a separate question altogether from the protection of the town and the preservation of order'.[218] Increasingly, uniformed policemen were perceived as unskilled in the 'detective instinct', so that their participation in crime investigation ended up with the loss of valuable time in tracking fugitive criminals and 'terrible bungling in the observation of little points of the utmost value as circumstantial evidence'.[219]

Most probably the majority of crimes in the land were unreported. Large sections of the population still refrained from recourse to the law. Many employers preferred to discipline and punish workplace offences, such as embezzlement and other acts of fraud, through internal mechanisms of justice, and many workers continued to settle personal disputes informally out of court.[220] Moreover, victims still depended heavily on private forms of detection. In fact, the number of private agencies actually rose in the latter part of the century, although none could be compared with the gigantic concern of the Pinkerton Brothers in America.[221] As an article in *Reynolds's News* surmised: 'It is doubtful if the public here would permit such a bureau of espionage to be controlled by private individuals.'[222] Some associations for the prosecution of felons continued their activity, though greatly diminished in number,[223] and the press kept carrying advertisements by private individuals who harboured grievances. However, the trend was towards greater official involvement in crime control and a differentiation in status between private and public detection. Although, owing to official efforts to save costs, the total number of prosecutions remained constant from 1857, police forces gradually took over their management and expense, and 'citizens increasingly oriented their complaints to the state and less frequently organised private responses or took steps on their own behalf'.[224] In 1880, the first director of public prosecutions was appointed, mainly to decide difficult cases. Even the working classes, who were generally sceptical of the official enforcement machinery, progressively took more advantage of it 'to prosecute thefts of private property', violent crimes, and other offences.[225] The law was becoming more available to people with few resources. If anything, private individuals and firms even paid for special services carried out by the public police. Although police instruction books time and again warned against permitting 'any enquiry of a private nature to be made', police detectives (and uniformed officers), with or without the consent of their superiors, worked for private people while in service and were at times officially loaned to companies, including the railways, for long periods of time.[226] All this testifies to the expansion of public policing into private arenas.[227]

Several factors helped reinforce the position of police detectives in society: a decline in the crime rate in the latter part of the century and the ensuing feeling of greater security among respectable people,[228] and the passage of additional laws such as the Criminal Law Amendment Act of 1885, which gave police, including detectives, new powers (in this case over prostitutes and homosexuals). Moreover, a new, widely disseminated image of the criminal as a professional implied the necessity for more sophisticated skills on the part of crime fighters.[229] Although by the late 1870s many detectives still had not incorporated such fundamental procedures as how to prevent confidential information from leaking to criminals, or how to shield the identity of informants,[230] nevertheless, a certain corpus of dos and don'ts had accrued. The circulation of senior officers with substantial detective experience, mainly from London, in the hierarchies of the various forces introduced basic detective practices and modes of operation.

In contrast to the Continent, where the detective branch was typically a distinct group 'working independently of the uniformed force and having little connection with its organization', in Britain the two branches were integrated, as were proactive and investigative tasks.[231] Reflecting the decentralized structure of the British police as a whole, where officers dealt with all manner of crime, the detective system was overall not conducive to the specialization of tasks. Here and there, certain detectives did develop special capabilities in specific areas, as did the criminals. The head constable of the Liverpool police observed in 1877 that some detectives were 'adapted more for one case than for another, one picks up a pickpocket, another goes in for a serious burglary, another goes into a bad Post Office case, and so on'.[232] Detective Inspector William Cozens of the same force acquired several specialities during his thirty-seven years of service (he joined as a constable in 1846), among them conducting police prosecutions in the police court and handling arson cases.[233] Other detectives—for example, W. Suckling of Birmingham—were in charge of betting and turf fraud cases.[234] Yet, these proficiencies were random, a product of local circumstances, chance experience, and perhaps natural inclination, rather than part of a built-in infrastructure.

THE SINGULARITY OF SCOTLAND YARD

A more systematic approach to expertise in crime detection did evolve, however, in Scotland Yard. One Yard man became a specialist in indecent literature and another in stage and theatre thefts.[235]

George Clarke (who was tried and acquitted in the scandal of 1877) had developed expertise in turf fraud cases. Detective John Taylor, known as 'Jack the Sleuthhound', confined himself almost exclusively to cases of housebreaking and burglaries.[236] Others specialized in company fraud, forgery, and coinage matters and in white slave trafficking.[237] In the process of trial and error, certain specialities took on an organized procedure and became the basis for departmental subsections.[238] Placing a premium on data collection and a knowledge of repeat criminals in order to single out such criminals and predict subsequent criminal behaviour, efforts were invested in devising methods for the retrieval of information. At first, the identification of criminals relied principally on the retentive ability of individual detectives, but, with the growing need to maintain surveillance of discharged criminals, the police tried new ways to classify and store information, leading to the formation of various repositories. Police forces aside from Scotland Yard also experimented with record-keeping and the organization and dissemination of knowledge about criminals,[239] but, as with many other facets of crime detection, Scotland Yard led the way. In 1880, a Convict Supervision Office was formed as part of the CID to deal with habitual criminals and supervise them after their release from prison, focusing on the collection of photographs (considered representations of the 'truth') and physiological and biographical records of recidivists and making them available to all borough and county forces.[240] By 1889, this office employed thirteen detectives.[241] From 1883 the Metropolitan Police took over from the Bow Street court responsibility for the regular circulation in the *Police Gazette* of particulars about crime, including wanted and apprehended criminals, throughout police forces in the country.[242] Such advances contributed to the emergence of Scotland Yard as an informal national resource. Not only did its staff provide expertise in provincial investigations, but it also kept a record of all known criminals in the country and acted as a clearinghouse for information and a centre of communications for the entire Metropolitan Police as well as for other forces.[243]

Nonetheless, the Yard faced difficult challenges during the 1880s. Intensive Irish terrorism during the first half of the decade, and the striking failure to identify Jack the Ripper in the latter part of the decade, hurt its reputation (see Chapter 5). The Metropolitan Police was governed in 1886–8 by Commissioner Charles Warren, who was no friend of the detective concept, opting instead to strengthen the uniformed force, although he was succeeded by James Monro (1888–90), who was a strong supporter of the detective branch.[244] Despite the adoption of new devices for the storage and transfer of knowledge, these advances were not advantageous in apprehending offenders in situations where no witness to the crime came forward. Although segments of information were coded in various ways (for example, classification by type of crime or distinctive physical marks, or listing criminals in alphabetical order) and collated in printed and visual portraits, the sheer volume of the data amassed over time limited its usefulness, as it inhibited quick and easy retrieval.[245] Additionally, identification based on personal recognition was bound to lead to errors.[246] On the whole, while in the vanguard nationwide, Scotland Yard was far from a pathfinder in 'the high science of modern crime-detection' and was widely regarded at the time as 'slow to adopt innovations' in comparison with various continental powers.[247] As methods of commission of crime became more refined, this backwardness was a serious check on crime control.

Nevertheless, Scotland Yard preserved its singular position in the English detective world and contributed significantly to the professionalization of the occupation. Although lagging behind the French and several other countries, in 1894 it adopted Alphonse Bertillon's anthropometric method of identification of criminals—namely, measuring certain parts of the body of the criminal to form a unique portrait (see Figure 2)—a reflection of the contemporary 'scientific' trend to identify common traits and hidden criminal tendencies in the criminal's physique.[248] The Habitual Criminals Registry, a central depository of criminal records that also employed forensic methods, was moved from the Home Office to the Yard in 1896 but served the entire country.[249]

Most importantly, a fingerprint bureau was created at Scotland Yard in 1901 and spread the knowledge of this technique to other parts of the country. At last, an (almost) infallible and succinctly stored proof of identity was available to English crime fighters. This greatly bolstered the English legal system, whose representatives time and again reiterated the necessity that the prosecution prove guilt beyond a reasonable doubt.[250] In fact, the notion that each individual was marked by unique papillary ridges, and the ability to authenticate personal identity through fingerprinting, were not new. A system of fingerprint identification of criminals developed by British scientists had been deployed in India in the latter half of the nineteenth

THE SYSTEM OF "ANTHROPOMETRY."

Figure 2. 'The System of Anthropometry', *Windsor Magazine*, 6 (June 1897).

century.[251] From the mid-1890s it was used in England alongside Bertillonage and other methods. Edward Henry, who was appointed assistant commissioner in charge of the CID in 1901, and became the commissioner in 1903, brought with him a more workable classification of fingerprint patterns from his service in India, a system he had helped develop while working in Bengal as inspector general of police.[252] At first it was viewed with scepticism by detectives and the public alike, but in 1905 it was accepted as irrefutable evidence in convicting and hanging the murderers of the owner of a paint shop and his wife in Deptford.[253] The Bertillonage system was henceforth discarded and the number of identifications by fingerprinting rose markedly. Fingerprint analysts, appointed on account of their speed, good eyesight, interest in their work, and mathematical and technical training, became specialists in their field.[254] Other techniques for identifying criminals were also proposed from time to time,[255] but the fingerprinters' proficiency proved to be so effective that police officials from all over the world came to train at Scotland Yard, which was thus responsible for the dissemination of fingerprinting worldwide.[256]

A SECRET POLICE BUREAU AFTER ALL

A milestone in the development of Scotland Yard as a centre of competence was the formation of a special unit that laid the groundwork for what would be known in time as the Special Branch, whose specific province was political crime. Unlike the practice on the Continent, the British detective system did not tend to organize separate units focused on particular types of crime. The Special Branch, however, was an exception. First called the Irish Branch or Irish Brigade, it was formed on 20 March 1883 by the Liberal Home Secretary William Vernon Harcourt as a subsection of the CID with the primary aim of suppressing Irish terrorist acts. In the past, the tasks of investigating political crime and protecting royalty and ministers of the Crown were initially discharged by the Bow Street Runners and later by detectives in the newly formed police forces as part of their other responsibilities. Except for a period in the 1850s when several Yard detectives were assigned the task of keeping watch on alien revolutionaries, usually in response to inquiries by other governments, no distinct unit existed for political purposes, although such an option was discussed by the 1868 committee.[257] After all, English police detectives preferred to be 'more earnest in their repression of small [property] crimes'.[258] The work of the Special Branch, in dealing explicitly with threats to establishment figures, to the elite in power, and to national security, 'was a thing apart, quite distinct from the ordinary criminal detection departments', a member of the Branch was to write years later, although the Home Office insisted at the time that it dealt with ordinary crime.[259] Its formation was perhaps the clearest sign of the acceptance of police detection in England, as tackling political crime was assumed to be the most 'unobtrusive' and 'unsuspected' and therefore secretive type of police activity.[260] It was impelled by the cumulative effects of events in the early 1880s that shattered the feeling of sanguinity of Victorian Britain and tilted the balance in favour of an institution present in many continental societies but shunned by the British authorities until then.

After more than a quarter of a century of relative quiet, during which most revolutionary activity in Britain was confined to clubs frequented by foreign refugees, the home-grown political scene awakened to the proliferation of socialist and anarchist groups calling for the radical transformation of the prevailing economic and political system. Although they were initially small numerically, the very founding of these groups, which made increasing inroads in the indigenous community, signified a rising tide of popular discontent in Britain, which from the mid-1870s until the mid-1890s was in the midst of an economic depression. At first, their fiery rhetoric was not interpreted by those in charge of public safety as constituting a hazard to the British government or to social stability,[261] but it did give rise to a climate of opinion more favourable to stiffened policing means. This was evoked in particular by the terminology of the firebrands, which was similar to that used at the time by groups responsible for the assassination of the Russian tsar in 1881 and several attempted assassinations of other heads of state and politicians on the Continent. As part of reinforced measures by the police, CID detectives, who until then had not been especially occupied by tailing revolutionaries, conducted inquiries into their whereabouts and helped convict several foreigners for seditious libel in 1881–2.[262]

Yet, the type of militancy displayed by the nascent variants of socialism on British soil was not in itself sufficient to promote drastic changes in policing at this stage, when liberal sentiments still governed attitudes to law enforcement. The major impetus behind the deployment of stricter undercover methods in an organized and exclusive fashion was the escalation of ominous activism by unbridled representatives of an old enemy—the Irish national movement. During the first half of the 1880s, following a period of relative lull, Irish extremists embarked on an intensive and indiscriminate campaign of terror on the British mainland, mainly concocted in the USA. The decade started with a gunpowder explosion at Salford Infantry Barracks in Manchester (14 January 1881), followed by a bombing at the barracks at Chester (7 May 1881), and the police station (16 May 1881) and Town Hall in Liverpool (10 June 1881). The Mansion House in London (seat of the City's lord mayor) was another target in 1881 (and again in 1882), albeit abortive. On 6 May 1882 Lord Frederick Cavendish, the new chief secretary, and Thomas Henry Burke, permanent under-secretary at Dublin Castle, were stabbed to death in Phoenix Park in Dublin. The years 1883 to the beginning of 1885 saw a series of bomb explosions, first in Glasgow (20 January 1883) and then in major strategic sites and symbols of authority in London, including the offices of *The Times*, the Local Government Board, and other government buildings on Parliament Street (15 March 1883), and, after the creation of the Irish Branch, in two underground stations (30 October 1883), the Victoria terminus (26 February 1884), the Carlton Club (30 May 1884), London Bridge (13 December 1884), and the Tower of London and the House of Commons (24 January 1885). Some of the bombs did not detonate, others caused some damage, while others cost lives and inflicted injuries and considerable material harm.

The press was filled with stories about the outrages, the attempts, and further plots and conspiracies, all of which exposed the limited ability of the police to carry out their task of safeguarding society. Particularly embarrassing was the explosion on 30 May 1884 in the building housing the headquarters of Scotland Yard itself, with the dynamite placed in a public urinal located under the room occupied by the Irish Branch. Human lives were spared, since the Yard's offices were empty at the time (only one constable was slightly injured), but this did nothing to stem the flood of criticism aimed at the detective department for a gross lack of vigilance.[263] The employment of dynamite—the explosive invented by the Swedish industrialist Alfred Nobel in the 1860s—which allowed the perpetrators time to deposit the device and leave the area unharmed—made these terrorists appear all the more potent. An attempt on the life of Queen Victoria in March 1882, albeit by a madman who used the traditional pistol, and was caught, did little to assure the British public that its own royal head was safe.

In the face of reinvigorated enemies and the destructive might of the new technique of political warfare, a growing number of officials and public figures came to the conclusion that, to be effective in preventing political violence and detecting perpetrators, police control had to be more prudent and kept under greater secrecy. They were supported by newspapermen who argued that 'the theory that the main function of the police is to keep order in the streets and regulate the traffic at crossings, and that every duty should be done in the same open fashion, must be given up'.[264]

Detectives in London and in the provincial cities had been customarily trailing and arresting Fenians in the early 1880s,[265] and some sort of Fenian Office was set up at Scotland Yard in 1881 mainly to garner intelligence on Fenian activity in London in cooperation with other individuals and bodies engaged in anti-Fenian pursuits.[266] However, only with the renewal of terrorist acts in London in early 1883 was a decision taken to institutionalize the police struggle against political subversion and build a separate branch within the CID, headed by Chief Superintendent Frederick Williamson. A circular was sent round to the various divisions of the CID asking for recommendations of Irish officers with knowledge of prominent Irish politicians in London to be sent to headquarters.[267] Twelve officers were chosen, and a special room was assigned to them on the east side of Scotland Yard.[268]

Notwithstanding the atmosphere of impending danger, the idea was not enthusiastically welcomed. Both CID Director Howard Vincent and Williamson himself were unhappy with the expense involved, especially the cost of paying informers.[269] Yet, their hesitation principally stemmed from the long-term aversion to clandestine methods, which still imbued public opinion, the Home Office, and Scotland Yard, whose officials looked upon the formation of the Branch 'as verging on the Continental system' to which they 'were avowedly hostile'.[270] Consequently, Vincent took little interest in its management, leaving it to Williamson, who was uncomfortable with secret law enforcement. James Monro (formerly chief of police in Bengal), who replaced Vincent in 1884 when the latter retired from office to compete for a seat in Parliament, was also unenthusiastic.[271] In view of these misgivings, the Branch was to be 'a temporary arrangement whilst outrages were being committed'.[272] Its manpower was minimal, rising to twenty-two by the summer of 1884.[273]

In fact, the Irish Branch was by no means the only, or even the major, agency dealing with Irish terrorism. A number of other governmental bodies were involved. Even before the early 1880s, the Home Office had operated a network of secret agents who led the offensive under the command of Robert Anderson, later assistant commissioner responsible for the CID (1888–1901), and continued to do so in parallel with the Irish Branch.[274] Members of the Irish Royal Constabulary were brought over from Ireland to lend a hand. In addition, uniformed and plain-clothes constables in London and the provinces routinely fulfilled duties related to the anti-Irish campaign, a good many guarding public buildings and politicians. Over fifty officers (not all of them in plain clothes) were stationed at various ports in Britain and abroad in 1884, working in tandem with the customs authorities to conduct 'a rigorous search of passenger baggage' and intercept explosives or identify Irish revolutionaries who attempted to enter the country.[275]

Perhaps partly as a result of this anti-terrorist front, the outrages receded during 1885. Since quite a few officials continued to be inimical to the idea of a political police, for reasons that also included manpower shortages and fiscal restraint,[276] it was 'even proposed to do away' with the Irish Branch altogether.[277] Nevertheless, the Branch acquired a momentum of its own and became a permanent feature of the Metropolitan Police, constituting an acknowledgement of its vital role in matters of internal security. In effect, its power and authority were to be extended. Both Liberal Home Secretary Harcourt and the Conservative home secretaries who followed him wanted to concentrate the anti-Fenian campaign in Scotland Yard, particularly if it imperilled the capital, and at the same time reduce the role of non-police secret agents and policemen who were not members of the Metropolitan Police.[278] These other operatives would assume the role of gathering political intelligence abroad.[279] Provincial forces would continue to take part in counter-subversive endeavours, but Scotland Yard had set the tone and was effectively becoming the centre of counter-terrorist operations in Britain.[280]

In February 1887, the political police force in the central CID was strengthened further with the creation of yet another counter-subversive unit, called the Special Branch (with no other adjective attached). In time, all three sections—the Irish Branch, the Port Police, and the Special Branch—would amalgamate into a single unit. The idea behind the inception of this new section was not only to replace the non-police Irish secret agents, and guard against any attempt on the life of Queen Victoria during her jubilee in 1887, but also to meet the mounting challenge posed by anarchists and other political agitators.[281] Chief Inspector John Littlechild (recruited to the Metropolitan Police in 1869) was taken from the Irish Branch and put at its head. In serving as a national body side by side with the other sections (and other CID officers), and in expanding the range of targeted groups, the Special Branch reinforced the status of Scotland Yard in the country, and its role as a nucleus of expertise.

The periodic suppression of anarchism on the Continent drew followers of the persuasion from nearly every corner of Europe to Britain, mainly to London. During the 1880s it was they, rather than the growing number of home-grown anarchists, who were the principal objects of police monitoring—to a large extent in response, albeit reluctant, to requests for information by foreign governments.

Although as an ideology anarchism had attracted only a handful of British subjects, by 1887 the community of believers was large enough to become a focus of police attention. In as much as anarchist meeting places hosted foreign as well as native activists, the Special Branch watched over both populations. On the whole, the indigenous movement placed primary emphasis on education, and in practice showed little inclination towards aggressive action.[282] But this relatively peaceful situation was interrupted in the winter of 1892 by the sensational news that six anarchists were found in possession of a bomb casting in Walsall, Staffordshire, and were charged with conspiracy to commit an unlawful act.[283] The public was alarmed that the anarchist danger had been brought home. On 15 February 1894, three days after a French anarchist, Émile Henry, had thrown a bomb into the Café Véry in Paris, a bomb exploded in London's Greenwich Park, allegedly planted by Martial Bourdin, a French anarchist who resided in London and was killed in the incident. He was suspected of planning to blow up the Observatory, although his actual motives were never revealed.[284] Between these two events, and immediately thereafter, minor incidents involving militant anarchists, along with recurring bomb scares and the occasional use of violent vocabulary by anarchists in Britain supporting or justifying 'propaganda by the deed', were widely interpreted as portending sinister threats. All this occurred against a background of escalating targeted stabbings and bombings by anarchists overseas as a means of hastening the revolution to come. Such leaders as President of France Sadi Carnot in 1894, Prime Minister of Spain Antonio Cánovas del Castillo in 1897, Empress Elisabeth of Austria in 1898, King Umberto I of Italy in 1900, and President of the United States William McKinley in 1901 were among the victims of anarchist outrages—not all of them known as tyrannical heads of state. Bombs also went off in various public places on the Continent, killing or maiming many innocent bystanders.

Although police vigilance regarding Irish militants lingered on throughout this period,[285] the anarchists now took up a good deal of police energy, involving uniformed officers, detectives in the central offices and the divisions both in London and outside the capital, and members of the Special Branch, although the intensity of such surveillance fluctuated. From the mid-1890s, the low incidence of anarchist felonies and misdemeanours in Britain, and the subsidence of anarchist appeals to emulate or excuse continental terrorists, gradually led the police to relax their scrutiny of native anarchists. However, the rejuvenation of anarchism a decade later, during the pre-war years, elicited renewed police attention. Anarchist papers once more reported 'an extra large number of policemen and detectives' at their meetings[286] and rejections by the police of requests for meeting permits.[287] Activists were again brought to trial, charged with obstruction, meeting without authority, and breach of the peace.[288] Still considered significantly more dangerous than the indigenous contingents,[289] foreign anarchists and other revolutionaries of varied nationalities who continued to seek asylum in Britain in large numbers were watched covertly by the Branch during this period.[290] Several criminal incidents involving foreigners associated with revolutionary activities both in Britain and abroad, which caused the death and injury of policemen and civilians and filled newspaper columns, confirmed the need for intense police vigilance.[291]

The presence of a large population of foreigners in Britain posed a problem for Branch detectives in yet another sphere: foreign spies, most prominently from Imperial Russia, whose activities did not necessarily agree with the priorities of the Branch or of the British government.[292] In the immediate pre-war period, the Branch also had to root out German spies, who threatened both the internal and external security of the country.[293] Exaggerated press reports and stories about their profusion and potential harm imposed extra duties on the overworked Branch, although it was not the only organization dealing with counter-espionage (MO5, the predecessor of MI5, was formed in 1909).[294]

The empire itself generated security issues not only overseas but also in Britain. For a long time, Irish republicanism was the primary source of such concerns in England, but in the early twentieth century nationalists from the other major component of the empire—India—demonstrated their own resentment in acts of violence in Britain. On 1 July 1909, Sir William Hutt Curzon Wyllie, a former official of the British Indian Government, was assassinated in London by an Indian student, who also mortally wounded a physician trying to stop him.[295] This outrage turned militant Indians in Britain into another target of the Branch's attention,[296] giving rise to another section in the Special Branch.

The scope of activity and numerical strength of the Branch also grew for purely domestic reasons in the years leading to the First World War. Anti-alien sentiment prevalent in certain social sectors in the wake of the massive immigration from Eastern Europe, mainly of Jews, between 1880 and the First World War, the resurgence of the

Irish question in Ulster, combative industrial protest, and the ascendance of militant suffragism combined to create a sense of acute domestic unrest and the need for heightened protection. While the Special Branch kept an eye on defiant labour activists and on intransigent socialists of varied types to gain intelligence about their intentions (alongside other CID agents and plain-clothes officers),[297] it appeared to be more preoccupied with the movement for women's right to vote. Indeed, in 1909, assessing that the movement was showing 'signs of developing from mere disorderly behaviour into attempts to do actual personal injury', yet another specialized squad was created within the central office, dedicated to the surveillance of bellicose women in London and the provinces.[298] Its aims were to prevent 'molestation of [government] ministers' and shield them from 'insult, annoyance and violence', as well as conduct inquiries 'as to the designs of the leaders and the agents they are likely to employ for militant propaganda purposes'.[299] Towards these ends, Branch officers, alongside other detectives, guarded politicians, trailed activists in the Women's Social and Political Union, searched their premises, intercepted their mail, tapped their telephones, and frequented their meetings and assemblies, reporting what was said.[300] They also assisted uniformed policemen and other detectives in preventing obstructions of the peace and keeping the kind of order mandated by the authorities.

Branch detectives were also required to protect foreign kings and queens who visited Britain, often jointly with the dignitaries' own detectives.[301] Detective Inspector Herbert T. Fitch boasted (in 1936) that 'since the formation of the Special Branch no royal person has ever been hurt in Britain'.[302] Branch detectives also had to keep back 'over zealous loyal subjects' who tried to obtain interviews with their royal sovereigns, inter alia by calling at their domicile or attempting to waylay them when they left their residence.[303] The valuable gifts to royalty and other celebrities had to be guarded as well.[304]

Clearly, the span and ramifications of the activities of the Special Branch broadened significantly in the turbulent pre-war era, although the army and other police forces played an important role in quelling unrest, using their own covert agents. In tandem, the Branch, and therefore Scotland Yard, gained in strength and importance. Sections B and D of the Special Branch comprised 34 members by 1909; the figure rose to over 70 in May 1913, and to 81 in 1914 (plus 33 serving in the ports).[305] Compared to the 700 agents at the end of the First World War, these numbers were not impressive.[306]

Nonetheless, the steady increase evinced a greater determination by the government to defend itself against perceived foes.

POLICE DETECTIVES IN THE PRE-WAR PERIOD

Despite all these modifications, the basic organizational and ideological structure of police detection in England hardly changed in the two or three decades prior to the First World War. On the eve of the war, it was still exclusively an urban phenomenon. Only cities and large towns had their own CIDs, which were assisted by ordinary policemen in plain clothes.[307] Hence, the majority of police forces in Britain had no designated detectives. The overall size of the CID in the country had grown, as had the CID branch in London—the latter from just under 600 detectives in a force of 17,000 in 1908[308] to 729 in a force of over 21,000 (about 48 of them constituting the central office squad) in 1914.[309] However, prevention was still considered the primary duty of the police.[310] Suggestions were made from time to time to establish a national detective force, but 'policing was still a local function', with 'no direction from the centre'.[311] Every detective department remained a law unto itself, with no inbuilt coordination except when voluntary. 'Every chief or head constable has his own methods of . . . tracing and detecting criminals' and is under no obligation to arrest or search for a criminal who has committed a crime in another district, complained *The Times* a year before the outbreak of the war.[312]

In this context, the role of Scotland Yard as a source of information and professional know-how remained essential. This role was solidified in 1906 with the ratification by the Home Office of a plan to set apart five chief inspectors from the central branch (later known as the Big Five) to be on call to help provincial forces solve 'obscure cases of murder or other serious crime' and 'crimes of violence committed in railway trains'.[313] The premiss behind this move was that these forces were 'inexperienced', and that their investigations 'might be misdirected', and important clues lost, if the London CID did not intervene.[314] The Home Office sent circulars to chief constables in the borough and county police forces with details of the plan, and they supported it, although its implementation, and the leverage it gave to the image of the cadre at the head office, stiffened the existing animosity between centre and periphery.

The Yard's methods of linking the criminal to the crime (or vice versa) may not have been the most sophisticated,[315] but the challenges of the new century had enriched the experience of its personnel and deepened their understanding of workable investigative techniques. As more and more foreigners found refuge in Great Britain, a growing number of continental police officers, curious about the paucity of terror in the land, paid visits to the central CID and sought counsel and aid from its staff about detective methods and procedures.[316] This sign of Scotland Yard's international standing, enhanced by similar approaches by detectives from the empire, and by the Yard's expertise in fingerprinting, strengthened its prestige in England and beyond. The Yard's reputation, even if envied or resented by other detectives, spilled over to all police detectives and contributed greatly to a sense of shared vocation. By the outbreak of war, it had long been assumed that, even if private detection had a role to play in society, when crime called for a professional response, official detectives became essential.

This double-edged trademark of English police detection—local diversification on the one hand, and common values and practices across the country on the other—was also reflected in its selection procedures, conditions of service, and occupational culture. Each force with detectives had its own preferences and policies, but broadly they followed a similar trajectory, with London's CID setting the standard. The next two chapters will investigate this employment strategy.

2

FROM BOBBY TO DETECTIVE

The Victorian and Edwardian police did not recruit detectives; they made them. The occupation of detection also existed outside the state system, and individuals who were not policemen but called themselves detectives undertook investigative work for private people and companies as well as for public institutions such as the railway police and HM Customs.[1] However, it was within the modern police establishment that a recognized body of specialized knowledge and professional expertise gradually developed and a type of vocational training came into being. Significantly, police detectives themselves did not start their career as detective trainees; they generally had to spend a substantial period of time as uniformed policemen before being considered for permanent plain-clothes work.

Internal recruitment of detectives was a fundamental principle of the police organization throughout the period under review. Although there was no rule forbidding external recruitment, and the police leadership had the authority to pass over policemen in the search for detectives, the general practice was to rely on available sources within the force. Detective units were initially created in the big cities at mid-century, and in the course of their consolidation some units, mainly the central detective office at Scotland Yard, occasionally admitted outsiders. The topmost positions as well as clerical jobs in detective branches were also sometimes filled externally, but generally police detectives were former uniformed policemen. This norm was to be critical to the development of police detection, as it dictated the entire process of recruitment, which in turn determined the profile of the individual detective and the nature of the detective force as a whole. It also impacted on training, and reflected the police authorities' conception of the substance of the occupation.

The policy of internal recruitment was a component of the overall employment strategy devised by police decision-makers. In effect, no central body made organizational decisions about police detection; rather, local authorities had the discretion to adopt policies suitable to them. However, in many respects the structure and norms of the occupation, whether in London or in the provincial cities and towns, evolved along similar lines. Significantly, the British police force in the Victorian and Edwardian period was among a minority of employers in the country who invested considerable energy in planning and pursuing long-term systematic policies regarding their labour force. Moreover, while most employers in nineteenth-century Britain essentially externalized activity related to the workforce—hiring and firing at will, resorting to outside training, filling supervisory positions by external recruitment, and determining pay and conditions by market forces—the police forces adopted internal labour market techniques. These involved on-the-job training, secure employment, wages not directly influenced by competitive forces in the external market, and jobs within the police force filled by the promotion or transfer of workers who had already gained entry. This style of labour management and rule-based procedures was deployed to varying degrees by other state administrative bodies as well, such as the prison services and the post office, and by some other large public services, such as the railway companies.[2] However, the police applied this approach to labour relations more systematically.

Indeed, a close examination of police culture reveals that the occupation of detection was to a large extent shaped not only in conformance with the priorities of law and order, but also with the type of employee envisaged by the police bureaucracy. More precisely, the interplay between police thinking about the essentials of police detection—duties, targeted populations, and modus operandi—and the needs of the police as an employer, combined to create the image of the desired police detective, the selection process to recruit him, the training he underwent, and his conditions of service.

Curiously, the manpower strategy of the police contained an inherent contradiction. Central to police ideology from the beginning was the notion that detectives should be 'superior in intelligence' to, and more 'competent' than, the preventive branches.[3] If police management emphasized physical strength and a commanding appearance in seeking uniformed policemen,[4] 'intelligence' was the term repeatedly used in referring to the ideal detective recruits.[5] Detectives were expected to be 'shrewd and sharp' and display 'cool judgment', alongside being honest and steadfast.[6] Furthermore, whatever the prerequisite of basic literacy skills in the uniformed branches, undoubtedly, detective work (at least in the levels below chief inspector and superintendent) demanded a much greater reliance on reading and writing and therefore on general education. In fact, the entire apparatus was predicated on paperwork, as will be seen in Chapter 3.

More than any other unit, the detective cadre at Scotland Yard, which came to be viewed as the central detective branch in the Victorian state, was meant to epitomize the attributes associated with first-rate detection. Its members took on the more complex and sensitive crimes, including political investigations, and were therefore expected to be a 'superior class of men...with a certain turn of mind...men of intelligence as to the ways of the world...[who] can bring into a case an amount of knowledge and energy that is not in the division'.[7] This objective presupposed that to meet these standards, Yard detectives had to be 'the more educated type of character'.[8]

Nonetheless, almost all detectives were recruited from the uniformed ranks and had been subject to the same initial selection procedures when applying to police service. Since most uniformed officers had worked in manual labour prior to enlistment, detectives, too, therefore, were drawn nearly entirely from the lower classes of the population, a sector generally deprived in the realm of education.[9] The aim of targeting men of high calibre in the process of selecting detectives thus conflicted with other interests of the police authorities, so that in practice the system of selecting and training detectives was a compromise between several goals. The gap between the ideal and reality, and the fact that the principle of internal enlistment was integral in other basic aspects of police culture, rendered this principle a controversial topic that hovered over the evolution of police detection. An analysis of the ordinary process of recruitment from time of application for police service to appointment as a detective, on the one hand, and the ways in which police leaders reconciled their different priorities, on the other, is crucial to an understanding of the moulding of police detectives, the employment strategies adopted by the authorities, and the calculations that guided them.

To appreciate the resilience of the policy of internal recruitment, an examination of the circumstances in which a small minority of men entered the detective force *without* going through the established sequence of police enlistment is instructive.

MINIMAL EXTERNAL RECRUITMENT

The major reason for external recruitment into detective units was 'the necessity... of having men with a greater knowledge of foreign languages than is generally found in the ordinary police constable'.[10] With better means of transport and greater movement of people across borders in the second half of the nineteenth century, the need to cope with foreign criminal subversion—whether political or other—became more pressing. As a focal point for immigrants and for continental fugitives seeking shelter outside their country, especially after the 1848 revolutions, London in particular demanded personnel who could communicate with non-English-speaking suspects. Even so, whereas provincial police authorities recruited men from the outside only sporadically, the commissioner of the City of London Police, Colonel James Fraser (1858–85), whose detectives regularly went abroad to 'every part of the world', saw no obstacle in sending out men without the knowledge of a foreign language,[11] but, when necessary, hiring external translators. Senior officers of Metropolitan Police divisions inhabited by large foreign populations did advocate employing men who spoke several languages with a view to having them 'mix' with criminals or suspected criminals to 'hear their remarks'.[12] Yet the commissioners thought that linguistic proficiency was indispensable only for the central unit at Scotland Yard, which, apart from meeting the needs of London and the central government, also lent such services to provincial forces.[13]

Aside from dealing with foreigners suspected of crime, and keeping an eye on political refugees, Scotland Yard required agents with a knowledge of languages other than English to handle extradition cases, read documents written in a foreign language, inquire about people who applied for a certificate of naturalization, and conduct inquiries for foreign governments.[14] From time to time they were asked to aid or provide protection to foreigners who spoke no English.[15] Detective Inspector George Hepburn Greenham, who spoke fluent Italian, German, and French, and had some knowledge of other continental languages, was chosen for special duty at the residence of the former French emperor Napoleon III, who lived in exile in England from 1870 (when the Third Republic was proclaimed) until his death in 1873.[16] The work of these linguists also took them abroad to conduct inquiries of all kinds, accompany or bring back suspects or prisoners,[17] carry out surveillance at certain

French ports 'to cover the possible arrival of persons on an official "wanted" list', and escort dignitaries.[18] Greenham, for example, was assigned from 1879 to accompany Queen Victoria whenever she travelled to the Continent.[19]

Outside recruitment for the purpose of hiring people with a knowledge of foreign languages was implemented only for a short time. Begun in the 1860s, it was used sparsely until the report of the select committee on extradition in 1868 and the passage of the Extradition Act in 1870, when it became essential. The Act imposed a great deal of work with foreigners, whether criminals or members of police forces across the seas, at a time when it was difficult to find policemen who knew any foreign language.[20] One of the few exceptions was Nathaniel Druscovich, the son of an Englishwoman and a Moldovian man, who had been educated in England and then went to Wallachia, where he was employed for a while in the British consulate.[21] Druscovich also spent some time on board a trading vessel in the Mediterranean with his uncle, its captain. These experiences endowed him with a knowledge of several languages. However, he was accepted into the Metropolitan Police as an ordinary constable, and patrolled the streets for some twelve months before his special attributes were discovered by his superiors, and he was thereafter engaged in what were considered 'exceptional' or even 'superior' duties. He was first employed at the London World Exhibition of 1862, then as a clerk in the superintendent's office, followed by a job as a clerk in the detective branch at Scotland Yard. There he became a second-class detective sergeant (in 1865). Since a man with such qualifications was rarely found in the ordinary police ranks in the formative years of this detective branch, management was forced to recruit outsiders to do work requiring foreign languages.

The external recruitment of men with linguistic skills declined in the second part of the 1870s. More men were now found in the expanding ranks of uniformed policemen who could join the tiny coterie of linguists.[22] Furthermore, some senior officers in the Metropolitan Police objected in principle to the recruitment of men of foreign origin. James Thomson, superintendent of the E Division during the 1870s (who had served in the small detective group during 1862–9 and mastered several languages),[23] went so far as to oppose such a hiring practice, even if one parent was English, as in the case of Druscovich.[24] Probably influenced by the 1877 trial of Yard detectives who were complicit in the turf fraud, which had ended with the conviction of Druscovich and two other detectives (see Chapter 1),

Thomson claimed that 'foreigners are too cunning and too artful, and they outwit you in the end', and suggested using some of the many foreigners residing in London 'without having them in the police'.[25] Although some men of foreign extraction were employed by the Metropolitan Police on a permanent basis, 'engaged on some big Russian rouble note forgery or other foreign business', Thomson's line of thinking was generally adopted thereafter.[26] Police leaders could employ people temporarily as needed.[27] In any event, police recruits had to be British subjects, and only a small minority of officers were born abroad.[28]

Pressure to seek detective recruits in the public at large had yet another important impetus. Over and above the specific requirement of foreign languages, which by the 1880s had been partially solved by manpower within the police, there was a persistent undercurrent of unease with the quality of serving detectives, which periodically gave rise to considering the alternative of bringing in men from the outside. During the 1840s and 1850s, the small detective force at Scotland Yard was drafted from officers 'considered best qualified in the police force'.[29] Most applicants who wished to become detectives without first joining the uniformed branch were turned down. Yet, the unfolding reality of the establishment of new detective units in the country, and the increasing demands on the detective department in the Metropolitan Police, led some forces to fill a number of vacancies with men who had never worn a uniform but had the potential to improve the quality of the detective workforce.

This divergence from the usual practice heightened debate over recruitment policy. One of the major reasons for the 1878 commission, convened by the Home Office in late 1877, was to examine the pros and cons of this policy and to consider ways of attracting 'intelligence and energy' into the detective branch.[30] The witnesses called up by the commission consisted of the commissioner and one of the assistant commissioners of the Metropolitan Police, the commissioner of the City of London Police, five head constables (of the Birmingham, Bristol, Glasgow, Leeds, and Liverpool police forces), superintendents of divisions in London, and Superintendent Frederick Williamson of the detective department at Scotland Yard (later chief constable), as well as detectives of various ranks in the Metropolitan Police. When asked, all replied that internal recruitment should be continued, although they differed somewhat on the reasons for their support. Moreover, the majority—themselves mostly the product of internal selection—opted to rely on this system unreservedly. Most of those who did criticize the system did not propose replacing it by recruitment from other sources, but only opening recruitment to outsiders as well. Opinions among these critics ranged from a desire to create easier access to all detective units by means of external hiring, to restricting external recruitment to specific units, principally the central office at Scotland Yard. The polemic, therefore, was mainly one of degree.

There was also disagreement over the reasons for enlisting men without police experience. The minimalists, such as Superintendent Frederick Williamson and Major C. B. Greig, head constable of Liverpool, were satisfied with confining outside recruitment to men with familiarity with foreign languages and to 'very exceptional men for very exceptional purposes',[31] and not for the 'ordinary duties of a detective officer'.[32] Others—a small minority—were less restrictive. Concerned about the quality of many of the detectives, they wanted to make the system considerably more flexible in order to raise their calibre. Underpinning their drive was the awareness that the majority of police recruits both in London and in provincial cities and towns came from a background of agricultural labour, without 'very much of that shrewdness and sharpness' required by detectives,[33] or industrial work, with few educational qualifications.[34] George Greenham, one of the rare detectives who had been appointed directly to the detective department at Scotland Yard in 1869, was among the small group of advocates of the advantages of opening up the detective ranks to outsiders. Greenham believed that 'the general area of the public would furnish a better class of detectives than the limited area of the 10,000 men of the [Metropolitan] force'.[35] He had no objection to selecting recruits from the police force, but was convinced that widening the net would contribute 'greater intelligence' and 'greater education', and 'improve the detection of crime'.[36] There was also an awareness that many capable men refrained from applying to the police because they were unwilling to endure the drudgery of an ordinary constable's service.[37] Reinforcing his argument, Greenham noted that detectives 'need to mix themselves with all sorts of society', a task for which lower-class men were not prepared.[38]

A major question raised in this debate was the role of the initial uniformed stage in the training of detectives. The vast majority in the police leadership viewed it as mandatory. Even some who supported external recruitment insisted that all recruits first serve as ordinary constables for a short period.[39] Yet, other 'externalists', among them Greenham, were convinced that such service was redundant for a man 'with fair average intellect from the outside', for he 'would be equally able to pick up this [police] knowledge' by himself, as 'education would go a great deal in his favour'.[40] Edwin Coathupe, head constable of the Bristol Police during the inquiry (and formerly a member of the Yard's detective branch), also believed he had not 'suffered any inconvenience' in carrying out his detective duties 'from not having had the experience of a police constable', as he had acquired the necessary know-how, such as giving evidence and acquiring an awareness of the detective's powers of arrest, on his own.[41] Some commentators felt that the required uniformed phase was not only of no value to educated people; it could actually be disruptive to the performance of detective tasks. In particular, they feared that the time spent in the uniformed branch left such an indelible imprint on the policemen's habits and body language that, when they became detectives, their identity would easily be recognized.[42]

Concern with the quality of detectives was demonstrated by numerous observations of their low level of education both in London and in the provinces by supporters as well as opponents of outside recruitment. Evidence to this effect was amply apparent during the late 1860s and 1870s when low standards of selection at a time of rapid expansion brought in men with deficient literacy skills.[43] Testifying to the 1878 commission, the legal adviser of the commissioner of the Metropolitan Police described the divisional detectives in London as 'the least informed and the least educated' men on the force.[44] Superintendent Williamson attested that, owing to 'their want of education', they were 'useless' to him.[45] 'Very few of them can make a decent report,' he emphasized. Another observer, W. Harris, chief inspector of the Executive Department at Scotland Yard, gave the example of Detective Sergeant Butcher of the C Division, known as 'not a very good penman', who even found it difficult to fulfil the daily chores of writing simple reports in the detective register.[46] He would ask an inspector or a sergeant on duty at the station to make the entry for him, which he then signed. Even the central branch at Scotland Yard, considered 'the upper class of detectives', was not devoid of such problems.[47] High-ranking officers in detective units both in London and in the provincial cities and towns experienced similar handicaps.[48] The superintendent of the detective branch in the Manchester Police force 'could do very little more than write his own name'.[49]

The socio-economic profile of the six detectives accepted without any prior uniformed service into the central branch at Scotland Yard before the formation of the CID in 1878 reveals the type of detective recruit sought. George Greenham (see above) was born in Trieste and his mother was 'a most intimate friend of Queen Murat of Naples' during the queen's residence in Trieste.[50] He studied at the Polytechnic Institute in Vienna for three years, from age 14, and continued his education in England. At 20 he entered a marine engineering firm, where he worked as a draughtsman for ten years. He excelled at drawing, and his sketches appeared in several illustrated papers.[51] Edwin Coathupe (see above) was a qualified surgeon who graduated from the Royal College of Surgeons and was employed by the Apothecaries' Company.[52] James Henry Lambert had been an engineer in the railway service in Russia and, in addition, spoke French and German.[53] The other three were a businessman who had lived in France, a political refugee from a respected French family, and a commercial clerk.[54] As a journalist attested in 1872, these men 'would pass muster fairly enough in any assembly of gentlemen—and gentlemen, of a sort, some of them undoubtedly are'.[55]

Nonetheless, the high expectations from external recruitment did not materialize. Despite their testimonials of 'character and general intelligence' from respectable members of the community,[56] of the six recruited directly into Scotland Yard, one 'gave way to drinking' and committed suicide, another had to be pensioned off early after his health had failed, and another was notable for his 'bad conduct', including excessive drinking, unreliability, and writing false reports.[57] Edwin Coathupe resigned in 1866', after three years of service, when he realized he 'could scarcely exist upon the pay' and had to fall back on his own resources (though he later re-joined the police).[58] The disappointment with well-educated men was not confined to London. The head constable of the Liverpool Police had an unpleasant experience with a clever and educated internal recruit who took to drinking.[59]

In any event, the number of external recruits had always been very small.[60] Clearly, external recruitment was not a serious threat to the standard procedure. Not surprisingly, the final report of the 1878 commission showed unanimous agreement that, while greater inducements should be offered in order to obtain 'a higher and more efficient class of men as detectives', the principle of internal recruitment should be maintained.[61] Nevertheless, the commission left some scope for senior officers to bring in detectives from the outside.[62]

Indeed, it did not take long for Howard Vincent, the first director of the CID (1878–84) and an outside nominee without police experience himself, to exercise the prerogative of inviting certain 'gentlemen of good education and social standing' (including retired army officers) to work for the department without going through the customary procedure of serving as ordinary constables.[63] Convinced that detectives 'are habitually expected to accomplish impossibilities' with 'scanty and inadequate facilities', he believed that he was likely to get 'better and more reliable detectives' from this more sophisticated pool.[64] His step was also informed by a recognition that it is not easy to 'prove the legal guilt of a delinquent', and that detectives ought to possess 'considerable knowledge of the criminal law and practice' as well as 'considerable knowledge of the world, good education, good address, tact and temper'. Moreover, the occasional need for impersonation, mingling with high society, or taking part in gala events of the elite demanded social graces that a village boy lacked.[65] Like his successors, Vincent maintained that the 'best general groundwork' for police detection 'is to be found in the ordinary life of a constable in a large and busy town for two or three years', but in his search for 'good men' his initial instinct was to look for them in social strata above that of the typical policeman.[66] Significantly, he did not recruit more than six men of high social standing. His aim was not to abolish internal enlistment, but only to improve the elite squad—namely, the detectives in Scotland Yard.

However, Vincent's recruitment of gentlemen proved yet another failure. Retrospectively, he and most of his senior officers viewed it as 'eminently unsatisfactory'.[67] None of the six 'gentlemen detectives' had survived in the force for more than three years, about half having left during the first year.[68] On the whole they were found 'less trustworthy, less reliable, and more difficult to control than those who enter a calling such as the police in the ordinary manner'.[69] Years later, Basil Thomson, assistant commissioner of the CID (1913–21), explained that they simply did not 'like the work, loitering about the streets', and some were dismissed because they did not perform well.[70] In conjunction with the previous disappointing results, this experiment had a significant effect in enhancing the system of internal recruitment and reducing opposition to it. The highest positions in detective departments were later sometimes filled by men with no police experience. This was the case with Melville L. Macnaghten, an old Etonian who had been a landlord in Bengal for fifteen years and was then invited by his friend James Monro, assistant commissioner of the Metropolitan Police in charge of the CID, to be his assistant chief constable in 1889.[71] Yet, direct recruitment to the lower levels in effect ended following Vincent's venture.

Nevertheless, criticism of the low calibre of detectives, and attendant challenges to the wisdom of forcing newcomers to start as constables on the beat, continued, mainly on the part of observers outside the police.[72] The shortcomings of the system did not disappear. Literacy was still an issue. One of the superintendents of the London CID during the 1880s was uncertain whether to write the word 'very' with one or two 'r's, according to his boss, Macnaghten.[73] Critics still pointed to the crucial need for secrecy in respect of the detectives' identity and their ability to move unknown in criminal environments, a goal defeated by the reality of an ordinary English constable being 'on show. .. in a policeman's uniform, moving up and down eight hours a day thirteen days every fortnight for three long years in the presence of the criminal classes', as a writer argued in the *Pall Mall Gazette* in 1888.[74] 'By the end of that time', the writer commented, 'when it may be supposed every habitual thief and receiver of stolen goods in London knows his face and voice, he is allowed to become a detective'. Another recurrent, and related, motif was that during the years he served as a uniformed policeman he 'acquired the gait, the manners, and the little character-betraying habits of the constable; so that he can be identified at a glance by any experienced cracksman'. In the view of these critics, the uniformed phase for detectives undermined the effectiveness of police detectives (see Chapter 5).

The possibility of external recruitment resurfaced in the decade before the First World War when Edward Henry was commissioner of the Metropolitan Police (1903–18). Henry had started his career in the Metropolitan Police (in 1901) as an assistant commissioner in charge of the detective branch, and continued to show a deep interest in the department after taking over the commissionership. In light of innovations he introduced, notably the fingerprint system, the aspiration 'for the employment of a superior class of persons' appeared pressing.[75] Official police correspondence from this period is replete with observations that the educational qualifications of constables were 'too low for a Public Service like the Police'.[76]

Henry pleaded for Scotland Yard as a special case. As he explained in a letter to the Home Office, aside from its responsibility for the whole of London, the department was tasked with carrying out a considerable amount of work 'in all parts of the Country and abroad, and acting as a kind of clearing-house for information, and assisting as far as possible the Constabulary and foreign forces'.[77] He reminded the secretary of state for the Home Office that the presentation of criminal cases depended 'almost entirely on the Police enquiry being thoroughly, intelligently and honestly performed'. Detective work, he added, required special skills in dealing with figures and documents, knowledge of criminal law, and 'last but not least...tact and intelligence which will inspire confidence in the public who seek the aid of the department'.

The issue became urgent at that time because the CID suffered from a shortage of suitable candidates, as was the situation in the Metropolitan Police as a whole—a state of affairs partly created as a result of a new policy of granting an extra day's leave a month, and the consequent need to recruit more officers.[78] Henry proposed to raise the standard of candidates by improving the conditions of service and the chances of promotion in the detective department, thus attracting high-quality police officers, but other policy-makers contemplated searching for appropriate candidates outside the police. That the contemporary intellectual climate largely rejected the values of amateurism embodied in the English gentleman in favour of trained professionals, and greater professionalism in public service was sought increasingly,[79] might have influenced them in this direction. Winston Churchill, as home secretary (1910–11), had toyed with the idea of repeating Howard Vincent's earlier experiment in this area, but decided against it when he learnt of its poor results.[80] In 1912, addressing the need for 'really good men' to serve in the CID, the receiver of the Metropolitan Police deliberated whether the CID 'might not possibly be rendered more efficient if a certain proportion of the appointments were made direct from the outside world and without requiring previous service in the Force, thus admitting men of better social position and education'.[81] Nothing came of this suggestion.

That ordinary policemen and detectives had an interest in keeping the system as it was is no surprise, but the consistent support of senior management in London as well as in the provinces (many of whom were recruited externally) is intriguing. What made the system so resilient? What were the principles that underlay it and how was it explained by its supporters? How did the system of detective recruitment relate to the wider employment strategy in the police?

THE LOGIC OF INTERNAL RECRUITMENT

A combination of factors explains why most police employees supported a policy of step-by-step advancement towards permanent plain-clothes work. The guiding principle of this policy was the assumption that 'a certain amount of training in police duties was essential for detective work'.[82] Detective Inspector Harold Brust, who joined the Metropolitan Police in 1908, explained in his memoirs that 'as a patrolling constable one learns the bedrock facts about police work, one becomes part of the great machine which enforces the Law, and one sees aspects of life that otherwise would be missed'.[83] Given that detection was a speciality of the general police function, 'police knowledge' was conceived as 'the first essential for a detective officer'.[84] Giving evidence in court was considered an indispensable requisite of acquiring police experience, but central to the policy of internal recruitment was the idea that the policeman 'learns it so much better out in the streets rubbing shoulders with the public' in his daily beat. Most detectives in this period did not handle complicated investigations, nor did they commonly pursue long searches for clues or lengthy readings of crime scenes. Mostly, they gathered information and coped with petty crime. Although this was not the standard rhetoric, people involved in the criminal justice system assumed that for these tasks little 'ingenuity', 'extraordinary genius', or formal knowledge was necessary.[85] To fulfil their daily duties, detectives were expected primarily to become acquainted with the world of crime and its chief actors, with the devices used by veteran policemen to detect and curb violations of the law, and with criminal law. These requirements they gained while serving as ordinary policemen. Detective Cecil Bishop, who joined the Metropolitan Police in 1903, compared this system of preparation to the sons of businessmen 'going through the mill' and learning through experience rather than through formal education.[86] 'Scotland Yard has only one University, with Experience as its best professor. Detection is a profession... in which no amount of book learning or theoretical exposition can take the place of actual practice,' he asserted.

Many detectives referred in their memoirs to the usefulness of their early experience in routine police work for their later performance as detectives. Bishop described the benefit he had acquired from tailing a suspected murderer. Detective Superintendent Francis Carlin of the Metropolitan Police (joined 1890) stressed the opportunity he was given to learn the modus operandi of lawbreakers.[87] Detective Superintendent Percy Savage of the same force (joined 1900) emphasized building up 'a deep knowledge of human nature which cannot be gained in any other way'.[88] Service in rough areas, such as in the Whitechapel (H) Division, was viewed by George W. Cornish (joined 1895), later a superintendent in the CID, as 'the best in which to test the worth of a fledging constable... it certainly made a detective' of him.[89] Frederick Porter Wensley, also a detective in the notorious H Division and later chief constable in the Metropolitan Police (joined 1888), owed his success as a policeman 'to having got knowledge early in his career of all the East End thieves', carrying about with him 'a mental rogues' gallery of faces, with cross-references to their line of crime and generally all he had ever known or heard about them'.[90] That ordinary constables were sometimes employed in plain clothes, as when they had to observe prostitutes or bookmakers, prepared them in specific ways for the fight against crime.[91] The winter patrol, in particular, served as a kind of training ground for detectives.[92] Theoretical knowledge in the form of the police instruction book was not sufficient, police representatives asserted to the 1878 commission.[93] What detectives needed was practical knowledge—for example, whom to arrest and how.

Moreover, even if detectives were less likely than uniformed officers to find themselves in physical confrontations with rough elements, and were not charged with highly demanding physical tasks such as fighting fires or handling animals, as were the uniformed men, their work entailed 'very great physical labour' and 'physical strain'.[94] They had to be prepared for violent resistance while trying to make an arrest, and needed above-average physical stamina to endure the long hours and bad weather involved in the surveillance of suspects (see Chapter 3). It was therefore necessary for future detectives 'to learn the rough and tumble of Police duty' before they applied for a transfer.[95] This was particularly true for divisional detectives. Referring to them, Inspector (later superintendent) John Shore of the detective department at Scotland Yard stated in 1877: 'You do not want a vast amount of education for those men, that is to say, for the subordinates, but you want men who do not care how many hours they work.'[96] Experience as a patrol officer was thought to prepare the detective for the psychological as well as the physical hardships of detective work. Only 'the irksome tasks, the long hours, the hard and often successful work performed' by the uniformed police 'could discipline a man for the disappointments, the buffetings, and badgerings to be silently endured by one who has decided to follow the calling of a detective', observed Detective Inspector Robert A. Fuller in 1912.[97] Such experience also allowed the many officers who were country lads time to adjust to city life, as well as learn how to conduct themselves in relation to the police organization.

Internal enlistment also promoted other police goals. The employment strategy was governed by management's desire to exert total control over manpower and vocational norms. Years of police work were supposed to cause officers to internalize the values of discipline and conformity, which, by comparison, were difficult for gentlemen to incorporate.[98] A related objective was the premiss that a period of service in the uniformed ranks would enable superior officers to obtain 'a thorough knowledge of the men before they are entrusted with the important duties they have to perform'.[99] In keeping a close watch on potential recruits and appraising their abilities, management could sift out those they thought to be the most adept among the uniformed policemen, thereby meeting the major goal of internal recruitment.[100] Moreover, apart from facilitating a more judicious selection, this policy put discretionary power in the hands of supervisory officers. Such power constituted another reason for superintendents or inspectors of divisions, who recommended divisional officers for detective work, as well as policy-makers, who aimed at using the system of internal selection to strengthen the hierarchical structure, firmly to support the principle of internal recruitment.[101] Not every policeman viewed transfer into the detective ranks as a promotion.[102] In addition to certain arduous conditions of service (see Chapter 3), contact with the murkier side of life could appear distasteful.[103] But, for those who did, the knowledge that the transfer depended on good conduct could be utilized by commanding officers, even below the rank of superintendent, to foster obedience and punish those aspirants who were not sufficiently deferential. Internal recruitment thus allowed for both a considered selection and better control in the workplace.

Bolstering employee morale and esprit de corps was another major aim of the police authorities. Hiring from within, according to this thinking, promoted better understanding and unity in the force, and diminished tensions between the uniformed and non-uniformed branches.[104] Chief police officers were generally of the opinion that importing people from the outside would be unpopular both with the detectives, who saw them as intruders, and with the uniformed police, some of whom were 'waiting their turn' in a 'long waiting list' to go into plain-clothes service.[105] This assessment was based on experience. The 1878 commission heard evidence from 'outsiders' about how discourteously they had been received.[106] George Greenham found 'a tremendous amount of jealousy' when he entered the force: 'Everyone was looking at me with disdain, and was sneering at me', he recounted.[107] William Henderson, head constable of Leeds in 1877, who years before had joined the detective branch in Manchester without having served as a constable in uniform, divulged that he had suffered 'a terrible amount of jealousy from the superintendent down to the lowest man' and was 'sat upon in every direction'.[108] He likened the detective force to a trade union whose members were reluctant to admit outsiders, and informed the commission that even his superior officers 'tried to make it as unpleasant as possible' for him.[109]

Underlying the strategy of internal enlistment, therefore, lay an attitude of looking inward, relying on the familiar community of policemen to meet the manpower needs of the organization. This attitude also explained the system of upward mobility in both the uniformed and detective police. Although the few topmost positions were often filled by men with no police experience, all the other hierarchical levels were filled from below.[110] Those who aspired to climb the ladder had to start at the bottom as ordinary constables and slowly make their way up through every rank. Beyond the notion that the experience involved in ordinary police work was necessary to prepare an officer for any post in the force lay the readiness to advance men who had proven themselves adaptable and receptive to police culture.[111] This outlook posited a stable community of policemen who, if in tune with police norms, would work together until retirement with the potential of benefiting from upward mobility to supervisory positions—both uniformed and detective.

Conceivably, a certain reverse class bias is detectable in this policy. Since the uniformed ranks were mainly recruited from low-income groups, choosing candidates among them to assume the more prestigious positions in police service signified that, in contrast to the minority of externalists who distrusted the potential of the working class to acquire high professional standards, the internalists believed in the ability of this class to produce able detectives who would give adequate, and even excellent, service. Imbued with this confidence, and with the recognition that the bulk of the work of detectives did not require extraordinary skills, the police leadership resisted pressures to turn to the educated classes for recruits. This decision was grounded in a set of rhetorical arguments that elevated the status of police detection. Describing detectives' necessary qualities as 'native gifts',[112] police discourse contended that to be successful as a detective one 'must be born with the detective instinct'.[113] Assistant Commissioner Melville L. Macnaghten would often say: 'You can't make a detective unless he has got the necessary ability in him.'[114] The implication was that such ability was unrelated to class, upbringing, or formal education. Since the natural gift of intelligence, common sense, and a good memory inheres in all classes, shrewd and sharp men could be found among uniformed policemen.[115] The message conveyed was that, if a man had a talent for police detection, he could transcend the limitations of his origins, nurture his innate gifts in the police environment, and acquire the tools of the occupation through experience and hard work.[116] Even if this view was aired for rhetorical purposes, it was enthusiastically adopted by the rank-and-file detectives. The rhetoric undoubtedly contributed to the prestige of police detection.

Weighing the pros and cons of internal recruitment, police leaders calculated that in waiving the employment of middle-class men they gained many advantages and served various other police interests. Beyond the early experiments with external enlistment, which taught them that, while gentlefolk could perform managerial tasks in detective units, they failed abysmally in ordinary duties, working-class men seemed better disposed to meet the needs of the rigidly hierarchical bureaucratic machinery for a disciplined, strong, and cheap labour force. Gentlemen were also not expected to be prepared to mix with the lower classes, in particular with the criminal elements among them, nor to be able to do it successfully.[117] Therefore, side by side with appeals to draft 'great detectives' with the 'best brains', particularly for the CID at Scotland Yard, arguments ostensibly incompatible with this objective were also heard. William Chamberlain, a detective sergeant in the L Division of the Metropolitan Police, asserted in 1877 that it was not the men of first-rate education who caught thieves.[118] Admitting that some detectives wrote poorly and knew little arithmetic, he put his faith in tried and true methods of overcoming these shortcomings, such as having other officers draw up the reports for those who were not good at it.[119] At the other end of the hierarchical pyramid, Sir Melville Macnaghten, too, deemed schooling 'almost a negligible factor' in detection,[120] pointing out that one of the finest detectives he had ever known started as a farm hand.[121] Proper manners did not seem to him to be necessary in the making of a detective, and he was not unduly concerned that some of his detectives were unpolished.[122] In his opinion, the fact that they could not write reports well did not prevent them from doing the most responsible work. To counter arguments that some detective tasks required breeding and manners, in order, for example, to deal with upper-class criminals,

Superintendent Frederick Williamson affirmed: 'Our men communicate constantly with the highest people in the realm.'[123]

The conviction thus became entrenched that only men with the stamina to endure police life over time were capable of detective work. This notion was cardinal to the police employment strategy, which viewed a stable workforce as a high priority (see Chapter 3) and was guided by the experience that policemen of working-class origins tended to be longer-term employees than officers from higher social sectors.[124]

No less important in reinforcing the policy of internal enlistment was the economic factor. The heads of police operated under continual directives by central and local governments to curtail expenses.[125] Although no explicit documentary evidence has been found in this connection, clearly internal recruitment was adopted as a policy, in part because of a fear that the entry of middle-class employees into police service would create pressures to raise pay in accordance with what was customary in the labour market for people of such background. The correspondence during this period between the Home Office and the various commissioners of the Metropolitan Police, deposited in the National Archives, abounds with exhortations to exercise financial constraint. Budgetary considerations systematically dictated low wages for uniformed policemen, despite the support of certain police officials and opinion leaders for 'adequate remuneration' for them.[126] Senior officials acknowledged that, because of the low wages of constables, they could not expect to draw men from the educated classes, but they acquiesced with the consequences.

These considerations shed light not only on the preferred labour force for detective departments but also on the prevalent concept of the essence of police detection. Generally, advocates of bringing in fresh blood essentially defined the occupation of detection as necessitating a middle- or upper-middle-class upbringing and formal education. In an article published in the *Daily Mail* in 1906, author and journalist Frank Dilnot promoted the view that detective service merited a different type of person from those currently employed, and urged replacing them with men who 'combined the acuteness of a successful barrister with the professional knowledge of a doctor… equally distinguished in the study of science and of human nature, and [with] abnormal tact [and] the mental agility of the chess player'.[127] While conceding that two or three of the chiefs at Scotland Yard would be prominent in any detective force, and that some police detectives possessed 'extraordinary ability', he found the majority handicapped by their 'early environment' and 'lack of opportunity'. People subscribing to his way of thinking perceived police detection as tackling serious, or at least complex, crime and dealing with sophisticated criminals, a task for which men of lowly origins were not suitable. Probably also envisaging white-collar crime or other crimes involving the 'respectable' classes, Frank Dilnot recommended that crime investigators possess 'ready tact and pleasant manners'. Notably, however, like many reformers who advocated recruitment from the higher echelons, Dilnot was not as concerned about ordinary detectives as with the central CID, which he wished to man with Holmes-like professionals.

No doubt, the decision-makers in police matters also paid special attention to the detectives at Scotland Yard and were united in their view that the department should incorporate men whose talents and intelligence shone,[128] but their overall conception of police detection signifies that they shaped it as more akin to a manual occupation. Not only did its personnel largely come from a manual background, but the nature of detective work was to a great extent structured as such. Despite the requirement of absolute literacy for the performance of tasks, it reflected emphases on physical strength, knowledge of street life and the criminal world, contacts with informers and informants, and a sustained ability to face grave risks and physical difficulties. George Dilnot, who published a booklet about Scotland Yard in 1915 (and a much larger volume on the same topic in 1927), epitomized this approach in 1915, describing CID men as 'engaged in business pure and simple, not in making shrewd detective deductions'.[129] The working-class population was the main target of their surveillance and investigation, and management wanted people of a similar background to police this population. Indeed, most senior officers consistently underscored the significance of patrol duties in detective work.[130] Selecting employees from the lower rungs of society thus made good sense.

Beyond promoting the many benefits of internal selection, senior officers claimed that the hiring system did in fact allow them to fill the ranks with men of 'superior intelligence' and natural gifts who could 'fish up' particularly shrewd criminals.[131] After all, the potential pool of policemen was quite large and varied, and the number of detectives to be selected small. This method of selection, however, was not always satisfactory. The police authorities were at times unhappy with the results of internal recruitment.[132] Their dissatisfaction was heightened by periodic criticism in the press of the investigative talents of police detectives, especially against the backdrop of striking failures to solve well-publicized crimes (as will be evident in Chapter 5). The internalists would tend to retort that the problem was not the quality of uniformed policemen, who constituted the pool of potential detective candidates, but the reluctance of the best among them to apply for detective service. In their view, the most effective measure for attracting 'the best intelligence of the police' was to offer detectives 'greater inducements, like a pay rise'.[133] Police leaders were only occasionally successful in convincing those responsible for police budgets to ameliorate the conditions of service for detectives, but this, and not external recruitment, was their argument in response to the tension between reliance on a working-class pool and the need for detectives 'with their wits about them'.

The examination below of the process of recruitment illuminates the profile of detectives and the contributory factors that enabled them to be part of the world of detection.

SELECTION PROCEDURES

The requirement of spending a period of time in the uniformed police before being eligible for acceptance in the detective force implied that even those who aspired from the start to serve as detectives had to go through the standard procedure of initial constable selection. Apart from the very top ranks, appointment in the police force was governed by objective rules based on merit rather than on patronage or political connection. Police authorities postulated that the tasks of uniformed policemen required only general skills and physical endowments. These criteria were essentially similar in the various police forces, although certain details varied. In general, candidates had to be tall young men, of British extraction, able to read and write, and not burdened by a large family. In the late nineteenth century, candidates to the Metropolitan Police had to be at least 5 feet 9 inches in height,[134] between the ages of 20 and 27,[135] and having no more than two children. Candidates also had to produce testimonials of a flawless character. Those who satisfied the prescribed standards were required to undergo a series of examinations testing their physical fitness and their literacy. In adopting the principles of merit and exam-based competition, the police organization was a precursor of modern employment norms. Certain departments of the civil service also followed such guidelines in the course of the nineteenth century, but they became standard practice only after the civil-service reforms of the 1870s.[136] Otherwise, as noted by historian David Vincent, 'very few working men ever had to write anything down when seeking employment'.[137]

However, while police work demanded both physical fitness and literacy, the screening procedure put a far higher premium on the former. An impressive build, so as to be conspicuous in the landscape, as well as physical strength and stamina, were viewed as central to the strategy of deterrence and public service. Accordingly, candidates had to be fit, free of any bodily ailment, and of a strong constitution.[138] Detective Sergeant Benjamin Leeson of the Metropolitan Police 'was amazed to see the number of apparently fine specimens of manhood rejected'.[139] Their physical prowess was thoroughly investigated. The first question Detective Chief Inspector Tom Divall was asked when he applied to the Metropolitan Police in 1882 was 'Can you fight?'[140] Arthur Fowler Neil, a future superintendent of the Metropolitan Police, was rejected at his first try to enlist in the City of London Police when the examining inspector, looking at his hands, suspected he had heart disease.[141] In fact, the physical examination conducted by the police constituted one of the most stringent employee-selection procedures in the country.[142] The standards adopted called for physical qualities considerably superior to those of the average working man.[143] The day Jack Henry (later detective inspector) was examined by the Metropolitan Police on the eve of the First World War, only 10 applicants passed out of over 100.[144] Moreover, looking ahead to a long period of service, the authorities were determined to make certain that the enlisted men remained 'fit and sound for 25 years'.[145] For this purpose, the candidates' previous medical history was examined in detail.[146] At the same time, little attention was given to the schooling of the applicants, and the literacy test expected them to show no more than a basic ability to read and write and sometimes to keep accounts. Not surprisingly, then, the great majority of rejections were due to inability to meet the physical standards, while only a small proportion of the applicants failed the education test.[147] Drawn from the uniformed ranks, detectives were well built, strong, and tall.

Being part of all-male police forces, all detectives were men. Women—often the wives of police officers—were on occasion employed in jobs deemed inappropriate for men, such as guarding female prisoners, conducting searches of female suspects, and taking statements from children, female offenders, and victims of sex offences.[148] They also provided distinctly detective services, such as obtaining information and incriminating evidence, particularly in cases where their gender gave them an advantage over (male) detectives.[149] Yet women were never part of the ordinary police workforce in the period under discussion.

No requirement was made regarding the social or occupational background of police recruits. Every young man who conformed to the physical and literacy entry criteria could gain admittance into police service regardless of class or skills. Indeed, the occupational experience of entrants varied greatly. As Detective Sergeant Benjamin Leeson recalled in his memoirs, the men who enlisted with him in 1890 were 'a mixed lot, farm labourers, ploughmen, waggoners, and the like from every county in the British Isles'.[150] If anything, senior officers favoured rural workers (albeit unofficially), particularly agricultural workers, whose educational record was one of the poorest in the country. Despite occasional reservations by commanding officers about rural recruits, and disparaging remarks that they had 'bumpkin brains' and suffered from a 'lack of smartness',[151] the dominant attitude was that the qualities associated with rural workers—pliability, obedience, physical strength, endurance, and low economic expectations[152]—were far more beneficial to police service than a higher level of education or urban experience. As late as 1908, former CID Director Howard Vincent reiterated that 'the best police recruits perhaps are men from the country unacquainted with town tricks', even though he was not unaware of their meagre intellectual accomplishments.[153] Such an awareness, however, did not prevent police decision-makers from exerting concerted efforts to attract recruits from the country. Even if the entry regulations contained no instructions regarding either geographical or occupational origin of potential recruits, the preference for country folk appeared to have influenced the selection process. In fact, during 1909–14 Metropolitan Police recruiters periodically travelled to the countryside with the explicit aim of reducing the proportion of city-bred policemen in the force and encouraging rural workers to join,[154] as city people, notably Londoners, were generally perceived as physically feeble, undisciplined, and, above all, conceited.[155] The outcome was that the reservoir from which detectives were chosen was made up of a majority of men of working-class origin and a small minority of petite bourgeoisie.

The procedure of detective selection that followed was neither short nor easy. The period of time that every officer had to spend working the beat was rarely brief. In principle, policemen could be moved to detective departments after only a few months of street duty in uniform. Although Charles Leach had served only twelve months in uniform before he was transferred to plain-clothes duty in the Convict Supervision Office of the Metropolitan Police, and there were others who served even less, it usually took several years before officers could become candidates for police detection.[156] In Liverpool during the 1870s, two or three years passed before a policeman was considered ready for detective service, although a few served less.[157] In the Metropolitan Police it took even longer—three to four years' service during the 1870s,[158] and four to six years, and sometimes longer, in the pre-war period.[159] The requirement to don the helmet was not designed to be a temporary stage on the path to detective work, but a substantial element in the making of a detective.

Seniority in itself was no criterion for advancement. Even after a long wait, becoming a detective was no simple matter. In the early decades, the initiative was taken almost exclusively by the authorities.[160] Police Orders in the Metropolitan Police requested the superintendents in 1867 'to send in the names and particulars of any sergeant or constables' whom they could recommend for detective work.[161] In other forces the choice was often in the hands of the head constable or the watch committee. Later, enlistment became more self-motivated. In the latter part of the century Metropolitan Police regulations stated that any sergeant or constable of the uniformed branch 'desirous of becoming a candidate for the CID must make an application in his own handwriting'.[162] Police Orders included announcements requesting volunteers for the CID, and uniformed officers responded. However, as in every other stage of advancement, the role of supervisory officers was central, since only with their goodwill and recommendation could a police officer become a candidate for detective work.

Many a detective had tales to tell about the special circumstances that steered him towards detective service. A conspicuous act of bravery could advance an officer's chances.[163] James Berrett, who was to rise to the rank of detective chief inspector in the Metropolitan Police, came 'under the notice of the great ones at Scotland Yard' as a result of saving a man from drowning.[164] More commonly, senior officers were impressed by men who were 'sharp in looking after thieves' and 'in making arrests'.[165] Detective Cecil Bishop recounted that after two months in uniform he caught two well-known East End pickpockets, a feat that, in conjunction with his interest in investigating crime in preference to other duties, brought him to the notice of the local detective inspector.[166] Bishop was one of the lucky few to serve as little as three months in uniform. Charles Stroud, in 1877 detective inspector of the Birmingham City Police, also manifested his ability in a series of captures of criminals.[167] 'Conduct in the courts' was also important for advancement.[168] A policeman who was 'unable to present his evidence clearly, or deal with and bring up witnesses in their proper and most useful order cannot hope for much success', Detective Superintendent G. W. Cornish of the Metropolitan Police observed in his memoirs.[169]

Periods in which policemen were asked temporarily to perform tasks in plain clothes allowed senior officers further to examine the suitability of the patrolmen.[170] Often, these stints served as an intermediate stage en route to detective service. The London Metropolitan Police and the City of London Police, for example, required the officer 'who shows superior intelligence', 'has a turn that way', and is put forward by his superior officers, to 'be employed as an acting plain clothes patrol' specifically in order to examine his likely performance as a detective.[171] In some forces the candidates were forbidden to conduct any sort of investigation at this stage; they could only patrol the streets in the evening and at night under the direction of experienced officers.[172] The underlying premiss was that 'receiving persons into custody as a constable in uniform does, is a different thing from investigating a case and tracing it out'.[173]

Thus the talents of those who became detectives and even rose through the ranks had been noticed while they were still in uniform. Conspicuous in their aptitude for the job, it was natural that the path to detective work was open to them. Selection, though, did not always measure up to police needs. The cardinal role superior officers played in the selection of plain-clothes officers resulted at times in the recruitment of favourites, or 'good stupid men who have never got into trouble, rather than in that of men specially fitted for the purpose'.[174] Indeed, while the memoirs of police detectives are replete with stories of the crucial role senior officers played in their recruitment into the detective branch, some detectives told about supervisory officers who had halted their advance, even if they had already earned several commendations.[175] Clearly, it was not sufficient to prove adept at plain-clothes duty. Uniformed officers had to be approved and suggested both by their immediate superiors and then by the senior detective officer of the division or the central department. Only then could they apply for a permanent job as a detective when a vacancy occurred.

THE ROLE OF BACKGROUND AND MOTIVATION

Although candidates for the detective branch did not have to compete with men from outside the force, they still had to demonstrate that they had an edge over their fellow officers. Some entered police service better qualified than others. Speaking foreign languages initially brought external recruits to Scotland Yard, and later on was an important criterion for enlistment into the Special Branch. The Special Branch also looked for Irishmen, of whatever background, preferring Roman Catholics, since most of the Fenians belonged to this faith.[176] Certain occupations led almost naturally to detective work. Harold Brust's biography before he entered police service pointed to useful, though by no means typical, work experiences that helped propel him in this direction. Brust, who later became detective inspector of the Special Branch, where he served as a bodyguard of kings, had been employed in his early twenties as the personal attendant of the British ambassador to Portugal, in which capacity he had the opportunity not only to observe the work of detectives who guarded the Portuguese royal family, but also to thwart an attempt on the life of the Portuguese king by an anarchist in 1907.[177] This proximity to protective surveillance fascinated him and evoked an awareness that 'here was a new field of activity, and avenue of service which I might explore myself'.[178] Before making a move in this direction, he met Superintendent John McCarthy, a famous Scotland Yard detective, who was visiting the British Embassy in Lisbon, and on hearing of Brust's exploit in foiling the anarchist plot suggested that he join the CID.[179] Significantly, Brust's boyhood and adolescence 'had been spent in travel, in college tuition, in learning European languages, and in working as assistant to a Parisian jeweller'.[180] His many visits to the Portuguese palace and his conversations with King Carlos and his heir had acquainted him with the ways of royalty and the political elite. Equipped with letters from the British ambassador to the home secretary and to the commissioner of police in London, he faced no difficulty in being accepted to the police. He did, however, have to work initially as a man in blue—walking along 'dirty pavements, sordid streets, malodorous back-alleys' in 'grey river-mist'—a 'startling contrast to the discreet, carpeted environment of the British Embassy in Lisbon, to the Royal Palace of the Necessidades, to all the suave atmosphere and trappings of regality and diplomacy' in his previous employment.[181]

Although police detection demanded intense physical exertion, and was populated by men of humble origins, concurrently it appealed to certain people from a non-manual background. Dealing with crime and the protection of society, and attracting extensive coverage in the press and literature, it attained a distinctive aura that combined adventure, excitement, and public service, exercising a special pull on young Victorians whose lives were quite different.[182] This glamour explains why some men of means and high prospects, aware that the job was difficult and not well remunerated, nevertheless set their minds on it,[183] although the majority of these abandoned the idea once they learnt that they had no choice but first to spend time in the uniformed ranks. Here and there, men belonging to this category did start at the bottom, such as Robert Sagar, later to become one of the most successful detectives in the City of London Police, who as a medical student had shared lodgings with a detective who convinced him to leave his studies and enter the police.[184] Such backgrounds were probably regarded by superior officers, who were pressured to raise the intellectual level of detectives, as desirable. At the same time they provided recruits with the kind of education, advanced literacy, or work experience that better prepared them for detective service than the average policeman.

Yet, while the system of recruitment into the detective force tended to favour the better off, it allowed the considerably less well off to advance as well. True, quite a few detectives descended from or were themselves skilled workers before they became policemen, but agricultural workers or men with an unskilled or semi-skilled past also succeeded in making their way into the exclusive coterie of detectives and in gaining promotion. Detective Inspector Samuel Bootman of the Rochdale Borough Force (born 1846) had worked on a farm before joining the police, and had 'only a limited education'.[185] For Detective Superintendent G. W. Cornish, born in 1874 and brought up on a farm in Wiltshire, going to London to enlist in the Metropolitan Police 'was the first time that I had been to London, or indeed far from my father's farm'.[186]

Notably, an unskilled or semi-skilled occupation did not invariably mean fewer years at school or a poor education. In some cases, the opposite was true.[187] Even those originally located on the bottom rungs of the labour ladder might have been exposed to an educational environment. Moreover, learning to read and write was often a long process, not necessarily linked to an educational institution.[188] Many working-class families who did not send their children to school nevertheless taught them reading and writing at home.[189] In effect, the majority of men in the country knew how to read and write before the Education Act of 1870, which introduced universal elementary education in England and Wales. Schooling thus seeped down through the social scale and widened the pool from which occupations depending on literacy could draw. By the end of the nineteenth century the literacy rate covered 95 per cent of the population.[190] Further, having to work from an early age did not necessarily imply that the ill-educated were detached from the world of learning. Material scarcity did not inevitably entail cultural deprivation. In any event, 'the great majority of the "literate" working class were never taught anything more than a basic manual dexterity with the pen', as David Vincent points out.[191] Many working-class children, whether attending school for many or a few years, developed a strong fascination for the written word and became autodidacts. The memoirs of detectives, including of those who lacked a substantial formal education, often display book knowledge and are filled with references to the classics, contemporary literature, and philosophical, geographical, and historical sources in English and other languages.[192] While such references may have been inserted to show off, the memoirists did not represent average detectives, but those with special writing skills and literary ambitions, who may have widened their erudition while in service. Still, they considered it important to demonstrate access to wider knowledge, or at least a respect for scholarship. Thus, the fact that some detectives sprang from the lower stratum of the working class did not imply that they had no education, formal or informal.

A significant number of detectives were sons of policemen—'pups of the truncheon', as they were called.[193] Such close proximity to police culture, and to crime investigation in particular, prepared the ground in many respects. Detective Sergeant Leeson, whose father had been a policeman who was associated with famous criminal cases, surely heard a great deal at home about crime investigations.[194] When Divisional Detective Inspector Charles Leach, who joined the Metropolitan Police in 1901, was only 12, he helped his father, Superintendent Alfred Leach, with certain investigations by performing routine detective tasks such as trailing men in whom the police were interested or carrying a message to a person who was associated with the criminal world.[195] He was not the only youngster to do so. In several instances he was accompanied by the son of another detective in watching a shop about to be visited by a man suspected of robbery, keeping track of a suspected thief, or gaining evidence that would stand up in court.[196] Not surprisingly, some of these young observers of police work felt destined to be police officers, not unlike other youngsters who followed their fathers' career patterns.[197] Although Leach was sometimes 'left to pace the streets' of 'an extremely rough neighbourhood', such as Clerkenwell, 'from early morning until close on midnight, with neither food nor the wherewithal to purchase it', and on occasion found himself in dangerous circumstances, he felt that 'all this early training with my father had...heightened an innate taste for police work'.[198]

Yet, background was not enough. Clearly, detectives also had to be strongly motivated in order to transcend the boundary between uniformed and non-uniformed policing, and ultimately to attempt to be admitted to Scotland Yard, considered the 'summit of the constable's ambition'.[199] Men who grew up in conditions of deprivation and attended school for only a few years had to be particularly ambitious. Contemporary photographs of police detectives showing smart dress and prideful deportment provide an indication of their social aspirations (see Figure 3). Whether endowed with the background that eased their way into detective roles or not, quite a few memoirists emphasized the abiding attachment they had formed to the occupation long before they could apply to police service, although it has to be remembered that detectives' memoirs were written years after enlistment and were hence coloured by the passage of time and authorial intention to convey a certain message to the public about their choices.

Some detectives referred to their strong interest in this branch of police work in their youth. Chief Constable Frederick Porter Wensley, who joined the Metropolitan Police as a constable, had 'a boyhood ambition to become a detective'.[200] Purportedly, 'the thought of exciting adventures and imagining myself bringing off the capture of some notorious criminal' was what motivated Francis Carlin to become a member of the Metropolitan Police at the age of 19.[201] Jack Henry, who joined the Metropolitan Police in 1913, 'had visions of clue-hunting with large magnifying glasses, bloodhounds and the general paraphernalia of detectives of fiction'.[202] Both Frank Bunn, who joined the Metropolitan Police in 1911, and Fred Cherrill, who

MR. WM. RECORD,
Ex-Detective-Sergeant, D Div., Metropolitan Force.

Figure 3. 'Portrait of Ex-Detective Sergeant William Record, D Division, Metropolitan Force', *Police Review*, 24 Oct. 1902.

joined the same force in 1914, also recalled devouring such tales, and as adults were prompted by them to enter police service and become detectives just like their childhood heroes.[203] If all such accounts are true, there have been few occupations in which fiction played so conceptual a role.

Some detectives recounted real encounters with the world of crime and detection in their youth. Such encounters were not always positive: Chief Inspector Walter Dew of the Metropolitan Police (recruited in 1880) admitted that he 'had an instinctive dread of the London policeman, which lasted more or less until I became one myself'.[204] Yet for some youngsters such encounters served as a rite of passage, igniting a passion for the occupation, or at least they were described as highly formative in the young men's decision to become a detective. Detective Inspector Joseph F. Broadhurst of the Metropolitan Police, for example, had witnessed the arrest in London in 1896 of Albert Milsom and Henry Fowler, the infamous Muswell Hill murderers, when he was 16.[205] He depicted the Scotland Yard men who effected the arrest as 'two impressive giants in silk hats', whose confident and forceful behaviour had fired his imagination and caused him to make up his mind immediately to pursue a career in the Yard.[206] He promptly 'read up everything I could about the process of skilful deduction that had put the CID men on the trail of the murderers'. The trial 'more than confirmed me in my desire to become a police officer', although Broadhurst was under age and therefore found work at first with the police of a large railway company.[207] His work there was dull and burdensome, and he waited 'in vain for the big moment', as petty pilfering and excess charges were all the crimes he encountered in this place of employment. His monotonous work was only seldom interrupted by an exciting event, such as when he caught a thief (stealing potatoes) red-handed. When he finally donned his uniform at the Metropolitan Police in 1900, at the age of 21, he felt proud.[208] In his words, 'the dream of my childhood was true, and the small boy who was threatened with the police by his fond aunt, was now a policeman himself'.

If observing detectives in action sparked Broadhurst's desire to emulate them, Charles Arrow's main motivation, as depicted in his memoir, was an episode in which he took part in law enforcement at 17, and the sequence of events following this episode.[209] Together with other pupils at the school he attended (in a village a hundred miles from London but within the Metropolitan District), he chased two men who tried to steal coats from the school lobby. One was caught, the other escaped. It was Arrow, assisted by a friend, who pursued and captured the escaped offender. The local policeman who arrived on the spot, a beat officer, impressed Arrow with 'the business-like "rough and ready" style' with which he handled the affair. Arrow also recalled his admiration for the policeman's uniform. Later, at the police station, he was given a chance to become acquainted with the process of charging, searching, and measuring the suspects—an experience that proved unforgettable. In recognition of their act, he and his friend were awarded the sum of 10s. by the commissioner. This dramatic first exposure to a police environment had crucial consequences for Arrow's future; from then on the local officers 'made much of me, and many a long walk and talk I had with them on their lonely country beats'.[210] By then he was 'trapped', but had to overcome the opposition of his parents, who had planned an illustrious future for him in the civil service. In the end, they abandoned their dream and reluctantly consented to his wish to join the police, although they were certain he had wasted a good education (until age 19) by doing so. Arrow joined the uniformed branch (in 1881) with a view to becoming a detective, eventually serving as detective chief inspector of the Metropolitan Police until 1907.

Despite testimonies by memoirists about planning their detective careers in advance, it is likely that a greater number of men discovered the lure of detective work only while in uniform. Some considered patrol work so demanding and uneventful that they were determined to escape it—not to another place of employment but to the detective ranks. When pacing the lonely beat, Ernest Nicholls (a City of London Police detective for over thirty-four years who reached the rank of chief inspector) resolved (in 1899) 'to carry out my duties [so] as to quickly lift me out of the rut of being a mere constable known by a number'.[211] Within twelve months of entering the police, he was a plain-clothes officer. The relief felt by those who moved from beat patrol into detection jobs was shared by Londoners and provincial detectives alike. According to Major Bond, head constable of the Birmingham Police, the men liked detective work 'infinitely better' than 'the monotonous executive duty of marching up and down the road' of a uniformed officer.[212]

Quite often detectives were impelled not only by push but by pull. Detective work was regarded by many, though not all, as not only preferable to trudging the beat, but compelling in its own right. Aside from better material rewards, detectives also enjoyed a certain amount of autonomy and a more prestigious and exciting job (see Chapter 3). Aspiring policemen went to great lengths to achieve this end. They knew 'you should show some aptitude and ability for detective work before you could hope to be recommended for duty in the CID',[213] and acted accordingly, even at the expense of family life.[214] Chief Inspector James Berrett of the Metropolitan Police, for example, preferred the more difficult night shift, as 'there was a better chance of finding thieves and, more particularly, of pulling up people carrying stolen property'.[215] Aside from trying to catch the eye of superior officers in their daily performance of tasks, they used their spare time to improve their education and literacy skills, well aware of the widespread criticism about the lack of such accomplishments among policemen,[216] and of senior management's dictum that 'a man is always a better man for being able to read and write'.[217] The generally long intervening period between entry into the police and appointment to the non-uniformed service allowed ambitious and hard-working officers to embark on a process of self-education, enhance their intellectual capabilities, acquire missing skills, and sharpen their urban sensibilities, all of which were useful in gaining a foothold in the detective world. With this in mind, some Metropolitan Police aspirants attended instruction classes in the divisions.[218] Prospective detectives also realized that knowledge of the theory and practical implications of criminal law helped detectives in their work, particularly in the preparation of admissible evidence in court. Hence, enterprising policemen 'used to attend the police court twice a day to listen to cases and see how they were conducted'.[219]

Libraries and reading rooms in police stations contained useful textbooks on law and police procedure for those inclined to self-education.[220] Tom Divall (later detective chief inspector), unable to join the CID because his education was deemed insufficient, could work in plain clothes only as a supernumerary.[221] He was employed in this capacity for four years, during which he dedicated 'every minute' of his spare time to 'bettering his education' and 'attending Board Schools and every possible place where I could learn something to my advantage'. Towards this end he sometimes studied until 3 a.m., or was up at 5 a.m., 'practising writing, spelling, etc., whilst my wife and kids were asleep and snoring', until he was in a better position to respond to the commissioner's call for recruits in the London CID. Edwin T. Woodhall (b. 1886 in Scotland), who joined the Metropolitan Police in 1906 and eventually became detective inspector, 'read all the works on criminal detection which were regarded as classics on the Continent and in America, as well as those published here'.[222]

By the beginning of the twentieth century, candidates in London were expected to pass a written and oral examination at the central office before being confirmed in the department, demanding further proof of officers' literacy skills.[223] The examination tested their knowledge of the police instruction book as well as their 'general intelligence and aptitude for the special duties' they would be called upon to perform.[224] Examinations for promotion to the rank of sergeant were also held; the subjects were the same as for appointment, but the questions were 'of a more searching character'.[225] As at any other point in the process, here, too, certain police officers displayed particular determination to pass the examination, sometimes paying a shilling a week to a schoolmaster to give them lessons.[226]

If a candidate did pass, he often found that there was a long waiting list ahead of him,[227] and, even when his turn came, a detective career was not guaranteed. Candidates in the Metropolitan Police were accepted on probation, usually for three months, although this could be extended to six, nine, or even twelve months at the discretion of the assistant commissioner.[228] Ultimately, the decision to allow a novice detective to remain in the detective force depended on 'the skill and vigilance shewn by each man, and above all by his success in following up crime and criminals'.[229] If the detective was found unsuitable, management had the prerogative of turning him back into uniform.[230]

INTERNAL TRAINING

At no stage in the process of selection during the Victorian period were candidates for the detective branch obliged to undergo any special course of study. The tacit assumption was that training was not confined to a specific period, and that it in fact started with the candidate's entry into the police. Even if a policeman did not initially intend to become a detective, the experience and knowledge he had gained in the force was thought to provide him with all-round policing skills and to serve as the best educational basis for detective work.

This meant that the initial training of a uniformed officer was in fact part of the training of the prospective detective. In the pioneering days of professional policing, and in many small forces even thereafter, newly arrived recruits, most of whom had no skills related to the work ahead of them, were given no formal training. Uniformed novices learnt their new vocation from their superior officers.[231] Soon, however, the large urban forces felt the need to give the newcomers more focused preparation in the period immediately following their acceptance into police service. No recruit was exempt. Since there was no uniform system of training policemen in England, each force made the arrangements that its senior management required.[232]

The Metropolitan Police had the most regulated system of instruction. The period of training was short—from a few days in the formative years of the force to three weeks by the end of the nineteenth century. The training programme included only scant instruction—albeit increasing over time—in vocational skills, while relying heavily on drilling exercises.[233] Detective Inspector Edwin Woodhall recalled that, 'as recruits to the police, a squad of us would parade every morning at nine o'clock, drill and listen to instruction until twelve. Then came a two-hour interval for dinner and at two o'clock we paraded again until five'.[234] Apart from the need to provide exercise to police officers whose tasks demanded bodily sturdiness and the use of physical force, the intense drilling was intended to socialize the recruits in police culture. The emphasis on drill stemmed from the belief that training was designed above all to instil discipline and orderly habits in the recruit. Regulating his body and inculcating suitable behavioural attitudes were thus considered more essential than the development of the recruit's theoretical or practical knowledge.[235]

This short programme was not intended fully to train the policeman to perform his tasks. Certainly it supplied little preparation for criminal investigation. Presumably, the authorities preferred lower productivity to investment in a longer training period. The policeman was expected to continue his studies and perfect his vocational skills on the job.[236] Hands-on practice was at the core of the training system, with accompanying officers when the recruits went out into the streets providing crucial instruction. It was they who were responsible for demonstrating police practices and for transmitting informal traditions. Some served as models worthy of imitation. The veteran constable who in 1895 walked the beats with G. W. Cornish and other recruits in the Metropolitan Police taught them 'not only a great deal about our work and its pitfalls, the neighbourhood and the type of people who lived there, and when and where trouble usually started, but also what was of almost more use to us, the various peculiarities and idiosyncrasies of our immediate superiors'.[237] The beat, and the knowledge passed on by veteran officers, also guided recruits in how to cope with the criminal world. The 'gnarled, rugged old "bobby"' who tutored Harold Brust gave him 'many tips which subsequently proved of the greatest value in dealing with the petty crooks'.[238]

This method of learning the secrets of the trade on an ongoing basis was deemed a cornerstone of the policy of internal recruitment.[239] Whatever the detective did not pick up as a patrol officer, he would, it was assumed, learn in his work as a detective once he had been drafted. The indifferent attitude towards the educational background of police recruits, combined with the belief that inborn talent was a key to the skilful detection of crime, further explains the reliance on on-the-job training. Consequently, no formal training time for detectives was delineated. Once again, the role of veteran officers was vital.[240] Newly appointed detectives in London and the provincial cities were paired with experienced detectives who, while monitoring their actions,[241] taught them 'what inquiries they should make, what steps they should take to apprehend criminals, and as to their duties generally'.[242] They also imparted knowledge of criminal law, how to gather information and assess its validity and to examine the crime scene. The task of new detectives was 'to gain an insight into the working of the detective system' and 'practical experience of the work of the department, and of the way in which cases were conducted there'.[243] Detective Inspector Charles Leach recalled being called to the superintendent of the CID, Frank Froest, on one occasion, and told quite casually: 'There are one or two smart young fellows just come into the Yard. I want you to take them in hand and... break them in'.[244] One of the first jobs Leach assigned to them was to follow several burglars, in the course of which the newcomers were violently attacked. One of them never recovered and had to retire from service. The probational period thus served as a special in-house training course during which officers had to prove not only that they were capable of detective work, but also that they had learnt the hard facts of detective life.

Still, there were aspects of detective work that the trainee did not master. What he learnt was what he happened to encounter in his work. Commentators criticized the unstructured approach to teaching the vocation and charged that the lack of formal training was responsible for the escape of criminals from justice.[245] More and more voices demanded a more rigorous and specialized form of training for both uniformed and plain-clothes officers.[246] A growing need to cope with white-collar crime and the greater resort to scientific and technical means in criminal investigations in the late nineteenth and early twentieth centuries constituted a further impetus in this direction. The considerable growth in technical education in the country at large in this period added momentum to the criticism.[247] Many of the critics upheld the system of internal enlistment and in-house training, but wanted to equip the workforce with more professional education.

The entry of Edward Henry into police service as assistant commissioner at the beginning of the twentieth century changed the training system in the Metropolitan Police dramatically. Convinced that 'any attempt to impose a higher test of education would only result in the loss of a half, if not more, of the men' recruited to the Metropolitan Police, he fought instead for better employment terms for detectives (see above), and devoted his energies to raising the level of the recruits' preliminary training.[248] Given the existing self-imposed constraints, this measure seemed the obvious solution to the problem.

As commissioner, Henry established a police-sponsored school for new police recruits in 1907. Drill was still an important part of the programme, but more time was set aside for 'learning the thousand and one laws, written and unwritten, that a policeman has to obey' and 'every contingency that a constable may have to face'.[249] Instruction was conveyed by means of considerable simulation, and greater stress was put on improving writing skills and 'wearing away [the recruits'] rough edges'.[250] Lectures were given on topics such as the law of evidence or police regulations, and recruits were taken to police courts and the Black Museum at the Scotland Yard headquarters, where exhibits relating to various crimes were stored.

As assistant commissioner responsible for detective matters, Henry had established a kind of school for detectives in 1902, and in 1913, as commissioner, he extended its curriculum. There was now a fixed time for the acquisition of professional competence by means of regulated training standards. The programme was systematic and planned in advance. The school exposed candidates to a higher degree of vocational knowledge and a more sophisticated form of training. Trainees were given lectures on law, with special emphasis on criminal law, and 'taught the methods of criminals, from gambling sharps to forgers, from pickpockets to petty sneak-thieves'.[251] They were also introduced to the latest technical measures adopted by the CID, principally fingerprinting, and were instructed by means of innovative techniques, such as lantern slides. As a result, officers acquired better know-how of both the practical and theoretical aspects of detection, although vital investigative skills, such as interviewing, were not developed.

No other detective training school existed in England in the period under review, but some forces sent their detective candidates for training in the CID at Scotland Yard.[252] Others still relied on practical experience obtained in the ordinary course of duty.

No doubt, the change in the transmission of occupational skills in the Metropolitan Police constituted a step forward in the professionalization of the detective branch. It was now officially recognized that detective work rested on a body of specific knowledge and that this knowledge had to be imparted through a course of instruction in which the trainees dedicated all their time to their studies. The establishment of a special training programme for detectives also implied a growing separation between uniformed and detective service. No longer was the work experience of an ordinary policeman considered sufficient to turn him into a detective. Even though police training continued to evoke criticism even after the establishment of these programmes (see Figure 4), a more complimentary attitude gradually surfaced in public discourse.[253] Still, the training courses for both branches were quite short (eight weeks for uniformed service and four for detective work), with the bulk of vocational training acquired only after this brief period of instruction. The system, with its focus on work experience as the best source of professional expertise, was apparently still considered to be the most effective for men who did not excel at absorbing theoretical material or at passing formal examinations.

Trainees who completed their formal course of study successfully became fully fledged members of the CID. That was when the career of a detective began, whether as detective constable or detective sergeant, although the commissioner or head constable could return a detective to uniform duty at any time. Usually, but not always, officers began working as detectives in a division, and only after further years of service and proof of ability could they apply for work in the more prestigious central branch—and that too only when a vacancy occurred.[254] In London there were other possibilities: the specialized offices or branches, most prominently the Special Branch.

Writing retrospectively, detectives depicted the move into the detective branch in superlatives. Walter Dew recounted 'the natural elation with which I viewed my promotion' in 1887.[255] 'My real life work had begun', Harold Brust wrote about his transfer in 1909 to the Special Branch, referring to it as 'the higher service of detectivedom'.[256] Similarly, after four years in uniform, Detective Inspector Woodhall described his promotion to the Special Branch in 1909 as 'a red-letter day in my career'.[257] 'It was the realization of my hopes. Often as I had patrolled my beat...I longed for the day when I might exchange my somewhat monotonous routine (as I thought at the time) for the more exciting life of a Scotland Yard detective.' Some may have missed the esprit de corps of the culture of ordinary policemen: when Charles Arrow moved to the CID, he ceased 'to feel that

Figure 4. 'How Scotland Yard Detectives Are Trained', *Punch*, 12 Mar. 1913.

he [was] one of the vast uniformed organisation, every member of which [would] support him', and regretted 'the loss of the protecting powers of his uniform'.[258] However, for many, the transfer from the uniformed to the detective branch was a significant change for the better. As a constable on the beat, Joseph F. Broadhurst's main duty had been to arrest drunkards and escort them to the station, but in his heart he was crying out for 'bigger things'.[259] Shortly after Broadhurst had been recruited to the force, he was appointed a plainclothes probationer and stationed at Deptford—considered 'the blackest spot in London at the time'—as a detective constable.[260] He soon had a taste of the kind of events that gave the place its reputation and himself the excitement he had craved: first, the murder of an entire family, and then (in 1904), the Deptford murders (see Chapter 1).[261] These were, at last, 'the real thing'.

Admittedly, such heartfelt expressions came from those who had developed long-term careers as detectives, and therefore had reason to feel this way, but other indications, too, suggest that detective work was conceived as far more interesting and satisfying than beat work and that detectives felt they had gained more than they had lost by becoming detectives (see Chapter 3). To revert to a uniform was regarded as degrading, a form of punishment, even for many of those who were not permanently employed as detectives.[262] In short, detection became not just another occupation in a long sequence of jobs, but a magnet, and the promised land, for many, a place of employment for ambitious and enterprising men to be secured entirely by single-mindedness and perseverance. This kind of attitude was exactly what the police authorities expected of their employees—men 'who possess a peculiar attachment to the duties, and are resolved to work a case out'.[263]

3

THE DETECTIVE AS WAGE-EARNER AND OFFICIAL CRIME FIGHTER

As policemen, detectives were part of the overall work culture designed for the uniformed police. While some of their conditions of service changed upon their being transferred to the detective branch, they continued to function in the same milieu as uniformed officers and were broadly subject to the same employment strategy.

Despite local variations[1] and the decentralized nature of the police network in England, a dominant organizational approach was gradually built up—the result of procedures developed by disparate local authorities over the years, merging aspects of traditional aristocratic paternalism with modern middle-class notions of efficient management.[2] In fact, the paternalistic approach was redefined to suit the particular interests and bureaucratic administrative style of the police. Focusing their labour policies on an internal market orientation, the police adopted a long-term strategy and elaborate standard procedures regarding not only selection but also rewards.

A COMMON POLICE CULTURE FOR UNIFORMED AND PLAIN-CLOTHES POLICEMEN ALIKE

In shaping work regulations, the police hierarchies were guided by three interrelated objectives: ensuring the compliance of police employees; inculcating police norms and goals; and promoting long-term commitment to the workplace. Together, these were intended to mould an efficient police force. To attain an obedient and deferential workforce, police decision-makers designed a bureaucratic structure based on domination, subjecting officers to a harsh and rigid disciplinary regime.[3] Supervision extended to after-work hours and to the family.[4] Trade unions were banned and no representative body was permitted to voice the grievances of the workers. Moreover, despite the semblance of unified standards governing the newly emerged police organization, personal bias and favouritism often marked the methods of control by supervisory officers all along the chain of command. The wage scale did not compensate for this demanding regimen for constables, who constituted the vast majority of each police force. At the insistence of both central and local government to reduce expenses, pay was low, if steady. In many forces, it was not significantly higher than that of agricultural labourers—widely viewed as a measure of a poor income—and it was considerably less than that of skilled workers. In the first few decades of the existence of the modern police, newcomers to the Metropolitan Police and to forces in boroughs with populations of 10,000–30,000 earned about 19s. a week, and, in boroughs of under 5,000, 14s. a week (when the weekly earnings of farm labourers ranged between 8s. and 18s., and of skilled engineers in Manchester and its environs between 28s. and 34s.).[5] County forces offered even less. It took years for a constable's wage, which rose incrementally, to reach the level of skilled workers.

These conditions clearly conflicted with the stated aim of employee retention and hence the formation of a highly motivated labour force. For many years, although they enjoyed regularity of income and faced the prospect of job security, large numbers of novices left the police almost as soon as they joined it, and many others departed within the first or second year of service.[6] That initially many officers were punished by dismissal exacerbated this exodus. Carolyn Steedman calculated that nearly 48,000 men joined county forces between 1839 and 1874, of whom over 24,000 resigned and 12,000 were dismissed.[7] Yet, high turnover rates were commonplace in the Victorian world of work. In fact, the police were among the pioneering employers to set their sights on creating a steady workforce, realizing that, the longer policemen served, the greater their value to the force. Several reasons informed this judgement. An outflow of workers was incompatible not only with the need to provide continuous service, but also with the fundamental reliance on cumulative experience as the key to the acquisition of job-specific skills. Further, only with time could employees become instilled with the hoped-for identification with the police ethos. Premature departure was also costly, for the police invested a good deal of money, time, and energy in recruiting, selecting, and apprenticing their employees. Additionally, it had a negative effect on the morale of the officers who remained.

With a view to developing lifetime police careers and fostering the assimilation of officers into police culture, compensation in addition to pay was offered. Even in the embryonic stages of the police, the authorities balanced sanctions with incentives based on both monetary and non-material rewards.[8] Intrinsic to this system was the assumption that certain working conditions would produce desirable behaviour. Under this paternalistic bargain, many officers were furnished with a degree of welfare, thus easing the burdens of the ordinary contingencies of life, such as old age and disability, and offering some security against income loss. The programme variously included free medical care, sick leave with pay, and a gratuity if an officer became unfit for work.[9] Some policemen, primarily in London, received a pension when leaving the force following at least fifteen years of work, if certified unfit for service.[10] They were also granted diverse combinations of non-cash inducements, such as a lodging allowance or inexpensive accommodation in police quarters (where these existed), clothing, boots, or supplies of coal.[11] Significantly, these protective measures were available to policemen at a time when few employers offered manual workers welfare in times of need.

Such assistance was not given randomly, but was presented as an ingrained component of the terms of work. However, because of the overriding policy of minimum expenditure, and the linkage (at least in practice) of benefits to good conduct, many promises were not kept and their provision was selective, contingent upon the good will of the superior officer, chief constable, watch committee or county magistrate. Only in the late nineteenth century, in response to continuing high labour wastage and periodic (albeit uncoordinated) police agitation, the social-security safety net became less discretionary, and employer-sponsored benefits expanded, among them the establishment of recreational rooms and convalescent homes for policemen and orphanages for their children. The Police Act of 1890 made pensions for policemen mandatory after twenty-five years of service (unless dismissed) and without the medical certificate previously required. Given the meagre prospects of a large portion of the working class if found unable to work—essentially dependence on relatives or the poor house—this was an impressive achievement for policemen. Under constant pressure to find ways of appeasing and retaining police officers, management now took greater care to attain an effective compromise between its aims and labour aspirations. Low wages and harsh discipline continued to govern labour relations during the rest of the period under review,[12] but these were counterbalanced by diverse perks and improved chances of security of employment.[13]

Another uncommon incentive held out to these working-class officers was the possibility of upward mobility through promotion, entailing an incremental increase in wages and enhanced prestige (see Chapter 2). Most officers managed to make their way up the various constable ranks only, which resulted in bitter complaints about slow or blocked progress through the different grades of sergeant and inspector, and ranks above these two.[14] Still, in principle, these positions were available through promotion, while only the very top positions in some forces were open to men from outside the police or to police officers who had not risen through all the ranks but came from other forces.

The amelioration of conditions did not entirely remove the causes of disaffection, and expressions of profound discontent by police officers continued throughout the period, culminating in strikes in the Metropolitan Police, in 1872 and 1890, and action in other forces around the country.[15] Undoubtedly, however, the fear of potential loss of guaranteed income and accumulated benefits served as a powerful deterrent to early departure.[16] The percentage of resignations declined in the last decades of the nineteenth century and the police workforce became more stable.[17] In tandem, with the mounting realization by management of how damaging expulsion was to the objective of low turnover, other penalties, such as fines, reprimands, and demotions, were more commonly used, ultimately leading to a growing body of veteran officers. It was from this pool that most detectives emerged. They were among the prized policemen, whose loyalty was secured and who had endured in service despite the difficulties, under the premise that it was worth their while to stay.

These detectives, particularly in the divisions, worked in league with uniformed and plain-clothes officers who were not detectives. After all, both branches were entrusted with crime control, though the detective branch was exclusively so. There was no precise job definition of police detection. Detective assignments depended on many factors, contingent on place and time. Generally, detectives concentrated their efforts on more serious offences than ordinary policemen, but, because of their common cause to fight crime, and the nature of English policing, many of the tasks of the two branches overlapped and, moreover, embraced both preventive and detective functions. Thus, while uniformed officers chased offenders, carried out arrests, and even investigated cases,[18] most detectives engaged in a certain amount of patrol, deterrence, and other duties associated with beat officers. Senior officers themselves acknowledged that 'a great deal of quiet inquiry and observation [was] left to the uniformed men'.[19] Patrolling beat officers, upon discovering a dead body, would sometimes immediately set out to locate the trail of the suspect.[20] Only after preliminary work had been done by the uniformed men would detectives take charge of the case. As Superintendent George Turner of the K Division of the Metropolitan Police told the 1878 commission: 'The duties are so mixed together that I cannot tell how we could separate them.'[21]

Occupied with stemming outdoor violence and disorder and ensuring street safety, officers of both branches roamed the roads, whether with a specific purpose in mind or simply searching for lawbreakers. They scrutinized racecourses and prize rings in attempts to detect swindlers, pickpockets, and other tricksters, and were 'on the alert to prevent any breach of the peace which might occur when the audience disperses'.[22] In the course of these activities, they recovered stolen goods, prevented acts of vandalism, and arrested criminals and suspected criminals (see Figure 5).[23] They also collaborated in guarding public houses, raiding gambling clubs, and surveying theatres, music halls, saloons, shelters, common lodgings, pubs, and beer houses, 'where large numbers of the poorest classes are to be found'.[24] Detectives took along uniformed policemen for assistance when the use of physical force was anticipated, for monitoring political activities, and for intelligence-gathering duties. They certainly worked together to quell public-order disturbances.[25] In forces with fewer detectives than in London, joint assignments were more common. The two branches met at police stations during work, and in police living quarters outside working hours. They also spent leisure time fraternizing and taking part in the growing array of recreational activities and special events organized by and for the police.[26]

Moreover, the shift into detective service was not necessarily permanent. Detectives who did not prove competent for the job were asked to return to uniformed service, while others left of their own accord, unable to cope with assigned duties or dissatisfied with the terms of employment. Officers who climbed the hierarchical ladders, especially outside London, often moved between the two branches.[27]

Notwithstanding this shared occupational ambience, those who shed the policeman's uniform were generally viewed as a distinct

Figure 5. 'Uniformed and Non-Uniformed Policemen in Action', *Illustrated Police News*, 25 Jan. 1868.

entity. Over and above the different attire, detectives were expected to be more professional in fighting lawbreaking and better equipped—by nature and experience—to do it.[28] They also enjoyed certain privileges denied to uniformed policemen. Further, although all police employees viewed themselves as police officers, and camaraderie developed between uniformed and plain-clothes policemen, a sense of separate identity evolved in each group, with the lines of demarcation becoming more pronounced with time, principally in London. This was not the only dividing line within the force. Divisions were also present between policemen and civil servants who worked for the police, between the rank and file and senior officers—in Scotland Yard itself as well—and between London and the periphery.[29] Friction also existed between divisional and central detectives. According to the author of an article titled 'Detectives', which appeared in the *Saturday Review* in the winter of 1884, 'the very mention of their [central detectives'] names to a district detective fills his heart with exceeding bitterness... when [he] sees the fruits of his labour seized at their ripest by the person he styles "a swaggerer from headquarters"'.[30] Yet it seems that the distinction between uniformed and non-uniformed officers was more palpable.

THE DISTINCTIVE OCCUPATIONAL CULTURE OF POLICE DETECTIVES

Although individual detectives had diverse work experiences in different jurisdictions—whether in Scotland Yard, the London divisions, the City of London Police, or the various forces in provincial England—they shared a particular occupational culture. By all accounts, much of their work entailed arduous physical labour. Pounding the beat was generally regarded as dreary and debilitating,[31] but detectives, too, even in the prestigious rank of inspector, were often compelled to walk for many miles.[32] Merely shadowing a suspect could be an exacting task, demanding a man's full energy.[33] When making bids for extra staff in London, commissioners emphasized the long work hours of detectives, averaging between ten and eleven hours per day.[34] Periods of intense pressure to resolve an intricate case involved special toil. During the hunt for Jack the Ripper, Detective Inspector Frederick G. Abberline, one of the chief investigators of this infamous mystery, after commanding his staff for a whole day, would 'pass his time in the streets until early in the morning, driving home, fagged and weary, at 5 a.m. And it happened frequently, too, that, just as he was going to bed, he would be summoned back to the East End by telegraph, there to interrogate some lunatic or suspected person.'[35] In such cases detectives sometimes did not remove their clothes for days.[36]

What marked detective work in particular, and burdened the detectives, was the irregularity of their daily schedule, in contrast to their uniformed counterparts, whose hours on duty were 'strictly limited to a fixed period each day', generally allowing them to have 'a reasonable amount of leisure' to 'devote to their own concerns'.[37] Detectives were expected to 'go where the enquiry leads' and pursue it to its conclusion.[38] As Detective Inspector John Sweeney of Special Branch put it: 'At any hour of the twenty-four I might be on some errand, nor could I even go away on furlough without feeling that at any moment I might through some pressing need be prematurely summoned back to headquarters.'[39] Special Branch officers guarding the safety of dignitaries, too, were liable to be overworked by putting in irregular hours. 'No one can tell when a member of a visiting royal family may choose to move from one house to another, and I have spent many weary hours trying to look inconspicuous near the garden gate of some fashionable house,' Detective Cecil Bishop observed.[40] He revealed that keeping a watch on Asquith was particularly toilsome, as the prime minister (1908–16) slept little and worked long hours, and Bishop had to get used 'to sleep[ing] in any odd corner and in any chair'. The workload could interfere with family life severely.[41] One could 'never arrange with any degree of certainty any pleasure or recreation with [one's family]', Assistant Commissioner Basil Thomson noted to the Desborough Committee in 1919.[42]

Whether engaged in the detection or the containment of crime, a great many detectives spent the bulk of their work time in the open in areas of squalid deprivation and sordidness, and often in the company of drunks, informers, and petty thieves. Seeking evidence or information, detectives frequently entered the 'lion's den—the "hot" quarters of their divisions'.[43] Their presence in venues where violence was not uncommon and where they were perceived as threatening rendered them susceptible to rough treatment. Typically, they would be attacked when trying to arrest a reluctant suspect, and have to fight off his or her friends or the crowd who would rush to his or her defence.[44] Detective Inspector Charles Leach 'was black and blue all over' as a result of an encounter with pickpockets; it was 'some weeks before the effects of the fight wore off'.[45] According to their recollections, many detectives carried the scars of such confrontations for life,[46] and in certain situations were 'lucky to escape' alive.[47] In one case, during a struggle with a suspected 'loan-office swindler', John Littlechild's head was within three inches of a passing tram car.[48] Hostility to the police in the dockers' strike of 1893 in Hull concentrated on two detectives, who had to be rescued from a building surrounded by an angry crowd determined to get at them.[49] Some criminals carried weapons, and detectives (as well as uniformed officers) were at risk of being stabbed or shot.[50] More than a few detectives ended up in hospital, or were forced to retire as a consequence of their injuries.[51] Some encounters ended with the death of the detective.[52]

Special Branch officers liked to tell stories about their clashes with female suffragettes, who, though by no means the most threatening of their enemies, seem to have injured their manly pride. They 'drove us crazy', Detective Inspector Harold Brust recalled.[53] In one inglorious incident, when a suffragette who intended to present a petition at Downing Street was seized by Detective Sergeant William C. Gough, her friends sprang 'from all sorts of odd corners and doorways where they had been hidden' and began stripping off his clothes.[54] He was forced to release the prisoner when, with him 'in shirt-sleeves, his face one crimson blush', they began 'to unfasten his trouser-braces!' Detective Bishop, because of his large size, was an easy target for the suffragettes' 'missiles...both material and verbal'.[55] Incidents such as the auctioning by suffragettes of police trophies—for example, hats and sticks—that they had managed to snatch from detectives in one of their confrontations, the proceeds going into a special fund, affronted the detectives' dignity and heightened their animosity.[56]

Another difficulty was the psychological strain inherent in detective work. For Charles Leach, nothing was 'more annoying or disappointing than to be on a case for some two or three weeks and, after long hours of patient watching and following up clues, to come to a fruitless end'.[57] Frustration at not achieving results, or at criminals evading punishment, was acute, as this was the principal measure of their effectiveness in the eyes of their colleagues, senior officers, and the public.[58] Their frustration was compounded by a prevalent feeling that detectives were 'terribly crippled in their attempts to grapple with a wily foe' (in this case the Fenians) because of safeguards that 'the existing law extends to all citizens, however unworthy', or by court procedures unfriendly to detectives.[59] Facing gruesome crimes could also prove markedly stressful. Detective Chief Inspector Walter Dew depicted his intense investigation of the Ripper murders—Scotland Yard's most famous failure—as 'wretched days'.[60] The hunt for the killer became an obsession, and he spent 'long, long hours on duty, only to return home worn out but sleepless'. As he recounted: 'Night after night I tossed about on my bed seeing again and again the terrible sights I had witnessed.' Food sickened him, as did the sight of a butcher's shop.

Despite such dramas, some detectives professed that their work was not infrequently boring.[61] 'Watching is always a tedious business,' Detective Inspector Andrew Lansdowne admitted.[62] Even Special Branch officers, such as Detective Inspector Edwin Woodhall, described their job as involving 'a great deal of routine work', much of it consisting in reporting 'from day to day on a certain district or a certain number of individuals, however little there may seem to be to report'.[63] The work of guarding dignitaries, Bishop observed, was mostly 'as dull as anything I know'.[64]

A frequent grievance was slow promotion and the paucity of opportunities for advancement.[65] While the move to the detective branch was widely seen as a 'much coveted promotion',[66] detectives complained that men in uniform had greater prospects of rising up.[67] Indeed, many detectives reverted to uniformed ranks to attain upward mobility. Frederick Abberline, who had served as a divisional detective sergeant for two years in the early 1870s, re-entered the uniformed branch as an inspector, only to return to the CID as a local inspector in 1878 at the personal request of CID director Howard Vincent.[68] Such a shift was even more common in provincial forces.[69] Grievances concerning promotion to the CID in the Metropolitan Police were supported in 1912 by Commissioner Henry, who affirmed that 'for a young constable of more than average attainments the most attractive avenue...is—at present—in the uniform side'.[70] In his opinion, the 'slowness of promotion' in the detective branch, and the fact that 'men are on duty, in trying conditions, for very long hours and with no regularity', explained the difficulty experienced at the time 'in obtaining candidates either in sufficient numbers or of the best kind for admission to the department' (see Chapter 2). It is only reasonable to assume that both the commissioner, who wanted to induce applications to the CID, and the detectives, for obvious reasons, had an interest in amplifying the issue of promotion. Uniformed officers actually voiced the opposite view, that they were the disadvantaged party.[71] Whatever the case, since many detectives were propelled by a strong career drive, merely to become a CID constable was insufficient to satisfy their ambition, especially as the detective constable enjoyed only a few of the privileges possessed by CID officers above his rank. In 1912, CID constables had to wait about four or five years before promotion to third-class sergeant was at all possible, in addition to the initial four to six years that the majority had served in uniform. During this period, six third-class sergeants awaiting promotion had an average of sixteen years' service, and six second-class sergeants who were recommended for promotion had an average of twenty years' service. For men who repeatedly heard from police heads that they constituted 'the best material in the police force', the way up appeared disappointingly arduous.[72]

Remuneration

Notwithstanding these drawbacks, and although details of the employment structure varied between forces, on the whole detectives had better conditions and seemed to derive greater satisfaction from their work than uniformed officers. Regarding themselves not only as brighter and more capable than uniformed policemen, but, increasingly, as specialists whose role in the police demanded greater responsibility and mental aptitude (for example, in preparing a case for prosecution), they felt that they were indeed entitled to enhanced compensation.[73] This conclusion was shared by many non-detectives, who from the outset held that this was the way to meet the unremitting ambition within police circles for detectives who were qualitatively superior to uniformed policemen. Even before the establishment of distinct detective units, suggestions in the press to create such a unit in the Metropolitan Police advocated higher pay for its officers so as to attract 'men of talent and integrity'.[74] The commissioners of the Metropolitan Police concurred, and, in an appeal in 1842 to Home Secretary James Graham to establish a detective force, asked to hold out 'adequate inducements for the most competent men to enter this branch, and forgo the hopes of promotion except in it'.[75] The request for higher pay was granted. The two inspectors who formed the detective branch in 1842 had their salaries raised from £116 to £200 a year, and sergeants earned £10 more than their uniformed colleagues (£73 a year, jumping to £109 in 1851).[76] Commissioner Richard Mayne was still dissatisfied. In a memorandum to the Home Office in 1844, he argued that to keep a competent officer permanently as a detective and prevent him from reverting to uniform, his salary should be further augmented (in the case under discussion then, the salary of the officer involved, Detective Inspector Nicholas Pearce, would be raised from £200 to £250 a year).[77]

Twenty-five years later, in 1869, the salary of Superintendent Frederick Williamson was £300 a year (rising to £400 by 1871, and £550 by 1877); detective chief inspectors were paid £250; detective inspectors £200; first-class detective sergeants £150; and second-class detective sergeants £110—all in Scotland Yard.[78] The rates rose further in the 1870s. Divisional detectives, however, were entitled to less: in 1877 detective sergeants earned about £104 a year (40s. a week) compared to £88–£93 for ordinary sergeants; and constables £83 4s. (32s. a week) compared to £62–£78 for ordinary constables.[79] The estimated median weekly adult man's wage in the United Kingdom at the time was 24s. 3d., and the estimated median weekly income of a head of household was 26s. 6d. (policemen's wives were not allowed to work in most forces, though some did, particularly in borough forces).[80] Yet, commentators within and outside the police periodically protested that the remuneration was insufficient to bring 'persons of superior social standing' and 'higher education' into the detective branch.[81] The turf fraud scandal of 1877 was attributed by some journalists to the low salaries awarded to detectives, which 'laid them open to great temptation',[82] even though the two chief inspectors and one inspector who were convicted earned £276 and £225 per annum, respectively, and the inspector also drew an allowance from the Midland Railway Company, which brought his salary to £300—a middle-class income.[83] *The Times* claimed that 'the detective officers ought to receive larger salaries'.[84] The concluding report of the 1878 commission pointed to inadequate remuneration above all in the divisions, where detectives were paid only a trifle more than uniformed policemen, as one of the major causes of the poor calibre of manpower recruited into the branch, and strongly recommended a higher pay scale.[85] Sharing the belief in the innate link between economic incentives and the quality of detectives, Howard Vincent, the director of the newly established CID, carried out the recommendations, as shown in the 1881 CID payment scale (see Table 1).

In line with the 1878 commission's recommendations, and in contrast to pre-CID practice, constables recruited into the CID did not enjoy higher pay than their counterparts in the uniformed branch. In the view of the commission, a 'real detective career' began with the rank of sergeant.[86] Consequently, when appointed to the CID, constables were not formally designated as 'detectives', but rather as 'P.Cs., CID'. Indeed, the rank of sergeant was the most common in the force, unlike in the uniformed hierarchy, where the predominant rank by far was constable, as demonstrated in Table 2.

The disparity in the rates of pay of the uniformed and detective branches in the Metropolitan Police was maintained until 1919 (when pay and conditions were unified nationally), though the gap varied with rank. Outside the Metropolitan Police, opinions about detective pay were more divided. The commissioner of the City of London Police and the head constables of the Birmingham, Liverpool, and Leeds police, who apparently experienced no difficulty in attracting men with special aptitudes for detection in their territory (and were willing to sustain their departure to higher uniformed ranks), argued in 1877 that uniformed officers joined the detective force because they viewed detection as more 'pleasant' work, and transfer as 'a mark of distinction'.[87] They saw no reason, therefore, to furnish detectives with higher pay. Yet, either then or thereafter, most of the large forces closed ranks with the Metropolitan Police and granted

Table 1. Distribution of the CID detective hierarchy and annual wages in the Metropolitan Police, by rank with annual increments, 1881

Number of officers	Rank	Annual wages
Annual increments of £10		
1	Chief superintendent	£450–£550
3	Chief inspectors	£300–£350
1	Chief inspector (convict office)	£226
Annual increments of £5		
3	First-class inspectors	£200–£250
14	Local inspectors	£180–£230
17	Second-class inspectors	£150–£180
31	First-class sergeants (5 ranking as inspectors)	£130–£150
33	Second-class sergeants	£110–£130
103	Third-class sergeants	£100
85	Patrols	1s. a day added to pay of their class

Note: For a comparative table for 1912, see E. Henry to Under Secretary of State, 13 May 1912, HO45/11000/223532.
Source: C. E. Howard Vincent, *A Police Code* (London: Cassell, Petter, Galpin, 1881), 91.

Table 2. Distribution of ranks in the uniformed and CID branches within the Metropolitan Police, 1912 (%)

Rank	Uniformed	CID
Inspectors	2.75	10.53
Sergeants	12.00	48.32
Constables	85.25	41.15

Source: E. Henry to Under Secretary of State, 13 May 1912, HO45/11000/223532.

detectives wages in excess of those of their uniformed counterparts—if not always as an inducement to become and remain detectives, then to reinforce their motivation to catch criminals.[88] In addition to the skills that they had acquired, detectives were an asset as long-serving men, which demonstrated their suitability and adherence to police objectives. Retaining them permitted the authorities to maintain their policy of internal recruitment and select the best men in the essentially working-class forces as detectives, without having to entice outsiders who would make much greater demands on public money. Furthermore, raising detectives' wages did not place an especially heavy economic burden on those holding the public purse, since detectives constituted only a small percentage of every force, and not everywhere was the gap between the wages of the two branches significant. Some advocates also contended that higher remuneration would prevent detectives from taking bribes.[89]

Most authorities thought not only that detectives deserved higher pay than ordinary policemen, but that, if police aims were to be attained, it was advisable to grant them allowances over and above what ordinary policemen were getting. To meet the wear and tear of the attire of these non-uniformed policemen, who 'must wear different clothes according to circumstances', and enable all ranks 'to dress neatly and properly', a plain-clothes allowance was administered.[90] In 1877, a £10 plain-clothes annual allowance was given to all ranks at Scotland Yard, though only £5 to divisional detectives.[91] Defraying travel and refreshment expenses incurred by distant assignments was recognized as a right from the outset.[92] The police leadership also promised to cover other incidental expenses. A particularly heavy cost was incurred by the task of obtaining information. Relying liberally on informers, detectives had to loosen their purse frequently, sometimes paying large sums.[93] Detectives were obliged to hand over 'judicious tips' to criminals and former prison inmates as well as to lodging-house keepers and others who might be of help, such as pawnbrokers, cabmen, or railway porters.[94]

Guided by the imperative to control costs, the authorities demanded justification for every penny spent. Often, superior officers judged that the expenses were unnecessary or suspected they were overblown, especially as on many occasions detectives had difficulty accounting for them and remembering 'how many pints of bitter you had to give an informant before he would open his mouth!', or had to spend cash without authorization in advance.[95] Faced with constant questioning, which they interpreted as indicating a deep lack of trust,[96] detectives complained that their allowances were insufficient or that often their expenses were not recouped in full.[97] As a consequence, they argued, they had to spend money out of their own pockets, sometimes amounting to 'many pounds'.[98] Detective Inspector Maurice Moser went so far as to describe their loss of income as 'one of the crying evils of the day'.[99] At times, the issue hampered their work. Detective Sergeant William Chamberlain revealed to the 1878 commission that detectives would not use devices such as the telegraph, even when imperative, on account of the expense.[100] Others avoided seeking information that involved payment.[101]

Apparently, for many detectives an important part of their compensation lay in special payment received for meritorious acts or the successful resolution of a case.[102] Uniformed men, too, were occasionally given gratuities—for example, for late meetings, attending parties, and their presence in criminal inquiries[103]—but detectives had far more opportunities to augment their income, particularly those who worked at Scotland Yard.

Although detectives were accorded regular wages, during the first few decades of the department they were allowed to accept gratuities from the public—individuals and companies alike—in recognition of their services.[104] Foreign governments were also a source of remuneration. The Belgian and French governments, for example, paid £10 and £12, respectively, for every person apprehended in extradition cases.[105] However, unlike the pre-1842 system, when thief-catchers were rewarded directly by the victims, each gratuity had to be approved by the superintendent of the Metropolitan Police and sanctioned by the commissioner, and in the provinces by the head constable or watch committee.

Senior officers, however, were deeply concerned that this type of inducement—which brought to mind the old-time thief-taking practices (see Chapter 1)—prompted detectives to pursue cases where the reward was guaranteed, and to neglect others.[106] Several witnesses at the 1878 commission indeed admitted that the 'men looked too much to gratuities from the public', and that, as a consequence, 'zeal was often not thrown into the work till a reward was offered, thus justifying the not uncommon idea that the poor man does not always get his case so carefully attended to as the rich'.[107] Partly for this reason, from November 1877, Metropolitan Police detectives were forbidden to accept gratuities from the public.[108] Instead, money offered in gratitude for services rendered was paid to a central fund, supplemented by a grant from the police fund, with the commissioner deciding how the sum was to be dispensed. Under this practice, the detectives were allotted only small sums, if any, unlike previously when the entire gratuity went to them.

Although the testimonies to the 1878 commission reflected a certain unease that a public servant whose wages were fully paid by the public purse should accept additional payment for doing his duty, the general feeling was that the promise of rewards was essential to keep the men motivated.[109] Consequently, the Metropolitan Police authorities opted to maintain the reward fund and, as before, obliged detectives to hand over gratuities to the authorities at Scotland

Yard, who would 'communicate with the donor, enquiring for what specific service the gratuity is given, and whether the sum specified is the whole of what was given'.[110] It was also determined that three-quarters of the amount would either be handed over to the officer who performed the service or distributed equitably among all those involved, while the remaining quarter would go to the fund.

Channelling gratuities through a police fund strengthened the authority of the supervisory strata but it did not put a stop to practices associated with traditional thief-taking. *Reynolds's News*, known for its critical attitude towards the police, accused Scotland Yard of consciously holding out 'every inducement to policemen to trump up charges in order to obtain the rewards that are given to those who procured most convictions'.[111] Evidence of the negative effects of the culture of rewards also emanated from within. Detective Sergeant Benjamin Leeson divulged that detectives were much more interested in tracking down smugglers than looking for thieves because of the sizeable rewards granted by the excise authorities.[112] Abuses of the system of rewards offered by the Home Office led Assistant Commissioner James Monro to reconsider this practice in 1884, though not to abolish it, as it had proved an effective device in the overall strategy of control and inducement.[113] Rewards were also initiated by senior officers in order to encourage detectives to make special efforts. Bearing out the adage 'reward sweetens labour', detectives indeed worked harder in order to gain gratuities, a practice that may be ascertained from their memoirs.[114]

Gratuities were thus a regular feature of detectives' remuneration. They were granted for a variety of services, including showing 'special skill' in recovering stolen goods; apprehending notorious criminals, escaped convicts, Irish terrorists, or anarchists who were subsequently convicted; or demonstrating courage in the face of danger.[115] Rewards also came from abroad—from foreign governments, public services, private companies, and individuals.[116] The sums ranged from the typical few shillings to a hundred pounds and more,[117] depending on factors such as the particular force, the type of crime investigated, the detective's position in the hierarchy and his relations with the officers allocating the jobs. Detectives in London—both in the Metropolitan and the City police forces, principally in their head offices—who were more likely to handle local and international crimes involving substantial financial and political interests, had the best opportunities to benefit from this system. When Detective Inspector Robert Outram retired in 1895 from the City of

London Police, where he had dealt mainly with charges of fraud, forgery, embezzlement, and robbery, he received a gold lever watch and a purse containing £52 10s. (representing approximately a quarter of his annual salary and half of his annual pension) from members of the Stock Exchange and bank managers.[118] The sums could add up to a significant amount over the years. During his forty years of service in the Metropolitan Police, John Shore, chief superintendent of the CID department at Scotland Yard, accumulated over £1,000 in reward money.[119] The higher the rank, the greater and more frequent was the compensation. A rare glimpse into the system of rewards at Scotland Yard was provided by ex-Detective Sergeant William Henry Harris, who, by his own admission, had left the CID in the early twentieth century in acrimonious circumstances (see Chapter 5). In an article published in 1910 in the radical *Penny Illustrated Paper*, he recounted several cases illustrating how his superior officers, ranging from inspectors to the superintendent, made sure they received the lion's share of this additional source of income.[120] In one case, of the £640 allocated as a reward by a Frenchman for the return of stolen bonds, the sergeant who had uncovered them was given only £40, while the inspector and the superintendent shared the rest. If this was the tip of an iceberg, then gratuities were a way of raising detectives' salaries markedly.

Socio-economic status

With a significant sector of the detective force originating in the countryside and from the less privileged strata of the population, work in the CID—considered a position that was, at the very least, skilled—meant for many a rise in social and economic standing. Detective sergeants, who belonged to the lower reaches of the detective hierarchy, could earn lower-middle-class wages (starting with a weekly wage of £1 18s.6d. (about £100 per annum) in the Metropolitan Police in 1888),[121] particularly with long service and the various perks of the job. Since the majority of CIDs reached this rank (at least in the Metropolitan Police), detectives generally moved up the social ladder in financial terms. Their remuneration exceeded that of even the best-paid artisans and compared favourably with the earnings of the expanding black-coated sector and the lower professions.[122] The economic position of some inspectors, and markedly chief inspectors, of whom there were only a few, took a significant turn for the better. They actually managed to secure a place in the middle class proper and advanced their standard of living substantially. This was all the more true for superintendents, whose annual salaries were in the hundreds of pounds. If middle-class status was measured by the employment of servants, then these ranks could afford to hire more than a single housemaid. For example, William Melville, head of the Special Branch (1893–1903), who had risen through the ranks, kept two live-in maidservants.[123] It is difficult to fit police detectives neatly into the established social structure, as they constituted a distinctive example of upward class mobility. Still, it may be safely said that many could afford to maintain standards well above those to which they had been born, although some may have chosen to maintain their original class affiliation.

The detectives' tangible benefits extended beyond their service in the police. Their work as policemen provided them with security of employment and a pension, guaranteed after the passage of the Police Act in 1890. In the light of their higher salaries, as compared to uniformed officers, their pensions were larger as well. Some detectives served well over thirty years in the police, but others opted to leave the police soon after they had served the minimum period required for receipt of a pension (typically twenty-six years), even though their pension covered only two-thirds of their annual pay, for fear that 'a single error of judgment' thereafter might result in forfeiting this 'reward for... life's service'.[124] Apparently, they preferred the certainty of a pension to full pay with a risk of dismissal, aware that their long-term experience as police detectives offered them job openings after retirement. Frederick Jarvis, chief inspector of the Metropolitan CID, who retired in 1897, received over £200 per annum after twenty-seven years of service.[125] A second career was likely to provide him with the income to which he was accustomed, if not a higher one.

Some detectives had accumulated the capital necessary to open public houses or other businesses.[126] Detective Inspector G. Godley of the Metropolitan Police took up a position with an insurance company.[127] Superintendent Jerome Caminada, who retired from the Manchester Police in 1899 (at the age of 55 after thirty-one years of service), became an independent candidate in the municipal elections in Manchester, which he won, and served on the city council during 1907–10.[128] More often, though, detectives made use of the particular skills they had acquired in the police. Former detectives from the Special Branch, as well as others, would on occasion be hired by foreign governments to help them with their security problems.[129]

Detective Chief Inspector Charles Arrow, who retired from the Metropolitan Police in 1907, was invited to Spain to organize a secret service to combat the rising tide of anarchist terrorism in the country (particularly in Barcelona), at a salary of £800 in the first year, £900 in the second, and £1,000 in the third.[130] Detective Chief Inspector Frederick G. Abberline went to work in a casino at Monte Carlo (declining, as he put it, 'domestic matters such as divorce cases as they were repugnant to my feelings'), and John Tunbridge served as commissioner of the New Zealand Police after leaving the Yard.[131] Henry Moore of the Metropolitan Police became a superintendent of the Great Eastern Railway Company's police, and Detective Chief Inspector Divall kept order at racecourses.[132] A more common option for detectives was to work as private detectives. Some, like Detective Inspector Maurice Moser, could afford to run their own agency.[133] Others were employees of such agencies, or of private people such as solicitors and well-off individuals who wanted their valuables to be protected professionally.[134] The practice of moving from public to private service had a long tradition, going back to the Bow Street Runners and to Charlie Field, one of Scotland Yard's early detectives, who had joined the Metropolitan Police before the detective department was formally organized.[135] Even Inspector John Meiklejohn, who was convicted in the turf scandal of 1877, found a job as a private investigator after his release from prison. Former police detectives John Littlechild, John Sweeney, Walter Dew, Benjamin Leeson, William C. Gough (and many other police detectives after the war, including Francis Carlin, Harold Brust, Cecil Bishop, Ernest Nicholls, and Herbert Fitch) followed this path. In 1898 Abberline replaced Chief Superintendent John Shore as the European agent of the famous American Pinkerton Agency.[136]

Retired detectives' contacts in the police gave them an advantage over other private detectives. First and foremost, they could get tips from their former colleagues about ongoing cases.[137] They were also given assignments that the police did not want to pursue.[138] According to information alleged in a newspaper report, as a trade-off, senior officers would be paid by the retired detectives for providing them with work.[139]

Although detective work was on the whole mundane and entailed a great deal of physical and psychological stress, it also embodied a potential source of deep satisfaction. Beyond extra earnings, detectives sometimes received presents and prizes as a token of appreciation beyond the usual retirement gifts common to both uniformed and non-uniformed officers. The item could be a gold watch, but it could also be much grander.[140] The few Special Branch officers who guarded British and foreign sovereigns (see Figure 6) and other distinguished personalities had gifts, awards, and decorations of considerable value and prestige lavished upon them.[141] Detective Inspector Herbert Fitch was vested with the famous Order of Officer of the Red Eagle of Prussia—a jewelled decoration—awarded by the German Kaiser, and the highly prized Order of Isabella the Catholic awarded by the Spanish King Alfonso.[142] King Manoel of Portugal, King Ferdinand of Bulgaria, and King Chulalongkorn of Siam decorated him with other medals.[143] For his services to the 'various royalties of Europe', Detective Chief Inspector George Greenham was awarded a decoration by the Grand Duke of Hesse, a gold medal by Tsar Alexander II, and many other tokens of esteem.[144] These tributes conferred fame on the recipients, and were 'a feather in their cap'.[145]

So were commendations by public persons such as judges, magistrates, coroners, the director of public prosecutions, local leaders, and police heads, for the satisfactory manner in which detectives had discharged their duties.[146] Some crime fighters, such as Detective

Figure 6. 'Detectives who Guard King Edward', *Penny Illustrated Paper*, 21 Sept. 1907.

Chief Inspector Walter Dew of the Metropolitan Police (who served during 1880–1910), were honoured by as many as 100 commendations in the course of their service.[147] These were often bestowed at special ceremonies in police stations or public venues in the presence of large crowds, local celebrities, and the press.[148] The attendant speeches usually praised the recipient as an accomplished and industrious public servant who shielded the local population from wrongdoing.[149] If detectives were sometimes 'shot at' by the courts for not presenting a case properly,[150] they also heard many pleasing words about their achievements in these very same locations.[151] The commendations were entered in the Police Orders and the officer's sheet. Uniformed officers, too, were commended on public occasions, but detectives received many more such expressions of approval and were depicted in more heroic terms.[152] Few others from their social backgrounds were applauded in like fashion by the elite of the country for doing their duty.

Detectives who were considered especially capable occasionally had the prerogative of journeying abroad to track or bring back a suspect or to make inquiries. Detective Sergeant Maguire of the Liverpool Police went to Queenstown in Ireland to arrest a man who had embezzled a large sum of money from his employers—merchants in Liverpool—and tried to secure passage to New York.[153] However, as with most other bonuses, detectives in Scotland Yard and the City of London Police had greater opportunities to see the world. Chief Inspector Frederick Jarvis of the CID at Scotland Yard was described as a man of the world 'who knew his New York quite as well as his London'.[154] Detective Inspector Charles Richards of Scotland Yard travelled extensively in France, Germany, Holland, and Switzerland, and as far as South Africa and India, as did Detective Inspector Andrew Lansdowne of Scotland Yard and Detective Sergeant Hancox of the City of Londan Police, who had circled the globe in search of suspects.[155] Some of these detectives availed themselves of the opportunity—rare for people of their class—to visit world famous sites.[156]

The chosen few who guarded persons of importance at times accompanied them on their tours.[157] In fulfilling the task of royal guard, Special Branch Detective Inspector Herbert Fitch stayed in palaces and accompanied the king 'to the amusements which lighten his leisure hours'—yacht and horse races, Epsom Downs, and the theatre.[158] Describing the privileged moments of the few detectives who were able to rub shoulders with the high and mighty in an ambiance of luxury, the journal *Dark Blue* offered its readers a glimpse of how these de facto commoners spent their time:

> At noblemen's balls helmeted policemen keep the doors, but the detective, in dress coat and kid gloves, enters with the company. It is not generally known that even at balls given by the highest nobility, by ambassadors, and the most exclusive of the 'Upper Ten', a detective, in evening dress, with a bland smile on his face, and his moustache curled in the most aggravating fashion, stalks about, and makes a note of diverse things.[159]

Proximity to the upper echelons enabled the assigned detectives to socialize with all sorts of personalities—old and new elite alike—whom they might not have met otherwise. As recalled by Special Branch Detective Inspector Edwin Woodhall: 'Being in the vicinity of Downing Street day after day for many months, I naturally got to know many people—photographers, "star" men and reporters from the various newspapers and press agencies, couriers of the Foreign office, King's messengers, and many other interesting and important people.'[160] Charles Arrow, in his capacity as a local inspector in the C Division in the West End, had a 'full share' of the London season and 'attended many of the afternoon garden-parties and some of the balls, always as one of the guests and dressed accordingly'.[161] Nonetheless, his day-to-day routine demonstrated that detective work inevitably touched the disreputable, less illustrious side of life. Even in his privileged location in the better part of the metropolis, Arrow's work obliged him 'to mix with the crowd in the streets and in the larger shops, for wherever wealth is gathered, criminals congregate like birds of prey'.

Other rewards

Detectives benefited from better treatment in yet another important aspect of police work. In contrast to uniformed policemen who trod defined beats and were expected to be at specific points at given times, thereby enabling supervisory officers to monitor their activities, detectives had a great deal more control over their time and movements.[162] If at times they had to work very hard during long hours, they could also take their time on occasion. The unpredictability of pursuing investigations could take them to places far from the gaze of their superiors, sometimes outside the city, and even abroad, where they could manœuvre between their duties and whatever else they wished to do.[163] Uniformed officers indeed complained that 'discipline in the CID is at a low standard' and that punishment was lighter there than in their own branch.[164] Moreover, the prevalent opinion was that detection should be left 'to individual experience and discretion', and that the detective was a 'free agent', exercising his judgement about how to pursue a case.[165] Therefore, 'the detective must be left in a certain measure to his own devices, and must be put in some degree upon his honour and integrity'.[166] This relative independence, apart from creating a more congenial work environment for detectives, earned them higher esteem. In essence, their semi-autonomy brought them closer to the ideal of a professional, for whom freedom of choice was an essential component. Indeed, time and again this characteristic of detective work was presented as distinguishing detectives from uniformed officers and as a powerful incentive for policemen to join the detective branch.[167]

If detectives derived a sense of empowerment from the relative freedom they possessed, senior officers felt threatened by it. Commissioner of the Metropolitan Police Edmund Henderson (1869–86) preferred employing uniformed to plain-clothes men precisely because of the difficulty of disciplining and controlling the plain-clothes detective.[168] Police management wanted detectives to exercise sound professional judgement but also to know their place. As early as 1845, senior officers in the Metropolitan Police complained that detectives were 'showing want of due respect to their superior officers'.[169] Particularly vexing was the trouble involved in keeping a tight watch on the behaviour, performance, and expenses of detectives, as it was suspected that they often 'slop their time away doing nothing'.[170] No less anxious was the police hierarchy about what detectives were liable to do, given their clandestine work style. Henry Smith, commissioner of the City of London Police (1890–1902), acknowledged that 'hundreds of time I have wondered how they got their information, hundreds of times I have hoped it was in a legal way, and hundreds of times I have refrained from asking any questions on the subject'.[171] The turf fraud scandal of 1877 revealed the potential for corrupt dealings and illicit practices when no systematic monitoring was in place. Indeed, the 1878 commission, convened immediately after the trial ended, focused on the question of authority over detectives, and a major impetus in the subsequent restructuring of the London detective force stemmed from the urge to 'render the supervision of the detective officer more stringent and severe'.[172]

This drive underlaid the build-up of an elaborate system of knowledge control in the various police forces in the late nineteenth century, a reflection of the steadily expanding bureaucracy of the Victorian state generally and its improved methods of data collection regarding its population. In line with these broader political trends, the police authorities surveyed diverse aspects of the duties, welfare, and turnover of policemen, such as number of arrests, officers' state of health, and manpower effectiveness, which were utilized to gain a detailed overview of the work process, to assess performance, and to wield firm administrative control over the men. To enhance the dual goal of efficiency and supervision, the police officers themselves became participants in the production of information.

A major tool in this configuration was extensive paperwork. All officers were required to document their daily activities,[173] but the issue of documentation was considered of greater urgency in the case of detectives, owing to the nature of their job as well as the difficulties in monitoring the specifics of their workday.[174] In fact, written records, according to the findings of the 1878 commission, constituted 'considerable facilities...for observing the manner in which [their] inquiries are carried out'.[175] The shock of the turf affair led to a tightening of the observation system in the Metropolitan Police. 'There was scarcely a book or a printed form used in the service that was not subject to some sort of change, and not an office or an officer that did not come under close scrutiny' when the CID was created in 1878.[176] Not only was it obligatory to file and report the facts of the crime, but 'every officer employed on detective, convict, and other special duty' was instructed to enter many more particulars in his daily diary than prior to 1878—the places he visited, the objectives and results of the visits, the people he saw, their addresses, the substance of his interviews, and 'personal observations upon the subject matter'.[177] The entries had to record the time that the various duties were performed and the time spent on each.[178] Any change had to be initialled and dated, and daily expenses noted. The diaries were carefully examined by the local detective inspector at least twice a week and by the superintendent at least once a week. The local detective inspector was asked to keep an independent record of the doings of his men in order to verify their own accounts.[179] Written communication was supplemented by oral questioning. CID officers (except for local inspectors and officers on duty at the head office) were required to report to the officer in charge of the police station upon going off duty, and those at the exterior stations upon going on and off duty.[180] Supervision did not stop in the divisions. As part of the centralizing tendency and hierarchical control, local inspectors had to forward divisional reports to the central office every morning, and submit their own and the detectives' diaries to the scrutiny of the director of the CID within a week of the end of each month.[181] Provincial forces adopted similar methods.[182]

Police leaders did not hide their motivation to control the men. While such detailed written accounts did provide 'protection to the officer himself, in the event of any question arising thereon', as Howard Vincent observed,[183] they were clearly intended 'to keep a check on... proceedings and expenses'.[184] Written reports also bridged the time gaps when no supervision was possible. Literacy thus served as a powerful agency of social and cultural hegemony over the entire hierarchy of police ranks. The various paperwork requirements, which were indispensable in the detective's day-to-day routine, were not effortless for men with limited schooling to fulfil, and many bemoaned this burden as irksome (as did uniformed policemen).[185] Some critics felt that the bureaucratic procedures hampered detectives' work, as 'all they do is buried in "reports" which they send to Scotland Yard, where their chiefs sit at ease and read them'.[186]

However arduous, these demands nevertheless underscored the uniqueness of the detectives' occupation and their social standing. While the middle classes habitually pursued reading and writing in their work, police detection was quite exceptional among occupations based on working-class employees in the amount of reading and writing it entailed. Although employers of working-class men (not only in the government sector) progressively expanded their administrative systems and produced materials concerning 'time-keeping and conduct within the factory', which demanded reading and some writing from their employees,[187] the extent was far less than in the police. Even if detectives did not sit 'all day long in an office writing',[188] much of their livelihood depended on reading and writing ability. In addition to extensive reading and writing of letters and reports, detectives ordinarily took notes when collecting evidence, interviewing suspects, or preparing cases for prosecution.[189] Record-keeping also took other forms.[190] So considerable was the amount of paperwork that, as reported by the first director of the CID, Howard Vincent, the criminal administration of the Metropolitan Police dealt with 40,128 official letters and special reports in 1879 alone.[191] The higher the police officer rose in the ranks, the greater the requirement to submit written materials and handle documents. This was particularly demanding for detectives who worked in the central CID in London, which pioneered various methods of compiling knowledge and served as a central storehouse of information for the use of all other police forces. Even Robert Anderson, assistant commissioner and head of the CID (1888–1901), complained about the red tape in the office.[192] Nevertheless, while reading and writing in no way afforded an escape from manual duties, it did elevate detectives above ordinary policemen and above many other workers of humble origins.

Their superior remuneration may have given police detectives a sense of fulfilment, yet it distanced them from their uniformed colleagues. The disparity in employment terms caused animosity among uniformed policemen, who demanded that they all share the same wage scale and non-wage benefits.[193] In the eyes of the ordinary policemen, to be a detective was 'not only to be classed as a sharp and responsible man, but to be lucky and a money-making man'.[194] A letter to the *Police Review* in 1893 arguing that the 'uniform branch are at a great disadvantage with the CIDepartment, who obtain many rewards by the mysterious words "From information received"' was typical of how they felt.[195] The power relationships between the lower levels of the two branches heightened this discontent. While detectives were entitled to ask for the assistance of a uniformed officer at any time, the reverse was not the case. Moreover, as Colonel James Fraser, commissioner of the City of London Police in 1878, pointed out, 'a plain clothes man would [not] consult a uniform man as to the steps that he was to take'.[196] Similarly, the uniformed man had 'to tell the CID all that he knows, and not vice versa'.[197] To cap it all, this division of labour allowed detectives to take all the credit,[198] even if 'the most important part of the business' had been done before the detectives took over.[199] Conceivably, the wedge driven between the two branches strengthened the particular identity of detectives. Although they worked in close collaboration with uniformed officers, and some of their assignments overlapped, they evolved a distinctive relationship with the public, which is explored in the rest of the chapter.

THE INTERRELATIONSHIP BETWEEN DETECTIVES AND THE PUBLIC

As with other policemen, detectives did not necessarily enforce the law every time it was broken. Discretion was exercised at all levels of command as to which complaint or offence merited a response, and the kind of response it was to be. Detectives had to balance the limits on police behaviour imposed by law, the bureaucratic rules of conduct, and the need to be attuned to public sentiment. Furthermore, the instructions were not always unequivocal.[200] Inherent contradictions existed between adherence to the letter of the law and the imperatives of the given situation, manifested, for example, in close relations cultivated with criminals and informers, or, by contrast, in physical confrontations with suspects. Superior officers contributed to this ambiguity by changing policies or informally recommending actions that ran counter to official procedure. Additionally, as historian Robert Storch points out, the police 'had to adjust to frequent changes in the interpretation of the law by the magistrates'.[201] Still, despite indistinct boundaries, detectives knew—broadly—what was considered acceptable behaviour, though this did not prevent them from disregarding legal restrictions and the directives of police management, sometimes with the tacit collusion of their commanding officers.

Evidently, the detectives' conduct was a function of the particular social group they confronted. Like the uniformed police (and the magistracy), they showed greater lenience and sensitivity towards suspects from the property-owning classes.[202] The crime scene had 'a very fair share of polite and well-dressed swindlers and confidence men', and dishonesty in business was far from rare.[203] In fact, not only was middle-class crime 'of a greater magnitude, in monetary terms, than the crimes of the other groups', but, in contrast to a general drop in crime rates in the second half of the nineteenth century, it was on the rise.[204] A contributor to the journal *Dark Blue* tellingly observed in 1872: 'Even in the very highest ranks, the mania for picking and stealing is not always undeveloped. Gentlemen with immense rent-rolls have been known to pocket a watch, abstracted from the belt of a lady with whom they have been waltzing. Even noblemen are not always above this incomprehensible weakness.'[205] Yet, the writer added, 'if an act of this kind happen to be effected under the eye of the representative of the law, one thing is certain not to follow—the arrest and exposure of the culprit. That would make a scene, and well-bred society abhors scenes'. The following morning the gentleman's valet would 'find himself approached in a very diplomatic manner, and solicited to request the return' of the stolen goods.

Even when detectives were reluctant to follow this informal code, senior officers often made sure they did. Detective Chief Inspector Arrow relates how his police career nearly came to an end when the chief of his department felt that Arrow 'had endangered the reputation of his department' by 'caus[ing] the arrest and detention of an American millionaire and his wife on a paltry charge of theft'.[206] The US ambassador himself appealed on their behalf to the Foreign Office, which rebuked the Home Office, and it in turn immediately ordered the commissioner to rectify the 'mistake'.[207] Middle-class offenders, aware of the weight of their status, often threatened officers who attempted to arrest them with initiating proceedings against them.[208] In his memoirs, Detective Chief Inspector John Littlechild described a parallel occurrence—namely, the bullying ordeal he endured after wrongfully arresting the son of a respectable gentleman.[209]

Detectives seem to have been less constrained when dealing with members of the privileged strata suspected of 'unacceptable' behaviour, such as homosexuality, or participating in radical protest. Middle-class women became the target of forcible intervention when taking part in the suffragette campaigns for the women's vote in the early twentieth century. In a memorandum by the Parliamentary Conciliation Committee for Woman Suffrage presented to the Home Office in 1911 concerning police treatment of women's deputations, detectives were said to have 'vied' with uniformed policemen 'in violence'.[210] Similarly, class distinctions were not made when it came to militant middle-class campaigners in the 1870s and 1880s seeking the repeal of the Contagious Diseases Acts (requiring prostitutes to undergo compulsory medical examination and treatment in order to reduce the levels of venereal disease in the armed forces), who were subjected to harsh police measures.[211]

Nonetheless, despite such instances of class-blind enforcement, more often police detectives betrayed a class-related bias against people of their own stock. Underlying urban policing was the presupposition that crime was largely a working-class phenomenon, especially connected with the lower rungs of this stratum.[212] Thus, the notion of 'the dangerous classes' applied not only to the criminal elements in society, but predominantly to the casual and unskilled poor who inhabited England's inner cities, vacated by the middle classes, who moved out to the suburbs in the course of the nineteenth century.[213]

The habitual criminals among them were considered the prime menace to the well-being of society, especially after the decline of penal transportation; hence they were the objects of attention by a growing number of detectives and temporary plain-clothes officers (see Chapter 1). Although towards the end of the century 'the image of a dangerous army of professional criminals faded from official, and public, discourse', replaced by a less threatening version, repeat offenders continued to be the objects of police concern, particularly as their number rose, owing, inter alia, to reduced durations of sentences.[214] Arthur Harding, a habitual thief who operated mainly in London's East End and who was in and out of prison in the early part of the twentieth century, left tape-recorded memoirs providing invaluable insights into the life and viewpoint of people of his kind. In his own words: 'Every known thief is a suspected person and every policeman knows that a convicted person is easy target for a suspected person charge.'[215]

Notably, habitual offenders were not necessarily professional or hard-core criminals; in fact, the professional criminal was rarer than was assumed by contemporaries.[216] Most defendants in court were tried summarily and were ordinary men and women who were driven to crime by deprivation and economic want. Mixing casual work with petty theft, they lived on the edge of acceptable society and functioned on the fringes of legality.[217] They were the most susceptible to close police watch, a practice that contributed to the entrenchment of a link between poverty, class, and crime.

High on the police agenda was the prevention of petty crime and regulation of behaviour in the streets. In pursuit of these ends, even persons who had not been accused of any offence in the past but were associated with the street culture in the major British cities could be the objects of close surveillance. In keeping such populations under supervision, beat officers and detectives encroached upon the liberties of all kinds of people—pickpockets and bookmakers, but also petty vendors, the Irish poor, and working-class youngsters.[218] A great many arrests were made for loitering, drunkenness, and suspicious behaviour.[219] Drink, in particular, was considered a path to lawlessness and therefore deserving of attention by uniformed as well as plain-clothes officers. In these attempts to control public comportment, police often harassed prostitutes, even if detention did not result.[220] Women who were never part of the sex trade were also pestered, stopped, or apprehended solely because of their less-than-respectable appearance, or simply their presence in the streets, especially if unchaperoned.[221] By and large such women belonged to the lower classes and were in the street earning a living as peddlers, as other types of small enterpreneurs, on the way to or from work, or in search of some entertainment with their mates. Clearly, many detectives (and other police officers) were influenced by the prevailing notions of gender, and thought (or were instructed to think) that women should stay in the private sphere.

Even without resort to harsh measures, a great deal of detective work involved some degree of intimidation. The very fact of intrusion into people's private lives when conducting an investigation could be viewed as a threat, whatever the class origin of the subject. However, judged by contemporary evidence, detectives harassed working people above and beyond the demands of the job. Arbitrary arrests, unsupported by reasonable suspicion, were not infrequent. Arthur Harding, though by no means an unbiased observer (see above), in his taped memoirs had a host of stories to tell of the heavy-handed approach, frame-ups, and fabricated charges employed by detectives when they wanted to pressure, trap, or teach someone a lesson.[222] Ticket-of-leave men (paroled prisoners) complained of being hounded by detectives even in their newly acquired places of employment.[223] Violence, too, was not shunned. Some detectives were known for their rough manner and abuse of position. Detective Cecil Bishop conceded that he 'on occasion hit some crooks very hard when my blood has been up', although he had 'always tried to get them compensation for their black eyes and sore chins when they have come up for sentence'.[224] On rare occasions excessive force caused the death of a suspect.[225]

Prevalent biases aside, individual policemen held varied views on moral and political issues and therefore acted in diverse ways. Contrary to what some radicals thought, policemen were not merely a tool in the hands of the governing classes to serve the interests of the elite. Some policemen even shared the objectives of demonstrators, ranging from suffragettes to the unemployed or to supporters of home rule for India.[226] Moreover, favourable discretion was shown by police not only to well-placed persons in society. The memoirs of detectives are replete with accounts of personal goodwill towards suspects and criminal elements, with aid extended to them and their families. A recurrent motif in these accounts is the detectives' active participation in the rehabilitation of former convicts, helping them reform and avoid returning to prison, usually by finding them work or interceding with the authorities on their behalf.[227] Police instruction books stressed the 'importance of rendering every aid to those who show a disposition to lead an honest life' and of making them feel, that 'as long as they do well they have in the Police a disinterested, kind, and powerful protector'.[228] Top police officials, such as Director Howard Vincent, made a point of publicizing efforts by detectives to assist discharged prisoners 'win an honest living'.[229] *The Times*, too, deemed it important to convince its readers that detectives sometimes went out of their way to do ex-convicts 'a good turn' by using their influence to procure support for their families during their 'retirement', or enabling them, after their release, to obtain assistance from a prisoners' aid society.[230] Aid also took other forms—for example, the acquisition of a sewing machine for a released female criminal,[231] or the kindness of Detective Inspector Nelson of the Birkenhead Police in the mid-1870s who, as a single man, took in a male child of 3, left at the station by a baby farmer.[232]

The repeated references to such good deeds were very likely designed to promote an image of the police as benevolent and dedicated public servants. Yet, even so, contacts between detectives and criminals, or those considered as potential offenders, sometimes evoked nuanced, and at times even warm, mutual relations. Formal arrangements existed in some police forces—due either to utilitarian considerations or to social trends—to assist repentant criminals, particularly from the 1870s onwards, when the role of the police regarding former convicts began to shift from deterrence and control to a broader conception of social aid.[233] If formerly the care of released convicts was largely left to churches and private philanthropy, by the late nineteenth century the state was increasingly viewed as responsible for the reform and welfare of delinquents.[234] Assistant Commissioner Robert Anderson, although advocating stern treatment of habitual criminals, pointed out with pride that the CID acted as a prisoners' aid society, negotiating between released prisoners and employers, and that the heads of the CID kept a special fund for convicts to assist them until they settled.[235] The fund consisted of the proceeds of the sale of unclaimed property taken from criminals.[236] The plan was to give ex-convicts some money (from £2 to £4) to enable them to make a fresh start.[237] These endeavours were significant, even if such arrangements were part of a system of close control.

Some levels of crime were tolerated and many criminals got away without prosecution, in as much as the police lacked resources, or thought it more advantageous not to interfere for practical considerations, such as when facing the threat of violence.[238] Yet, a certain measure of sympathy could also be a factor.[239] Offenders sometimes broke the law for reasons that were understandable to those detectives who came from the same background. Presumably, this applied primarily to petty offenders, particularly those who wanted to have some fun drinking and gambling. Apparently, criminals were well aware of some of these ambiguities. No less than detectives, they carefully studied their adversaries and could tell them apart. Arthur Harding intimated that his associates distinguished between fair and unfair detectives and that this knowledge affected their behaviour.[240]

Detectives also showed indulgence towards delinquents on the premiss that it would pay useful dividends. After all, their success in quelling illegality depended to a large extent on informants ('narks' or 'noses', as they were often called), many of whom led a life of crime.[241] Aiming to gain the willing or unwilling cooperation of these 'spies in the pay of the police', in addition to threats and payments, detectives traded enforcement for information, promising to overlook offences and grant immunity from legal procedures.[242]

THE BUILT-IN BOUNDARIES OF THE ENGLISH DETECTIVE

To understand the essence of the English detective more fully it is necessary to assess whether the long-standing fears of what plain-clothes law enforcers might do were justified. Did detectives resemble the presumed figure of a spy?[243] An examination of some of the activities of the Special Branch, whose detectives were more closely associated with such a figure, and hence with disguise and a threat to the values of freedom and privacy, is instructive. The tasks of the branch included investigating suspects of politically motivated crimes and unresolved cases with a view to apprehending and prosecuting the guilty party. But, if in ordinary detection the dominant approach was reactive, in the Special Branch it was primarily pre-emptive. Its principal strategy tended to be anticipatory and intelligence based, entailing monitoring and assessing political populations considered risky in order to warn the authorities of their potential to disrupt the social order or harm political leaders. Unlike uniformed policemen, the activity of Special Branch detectives focused on small communities—initially almost exclusively on Irish revolutionaries, later principally on anarchists, and then on other foreign revolutionaries and German spies. Their evident role as protectors of state interests, and assumptions about their contacts with foreign secret agents and governments known as oppressive, created a conceptual suspicion of governmental abuse of power. As their work was less overt than that of ordinary detectives, only faint traces of the measures they employed can be gleaned from written records. From what is known, it transpires that their methods were indeed more deceptive and elusive, as was anticipated by the early opponents of the police, with less supervision and accountability than was customary in detective branches. Much that was done covertly accorded with strictures of the law, but, as Bernard Porter aptly showed in his detailed book on the evolution of the Special Branch, the rules guiding the conduct of Britain's secret police were sometimes seriously bent, with or without the consent or knowledge of those in command.[244] In fact, under the leadership of William Melville (1893–1903) and his superiors, the Branch gradually became less mindful of constraints and more likely to engage in malpractices.[245]

The confrontation of detectives with anarchists during the 1890s illustrates how they coped with the perceived major challenge to the established order of the time. To keep internal security intact, Branchers trailed individual anarchists, raided their rendezvous and homes, confiscated their literature, arrested and detained suspects, and brought some to trial for inflammatory speeches and articles.[246] They also attended meetings and took note of speeches to serve as incriminating evidence,[247] and tracked certain anarchists outside the British mainland.[248] As a by-product of their extensive intelligence work, Branch detectives knew the addresses of anarchists and where they worked.[249] Detectives also made use of more furtive measures, gaining information by masquerading as sympathizers of the cause, and paying informers from within the anarchist ranks, who were sometimes revealed to have provided grossly exaggerated or incorrect information and fabricated evidence and scares.[250] Periodic exposures of police spies,[251] testimonies in anarchists' trials, and partial admissions by the police themselves,[252] verified the anarchists' suspicions of these tactics. The concerted efforts to hold anarchism in check also led the Special Branch to enlist the services of at least one agent provocateur, whose employment was considered by large segments of the public as well as by some heads of the police (at least rhetorically) as overstepping any permissible limits.[253]

That agent, whose ventures made headlines, was a Frenchman, Auguste Coulon, who had been in contact with anarchists in Britain since 1886 and arrived there four years later.[254] A vigorous activist, he preached brute force openly in talks and lectures across the country, distributed a book in French containing detailed instructions on the manufacture of bombs, extolled terrorism in the anarchist journal the *Commonweal*, and conducted chemistry classes.[255] Conceivably, his initiatives magnified the impression of an entrenched commitment to violence by the anarchist movement,[256] although in fact he encountered little positive response from anarchist exponents.[257] French archival evidence confirms the allegations of his comrades, and those of a Special Branch detective sergeant, Patrick McIntyre, that in late 1891 he managed to set a trap for anarchists in Walsall by enticing them to produce explosive devices, leading them to believe that they were to be used against the despotic government in Russia, whose victims elicited their sympathy (see Chapter 1).[258] This was a case of provoking a crime that might not otherwise have been committed. Presumably, the Special Branch was actively involved, as Coulon had been in its pay as early as July 1890 (an arrangement that would continue until 1904).[259] By all accounts, the person behind the scene was William Melville—at the time a highly energetic detective inspector in the Special Branch, known for dirty tricks.[260] Melville 'would not swear' at a magistrates' inquiry at Walsall in early 1892 that he had not employed Coulon.[261] Moreover, a biography of Melville refers to an assessment by a contemporary French agent that Coulon had been Melville's 'unwitting accomplice'.[262] Whatever the case, according to Detective Sergeant McIntyre's testimony, police authorities in London were aware of the affair during its various phases.[263] They may not have been conscious of Coulon's or Melville's stratagems, or they may have simply turned a blind eye to what was inconvenient for them, but they did not recoil from taking advantage of the questionable plot to cut short anarchist activities and hamper the advance of anarchist tenets in the country.

Much of the work of the Special Branch in this period may be viewed as a professional response to a potential threat to life and property posed by anarchist agitation. Prosecuting anarchists for seditious language, incitement to murder, and disorderly conduct, raiding the office of a major anarchist organ (the *Commonweal*), and breaking up and banning anarchist meetings[264] were justified by the police as legal actions designed to prevent serious harm to society. Yet anti-terrorist measures cannot be easily separated from the intent to curtail political activity. Available evidence indicates that the police intimidated and harassed the anarchist community even in situations when no danger to law-abiding citizens was perceived.[265] Allegedly, the police intruded into the private lives of anarchists in domains totally outside routine procedure. The anarchists claimed that anonymous letters were written by the police to their employers, and that officers sometimes called in person to inform them that their employee was a 'dangerous character'.[266] The police also attempted to persuade printing houses to refuse their services to anarchists.

Other evidence shows that on occasion the Branch invested energy in stifling non-conformist opinions on a variety of topics when no physical risk of any sort was discernible. The Legitimation League, formed in 1893 with the objective of securing rights of inheritance for illegitimate children, sparked polemics about legal marriage and the state's functions in general, attracting the attention of Individualist-Anarchists, who consistently eschewed abrasive rhetoric. As the decade wore on, the League veered towards a free-love position.[267] In mid-1898, the editor of its paper, the *Adult*, was arrested for publishing and selling obscene literature—namely Havelock Ellis's polemic *Sexual Inversion* about homosexuality. As a result of the single-mindedness of Special Branch Detective Inspector John Sweeney, who attended the League's meetings in disguise, the police were provided with the opportunity to prosecute the League on what would appear plausible grounds to the public, rather than infringement of the right of free speech,[268] and the League soon became defunct. Conceivably, the Branch would not have become involved if the League's areas of concern had not overlapped with certain anarchist ideas. Sweeney, the chief protagonist in the affair, admitted that the police became interested in the League once there 'was good reason for believing that Anarchist proselytising took place over and over again' at its meetings.[269] He noted with relief that police action had suppressed the 'growing evil in the shape of a vigorous campaign of free love and Anarchism', and that Britain was saved from 'the growth of a Frankenstein monster wrecking the marriage laws of our country, and perhaps carrying off the general respect for all law'.[270] His comments imply that the anarchist threat was perceived not only in terms of physical safety, and that some Special Branch officers interpreted maximum protection of society as extending to the realm of political thought.[271]

It is impossible to say how prevalent such excesses were. Branch detectives felt a certain freedom to intrude in the alien fringes of British politics,[272] but if anarchism was the ultimate test case for the police, it seems to have pushed them to the threshold of political repression though not beyond. Except for minor incidents, Bernard Porter, in his study of the Branch, found no discernible evidence that it had shadowed or infiltrated other English left-wing organizations during the 1890s, even though certain policy-makers saw these organizations as posing a serious danger to the welfare of British society.[273] When researching a clandestine institution of this kind, no firm conclusions can be reached. The British state of the early twentieth century was more interventionist in social and political life and less inhibited in using spies and spying measures than in the past. However, as much as can be judged, the typical English detective bore little resemblance to the figure of the dreaded continental spy.

Certainly, wearing plain clothes allowed police detectives to engage in all kinds of activities that would otherwise have drawn considerable public censure. Apparently, some detectives exploited their special position in society for personal gain. Critics who warned that close contacts with the underworld and mixing in 'very bad company to obtain information' would posit dangerous temptations for detectives were right.[274] Proximity to the underworld did lead to corrupt collaborative dealings. Not surprisingly, there is only scattered evidence for this, but it is sufficient to suggest undercurrents of collusion of various degrees throughout the period.[275] The most famous case was the turf fraud that exploded in 1877; other instances of illegal conduct by police detectives also reached the press,[276] but many did not gain publicity. Most probably, minor breaches of the law were quite routine in the metropolis and in other cities, with money and other favours changing hands regularly. Arthur Harding attested that in certain areas thieves 'did a lot of business with the police'.[277]

Some officers paid dearly for alleged misdeeds, even if they had an impressive record. Detective Inspector John McCarthy, who had served in the Metropolitan Police for twenty-three years, was dismissed in 1904 on the grounds that he had accepted bribes from bookmakers in return for favours in the discharge of his duties.[278] In 1906 an unnamed detective sergeant, reputed to be an exceptionally clever officer with a first-class education and rapid promotion, was forced to leave the Metropolitan Police for preferring a false charge against two men with whom he had quarelled.[279] Many others, however, survived unscathed, or at least were not sacked. According to ex-inspector John Syme, who was discharged from the Metropolitan Police in 1910 for insubordination, and conducted a life-long campaign to clear his name, 'the Commissioner is aware of many of the lapses from the honest path, but, unlike the uniform branch, the detective receives for some unknown reason more lenient treatment'.[280] If so, the police heads had learnt to live with a certain level of unlawful behaviour among detectives. Yet, contrary to assumptions of critics of police reform, as far as is known, the gravity of the turf fraud case was exceptional, and complicity between detectives and criminals was not carried out on a large scale. Syme himself acknowledged that there were 'many honest and straightforward men in the detective department'.[281]

As shown, detectives, whether investigating political or ordinary crime, sometimes breached civil liberties and invaded the privacy of individuals to attain professional goals, primarily in communities considered marginal or disposed to crime. Without delving into their methods of interrogation, it seems that they did not refrain from extracting confessions or statements from prisoners, although this was considered improper in the English criminal system.[282] They also resorted to pressure, coercion, and informers implicated in crime to obtain intelligence or evidence, and infiltrated targeted groups. Further, they employed agents to entrap suspects in ordinary crime as well. A publicized example was the case of Thomas Titley, a chemist who sold abortifacients (drugs that induced abortions), who was entrapped by disguised CID agents, and was then arrested and accused of supplying noxious drugs with criminal intent (see Chapter 5).[283] Nevertheless, neither detectives nor beat officers constituted a network of agents who systematically scrutinized citizens of all ranks of society. In particular, they did not meddle in the private affairs of the privileged members of society unless they were under strong suspicion, and even then they did so with great care. Inter alia, they did not have the manpower or the technology to exercise this type of control.

Moreover, English detectives did not routinely adopt clandestine means in carrying out their duties. If anything, often they were the object of criticism for being too visible, as will be seen in Chapter 5. Given the police occupational culture in Victorian England, the visibility of police detectives was inevitable. As Detective Sergeant Charles Leach confirmed to the 1908 royal commission: 'When we take a thief to the police court we are in the police court, which is open to the public, and there may be at least 20 or 30 of the prisoner's confederates, and they would all have an opportunity of seeing us.'[284] Divisional detectives could easily be seen entering and leaving police stations, patrolling the streets, or visiting prisons or venues frequented by suspects or informants. Special Branch officers, too, commonly functioned in the light of day, confronting and arresting suspects in front of crowds, appearing in court, serving warrants, and searching baggage in main railway stations. Their names were mentioned in the press, at times even accompanied by a photo or illustration. Certainly detectives who guarded dignitaries or kept watch at ports were bound to be recognized by the public.

The very policy of internal recruitment was commonly blamed for exposing English detectives. Not only did detectives become known in the areas that they covered, but the body language and mannerisms acquired during their generally long-term service as uniformed policemen allegedly made it impossible for them to mask their connection with the police (see Chapter 2). As a writer in the journal *Dark Blue* affirmed, although 'they go out dressed up as sailors or labourers, or others', 'the cleanliness of their faces and the severe cut of their hair, to say nothing of their methodical tread', betrayed who they were.[285] In addition, the selection criteria for height in all police forces caused detectives, like their uniformed counterparts, to stand out as particularly tall men.

The argument that policemen 'cannot get rid of the unmistakable manner and carriage which they have acquired, which cause the criminal population to know them at a glance at any distance', and that it was difficult to eliminate the effects of the considerable amount of drill they once performed,[286] was countered by some observers with outright denial,[287] while others viewed the conspicuous presence of detectives as an asset. Given that the major strategy of crime control in England was preventive, and that detection was also meant to discourage people from violating the law, the deterrent element in detection was contingent upon public awareness that detectives were around and about, active and doing their job. Further, even though recognition by criminals could seriously undermine crime control, the visibility of detectives reassured the public that they had 'the law at their backs', and carried 'moral weight'.[288] Not infrequently, assertions were also made that, had the populace not known who they were, detectives might have been indistinguishable from the criminals they were pursuing, and hence be vulnerable to attacks.[289] In addition, the ability to identify detectives was not necessarily an impediment, as informers and informants could recognize them in order to sell them information, and citizens could approach them for help or to offer clues or evidence.[290]

Yet, over and above these factors, many English police detectives simply showed limited enthusiasm for surreptitious means. Howard Vincent noted in the first edition of the *Police Code* (1881) that 'the idea that a detective, to be useful in a district, must be unknown, is erroneous in the great mass of cases'.[291] The unease with secrecy was reflected in the manner in which the resort to disguise was discussed. Although certain detectives openly acknowledged its use, and even boasted about how skilful and effective it was, others disapproved of it altogether or in any event underplayed its prevalence.[292] In his testimony to the 1868 departmental committee, Frederick Williamson asserted that, if a detective 'went in his ordinary clothes, and trusted to his own tact, he would be much more likely to get what he wanted than if he went in disguise'.[293] Another witness gave the same view: 'The less you disguise yourself, and the more you appear like other people, the better I think for Detective purposes.'[294] Questioned about whether detectives used very much disguise, Detective Superintendent John William Hallam of Manchester replied: 'No, practically none. A man may be a Detective all his life and never have a disguise.'[295] An article in the *Daily News* in 1886 about detectives in the Metropolitan Police stated that the practice of disguise had been abandoned by the police long ago, adding: 'Though circumstances may arise under which it may be expedient, or even necessary, for a detective to conceal his identity, such cases are very rare.'[296] In the early days, at least, it appears that certain detectives were quick to resolve this dilemma by utilizing the services of 'traitors to their own friends'[297] in the belief that it was better to use outside agents to spy on suspects or potential criminals, not only because they attained quicker results, but also because, if exposed, the police would not be tainted with espionage and would avoid denunciation 'from the Bench' for 'assuming a character'.[298]

As the century wore on, and Britain faced grave international and domestic challenges, the detective police were more willing to endorse secretive techniques. After the founding of the CID, greater thought was given to fashioning codes of practice to guide its members. The *Police Code* advised detectives on how to shed their police identity: not to walk together with police in uniform, not to walk in step with each other or in drill style, nor to wear 'very striking clothing, or police regulation boots', and not openly to recognize constables in uniform or salute superior officers.[299] Experience taught detectives how not to be seen as linked to the law. William Suckling of the Birmingham Police, an expert in rooting out illegal betting, refrained from coming close to the police station, and delivered his reports to a designated meeting place.[300] Signs were invented for communication among detectives when shadowing a suspect.[301] In a similar vein, family members were used as decoys. In one case, in Birmingham, when the greatest caution had to be used, the children of policemen were sent out to play in the street, observe the whereabouts of the wanted man—a Fenian terrorist—and communicate the information to nearby detectives by signalling in code.[302] Moreover, however problematic, camouflage was progressively utilized,[303] even in forces without a detective unit. Taking on a new identity could last some time. For example, in order to track down the author of a threatening letter sent to a policeman in Buckinghamshire, John Pearman, an acting sergeant from another part of the county, lived the life of a vagabond for three weeks—'dressed in rags', selling writing paper, and begging.[304]

There were no hard-and-fast rules about the sensitive issue of disguise, but, all in all, the English police detective preferred impersonation to merely putting on 'make-up' such as a beard, a moustache, a wig, or whiskers, especially in daylight (see Figures 7 and 8).[305] George Dilnot, author of several books on the police, explained that 'the real detective does not disguise himself in any elaborate or melodramatic fashion'.[306] He opted instead for a 'natural disguise'.[307] The premiss was that the best disguise was 'an easy and unconcerned appearance, that is to say, not likely to attract any particular notice', and that 'a zealous detective officer, in a general way, need wish for nothing more suitable for his purposes than to be taken for an ordinary member of the public'.[308] This type of disguise was considered 'more impenetrable because there is nothing that can go wrong with it'.[309] No one would spot the detective beneath the cover. Assuming a different character and blending in completely with the environment increasingly demonstrated the detective's skill and intelligence.[310] Furthermore, in a milieu that conceivably harboured spies—chiefly German, on the eve of the First World War—dissembling was no longer seen as out of the ordinary. Scotland Yard kept a 'make-up' room in this period, where a novice detective in the Edwardian period learnt 'how a difference in dressing the hair, the combing out or waxing of a moustache, the substitution of a muffler for a collar, a cap for a bowler, will alter his appearance', although this was used 'not half a dozen times in a year'.[311]

Such random devices, however, were only partly successful. Throughout the period, the English detective was widely regarded as working 'a little too openly', which prompted intense debate about the pros and cons of this propensity.[312] It seems that in the majority of assignments, no serious attempt was made to hide the fact that detectives were police officers. Notwithstanding the greater trend towards keeping a low profile, detectives were so familiar in their

SERGT. RECORD IN HIS "SCRAPS" COSTUME.

Figure 7. 'Detective Sergeant William Record in his "Scraps" Costume', *Police Review*, 24 Oct. 1902.

communities that they were given nicknames.[313] Most important, vigilant criminals developed a special sense of recognizing 'the policeman at a glance, through the thin disguise of private clothes', and would alert their friends.[314] One criminal boasted that, whereas he knew all the detectives, they knew so little of him that he had the audacity to live over a police station.[315] Even when obscuring their affiliation, detectives were often spotted by the subjects of their surveillance, who sometimes threatened vengeance. In response to reminiscences by Detective Sergeant McIntyre in *Reynolds's News* in 1895, a correspondent, identifying himself as 'The Watch', claimed that 'the Fenians quite as frequently and quite as successfully

SERGEANT LEESON DISGUISED AS A "TOUGH"

Figure 8. 'Detective Sergeant Benjamin Leeson Disguised as a "Tough"', in Benjamin Leeson, *Lost London* (London: Stanley Paul & Co., 1934).

"shadowed" the detectives'.[316] Anarchists, too, became experts in spotting disguised Yard men.[317]

While individual detectives and police officials may have harboured genuine misgivings about covert policing, an overt style of detection conformed with the fundamental aim of police ideology to dispel the popular conception of the detective as 'a man whose avocation it is to prowl about in various disguises, with unlimited means at his command, and with no kind of supervision'.[318] Whether consciously or not, it seems that in practice English police detectives as an organized body projected a message that they had nothing to hide and were accountable for their deeds. In working openly with uniformed officers, they reinforced this message. Their uneasy approach to disguise conveyed the impression that limits were placed upon the scope of detection and that detectives would fully conceal their identity only when it was vital for the criminal justice system or the security of the state. The second part of the book investigates the roots of the priority to calm and appeal to the public, and traces the changing image of the English detective in the print culture of the time.

PART TWO
DETECTIVES AND THE PRINT MEDIA

INTRODUCTION

Few occupations in the Victorian and Edwardian period were as exposed to public scrutiny as police detection, and few were as greatly affected by their image in, and their relationship with, the media of the time. Almost from the outset, police detectives were put under a magnifying glass by all types of published material. These close links with the communicators of information, so atypical of an occupation largely manned by working-class people, did not necessarily impinge upon the life of each and every detective, even if quite a few detectives elicited media coverage. Yet, over and above the specific experience of individual police detectives, these relations had a crucial impact on the development of police detectives as a collective. This curious phenomenon raises many questions, the first of which is why the detective's image was of such consequence.

The image of police detectives cannot be separated from that of the police as a whole. Many public discussions treated the two branches as one, using the term 'policemen' with no special reference to detectives even when they had them in mind. This was the case especially in the initial stages of the formation of detective departments. Still, detectives soon constituted the focus of public attention to the exclusion of their uniformed counterparts, perceived by many as much more compelling than the uniformed policemen. Moreover, plain-clothes work was more vulnerable to public sensibilities and censure than ordinary patrol work. Detectives were expected to prove that existing fears of plain-clothes policing were unjustified and that their actions diverged sharply from those of their predecessors in England—namely thief-takers; from spies; and from continental law-enforcers. Even after their legitimacy was secured and the extensive attention they received worked primarily to their advantage, detectives remained objects of some distrust, even by other agents of the criminal justice system, such as magistrates and judges.[1] Their inevitably intimate contact with criminals and persons living on the edges of the underworld constituted a constant threat that the borders between crime and law enforcement could be transcended without difficulty.[2] Even police officials habitually referred to the 'many temptations' to which detectives were exposed.[3] Precisely because plain-clothes officers were not as easily identifiable as ordinary policemen, and their whereabouts and behaviour could not be readily supervised, they were suspected a priori of shady practices.

This lingering scepticism carried over as well to private detectives, whose reputation was essential to their commercial success. However, the dominant view of police officers was as public servants, and they were therefore held to a higher standard. Demands by the public that government offices, whether national or local, should cater to its needs and that taxpayers should get good value for their money grew more vocal as the century progressed. Furthermore, detectives were perceived as public servants of a special kind, belonging to an institution whose designated tasks were to protect the public in the sensitive areas of crime and safety, to embody the rule of law, and to be committed to maintaining justice. Moreover, in contrast to private agents, police detectives, in addition to tackling property offences, also dealt with life and death issues, including the most terrible of all transgressions—murder—thus touching upon the very core of human fears and anxieties. As policemen, they were meant to serve the common interests of every member of the community regardless of class, income, or gender. In an age increasingly exposed to the pressures of democratization and public debate, these public servants were constantly examined to see if they had fulfilled their duties to society, unlike private detectives who served the needs of private individuals or institutions and were responsible to them only. Many police detectives shifted to the private sector upon retirement, and some detectives, as well as uniformed policemen, took on private work while in police service. Still, the police singled themselves out as the experts in the fight against crime and as *the* body that could best stamp out crime and enforce the laws of the state, thereby meriting the reinforcement of their authority and their means of surveillance.

To attain this power and status, police detectives needed to be widely appreciated not only as honest, disinterested, and non-intrusive public servants, but, no less importantly, as good at their job. As Melville L. Macnaghten, head of the CID (1903–13), affirmed, failure to find the culprit could put the honour of detectives at stake, while succeeding could strengthen public regard for them.[4] Their professional status depended on it. Moreover, although the media emphasized the special abilities of detectives as the key to solving crimes, in practice, access to information about the circumstances of a reported crime, the local underworld, or other suspicious elements was the most crucial factor. Apart from informers and informants, the steady advance of cases and breakthroughs in investigations rested to a large extent on unpaid and disinterested cooperation. Detectives, and the police in general, relied on the public, whether they were pawnbrokers,[5] shopkeepers, stationmasters, railway porters, bus conductors, newsboys, bank and post-office clerks, hotel or club managers, to provide evidence. Neighbours, landladies, servants, bystanders, newspaper readers, and the victims or accomplices of criminals were other sources of valuable knowledge.[6] Neither the uniformed police nor the detective branch had sufficient manpower to cover crime-ridden areas adequately, and, even if they had, some crimes would always occur far from the gaze of police officers. In fact, the patrolling role of the police, whether in uniform or in plain clothes, was designed at least in part to motivate the public to report about crime. Ordinary people could supply clues, identify a suspect, or catch a criminal in the act. In addition, the legal system required members of the community to testify in court to corroborate police testimony.

There were thus mundane reasons not to antagonize the public. In his book *A History of Police in England* (1901), W. L. Melville Lee, a former army captain, articulated this message succinctly.[7] Believing that 'the actual continuance of the English police is...dependent upon the consent of the people', he held that popularity was 'of the utmost value to the police', since public assistance was crucial for efficient police work.[8] Representing the police perspective, he wrote:

It is only on the rarest occasions that a policeman is actually the eye-witness of a crime, nor in the nature of things is he likely to be in the confidence of the criminal. As a rule he must rely on information, and generally speaking the public is the only source from which the necessary knowledge can be obtained. If the public are hostile, the one source of information is closed, and the police are rendered powerless.[9]

Public esteem was also meant to convince reluctant victims to come forward with information. Hence, there was a certain mutuality in the relationship between the public and the police: while the public depended on the protection of the police, the police, in turn, needed the cooperation of the public. Moreover, it was essential that support by the public be given unreservedly. As Lee noted, if every act of the police officer is questioned, and 'if at every turn he has to surmount some obstacle set up to annoy and discourage him', this will affect the results of his labours.[10] In sum, establishment figures like Lee were anxious to inculcate a positive image of the police in the public mind and to persuade the public that:

> The police are not the representatives of an arbitrary and despotic power, directed against the rights or obtrusively interfering with the pleasures of law-abiding citizens: they are simply a disciplined body of men, specially engaged in protecting 'masses' as well as 'classes' from any infringement of their rights on the part of those who are not law-abiding.[11]

Detectives recognized the possible drawbacks of relying on information emanating from the public. Notably, during scares and alarms, the CID was flooded with letters offering information, as, for example, at the time of the Jack the Ripper murders (31 August to 9 November 1888), when the public inundated the police with letters suggesting clues, suspects, or solutions to the crimes (see Chapter 5). In a less-well-known, though sensational, case, the Boulton and Park affair, Superintendent James Thomson of the Metropolitan Police E Division 'had in his possession over 2,000 letters'.[12] Even if some of the information provided by the public was time-wasting or even misleading,[13] detectives believed that the public assisting the police with information-gathering contributed to the reduction of crime.[14]

Police officials who called for public cooperation did not have notions of neighbourhood watches or community policing in mind, nor did they aim to encourage self-help or traditional forms of informal control by the community. They wanted the public neither to engage in actual policing functions, nor to be party to decision-making. If policing in the eighteenth and early part of the nineteenth century relied to a large extent on the initiative of individuals or associations to cope with crime, now the administrators of the criminal justice system aspired instead to aggrandize the authority and status of the police in society, thereby enhancing the role of detectives as well. The police were to be the principal enforcers of law and order, with the public contributing its share in assisting this body strictly in accordance with the requirements of officialdom.

Such expectations imposed the burden of sustaining the confidence of the public on the police. Aiming at achieving compliance not through the use of physical power or the threat of violence—although these, too, were employed—but by voluntary consent, the British establishment valued a police image that persuaded the public that suppressing certain forms of behaviour was justified and that the means adopted to fight crime were appropriate and effective.[15] The heads of police also came to believe that the 'public judges of the efficiency of the Police generally largely on its detective work'.[16] Ultimately, police popularity reflected on the image of the state as a whole. While the nineteenth century saw the growing intervention of the state in the life of the people, whether in their homes, beliefs, schooling, health, or leisure activities, the state itself steadily became an object of investigation and inspection. As an arm of the state, the police in general, and their role of crime investigation more specifically, needed to be seen not only as necessary but also as benevolent. A favourable image of the police could generate satisfaction with the established order and foster an alliance between the state and the law-abiding public.

Sensitivity to public opinion, however, was not solely impelled by the desire to accomplish tangible gains; it was also related to the motivation and self-esteem of policemen, whether uniformed or not. Eight years before the Metropolitan Police was created, George B. Mainwaring, a magistrate for Middlesex, had espoused the formation of a force that would not only be untainted by criminality, seen, known, and expected anywhere—but would also 'feel the public interest to be... [its] own', as he wrote in a pamphlet titled *Observations on the Present State of the Police of the Metropolis*.[17] In time, policemen who, increasingly, became long-term employees, did indeed develop a strong identification with the ethos of service.[18] Attaining public recognition and respect was integral to this process.

However crucial public opinion was to detective work, a gap existed between how the police wished to be seen and some of their practices. As discussed in Chapter 3, many detective activities were inconsistent with the letter of the law and impinged on British civil liberties. The communities that were more closely policed—particularly those who were not identified with 'public opinion'—were susceptible to abrasive enforcement practices. Given the nature of the occupation, many more such activities—unrecorded or unavailable to researchers—probably took place at the time. Had these been known, they would have come in for heavy criticism and eroded public confidence. Equally, decision-makers were sensitive to public sentiments, and this too impacted on the evolution of police detection in Britain. As shown in Chapter 1, the birth of the modern police itself was delayed out of fear—less of uniformed patrol officers than of a 'secret service' composed of individuals whose occupational identity was unknown and who could therefore engage in the dreaded acts of spying and provocation associated with continental policemen or indigenous thief-takers.[19] The same widespread fear explains, at least in part, why no distinct detective department was formed in the Metropolitan Police of London until thirteen years after the establishment of the force. The ongoing distrust of undercover policing also accounted to a great extent for the minuscule size of detective units for years after its formation in 1842. Evidence shows that senior officials were often guided by the desire to avoid alienating dominant opinion when deliberating policies or making decisions, or they used it in their rhetoric as an explanation. For a long time, the British police were reluctant to work together with foreign police agencies to monitor militant political refugees living in London—although on occasion they did so[20]—inter alia because of the possibility of provoking an angry public response.[21] When augmenting the Special Branch to deal with the radicalization of the women's movement before the First World War, police officials were determined to employ only 'men of practical experience ... as any tactical mistake would be much criticised and would have the effect of promoting ... the progress of the Suffragette propaganda'.[22] The impetus to gain public support for the forces of law and order was in fact at the root of many of the compromises reached in the police world.

Mindful of the continuing deep-rooted suspicion of the propriety of detective work, the police leadership tried to inculcate habits in detectives that would improve their image. The first director of the CID, Howard Vincent (1878–84), anxious to elicit public endorsement of the new body, ordered detectives to attend to their attire so as not 'to lower themselves, and the service, in the estimation of the public'.[23] Behaviour was equally important. One of the first Police Orders addressed to detectives stressed 'the great importance of not using any irritative language or expressions even towards those who may be offending against the laws. The more good temper and coolness shewn by the police ... the more readily will all the well disposed assist them in preserving the public peace, and securing any riotous or disorderly persons.'[24] The same message was reiterated in different formats throughout the period. Uniformed constables, too, were instructed that 'good temper is almost as essential as sobriety' and that they must be mindful that they were public officers, but the basic assumption in the police forces was that 'a Detective Constable should, of all others, be a man of temperate habits'.[25] In a report to Parliament for the year 1882, Superintendent James Thomson of the Metropolitan Police E Division declared that detectives 'must temper their zeal with discretion and integrity, or they will never honour the Police service'.[26] *Snowden's Police Officers' Guide* of 1897 emphasized that every officer engaged in detective duty 'must carefully avoid in any way compromising his own position, or the credit of the service to which he belongs'.[27] The Police Orders of the Metropolitan Police reminded CID officers in 1907 that it was 'specially incumbent on them to avoid conduct likely to bring discredit or suspicion on them'.[28] Each detective was thus made to feel responsible for the reputation of the police service as a whole.

Predictably, shaping the image of police detectives greatly depended on their interaction with the public. However, most of the public had no direct knowledge of or contact with detectives. Detective departments existed mainly in the big cities, where the chances of coming across a detective were minimal for those living in respectable areas. As the nineteenth century wore on and the population expanded, more and more people lived in large cities and towns where face-to-face interaction gave way to virtual experience. Those who did come in contact with detectives were mainly criminals or residents of neighbourhoods that were particular targets of detective attention. Here and there other people encountered plain-clothes policemen, either because they sought this contact—such as informants, journalists and reporters interested in crime, ordinary people who packed galleries in the courts, and participants in the proceedings—or because of circumstances beyond their control—such as street walkers or onlookers who found themselves unexpectedly embroiled in the investigation of a case.

Most people, however, learnt about the day-to-day business of detectives from the printed word. Since every form of media devoted space to detectives, readers of all social groups and inclinations got to know something about them. In fact, the battle for the reputation of detectives was mainly waged there. The print culture in the Victorian and Edwardian period was a location in which writers of all sorts, including several police detectives themselves, conducted an ongoing multifaceted dialogue about detectives and argued for and against certain depictions of them, whether explicitly or not. The emerging image was not homogenous. Part Two of the book explores the image of detectives as it appeared in the press, in fiction, and in the detectives' own memoirs, each format reflecting different emphases. An exploration of the information about detectives that reached the public through each of these media helps answer the following questions. What topics and messages constituted the main focus of attention? Did the dominant presentations appearing in the contemporary media support detectives and override initial objections? How was the occupation perceived? We know from existing scholarly works that the image of the police improved significantly in the course of the period.[29] What role did detectives play in this process? Did they manage to win over respectable opinion and pivotal cultural agents?

While depictions of detectives in fictional literature surely had an effect on public perceptions, and detective memoirs also contributed to the formulation of the detective's image, the present volume contends that the press served as the principal mediator in the interaction between detectives and the public. By its nature and role in society, the press was the primary disseminator of information about the authentic world of crime prevention and detection. Further, in its task of reporting real events and covering actual issues, the press was the major channel through which the public believed it truly learnt about real-life detectives. That press reports and commentary described, and more importantly moulded, reality was also the prevalent perception in the nineteenth century in the press community, including advertisers.[30] Admittedly, over the course of the nineteenth century commercial interests in the press grew in importance, and selling newspapers became a more dominant impetus than educating the public.[31] Yet, the transmission of news and commentary retained its educational value. The result was that 'the press, in all its manifestations, became during the Victorian period the context within which people lived and worked and thought, and from which they derived their... sense of the outside world'.[32] In addition to publishing extensive reports about police detectives and their work, journals of all descriptions frequently commented on the police image as it unfolded in the press. Consequently, the detective departments, and the police as a whole, depended heavily on the press for their reputation.

Journalists thus played a major role in shaping opinion about detectives in Britain. Yet, the relationship was not one-sided. In turn, media personalities developed a certain dependence on detectives. In fact, the relationship between members of the two occupations was unique as well as complex. In this context, an analysis of the evolving relations between formal criminal investigators and agents of the press is needed. What were the points of contact between them and how were they manifested? How was information passed on to journalists and how did journalists and detectives regard each other and exchange services? Lastly, did they benefit each other and meet each other's expectations? Chapter 4 highlights these issues.

4

THE UNIQUELY SYMBIOTIC RELATIONSHIP BETWEEN DETECTIVES AND JOURNALISTS

Detectives and journalists had much in common. The essence of their work relied on investigation and information-gathering—that is, probing and then exposing. Indeed, journalists often called themselves 'investigators'.[1] In their professional capacities both developed the skills of taking evidence, interviewing witnesses, and, on the basis of scattered pieces of information, constructing a narrative, sometimes explaining a perplexing issue. Their professional status depended on their ability to perform these tasks repeatedly and successfully. The limited use of scientific means in investigations in Victorian and Edwardian England meant that individual acuity was prized. Accordingly, both detectives and journalists were increasingly expected to possess a distinctive mix of qualities to fulfil their jobs adequately—determination, persistence, an inquisitive and analytical mind, and sharp observation. Moreover, although journalists worked for private organizations, they increasingly perceived themselves as advancing the public interest, as did detectives.[2] Both occupations aimed, at least in theory, at getting to the bottom of things and revealing the truth.[3] If police detectives, as functionaries of law and order in society, were also known as agents of social control, this was also true to some extent for journalists, notably those who worked for the mass-circulation dailies.[4] An additional similarity was that neither group had formal professional training, and acquired their skills on the job.

So overlapping were their tasks that at times they exchanged roles and crossed into each other's domains. Some journalists, like detectives, wore a disguise when they searched for information and wanted to hide their identity.[5] On occasion, each party would actually pass itself off as the other. An early example was Inspector Joseph

Todhunter of the City of London Police, who adopted the role of a reporter in order to penetrate Chartist circles in 1839.[6] A few decades later, Detective Sergeant Patrick McIntyre of the Special Branch did likewise when shadowing a French colonel living in London, who allegedly was sending arms to an African sultan, to the consternation of the French government.[7] Special Branch detectives pretended to be journalists in order to attend suffragette meetings without encountering animosity.[8] Conversely, J. Hall Richardson and Ashmead Bartlett, both of the *Daily Telegraph*, pretended on different occasions to be Yard men in order to gain entry to crime sites and obtain a good story.[9] Their methods and the objects of their investigations were at times so similar that journalists were suspected of being detectives even when they were not impersonating them.[10] The similarities between detectives and journalists did not escape the notice of perceptive contemporaries. The journalist J. Hall Richardson described his forty-five years of reporting about crime as 'press-detective work'.[11] In 1904, the *London Magazine* published an article entitled 'Newspapers as Detectives', featuring accounts of pressmen acting as crime fighters.[12]

Not only were both occupations alike, they also evolved in parallel. Each had existed before the nineteenth century, but for both the 1840s constituted a turning point. Similarly to detective work, journalism as a profession began to develop during the eighteenth century,[13] although journalists then did not yet operate in the role that evolved later of 'professional processor[s] of information' who 'tell the truth only'.[14] From approximately the mid-nineteenth century, journalism was widely viewed as a distinct profession;[15] its linguistic style coalesced, and a more clearly defined occupational identity for newspaper reporting emerged.[16]

Both occupations made considerable strides during the Victorian period. Although detectives formed only a fraction of the total number of policemen and of each individual force, and their number *in toto* was never large, their growth rate was dramatic in the latter part of the nineteenth century, as seen in Chapter 1. For its part, the press underwent a process of unprecedented growth at about the time detective departments were formed in the metropolis in the mid-nineteenth century.[17] Technological advances in printing, the abolition of various duties on the transmission of information in the course of the 1850s and 1860s (like the advertisement tax in 1853, the stamp duty in 1855, and the duty on paper in 1860), and a drop in the costs of paper and newspaper production gave rise to a mass-produced commercial press. A further expansion occurred at the end of the century with the advance of the half-penny press. Integral to this process was a substantial expansion in the number of journalists.[18]

Both detectives and journalists struggled hard to secure recognition and respectability during the course of the nineteenth century. The attitude of the public to press reporting during the eighteenth and early nineteenth centuries reflected a mix of cynicism and an awareness that it was informative and useful.[19] However, in parallel to detection and detectives generally, 'before 1840 the reputation of the press was low' and journalists 'were regarded as hacks or as demagogues'.[20] By the end of the century, both vocations had gained considerably in credibility and status,[21] although both groups felt that much remained to be accomplished in this area.[22]

RECIPROCAL ADVANTAGES

Evolving side by side, the two occupations developed a certain mutuality and even interdependence, as the links between them were potentially advantageous to both. Clearly, detectives badly needed positive exposure in the press for the many reasons discussed above. The power of journalists to influence, if not mould, opinion could help dispel distrust and win support, especially since most of the public formed its evaluations largely on the basis of information given in the press. No less conspicuous was the dependence of many journalists on policemen engaged in the struggle against crime. Although these journalists might seek out material on crime from varied sources, the cooperation of the police was indispensable—a dependence that was the direct product not only of the growing role played by the police in crime control, but also of the immense public interest in it.

Crime had long been a serious matter of concern. In varying degrees, the fear of crime was a component of people's mental world then, sometimes generating lasting anxieties. If not anxious about physical harm, the property-owning middle and upper classes, as well as groupings lower down the social scale, expressed apprehension about property crimes. Yet fear was not the only source of interest in crime. The novelist and journalist Edward Bulwer-Lytton observed in the early 1830s that a notorious characteristic of his countrymen was their 'love for narratives of terror', noting that 'it is exactly from our unacquaintance with crime, viz., from the restless and mysterious curiosity it excites, that we feel a dread pleasure in marvelling at its details'.[23] Whether the preoccupation with crime was personal, theoretical, or of interest only for its entertainment value, the press satisfied this curiosity best of all on a day-to-day basis.

Newspapers and periodicals had long shown a close observation of the world of crime.[24] The press in the early decades of the eighteenth century was 'infatuated with the representation of criminals. It gave prominence to accounts of remarkable individuals, but also provided an extensive underworld context in which criminal activities made a kind of sense.'[25] London led the way. By the end of the eighteenth century, most of the London papers regularly published articles about arrests and detection activities drawn from the hearings of the summary courts, particularly the Bow Street Office.[26] In addition, the press published detailed accounts of such activities based on sensational cases at the Old Bailey.[27] As Peter King has postulated, by then, newspapers were 'the most widely read source of printed information about crime and justice'.[28]

The public's curiosity kept growing during the nineteenth century. With the expansion of the reading audience in the second half of the century, reports about all manner of crime became more popular. As part of their mandate to acquaint the public with recent events, newspapers were obliged to report about crimes and trials, yet the coverage of these topics was propelled by a far stronger drive than the obligation to disseminate news. The aim was to satisfy the seemingly insatiable interest of the public in the criminal justice system and to profit commercially thereby. If 'the comprehensive reporting of recent crimes and disasters now became a staple of the cheap newspapers', some of the older general papers also 'made profitable specialties of "criminal intelligence", and one or two other papers...printed little else'.[29] The popular Sunday papers, read by many workers on their day of rest, and 'the weekly miscellany-*cum*-sensational-fiction paper which was issued on Saturday' accorded considerable space to crime.[30] The periodical press, focusing on opinion rather than on news, was also preoccupied with various aspects of this subject. Writing in depth about crime and punishment, contributors to periodicals had to be in touch with sources that would supply them with knowledge and insights, albeit less urgently than newsmen who were dependent on speedy and regular access to crime news.

Throughout the century newspapers continued to derive much of their information about crime from court proceedings, where details of cases, from the perpetration of the crime to its punishment, were unfolded. In this they were not dependent on police cooperation and could gain information about the process of an investigation simply by having representatives in court. However, as the century progressed, the commercialization of the newspaper industry generated a growing demand for a broader range of material about crime, while at the same time the expansion of detective departments in the big cities made their work an attractive subject for the press. To be topical, newspapers were increasingly required to report about the progress of investigations before the results reached the courts, making the press ever more dependent on police sources. In addition, growing emphasis in the last two decades of the century on news rather than opinion and commentary, which heightened the role of news reporters, created greater urgency for the press to obtain easier access to information.[31] The feeling among many journalists at the close of the nineteenth century was that 'the discussion of public business... must give way to a lively demand for matters of "human interest"'.[32] A large portion of this demand was vigorously met by covering crime and detection. Contact with crime investigators thus became essential to journalistic work.

A CULTURE OF EXCHANGE

A web of mutual dependencies between detectives and journalists interested in crime was created, propelled by a dynamic relationship moulded by the internal changes taking place in both occupations. No set procedures regarding the transmission of information to journalists, and no routine system of briefings, or press officers, existed in the police in the period under review. Relations developed haphazardly and were unstructured. However, these links gradually became more intensive, albeit not always smooth, as will be shown below.

Benefits to journalists

Circulating in the proximity of law-enforcers, who would feed them information, insights, and good stories, journalists and reporters gradually cultivated a wide range of contacts with detectives, from the topmost to the lowest levels.[33] This was particularly true for the growing number of reporters who became experts on crime news towards the end of the century.[34] A small number of prominent journalists had social connections with politicians and officials, including those working for the police both in London and the provinces, whom they met in gentlemen's clubs and other social venues and could tap for information.[35] Nearly all the editors of *Punch* were members of the Garrick Club, as were such police officials as Melville L. Macnaghten (assistant commissioner and head of the CID at Scotland Yard, 1903–13), Basil Thomson (assistant commissioner of police and head of the CID at Scotland Yard, 1913–21), and Nevil Macready (commissioner of the Metropolitan Police, 1918–20).[36] The most productive interaction, however, was between journalists and officers lower down the hierarchical scale, who were more likely to serve as sources of updates and piquant information. In their memoirs, George R. Sims—journalist, author, playwright, and poet—and the journalist J. Hall Richardson describe the cooperation and close contact they had with both the rank and file and those higher up in the Metropolitan Police and other police forces in reporting extensively about crime.[37] Reporters hung about police stations, especially during interesting inquests, in the hope of gathering clues and leads. Others sought the company of detectives in a more methodical manner in order to hear about their experiences. Charles Dickens's open channel of communication with the small number of detectives in the formative days of the detective department in London is well known and is detailed in Chapter 5. As founder and editor of the popular magazine *Household Words*, established in the early 1850s, he hosted crime fighters employed in the Metropolitan Police headquarters and listened attentively to their stories of crime and criminals, which they were only too happy to divulge.[38] If not with the same intensity, many other journalists invested time in listening carefully to police discourse and publishing the results.[39]

Yet, writers without these connections also knew whom to seek out for on- or off-the-record commentary, in the same way that detectives knew whom to approach and tip off regarding information they wanted published. In their pursuit of news, journalists relied as well on 'the gossip of a police subordinate' and were innovative in loosening his tongue.[40] In their efforts to gain information denied them by the detective in charge of a case, they sometimes plied 'him with drink'.[41] 'Money bribes' were also utilized.[42] Commissioner Nevil Macready revealed in his memoirs that leaks of all kinds related to the police in the metropolis were rife, 'partly due to the temptations offered to the police by people connected with the press, who paid either in cash or in kind for the information, often inaccurate, which they extracted'.[43] Retired detectives and police officials were another fertile source.[44] Journalists and reporters thus obtained inside information about the goings-on in detective departments, although most often they could not disclose their sources.[45] They knew about internal conflicts and proposed changes, had access to certain formal reports and documents, and were cognizant of the feelings of the police rank and file. They also offered recommendations for change and took sides on controversial issues.

A strong undercurrent of favouritism typified these relationships. Close contacts and amicable relations sometimes developed between detectives and journalists,[46] which in all likelihood quickened the flow of information to journalists and facilitated access to data, exclusive news, and even material considered confidential. As the journalist Frederick J. Higginbottom recounted:

To be suddenly ordered to follow up a murder inquiry or a police investigation of any kind meant a succession of rebuffs to the reporter who was unknown to the officials concerned. It was no use demanding information as a right. It could only be obtained as a favour, and this meant the employment of diplomatic art, sometimes aided by hospitality, that brought into play the reporter's most ingenious faculties.[47]

The privileges enjoyed by journalists were an integral part of the culture of exchange that developed between reporters and the police. Both official and unofficial sources of knowledge presumably passed on information more willingly to journalists who were known as effective spokesmen for police interests and inculcated a positive image of the police in the public mind. In turn, police officers and officials were sometimes allowed to censor material damaging to the reputation of the police. According to former policeman John Syme (see page 136), a leading newspaperman, upon receiving a pamphlet Syme wrote detailing the wrongs done to him by the heads of the Metropolitan Police, actually approached the commissioner and asked him whether he had any objection to the publication of the damning piece.[48]

Detectives also agreed to offer their services to journalists in less conventional contexts. Notably, they were sympathetic to requests early on by journalists seeking personally to experience what it meant to work as a detective.[49] Dickens was one of the first journalists to be granted such a privilege. Unsatisfied with a reliance on interviews only, and having a deep affection for detectives, he arranged to accompany them on their routine tours. One result of his explorations appeared in *Household Words* in June 1851 in an article titled 'On Duty with Inspector Field'.[50]

Aside from providing journalists with the opportunity to observe detective work in action, individual detectives would escort members of the press on investigative visits to poverty-stricken areas, thus reinforcing a vogue among journalists and men of letters, begun in the 1830s and accelerating during the middle decades of the century, to explore lower-class life.[51] In contrast to Dickens—one of the pioneers of this trend—the interest of the journalists was not necessarily in detectives *per se*, but in their services as guides. As one scholar commented: 'Much Victorian journalism was a literature of voyeurism, revealing to its middle class audience a hidden life of the city which offered... illicit enjoyment of the forbidden "Other" that was so close to, yet so far from, the Victorian bourgeoisie.'[52] Aiming to observe life in all its variety, journalists focused on the conditions of the labouring population in darkest London and in other urban environments. In this context, a new task assigned to the police by the Common Lodging Houses Act of 1851—supervising London's lodging houses partly with a view to keeping an eye on criminal suspects—was particularly appealing to the journalists.

Aspiring to alleviate misery and prevent crime, and in the belief that accurate knowledge of the life of the poor is essential to attain these aims, the well-known journalist, playwright, and novelist Henry Mayhew and his assistants roamed the streets of London in mid-Victorian times to interview a broad spectrum of lower-class men and women and collect evidence of deprivation and crime.[53] To help him in this mission, on several occasions, uniformed and detective officers accompanied his team on its investigative quests in the slums and criminal haunts of the capital, as they did with many journalists thereafter.[54] In 1869, the novelist, playwright, and journalist Blanchard Jerrold suggested to the famed French illustrator Gustave Doré, who was on a visit to London, that they work together to produce a panoramic portrait of London.[55] To cover working-class London, they approached the police to take them around. The result was the book *London: A Pilgrimage*, which 'soon came to be recognised as the greatest of all Doré's achievements in illustration' and one of the best guides to Victorian London.[56] This type of service was also used by foreign journalists. At about the same time, the French author, philosopher, historian, and journalist Hyppolite Taine asked detectives to lead him through the 'disreputable quarters' of Manchester.[57] The outcome is to be found in his book *Notes on England*, which appeared in 1872 in England and under the title *Notes sur l'Angleterre* in France.

Describing how this process worked, Blanchard Jerrold wrote about his tour of the East End of London thus:

> You put yourself in communication with Scotland Yard to begin with. You adopt rough clothes. You select two or three companions who will not flinch even before the humours and horrors of Tiger Bay; and you commit yourself to the guidance of one of the intelligent and fearless heads of the detective force. He mounts the box of the cab about eight o'clock: and the horse's head is turned—east.[58]

Jerrold narrates how the cab left Fleet Street for the crowded, dark, noisy lanes of the East End, where 'groups of gossiping or quarrelling men and women block the road'. Apparently, the two men sought assistance not only from Yard detectives but also from local police officers with a particular knowledge of the locality, stopping at the Whitechapel police station 'to pick up the superintendent of savage London'.[59] The cab was then dismissed, as 'it would be useless in the strange, dark byeways, to which we are bound', and the walk through the mean streets of the East End began. At the end of the tour, Jerrold and Doré, shaken and exhausted, hailed a cab and 'buried' themselves in it with relief.[60] 'It was two in the morning when we got clear of the East,' Jerrold concluded.

Such ventures became something of a long-standing tradition. Aaron Watson, a freelance journalist in London in the early 1880s, made 'many plunges into the obscure places of London life' in the company of police officers.[61] Watson also asked the police to take him on a round of the West End, and was obliged.[62] The journalist Charles Williams, then editor of the *Evening News*, suggested that Watson should look up a Yard inspector, a friend of Williams, and 'go with him on some of his rounds'.[63] It seemed the natural thing to do for journalists interested in inspecting lodging houses, poor houses, gambling sites, thieves' dens, 'opium smokes', and other places that were not part of their natural environment. In the event, Watson, too, became 'great friends' with the inspector. That these tours were conducted while the officers were on duty was not considered at all odd. Officers took their task as guides seriously, recommending to journalists what they ought to see and where they ought to go, then taking them there. Sometimes in these joint ventures, both officers and journalists put on a disguise. The symbiosis on these occasions was close to perfection.

Foreign visitors also continued to enjoy such services. An American journalist who arrived in London to research the Whitechapel murders in the summer of 1889 was escorted to the scenes of the crimes by Inspector Henry Moore, who was in charge of the inquiry from the beginning of 1889, and was invited by the head of the CID, Robert Anderson, to view the lodging houses and narrow passageways in the area.[64] In the early 1890s, Joaquim Pedro de Oliveira Martins, a Portuguese historian and writer (later Portuguese finance minister), was taken by a detective on a guided tour of the area where the Jack the Ripper murders had taken place.[65] Part of the tour also included entering a tenement building inhabited by a family of impoverished drunks to show the guest the lower depths of English society.

Journalists were not necessarily passive observers who accompanied detectives in order to report about what was shown to them. At times their preferences dictated the itinerary. While detectives may have performed investigative duties in the course of these rambles—examining reputed criminals and suspects, visiting venues known to harbour lawbreakers, and even capturing offenders—it was not uncommon for them to arrange their routine to suit the needs of the journalist in question.[66] The practice of 'letting the police serve as guides to slumming parties' was so ingrained in their occupational culture that 'the police were practically keeping certain places open in order to have something ready and handy to show to strangers', as observed by Sir Edward Bradford, commissioner of the Metropolitan Police (1890–1903), to Josiah Flynt, an American journalist on a visit to London, who had requested such a tour at the beginning of the twentieth century.[67]

Most of these journalists viewed detectives as a means to an end. The assumption was that an acquaintance with the poor inevitably entailed some contact with crime and vice versa. Detectives had the know-how to provide an insider's view of the margins of society. As law-enforcers, they were empowered to visit—'at uncertain periods and at their own discretion'—the locales where the 'dangerous classes' lived and spent their time, and where 'persons wanted' could be found.[68] Together they examined the lives of the poor and desperate in the slums and rubbed shoulders with them. With the aid of detectives, journalists learnt how to see things that others could not—for example, identifying disguised criminals and habitual thieves.[69] Detectives imparted knowledge that only they possessed, and that journalists could then convey to their readers. In this manner, detectives served as mediators between print agents and information, and in fact between representatives of different classes.

An added benefit was that, though detectives did not wear uniforms, they were recognized in the neighbourhoods visited, thereby providing protection and a sense of security to the investigative journalists who accompanied them. Indeed, there were good grounds for fear. As Jerrold and Doré and their police guides walked through the dark byways of the East End in the early 1870s, the cockneys looked at them 'as the Japanese looked upon the first European travellers in the streets of Jeddo [Edo or Tokyo]'.[70] Furthermore, 'lowbrowed ruffians and women who emphasize even their endearments with an oath' scowled at them in threatening groups as they passed, 'keeping carefully in the middle of the road'. The escorting officers—whether in uniform or in plain clothes—aware of the danger, cautioned the journalists that a lone wanderer who found himself in these regions unprotected would be 'stripped to his shirt'.[71] The guides, therefore, took extra care of the group, urging its members to 'stick closer together' in rough parts, while they themselves walked both in front and behind the journalists, now and then placing one of their number at strategic points to protect the advancing party and keep the road open behind them.[72] What better protection could the journalists have?

In his memoirs, Detective Cecil Bishop provides a similar impression, over thirty years later, of the dangers posed by locals to strangers roaming the slums. He was assigned to escort George R. Sims, who was writing a book about London and 'wanted to see some "low life" ... the real thing and not the fancy stuff that's usually written'.[73] Bishop chose to tour his district, Seven Dials, 'one of the roughest districts in Britain', but, he recalled, Sims was so alarmed by what he saw that he soon asked Bishop 'to conduct him back to civilisation'.[74] This is surprising, since Sims was accustomed to the perils of journeying into the 'dark side of life', where 'life... [was] held of little account' and strangers would routinely be 'hemmed in down a blind alley by a crowd of roughs' who would throw half-bricks at them.[75] Sims seemed to have thought that the presence of law-enforcers on the tour put outsiders at a greater risk. Experience had taught him that it was 'unpleasant to be mistaken, in underground cellars where the vilest outcasts hide for the light of day, for detectives in search of their prey', and that he and his company could 'pass without let or hindrance where it would be dangerous for a policeman to go'.[76]

Benefits to detectives

That police officers willingly consented to offer such services, and that publishers and journalists were grateful for them, is evident in the resultant accounts. By way of example, the preface (entitled 'Advertisement') to the fourth volume of Henry Mayhew's *London Labour and the London Poor* contained explicit thanks to Richard Mayne, commissioner of the Metropolitan Police at the time (1829–68), and to the authorities at Scotland Yard, for information and assistance extended to him.[77] In return, the press offered services to detectives that were vital to the success of their work. While the contribution of journalists was by no means uniformly advantageous to detectives, gradually, more articles portrayed the police, and police detectives, in a positive light.

Some journalists also published books that improved the police image.[78] Notably, the socially conscious writers who visited crime-ridden locales in the company of detectives played a fundamental role as such image moulders, albeit not always intentionally. One of these was Henry Mayhew. His monumental *London Labour and the London Poor* contained, in addition to three volumes on the labouring population of London (published in different formats between 1851 and 1861), a fourth volume on 'those that will not work' (focusing on prostitutes, thieves, swindlers, and beggars). Published in 1862, it incorporated abundant references to detectives and uniformed policemen.[79] The officers were described as well informed, 'bold and adroit',[80] assertive, confident,[81] 'experienced and able', and physically alert and strong.[82] On the whole, their manner of detecting crime 'was very ingenious, and reflected high credit' to them.[83] They worked hard and were effective in making arrests as well as in securing convictions. Acting on the basis of accumulated information—very much like Mayhew himself—police detectives were portrayed as more than a match for clever criminals, and as rational reformers working for the betterment of society at large.

Hyppolite Taine, the French social eyewitness who published in both England and France, noted that his police escorts in Manchester were 'serious, sensible, prudent men' who 'made no parade of their talents', spoke little, and answered questions always to the point.[84] Moreover, in remarking that, 'with their impassive countenance and their meditative expression, they inspired confidence and had an air of dignity', he reassured readers that Manchester residents were protected by responsible as well as thoughtful and respectable officers.

Blanchard Jerrold, in *London: A Pilgrimage* (published in monthly instalments in 1872 and as an entire volume that same year as *Notes on England*), provided many flattering descriptions of both uniformed and plain-clothes policemen on land and on the river. The 'stern-faced' Thames Police whom his party had set out to visit are sketched as going about their job industriously, and the police officers whom they met during their foray into darkest London as knowledgeable in the ways of crime, and familiar with 'notorious rogues' as well as with the landlords and inmates of common lodging houses, which are under 'severe control'.[85] Creating a sense of minute-by-minute reality, Jerrold, like Dickens, with whom he was well acquainted, portrays police officers as fully in command of the areas toured, respected or feared by the inhabitants, some of whom are violent and desperate.[86]

Ironically, Jerrold singles out Detective Sergeant Meiklejohn for praise as 'an intelligent, a reflective, and courageous professional student of the criminal classes'[87]—the very same Meiklejohn who at the same time became embroiled in the affair that in 1877 would disgrace the police when he and two of his colleagues were found guilty of perverting the cause of justice (see Chapter 1 and below). Apparently, Meiklejohn so impressed Jerrold with his expertise in matters of crime that the writer recommended to 'gentlemen who are anxious to get at a true idea of the causes of crime; of the influences which foster it; of the nature pronest to it; and of the surest means of reducing its extension and its gravity' to listen carefully to Meiklejohn's 'instructive' stories and explanations. 'Such education on the spot would be worth more to our legislators...than any number of attendances at Congresses, Charity Organisation Associations, committees, and lectures,' Jerrold counselled.[88]

The input of journalists was also of direct value in their participation in the fight against crime. The very fact of the appearance of crime news in newspapers disseminated information to the public and made every reader a potential informant. The help of the public in identifying suspects was valuable, and at times crucial, in bringing about a culprit's arrest. One remarkable example was the case of the murderer of Lord William Russell in 1840, when the identity of the culprit—the victim's Swiss valet—was confirmed by a French restaurateur who found jewelry in a parcel he had left with her, and associated it with Russell's murder after reading details about it in the French press. Another was the case of Percy Lefroy, who murdered an elderly gentleman named Isaac Gold in a railway carriage on the Brighton line in 1881, and was arrested after his landlady saw his portrait in the *Daily Telegraph*.[89] The police, too, sometimes noticed incriminating details which they had previously overlooked, in photographs published in newspapers.[90] The press also served as a mediator between persons with information and the police in more active ways. As far back as the eighteenth century, John Fielding utilized a government grant to advertise descriptions of suspects and offers of rewards in the press.[91] Law-enforcers and victims in provincial England at the time also resorted to newspaper advertisements to circulate and acquire criminal intelligence.[92] Admittedly, although this detection technique had proved relatively successful in bringing cases to court and retrieving stolen property, the new police forces of the nineteenth century would use the press less extensively, preferring to circulate criminal intelligence internally within the law-enforcement system, 'with less and less emphasis on the broadcasting of information to the public'—a reflection of the shift from reliance on the randomness of private initiative in detection to systematic official procedure.[93] Still, the pages of Victorian newspapers carried portraits of wanted criminals and many advertisements requesting information.[94] Occasionally, journalists would pass on the results of investigations they pursued on their own to the police, providing potential clues in baffling cases. Detectives acknowledged—though at times grudgingly—that information published in newspapers was in certain cases essential to the resolution of a crime.[95]

The press could be beneficial not only to detection generally but to individual detectives in particular. Journalists showed curiosity about detectives from the earliest period of detective departments and began sketching their profiles.[96] Such interest kept growing with time. Heads of police and top-ranking CID officials were natural subjects for interviews and reportage, enjoying exposure in the press both in Britain and abroad. Their names, opinions, and feats became known to a broad audience.[97] With the entrenchment of the journalistic interview format in the last two decades of the century, these personalities benefited extensively from such exposure, which allowed them not only to communicate their personal story but also to represent the institution as a whole in a positive light.

Significantly, detectives lower down the hierarchy also gained personal publicity. From the outset, they won a permanent place in press reports as witnesses in court proceedings, which were covered routinely. Although the defendant and the representatives of the legal system—the judge, the prosecutor, and the defence counsel—took centre stage in court, the detective, sometimes identified by name, was often an integral component of the courtroom scene and his statements were quoted, paraphrased, or most often summarized.[98] Detective Andrew Lansdowne, in his memoirs, showed that detectives knew how to conduct themselves in court and what to say.[99] Not infrequently, their testimonies revealed them to be enterprising and resolute, possessing skills that were instrumental in bringing the accused to trial.[100] It certainly paid to be a favourite of the press.

Detectives also acquired fame while conducting investigations. Generally, the press focused on crimes against persons, with murder—the ultimate social sin—occupying pride of place, especially if it incorporated shocking elements. The rare serial killings, naturally, captured headlines. By contrast, most criminal acts did not gain nationwide publicity.[101] As L. Perry Curtis, Jr, points out, national or in-depth coverage 'depended on the social standing of the principals and the amount of violence, intrigue, or mystery that reporters could wring from the story. If the method and motive of murder seemed too ordinary, or if the police arrested the perpetrator right away, then the case might earn only a few lines of print at the bottom of a page devoted to domestic news.'[102] Since the national press did not usually bother with the labours of detectives tracking down petty crime, the only detectives likely to appear in it were those pursuing daring or scandalous offenders and involved in exciting tales of their capture. For these reasons, Scotland Yard detectives gained disproportionate attention in the national press. Moreover, various news items and articles appearing in the London papers were often reprinted in provincial organs, so that crimes in London, and the people associated with their resolution, continuously enjoyed national fame.[103] In any event, while only a minority of local events managed to draw the attention of the national channels of communication, the flow of crime or police reports from the metropolis outwards was more certain.[104] In addition, since the detective unit at Scotland Yard functioned as a kind of national body, extending assistance to provincial police forces, it attracted further notice by the provincial press. Inevitably, the perception of the English detective by the public principally relied on what it knew about Scotland Yard, or at best about detectives operating in London.

Increasingly, detectives were also described as colourful and imposing characters in impressionistic journalistic pieces about life in London's slums or in its prisons, and about the daily routine of patrolmen, which usually appeared in the literary periodicals.[105] This popularity spurred press interest in the life stories of detectives. The police trade journals—the *Police Service Advertiser* (established 1866), *Police Guardian* (1873), *Police Chronicle* (1888), *On and Off Duty* (1883), and *Police Review* (1893)[106]—in publicizing the progress of police careers around the country, complete with a photograph of the subject, seemed to give pride of place to detectives, certainly beyond their proportion in the various police forces. Naturally, the accounts were unreservedly laudatory. Interestingly, national papers, too, sometimes dedicated space to the occupational histories of detectives and even to lists of promoted officers, though it was mostly the local papers that wrote up native sons, not only when detectives were successful in solving cases, but also at milestones in their careers.[107] For some detectives, coverage in the local and even the national press was not a one-time occasion but occurred repeatedly. Richard Jervis won the acclaim of the local press upon every significant move he made: when appointed inspector of Southport and district (1857), when transferred to Lancaster (1866) and then to Ormskirk (1877), and on other occasions.[108] When Detective Inspector Frederick Abberline left the H Division in London's East End in 1887 and joined the central office in London, the *East London Observer* paid him tribute as 'the very ideal of a faithful, conscientious, and upright officer',[109] and, in 1892, several distinguished journals covered his retirement from Scotland Yard after thirty years. Every reference praised him as remarkable.[110] As a consequence, detectives became well known as stars or heroes, at least in their local communities.[111] Some, principally those working in the central office at Scotland Yard, turned into national celebrities, particularly if they worked on sensational cases. Detective Superintendent William Melville, known for his resourceful and courageous encounters with dangerous revolutionaries, became a celebrity not only in England but also in France (see Chapter 3).[112] Some were perceived as experts whose opinion and advice should be sought, and merited reporting, even after their retirement. Detective Sergeant Patrick McIntyre of the Special Branch, who was demoted to the rank of constable and left police service as a result,[113] was interviewed thereafter by *Reynolds's News* (which had also published his memoirs in 1895) and was described as 'well informed...on all points related to subterranean movements'.[114] Similarly, the *South London Chronicle* quoted his opinion about safety in southern London.[115]

Quite a few detectives tended to be notorious self-publicists, going back to the days of the Bow Street Runners, who were adept at press manipulation.[116] Articles in the press and books about crime were replete with stories volunteered by detectives about their work. Their eagerness to be heard is consistently manifested. A *City Press* representative recounted how a detective inspector pleaded with him to hear stories of the successful cases he had handled.[117] Much of the limelight attained by William Melville was the outcome of his own efforts with the press.[118] Detectives avidly read all communications about the police in the press, keen to know what was written about them and about Scotland Yard generally.[119] Some detectives were mentioned in print so often that they adopted the celebrities' habit of collecting newspaper clippings about themselves.[120]

Senior officers did not necessarily approve of the publicity accorded to their subordinates. In his *Police Code*, Howard Vincent, first head of the CID, included 'an absence of craving for individual credit' as an important factor in the success of detection, though this did not stop detectives from seeking publicity.[121] Edward Henry, as assistant commissioner of the Metropolitan Police responsible for the CID (1901–3), had to caution an American journalist who wanted to become personally acquainted with detectives in the central office not to cite their names.[122] 'We are very hard on men whom we suspect of looking for notoriety', he explained, 'and we do not like to see their names in the papers when they can be kept out. We are not seeking any advertisement whatsoever.'

THE SPARING RELEASE OF INFORMATION

Notwithstanding the mutual dependence between journalists and detectives, their interaction was also characterized by conflicts of interest and mutual suspicion.[123] Tensions derived mainly from the manner in which police authorities released information about the progress of investigations, especially when culprits had not yet been discovered. To a large extent, the negotiations between the two sides depended on the standpoint of the senior level in each force and on the personal relations that developed between reporters and police officers. Still, Scotland Yard, the force with the most complex and precarious position regarding public opinion, was notorious for its reluctance to share the results of its investigations with journalists. Contemporaries complained that, if reporters made inquiries, they were 'invariably fobbed off with the kind of "cock-and-bull" story which is dealt out to too inquisitive little children'.[124] A member of the Institute of Journalists was quoted as saying: 'At Scotland Yard there is a law, which is supposed to be as unalterable as that of the Medes and Persians, forbidding the communication of intelligence to the Press.'[125] By comparison, the City of London and provincial police were on friendlier terms with the press,[126] although they, too, denied information to the press when they did not want it published.[127] This widely accepted practice, referred to by both detectives and journalists as the 'policy of reticence',[128] created tension between them and undermined their relations.[129]

Police employees did communicate with members of the press about ongoing cases, and sent releases with the basic facts to news agencies,[130] but they tried to do it meagrely and only to the extent that it suited their interests. In cases such as the Whitechapel murders (1888), where the identity of the perpetrator was not known and no serious clues were available to the police, Scotland Yard was even more uncooperative in divulging details to journalists or letting them interview suspects and detainees.[131] As a reporter for the popular evening *Star* complained bitterly following the second Whitechapel murder, 'not only have their [the detectives'] superiors grossly mismanaged and neglected their duties, but they have encouraged their subordinates to treat the newspapers in a manner to which no other press in the world but that of Russia and Germany would submit'.[132] In another article, published in response to the murder of Mary Jane Kelly (now generally considered to be the last Ripper victim), the same paper protested that 'the police had orders to refuse the newspapers every information', were guilty of 'endless prevarications', gave false information to reporters, and, with 'honourable exceptions', treated them as 'interlopers or pickpockets'.[133] According to two contemporary writers, one of them a journalist, 'the detectives refused information even to the accredited representatives of London papers'.[134] The response of the police may have been particularly severe because of the horrific nature of the case and the striking lack of success in finding the perpetrator, but the policy of reticence was by no means new, nor did it disappear thereafter.

This policy had several causes. Civil service rules limiting communication with the press resulted in the sparing release of information by officials generally in the Victorian period, especially with the passage of the first Official Secrets Act in 1889.[135] Police officers, likewise, were careful not to violate the sanctity of official secrets.[136] They also had more specific reasons to withhold information from the probing eyes of the press. Much like the admiralty and the army, the police, and especially their detective branches, operated in an environment of secrecy, which complicated relations with industrious journalists and reporters. In the case of crime investigations specifically, the details of certain cases were withheld, either because disclosure was explicitly prohibited or because revelation could jeopardize the progress or results of an inquiry and enable criminals 'to evade justice more easily'.[137] Informers were liable to be exposed. Howard Vincent instructed his officers not to 'give any information whatever to gentlemen connected with the press relative to matters within police knowledge, or relative to duties to be performed or orders received, or communicate in any manner, either directly or indirectly, with editors or reporters of newspapers... without express and special authority'.[138] His initial motivation was most likely to monitor the information flowing from officers to the press, knowing too well the tendency of detectives to call attention to their exploits, but he was also concerned that 'the slightest deviation from this rule may... defeat the endeavour of superior officers to advance the welfare of the public service'. Indeed, several prominent police officers alleged that in certain incidents 'the premature or injudicious disclosure of facts obtained in the progress of investigation has led to the escape of criminals'.[139] Sometimes the divulging of certain information was designed to baffle inquisitive reporters who pressed for news that could be disruptive to the investigation.[140] It was also feared that publicizing details in such vile cases as the serial murders at Whitechapel could 'foster panic' or 'inspire imitators'.[141]

The restrictive attitude of the police to journalists was also rooted in more prosaic reasons. Police sensitivity to press criticism, and the crucial importance of good publicity, have been noted. Although police leaders defended their position regarding secrecy with rhetoric about the public good—namely, that public safety demanded that particulars not be released, or that 'public distrust of the police force' must not be aroused[142]—their selective release of information was also a function of their desire to hide data harmful to their own reputation or to that of the police as a whole. A major problem was that certain methods used by the police to obtain evidence sufficient for conviction were unsavoury and invited scathing press responses.[143] Another acute problem for the police was handling the coverage of failures in the conduct of investigations. As one journalist argued, reporters' requests for particulars of a case were rebuffed when the police were anxious to hide the fact that 'in many instances the supposed sagacity of the police in the detection of crime is a little bit of modern mythology', and that criminals were often caught 'by means of some outsider'.[144] Understandably, detectives disliked press reports that emphasized their inability to stop crime and catch criminals, or exhorted them to take more vigorous action and improve their performance.

Moreover, the detectives' suspicion of journalists masked deeper and more complex sensibilities related to professional pride and the protection of their occupational status. In effect, underlying the withholding of news stories by detectives was an undercurrent of competition. On the surface, journalists and detectives were preoccupied with their separate vocational tasks, however much they resembled and needed each other. In reality, they were sometimes locked in a form of latent rivalry that generated bitterness on both sides. While the detectives' task was to solve legal cases, the journalists' main objective was to write a good story. Each dealt with the reconstruction of crimes, yet the police postulated that detectives, as the experts in cracking cases, must necessarily lead the investigations, while journalists should be satisfied with reporting about them. Nonetheless, many reporters (and press photographers), partly because they were forced to cope with the policy of reticence, conducted their own investigations, dredging up their own clues and forging explanations to difficult cases, a practice that reached new heights during the Ripper murders.[145] In their search for leads that could help them report their version of events, they learnt to hasten to the crime scene in order to gather interesting items and interview eyewitnesses, bystanders, and anyone else who could provide details. They also followed detectives at work and used informers.[146] Reporters would sometimes go without sleep all night, just like detectives, waiting for a suspect to appear, or would employ the services of private detectives for investigative purposes.[147] So intense was the involvement of journalists in detection during the serial killings attributed to Jack the Ripper in late 1888 that some were mistaken for the Ripper himself.[148]

Such behaviour aroused the indignation of police investigators, who would at times protest against the persons involved.[149] Moreover, if the police could barely tolerate the journalists' habit of reminding their readers that 'the press is the detectives' best friend' and 'of inestimable value' in the solution of crimes, the recommendations and advice offered by newspapermen in print in the course of investigations were overtly disturbing.[150] The entire article 'Newspapers as Detectives' published in 1904 was devoted to showing how the press could be a useful guide to crime fighters and even teach them how to operate.[151] Further, journalists competed not only with one another but often with police investigators as well in being the first to find clues and sources or to convey information to the public.[152] Some journalists presented themselves as better at detective work than professional detectives.[153]

Detectives were used to being attacked in the press, yet the harsh criticism sometimes voiced by newspapers and periodicals heightened feelings of animosity. Police annoyance with the press was well known, reflected, inter alia, in fictional works in England and abroad. In the prologue to *Cleek of Scotland Yard*, a detective novel published in England and the USA not long before the First World War, Superintendent Maverick Narkom of Scotland Yard airs his exasperation at 'the sneers of carping critics and the pin pricks of overzealous reporters, who seemed to think that the Yard was to blame' if every evildoer was not immediately caught, ignoring past 'brilliant successes'.[154] He would have 'given his head' to 'make those newspaper fellows eat their words'.

In this atmosphere, it would not be surprising if the denial of access to information, even to journalists who usually enjoyed police cooperation, was the outcome of a punitive attitude on the part of the police. The authorities, after all, were entirely familiar with the material appearing in the press about the police. Richard Mayne, the first commissioner of the Metropolitan Police, was in the habit of collecting information on people's attitudes towards the police, 'filing away praise and criticism and combing newspapers for relevant letters and material'.[155] He and his co-commissioner, Charles Rowan (1829–50), were in direct contact with the editors of all the major dailies in London, checking and then responding to unfavourable reports in an attempt to counteract bad publicity.[156] A survey of the National Archives shows that many of the official reports by detectives on assigned cases referred to press articles, often in an apologetic tone, as if to justify their moves to their superiors in the face of press criticism.

A number of journalists were victims of retribution by the police. George R. Sims temporarily lost the friendly rapport he had with Scotland Yard when in the summer of 1904 he took up the case of Adolph Beck in the *Daily Mail*.[157] As he recalled: 'For a little time... Scotland Yard ceased to smile upon me. Certain statements that I made were regarded as reflecting upon the Yard methods.' Possibly, too, the Yard had not forgotten his vocal criticism of the force during the Ripper days.[158] However, mutual dependence, and perhaps Sims's long friendship with a host of police detectives, outweighed these resentments and 'the hatchet was buried, the pipe of peace was smoked, and we once more "spoke as we passed by"'.[159] Other *Daily Mail* journalists experienced a similar loss of goodwill on the part of the police a few years later, when the paper 'dared to make certain pertinent remarks about the Scotland Yard sleuths and their methods in regard to the Crippen case' of 1910.[160] To judge by the testimony of a reporter who had been a victim of the policy of reticence, 'playing off one paper against the other—by supplying one with news and withholding it from the other, because the reporter of the other determines to report police cases impartially'—helped the police 'teach the Press "to know its place"'.[161]

The police used other means apart from 'reticence' to restrain journalists and censor harmful publication. Journalist Aaron Watson recounted that he was invited for an interview with Commissioner Edmund Henderson and Howard Vincent, then head of the CID, after he had published an article in the *Pall Mall Gazette* (in the early 1880s) on criminal gangs, which the police claimed 'were an invention of the newspapers'.[162] In Watson's opinion, the purpose of the interview was to catch him out in 'something which might supply an occasion for the contradiction of my whole narrative, and the exposure of myself as a liar and impostor'.

A DEGREE OF CHANGE IN POLICE POLICY

The pattern of grudging and partial cooperation with journalists continued throughout the period under review. However, at the turn of the century, following the example of other government departments, the police developed a more acute awareness of the power of the press and a determination to be more forthcoming towards its agents. Although officers of the law had long understood the value of positive publicity in newspapers, a half-century of interaction sharpened its ramifications and heightened their appreciation of the entire spectrum of services that men of the press could provide.

Definitely, the civic climate in the country was an important factor in this change. Admittedly, the Official Secrets Act signified that the political elite was determined to enhance its control over the dissemination of official information in the face of increasing democratization and the growth of the commercial press.[163] At the same time, however, the expansion of the electorate through wider enfranchisement during the closing decades of the century, in conjunction with reinforced notions of the obligation of officials to work for the public good, and the public's right to information, elevated the importance of public opinion. Progressively, officials in various departments of state were prompted to provide journalists with reports about the activities and policies of their offices on a regular basis and to establish systematic channels for a smoother flow of information.[164] All this steered the police towards greater attentiveness to the demands of the press. The change of attitude in the Metropolitan Police might also have stemmed from a change of personnel at the top. In 1903, Commissioner Edward Bradford, who in 1897 had issued an order prohibiting giving information to the press under any circumstances,[165] and who tried to put a stop to the habit of detectives escorting journalists on their social explorations,[166] was replaced by Commissioner Edward Henry (1903–18) who, along with Assistant Commissioner Melville L. Macnaghten, favoured a more open approach to journalists.[167]

Perhaps even more important in the emergence of a spirit of greater collaboration were the contribution and status of the journalists themselves. As a body, they played a meaningful role, directly or indirectly, in altering police perceptions, even if at times inadvertently. Although detectives disliked the tacit competition and the haughty tone of some journalists when reporting about criminal investigations, they could not avoid appreciating the services provided by the press. Positive reporting, whether about the police as an institution or about individual detectives, constituted a clear-cut reason for indebtedness. Journalists did not necessarily seek any favours in publicizing the exploits and achievements of individual detectives: the readers enjoyed such material. However, it stands to reason that detectives craving publicity were likely to be better disposed to requests for information by reporters, and that the publicity generated a friendlier disposition among detectives in their dealings with the press. Furthermore, growing public interest in journalists as individuals, and the gradual acceptance of journalism as a profession towards the end of the nineteenth century, also contributed to the shift in attitude.[168]

Journalists also played an active role in eliciting a changed relationship with the police. Challenging the poor treatment they received at the hands of Scotland Yard, they reprimanded the Yard for withholding information useful to the press.[169] Journalist J. Hall Richardson, in his book *Police!*, written in the late 1880s jointly with a former police officer, drew attention to the 'brusque impertinence' frequently shown by police officers to journalists.[170] Although the authors did not fully endorse the views expressed in an article in a leading newspaper on the subject, they quoted extensively from it. One quoted allegation was that 'the less the police have to communicate the more desirous they are to enshroud their ignorance in mystery'.[171] Another quoted passage intimated that the police were ungrateful to the press for rendering 'substantial assistance' to the cause of justice 'by affording publicity to the most intimate details of crime', accusing the police of jealousy. Bluntly dismissing the policy of reticence as 'a stupid dog-in-the-manger one', the quoted article charged that 'it suits official uppishness and the pride of police subordinates dressed in a little brief authority to snub and to thwart the representatives of the press, and to be either sulkily silent or barrenly communicative'. Such complaints were voiced repeatedly. In 1910, the *Penny Illustrated Paper* criticized 'the extraordinary attitude of the London police towards the Press', accusing the CID of raising a 'stone wall' when journalists demanded news updates and of lagging significantly behind practices customary in France and the USA.[172]

In these remonstrances, the journalists, much like the police spokesmen themselves, claimed to represent the general good, contending that by their actions the police deprived the public of useful information, and that 'every report of a crime made to the police should be at the service of reporters'.[173] They assured the authorities that 'treating authorized pressmen with uniform courtesy' would be 'greatly to their advantage', pointing to examples in which the 'minute chronicling of the incidents surrounding a crime has...tended directly to the discovery of the criminal'.[174] Some journalists, conceding that the police had a right to keep information to themselves, nevertheless objected to their placing obstacles in the way of the press in pursuing independent inquiries.[175] One journalist proposed taking an example from the chief of detective police in Paris, in telling reporters 'all that they would inevitably discover if they set to work making inquiries of less discreet subordinates', without revealing anything that might be of use to criminals.[176] Journalists also warned that 'an energetic pressman, when rebuffed by the police', would not consult with them 'as to the expediency of publishing or withholding the information he obtains by personal inquiry'.[177] The strident criticism levelled periodically at the police for their lack of transparency, and the impact this had on the public, were a constant and painful lesson in the power of the media.[178]

Indeed, the solution to the lack of cooperation from the police was for journalists to help themselves in filling in the gaps and finding material for their speculations and reports by assuming the role of detectives. Although deeply offensive to official crime investigators, this kind of unintended pressure seems to have worked. In his memoirs, Melville L. Macnaghten disclosed the annoyance of the police leadership with journalists-cum-detectives but also the impact of these practices on police calculations, observing:

> The old idea used to be that detectives best served the interests of justice by keeping journalists at a distance, with the natural result that pressmen, being under the necessity of reporting something, used to string together unreliable stories, and to set about investigations themselves in a manner very maddening and handicapping to the detective officers who had the handling of the case. It seemed well, therefore, in many cases, to give fully and frankly such information as could be used without hesitation, and at the same time with profit to the public and to the police.[179]

Indeed, in an interview in the *Daily Mail* in 1913 upon his retirement from the police, Sir Melville was credited with breaking 'down the barrier of secrecy between the police and the Press'.[180] Notably, challenges by journalists produced results even from a more implacable police manager, Robert Anderson, Macnaghten's predecessor, who admitted in his memoirs that his change of attitude towards journalists stemmed from a cold calculation of how best to serve police interests: 'I ought to have snubbed all pressmen and had them "chucked out", treating them in fact as the Cabinet Ministers have treated the suffragettes. And they would naturally have declared war upon me, to the detriment of my work, whereas I had not a single enemy among the journalists of London.'[181]

Nevertheless, changes in the attitude of the police towards the press, such as they were, did not meet the expectations of journalists.

Aside from their continuous complaint that the police released information sparingly, throughout the period under discussion they fought to be accepted as a permanent professional presence in police territory, as distinct from ordinary citizens.[182] Their aim was to create fixed standards of negotiation anchored in uncontested privileges, independent of the random goodwill of officers, whether uniformed or not. Towards this end, journalists tried lobbying tactics. During the period when Charles Warren was commissioner of the Metropolitan Police (1886–8), the National Association of Journalists attempted to win official recognition for reporters and some protection from the police 'during periods of popular excitement'. Commissioner Warren, however, 'returned a dry curt answer that he saw no reason for interference with the existing relations between the Press and the police'.[183] Efforts were also made during the period of his successor, James Monro (1888–90), who was known to be more moderate, to impress him in particular with the journalists' need for a permanent pass 'to be used at public functions, street parades, fires, and all occasions when the ordinary public is debarred from free locomotion, and the reporter has difficulty in persuading zealous constables that he has a title to be considered a privileged person'.[184] These attempts failed as well.

Efforts by journalists to gain special prerogatives and status continued in the twentieth century. In 1910, the Central London branch of the National Union of Journalists communicated with police officials and journalists' associations abroad to find out what systems prevailed there.[185] Individual newspapers, too, joined these efforts. To advance the cause, the *Penny Illustrated Paper* sent a journalist to Superintendent Frank Froest, 'the power behind the throne at Scotland Yard... in all matters concerning the Criminal Investigation Department', to inquire why journalists did not get renewable passes, as was the practice throughout America. The paper further inquired:

If, because of the peculiarity of the police system throughout London, it is thought advisable not to let the Press into the police stations to examine charge-sheets, why not adopt the system in vogue in Paris, where the Press people are granted identification cards, are not moved on by the police, and have come to a semi-official understanding with the police commissaries.[186]

According to this unsigned article, the problem was unique to London, as the provincial police had reached an understanding with the press whereby reporters were tolerated, allowed to see charge-sheets, and given 'correct and reliable news'. The article maintained that the provision of such services to the press in London would assist the police with their investigations and keep the public reassured as to their efficiency, while it would also 'keep check over the police and see that the guardians of the peace do more than arrest "drunk and disorderlies" and unfortunate women'. Froest had asserted, in a manner typical of the London police, that the Metropolitan force was a governmental, not merely a municipal, organization and that all information received or gathered by it became governmental information. Divulging this material constituted 'a very serious breach of the Official Secrets Act'. Dismissing such arguments, the article contended that the reluctance of the police to agree to requests by journalists stemmed from their fear that this might 'disturb the reputations for detective prowess held by a few members of the Force'. The supposedly 'brilliant arrests' made by London's detectives, he scoffed, were usually no more than the result of information provided by narks or informers.

The journalists' ongoing campaign enlisted support from an unexpected quarter—William McAdoo, a former New York City police commissioner, who considered the more forthcoming approach of the London police in 1909 still a far cry from the situation in his own city. Baffled by the nature of the interaction between police and journalists in England, he shared his surprise with readers of the American journal *Century Magazine* that no newspaperman was present in the anterooms of the headquarters of the Metropolitan Police and, worse still, that none was permitted in the building.[187] Significantly, he did not find a single interview with a police official in any of the London newspapers 'during the investigation of three sensational and mysterious crimes', and was 'more than astonished that the police admitted repeatedly that they had no clue whatever' about the perpetration of a murder 'which startled and horrified the whole kingdom'. He could not think of 'any New York official, commissioner or other, making such an acknowledgement!' On the whole, he found press coverage of the police in New York to be much more extensive than in London, where 'the internal workings of the machinery are not exposed to public view', and 'millions of people may live...all their lives and never know the name of a commissioner so far as the newspapers are concerned'.[188] As a result, he surmised, 'the police are not held to the same direct accounting as in New York'. Clearly, in his view, the police in London neither provided service to the press in a satisfactory way nor learnt how to utilize what the press could offer.[189]

THE INTRICATE RELATIONS BETWEEN DETECTIVES AND PRESSMEN

Evidently, during the formative period of both occupations, journalists and detectives came to recognize their own and each other's strengths along with their interdependence. Yet this mutuality did not result in a consistent approach. Detectives (and uniformed policemen) quite often disobeyed the directives of senior management vis-à-vis newspapermen, communicating details of ongoing inquiries to them informally and allowing them special privileges. Moreover, some detectives, motivated by grudges against their bosses or their conditions of service, made damaging statements to representatives of the press (anonymously, while in service).[190]

Journalists, for their part, sometimes added their voice to police criticism of journalistic practices, objecting to sensationalism or to irresponsible coverage of criminal investigations by some of their colleagues. *Punch*, in addition to ridiculing policemen and detectives, satirized journalists as well. It published a biting sketch in 1882 entitled 'The Police, the Press, and the Public', consisting of five 'theatrical' acts in which hard-core criminals benefited from detailed information published about them and their whereabouts in the press, allowing them to escape and evade justice, which prompted the press, in the sketch, to disparage the police for failing to capture the criminals and to refer to them as stupid and disgraceful.[191] *Punch* returned to the theme of the disruptive role of the press with renewed vigour during the Ripper investigations, but also mocked detectives for following useless press leads. On 22 September 1888, an article entitled 'A Detective's Diary à La Mode' lampooned the British press for its repeated mistaken speculations about the identity of the murderer, and contended in jest that the investigating detectives were arresting suspects based on these speculations. *Punch* sneered that, after a certain periodical suggested that 'the Police may have committed the crime', the detective on the case arrested himself.[192]

Less than a month later, the magazine carried two illustrations captioned 'Is Detection a Failure?', and the answer that failure is attributable to the sensationalist reporter who, by dogging the detective's footsteps and publicizing his moves in the daily newspapers, serves the interests of both the gutter press and the criminal classes (see Figure 9).[193] In the same issue the paper published a short satirical

IS DETECTION A FAILURE?

In the interests of the Gutter Gazette and of the Criminal Classes, the Sensational Interviewer dogs the Detective's footsteps, and throws the strong light of publicity on his work. Under these circumstances, it is not surprising that Detection should prove a failure.

Figure 9. 'Is Detection a Failure?', *Punch*, 20 Oct. 1888.

play entitled *The Detective's Rescue*, in which 'sensation-mongers' threateningly pursue a detective in their 'morbid hunger' to get hold of details of an investigation regardless of the detective's plea that it would be unwise to divulge his plans and drop his disguise. This arouses the anger of the criminal, who cannot operate successfully without such detailed press reports, and of the correspondent and the subeditor of a daily paper, who depend on them 'to feed the daily scare' and tickle 'the public taste'.[194] Similar criticism was expressed by various journalists regarding minute details of criminal charges given in press reports with striking headlines and suggestive comments that were likely to 'produce morbid interest' among readers.[195]

Attitudes in both occupations ranged from criticism of their own and the others' practices to recognition of the benefits of reciprocal exchanges.[196] Yet, despite this diversity, a certain pattern of behaviour was discernible. On the whole, the police were stingy in releasing information about the state of an investigation and did little to systematize relations with journalists. No special facilities or personnel existed in the Metropolitan Police during this period to deal with journalists, nor was there any formal agreement on the issue. Detectives in some provincial cities and towns were more accommodating than Scotland Yard men, but the importance of smooth interaction between journalists and the police of the metropolis was infinitely more vital for both occupations. Members of the press did not accept this situation and campaigned continuously for special privileges and greater accessibility of information. Their success, however, was partial. By the start of the twentieth century, detectives had become more sensitive to journalists' demands for information about investigations, and the atmosphere improved, yet the level of cooperation did not meet the expectations of many journalists. Only in 1919 did Scotland Yard establish a press office, which twice daily communicated information gathered from all police departments. This development arose not from a recognition of the public's right to information, but principally from fears of a public scandal if unauthorized leaks resulting from pressmen bribing policemen became known.[197] Throughout the period, the police were resentful of press criticism and the sensationalism of some of the papers, and were displeased as well by the journalists' competitive stance.[198]

Nonetheless, each group learnt to use the benefits it was able to exact from the other more effectively, albeit with underlying misgivings and not entirely to the satisfaction of either journalists or police officers. Each side held that its stance stemmed from professional values and principles, yet both were also driven by pragmatic considerations. From the perspective of people like the American law-enforcer William McAdoo, the Metropolitan Police did not know how to market themselves by means of the press. Yet, scrutiny of their conduct reveals that they did assign importance to their relationship with the press, and increasingly so. They may not have been as proactive in their public-relations activity as the New York Police, but many of the steps they took were guided by the desire to gain supportive press coverage. Rewarding journalists who worked hand in glove with the police was certainly part of their overall strategy. Responding positively to requests by people central to the media world and providing them with guidance in their slumming tours was a reflection of this effort. Indeed, the police continued the practice of guiding journalists in their forays 'into the under-world of London' throughout the period.[199] Police authorities understood that the release of some information was preferable to letting journalists discover it by themselves or, worse still, inventing it. Moreover, if on certain occasions detectives were reluctant to reveal information, at others they were as keen as journalists to make information available to the public. In parallel, journalists came to recognize the benefits of avoiding antagonizing detectives and other policemen. Critical comments in the press about detectives notwithstanding, journalists were instrumental in diminishing the initial opposition of the public to the existence of plain-clothes officers, and later in entrenching a positive image of them as protectors of society (for details, see Chapter 5).

To all appearances, then, despite an abiding element of distrust, detectives and journalists benefited from a tacit give and take that developed between them. Both the field of journalism, emerging in the second half of the nineteenth century as a profession, and detective work, emerging as a skilled occupation, relied on this reciprocity, which helped confirm them as essential to society, designating a public role for them as professional fighters for the public good. The upshot was that, by the end of the period under discussion, the two had attained a stature of importance and become figures of authority in society.

Given the special interaction between detectives and journalists, how did journalists portray detectives, and what image of detectives emerged from this reportage? Chapter 5 surveys the changing image of police detectives as reflected in journals of varied cultural and political orientations in the period under review, with brief references to the representation of the police as a whole.

5

THE CHANGING IMAGE OF POLICE DETECTIVES IN THE PRESS

The first modern police force in England—the Metropolitan Police of London—came into existence in 1829 in an atmosphere of hostility. A petition to the king declared that the Police Bill was a violation of the 'English constitution's spirit'.[1] So unwelcome were the new police that constables were 'followed by crowds hooting at them, and calling them by the obnoxious names of "Peelers", raw Lobsters, Crushers, Bobbies, etc.'.[2] Various forms of popular entertainment reflected these public sentiments. The journalist George Augustus Sala recalled how as a boy in the 1830s he attended the Brighton pantomime, where one of the comic tricks was 'the metamorphosis of a policeman into a lobster'.[3] The popular press added its voice to the gallery of opponents by headlines such as 'More Police Tyranny' and 'More Disgraceful Conduct of the New Police'.[4]

Yet, as police historian Wilbur R. Miller observed: 'The period of almost universal opposition to the new police was brief.'[5] The upper and middle classes, whose views after the Reform Act of 1832 grew closer on many political issues, including their support for the existing social order, were the first to welcome the new policing arrangements.[6] The police began to appear not only as far less threatening than the dangerous classes, but as a legitimate and morally correct weapon, if not always the most efficient one, to meet their objectives. Miller notes: 'The middle classes came to depend for protection and order upon an institution which fostered social stability by restrained power and in many small ways helped discipline an unruly population being transformed by industrialization.'[7] During the late 1830s and 1840s, the new police seemed to meet the Chartist challenge to those who wanted to sustain the status quo. The fact that, except for truncheons, policemen were usually unarmed when carrying out routine duties reinforced their image as citizens in uniform.[8] The donning of a uniform itself allayed fears that officers would engage in sinister activities. While members of the working classes continued to resent the new forces of law and order, criticism of the police from more prosperous quarters gradually shifted from the use of arbitrary power or brute force to the scarcity or unavailability of policemen when needed.[9] Even if at times middle-class contributors to journals continued to urge the public to take measures into its own hands to protect itself, as in the past, more often they used the press in order to pressure policy-makers to impose greater control.[10] In this context, how did the press react to the creation of the detective department in London, and how did it cover the evolution of non-uniformed officers?

THE DETECTIVE'S IMAGE IN THE EARLY DAYS OF POLICE DETECTION

By the time the first detective department was formed in 1842 in the Metropolitan Police of London, the climate of opinion regarding the new police generally had become more accepting.[11] Still, the department met with a mixed response. Growing numbers acquiesced with the need for it, but many still felt uncomfortable with the implications of a non-uniformed police branch—a divergence of opinion that was reflected in the press. *The Times* held that the war against crime obliged the police, both uniformed and plain clothes, 'to be about, and to have their eyes about them—to hang about popular meetings and suspicious corners—to collect rumours, and recollect misdemeanours—to watch and store up random words and unintended disclosures—to find out what they were never intended to know, and to make instant communication, and, if necessary, use of it'.[12] Those who opposed such methods feared that the detective department would do just that and thereby become a dreaded network of all-pervading surveillance of citizens of all classes. The liberal *Examiner*, which had concurred with the 'appointment of a detective police',[13] nevertheless charged that the means advocated by *The Times* suggested a treacherous system of espionage of the kind created by the notorious French police minister Joseph Fouché, which poisoned 'the intercourse in society' and destroyed 'the confidence between man and man'.[14] Wearing a disguise, in particular, was regarded as a 'mischievous' practice, even by *The Times*, which preferred to risk attaining 'good ends' or even to dispense with a detective department altogether than to employ this 'evil means'.[15] This debate was symptomatic not only of the aims of the supporters and the fears of the opponents of the new department, but also of the persistent tendency to refer to France in discussions about the best law-enforcement system for Britain, although police forces in states considered tyrannical, most prominently Tsarist Russia, were also mentioned.

What frightened or at least troubled people across class boundaries was the figure of the spy, the invisible policeman who eavesdrops and pries even into the lives of the innocent (see Figure 10). The connotations of such a figure had constituted a principal objection to the idea of the police in the first place. *The Times*, too, admitted that there would always be 'something repugnant to the English mind in the bare idea of espionage', in that it is 'liable to great abuse'.[16] Typically, an open-air Chartist meeting in the summer of 1842 called for adopting the Charter in peaceful ways so as not to encourage the 'system of espionage' of the new detective force.[17] Indeed, while the word 'detective' gradually acquired a positive, or at least less loaded connotation, 'spy' and its linguistic derivatives remained a pejorative term.

To fulfil their duties, detectives simply never put on a police uniform. Yet, for significant sections of the public, wearing ordinary attire, especially after the creation of the uniformed police, was in itself an indication of fakery and dishonesty akin to spying. The condemnation of any camouflage of police identity was flaunted in popular poems about ladies and gentlemen being closely watched, censured, and even apprehended by the police for singing a song in a tavern at midnight deemed indecent by the law-enforcers.[18] Fears of an impending atmosphere of suspicion and deceit were exacerbated by circulating reports that unidentified police officers and other agents of the state engaged in subversive practices, not only spying on political dissidents but attempting to entrap and provoke them to commit unlawful acts.[19] The uniformed police could also be oppressive, encroach on the life of people and undermine British liberties, but the presupposition was that the systematic concealment of the identity of law-enforcers facilitated a much wider scope for devious activity.[20] Proposals to base the new detective police on the Bow Street Runners because of their experience and knowledge of criminal haunts and habits were criticized as 'highly objectionable', because this would tend to re-establish the thief-taking system of 'partial

Figure 10. 'One of the Detective Force', *Cleave's Penny Gazette of Variety and Amusement*, 15 Oct. 1842.

connivance' with criminals and 'subject [the public] to much greater evils, by the treacherous and immoral system of *blood-money*, or by the intolerable tyranny of domestic *surveillance*'.[21] This array of perceptions underlay much of the antagonism towards detective work in the press.

Mitigating such fears was the mounting endorsement of the police as a whole by the middle classes, which gathered momentum within a few decades, as reflected by articles about the police in the press.

In 1852, an article entitled 'The Police System of London' in the pro-Whig *Edinburgh Review* opened by complimenting the new arrangements for the internal security of the nation, stating that the complex police machinery in London was so good that 'people begin to think it quite a matter of course, or one of the ordinary operations of Providence, that they sleep and wake in safety in the midst of hordes of starving plunderers'.[22] The Tory *Quarterly Review* confirmed that the police 'are now looked upon as a constitutional force, simply because we have got accustomed to them'.[23] The acceptance of the police was also manifested in comparisons between the old and the new police, favouring the latter, and in distinguishing the new police from continental law-enforcers. An anonymous writer in the family weekly *Leisure Hour* in 1858 praised the new police as the 'servants as well as guardians of the public', who used force only as a last resort, unlike the continental forces who oppressed the population and were 'universally political spies, paid for espionage rather than for municipal service'.[24] Periodic outbreaks of garotting (mugging) scares during the late 1850s and 1860s;[25] riots in Hyde Park in 1866 for free speech and parliamentary reform, resulting in many casualties; and Fenian militant agitation in the same period 'shocked Londoners who had relaxed during the peaceful fifties' and fuelled sharp criticism of police inefficiency.[26] At the same time, however, they evoked widespread public demands for the extension of police powers.[27]

Mainstream journals reported with pride that foreigners, too, had an elevated image of the British police. In an interview with an English journalist in 1863, Emperor Napoleon III of France 'expressed himself in the highest terms of admiration' about the London police, impressed, ostensibly, with their restraint and their record of rarely abusing their power.[28] The same journalist, dining with the French president, Adolphe Thiers, in 1871, said he heard a similar appreciation from him. Both these personalities allegedly based their judgements on their stays in England.[29] An anonymous writer in the prestigious literary *Cornhill Magazine* (1881) observed:

The Continental conspirator, who has fled from justice, or injustice, in his own country, and has found no rest for the sole of his foot in any other state abroad, is delighted, on landing in England, to find himself free from every sort of surveillance. He is not asked to exhibit a passport or papers of identity; he may lodge where he likes, and under any name he pleases, without being required to register his name, profession, and previous dwelling-places.... So long as he avoids breaking the law, he and the police need never come into contact; and the law allows him exactly the same privileges as to a born Briton.[30]

Notable foreign refugees residing in London such as the shah of Persia, or radicals such as Louis Blanc and Giuseppe Garibaldi, had come to believe, the *Cornhill Magazine* reported, that 'the ideal police is that of London'.

The lower orders took longer to concur with the presence of the police in their midst, and, when they did, it was only grudgingly. Not only were members of the working classes subjected to the heavy hand of the police, but they shared a deep-rooted belief that the law was not imposed equally on all inhabitants, and that the propertied classes enjoyed better treatment and greater protection against crime.[31] Resentment was manifested in daily assaults on the police, some so violent that every year several Metropolitan Police officers had to leave the force on account of injuries on duty.[32]

Still, more and more working-class people began to recognize the police as an indispensable agency in society. The demise of the Chartist movement and the rise of working-class reformism during the 1850s led to a reduction of class tensions, accompanied by an increased acquiescence in the police presence. A growing number of those who had viewed the police as serving the interests of the privileged classes pre-eminently now wanted the police to handle law violators who disrupted their own lives too. Apart from bringing about greater order in the streets, the police undertook the provision of various services to the community, such as returning lost children to their parents and saving people from drowning or from accidents, which made them all the more acceptable to the less poor strata of society.[33] Such 'fragile toleration... broke down in periods of political crisis when workers saw the police as an instrument of oppression', but it constituted 'an improvement over the violent opposition of the thirties', as Miller points out.[34]

In time, an ever-growing number of journals of opinion were drawn to the topic of detective work specifically, with Scotland Yard becoming a prime object of attention. Periodicals in effect became sites of contesting views about detection. An article in *Dark Blue* in 1872 claimed that the police were widely regarded as 'able-bodied fools, dressed up in blue', and the detective as 'employed in letting murderers slip through his fingers'.[35] On occasion, nostalgia for the good old days of the Bow Street Runners was expressed.[36] Concerns about the detectives' secret methods were still voiced in the press and other platforms, and radicals continued to raise the spectre of the police as an espionage network.[37] Nevertheless, the periodical press also reflected a consistent perception of the emerging detective departments in London and in the provinces—whether more efficient or less—as integral to the urban management of law and order and as an incontrovertible agent of justice.[38] Scotland Yard detectives were acknowledged in the *Quarterly Review* in 1856 as a necessary 'wheel in the constabulary machinery'.[39] Around the same time, an anonymous writer in *Leisure Hour* declared that uniformed policemen were not qualified to discover serious offences and that only detectives possessed this expertise.[40] Although some people recalled the Bow Street Runners as a worthy force years after it had been disbanded, others held that 'as a Preventive Police they were utterly ineffective, and as a Detective Force were very loose and uncertain in their operations'.[41] With the passage of time, fewer and fewer commentators evoked them as preferable to the new detectives.

Increasingly, detectives were judged in the press on their merit, complimented in cases of the successful resolution of a crime,[42] while derided when less successful.[43] In time, even the radical mass-circulation Sunday paper *Reynolds's News*, which appealed to a working-class readership, accepted the legitimacy of detective departments, though not without strong reservations.[44] Referring to both the uniformed and detective branches, the paper rebuked the police for its inability 'to cope with the evils for the correction and prevention of which it was established', and, characteristically for this type of paper, proposed that the police should concentrate on bringing lawbreakers to justice rather than using officers to intervene in lawful political assemblies.[45] Such rhetoric inadvertently signified that opposition to the idea of organized policing—whether uniformed or plain clothes—had waned, conceivably easing the way in 1869 for Commissioner Edmund Henderson to institute changes in the detective structure that included significantly increasing the number of both plain-clothes and patrol officers in the Metropolitan Police (see Chapter 1).

Moreover, criticism of detective branches prompted various journals to attempt to modify their questionable image. An anonymous writer in *Leisure Hour* asserted unequivocally in 1857: 'So perfect is the system, and so successfully is it carried out, not only in London but throughout the whole country, that among the tens of thousands who live by rapine in England, there are but a few exceptional individuals unknown to the agents of the law.'[46] If detectives were not successful in catching criminals, the writer argued, this meant that 'nothing could be done'. Some journalists reinforced such statements by attributing a decline in crime during this period to the police system.[47] A dynamic discourse thus developed in the press between defenders and critics of the detective branches.

DICKENS'S ROLE IN ELEVATING DETECTIVES

Despite the ongoing tension between reporters and detectives, an important aid to the crusading journals in highlighting the work of detectives and tilting the balance in favour of a more pronounced acceptance of their role was the active support of certain journalists. Some developed personal relations with detectives. The most distinguished of these was Charles Dickens, the acclaimed novelist who was also an editor and proprietor of several journals and who pioneered the role of the journalist as an investigative reporter. In all these capacities he used his position to enhance the soothing image of police detectives.

Dickens was singularly engrossed with every aspect of the world of crime. He 'frequently attended the London magistrates courts and was present at a number of important murder trials', in addition to showing a close interest 'in several of the most notorious criminals of the day' and in the theory of penology.[48] He chose to witness public executions, visited prisons in Britain and abroad, and, according to his friend and colleague George Augustus Sala, among his favourite topics of conversation were the latest exciting trial, police case, swindle, and, especially, murder.[49] Based on his vast knowledge of the criminal world and the administration of justice, he developed strong opinions about crime and punishment, which he aired in the various channels of communication at his disposal. His thirst for knowledge about this world propelled him to direct his attention to the men assigned the task of suppressing crime. Sala attested to Dickens's 'curious and almost morbid partiality for communing with and entertaining police officers'.[50] He expressed a deep interest in uniformed policemen, but what fascinated his inquiring mind were the less visible policemen. This inquisitiveness was manifested in his fictional work, which is populated with detective characters, in several of his articles and in articles written by others under his supervision.

Apart from a personal attraction to the subject of detection, Dickens understood its value as a commercial asset relatively early, which was an added incentive in making it an object of intensive inquiry. His interest in detectives peaked in the early 1850s during his first years as founder, editor, and part owner of the weekly periodical *Household Words*. The title of the journal reveals his determination to appeal to a wide public.[51] The very first article in *Household Words* (30 March 1850) contained his stated intention to bring 'into innumerable homes' the 'stirring world around us, the knowledge of many social wonders, good and evil'.[52] In his perceptive mind, the world of detection met this objective. The particular terminology employed in the texts, however, shows that Dickens set out to enlighten his readers specifically about the Metropolitan Police, clearly the focal point of his interest in the forces of law and order.

Dickens had referred to detectives in his journalistic reports before 1850, but in that year he was responsible for the publication of several articles centred exclusively on them. On 13 July, *Household Words* published an article entitled 'The Modern Science of Thief-Taking', introducing the Metropolitan Police detective branch, which had been established only eight years earlier. This piece was written not by Dickens, but by his sub-editor, William H. Wills, an experienced journalist himself, known to have faithfully followed Dickens's ideas, 'tastes and methods'.[53] Notably, the article still used the old-fashioned term 'thief-taking' side by side with 'detection'. It presented subtle thieving as a fine art, while defining thief-taking as a science, implying precision, practicality, and systemization.[54] By referring to detection in this way, the article raised the ideals of detective work to new heights for its time. In the author's view, the higher branches of thieftaking demanded

> all the thief's ingenuity; all his knowledge of human nature; all his courage; all his coolness; all his imperturbable powers of face; all his nice discrimination in reading the countenances of other people; all his manual and digital dexterity; all his fertility in expedients, and promptitude in acting upon them; all his Protean cleverness of disguise and capability of counterfeiting every sort and condition of distress; together with a great deal more patience, and the additional qualification, integrity.

Apart from perceiving detection as an elevated scientific task, the very description of certain forms of thieving as a sophisticated art *ipso facto* heightened the value of the pursuers in the public eye. Furthermore, the article exalted detectives over patrolmen in skills as well as status. Detectives were 'a superior order of police' and performed the 'most difficult operations of their craft', handling 'tricks and contrivances' of sophisticated criminals, while their uniformed colleagues dealt with ordinary pickpocketing and thieving. Moreover, in contrast to the limitations of the uniformed man, the detective also acted as a preventive agent, thus carrying out the two functions necessary to stamp out crime. The article described detectives not only as highly perceptive and effective, with knowledge of criminals and the ways of crime, but also as honest.

Wills's article served as a prelude to several other favourable accounts of detectives by Dickens and his sub-editor. On 27 July 1850, an article by Dickens titled 'A Detective Police Party' continued the focus on Scotland Yard detectives from the point where Wills's article had left off. This article, too, aimed 'to convey to our readers some faint idea of the extraordinary dexterity, patience, and ingenuity, exercised by the detective Police', assuring them that this description is 'a piece of plain truth'.[55] To lend legitimacy to the new detective department, Dickens tarred the reputation of the old Bow Street Police, noting their habit of consorting with thieves and caring for their own interests. They stood in marked contrast to the new detective branch, presented as 'well-chosen and trained', systematic and efficient, and 'steadily engaged in the service of the public'. The missionary zeal reflected here is evident.

Dickens's initial interest in detectives, and his feeling that 'the public really do not know enough' of the useful public service provided by detectives, impelled him to seek them out personally. With this in mind, he requested the authorities at Scotland Yard to allow him to interview detectives in the office of his journal in the Strand, to which the authorities willingly acceded. Seven detectives—two inspectors and five sergeants—arrived at the author's office.[56] The encounter was amicable, and Dickens liked them at first sight. Seated leisurely in a semi-circle near a table laid over with glasses and cigars, the men were depicted in detail one by one. Each had his own character, unique features, and occupational speciality, but in Dickens's view they shared much in common. They were

> one and all, respectable-looking men; of perfectly good deportment and unusual intelligence; with nothing lounging or skilling in their manners; with an air of keen observation, and quick perception when addressed; and generally presenting in their faces, traces more or less marked of

habitually leading lives of strong mental excitement. They have all good eyes; and they all can, and they all do, look full at whomever they speak to.[57]

Though they had different tasks, they assisted each other and expressed their mutual solidarity whenever necessary.

Dickens was one of the first pressmen to appreciate the value of interviews. Not satisfied with an intellectual interest from afar, he wanted to base his understanding on first-hand testimony. He therefore conducted a probing and lively dialogue with detectives, questioning them about their work and learning about the behaviour of both law-enforcers and offenders, about different types of lawbreaking, and about celebrated crimes. According to George Sala, who was present at the meeting described above, 'Dickens seemed always at his ease with these personages'.[58] During the exchange, he became alive to the detectives' strong desire for exposure and their fondness for describing their adventures. Thus, what began as a dialogue changed to a forum in which the detectives recounted graphic particulars of cases in which they had been involved, and Dickens was all ears. Their stories entrenched the impression created in previous descriptions in *Household Words*, painting a picture of singularly fair-minded men. The issue of 27 July contained two such accounts, one by 'Sergeant Whichem' (pseudonym for Inspector Jonathan Whicher of the infamous Road Hill House murder, who had enjoyed considerable previous exposure in the press for the many other cases he had handled), the other by 'Inspector Wield' (pseudonym for Inspector Charlie Field), concluding with the promise of more to come.

Indeed, on 10 August of that year, another article appeared under the same heading, 'A Detective Police Party', with two more stories by detectives. Dickens inferred from these accounts that the detectives were 'for ever on the watch, with their wits stretched to the utmost... [setting] themselves against every novelty of trickery and dexterity'.[59] At the end of the second article this impression was somewhat marred by the revelation that on the way home at midnight one of the sharpest detectives (Whicher) was pickpocketed[60]—ironically, the detective best acquainted with this type of crime. Significantly, the accounts reveal that the detectives engaged in activities associated in the public mind with spying: they frequently hid their identity or assumed a false one. Yet, far from condemning these measures, Dickens sees them as appropriate to enforce social order. In contrast to thief-takers, detectives are imbued with a social conscience and the motivation to do good without a corrupting reward, as part of the ongoing reform in the country.

The next article, 'Three "Detective" Anecdotes', which appeared on 14 September, indicates that Dickens had kept in touch with the detectives.[61] He had continued listening to their tales on yet another evening in his office, and then published them in his journal.[62] Once again, the detectives were portrayed as highly intelligent and perceptive. A week later, the journal published an article entitled 'Spy Police', which commended the London detectives and the political culture that had bred them, and emphasized, as in many of his other texts, how different these police officers were from law-enforcers abroad. 'We have no political police, no police over opinion', the article stated.[63] 'The Detective Police... is solely employed in bringing crime to justice.' In contrast to practices across the Channel, 'the most rabid demagogue can *say* in this free country what he chooses, provided it does not tend to incite others to *do* what is annoying to the lieges.... He dreads not to discuss the affairs of the nation at a tavern, lest the waiter should be a policeman in disguise; he can converse familiarly with his guests at his own table without suspecting that the interior of his own liveries consists of a spy.'

The following year Dickens decided to shift his focus from detectives to the uniformed police, here again advertising their 'patience, promptitude, order, vigilance, zeal, and judgement'.[64] The immediate impetus for this account was the need he perceived to dispel widespread concerns that the forthcoming Great Exhibition (in 1851) would draw criminal elements from around the country and abroad to the metropolis, who, together with local offenders, would threaten not only the property of the respectable public but also the lives of foreign notables and the viability of the British constitution itself. Dickens set out to convince those who harboured such fears that the police force of the metropolis was well prepared to deal with these dangers. To this end, he decided to spend a few nights at police stations and feel the pulse of police life.[65] The outcome was an article in which Dickens and his sub-editor, William H. Wills, who accompanied him, left not a shred of doubt about the efficiency of the force:

We have seen that an incessant system of communication, day and night, is kept up between every station of the force; we have seen, not only crime speedily detected, but distress quickly relieved; we have seen regard paid to every application... [and] that everything that occurs is written down, to be forwarded to head quarters.[66]

Dickens and Wills could thus safely assure a nervous public that they were well protected and hope that the rate-payers would be convinced to pay the rates ungrudgingly.

Later in 1851 Dickens returned to his interest in detectives. This time he was not satisfied merely with listening to them recount various episodes from their working lives in the shelter of his office. Imbued with a pioneering and enterprising spirit, he repeated his experiment with the uniformed police, and arranged to be taken by several detectives and uniformed men to inspect the terrain that nurtured much of the crime in London. Frequenting the streets and observing its people had long been his habit. Now the detectives helped him discover parts of the city that were more hidden. He accompanied them for several hours in the darkness of night to the worst slums in London, visiting pubs, common lodging houses, and thieves' dens and experiencing the detective's work at close quarters. His intention was to produce a narrative of these events. The pivot of this narrative, published in *Household Words* in June 1851, was Inspector Charlie Field, described as 'sagacious' and 'vigilant', with a 'shrewd eye' and 'a burly figure'.[67] Above all else, Field seemed highly familiar with the seamy side of life in London. He knew the people who inhabited the filthy, crowded lodging houses and they knew him, although the relationship was by no means equal. Field was undoubtedly the powerful party, standing in one of the thieves' dens as 'the Sultan of the place'.[68] As a benevolent patron he assisted the inmates of such venues, but when necessary he exerted his authority as the representative of the law. His role was to care and protect, but in turn he demanded obedience. They recognized his might and dared not go against him, even if his party was outnumbered. They treated him with awe and also with respect. 'Every thief here cowers before him, like a schoolboy before his schoolmaster. All watch him, all answer when addressed, all laugh at his jokes, all seek to propitiate him.' In pubs he 'is received with warmth. Coiners and smashers droop before him; pickpockets defer to him; the gentle sex (not very gentle here) smile upon him.'[69] The general impression conveyed of Field's tour of the most dangerous locations in the vast city was that, with the detective branch made up of people like him, London was under efficient control, and respectable society could sleep in peace.

In an article titled 'Down with the Tide', published in early 1853, Dickens directed his attention to the Thames River Police, and, although no specific reference was made to plain-clothes men, his account focused on officers engaged in the detection of crime. To observe their work, he again left the comfort of his middle-class ambiance to join them on one of their regular excursions, this time on the river on a cold and windy night. He blended well with the men, lying 'in the deep shade as quiet as mice', conversing in whispers.[70] He was the amateur observer asking questions, while they were the professionals who had the answers. Dickens indeed learned a great deal about crime on the river and on shore, including the secrets, hardships, and risks in enforcing the law in this particular venue. Here again the reader could not but be impressed with the wily practices adopted by the Thames Police, far from the public eye but revealed by Dickens's pen.

Dickens established such good relations with the police that when, in 1855, a banker friend of his from Genoa visited the British capital and 'had a great desire to see some of the low life in London', Dickens considered it natural to arrange a tour with the police.[71] He invited other acquaintances, including Edmund Yates, who was to become a well-known journalist.[72] The party dined, then set out to '"go the rounds" of the thieves' quarters in Whitechapel, the sailors' and German sugar-bakers' taverns in Ratcliff Highway, the dens of the Mint, etc.', apparently seeing as normal '"slumming" expedition[s]' in the company of detectives.[73]

Clearly, Dickens's descriptions were extraordinarily flattering. Other journalists extolled detectives at the time, but none gave them such an extensive and favourable press. Dickens praised detectives in article after article. His approach seems exceptional, especially in view of his criticism of other aspects of the legal system and his less than enthusiastic attitude to other public officials and agents of the law, such as magistrates.

The impact of a single figure on the public imagination is difficult to assess. Many journalists, editors, and publishers would later adopt a commendable view of detectives. However, Dickens was already famous by the early 1850s, and his journals, *Household Words* and *All the Year Round*, were widely circulated. Undoubtedly, the fact that these prose sketches about detectives were written by Dickens (although unsigned) and published in these journals exposed them to a large public, both at the time and afterwards. Indeed, the articles are quoted time and again in books and articles written later in the century.[74] His repeated commendation of their qualities in each printed piece fused to create a persuasive narrative. One may reasonably conclude that Dickens's message left an imprint on the public mind of the period. Moreover, he was soon joined by other social explorers (discussed in Chapter 4), who, in describing their excursions in the streets of the expanding cities, all but praised the escorting detectives. Their books were widely advertised in the press, with quoted segments of them appearing in newspapers either before or after publication.[75]

These journalists-cum-writers, active during the 1850s–early 1870s when the image of detectives still evoked a measure of anxiety over secret methods of crime detection and the prevention of disorder, helped counterbalance negative impressions projected by other journalistic narratives. They depicted their experiences with detectives in a manner that not only popularized the topic of crime detection, but presented police detectives as guardians of the public good. Moreover, by frequently referring to the detectives who accompanied them as indispensable in the machinery of law enforcement and as possessed of special talents to discern lurking criminality, they confirmed the detectives' occupational credentials. Along with explicit compliments for detectives, the vivid depictions of the excursions, guided by detectives who see all and know all, conveyed an image of them as keen observers and controllers of modern urban life and as a cardinal source of knowledge about the world of crime—in short, as professional specialists. In contrast to radical portrayals of police officers as enemies of the poor and downtrodden, these sympathetic narratives typified them as caring and benevolent, and at times as instruments of progress.[76]

Admittedly, other readings of these sketches are possible. Some readers may have viewed the reality unfolded in them as justifying their worst fears. Exposés of detectives striding through mean streets as all-powerful representatives of the state, imposing disciplinary measures on the poor and powerless with a far from innocent gaze, may have signalled to readers that Jeremy Bentham's proposals to improve penal surveillance in prisons were being applied to society as a whole. Whether they recognized the detectives or not, the 'pack of boys and girls' and the 'sharped-eyed young thieves' attending the penny gaff (popular performances) in Whitechapel saw the respectable looking company of Jerrold, Doré, and the plain-clothes officers as 'unwelcome intruders'.[77] At least that is how Jerrold interpreted the feelings of the neighbourhood's inhabitants: 'We were to them as strange and amusing as Chinamen: and we were something more and worse. We were spies upon them; men of better luck whom they were bound to envy, and whose mere presence roused the rebel in them.'[78] His descriptions impart the impression that for locals the touring groups were patronizing outsiders whose presence, far from conducing to social progress, in fact provoked resentment and disobedience. Nevertheless, for the growing number of people who demanded more order and less crime, and were less concerned with the means to achieve these aims, the scenes Dickens and other investigative journalists portrayed, highlighting the efficiency of the police, were highly reassuring.

SETBACKS TO THE DETECTIVES' REPUTATION

Whether as a result of such media campaigns or not, by 1870 articles in the *Quarterly Review* and elsewhere pointed to a significant improvement in the image of the police, both uniformed and in plain clothes, in 'the respectable organs of the press'.[79] Detectives were portrayed as 'the exceptional men of the police, who are employed in the performance of special work, requiring the exercise of great experience, ability and skill'.[80] Although feelings of unease regarding the spying role of detectives were still articulated, plainclothes policing no longer appeared threatening to mainstream opinion. That no political police force was known to have developed in the detective branch—the main source of anxiety in this context—assuaged the fears of the liberal public.[81] Further, against expectations, during the first three and a half decades of its existence, 'there had been a striking absence of important allegations of corruption' against Scotland Yard detectives.[82] Even newspapers critical of the work of police detectives rarely accused them of such practices.

The trend was reversed in 1877 when newspaper headlines trumpeted the startling news that most of the senior officers in the detective unit at Scotland Yard had violated the law themselves and had helped other criminals avoid capture (see Chapter 1). The detailed coverage of the trial of public servants who had come to be regarded by many as the guardians of society shattered the growing confidence of the public in detectives (see Figure 11). In the words of the liberal *Daily News*, the detectives had 'flagrantly abused the trust committed to them'.[83] Detection now took up greater space in newspapers and journals than ever before, but not to the advantage of the force. *Punch* nicknamed the detective department at Scotland Yard 'The Defective Department' and 'The Criminal Instigation Department'.[84] The restructuring of the detective department in the Metropolitan Police

Figure 11. 'Bull's Eye on Bobby', *Punch*, 25 Aug. 1877.

that followed took shape in an atmosphere of public distrust and suspicion. Papers such as the Tory *Globe* retorted to an attack on the corruption of the detectives by Lord Truro in the House of Lords that it was unrepresentative,[85] and described the creation of the CID in 1878 as a clean start,[86] but the shady practices by several high-ranking detectives cast a dark shadow on all detectives and revived apprehensions about undercover policing. *The Times* proclaimed the uniformed branch to be the only 'protective police', though it still considered the office of detectives to be vital to the administration of justice.[87]

The early 1880s witnessed little improvement in the reputation of the London detectives. Although reports of detective corruptibility of a similar magnitude did not reappear, the press was now intensely vigilant and more readily took an offensive position against the detective police. Typically, it was the radical press that most closely monitored police departures from expected norms, but, when the police used agents to ensnare Thomas Titley to commit an indictable offence (selling drugs that induced abortions; see Chapter 3), the condemnation was much wider.[88] Although the defendant was known to be predisposed to commit such offences, and entrapment was employed in order to obtain evidence to incriminate him, such undercover means to arrive at the truth were widely seen as unfair deception, especially as Titley was reluctant to sell the drugs and had to be tempted several times. Notwithstanding, because of mounting Irish terror in the first half of the 1880s, and socialist and unemployment agitation, and the Ripper murders in the second half of the decade, the disapproval of detectives was aimed less at their infringements of civil liberties and the use of purportedly devious stratagems as at their failure to adopt methods of ameliorating police performance.

Against this background of growing political and social tensions, magnified by the press, which focused on the extent of poverty and deprivation in the country unprecedentedly, a need to re-examine the role of the police and the limits of their power and capabilities was felt in many quarters. The dailies continued to report and comment on detective activity extensively,[89] with deeper analyses of detective organization, tasks, and performance provided by the periodicals. In the 1860s, the most influential periodicals in the realm of political commentary were monthlies, but by the end of the century the significant vehicle of political commentary was the weekly, which, committed to 'topicality and day-to-day events',[90] reviewed diverse aspects of the world of detection almost routinely.[91] In particular, the *Saturday Review*, which, under the editorship of Walter Herries Pollock (1883–94), became 'a predictable supporter of the Conservative party',[92] and the liberally inclined *Spectator* (the leading Unionist weekly) showed a sustained interest in detection as a major public issue. As ever before, London detectives drew the bulk of attention.

Once again, the uniformed police were said to be the better branch. In an article in 1882 in the *Spectator* titled 'The Work of the London Police', an anonymous writer complimented the preventive police as 'the most successful in the world', while asserting that 'it is in detective work that the London Police shows least efficiency'.[93] When in 1884 a disguised detective in the Birmingham Police uncovered a nitroglycerine (from which dynamite was manufactured) canister buried in the garden of James Egan, an Irish revolutionary, certain journalists reached the conclusion that 'the police of the provinces... have set a good example of prudence to the force of the capital' (although Special Branch detectives had a hand in this successful operation).[94] Deriding the professional ability of the London detectives, the *Saturday Review* declared in February 1884: 'Low-class crime can be dealt with fairly well by our London detective.... In attempting to discover a murder or a burglary committed by an intelligent person, Mr Howard Vincent's "staff" are pretty nearly impotent.'[95]

A FOCUS ON THE FRENCH MODEL OF DETECTION

Incompetence was attributed to various causes. A repetitive motif was the system of internal recruitment in the police, which failed to bring into the detective force 'men of real ability and fair education' and instead promoted constables who were no match for a criminal of above-average intelligence.[96] However, more drastic means were now recommended in various organs of opinion, with criticism focusing on 'the reluctance of English officials to sanction the introduction here of the systematic espionage and the organised trickery which are habitually resorted to by the Continental detectives'.[97] Turning reflexively to the French model for direction and guidance, the press laid out a sheaf of comparisons between the two systems, some rejecting that model and others advocating its imitation. The *Daily Telegraph*, surveying the contemporary preoccupation with the comparison between the systems in 1882, concluded that for the most part it conveyed 'the impression that "they order this matter better in France"'.[98]

One of the contentious issues repeatedly raised in the contemporary press regarding the effectiveness of police detectives in England was their conspicuousness. Most articles, whether supportive of greater secrecy or not, admitted that the English detective was generally known to the public (see Figure 12).[99] In an atmosphere of mounting dissatisfaction with the performance of police detectives, this was widely seen as a disadvantage. The journalist M. Laing Meason, who had helped the Turkish government set up a police force in Syria in the 1860s, and appended his name to several articles about detective work, attributed the inferiority of the English detective

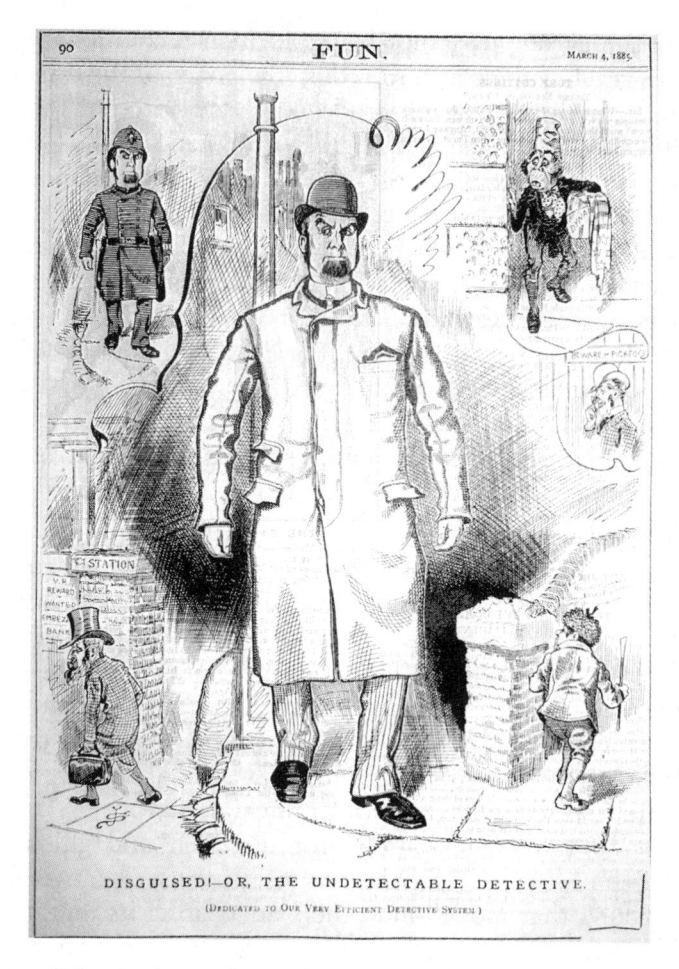

Figure 12. 'Disguised—or the Undetectable Detective', *Fun*, 4 Mar. 1885.

system above all to public prejudices against 'not doing everything in the light of day' and against 'the system of men going about disguised for the discovery of crime and criminals'.[100] Criticizing the police for acting upon these prejudices, he echoed similar disapproval voiced in secret-service circles at the time.[101] Except that they wore plain clothes instead of a uniform, he could discern no other difference between British detectives and ordinary constables, as they were as 'well known as if they were clad in blue tunics and helmets'.[102] The French way of doing things was far better, he thought. In particular, he was impressed with their special squad of detectives, who, apart from exceptional cases, did not visit headquarters (their orders were given in a letter in cipher), were never employed to make arrests, and rarely appeared as witnesses in court.[103] They only 'indicate where testimony to convict the offenders will be found; and there their functions cease'. As a result, the French criminal classes were 'utterly ignorant as regards the... [detectives'] names, personal appearance, and the places they frequent'.[104] Armed with this information, Meason preached that the only way to diminish crime in England was to choose 'intelligent, well-educated, practical men' who would disguise themselves and not be known to anybody except their immediate chief.[105] Moreover, in his opinion, the English should also copy the French practice of keeping these detectives as 'a body of men quite apart from the regular police', as in the relationship between spies and army generals in wartime.[106] Significantly, the sharp edge of criticism was now pointed less at the detrimental effects of the existence of secret agents and spies and more at the visibility of detectives.

Evidently, against a backdrop of anxieties over a rising tide of terror, socialist protest, and pressure by moralist groups, tactics that formerly seemed disagreeable—such as greater secrecy and powers to investigate, more aggressive measures, and subtler surveillance over the population—were seen as more plausible, or at least worth considering. At the same time, far from the readers' awareness, deliberations took place on various official levels to counter Irish terrorism with more covert action, of the kind suggested by Meason.[107] Most probably, a climate of opinion that kept referring to the French way of conducting investigations and fighting crime helped pave the way for the creation of the Irish Branch in March 1883. It was also an index of the growing willingness in society to accept the idea of disguise, and the confidence that, if detectives resorted to camouflage, it was imperative.

Nevertheless, although many commentators acknowledged that in certain respects the English might learn how to improve the system of detection from the French,[108] few articles gave the French system unqualified support. So challenging were the suggestions made by Meason that quite a few journalists engaged him in dialogue. Most seemed to agree that the French detective operations were 'very serviceable for the detection of crime', but that this success was attained through tight control over the population.[109] 'The whole of the French capital is subject to a sort of official espionage, very elaborately carried out,' the author of an article in the Tory *Saturday Review* argued. Moreover, many articles repeated the observation that the French method, 'good as it is', would not be tolerated in Britain.[110] Meason himself acknowledged that:

> there is in England such a strong... feeling against anything like secrecy, or not doing everything in the light of day, that if the French detective system were introduced into this country, we should no doubt have scores of petitions against it, and gushing letters and leading articles written to prove that it was in every way un-English and demoralising.[111]

In the event, it appears that the majority of those who took part in the debate about ways and means in this tension-ridden period opted for a middle position, proposing the adoption of only certain French methods of detection, either because they rejected the rest or because of their belief that a more wholesale adherence to the French system would alienate the English public. The late nineteenth century witnessed a period of considerable cross-fertilization of ideas between the liberal and conservative camps, resulting in convergence on a variety of issues. In this spirit, the dominant view on crime prevention and detection reconciled individual rights with order in varying degrees, advocating a compromise between expediency and morality, while shunning the use of the full coercive powers of the state.

Notably, blame for poor detection rates was not always attributed to the police, but rather to the criminal justice system and the general climate in the country, which were regarded as too liberal. The *Daily Telegraph*, which was moving towards the conservative camp in this period, asserted in 1882 that 'the disabilities of the British detective have been greatly exaggerated by his adverse critics' and that failures were the result not of any intrinsic shortcoming of his own, but of the deficiencies of the system.[112] The laws in England limited his powers. In contrast to the interventionist French agents of the law, who were free to practise any deception 'when actively engaged in the unravelling of a tangled political or criminal skein', in England 'individual privacy and personal liberty are hedged round with a hundred protective provisions, none of which may be infringed with impunity by police officers or magistrates'. In the columnist's view, the judiciary, too, failed to extend the necessary assistance to the detective in court. This attitude of exculpating the individual policeman was not uncommon. Even among those journalists who acknowledged the superiority of the French police and their methods of curbing crime, quite a few asserted that, in so far as the skills and ingenuity of individual members of the force go, the English are 'certainly equal to the French'.[113]

Discontent with the English legal system, however, did not necessarily constitute its rejection. Whether or not the individual detective was deemed efficient, criminal justice in England was regularly lauded as more distinguished than in France, if not in efficacy then in its moral principles. The monthly *Cornhill Magazine* argued that, to equal the French in effectiveness, the English would have to 'alter our institutions and sacrifice a good deal of that personal liberty which we esteem very precious'.[114] Further, in contrast to the French police, the English were 'servants of the public, not its masters'.[115] This was emphasized time and again. Thus, many articles that began with claims about the superiority of the French system often ended up extolling the English way of stamping out crime, or at least the priorities intrinsic in it. Meason himself declared that to a large extent the success of the Metropolitan Police 'in the cause of order, is owing to moral force'.[116] The controversy was not necessarily about facts; it was also about values and self-definition. Eschewing efficient detection results in the name of liberty and fair play was in itself cause for a sense of superiority of the English over the French system. It represented a triumph over French culture as a whole, as did the repudiation of plain-clothes policing in the early nineteenth century.

Moreover, as the decade of the 1880s wore on and terror subsided, enthusiasm for the French model diminished and press analyses now more often discussed its shortcomings. That some French agents of the law, including M. Gustave Macé, head of the Sûreté (1879–84), disapproved of aspects of French policing and celebrated the values of the English system of combating crime could only boost national pride.[117] Sharpening the national differences between Britain and France—the ultimate continental rival as the fountainhead of civic rights—served to balance criticism by radicals and socialists. The contest was not only between the two most famous detective departments in the world—Scotland Yard and the Sûreté—it was between the two nations themselves. If Britain was perceived as a stronghold of liberty and its culture as equalled by none, its detectives, by implication, personified this reality.

CRISIS IN THE LATTER 1880s

In 1886, the liberal newspaper *Daily News*, in an article devoted to the 'London Detectives', pointed out with satisfaction that the alarming predictions made in 1842 when the detective department was created that it would become 'a new system of espionage' were not fulfilled and that it had proven to be 'a very useful and a highly creditable branch of public service'.[118] However, events in the second half of the 1880s would continue to elicit dissatisfaction. If the crisis over the Fenian bombing outrages had abated, the mishandling of demonstrations by radicals, socialists, and the unemployed in London during 1885–7 again drew heavy fire aimed at the London police. Clashes with the police had the effect of swelling the ranks of the demonstrators, who accused the police of using heavy-handed methods, including the repression of freedom of speech, while other members of the public, shocked by the rioting and looting, blamed the police for not doing enough or for dealing with the riots incompetently.[119] As the focus of attention was neither crime nor criminal investigation, but the maintenance of order, detectives did not bear the brunt of the unflattering coverage. Yet, taking part in enforcing public order alongside their uniformed colleagues, and engaged in gathering information about the intended moves of the demonstrators, they too were subject to attacks—both by those alleging physical brutality and by those accusing the police of insufficient action.[120] The accumulation of events in which the forces of law and order appeared unskilful were highlighted by *Punch* in 1887 in a three-act sketch directed at both uniformed policemen and detectives. Titled 'The Detective's Triumph', it depicted an 'enterprising detective' instructing ordinary constables to find a man hiding in the district with no money 'within a couple of months'.[121] 'The Wanted One' had been trying hard to turn himself in for nine days, to no avail. Nothing helped—neither the informer, who pointed to the 'Wanted One', nor the culprit, who gave himself up to the men at Scotland Yard, nor his photograph, which was on display in Scotland Yard. After further effort, the 'Wanted One' finally succeeded in having himself arrested by the 'enterprising detective'.

Yet no event provoked so intense a reaction in the press as the series of murders perpetrated by Jack the Ripper in the poverty-stricken Whitechapel neighbourhood of London from August to November 1888.[122] Murder always touched a sensitive nerve in the community. It was also considered the ultimate criterion by which police competence was measured. A fivefold murderer in a period of ten weeks evoked panic and rage in the public, especially as widespread speculation kept raising the number of victims. The fact that they were prostitutes, and the ruthless and gruesome manner in which they were murdered combined to escalate the killings into a national disaster, perceived as an outrage both against private life and against the entire social fabric. The police failed not only to apprehend the murderer and put him on trial but even to identify him. As a result, the public was denied the calm of closure and remained fearful that the murderer might strike again.

The press did not always differentiate between the uniformed and the non-uniformed branches, as both worked together on the case, but, since the detectives' principal undertaking was the investigation of crime, they were a prime target of press attention. 'No one who was living in London that autumn will forget the terror created by these murders', recalled Assistant Commissioner Macnaghten, adding that 'leading articles appeared in nearly all of the principal papers, and feeling against the police in general, and the detective department in particular, ran very high'.[123] Still, the press responded to the lack of success in different ways. In his thorough research of the reaction of the press to the Ripper case, L. Perry Curtis, Jr, found that, typically, 'the Liberal and Radical press belabored the police and the government for their failings', while the Tory papers tended to defend police performance.[124] Yet, when the number of Ripper murders rose to four (on 30 September 1887) and then five (on 9 November), and no culprit had been found, some of the Tory papers, too, faulted aspects of the workings of the detective department, though most continued to exonerate the police. The *Saturday Review*, maintaining its defence of the police, inveighed against 'the wildest, most ludicrous, and most coherent ravings [against the detective police] ever remembered even in these days of "spread-eagle" journalism'.[125] Acknowledging that it, too, criticized the defects of the Metropolitan Police, the *Review* pointed out that it attributed these shortcomings not to the detectives but to those responsible for their small numbers—Parliament and the Home Office.[126] The journal nonetheless proposed certain reforms, among them the suggestion that 'within due limits we should not object to see women employed in the ranks of our *police de sûreté*'.[127] The Tory press consistently demanded 'more police, more surveillance and harsher sentences', but these demands were now also voiced by other papers.[128] Liberal and radical papers called for modifications in the organizational life of detectives, including relaxing the strict entrance criteria into police service regarding height to allow 'clever little ferrets of men' into the detective branch.[129] In its persistent campaign to show how unprotected the inhabitants of London were from criminal elements, the *Pall Mall Gazette*, claiming to reflect public opinion, depicted many constables as 'very "muddle-headed"' and detectives as not particularly intelligent.[130] It also reminded readers that detectives were prone to pocket a shilling and 'tip and treat' where they could.

GROWING SYMPATHY FOR DETECTIVES AT THE TURN OF THE CENTURY AND THEREAFTER

The passage of two or three years without another such sensational murder dulled the memory of the glaringly botched performance of both the City and the Metropolitan Police in dealing with the Whitechapel murders, although from then on many unsolved murders tended to evoke echoes of this failure.[131] If anything, the press became more indulgent towards detectives during the following decades.

To be sure, bungling in detection continued to draw derisive commentaries from journalists. When a murder case was not solved quickly and the public felt robbed of the protection it deserved, the press was filled with letters from readers with such signatures as 'Vox Populi', 'Disgusted', or 'A Taxpayer', questioning the ability of police detectives to bring serious law offenders under control.[132] Waves of panic, as when at the end of the century stories about hooligan gangs and street violence provoked fears for the morality of the youth and the safety of the population in urban areas, had immediate and severe implications for the reputation of crime fighters,[133] as did cases of imprisonment of innocent men, such as Adolph Beck (see Chapter 4). However, increasingly, much of the criticism that was levelled at official crime control came from the radical press, which continued to view unsolved crimes as symptoms of a much deeper malaise in the prevailing detective system, both in London and in the provinces.[134] A series of articles published by the *Sun* between 25 September and 1 October 1897 detailed the many instances of failure by the Yard, accusing it of inefficiency under captions such as 'The Decadence of our Detective System', 'Public Dissatisfaction Become General', and 'The Incapacity of our Criminal Investigation Department'. The series pointed to the senior management of the police, the military culture, conditions of service, an 'overdose of regulations and restrictions', petty jealousies, lack of municipal control over Scotland Yard, and internal recruitment as the major drawbacks responsible for the lack of success in combating crime. The

Special Branch was called 'a bureau of political *mouchard*', and its tasks 'espionage duty'.[135] The socialist and trade union activist John Burns (elected MP for Battersea in 1892, and appointed a member of the Liberal Cabinet in 1906) was quoted in the *Sun* as stating that, instead of tracking down criminals, detectives (and uniformed men) were 'used to help the employers to fight the workmen in a way [in] which [it] was never intended they should be used'. Burns also complained that officers were following him and other trade unionists wherever they went. Accusations of endemic corruption were also levelled by the radical press.[136]

In one respect the radical press adopted a new approach to detectives in the course of the 1890s: attuned to the progress of reform of all kinds, it became more attentive to the needs of the police rank and file. Adjusting to the spread of trade unionism and democratic notions in society, radical papers devoted more space to collective protests about conditions of service in the police and to individual detectives with grievances. Their stories illuminated what was happening within the forces of law and order. Apart from sympathetically covering national events such as the police strike in 1890, which was also reported extensively in the established press, radical papers on occasion interviewed officers, both uniformed and plain clothes—without revealing their names—to allow them to air complaints against their superiors.[137] The radical press also interviewed former detectives who held a personal grudge against the police, as in the case of ex-Detective Sergeant Patrick McIntyre, who over a period of seventeen weeks in 1895 recounted his experiences as a detective in the Special Branch, and the reasons for his departure from the police in *Reynolds's News* (see Chapter 4).[138] Another case was that of former First Class Detective Sergeant William Henry Harris, who had been dismissed from the detective department in London in 1902 after fourteen years of service. He took the opportunity given to him in 1910 in two issues of the *Penny Illustrated Paper* to accuse the department of various malpractices, including personal gain and favours.[139] Directly thereafter (15 October 1910), in an article replete with accusations of false charges, harassment, and whitewash by the police (with reference to the Royal Commission on the Metropolitan Police of 1908), the paper opened its columns to ex-Detective Inspector John McCarthy to explain his wrongful dismissal from the Metropolitan Police.[140] These detectives were projected as individuals in distress, in need of protection against a brutal employer. In the absence of a representative body of policemen to deal with complaints, these journals helped the aggrieved detectives publicize their plight, fight the bureaucracy, and espouse their cause.

Overall, however, the press in the late nineteenth and early twentieth centuries carried a larger body of articles conveying support for the police institution and its detective departments. Liberals and others condemned Victorian criminal policy for its severity towards former convicts, but a growing emphasis on the social and communal role of the police rather than on deterrence, and on care rather than punishment, strengthened the reputation of the official forces of law and order.[141] Periodic reports in the local press about the philanthropic activities of policemen and police forces enhanced their image as benevolent agents.[142] A comment in parliament by William Burdett-Coutts, Conservative MP for Westminster, that 'we owe the police much on account of the important duties they perform' reflected the opinion of many contemporaries.[143] Such support was helped by a reduction in the rates of crime, and particularly of serious crime, in the latter part of the century,[144] the solution of several high-profile crimes, and the handling of what was widely perceived as the 'anarchist threat' during the 1890s.[145]

The stunning news at the beginning of 1892 that several anarchists were manufacturing explosives in Walsall initially generated displeasure in some liberal papers and unequivocal condemnation in the radical and socialist press when it transpired that Detective Inspector William Melville of the Special Branch had used the services of a French–Irish spy, allegedly operating as an agent provocateur (see Chapter 3).[146] This was widely viewed as crossing acceptable boundaries, as they had entrapped the non-predisposed to crime, and, even if anarchists were considered to be potential saboteurs, this was a clear case of deceit, by an undercover, if unofficial, agent posing as an ordinary citizen not to detect but to create a crime. At the time, however, press reports of greater anarchist outrages on the Continent, often accompanied by illustrations and caricatures,[147] and prominent headlines and lengthy pieces focusing on the assassination of heads of state and on bomb explosions in public places abroad, had the effect of mellowing criticism of the police. In fact, the police gained in stature more than they lost from violent anarchist agitation, particularly once it spread to Britain. Readers of popular newspapers such as the conservative *Evening News* learned that detectives who shadowed anarchists exposed themselves to grave risks.[148] Moreover, precisely at a time when the Special Branch allowed itself to make greater use of means associated with more sinister spying, the press itself once again became more open to the use of such means against the enemies of society. By the mid-1890s, even papers not in the conservative camp were more willing to endorse secretive measures, albeit insisting they should not go so far as practices on the Continent.

The *Spectator* argued in 1890 that, 'in order to catch an offender, a detective has a perfect right to assume a character not his own, and in that capacity to lay a trap for the capture of the man he wants, even though in so doing he has to enter upon a series of deceptions'.[149] In reaction to the anarchist explosion in Greenwich in February 1894 (see Chapter 1), the liberal *Daily News* mocked Scotland Yard for having been 'caught napping' but otherwise gave the impression that the force was doing its job, was vigilant, and was familiar with individual anarchists and the movement as a whole.[150] It also congratulated the police for their caution and moderation in handling the anarchists and in shielding them from angry crowds.[151] By contrast, the radical *Reynolds's News* was of the opinion that foreign and domestic police alike were implicated in anarchist aggression,[152] but, in as much as most of the press portrayed anarchists as conspirators against humanity (and in conservative papers as foreigners, lunatics, and wild beasts),[153] the detectives, mainly of the Special Branch, were seen as its defenders. So noticeable was this change in the attitude of the press that the *Spectator* commented in 1893 on a 'tendency to glorify the detective's trade, and invest it with an air of romance'.[154]

In the pre-war years, industrial disputes outside London proliferated and police intervention was brutal, involving charges into crowds that provoked censure by some sections of the press.[155] The introduction of cars onto British roads at the beginning of the twentieth century also created tensions between uniformed policemen and drivers. The rates of serious crime rose again from the beginning of the century. Nonetheless, to middle-class observers, the bobby had long become 'the personification of an idealized image of the English legal system—impartial, and functioning with solemnity and a clockwork regularity'—and the new tensions did not seriously mar this impression.[156] Many working people still regarded the uniformed policeman as a man they feared 'very much indeed',[157] but by that time the policeman had also become a barometer of the respectability of the working-class family—a policeman's visit to a family in his capacity as a law-enforcer was considered 'a terrible thing'.[158] In the years leading up to the First World War, there were still streets that policemen refrained from entering on Saturday nights, even in pairs, because of the danger.[159] Yet, overall, physical attacks on policemen greatly declined in this period. Indeed, a significant index of the diminishing animosity towards policemen among working people was the decline by 64 per cent in the rate of trials for assaults on police officers from the late 1850s to the pre-war years.[160] Complaints about the police were often directed at the small size of the force and its damaging effect on police efficiency.[161] Working alongside the uniformed police, detectives, for better or worse, were influenced by what the different segments of the public thought about police activities.

Interest in police detection seems to have subsided slightly in the late 1890s and the early twentieth century, but it flourished in the years preceding the First World War with the renewal of social and political tensions in various walks of life (see Chapter 1). Even though relations between detectives and journalists were not invariably good, they improved in the twentieth century (as seen in Chapter 4), which may have had a moderating effect on the tone of press reports. The revived focus by the press on police detection produced the familiar mix of occasional blame with considerable sympathy and praise. Lingering preoccupation with anarchist activity continued to benefit Scotland Yard. 'Not much is heard of the vigilance of Scotland Yard, but it is perhaps not the less effective on that account,' the liberal *Daily Chronicle* reassured its readers in 1901.[162] In the wake of the Royal Commission, which examined allegations against the police (1906–8), publishing its report in the summer of 1908, *The Times* devoted an article to overcoming the public's prejudices against, and 'ignorance' of, detectives by laying out the 'true facts' about them. The article, published on the first day of 1909, titled 'The Plain-Clothes Man', commended various aspects of plain-clothes work, such as the selection of candidates, training, and examinations, and saluted the officers' intelligence, wit, and quickness of mind. The tenor of the article was that 'the man in plain clothes is under the same disadvantage as his helmeted comrade through the public which he serves being, as a rule, quite ignorant of his work and training and of the principles on which he proceeds to carry out his duties'.[163]

During the Houndsditch affair (1910), when three officers of the City of London Police were shot by a gang of foreign burglars (wrongly identified as anarchists), press reports assured the public that 'detectives keep a continuous watch' on anarchists and that 'information about... [anarchist] meetings was constantly leaked out and become known to the police'.[164] Against a background of vigorous public debate mixing issues of ordinary crime, political threat, and immigration, such confirmation must have set the mind of some readers at rest.

More than ever, individual detectives riveted the attention of journalists. Although detectives now operated in an increasingly bureaucratic organization, working within set rules and procedures, journalistic reports continued to highlight individual idiosyncrasies. The focus was on the detective's initiative, daring, and cunning. Despite bureaucratic constraints on his movements and decisions, he was viewed as the engine propelling the steps taken to combat crime—an ingenious individual who determined the course of action against crime. Moreover, the all-male character of the police labour force supported a powerful macho image of the detective in the press, with a focus on pursuit, action, the use of force, and recurrent confrontations with dangerous criminals. Uniformed policemen, too, were associated with hegemonic masculine qualities, but whereas they were identified principally with an impressive physique, detectives were seen as combining an imposing constitution with cerebral aptitudes.[165] Even though, as detectives, they had to shed their uniform—a symbol of authority—they acquired masculine attributes intimately linked to middle-class notions of manliness, which, in addition to brain power, included individuality, discretion, and relative independence at work. No doubt, the expansion of the popular press in the late nineteenth century, with its embrace of sensational reporting, fortified the drive to invent or search for exceptional individuals. As part of this trend, the public was fascinated with detectives not only as agents of the law, but increasingly as manly actors in dramas, especially when the investigations involved celebrities, incorporated thrilling elements, or were conducted worldwide.[166]

Even a daunting case such as the disappearance of Dr Hawley Harvey Crippen's wife in January 1910, in which the police groped blindly for clues and, upon finding her dead body, had to deal with the situation of an escaped culprit,[167] could, with the right kind of press coverage, turn into a victory for the chief investigator of this case, Detective Chief Inspector Walter Dew of Scotland Yard. He had been involved in the case from the moment the disappearance was reported to the police in late June, yet, when he finally caught Crippen, the murderer, at the end of July, he won mainly approbation.[168] Indeed, the Crippen affair contained elements that lent a certain mystique to detective work while glamorizing individual detectives. Crippen, an American doctor who lived in London, had poisoned his actress wife, mutilated her body, and escaped from England using a false identity. Crossing the Atlantic on a ship to Canada with his mistress, who was disguised as a boy, he was making plans for a new life, unaware that their identities had been exposed. Dew travelled to Canada on a fast boat to wait for them there, his progress followed avidly by legions of newspaper readers. The papers reported extensively on this stratagem, but left some of the details obscure, spreading rumours regarding the disguise Dew would assume and hinting that they relied for their information on unknown private sources. The use of a new technology—wireless telegraphy—allowed the story to be carried by newspapers almost in real time. Readers on both sides of the Atlantic waited anxiously for the encounter between the couple and the detective.[169] By then the readers had forgotten how unimpressively the investigation had been conducted in the first place, and focused on the drama of the approaching meeting between the criminals and their hunter.[170] Detective Chief Inspector Dew was now portrayed as highly shrewd, using 'every precaution' and planning ahead. Regardless of how the story began, it garnered widespread popular acclaim for Scotland Yard and for detectives elsewhere.[171] That Crippen was successfully brought back to England, found guilty, and hanged (in November 1910) heightened their prestige.[172]

As in the past, in many instances of criticism it was in fact the system of detection that was under attack, rather than individual detectives. Even the acrimonious series of articles published in the *Sun* in 1897 claimed that its attack on the detective force was against methods, not men, and that CID officers 'under altered conditions are capable of redeeming the character which Scotland Yard has lost'.[173] Detectives knew how to push themselves forward, and newspapers readily obliged, allocating considerable space to portraits of detectives and their life stories.

Still, for all the emphasis by the press on individual ability, Scotland Yard gradually acquired a collective image encapsulating the aggregate qualities of its officers, which passed on to other detectives. The introduction of fingerprinting into the technological arsenal of official crime fighters early in the twentieth century added an element of precision and sophistication to this image and strengthened its aura of professionalism.[174] The triumph of fingerprinting over Bertillonage not only in Britain but in other countries, including France itself,[175] cemented the superiority of the British over the French criminal justice system even in the domain of scientific methodology.

Several police officials made a point of publicizing the Metropolitan Police and their detective branch abroad as well. Howard Vincent, who had been a correspondent for the *Daily Telegraph* in the 1870s and had an appreciation of the power of the press, gave an interview in Paris in 1884 to the French newspaper *Voltaire*, in which he promoted his own image and that of the British police by highlighting the clever methods he had devised and his men had used to track criminals.[176] Ex-Commissioner James Monro, in an interview with the *North American Review* in 1891, ascribed the reduction of violent crime to the Metropolitan Police and their detectives and pointed out that the public should be indebted to the officers and men of Scotland Yard.[177] Edward Henry, as assistant commissioner responsible for the CID, discussed detective methods in London with the American journalist Josiah Flynt, later published in the *North American Review*.[178]

Former police commissioner of New York, William McAdoo, joined forces with British police officials, stressing the exemplary conduct of British detectives to foreign readers. Comparing Scotland Yard detectives with their counterparts in New York, he acknowledged that the prevailing opinion was that the ability of Scotland Yard was 'very much superior' (though he disagreed).[179] He did, however, add that 'the reputation of the London detective for honesty, whatever it might be for efficiency, is absolutely unquestioned by either the public... or the law-breakers against whom they operate', as were 'the honesty and integrity of the heads of the department', and he expressed the wish that the New York police would acquire this standing.[180]

Pictorial magazines devoted to sensational news stories, which proliferated from the mid-nineteenth century onwards, buttressed the prestige of police detectives. Depicting crimes based on recent events, the pictures staged the events as melodramatic chases and confrontations between a vigorous and determined detective and his opponent—the criminal—often in situations of risk (see Figure 13), injury, or even death to the detective. This visual material, sometimes filling a full page, enlivened the image of the detective (see Figure 14). Combining fact and fantasy, such popular magazines were read by a public that generally avoided the more serious critical press, with the result that some sectors of the public were exposed almost exclusively to a heroic portrayal of detectives. Photos and illustrations of detectives in other journals, highlighting their impressive physical attributes and projecting self-confidence, gave their image added strength,

Figure 13. 'The Arrest of Hudson for the Yorkshire Murders', *Illustrated Police Budget*, 29 June 1895.

especially against the backdrop of continual concerns about the deteriorating physical fitness of city-dwellers and the poor results of the physical examinations of candidates to the army during and after the Boer War.

Unsurprisingly, an exalted image of detectives was also promoted in police journals. In various ways, whether in captions such as 'Clever Capture' and 'Clever Arrest', in columns about successful solutions to crimes, or in accounts of the life histories of detectives, these publications underlined the achievements of detectives and unfailingly portrayed them as loyal and able civil servants (see Chapter 4).[181]

The standing of English detectives was enhanced from an unexpected quarter when in 1913 the Prince of Wales participated in a meeting of a debating society in Oxford at which he opposed the motion that 'this House considers that the English detective force is in a parlous condition'.[182] The prince's side of the debate prevailed.

Figure 14. 'The Arrest of Oscar Wilde by Two Police Detectives', *Illustrated Police Budget*, 13 Apr. 1895.

THE CONSOLIDATION OF THE DETECTIVE IMAGE IN THE PRESS

Clearly, the press conveyed competing approaches to crime-related issues. A fair number of references to detectives were not particularly laudatory, often charging them with unprofessional behaviour and poor performance. How then did police detectives eventually acquire a glamorous veneer of 'great heroism and coolness', as noted in a newspaper in 1910?[183]

Press coverage involved a considerable amount of omission. Although newspapers and periodicals purported to act as conveyors of information to the public, in practice the published material was the result of selection by those responsible for publication. In effect, all knowledge emanating from the press was constructed. Items considered not newsworthy, such as petty crime, were routinely ignored. Although most offences with which the detectives dealt were mundane, naturally newspapers preferred to dwell on the spectacular crimes, often stressing the detective's gallant exploits. Although murders were relatively uncommon, and only a few detectives were involved in the investigation of such crimes, it was they that won extensive press attention, while uneventful reality was sparsely covered. The detectives' wearisome, overlong days gained publicity mainly in the context of the hard work and self-sacrifice that characterized these loyal public servants. Glimpses into the everyday routine of detectives in books and articles by social explorers also tended to glorify them. Detectives were thus portrayed at once as brave, enterprising, hard working, and benevolent.

Their perceived role as watchdogs led reporters to expose police malpractice, illegal or otherwise, as a political and moral issue, but, if at the beginning of the period plain-clothes policing was the object of sharp criticism for its clandestine nature, in time it was more likely to supply compelling material for news. The underlying notion then was that covert tactics were at times unavoidable if the reduction of crime was to be accomplished, as long as the police did not overstep consensual boundaries, by adopting such doubtful methods as employing agents provocateurs. Corrupt practices were presented as exceptional, and the ease with which legal norms were bent and procedures broken was generally not made public. The resort to physical coercion by detectives only infrequently reached the press. It was principally the radical press, as well as socialist, anarchist, and occasionally liberal papers, that periodically exposed complicity between detectives and criminal elements, bribe-taking, and the use of unlawful means against those considered political subversives.[184] None of the newspapers held back from revealing examples of police inefficiency, but this did not undermine the overall positive portrayal. From a Tory perspective, to argue that the detective department did not operate competently was often to call for greater power for the police and for more resources, this last demand being put forward by other papers as well. In any event, as far as the Tory press was concerned, failures in policing were often the fault of the restraints imposed by the criminal justice system and not of the police themselves.

In addition to the selection process by proprietors, editors, and journalists, the police themselves played a significant role in determining the nature of the image projected in the press. If initially reporters derived much of their material about crime and punishment from their presence in courts, in the course of the century the police themselves became the major source of news and reports about crime detection and investigation. The information they possessed, and the reliance of reporters on their goodwill, endowed them with a great deal of power in choosing what to release to the press. Mindful that effective management of the flow of information could shape reality, they selected what they wanted to see in print and the messages they wished to get across, and screened information harmful to the police. The police withheld information on the progress of investigations, either to avoid undermining the investigation or to hide the lack of achievement from the public.[185] They also tried to conceal some of the more uncongenial investigative measures, such as the use of narks to frame criminals by enticing them to engage in criminal acts,[186] or the employment of certain means by Special Branch agents to spy on political dissidents. The police also manipulated crime statistics, thereby magnifying the impression of success.[187]

In the main, despite the latent tensions between the press and detectives, the press adhered to the perspective of the law-and-order camp. Conservative journals primarily, though not always, concurred that the good name of the detective should be protected, whether he was effective in his job or not. The book *Police!* (1889) by Clarkson and Richardson seems to have reflected widespread feelings not only of policemen but also of many journalists that to be over-critical of the police was not in the public interest. Although the book included complaints about the police 'policy of secrecy', the clear message was that policemen were the object of 'considerable misunderstanding', which was unjustified, and that they ought to be assured of 'public support' and 'friendly feeling'.[188]

Whether for these reasons or because many reporters depended on the cooperation of detectives and did not want to alienate them, or simply because they had formed cordial relations with them, some journalists became active participants in the cause of improving the reputation of detectives. By eliciting the readers' identification with formal agencies of crime control, journalists played an important role in disseminating a more consensual view of detective work. The fact that many newspapers in London and in the provinces derived their news from the same sources—news agencies—or copied from one another, meant that the same stories and personalities were featured in many publications, and that readers were exposed to similar messages.[189]

Apart from overt support for the forces of law and order, the journalistic mode of narration *per se* evoked an empathetic attitude towards the detectives' vocation. The accounts and illustrations generally presented detectives engaged in some action against crime, usually a serious crime, thereby heightening the sense of threat and the urgent need for the detectives' skills. In addition, while many undetected crimes were either never mentioned by the press or quickly forgotten,[190] the focus of the press on trials throughout most of the nineteenth century, and, therefore, on criminals in legal proceedings, served to exaggerate police success.

This is not to say that the press intentionally served as an instrument of the police, even if in individual cases it did consult the police and took their interests into consideration.[191] To be sure, journalists resented the paucity of details released by the police and fought against it, but on the whole they had no choice but to rely, at least partly, on the material they received from the police. In some cases, though, they conducted their own investigations. In sum, for disparate reasons, the press, although encompassing dissonant voices and different narrative styles, played a pivotal role in entrenching a tolerant attitude to official crime control.

There are no means of assessing how the reading public absorbed the messages in the press. Obviously, not all media information was believed. However, the predominant perception in the Victorian period was that events were what they seemed, and that the medium that transmitted their content to the public portrayed reality. This was particularly true for the transmission of news, which supposedly provided accounts of authentic people and events. The press may distort, it was believed, but does not invent. The diversity of opinion in the press about detectives, and the demands for reform and supervision of detective practices by an external body such as the press, only strengthened its position in society. Radical coverage throughout the period gave expression to dissenting voices, but at the same time created the impression of equal access to the media. Some readers may have been disappointed with police ineffectiveness, and their confidence in police ability may have been shaken at certain periods, but the overwhelming belief in the decency and commitment of detectives was stronger.

The press was not the only medium to be preoccupied with undercover policing. The world of fiction, too, devoted extensive attention to detection and its practitioners. Yet, unlike the press, which presumed to mirror reality, works of fiction were by definition products of artistic imagination. What then was the image emerging from this medium? The answer to this question is presented in Chapter 6.

6

POLICE DETECTIVES IN FICTION

Few occupations, if any, can claim so pervasive a presence in imaginative writing as detection. Detective figures emerged in ever-growing numbers in novels, serial runs, and short stories during the Victorian and Edwardian period, alongside their appearance in press reports. Abundant and insightful analysis has been devoted to the development of detective fiction in the Victorian and Edwardian period,[1] and no attempt is made here either to review this topic or to offer new research findings. The chapter's prime concern is rather briefly to outline the intriguing phenomenon of the deep penetration of the detective into the English literary world, and in this context to focus more specifically on the representation of the police detective—the subject of the present volume.

Curiously, although both private and police detectives are represented extensively in a vast array of fictional works, it is the private detective, whether amateur or professional, who outnumbers the official variety. Moreover, he also often appears as a more competent and praiseworthy figure. Evidently, the literary image of the police detective did not replicate his prevalent position and image in newspapers and periodicals. This needs to be explained. In short, why did not fiction writers project a sense of greater confidence in the official agency of law enforcement? Furthermore, if, as Foucauldian scholars have argued, detective fiction served to entrench practices of surveillance and regulation in Victorian society, as will be discussed below, an analysis of how the most typical agents of public control were represented in this fiction is relevant. The answers, gleaned from reviewing a varied collection of fictive texts, with particular attention to popular novels and stories not routinely studied or read, will evoke a greater understanding of the attitude of the public to police detectives and detection. They will also expand the discussion in previous chapters regarding the moulding of the detective's image in print culture and the involvement of detectives themselves in cultural production.

THE CRIMINAL AS LITERARY HERO

Tales of crime and punishment have kindled the imagination of humankind from the dawn of civilization. Myth-tellers and biblical authors repeatedly recounted the violations of the codes by which society is governed and the retribution that such criminal activity incurred. The demand for such texts accelerated with the proliferation of printed materials in the seventeenth and eighteenth centuries, and the criminal gained a position of cultural centrality. Whether real, imaginary, or a mixture of both, he or she exerted a distinctive fascination, surfacing in all manner of literary formats and projecting an image of society as filled with lawbreakers, deviants, and corrupt servants of the legal system.[2] Notorious criminals such as Jack Sheppard, Jonathan Wild, and the famous highwayman Dick Turpin struck a special chord with the best literary talents of the period, who awarded celebrity status to those who had trod errant paths.[3]

The appeal of crime literature kept accelerating in the nineteenth century across the class spectrum. Broadsides, pamphlets, and other publications depicting gory details of the trials and executions of criminals continued to serve as a moral lesson for readers to avoid crime; at the same time such writings placed the criminal at the centre of the narrative. Fact and fiction were magnetic in equal measure. During the 1830s and 1840s a series of melodramatic narratives, commonly referred to by contemporaries as the Newgate novels (after London's Newgate prison), prominently featured accounts about real criminals alongside imaginary ones.[4] In their critics' view, the Newgate novelists 'romanticised and glamorised crime and low life, and invited sympathy with criminals rather than with the victims of crime by making their criminal subjects the hunted object of a chase, by focusing on their motivation or psychology, and by representing them as the victims of circumstances or society'.[5] Furthermore, stage adaptations of these novels and similar themes, embraced by the rapidly growing penny press, had the effect of perpetuating the sentiments reflected in the Newgate novels.[6] Street ballads, too, 'implicitly or explicitly exculpated individuals of moral responsibility', most notably when the offence was one regarded sympathetically, such as cases of poaching.[7] The popularity of these texts filtered down to the more disreputable sectors of society with an effect deplored by their critics. The journalist James Greenwood claimed that at least 50 per cent of the young thieves incarcerated in mid-century admitted 'that it was the shining example furnished by such gallow heroes as "Dick Turpin" and "Blueskin" [Jack Sheppard's accomplice], that first beguiled them from the path of rectitude, and that a large proportion of their ill-gotten gains was expended in the purchase of such delectable biographies'.[8]

Criminals who did considerable harm to the community, yet were presented as defiant, gained the admiration of readers as daring and adventurous, even if depraved and threatening. Even when the criminal's guilt was incontestable—his penitent confession or last words proving blame beyond doubt—he was often posited as heroic, albeit deserving of punishment. By contrast, the crime fighter was a much less common figure than the criminal in crime literature before the middle of the nineteenth century. Often, the identity of the criminal was made known in the early stages and the plot hinged on his 'perverted psychology and actions' rather than on his capture.[9] In the event that he was brought to justice, this usually came about not through the action of a representative of the political authority but rather by coincidence, by providence, by a private person, a thief-taker, or the villain himself.[10] The writers manifestly expected little of the criminal justice system, which was often depicted as brutal, insensitive, and oppressive. Thief-takers were shown to symbolize the corruption of society and not the power behind the law. Outlaws like Jonathan Wild were at once criminals and legal agents.

THE ENTRANCE OF THE DETECTIVE

Gradually, however, the detective assigned to a case attained parity with the criminal as a literary character, and in time replaced him as a dominant figure in aesthetic discourse. Presumably, the greater attention in public discourse of the later eighteenth century to the need for more publicly employed crime fighters, and the alterations made in the policing system in London at the end of the century and thereafter, constituted the catalyst for the emergence of narratives centred on crime fighters who were firmly on the side of the law, though not necessarily employed by the legal system. Indeed, one of the earliest detective figures in English fiction, Caleb Williams, the lead character in the novel entitled *Things as They Are; or, The Adventures of Caleb Williams*, by the radical philosopher William Godwin (1794), was an amateur detective, driven by a private grievance and an inner determination to unmask the identity of the criminal.[11]

The vigorous public discussion of policing matters in the 1820s, whether supportive of or opposed to the formation of a new police force in London, may have prepared the ground for the appearance of a growing number of official law-enforcers in literary works in the late 1820s and the 1830s. The Bow Street Runners, London's major detective force until 1839, played a role in such novels as Edward Bulwer-Lytton's *Paul Clifford* (1830), about a gentleman-criminal, and Charles Dickens's *Oliver Twist* (1838).[12] A Bow Street Runner also assumed the central role in a three-volume pseudo-memoir of a detective published by an anonymous author in 1827, entitled *Richmond; or, Scenes in the Life of a Bow Street Officer*.[13] Significantly, Richmond is a rogue hero who, when 'sick of the uncertainty of a precarious livelihood', resolves to obtain a 'settled occupation' as a Bow Street Runner.[14] He and the other Bow Street Runners appear as decent servants of the public interest. Notably, while the book did not prove to be a great success, it was written in a style that had recognizable cultural forebears going back to fictitious accounts of highwaymen and thieves published before the nineteenth century, and would be adopted to a greater or lesser extent by both real and fictitious first-person detective stories later in the century (see below). Typically, the text begins with a chapter on the life and adventures of the protagonist before he was made an agent of the law, followed by a long exposé of the situations in which he found himself embroiled in this capacity. Interwoven in the memoir are efforts by the author to convince the reader that the stories he tells are firmly fixed in the context of the real world and are in fact based on Richmond's own 'private memoranda'.[15]

Another early text casting an official crime investigator in the lead role was the ghosted, edited, and translated memoir of Eugène-François Vidocq, published in 1828–9 in France. Vidocq was a French criminal who eventually, in 1812, established and headed the Brigade de la Sûreté, Paris's detective department (later known as the Sûreté), which he ran with the aid of ex-convicts.[16] The English publisher of his memoir apparently quickly recognized the commercial value of the narrative, which blended Vidocq's life story with gripping invented or highly embellished crime tales, as the English translation saw light in England soon after it was published in France.[17] Vidocq, as a thief turned detective who had served several prison sentences—a life experience he utilized for the benefit of the detective department when apprehending criminals—made a strong impression on audiences keen on reading about criminals and tending to romanticize crime fighters as heroes. Moreover, he was accused of continuing his collaboration with the underworld even when employed by the forces of law and order, thereby combining the identities of a criminal, an informer, and a police and private agent, which surely made his persona all the more alluring.

The texts by the anonymous author of *Richmond* and by Vidocq, however, were exceptional. Generally, both official as well as self-appointed detectives appeared as minor characters in literature at that time. In addition, although crime and crime investigators of diverse kinds also figured prominently in the 'shilling shockers' and the 'penny bloods' (precursors of the 'penny dreadfuls' popular during the 1840s), featuring grisly accounts of murders, betrayals, and low life, the total number of texts concerned with detectives and published in England before the establishment of the detective department in Scotland Yard in the early 1840s remained small. It was the criminal who still proved to be the more engaging character.

With the consolidation of detection as a distinct occupation within the British public service during the middle decades of the Victorian era, the theme of detection became more prevalent and detectives surfaced more regularly in British literature. Literary critic Ian Ousby persuasively argues that, in the mid-Victorian period, when most fictional detectives were secondary figures, their failures functioned 'as a convenient device for removing them discreetly from the action, leaving the hero and heroine to occupy the center of interest at the end'.[18] Ousby also points out that the writers of the period still relied on 'the abstractions of Providence and Destiny to dictate the progress of their plots and to bring the action to neat and satisfactory conclusions in which mystery is dispelled, the good rewarded, and the bad punished'.[19] The detective's discoveries were not integral to the progress of the plot, as in the later detective novel. These factors help explain why the sleuth in many of the early detective novels did not develop into more than an interesting supernumerary.

However, the number of detective characters in fiction, whether official or not, mounted progressively. More than any of his counterparts, the writer who heightened interest in police agents in this period was Charles Dickens.[20] At the time that he was on intimate terms with the flesh-and-blood group of detectives at Scotland Yard and accompanied them in their daily routine (see Chapter 5), he invented Inspector Bucket in *Bleak House* (1853), a full-blown figure of an official investigator, though not the narrative's central character.[21] Another celebrated author who wove police detective characters into the plots of several novels was Wilkie Collins, whose most famous fictional detective was Sergeant Cuff in *The Moonstone*, published in 1868 (where the crime was the theft of a precious jewel).[22]

A fair proportion of detective fiction published in Britain during these and the next two decades was imported, whether translated (mainly from the French), or written in English in the USA. Along with the various texts connected with Vidocq, which drew a mass audience,[23] and with other French writers, translations of the crime stories of the French author Émile Gaboriau whetted the public thirst for detective literature, reaching 'a very wide public'.[24] Gaboriau incorporated several crime investigators in his fictional tales and novels, but his police-detective hero M. Lecoq captured most of the attention.[25] The American publishing industry impacted on the evolution of detective fiction in Britain with the novels of Anna Katharine Green (notably *The Leavenworth Case* (1878) featuring an impressive female police detective) and the highly popular (and inexpensive) dime novels, which featured many detectives, most famously the serial character Nick Carter, private investigator, who first appeared in 1886.[26]

Despite the popularity of certain police figures in contemporary detective fiction, official detectives were usually not chosen to be the focal point of the plot in British texts, which typically portrayed detectives, whether public or private, as secondary characters (an exception was the pseudo-memoirs, discussed below). Besides Dickens and Collins, other established authors, such as Elizabeth Gaskell (in *North and South* (1855)), and Anthony Trollope (in *He Knew He Was Right* (1869), and *The Eustace Diamonds* (1873)), also introduced detectives into their plots, but none considered these characters sufficiently important to make them the focus of their novels. Furthermore, despite the impact of the detective department at Scotland Yard on the entry of detectives into works of fiction, police agents were apparently not the obvious characters to play the role of investigators. A large proportion of the new fictional crime fighters were unconnected to the official forces of law and order. Many of the texts with detection themes were novels and stories in which characters assumed the role of a detective without being designated as such, as in Elizabeth Gaskell's *Mary Barton* (1848). Overall, the sub-genre of sensation novels which flourished in the 1860s and 1870s, with Wilkie Collins as its prominent author, while replete with crime, mystery, social deviance, family melodrama, and the pursuit and exposure of villains, opted more frequently to picture amateur detectives in their plots. Writers such as Mary Elizabeth Braddon did include a few police detectives in their narratives, but a much larger proportion of the investigators in her texts were men and women who had never before engaged in such a task and took it up for ad hoc reasons, to unravel a mystery facing them; or were servants who played a detective role of sorts in the Victorian home.[27] Since transgressions in sensation novels usually took place in the families and homes of the more privileged sector of society, many of the investigations were conducted by family members or friends, far from a police environment. The setting in these works was an imagined society in which respectable citizens policed each other.

Gradually, a growing body of texts, including sensation novels, allotted the professional private detective—whether self-employed or in the service of a private agency—a greater role in the investigation of crimes. Sometimes these private individuals were sketched as more professional, not only in the sense that they developed an expertise in this role, but also in that they chose to do it as a vocation, not necessarily for a fee but in more than a single case. A significant contribution to this category was made in the early 1840s when the American author Edgar Allan Poe, considered by many scholars as the originator of detective fiction,[28] wrote four detective stories within a few years, three of them—'The Murders in the Rue Morgue' (1841), 'The Mystery of Marie Rogêt' (1842–3), and 'The Purloined Letter' (1844)—centred on the figure of Chevalier Auguste Dupin, a French private detective who operated in Paris. Such characters, however, were few and far between until the closing decades of the nineteenth century. In the majority of texts, the detective was neither the main character nor a career detective who is employed in case after case. Indeed, although Poe's stories were published in England during the 1840s and 1850s, they gained popularity there only from the 1870s onwards.[29]

THE EMERGENCE OF DETECTIVE PSEUDO-MEMOIRS

An important exception to the delineation of detective figures in various literary modes was the pseudo-memoirs of detectives. This distinct corpus of fictional texts emerged in mid-century using a memoir format that posited a detective as the central figure in a series of crime stories, each resolved by the actions of the detective-hero who speaks in the first person. This narrative strategy not only expanded the presence of the official detective figure in literature significantly, but also accorded him a central role in the plot. In some of these invented life stories the protagonist was a private detective,[30] but, as far as can be ascertained from surveying the fiction of the time, police investigators more often played the leading role—a contrast to their status in other types of literary texts of the period. The vast majority of these texts were written by authors who concealed their identity, sometimes using pseudonyms, or writing anonymously, allowing them the liberty to let their imagination run free of the dictates of social and literary conventions and create imaginary police-detective protagonists. In many of these seemingly factual accounts of detectives, as in the anonymously written *Richmond*, the protagonist's personal background is given at the beginning of the series, with brief references to his past and his family in succeeding instalments, which concentrate on his exploits. In addition to insisting that the narratives were penned by a real detective, authors employed another common device to confirm the authenticity of the pseudo-memoirs—namely, the inclusion of authentic events and personalities in the story (including mention of the commissioner of the Metropolitan Police by name and other true facts about the force). Many such fake memoirs were published first, or solely, as serial runs in journals (as many other works of fiction in the nineteenth century); some came out in journals as single stories;[31] and still others saw print in book format.[32] The texts were lightweight but gained considerable popularity, indicating the mounting interest in the topic of detection.[33]

Richmond (1827) may be viewed as an antecedent of this literary style, but, for whatever reason, it failed to make its mark with readers and publishers, and a quarter of a century was to pass before similar texts won wide currency. Possibly, the reissuing of *Richmond* in 1845 was a harbinger.[34] Several factors combined to promote the new trend of the pseudo-memoirs of detectives. Undoubtedly, the formation in 1842 of the detective unit at Scotland Yard, and the growing interest it stimulated in the press, inspired literary efforts. Police detectives were also gaining prominence in courtroom testimonies as distinctive representatives of the forces of law and order, as, in effect, they increasingly took over prosecutions (see Chapter 1), and their function became less controversial in respectable opinion.

Changes in the literary world, too, laid the groundwork for the rise of these fictional autobiographical texts. The 1830s saw an escalation in serials aimed at working-class consumption and in the publication of novels in weekly instalments.[35] Dickens, who was quick to grasp the potential of new literary modes, first published *Pickwick Papers* in serial form (1836–7), helping to make it an established publishing format.[36] The same period witnessed an increase in the publication of autobiographical accounts—both true and falsified—of ordinary people who did not lead a lofty life, as well as of professionals.[37] In addition, the reading public in the mid-Victorian decades showed a preference for texts that claimed historical authenticity, such as narratives based on the country's past.[38] During that period, too, in an effort to avoid the stamp duty levied on newspapers, publications such as the *Penny Sunday Times and People's Police Gazette*, which appealed to the lower classes, 'consisted entirely of fiction and fabricated police reports'.[39] Perceptive writers and publishers merged these trends to form the new pseudo-memoir narrative technique. Unfettered by factual constraints, and taking advantage of the growing acceptance of police detection, the writers of such 'memoirs' wove dramatic tales of crime and detection, which they presented as a sequence of episodes, a style highly suitable to serial publication. Pretending that the texts were self-revelations by established crime fighters, they insisted on accuracy of detail. For a few decades, starting from the mid-century, this fusion seemed to work, and writers with no experience in detection increasingly used their imagination, and the snippets of facts about detection that they had on hand, to produce the kind of fiction favoured by the reading public.

William Russell was one of the first authors to recognize the attraction of the detective memoir format. He wrote several such pseudo-memoirs, but the 'Recollections of a Police-Officer', published in *Chambers's Journal* between July 1849 (even prior to Dickens's efforts to promote detectives) and September 1853 under the pseudonym 'Waters', enjoyed immediate and sustained popularity, both in instalments and later in volume form. The protagonist, Waters, is a gentleman who has lost his entire fortune at gambling and as a last resort decides to join the ranks of the Metropolitan Police.[40] The first story relates how Waters ingeniously and boldly unravelled a mystery that led to the punishment of the perpetrators of 'an artistically-contrived fraud' and drew the attention of his superior officers.[41]

As a result, Waters became a police detective and is the hero of all the tales that follow. While the criminals in the stories frequently make mistakes and fall into traps prepared by the hero, he himself is nearly always immune to blunders.[42] Mostly he works alone, managing the investigation, questioning witnesses, examining the scene of crime, and searching for evidence, relying essentially on his intuition and personal ability. Only when the criminal is exposed and must be brought in does he require the cooperation of other police officers. He does employ disguise—and often—to set trap for the criminal and catch him. His memory is excellent, which aids in identifying suspects. Notably, not only is Detective Waters a member of the privileged classes, but the victims he helps—usually in cases of fraud and blackmail—are from the very same background. Hardly ever does he deal with the lower classes. He thus feels at home in the company of those he assists. In sum, the image of the detective derived from these stories is that of a respectable and competent professional whose work directly benefits the social groups to which most of the readership belongs. Moreover, the ending of each story confirms the victory of the criminal justice system: the criminal is always caught.[43]

An essential factor in the commercial success of Russell's 'Recollections' was the format and vehicle in which the series appeared. Each story was self-contained, published in its entirety in a single issue of *Chambers's*. Thus, if readers missed the subsequent instalment, they were not deprived of a closure, but if they were interested in further exploits by the detective-hero, their curiosity would be satisfied in future instalments. Moreover, *Chambers's Journal* (launched in 1832) was considered a journal of good taste, and hence was popular among the middle classes, though it also penetrated lower down the social pyramid.[44] By mid-century, it was one of the most popular family journals in England.[45] In the event, the stories had an impact beyond the readership of *Chambers's Journal*. In 1856, they were compiled in book form and published by J. and C. Brown under the title *Recollections of a Detective Police-Officer*.[46] In 1859, another volume was published in England with the same title and author, which included additional stories.[47] Thereafter, *Recollections of a Police-Officer* was published in various editions under different titles both in England and abroad.[48]

Adopting the contemporary trend of reprinting serialized texts in book form enhanced their status and longevity. The prefaces to the books also allowed the editors to focus attention on the messages they wished to convey. In such ways, even under an assumed name Russell helped build up the reputation of the English detective locally and abroad.[49] Apparently, the series was thought to be appropriate reading for police detectives: throughout 1877 the *Police Guardian* repeatedly advertised it to its readers.

The success of *Recollections* convinced Russell that he had a winning narrative strategy at hand. His *Experiences of a Real Detective by Inspector F.* (1862) faithfully replicates the formula that underlay *Recollections*.[50] Russell's central character, Inspector F. of Scotland Yard, explains at the start that '"detective" literature' is popular primarily because 'the stories are believed to be, in the main, faithfully-told, truthful narratives'.[51] In line with other familiar features of the pseudo-memoirs of detectives, each segment is self-contained, but promises another instalment. This strategy was repeated a year after the publication of *Experiences* with another fictionalized memoir by Russell, *Autobiography of an English Detective* (1863), which appeared in two volumes of over 300 pages each, again under the assumed name of Waters. This time the reminiscences are of a Bow Street Runner (and a stepson of a Bow Street Runner) who, when the Runners are absorbed into the Metropolitan Police, continues his service as an investigator in this force.[52] The ongoing appearance of Russell's fictional narratives in journals and books enabled them to reach a vast audience. That his fictional texts, which invariably complimented the police, inspired other such series served to publicize the role of detectives and to mould a favourable view of the profession.

By the early 1860s, when the sensation novel 'exploded onto the literary scene',[53] a number of other writers were using the formula of pseudo-memoirs of detectives with success. One of them was Charles Martel (a pseudonym for Thomas Delf), who wrote *The Detective's Note-Book* and *Diary of an Ex-Detective*, published by Ward and Lock in 1860. Claiming to be the true reminiscences of a police detective (and dedicated to real-life detectives), both volumes consisted of stories of murder, robbery, forgery, absconding debtors, and the pursuit of suspects through slums, lodging houses, and thieves' dens, all unified by the activities of a detective who speaks in the first person and generally deals impressively with any given situation.[54] Surprisingly, some of the pseudo-memoirs featured women detectives, possibly expanding the number of female readers.[55] One example is Mrs Paschal from Scotland Yard, in the unsigned *Revelations of a Lady Detective* (1864). She is portrayed, as many other protagonists in pseudo-memoirs, as 'well born and well educated', having joined the police after her husband died suddenly, leaving her badly off.[56]

Works based on the narrative conventions of the pseudo-memoirs continued to be published, and, following a certain lull during the 1870s, received a significant boost with the publication of *Brought to Bay; or, Experiences of a City Detective* in 1878 by James McGovan (pseudonym of William Crawford Honeyman), followed by *Hunted Down; or, Recollections of a City Detective* in 1878, *Strange Clues: or, Chronicles of a City Detective* in 1881, *Traced and Tracked; or, Memoirs of a City Detective* in 1884, and *Solved Mysteries: or, Revelations of a City Detective* in 1888.[57] As the author later related, he decided to write *Brought to Bay* when 'the Detective works of "Waters" and of my old friend M'Levy (a real detective who published detective stories in the 1860s (see chapter 7)) were all but forgotten'.[58] McGovan's books enjoyed tremendous popularity. Each saw a number of editions, simultaneously published in Edinburgh and London. They were also published in German and French, as well as in other English-speaking countries, selling hundreds of thousands of copies. Reviews appeared in many journals, referring to them as 'thrilling', 'exciting', and 'life like'.[59]

In as much as the pseudo-autobiographical texts teem with police detectives as main figures, they are usually charismatic and adroit. Although they may make minor mistakes, and perpetrators of crime might evade justice, the narrator–protagonists almost always excel at their job. In all of James McGovan's pseudo-memoirs, the central character and narrator is an Edinburgh policeman who is singularly humane and sensitive, while always managing to get a conviction. Mrs Paschal, in *Revelations of a Lady Detective*, alludes to her work as requiring such qualities as 'nerve and strength, cunning and confidence, resources unlimited'.[60] Waters is shown to be skilled at his job and confident of his abilities and methods. Some pseudo-memoirs present the police detective as empathetic and as instrumental in helping victims start a new life.[61] Waters and Tom Fox in *Tom Fox or The Revelations of a Detective* (1860)[62] are fair-minded public servants who do not hesitate to ask for clemency for transgressors or extend aid to them. Detectives thus play a role in the reform of society. Not only are individual members of the police commendable, but so is the organization as a whole. It is certainly infinitely better than the previous system.[63]

Victorian readers evidently welcomed this style of writing. Quite a few of the books had more than one edition.[64] Recirculation reached high levels as many pseudo-memoirs were published in different formats. However, by the end of the century, or even before, this narrative mode—sometimes referred to as casebook fiction—had largely lost its vitality. Although a number of series of imaginary texts written as reminiscences in the first person, supposedly by a detective, continued to be published, the bulk of narratives revolving around a detective were now written in other styles (see below and Chapter 7).

Further research is needed to explore the rise and fall of this distinctive literary mode and its impact on the history of detective fiction. Notably, the arrival of Sherlock Holmes roughly coincided with its decline. Conan Doyle published his first Holmes novel in 1887, but his great success with this captivating character came in the early 1890s, more or less at the time when pseudo-memoirs had lost their popularity. Conceivably, Holmes replaced that sub-genre in the readers' affections. While consciously or unconsciously adopting at least one attribute from it—placing the detective at the centre of several events requiring investigation—Conan Doyle had apparently devised a more attractive model for contemporaries and readers thereafter.

In any event, by the time the magnetic figure of Sherlock Holmes made his debut, an extensive body of work incorporating detectives had come into existence. In 1883, the *Saturday Review* could affirm that 'for a long time past fictitious detectives and their achievements have...interested the readers of novels'.[65] Many detective books began as serial runs in magazines. The *Westminster Review* estimated that in 1893, out of a total of 800 British weeklies containing serialized stories of one kind or another, no fewer than 240 published detective stories.[66] This genre, the article implied, increased their circulation. How the detective acquired this standing in the literary community is discussed in the next section.

THE ENTRENCHMENT OF THE DETECTIVE FIGURE IN LITERARY TEXTS

The attractiveness of the detective figure has elicited numerous interpretations, some pointing at a universal and enduring appeal.[67] Yet, in addition to universal elements, the vitality of the fictional detective figure in its formative period was the product of an intricate matrix of contemporary factors (only a few of which can be analysed in this section). Ample references have been made in the research literature to the many repercussions of an emerging industrial, urban, and commercial society, which explain the concurrent rise of the modern police. Critics have also referred to contemporary scientific thinking, combined with the legacies of the Enlightenment's emphasis on reason and empiricism and that of the Romantic movement's on the imagination, feelings, and spontaneity, as conducive to this phenomenon.[68]

Particularly noteworthy in the context of the present study are the pronounced modifications in the criminal justice system and the attendant transformation in public perceptions of law and order. As has been shown, many of the criminals, rogues, and deviants in the eighteenth and the first half of the nineteenth centuries elicited varied levels of sympathy both from the general public and from readers. Real-life criminals who managed to evade the law, attained a legendary aura. Since punishment often did not correspond to the severity of the crime, and petty offenders could find themselves on the way to Australia or even to the gallows, criminals were often depicted as victims of circumstances, or, worse, of the brutality of the authorities. With the dramatic reduction in the number of offences incurring capital punishment during the first half of the century (murder and high treason remaining practically the only such crimes after the 1860s), and the concomitant decrease in executions, the image of the law gradually seemed less cruel. As punishment came to fit the crime more closely and penalties that publicly humiliated offenders (including public executions) were abolished, the attitude to criminals in literature changed correspondingly. Although a certain sympathy for the criminal lingered, and he was sometimes presented as an outlaw brutalized by a harsh regime, more often he was someone who deserved what he got. Even if social factors or innate qualities were responsible for his actions, the accused was assumed to have at least a measure of free will. Against this background, commentators and opinion moulders increasingly denigrated the traditional tendency to dignify some lawbreakers in the print media. Even relatively harmless romantic rebels who rose up against current practices and behaved according to an inner code of conduct 'came to be perceived and represented as a threat to bourgeois society'.[69] The diminishing stature of the criminal in literary texts created an opportunity for the detective to take his or her place as a central character. In many ways, Vidocq's shift from criminal to head of the detective department in

Paris symbolized 'the transition from outlaw hero to detective-hero',[70] as did Richmond, the rogue hero who became a Bow Street Runner.

With growing demands by the establishment and the public at large for more adequate means to deal with crime and disorder, fictional works incorporated more figures who took this challenge upon themselves. In particular, these literary figures were shown to respond to greater intolerance to property crimes, the sense of insecurity in the anonymous city, and pressures to augment surveillance over the population. They also echoed the prevalent notions that, if harsh punishment was now no longer considered the principal deterrence to crime, and every offender had to be caught, then the men responsible for it should be adept at the mission, whether employed in a private capacity or officially. As pointed out by the literary historian Beth Kalikoff, if 'in the street literature of the [eighteen] thirties and forties, murderers are caught in the act or soon afterwards, incriminated by their own actions or by key witnesses', crime was now recognized 'as a significant problem that [could] not be solved by ordinary citizens' but by clever detectives.[71] These were meant to cope with sophisticated criminals nurtured by the modern economy as well as offenders, such as servants, who did not ordinarily follow a life of crime.

Moreover, literature portraying the detective as hero, or at least as a worthy character, was more likely to flourish after the objections to undercover policing had declined substantially in the second half of the nineteenth century. This was especially so in the circles from which most authors emerged, and in a society where the police were consensually accepted as a force for good and as a legitimate public service, even if at times they failed in their tasks. As a contemporary contributor to the *Spectator* explained in an article entitled 'Espionage as a Profession', the growing taste for detective stories in the period was due to the blunting of the previous distaste for espionage in a society that no longer felt the same dislike of such methods.[72] With respectability becoming a dominant social norm, and obedience to the law central to it, the criminal was perceived as an outsider to society—and therefore not frequently a main character in the plot—while the person charged with imposing the law was seen as necessary and even a benefactor.

Other changes in the legal system may have had an effect as well. With the entire procedure in court, and the detective's role in giving evidence, becoming more critical, the task of gathering information became more vital (although detective fiction concentrated on the process of investigation and not on the courtroom). As Foucault noted with reference to the detective genre: 'We have moved from the exposition of the facts or the confession to the slow process of discovery; from the execution to the investigation; from the physical confrontation to the intellectual struggle between criminal and investigator.'[73] The promise that the crime investigator knows how to make sense of scattered clues and construct a narrative that would defeat 'the truth' of the enemies of law and order and result in the triumph of good over evil provided readers with a sense of security.

Dramatic changes in the literary market in the second half of the century, manifested in an increase in the fiction readership and in published material generally, also provided fertile ground for the enhancement of the detective figure. Such developments as railway travel, widespread borrowing from circulating libraries, and the expansion of print technologies[74] prompted book and magazine publishers to experiment with new formats in order to augment their output and make it accessible to a broader population. In response to the growing demand for reading matter, new publishing firms were established, focused on disseminating 'an up-to-date and interesting product in a competitive market'.[75] With readers showing a special fascination for crime fighters, publishers sold large quantities of popular fiction and non-fiction featuring detectives,[76] benefiting, as did the press, from the rising purchasing power as well as the expanding leisure time and literacy of the lower-middle and working classes. A significant transformation in book production in the late nineteenth century was the replacement of the traditional three-volume novel by the less costly single volume. Texts revolving around a single detective character seemed to fit easily into such a format.

Most importantly, such texts filled the steady demand for entertaining and engaging reading materials no less than those focusing on the criminal. One of the reasons readers were drawn to detective fiction was that it mingled 'extravagant' elements with descriptions 'to some extent based on fact'.[77] Revolving around issues related to crime and deviance, and often set in exotic, sensational, or mysterious milieus, or, alternatively, in the homes of the rich and powerful, it offered escapism, drama, and thrilling moments. This proclivity for gripping themes accounts for the pronounced paucity of descriptions of the prosaic preventive tasks of real-life detectives, such as patrol work and guard duties. Yet, although the plots were fabricated, the issues and topics dealt with in the narratives related to contemporary actuality, thereby touching the hearts and minds of the Victorians, who preferred their fictional prose 'to be as close as possible to common reality'.[78] Various detective tales, besides pseudo-memoirs, referred to real persons, institutions, and events, mentioning dates and specific localities familiar to readers. They were also replete with implicit references to real crimes (particularly murders), which were widely reported in the press.[79] Fictitious detectives were often presented as working for Scotland Yard, an institution well known to readers by then,[80] and some were actually modelled on genuine personalities.[81] Perhaps the stress in detective fiction on the detective's search for fact, truth, and precision in the observation of reality also had special resonance among the intended audiences.

Readers could thus enjoy both worlds—fictional and factual—a good story, and some truths about the human condition. The distinction between fiction and non-fiction was further blurred by pseudo-memoirs and by the prevalent practice of publishing fictional tales as serial runs in periodicals, where they were laid out side by side with non-fiction content. The oscillation between the two satisfied the desire for flights of fancy as well as authenticity. So powerful was this interplay that readers sometimes responded to fictitious figures as if they existed in reality and as if the texts were documentary. Even before the advent of Sherlock Holmes—and a widespread assumption that he was a real person—the figure of Lecoq was treated as historically true,[82] and 'English detectives were advised to study the methods' described by his creator, Émile Gaboriau, on the occasion of an unsolved 'memorable murder'.[83] Real detectives and 'idealised types of detectives' were juxtaposed in literature, and their performance was sometimes compared.[84] While assertions about the superior quality of French detectives rested partly on the image projected by French detective fiction such as Gaboriau's,[85] the author and historian Lascelles Wraxall, in his preface to the *Autobiography of a French Detective from 1818 to 1858*, drew attention to the superiority of the English police system, urging the reader to compare the content of the autobiography written by Louis Canler, a former chief of the Sûreté, with the revelations 'so admirably described' in the pseudo-memoir *Experiences of a Real Detective by Inspector F.*[86]

The interest in the figure of the detective, which became entrenched in the pantheon of literary figures in both canonical and popular literature, propelled a dynamic process of cross-fertilization, which kept fuelling curiosity about the topic. In an attempt to copy real life, writers read actual detectives' reminiscences. Vidocq's memoir, for example, was a seminal text for many fiction writers, including Poe and Gaboriau. Further, not only purportedly factual accounts but fictional narratives, too, served as sources for authors of detective fiction: writers, journalists, and detectives themselves[87] avidly read detective fiction. The formative influence of Poe's Dupin and Dickens's Inspector Bucket in *Bleak House* on other writers is well known. Charles Gibbon freely adopted story lines, themes, and characters from Gaboriau. Arthur Griffiths, too, studied Gaboriau closely, as well as the French author Fortuné du Boisgobey and the American poet and detective novelist Anna Katharine Green.[88] Lowbrow narratives that were bypassed by arbiters of literary taste and did not appear in lists of recommended reading also contributed to the dispersion and circulation of detective texts among writers. Personal contacts between writers, and the close-knit nature of Victorian literary networks, where friendships frequently developed between diverse cultural agents, facilitated an exchange of opinions and stimulated ideas for motifs, characters, and plots.[89] The press itself served as a meeting point for writers of detective fiction. Certain journals, such as the *Strand Magazine* and the *Idler Magazine*, employed some of the best writers of detective fiction, many of whom established lifelong friendships with one another.[90] As a consequence, by the mid-1880s narratives with detective figures enjoyed 'sometimes phenomenal sales at low rates'.[91]

The meteoric rise of Sherlock Holmes—the best-known detective figure ever—and the establishment of a captive audience for Arthur Conan Doyle's works about him, thus marked the high point of a series of social and literary developments in nineteenth-century England. In turn, the Holmes figure impacted on the literary corpus and the representation of the detective in it. Whether as a result of the literary dynamics that had evolved before Holmes won public acclaim, and certainly in the wake of his success, books and stories featuring detective figures surfaced in ever greater numbers and in diverse modes of expression at the end of the nineteenth and the beginning of the twentieth centuries.[92] Books and stories dealing with uniformed policemen were published as well,[93] but the detective was a much more dominant figure. Detective figures persisted as minor characters in texts where the hero himself was a detective, and in those where the protagonist was not a detective. They continued to appear as central characters in single novels or stories, but their greatest blossoming was as centrepieces in serial literature, resurfacing in story after story.

The repertoire of characters in the detective genre became richer, and the plots more varied. The number of women detectives increased substantially, although in reality detective departments continued to hire only males.⁹⁴ By the First World War, the gallery of fictional detectives included a gypsy woman (*Hagar of the Pawn-Shop*, by Fergus Hume (1898)), a millionaire (Arnold Bennett, *The Loot of Cities* (1905)), an armchair detective who sits in the corner of a teashop solving cases that baffle the police and discussing them with a female journalist in *The Old Man in the Corner* (1909) by the Hungarian-born Baroness Emmuska Orczy, a Catholic priest (Father Brown, introduced by G. K. Chesterton in book form in 1911), a blind detective (in Ernest Bramah's *Max Carrados* (1914)), and a conspiracy of anarchists who turn out to be police detectives in pursuit of anarchists (G. K. Chesterton, *The Man Who Was Thursday: A Nightmare* (1908)). In *The Big Bow Mystery* (1891) by Israel Zangwill, the major character is a private detective, Grodman (formerly a police detective), who towards the end of the book confesses to being the murderer he is chasing.⁹⁵ Indigenous texts concentrated not only on English detectives but also on detectives of foreign descent, particularly French. Examples are Simplice Renaud of the Sûreté in H. F. Wood's *The Englishmen of the Rue Caïn* (1889), Arthur Griffiths' Floçon in *The Rome Express* (1896), Eugène Valmont in Robert Barr's *The Triumphs of Eugène Valmont* (1906), Inspector Hanaud of the Sûreté in A. E. W. Mason's *At the Villa Rose* (1910), and Hercules Popeau in some of Marie Belloc Lowndes's works.

DIVERGING IMAGES OF POLICE DETECTIVES AND PRIVATE DETECTIVES

The diversity of detective literature by the end of the nineteenth century meant that the fictional image of detectives, whether private or official, was never monolithic. However, an examination of detective fiction in the Victorian and Edwardian periods reveals broad patterns across the entire range of printed texts. Such patterns are discernible even before Holmes's advent in the late 1880s. The corrupt thief-takers had receded into the background, to be replaced by crime fighters who only relatively rarely associated with the criminal world for illegal purposes and private gain. This was particularly true for police detectives. Admittedly, some fictional policemen or ex-policemen strayed from the honest path, such as Paul Davies, the ex-Scotland

Yard detective in Joseph Sheridan Le Fanu's book *Checkmate* (1871), who was dismissed from the force and then tried to blackmail the person he was investigating.[96] Detectives and detection were still sometimes disparaged as unwholesome. In H. F. Wood's *The Passenger from Scotland Yard* (1888), Brother Neel, a suspect, has this to say about official law-enforcers: 'I regard the companionship of detective-officers as little less compromising than that of criminals. Who knows where detectives have sprung from? They do say that ex-thieves make the very best thief-takers.'[97] By the end of the century, however, such characters were in a minority. To a great extent this applied to private detectives as well, especially if they were the primary detectives in the plot, despite lingering perceptions of collusion between law-enforcers and lawbreakers reflected in the appearance of new (and sometimes admirable) criminal heroes in the publishing world. Examples are A. J. Raffles—a gentleman-burglar who sometimes dabbled in investigations (created at the end of the nineteenth century by E. W. Hornung, Conan Doyle's brother-in-law), and Maurice Leblanc's Arsène Lupin—another gentleman-burglar who 'devotes himself to correcting the blunders of the official police' (originally published in French in the early twentieth century).[98] Yet, on the whole, crime and law enforcement were now separate. Most fictional crime fighters acted in the spirit of the law. They may have resorted to manipulation, trickery, disguise, spying, and intimacy with criminal elements, but all these were to serve the ends of justice. However, the question of who was most qualified to engage in crime investigation, and in what framework it should be carried out, was less obvious.

The texts are replete with both private and official detectives, often juxtaposed in the same narrative. Skimming through a long list of detective publications, the *Windsor Magazine* concluded in 1895 that the detective, 'both professional and amateur, has been a prominent personage in fiction and on the stage'.[99] The distinction between them is not always clear. Sometimes it is not apparent whether the fictional detective works for private or public interests, partly because the texts accorded with the reality that police detectives were occasionally employed by private persons. Even so, although more and more fictional police detectives, especially from Scotland Yard, entered literary works (though most often not as central protagonists), private investigators predominated. More curiously, except for the pseudo-memoirs, the general impression is that the self-appointed detective—whether an amateur or a professional—outmatches the police detective. The detective genre may have heroized the agent of surveillance in his struggle against villainy,[100] but frequently this agent was not an official public servant.

To be sure, there are plenty of benign references to police detectives in detective literature in the Victorian period. Predictably, the life stories of detectives (whether real[101] or imagined) underscored commendable qualities. In fact, pseudo-memoirs were the most consistent in delineating police detectives as highly talented and benevolent, though non-formulaic texts also contained favourable references to police detectives. In Tom Taylor's play *The Ticket-of-Leave Man* (1863), a police detective named Hawkshaw helps an ex-convict who has been falsely accused to return to ordinary life.[102] Bradbury, a Bow Street Runner in Charles Reade's story 'The Knightsbridge Mystery' (1884), is a compassionate public servant who labours to save a criminal condemned to death and tries to fulfil his other requests.[103] Even in the more prestigious kinds of literature, the police detective who combats crime sometimes emerges as memorable. Dickens, through his literary weight and his impact on other writers, contributed both directly and indirectly to expanding the gallery of positive detective characters, mainly through the admirable figure of Bucket, who served as a model for other writers.

Nevertheless, with the exception of the pseudo-memoirs, the figure of the private detective gained greater, and on the whole more complimentary, attention in the total output of detective texts. Especially when private detectives work alongside police detectives, they are more likely to be painted as more rational, skilful, and effective than the official detectives. One of the first fictional detectives to embody this concept was Edgar Allan Poe's Dupin, who, although a foreign import into England, was a seminal figure in moulding the native British fictional detective. His American creator made a decision in the 1840s to elevate private detective Dupin over Monsieur G—, the prefect of the Parisian police. Dupin's most valuable resource for solving mysteries was his analytical faculty, which was far superior to that of the police, although the police detectives were not totally useless and showed perseverance and even a certain ability. Yet, they overlooked evidence, made wrong assumptions, and erred in their findings, while Dupin displayed outstanding skill in gathering clues and arriving at the right conclusions. Conscious of the intellectual gap between them, Dupin, an impoverished gentleman, had a low regard for police officers and treated them somewhat disdainfully. The Parisian police seemed cunning, 'but no more. There is no method in their proceedings, beyond the method of the moment. They make a vast parade of measures; but, not unfrequently, these are...ill adapted to the objects proposed.'[104] Dupin even disparages Vidocq, who, in his view, 'erred continually by the very intensity of his investigations'.

Whether following Dupin's ideas, or developing this theme independently, a trend evolved of portraying police detectives as not very discerning, and often as inept. By contrast, the private agent often shone. The concern expressed in the press that English police detectives were too visible and hence ineffective, especially compared with their French counterparts (see Chapter 5), was echoed in fictional works.[105] They are not devoid of good attributes, notably industriousness and determination, and they do their job diligently, following up on suspects and keeping watch on locations where criminals are thought to be, but these measures are no guarantee of success.[106] Even when they discover the identity of the murderer, they do not always manage to apprehend him, as in Mary Elizabeth Braddon's *Aurora Floyd* (1863). Sometimes they arrive at the truth purely by coincidence or because it is self-evident. 'You will see that the mysteries which the police discover are, almost without exception, mysteries made penetrable by the commonest capacity', says one of the characters in Wilkie Collins's *My Lady's Money* (1877) about the detective department.[107] Above all, they are overshadowed by the private detective's intelligence and reasoning, which explains why often they cannot accomplish their tasks without his help.

Not all private detective characters conform to the image of talented professionals, and many are neither brilliant nor triumphant sleuths. An example is private detective Green in Charles Reade's *Hard Cash* (1863). Still, despite the diversity of detective figures, a common conception in the evolution of detective fiction was the depiction of unofficial detectives as greater achievers than their opposite numbers in the police.[108] This vogue appeared to take a firmer grip on authors' minds as pseudo-memoirs became less popular during the closing decades of the nineteenth century. As a consequence, relatively fewer police detectives towered as heroic characters in the massive corpus of detective novels and short stories that was to flood the market by the end of the century. Giving greater space and weight to private detection was reinforced by narratives imported from across the Atlantic. The detective heroes of the mass-circulating American dime novels invariably came from the private sector.[109] No doubt the figure of Sherlock Holmes fortified this trend. His presence also sharpened the juxtaposition of public and private investigators to the advantage of the latter.

HOLMES AND THE REINFORCEMENT OF THE PRIVATE DETECTIVE'S SUPERIORITY

The success of the Holmes figure was unprecedented. The reasons for the popularity of this private detective who is an eccentric genius and a gentleman, as for other aspects of Holmes's literary impact, have been the subject of extensive commentary.[110] The salient question in the present context concerns the significance of the remarkable effectiveness of Conan Doyle's portrayal of Holmes in terms of the status of real-life police detectives. Why were the most reputable detective characters in fiction private agents whose biographical profile and lifestyle stood in stark contrast to those of real-life official detectives who were the designated crime fighters in society? The likes of Holmes were at best scarce in crime investigation of the period, yet they populated detective fiction disproportionately. What, then, can an ideological reading of Holmes and of similar literary characters tell us about public attitudes to police detectives, and to the system of law enforcement as a whole?

Gentleman-detectives were far from rare in literature before Holmes showed up. He was preceded by a long line of private detective figures who belonged to the leisured classes. In fact, a clear majority of detective protagonists came from an advantaged background. Many were financially independent and solved enigmas for various reasons: as a diversion or hobby, for self-promotion, to prove their intellectual superiority, to discharge an obligation, to assist someone as a favour or as a public service, or because they themselves were implicated in the case. Victorian Britain held up the ideal that 'public service was a burden which the gentleman was expected to shoulder for the sake of his country, without thought of gain and irrespective of hardship',[111] although in literature, as in reality, gentlemen or near-gentlemen gradually tended to work for material reward. A famous fictitious gentleman who chose to become a detective, Fanny and Robert Louis Stevenson's Somerset, goes so far as to declare in the prologue to 'The Dynamiter' (1885) that detection is the only profession for a gentleman, as it requires 'manners, habit of the world, powers of conversation [and] vast stores of unconnected knowledge'.[112] Even in pseudo-memoirs, which presumed to transform reality into fiction, the police detective heroes are often gentlemanly types, firmly grounded in middle- or upper-class manners, many of whom feel compelled to explain why they work at all, and in a workplace not considered prestigious.

Holmes is not flawless. In addition to being depressive—at the beginning of 'The Adventure of the Devil's Foot' (1910) he is on the verge of a nervous breakdown[113]—he is addicted to drugs, does not conform to the family values of Victorian society, does not always stick to the letter of the law, and fails to bring some cases to a positive resolution. In fact, he is an outsider—the Poe model, suggesting great anxiety about the state of the gentleman class. Yet, he is far superior to the police detectives in almost every respect. Holmes is attentive, observes every detail, and uses his powerful faculty of reason and logic to get to the bottom of things. He is a scholar whose knowledge is encyclopaedic, though not on every subject.[114] He is able to quote the classics and has more than a passing familiarity with the exact sciences. To add colour to his singular attributes, Holmes is depicted as personifying the ultimate British gentleman: he is courageous, never falters in the face of threat or danger, and is chivalrous towards women, while behaving with all the entitlement of an aristocrat.

It is impossible to rise above him in stature. While Conan Doyle presented an array of detective figures in his literary works, giving them varied and distinctive characteristics, he systematically posited the police as unequal to the private detective. Even when successful in their investigations, they are represented as conventional, distrustful of theory, and above all unimaginative and devoid of the mental acuity that characterizes Sherlock Holmes. Time and again they make wrong assumptions and deductions, arrest and otherwise harm innocent people, and are oblivious to critical clues that Holmes perceptively discerns by means of his special gifts. Holmes is always ahead of the police, anticipating events and seeing the details as well as the overall picture. Given their low level of education, it is not surprising that their reports are defective.[115] Their strength lies, rather, in their physique. Holmes does not spare police officers, including detectives, his condescending attitude and repeatedly berates them as lacking essential mental attributes.[116] He is only too conscious of his superior detective skills. In *The Sign of Four* (1890), he smugly avers about Scotland Yard: 'When Gregson, or Lestrade, or Athelney Jones are out of their depths—which, by the way, is their normal state—the matter is laid before me.'[117]

Holmes's attitude towards police detectives is not entirely negative. Sometimes, as in the case of Inspector Gregory in 'Silver Blaze', he admits that detectives are competent.[118] Moreover, recognizing that ultimately police detectives, as public servants, are required for crime investigation, he collaborates with them and assists them in their assignments, even if he does so in an arrogant and patronizing manner. Notably, when a mission is accomplished, he often leaves it to the police to make the arrest and lets them take the credit for getting at the truth. At the same time, however, the reader is made aware of who the truly effective figure is in the crime investigation. Many of the police characters themselves acknowledge Holmes's superiority and seek his help. They seem to be less and less jealous of him or perturbed by their dependence on him, and, like Inspector Lestrade in 'The Adventure of the Six Napoleons' (1904), they are sometimes pleased to work with Holmes and even view it as a privilege.[119] Inspector Martin of the Norfolk Constabulary ('The Adventure of the Dancing Men' (1903)) welcomes his intervention and willingly shares information with him. 'I should be proud to feel that we were acting together,' said Martin to Holmes, allowing him 'to do things in his own fashion', and contenting himself with 'carefully noting the results'.[120] Although policemen are the representatives of the criminal justice system, Holmes takes over the investigation. He directs it and decides what information to provide to the official detectives, sometimes keeping essential material from them. He is manifestly the boss, the person in command. In some texts police detectives revere him, as in 'The Adventure of the Six Napoleons', when Inspector Lestrade amicably declares: 'We're not jealous of you at Scotland Yard. No, sir, we are very proud of you, and if you come down to-morrow, there's not a man, from the oldest inspector to the youngest constable, who wouldn't be glad to shake you by the hand.'[121] The impression evoked in reading these tales is that the police detectives serve as a background or as a standard against which to glorify Holmes's achievements.

Detective stories by a contemporary of Doyle's, author Arthur Morrison, about the exploits of Martin Hewitt—invented a few years after Holmes was created—pursued similar themes. Hewitt, a private detective, feels it is natural for him as a private citizen to drop into a police station for a chat and to gather information,[122] and both sides frequently collaborate in trying to get to the root of mystifying crimes (see Figure 15).[123] In all points of contact the superiority of the private detective is unquestionable, even if Martin Hewitt is not quite

"'STOP, SIR! LET ME SEE THAT!'"

Figure 15. 'Detective Inspector Trusco about to Make an Arrest in a Joint Operation with Private Detective Martin Hewitt', in Arthur Morrison, 'The Case of the Dead Skipper', in *Adventures of Martin Hewitt* (London: Ward, Lock & Co., 1896), 105.

the superstar that Holmes is.[124] With his acute reasoning, he is better than the police at observing details, amassing evidence, and piecing it all together.[125] He also has considerably more general knowledge than they, and conducts independent inquiries in cases under their investigation.[126] Further, he is sure of his methods, while the police are often perplexed and uncertain about what should be done. Hewitt, therefore, can help them much more than they can help him. This is not to say that they are inactive or consistently inefficient. In fact, they are portrayed as trying their best. In 'The Case of the Lost Foreigner', plain-clothes policemen impressively surround and penetrate an anarchist club without being noticed. Yet, even when they follow significant clues, they often fail to construct the whole picture. Like Holmes, Hewitt is not immune to failure;[127] he is, however, the one who ultimately enables the police to make the arrest and prosecute the offenders.

Moreover, like Holmes, Hewitt is not only the most skilful detective but also manages the investigation. He is a friend of the police, willing to give them a hand; still, he is clearly the expert, the person who summons the police, gives them orders, questions them, and soon acquires all the details he needs, as if in the role of senior partner.[128] He listens to them but restarts the investigation from scratch, implying that he trusts no one but himself. As is often the case in this genre, the police comply and follow his instructions. Another well-established motif is his magnanimous gesture of leaving it to the police to make the final arrest.[129]

With certain variations, many other texts published during the 1890s reflected similar perceptions of the police. In two popular series by Headon Hill—*Clues from a Detective's Camera* (1893) and *Zambra the Detective* (1894)—Sebastian Zambra, the manager of a private detective agency in London and the protagonist of both series, views police officers somewhat condescendingly, though inoffensively.[130] He usually conducts his investigations on his own, but, when he does use the assistance of policemen, their help turns out to be deficient. In the story 'The Secret Armoury', in *Clues from a Detective's Camera*, the police treat Zambra with great respect and call upon his services. In 'The Infernal Machine', in the same volume, he saves the police from an explosion, although Inspector Wiggins objects to his participation in the inquiry and refuses to listen to him, which results in the failure of the mission. Another popular private detective character, Sexton Blake, created by Harry Blyth in the same period, comes from a well-established family and was trained as a doctor. He has a generally cordial relationship with the Metropolitan Police and their detectives, but, he, too, is more accomplished than they.[131]

Other examples abound.[132] Female private agents, too, are frequently much better at their job than police detectives. In the Loveday

Brooke stories, written by Catherine Louisa Pirkis, the police detectives do not excel in analytical skills and cannot bring an investigation to a successful conclusion.[133] They know how to follow suspects and to entrap, catch, and arrest criminals, but it is private detective Loveday who does the hard thinking. From Loveday Brooke's point of view, her work is done when she discovers the truth and hands the criminal over to the police. At that time, in the final stages of the investigation, the police are the more active partners.[134]

On the whole, the detective novels of the first decades of the twentieth century perpetuated the tradition of stereotyping police officers as 'conspicuously lacking in intelligence'.[135] The underlying conception remained that unofficial detectives were far more estimable than their equivalents in the police, and that they were pivotal in enabling the police to lay their hands on criminals and other offenders. Attitudes to the police in Arnold Bennett's *The Grand Babylon Hotel* (1902) are illustrative. Typically, the central mystery in the novel—the disappearance of a German prince and the murder of his relative—is solved by amateurs rather than by the police. Underlining the incompetence of the police, the chief characters unabashedly treat them with scorn. The American millionaire who owns the hotel observes that the police always have a clue but 'they seldom had more than a clue, and ... a clue without some sequel to it was a pretty stupid business'.[136] In a series of stories by R. Austin Freeman featuring the character Dr Thorndyke, a medico-legal forensic investigator, the police regularly appeal to the doctor to assist them with their investigations (see Figure 16). In *John Thorndyke's Cases* (1909), he willingly agrees to their requests and, despite minor differences, seems to enjoy the collaboration.[137]

Despite the persistence of the perception of the superiority of the private detective, a certain shift is discernible after the turn of the century towards greater appreciation for the performance of Scotland Yard detectives in literary works. In *The Chronicles of Addington Peace* by B. Fletcher Robinson (1904), the principal investigator is Inspector Peace of the CID, who is accompanied by an artist, Mr Phillips, a Watson-like friend who narrates his adventures. The inspector is highly intelligent, civil, and somewhat mysterious, a 'bachelor with principles' who in story after story unveils the identity of crime perpetrators.[138] Initially, the artist views Scotland Yard officers as tiresome, but he soon discovers their worth and begins to worship the inspector almost to the point of submerging his own personality.[139] Vivian Grey's *Stories of Scotland Yard* (1906) perceive

THORNDYKE'S STRATEGY.

Figure 16. 'Detective Dr Thorndyke in the Midst of a Forensic Investigation', in R. Austin Freeman, *John Thorndyke's Cases* (London: Chatto & Windus, 1909).

Scotland Yard as a 'great machine designed by society to uphold law and order', which works relentlessly 'in the never-ceasing campaign against crime'.[140] These stories cast police detectives as quick, clever, skilful, alert, zealous, and endowed with 'deductive faculties'.[141] At a certain point the author interjects: 'Too much praise cannot be given to the Scotland Yard authorities for the masterful way they handled what must have been a tremendous problem.'[142] Their task is to 'stand for ever in stately dignity to protect the children of the empire from the trespasses of evil-doers'.[143]

The softening of the detective image was reflected as well in Conan Doyle's shift in portraying them. As Christopher Clausen observes, by the time of the late stories—'The Adventure of Wisteria Lodge' (1908) and 'The Adventure of the Red Circle' (1911)—the image has improved to the point that 'they figure things out more thoroughly than the now superfluous Holmes'.[144] Possibly, the fact that police detectives were given a much better press in the new century was a factor.[145]

Nevertheless, the change of attitude before the First World War was slight. Considerably more fictional material adhered to the old line. As A. E. Murch reckoned, 'almost all the popular detectives of this period were amateurs'.[146] Moreover, private detectives were still considered to be more impressive characters, exhibiting superior intellectual acumen to that of police detectives.

EXPLAINING THE PREPONDERANCE AND SUPERIOR IMAGE OF FICTIONAL PRIVATE DETECTIVES

The prevalent portrayal of detectives in Victorian and Edwardian fiction may be dismissed as a literary preference or as the entrenchment of a trend that began with Poe's Dupin in the 1840s. It can also be explained in the light of contemporary developments in the world of policing, notably in London. If the improvement in the detective image in the press during the 1850s and 1860s coincided with the rise of the pseudo-memoirs and the publication of narratives featuring imposing police detectives, such as Inspector Bucket and Sergeant Cuff, as well as similar figures in other sensation novels, the specific historical juncture that first witnessed Holmes's appearance in print was not propitious to a police-detective hero. The revelation of widespread corruption in the central office at Scotland Yard in the late 1870s, and the generally negative press coverage of the detective department during the 1880s because of perceived ineffectiveness, may have discouraged writers from choosing a fictional police protagonist to enthral audiences. With the police seemingly incapable of coping with terrorism, political threats, and crime in the streets, authors may have decided to opt for private detectives as heroes. Notably, by then, the pseudo-memoirs, with their laudatory portraits of police detectives, largely depended on reprints.

Still, the mediocre image of police detectives in various forms of fiction continued even after the 1880s, when the press significantly softened its criticism of the police. Moreover, press coverage, even when critical of the police, cannot account for the superiority of the image of the fictional private detective and the better skills with which he is endowed in numerous narratives, as private detectives barely figured in press reports, and little was known about them and their work. Presumably, the public was aware that, in contrast to fictional tales, private detectives in this period were not in the forefront of the fight against crime in the country. Furthermore, their assignments in real life were on the whole less stirring than those of police detectives, especially in the central branch in London, as they were barred from dealing with serious crime—precisely the type to excite the public imagination. In any case, they generally did not get a good press, even when they were mentioned in newspaper reports.[147] Why, then, did the number of private detectives in fictional works far exceed that of police agents, and why were police characters portrayed as inferior to private detectives? Clearly, the two questions are related, as they indicate that a substantial body of literary texts accorded private detectives a leadership status in crime control in the country. Additionally, why was the fictional motif of close collaboration between the two so widespread?

One possible explanation for the preponderance of fictional private agents in relation to police detectives may be the lingering traditions of law enforcement in real life. Until the formation of the new police in the middle decades of the nineteenth century, society relied heavily on personal resources to employ individuals or privately organized associations to retrieve property and catch criminals, as seen in Chapter 1. The Bow Street Runners themselves were a semi-private organization. Often, victims had to rely on family, friends, or neighbours to do the job of detection. Besides, it was considered 'a man's duty as a subject and a Christian to bring all offenders before the law'.[148] Indeed, many of the characters who assist the aggrieved person in fictional literature are members of the community who are not detectives by occupation. The ubiquity of private crime fighters may also have reflected the survival of yet another old form of popular justice—that of reliance on communal sanctions and the settling of disputes outside the legal process.[149] Hence it was reasonable for authors in the early days of bureaucratic policing, at the start and middle of the Victorian era—when there were anyway very few permanent detectives in police forces—to adhere to old-style detection in their literary works.

Nonetheless, despite the consistent trend towards the greater involvement of government in law and order issues, and the subsequent appearance of more police detectives in works of fiction, unofficial investigators, while increasingly professional in that they either regularly engaged in crime fighting or derived their income from it, continued to predominate in literary texts. Although this picture by no means replicated reality, where the major force assigned to quell crime by then was the police, it did have some basis in fact. Amateurism still characterized many administrators of the law in the late nineteenth century, especially unpaid justices of the peace in rural England,[150] and private detective agencies proliferated.[151] Informal justice continued to be widely practised throughout the period, despite the principle that lawbreaking should be solved within the confines of the legal system, and the decoding of crimes depended to a large extent on information provided by different members of the public, whether for a fee or not. All this is echoed in the words of Thomas W. Haycraft, a barrister-at-law in the Inner Temple, who wrote in a scholarly study at the end of the century: 'The law of England encourages private persons to aid in the discovery and pursuit of crime and the maintenance of order, and considerable powers are, to this end, vested in the non-official citizen.'[152] In particular, police failures in solving crimes, most prominently regarding the mysterious Jack the Ripper, revived notions of self-help and private enterprise. Thus, the overwhelming presence of non-official investigators in literature may have communicated a subtle awareness that in actuality a significant volume of crimes were cleared up or punished not by the police but by members of civil society. The press, connected more closely to the political establishment than the literary world, related to the emerging tendency to depend on the police more readily, but works of fiction revealed that many people still thought in terms of self-help and the entrepreneurial sectors in society when it came to investigating crime. Nevertheless, this does not explain the qualitative discrepancy between the two major types of investigators.

The most relevant factor might be related to the social origins of the detectives in real life. All the evidence shows that the majority of police officers—and thus also most detectives, who were nearly always recruited from the force—originated from the working class, with a minority from the lower middle class. The sustained belittlement of the police detective in literature may have had its roots in bourgeois anxiety regarding the threat lurking from below to their own powerful, yet relatively newly created position in society, reflected, inter alia, in the extension of full citizenship to the majority of the male working class in the latter part of the nineteenth century and the growing tendency to recruit people to public service who inherited neither status nor wealth. To present lower-class people as potent representatives of the law was to invest them with menacing power that might strengthen their position in society.

An even more persuasive explanation might lie in a condescending attitude towards the background of real-life police detectives, and a lack of confidence in their ability to carry the heavy burden of guarding law-abiding citizens against evil. This was especially so since many fictional perpetrators of crime (and victims or potential victims) belonged not to the 'criminal classes', but to the property-owning and educated strata, thus presenting a more acute intellectual challenge to the forces of law and order. The contempt often shown by fictional private detectives to their equivalents in the police may have reflected this class bias. Police detectives were often depicted in literature as hard working, robust, assiduous, and duty-bound. They may attain good results in what they do, thanks to their natural intelligence, but they do not easily overcome their humble background. They can only infrequently achieve the excellence and authority of the well-born, being limited by an invisible but abiding barrier. Apparently, readers and authors were not wholly satisfied with this type of crime fighter, despite his determination, cunning, and common sense, and sought a more ingenious figure. That is why the private detective, who was not associated in real life with any particular class, was commonly portrayed in literature as a gentleman or gentlewoman, especially when cast as the central crime investigator. Members of the privileged classes were regarded as more likely to have the sharp intelligence and the wide knowledge to infer signs of criminality from minute clues, and to restore order to society. Because of their class, their amateur status did not undermine their prestige. Quite the opposite, the heroic private detective in fiction often embodies all that is good about the nation, personified in the patriotic, fair, and courageous English gentleman, the linchpin of the social order. However hard a police detective tries, as a commoner he can never become a real gentleman. Wilkie Collins articulates this openly when describing a police detective in *The Fallen Leaves* (1879): 'He was well dressed; his manner was quiet and self-possessed—and yet he did not look like a gentleman. In fact, he was a policeman of the higher order, in plain clothes.'[153] Moreover, for the largely middle-class readership, if someone had to enter their homes, observe the private affairs of the family, and reveal guilty secrets, he or she might best be someone of their own class. Even if eccentric and not devoid of weaknesses, as was Holmes, in sharing class norms with them, he or she could be trusted to be more discreet and sympathetic.[154]

To all appearances, the literary world found it more difficult than the press to imagine memorable police detectives of working-class lineage. A few fictional detectives of humble birth, such as Hawkshaw in Tom Taylor's *The Ticket-of-Leave Man*, Cuff in *The Moonstone*, Bradbury in 'The Knightsbridge Mystery', and the protagonist in the pseudo-memoir *The Detective's Note-Book*, did attain a commanding stature, but these were a minority. The rise of realism meant that 'the lower classes were no longer portrayed in literature as buffoons but were now treated with imaginative sympathy', and that 'the nascent voice of the lower classes was heard most powerfully via the new literary dominance of the middle class'.[155] Yet the authors who catered to mass audiences knew that the readers would not accord equal reception to a hero of modest origins. Gentlemanly heroes had much greater potential appeal.

The anonymous authors–narrators of the pseudo-memoirs, and a handful of other fiction writers, overcame the constraints of the humble parentage of real police detectives simply by upgrading the background of various police characters and transforming them into persons of a higher social position, even if that of gentlemen or gentlewomen in difficult straits. Their invented elevated origin was a guarantee of their ability to stand up to wrongdoing, especially if faced with a dangerous criminal. That this accorded with authentic police life only in the most senior ranks, or in a few exceptional cases (see Chapter 2), was a marginal consideration compared to the appealing aura of self-confidence and status that such characters exuded. In some cases these fictional gentleman-detectives are reduced to joining the police because of such human frailties as drinking, gambling, or lack of self-discipline. Detective work thus becomes a form of rehabilitation, akin to a secular penitence. In joining the public service, now constituting a kind of replacement for the church, the reformed gentleman becomes its faithful servant.

The portrait of the police detective in literary works also echoed the scruples of certain opinion leaders—mostly outside the police— regarding the wisdom of recruiting detectives from the uniformed ranks, and its most obvious consequence—the low educational level of detectives. As discussed in Chapter 2, from time to time debate surfaced in the press and in police circles over the question of whether to allow candidates to skip this customary procedure. To a large extent, the division of opinion was about the relationship between qualitative detection and social class. Direct entry, in the view of the 'externalists', would bring in educated and more sophisticated men—that is, from the middle class—who were unwilling to serve first as ordinary policemen, and who would significantly improve the performance of the detective branch. Many fictional narratives shared this perception that the lowly origin of most detectives was the reason for their unsatisfactory achievements. Some fictional characters even joined the public debate in suggesting that entry to the detective ranks be based on more selective criteria. An MP in H. F. Wood's *The Night of the 3rd Ult* makes the following observations:

> How is a Detective Force, I ask, to adequately answer the very purpose for which it has been created... when the men who enter the force must first have belonged to the Constabulary! That is to say, the detectives are chosen from among the constables—it doesn't affect my argument to tell me that the constable may have been promoted sergeant or inspector. What percentage of superior material do you get in this way, or are you ever likely to get? They reply to you that, as a rule, promotion comes quickly, and that it is a man's own fault if he does not rise. But what procures him his promotion? He is to be steady, capable, and fit to be trusted... And out of that material we manufacture our detective officers. A man stamped head to foot a constable goes out in what they call plain-clothes, for the detection, pursuit, and capture of daring and astute criminals.[156]

In the same novel, police inferiority is also attributed to other aspects of police culture. Sergeant Vincent Erne is employed essentially by a large bureaucratic machine—the London Police Detective Force—confined to rules and regulations (in itself not the obvious formula for stardom), unlike the private detective who is at liberty to decide what case to handle or what means to employ without owing anyone an explanation. A private agent remarks to Erne: 'Under the circumstances, I don't see how you are to accomplish anything that lies out of the beaten track. You are not a free agent; you have not a free hand. You are tied down by routine, precedence, interest, envies.'[157] Yet, although fictional characters sporadically complain about the constraints imposed by the British legal system, or interpersonal relations within the police hierarchy, more often the reason for their failure in literary works is neither the bureaucracy nor the norms of the criminal justice system, but personal shortcomings, lack of vision and education, and insufficient professionalism—norms inimical to what the bourgeois ethos held dear.

Seen in the aggregate, detective texts seem to endorse middle-class individualistic and voluntarist attributes in the best detective characters. It is the private detective who symbolizes the virtues of individualism and is the natural carrier of bourgeois ideology (though not in every respect—for example, private detectives are not always patriarchs of a family). The emphasis is on detective activity that stems from freedom of action and private enterprise; from individual action based on an innate drive rather than external pressures emanating from bureaucratic regulations. However, the police detective figure is also increasingly endowed with qualities associated with bourgeois society. Certainly Lady Molly, head of the Female Department at Scotland Yard in *Lady Molly of Scotland Yard* (1910) by Baroness Emmuska Orczy, who is a high-born, talented individual, is depicted as an agent free of institutional bureaucracy and, when necessary, of legal strictures.[158] When left to her own devices, and allowed full control over her intellectually and socially inferior subordinates, she achieves good results. Similarly, though, police detective Clutch, in the anonymous 'Tale of a Detective', who does not share her background, reports to his senior officer about the process of an investigation only when he is about to make an arrest and requires an additional policeman to help him do it.[159] In fact, police detectives are not ordinarily portrayed as typical bureaucrats filling in forms and consulting with or reporting to their senior officers on their moves—as in real life—but as self-motivated crime fighters pursuing criminals in a manner similar to detectives working outside official organizations, even if their results are meagre. Although the chief investigators do not necessarily work alone, they rely on their own intuition and judgement. Broadly, the organization in which police detectives operate, whether it is Scotland Yard or other detective departments, serves mainly as support, providing assistance when necessary. Still, the combination of rational ability, an analytical mind, special knowledge, and expertise remained intimately linked to a middle-class background.

Some texts give the impression that only the exceptional individual, the ultimate maverick, driven by his own inner voice and propensities, can, in addition to satisfying the readers' thirst for heroic figures, serve as the best saviour of society. In *Prince Zaleski* by Matthew Phipps Shiel (1895), the Russian exile often conducts his investigations without leaving his house, applying his superhuman intellect to tackling intriguing puzzles.[160] Holmes, of course, is another example. This image of the unfettered individual who rises above the average person in almost every respect and is answerable only to himself is replicated in many other contemporary texts and genres. Such an individual was a familiar figure in the proliferating adventure, imperial, spy, and 'invasion-scare' narratives of the period, fighting to save Britain and the Empire from internal and external threats and decline, and articulating deeply held patriotic sentiments. These unconventional figures are so brilliant that they can impersonate any character, and, like detectives, often use disguise to accomplish their aims.[161] That Holmes is a bachelor and unbeholden to others strengthens his individuality and independence. So unbridled is he that in his search for justice he feels free to allow guilty people to escape the hands of the police without being held to account, yet his nonconformity does not tarnish his reputation. The police keep calling for his help, as for that of Loveday Brooke and many other private agents. Yet less outstanding private detectives also outrivalled their official counterparts.

THE INTERDEPENDENCE OF POLICE AND PRIVATE DETECTIVES AS AN AIM

The broader implication might be that private detection was perceived not only as more efficient but even preferable to an official force of crime fighters. Certain texts indeed conveyed this idea. Yet, a survey of the cumulative message of a large array of detective narratives—many of them best-sellers that did not survive the test of time—suggests that the tacit inclination of most authors was not to dispense with official authority. Residual opposition to the police concept might exist here and there, as well as a belief that it may be better for the community to police itself, but basically the texts accept the police as a given. Even when the police are criticized, the narratives only rarely question the need for official societal control. Rather, the prevalent view is one of impatience, or even strong impatience, with police performance. Fictive police detectives may occasionally abuse their powerful position and conspire with criminals, but, as the century progresses, most are no longer tainted with illegality. Police detectives make many mistakes, but they are on the whole industrious, moral, and devoted public servants. One of the few exceptions to this rule, Mr Gregory, the dishonest police detective in 'The Great Ruby Robbery' (1892) by Grant Allen, is caught in the end and brought to justice by the very force in which he serves.[162] The rule of law is generally preserved with reasonable impartiality.

Still, this level of performance is not deemed sufficient. The sustained focus on police incompetence seems to call for amelioration. Indeed, the texts do not leave the problem of police functioning unresolved, but offer a solution as to how to improve it. In addition to the recruitment of men from a higher class and education, and a more intensive resort to middle-class values—solutions that many texts evidently advocate—another implication is that police detectives could achieve much better results by cooperating with entrepreneurial elements outside the force and listening to their constructive ideas. More specifically, if inadvertently, the coexistence of private and official detectives in many texts indicates an underlying premiss that effective crime investigation requires the input of the commercial sector even in a sphere progressively recognized as dependent on state coordination and control and on the use of a collective and impartial force serving the entire population.

Such cooperation was not entirely imaginary. The police consulted private individuals for professional advice—for example, in the field of medicine—and sometimes worked with private agents who were retired police detectives. The Pinkertons—the famous American private agency—were in touch with Scotland Yard.[163] However, such contacts did not point to a significant role for private enterprise in official crime control. If anything, police detectives were not infrequently hired by private people and establishments. Therefore, what can be said with certainty is that, predicting a trend in policing that was to become dominant in the late twentieth century, the texts advocated a closer alliance between private and public detection as a more workable alternative to dependence on one alone, without specifying a precise balance between the two. Neither sector has a monopoly over law enforcement, even if sometimes, as in certain incidents involving Sherlock Holmes or Max Carrados, one element manages to mete out justice by itself.

Furthermore, what many literary texts seemed to be saying is that stemming crime requires not only the combined efforts of the state and the paid service of private agents, but also the involvement of the community at large, and especially the initiative of individuals who take it upon themselves to defend their home, family, or property, society as a whole, and sometimes the Empire itself. In stories written during the 1860s and 1870s, exemplified by 'The Mystery at Number Seven', written by Mrs Henry Wood (1877), and Richard Dowling's 'The Going Out of Alessandro Pozzone' (1878), it is often a private person, and not an investigator or the police, who discovers the identity of the murderer or the villain, or produces the incriminating evidence.[164] Similar conventions are inscribed in texts written during the 1890s,[165] but to a lesser extent, as authors increasingly positioned police detectives side by side with career private detectives. The presence of the sparkling private detective, therefore, does not generally translate into an alternative to the official investigator, but conveys an impulse to reform the service.

Beyond the notion that cooperation with (and absorption of) individuals with high intelligence, wide knowledge, and bourgeois norms of behaviour would significantly raise the personal level of English crime fighters, the recommendations embedded in detective fiction signalled the need for more professional detection. Clearly, most of the fictional police detectives were not sufficiently skilled to root out crime by themselves and needed vocational advice. The introduction of private detectives with impressive scientific knowledge into imaginative literature at the turn of the century, notably Sherlock Holmes and Dr Thorndyke, point in this direction.[166] Moreover, a significant number of fictional private investigators who were not detectives by vocation were professionals in some other field—lawyers and doctors, for example. Journalists, whose professional status rose significantly during this period, also acted as investigators in a number of literary texts, although some of these texts mirror the contemporary tensions and power struggles between police detectives and journalists (as analysed in Chapter 4), and portray the collaboration as unproductive in terms of results.[167] This insistence on the professionalization of the police conformed with pressures exerted in the period both to fill positions in the public service by merit and to enhance 'national efficiency', reflecting the growing belief in the role of the expert to present solutions to social problems. Although certain intellectual and artistic circles began to question long-established scientific certainties and to undermine confidence in the power of human reason, the application of a scientific and a generally professional approach was increasingly widespread in many spheres. The formulas embedded in detective fiction bore the imprint of these changes.

Ultimately, the motif of collaboration in some texts may have transmitted explicit class interests. In plots where the private detective comes from a middle-class or even higher background, his assumption of the management of the inquiry, and the submissiveness of police detectives, indicate a desire, or perhaps an implicit dictate, that the police should consistently adopt the order of priorities of the country's elite, and for that purpose specifically become more professional. At the same time, and without any contradiction, such an alliance between crime fighters from diverse backgrounds could be interpreted as a way to ease interclass tensions, echoing the aim of many contemporary social reformers to promote more contact between the classes and lower the barriers between the propertied and the propertyless, thereby also promoting a common patriotism. In this, police detectives, who were respectable and upwardly mobile citizens—not inhabitants of slums—could play a useful role, as they shared a common enemy in the Victorian and Edwardian underclass.

THE IMAGE OF POLICE DETECTIVES AS REPRESENTING THE STATE

The association of police detectives, as employees of central or local government, with the political establishment must have been clear to both writers and readers, who, whether consciously or not, viewed their behaviour in fictional works of the Victorian and Edwardian period as representing official Britain. Although the sensationalism of many detective tales had the effect of depoliticizing the public–police relationship to some extent, certain recurring tropes in detective fiction may be seen to express an ideological view of the state and its relationship with the individual and the community.

By virtue of their respective ideological configurations, both Marxist and Foucauldian critics have devoted some attention to this aspect.[168] Briefly, in viewing politics through a class perspective, Marxists generally postulate that detective narratives promote the hegemony of bourgeois values and modes of conduct and hide the contradictions inherent in capitalist society. Foucauldians, who conceive modern society primarily as 'a society of surveillance... penetrated through and through with disciplinary mechanisms',[169] concur with Marxists that the state acts as a coercive apparatus, even if subtly and with the object of reform rather than punishment. Although Michel Foucault did not accord literary texts a central place in his analysis of the disciplinary process, literary critics indebted to him contend that detective stories (and the novel in general), in making strict distinctions between normative and deviant behaviour, function as a political and cultural force, enhancing not only external control but also self-control.[170] Indeed, D. A. Miller, arguing from a Foucauldian point of view in his seminal work *The Novel and the Police* (1988), focused not on the institution of the police *per se* but rather on the less visible, dispersed modes of social discipline that moulded Victorian society and regulated the life of the people, defined as 'the policing power that never passes for such'.[171] In his opinion, the novel's narrative technique was just such an expression of power (defined by Foucault as producing behaviour), instilling support for the practices of surveillance and regulation.[172] Because of the pervasiveness of these disciplinary forces in society, the role of the police was actually peripheral, according to Miller. Significantly, the official and the private systems of detection assist and support one another in the novel, and 'the work of detection is frequently transferred from the police to a private or amateur agent', as the police are not the most important instrument of control.[173] In other words, the Victorian public had internalized the values of obedience and learnt to police itself in many other ways, outside the sphere of activity of the police.[174]

Broadly, the present reading of the texts lends support to Marxist and Foucauldian interpretations in the sense that detective fiction of the period not only upheld hegemonic middle-class norms but also celebrated the notion of the centrality of surveillance in the new urban and industrialized milieu, whether executed by private or official agents or both.[175] Nevertheless, the role of the police in imposing control remains cardinal in this fictional genre, albeit alongside other social forces, and this presence can hardly be ignored. In effect, interwoven in the narratives is the crucial need not only for law and order but specifically for the detective police. Moreover, if the novel indeed has the power to influence public opinion, as assumed by Miller, considerable weight should be assigned to the novelistic representation of the detective police. Our survey of detective fiction reveals that the state agency of control does not usually appear as an intrusive body with unlimited powers, either in its preventive or its detective capacity. Even if the ascribed role of the police may be the constant monitoring of the population, they do not commonly act towards this end. On the contrary, as discussed above, most writers of detective fiction articulated deeply felt concerns that official social control, as it was, was not sufficiently resolute and was often in the hands of ineffectual agents.

Admittedly, many scattered references to the police as an invasive institution may be found in detective fiction throughout the period. Fictive texts published nearer in time to the formation of Scotland Yard in 1842 reflected the widespread association of detection with spying and surveillance more intensely, and expressed the fears of a large part of the population who were still suspicious of plain-clothes policing. In particular, such texts present the policeman as 'a threat to the privacy of the middle-class home'.[176] As Anthea Trodd has shown in her *Domestic Crime in the Victorian Novel* (1989), contemporary writers supported the policeman in his attempts to control the 'dangerous classes', but when his 'enquiries took him to the door of the middle-class home... he became a different figure'.[177] In the same vein, D. A. Miller observes that police intervention in bourgeois domestic settings in *The Moonstone* constitutes an affront to the community.[178] As he puts it: 'Not only does an outsider watch what is not supposed to be watched, but he also construes what he sees by other rules than the ones this community uses to regulate itself.'[179] Another random example is 'Tale of a Detective', published in the early 1870s, in which the police detective, Clutch, conducts the investigation of a robbery in a sophisticated but invasive manner. As an agent of the state he penetrates the household of the victims (who in the end turn out to be the robbers), feigns an identity, preys upon the inhabitants, and follows the suspects incessantly. This theme of police intrusion recurs in later works as well, such as Grant Allen's story 'The Great Ruby Robbery' (1892), in which Lady Maclure is convinced that no one, whatever his or her social position, is safe from the Scotland Yard detective, who suspects (or pretends to suspect) everyone and whose questions invade the privacy of the individual in the name of public duty.[180]

Such episodes, however, do not pervade the genre. Overall, detective texts do not send a message of alarm about the repressiveness of police detectives, and in fact do not depict them as fearsome. The middle classes may resent police interrogation and the presence of a policeman in their homes, but the watchful eye of police officers is by no means omnipresent. If anything, in many instances, just when people need the police, they are absent, which is why victims are forced to hire the services of a private individual who slips easily into the vacuum created by the police. This means that the police cannot defend the citizens properly, and that quite often the criminal goes free, but it also means that the police do not use as much force as they might. The pervasive presence of private detectives in the vital role of preserving law and order in works of fiction implies that the elites have not invested all their power in enhancing formal control. Significantly, police detectives themselves are sometimes subject to monitoring—certainly by the reader who studies their performance and is guided by the author to doubt their effectiveness and ability.

This literary convention may be interpreted as a call for stronger or at least more effective police. In this sense it reinforces Foucauldian contentions about the disciplinary role of detective stories. Yet by no means do the texts advocate a panoptic type of police of the kind associated with continental societies. They may aim at shaping behaviour, inter alia by deliberately depicting the police as conspicuously incompetent and therefore as unthreatening,[181] but not at maximizing the regulatory powers in society. By implication, the state in most of these books is not ever present. The discussion of the texts in this volume suggests that most writers of detective fiction did not view contemporary society as subject to overall and unremitting official surveillance. State agents are surely not commonly invisible law-enforcers. On the contrary, the detective texts convey the sense that the state is incapable of, or unwilling to attain, complete control and that the enforcement system is imperfect.

While no single coherent ideology marks detective fiction, a general tendency does emerge from the texts surveyed. Essentially, what detective fiction offers is a kind of middle way—an equilibrium between reliance on the individual and the state. It grapples with the interconnecting and shifting relations between self-interest and social responsibility by negotiating a reconciliation between personal freedom and centralization. If, in mid-Victorian Britain, the popular premiss was that 'central government, even if it did try to interfere for the best of motives, was incapable of fulfilling the task [of solving economic or social problems] and would become overbearing', and that 'individuals could do the job better than the state',[182] in the last years of Victoria's reign the state increasingly appears as the embodiment of the common will, having the right to coerce the individual to obey the law and state regulations for the good of society. In this sense its activity cultivates social discipline. Yet, concurrently, in a variety of ways, the state takes the aspirations of the individual into account. Moreover, it allows, if sometimes reluctantly, certain above-average individuals the freedom to operate outside the parameters of the state and in fact even to guide it.

Middle-class virtues such as self-help, self-reliance, and voluntarism are encouraged, but within limits. Most detective initiatives must ultimately be resolved within the confines of the law. This is the sort of bargain detective texts endorse.

Holmes and police detectives may thus be perceived as complementary, not only as representatives of civil society and government, respectively, but also of the private and public sectors. The ongoing intellectual ferment discernible in the liberal camp of the late nineteenth century—but also outside it, and cutting across party lines—regarding the desirable balance between individual freedom of action and state regulation undoubtedly penetrated the literary world.[183] During the last two or three decades of the nineteenth century, a certain shift away from laissez-faire individualism and a growing acceptance of state authority and its ability to contribute to the common good was evident in liberal thought and in the policies of the various governments in power.[184] One of the most prominent liberal thinkers of the period, L. T. Hobhouse, asserted that the theory of collective action was 'no less fundamental than the theory of personal freedom'.[185] He, and J. A. Hobson, another notable contributor to the theory of social liberalism, articulated notions about harmonizing individual and social aims in language strongly evocative of the messages in detective fiction.[186] Imperialist Tories, of course, did not need convincing that Britain required a more powerful state.

The appearance of a growing number of police detective characters in the literary corpus, even if not as central figures, may be read as a metaphor for this shift in attitude towards a more conscious advocacy of state collectivism as a necessary instrument for attaining social justice and defending society's interests. The police might not perform their tasks entirely laudably, but they are relied on increasingly when disorder and crime occur. This was, after all, the period of the creation of the CID and the Special Branch, and the adoption by the latter of more stringent measures than had been acceptable until then. With this, the superiority of private over official detectives in the literature of the time reflects the countervailing impulse in intellectual circles and in public rhetoric to value the supremacy of individualism over government regulation. A broad repertoire of images encodes this duality, with the fictive solution pointing to the impulse to reach some kind of resolution.

No less tellingly, the interplay between police and private detectives, and the inadequacy of the police as major themes in a plethora of fictional texts, may be seen as a paradigm of underlying concern with the instability of the political order, as manifested in the incompetence of the police detective. The consolidation of detective departments in the country and the popularity of detective fiction coincided with the appearance of cracks in the façade of Victorian optimism and complacency. While many politically minded thinkers in late Victorian Britain continued to believe in the force of progress as an inevitable harbinger of greater good, others were less optimistic and detected worrisome developments. They did not constitute a single camp. Certain intellectuals viewed the substantial growth in state power, embodied by an expanded bureaucracy and its attendant legal entitlement to intervene in areas previously considered the province of the individual or the family, as a bad omen for society.[187] Indeed, Conan Doyle's Sherlock Holmes and Arthur Morrison's Martin Hewitt may both be perceived as manifesting anti-state sentiments. They accept the need for law and order but not all the practices that go along with it. The challenge to state decisions, exemplified by the private detective who time and again questions official measures and observations, appears beneficial to society, since police detectives are often wrong. Thus, side by side with a justification of the maintenance of order, the texts also propose resistance to state power. Moreover, they generally do not recommend strict bureaucratic means, but a reliance on individualistic norms.

For other commentators, the enemy was not the state but those who threatened its foundations. The late nineteenth century experienced economic uncertainty and mass unemployment because of increased foreign competition with Britain in the international market. The mood, consequently, tended to question the advance of liberalism and industrial capitalism, and with it the future of Britain as a world power, although this was a time of great expansion for the Empire. The period also saw the rise of socialism, which contained elements that called for radical change and the eradication of existing precepts, and the women's movement, which raised the spectre of undermining patriarchal values. The riots and disturbances that accompanied these developments seemed to confirm existing fears.[188] A current of anxiety regarding the detrimental effects of pervasive urban poverty, as epitomized in the slums of the East End and in the distressing results of the medical examinations of recruits to the Boer War, added to the pessimistic mood. Furthermore, Fenian terrorism in the 1880s and continuing problems in Ireland loomed unremittingly, eroding confidence in the government, as did fears of a foreign invasion on the eve of the First World War. The stories that appeared both in the press and in fiction are fraught with anxieties that the state would be unable to meet the new challenges, exacerbating fears of the weaknesses of the modern bureaucratic state and the underlying need to improve it.

The body of literature discussed here reveals that, while the detective fiction genre may have exerted considerable pressure to reinforce the established social order and bourgeois norms, it also seemed to accommodate diverse prescriptions that do not accord with the image of society as governed by networks of social discipline. If, as is contended here, detective fiction celebrated individualism, choice, and the circumscription of state power, while at the same time largely accepting the authority of the state, it also advocated moderation and restraint, even at the expense of efficiency, and a reconciliation between liberty and security. This overall portrayal may be seen as an expression of faith in tolerance, a value espoused by the press and a source of pride to the British public, especially when its system of law enforcement was compared with that of France and the rest of the Continent. In such an uncertain world, with rising scepticism, a questioning of the status quo, and a bewildering suspicion that what one sees and is being told is often not the case, as exemplified in the celebrated novel *The Strange Case of Dr Jekyll and Mr Hyde* by Robert Louis Stevenson (1886), the detective figure provided some reassurance that with combined effort truth can be revealed and internal peace maintained.[189] Arguably, the fictional figure of the police detective defies generalizations, yet this figure, which in the first half of the nineteenth century symbolized the notion of concealed identity and spying, was now perceived as a vehicle for exposing evil for the benefit of the public. It was precisely this police detective, depicted as visible, unextreme, less resolute, or effective than French detectives, but guided by moral principles and constrained by precepts of collaboration with the private sector, who symbolized what many regarded as the quintessence of Englishness in the late Victorian and Edwardian periods.

7

POLICE DETECTIVES AS AUTHORS

The literary image of police detectives as mediocre in intelligence, judgement, and performance evoked some commentary in the printed media, protesting against the portrayal as unfair and a grave injustice to the police. Even if official detectives were depicted as loyal, law-abiding, generally decent, and not particularly intrusive, the literary trend that projected private detectives as the true heroes in protecting society against criminals constituted an affront to police professionalism. Increasingly during the latter half of the nineteenth century, commentators criticized this image as distorted and pointed to its injurious consequences for the forces of law and order. Unexpectedly, these largely middle-class commentators were joined by a number of retired police detectives who published their memoirs—works that served to highlight the discrepancies between genuine and imaginary detectives and to enhance the police detectives' professional status.

DETECTIVE FICTION UNDER ATTACK

Pinpointing the gap between the portrayal of detectives in fiction and the reality began when detective fiction was still in its infancy, and not necessarily with a view to elevating the status of police detectives. An article in the *Saturday Review* in 1864, written anonymously by the distinguished judge, legal historian, and thinker James Fitzjames Stephen, focused on the fallacy of depicting both private *and* official detectives as 'ingenious' and 'remarkable' in Poe's works and in 'all forms of sensation novel-writing' (probably also including detective pseudo-memoirs, the literary sub-genre that presented police detectives in a favourable light; see Chapter 6).[1] From the point of view of someone acquainted 'with the proceedings of detectives and with the transactions which they try to detect', Stephen maintained that 'there is hardly anything that can be fairly described as remarkable or even peculiar ability' in the work of police and other detectives. In contrast to literary texts, many of the crimes went undiscovered or even unsuspected, and 'thousands of professional thieves, robbers, burglars, and coiners, to say nothing of people who make a living by extortion', operated in England. Typically, he did not blame the police, but the liberal 'system of law and rules of evidence', which give 'little scope for the sort of cunning' ascribed to detectives by the novelists he attacked. He particularly complained that the system had 'no power to keep suspected persons in prison, and constantly worry them by interrogation . . . [that] every form of hearsay is rigidly excluded from consideration' and that 'nothing is allowed to be given in evidence which is not immediately connected with the very point at issue'.

Other mainstream periodicals, seeking to portray detectives as they were, discredited the pseudo-memoirs of detectives, with the intention of heightening the esteem of real-life crime fighters. In a typical article bearing the apt title 'Detectives as They Are', published in 1870, *Chambers's Journal* warned readers of 'highly-spiced fictions purporting to be reminiscences of detectives' not to 'take it for granted that a halo of romance o'erhangs the life of a professional taker of thieves and murderers', for 'in actual experience it is not so', but 'contrariwise, the life of such a man is rather prosaic than otherwise'.[2] It also pointed out that detectives did not 'go about in those wonderful disguises the books we have referred to so enlarge upon—disguises only to be met with on the stage, and in novels'. To illuminate the unreliability of these pseudo-first-person accounts, the article proceeded to recount the actual, and generally effective methods used by plain-clothes policemen, suggesting that in many cases the perpetrators of crime, who were anyhow far from sophisticated law-breakers, were caught almost immediately, leaving no room for the kind of intricate detection depicted in detective fiction. The author's source was his neighbour, a detective sergeant who was 'an intelligent man, who has seen more of the world and its ways' than most men, and who, although he 'is up to every trick and dodge that ever sharper knew or dicer played', is 'unstained in morals'. Real-life police detection, even if devoid of glamour, was in reliable hands.

With the proliferation of detective fiction in the final two decades of the nineteenth century, literary works were increasingly viewed by champions of the police as bearing a significant responsibility for the unrealistic expectations the public had of police detectives. In 'Detectives and their Work', the journal *All the Year Round* (1885) gave its version of the power of fiction to mould opinion about official investigators and the differences between image and reality:

> In judging detectives and their work, many people are apt to take the detectives of the stage and of fiction as their standards of comparison, and compared with Vidocq, Hawkshaw, Mr Bucket, or the still more marvellous detectives of Poe's stories, the plain-clothes men of real life are unquestionably an inferior race.... [While] the playwright or novelist is very much master of the situation, [able to] control circumstances, and make everything fit in... [the] detective of everyday life is controlled by circumstances, and about the worst fault he can have is to try to make things fit in to his foregone conclusion of the explanation of any more or less mysterious crime.[3]

Fantasy is not bound by facts, but police detectives are, it seemed to say. In the same vein, the author of an article titled 'Detective Fiction', which appeared in the *Saturday Review* in 1886, pointed out that 'it is only in pages of fiction that the detective almost invariably triumphs. The reality falls far short of the ideal.'[4]

With unflattering treatment of police detectives in fiction falling into a distinct pattern by the turn of the century, the pejorative impressions conveyed by the texts were increasingly the target of attacks. *The Times*, a long-standing defender of the British police, published a series of articles about the Metropolitan Police in 1908–9 with an instalment on 'The Plain-Clothes Man', focusing on the helplessness of police detectives vis-à-vis their literary avatars and the ease of persuading gullible audiences of their incompetence (see Chapter 5). The author's anger at the mistreatment of police detectives is evident from the beginning, when he charges:

> There are some departments of police work which suffer from lack of public interest, and there are others which suffer from too much. The men in plain clothes are the victims, not to say the martyrs, of a notoriety which is without mercy, knowledge, or even common sense. Let the way in which they are treated by the popular writers of 'detective' tales bear witness. They have no power of defence of any kind.... Month after month there are published in the magazine, and in luridly-illustrated paper covers, thrilling, hair-curling stories, generally written in the first person, of dark and mysterious crimes concerning which professional detectives invariably display invincible ignorance, crass stupidity, and frequently an imbecility calculated to draw tears from any credulous, unreflecting taxpayer—and there are many of these—when he considers how quickly hard-earned money goes to pay the salaries of these poor boobies.[5]

Mocking the laudatory portrayal of the private detective, the author continues:

> It is only the amateur detective, these authorities assure us, who is capable of intelligent criminal investigation. This genius of modern times—he has not been in vogue many years—is generally addicted to cigarette smoking and dressing-gowns and slippers, and is roused to action by seeing a headline in his morning newspaper announcing the failure of the police to find something—a murderer, or a bag of diamonds, or a distinguished diplomatist. Upon this he rings the bell, instructs his confidential servant, and—we know the rest.

Coming out decidedly on the side of real police detectives and their contribution to society, the article emphasizes how strenuous their job is and how grateful citizens should be to them:

> Our business is solely with the real plain-clothes men, who, notwithstanding the scorn of the writers of shilling shockers, sixpenny dreadfuls, and magazine stories, strive not without success, by day and by night, through the best years of their lives, under guidance of leaders who have been trained in sterner schools of criminal investigation than are to be found in our mild and orderly Western civilization, to make the life of the man who preys upon society a hard and dangerous one, and preserve us all in peaceable possession of our propriety, be it great or small.

Commentators with strong sympathies for the contemporary system of criminal justice also voiced their reservations about the fictional image of police detectives in non-fiction books. Inter alia, one of the themes they raised was the role fictional writing played in shaping the contentious but widespread supposition of the superior ability of the French police. Major Arthur Griffiths, in a two-volume history titled *Mysteries of Police and Crime*, published in 1889, blamed French 'romance writers, the Gaboriaux, Boisgobeys, and Chavettes who have invented such types as PèreTabaret and Monsieur Lecoq', for attributing greater 'astuteness in detection, deeper insight, more scientific analysis, [and]...better skill in reasoning' to French detectives than to their English counterparts.[6] English novelists, too, he asserted, helped 'belittle the usefulness of the English police'.[7] In his opinion, so effective was 'the latest detective fiction' that it managed to efface the memory 'of such remarkable characters' as Collins's Sergeant Cuff and Dickens's detectives. Defenders of the police were also engaged in a kind of competition with fiction writers as to which detectives, and books, were more 'absorbing'—the authentic documentary or the fictional. To Griffiths, the answer was incontrovertible: real-life detection 'is better than anything invented by the detective novelists' and 'truth is far stranger than fiction'.[8]

The House of Commons itself served as an arena for airing qualms about the validity of the literary image of police detectives. Addressing the House in the early 1880s, Home Secretary Sir William Harcourt assured its members that 'mysterious and fanciful Lecocqs [did] not exist at all'.[9] Altogether, these spokesmen drove home the idea that police detection, though less mysterious, was a much more complex business than that which emanated from the pages of fiction, and that the public should refrain from judging detectives unduly harshly.

Not surprisingly, police journals also joined the fray, with the *Police Review* singling out Conan Doyle as their main target. In January 1893, the paper triumphantly reported that Doyle had visited the Black Museum of Scotland Yard, commenting that he 'has much to learn'.[10] Referring to Doyle's 'sarcasm at the expense of Scotland Yard'—an especially sore point—the reporter acknowledged that the famous writer's attitude 'is mellowing now', and that lately he had even bestowed 'some praise on the representative of the official police'. A few weeks later, however, the tone of the paper became harsher, accusing Doyle of 'circulating mischievous popular fallacies', and devoting an entire article to deriding the figure of Holmes and his style of detection.[11] It was a system that worked backwards from the discovery to the clues, instead of forwards from the clues to the detection. In particular, the author inveighed against Holmes's description of the 'official police' as lacking in imagination, reminding the readers of the importance of hard work as opposed to sitting by the fire spinning fine theories, and of having the luxury of 'legal evidence of facts before embarking on a prosecution'.

A METAMORPHOSIS FROM POLICE DETECTIVES TO AUTHORS

Clearly, those most affected by the adverse literary image were the detectives themselves, but so long as they were in service they could do little other than contribute articles to police journals. However, after they had retired, several police detectives were able to publish their memoirs, and used this vehicle to advance their cause.[12] Until then, police crime investigators influenced print culture only indirectly, whether through their contacts with journalists, their leverage on what was allowed to be passed on to the press, or their inadvertent impact on fictional literature. Yet, when reputable publishing houses in both Britain and the USA published detectives' memoirs as full-length books (from the late nineteenth century), detectives had an opportunity to communicate directly with the public and portray their occupation in the way they saw fit.[13] This platform also allowed them to speak out against those who gave them a bad name.[14] The publication of memoirs by detectives, most of whom had grown up in working-class homes, was an achievement in yet another respect. Although autobiographies were written by working-class men of various backgrounds, ranging from tramps to skilled workers, political activists and public figures, mainstream publishers were not inclined to publish first-person accounts by people of this class.[15] Nonetheless, plain-clothes law-enforcers entered print culture in growing numbers, starting a trend that soon became apparent.[16]

Notably, most of the published police memoirs were written by detectives who had served in the Metropolitan Police of London, and, moreover, most of these authors had worked in the prestigious and in many respects atypical detective unit at Scotland Yard, thereby representing the collective voice and experience of these officers in particular. It is reasonable to assume that this exposure reinforced the special status of Scotland Yard in the police and, perhaps more importantly, in society, yet it also supported a tendency to regard the life of Yard men as typical of English detectives as a whole.

The rest of this chapter aims to explain how various detectives managed to publish these memoirs and what they did with the opportunity given to them. Aside from illuminating an additional dimension of the relationship between detectives and the print media, the discussion reveals how police detectives viewed themselves and their work, and how they wanted the readers to view them, thus enhancing an understanding of their world.

EARLY PUBLISHED MEMOIRS

Few police detectives in the British Isles published books relating to their work experience before the 1880s. One of the rare exceptions was the Edinburgh police detective James McLevy, born on a small farm in Ireland, who became a famous detective in Edinburgh and beyond.[17] During the 1860s, following his retirement, McLevy published a series of books based on cases he had handled over his long career, which had begun in 1833 (he had entered the force three years earlier as a nightwatchman).[18] The books were published both in Edinburgh and London and were reprinted several times. To render the texts more alluring, imaginary details were interwoven in them, creating a romantic halo surrounding detectives.

Memoirs by foreign police detectives circulated in translation before the 1880s as well, and attained popularity. Apart from the memoir by the noted French detective Eugène-François Vidocq, which came to light in various versions (see Chapter 6), the French exported other texts by former chiefs of the Sûreté, recounting encounters between crime fighters and offenders in France. In 1862, an English translation of Louis Canler's memoirs as *Autobiography of a French Detective from 1818 to 1858, Comprising the Most Curious Revelations of the French Detective Police System*, was issued by Ward and Lock, a publisher with an eye for such texts. The initiative to publish this memoir came from the English author and historian Lascelles Wraxall, who found much merit in 'offering to English readers the true and ungarbled experiences of a French detective police officer'.[19] The reader was informed in the preface that in France the book had gone through three editions in a fortnight, and that immediately after the appearance of the third edition it was suppressed by the French government, which was 'ashamed of the Revelations which Canler does not hesitate to make about the working of the Police system in France, which countenances criminals in the hope that they may betray their companions'. This was probably meant to enhance its appeal. The translation was also intended to demonstrate the superiority of the English police system.[20] Yet only around the time of the appearance of the figure of Sherlock Holmes (1887), which (in the early 1890s) raised popular enthusiasm for the fictional detective character to unprecedented heights, did the trend of police memoirs gain a certain momentum in Britain.[21]

That a growing number of police detectives saw their life stories in print in this period was the product of both a convergence of developments in the publishing world and the nature of police culture.

DEVELOPMENTS IN THE BRITISH PUBLISHING WORLD

Undoubtedly, writers benefited from the improved market conditions brought about by rising income in the reading public, the declining prices of books, and the near total elimination of illiteracy in the late nineteenth century. From 1880 onwards, publishers 'began to look beyond the middle classes towards a mass audience', catering to newly educated readers and semi-literate labourers.[22] As businessmen whose aim was to make a profit, they had to be convinced that narratives by unproven writers were saleable before they were willing to stake an investment in such books. Many indications point to the readiness of the market for detectives' life stories. Clearly, the subject of criminality had become steadily more topical in all print formats in the course of the nineteenth century. According to an article entitled 'Crime in Current Literature', published in 1897 in the *Westminster Review*, there had never been 'so many pens engaged in dealing with crime and criminals as at the present time'.[23]

The vogue for Sherlock Holmes in the last years of the nineteenth century was a symptom of the overwhelming interest in solving crimes in the realm of the imagination, yet the period also saw a demand for authentic accounts that would illuminate the lives of real detectives and give the public 'an opportunity of judging between the romance and reality of the Criminal Investigation Department'.[24] As described previously, such interest was not new. The press had devoted considerable space to the true nature of police detection earlier, while publishers and authors of pseudo-detective memoirs also understood the importance of stressing the veracity of detail in these texts. However, the popularity of fictionalized detective memoirs was waning towards the end of the century. Perhaps, just as pseudo-memoirs had preceded and promoted the rise of Holmes, and then vacated the literary stage for him, so they did for real-life memoirs of detectives. In short, the stories revolving around Holmes and similar fictional characters, and the life histories of real detectives replaced the pseudo-memoir genre. The reading public continued to hanker after the imaginary, yet was eager, too, to read about the here and now.[25] An article published in the *Windsor Magazine* in 1895 points to a certain satiation with seemingly documentary, but fictional, narratives about the world of detection, and an appetite for memoirs based on actual experiences, observing:

> it may be doubted whether imagination has outdone reality, whether fiction is equal to fact, whether the ideal is as interesting or even accurately resembles the real detective officer. No detective stories are stranger than the personal records and reminiscences of the men themselves.... The same superiority may be claimed for authentic portraiture as compared with the many imaginary characters so freely invented of late. A picture taken from life cannot but possess a certain truthfulness. It may possibly caricature, exaggerate, even mislead—so do photographs; but they are still the real thing, not fancy-drawn sketches, and must exhibit some actual phase in the aspect of the sitter.[26]

In the same year, an article reviewing Jerome Caminada's memoirs for the *Morning Post* professed that, 'after so much fiction about crimes and their detection, a volume of facts on the subject ought to be especially interesting'.[27] The *Birmingham Daily Post* reiterated the same message—namely, that, because Caminada was a real detective, his memoirs 'should make racy and instructive reading'.[28] Evidently, there was a growing demand for detective texts of all types, whether fiction or non-fiction, but the public and the publishers now favoured a clearer distinction between the two.

The Victorian fin-de-siècle thus witnessed a split in the publication of crime writing into two parallel genres, each with its own conventions, though by no means comparable in quantity or impact. One relied on the imagination of the author to delve into the world of detection, and the other presented the true-life experiences of the author–detective. The two trends established, or more precisely consolidated, identifiable narrative modes: what is generally termed the detective genre, and autobiographical texts by police detectives. The print market, both the press and books, produced an ever-growing body of fictional detective stories with the detective as the central character, sometimes in a series featuring the same hero, alongside authentic detective memoirs, notably structured in a similar manner—namely, a detective engaged in a sequence of criminal events.

Like all autobiographical narratives, genuine detective reminiscences contained some fictitious elements—possibly more than other such kinds of narratives in view of the dramatic nature of their occupation and the engagement with crime. What differentiated these narratives from pseudo-memoirs was that they were signed by authors who had on occasion been mentioned in the press, as in the cases of detectives

Jerome Caminada, John Littlechild, and John Sweeney, and their depictions were anchored in verifiable facts. Moreover, their accounts of criminal cases were often familiar to the reader from news columns. As full-length books, these memoir volumes also offered many more autobiographical details than any journalistic sketch of detectives. Admittedly, some readers may not have been aware of the difference between genuine and pseudo-detective memoirs, and the fact that pseudo-memoirs were not the real stuff, but, despite the similar format, many readers were aware of the distinctions, as is evident from reviews of the latter and contemporary comments by literary critics. Perpetually looking for new manuscripts, publishers discovered a new, albeit limited, niche in the appeal of detective memoirs. The circulation of *Reynolds's News*, the newspaper claimed, had 'gone up by leaps and bounds' when it published the entire memoir of Detective Sergeant Patrick McIntyre in 1895.[29]

While detective memoirs in book form served the publishers' interests, their monetary potential does not fully explain their expansion. Potential author–detectives had to have the impulse, the ability, and the conditions to undertake such an unfamiliar venture. They also had to have confidence in themselves, along with an understanding of market trends and a sense that the expanding mass culture promised opportunities for new writers.[30] Fulfilling these requirements, a small number of detectives took the deliberate step of entering the publishing world.

THE ROLE OF POLICE CULTURE IN THE EMERGENCE OF AUTHOR–DETECTIVES

This phenomenon started in the late 1880s. Earlier, detectives may not have been convinced of their aptitude as writers. When they did commence writing, some may have been discouraged from publishing their memoirs. As Chief Inspector Frederick G. Abberline of the London CID explained in his unpublished memoirs, 'the authorities were very much opposed to retired officers writing anything for the press as previously some retired officers had from time to time been very indiscreet in what they had caused to be published', and, to his knowledge, 'had been called upon to explain their conduct and in fact... been threatened with actions for libel'.[31] This was the reason he gave for not publishing his own reminiscences after he had retired from service in 1892, contenting himself with a third-person journalistic account of his occupational life published in the press (see Chapter 4). Still, some pioneers, aware of interest in their life stories, set about satisfying this curiosity by producing authoritative versions of detective reality. These author–detectives seemed to have been a select group of individuals with initiative. Yet, it was police culture that had, however inadvertently, provided them with the tools and opportunities to fulfil what for some became a long-standing ambition or a challenging undertaking in a new domain.

First and foremost, perhaps more than any other occupation that drew its manpower primarily from the working class, police detection fired the imagination of both publishers and readers, constituting a built-in professional advantage. Detectives did not have to make up stories. The thrilling moments in detective work a priori made for a good read, though their memoirs suggest that the author–detectives also tended to give free rein to their imagination. Furthermore, beyond the obvious appeal of the occupation, retired police detectives had acquired the economic means, along with the leisure, to engage in writing, and did not have to live by their pen. Under certain circumstances, detectives, as all veteran policemen, benefited from some form of pension before 1890, and, following the Police Act of 1890, all police employees had the right to retire in their late forties or fifties with a guaranteed pension (see Chapter 3), which allowed those who wished to document their working lives to do so in relative comfort. Moreover, almost without exception, the police detectives whose personal reminiscences saw the light of day were men who had managed to rise in the police hierarchy, had become senior officers with the rank of inspector or higher, and were therefore entitled to a more comfortable pension than average. Since many police detectives became private agents upon retirement, or engaged in other remunerative jobs, their income when they were writing their reminiscences rose even higher. Such privileges were denied to most working people.

Detectives' life-writing also gained from the bureaucratic nature of their work and the constant documentation required. Some police detectives published their retrospective texts long after retirement, such as Detective Chief Inspector Tom Divall, who had left the London CID in 1913 but saw his life narrative in print only in 1929. But even those who wrote their reminiscences soon after retirement still faced the difficulty of reconstructing the details of the distant past. Some claimed that they drew on their recollections almost entirely, thus assuring the public that they had a good memory (and hence that their accounts were reliable).[32] The truth is that they did not have to rely heavily on recalling details from memory, as they had access to documents that could help them refresh it. For cases covered in the news, they could resort to press cuttings, which some detectives habitually collected. In addition, some officers retained their original notes.[33] Possibly, those who kept in touch with their fellow officers could also examine archival police reports. Of course, this did not prevent some author–detectives from reinventing parts of their past, at least to some extent.

Many author–detectives probably utilized the services of professional writers, who, to varying degrees, edited or even fully ghosted their memoirs.[34] Other types of authors—even more than a century previously[35]—had used such services, so it is likely that police detectives, especially those who were not gifted writers, availed themselves of the talents of others. Fictional stories offer additional insights into such assistance. In the pseudo-memoir *Tom Fox or The Revelations of a Detective* (1860), the protagonist, a police detective, has the attentive support of his host and his host's wife, who urge him to put his stories 'on print', and, educated in an environment that nurtured literary proficiency, they offer to edit them.[36] The author of this book affirms that 'rough "mems" [memoranda]' must be edited as well as be intriguing. Evidently, the idea of outside assistance for ambitious crime fighters seemed natural, even then.

Nevertheless, detective duties surely improved the literacy skills of police detectives, many of whom grew up in homes where education was not promoted, although a few of the memoirists actually came from a lower middle-class background, had worked in a clerical position, or had otherwise expanded their literacy and education before joining the police (see Chapter 2). Policing generally, and crime investigation in particular, were among the non-middle-class occupations for which literacy was a condition of employment. Additionally, there was a strong clerical component to their tasks. Such experience could have been useful to detectives in the initial stages of writing their own personal narratives, strengthening their resolve to embark on compiling their work reminiscences before seeking professional assistance. It may also have enriched their vocabulary and refined their literary skills, as well as inculcated in them the habit of editing. In presenting reports in 'good form' during their working years, they had been required to copy them from pencil to ink, put them 'in a grammatical form', and rewrite them.[37] All this does not discount the possibility that some author–detectives had a natural talent for writing.

The police detectives' writing experience also assisted them in structuring the narrative in the particular format prevalent in most of their memoirs—a sequence of stories based on the cases they had investigated. Narration, in fact, was at the core of detective work, particularly for those engaged in investigation. The guiding principle behind the vocation was the aim of formulating a coherent story from observed signs. In practice, detectives functioned as serial storytellers. Their occupational duties forced them to chronicle the episodes in which they were involved and narrate a series of events comprehensively. Although many cases were not solved, those that were had to be recorded as a narrative with a beginning and an end, with detailed descriptions of the process of detection. As they were to do later in the memoirs, they had to select and organize the events in a particular order, highlight some, indicate their importance, and reach conclusions. Repeating the process time and again, they became adept at it and were prepared in this respect for their literary undertaking.

Furthermore, police detectives acquired the habit of recounting their exploits to an attentive audience, whether at work or outside it.[38] Accounts of the goings-on in police headquarters or stations show that detectives were fond of chatting about crime and law enforcement.[39] In effect, to a significant extent, the legal system depended on the storytelling capacity of the detective to construct a reliable narrative. He often became the principal source of information as to what had happened in situations that necessitated the intervention of the law. This role trained him for the writing of texts in which such stories comprised the inner rhythm, and perhaps also enhanced his reliability as an autobiographer. In sum, for people who were not educated to write for publication, detectives did quite well, largely because of a work environment that assisted them in compensating for the absence of educational opportunities. Many had no liking for the bureaucratic demands of the job, but, when it came to writing their memoirs, they may have appreciated the benefit of having mastered the art of narrating a succession of tales.

These aspects of detective work, which became more entrenched with time, combined towards the end of the century to provide detectives with an unanticipated commercial edge. By that time, the pool of retired detectives was large enough to produce more than the odd memoirist. A growing number of police detectives decided to embark on a path of self-presentation and exhibited a professional approach to writing that cannot be explained solely by the skill or assistance of editors. Most likely their close links with the media, particularly in London for those located at Scotland Yard, exposed them to essential contacts with the publishing world and to contemporary publishing trends. They appeared to have become conscious of public taste and the need to construct a compelling narrative, although each detective wrote no more than one, or at best two, books. Typically, Detective Chief Inspector John Littlechild made special efforts 'to avoid repetition, for necessarily much of the experience which I have gained presents features of similarity'.[40] Detectives understood that the 'commonplaces of a detective's experience' could weary the average reader; hence they selected 'incidents of a somewhat unusual character' and stories with the potential to engage the public.[41] They combined melodramatic elements of murder, burglary, and fraud with accounts of everyday persons, events, and minutiae. They provided detailed information on the way criminals plan and execute their crimes, and also on how they fail; on women who live in highly unconventional ways, and on female criminals; on exotic foreigners from faraway countries and on other social groups far removed from the life of the average reader. Their books also told tales about foreign governments and distant places where British police detectives arrived in search of a missing clue or a criminal.

THE UNDERLYING IMPULSE TO WRITE

Over and above a financial impetus, a desire for self-promotion, or perhaps a wish to make up for the education denied them in their youth, there seems to have been yet another explanation for the detectives' impulse to write. Detectives had a unique opportunity, given their lower-class background, to represent their occupation to a vast audience, and in their own words, and some took it up. This impulse is reflected in the structure and themes that mark the texts: a brief introductory section, in which the author divulges a few biographical details and his reason for writing,[42] followed by a long section devoted to his work experience. The latter section, which constitutes the bulk of these books, barely alludes to domestic circumstances, social relationships, leisure activities, or views about issues other than law enforcement. In fact, the memoirs do not proportionally relate to the narrators' entire life at all, focusing on their lives as detectives only. Each book is taken up by episodes and cases that occupied the author on the job.[43]

The adoption of this paradigm may have reflected a commercial decision to provide what interested the public most—stories about crime detection. It was long understood in literary circles that inserting detective segments in texts, even in non-fiction, was a formula for success. The journalist J. Hall Richardson reveals in his memoirs that he was advised to include 'a good detective story' in his book *Police!* (1889), about the history of the police in Britain, and that he regretted not having acted upon this 'invaluable hint'.[44] The format also suggests that retired author–detectives were attentive to generic precedents. While police detectives may have been ignorant of the many fictitious accounts of highwaymen and thieves written in a strikingly similar narrative mode as early as the seventeenth century—a few personal details about the protagonist's origins, followed in the rest of the text by a 'string of episodes' about his life of crime[45]—they certainly read contemporary narratives that adopted the same pattern. Judging by Detective Superintendent Jerome Caminada, the author–detectives were familiar with pseudo-memoirs of detectives that used this specific strategy of self-fashioning, and took their cue from them.[46]

Yet, the repeated use of this structure may betray deeper, perhaps less conscious, sensibilities. The omissions in these discourses were as revealing as their emphases. The authors' relatively cursory attention to their life before they joined the police, and their silence regarding family, economic circumstances, and leisure activities outside the police force point not to indifference to these aspects of their existence but to the overriding significance of their work to them. Detectives appear to have derived a deep sense of fulfilment and satisfaction from their vocation, even if their occasional effusive pronouncements about their feelings must be taken with qualifications. The occupational self clearly dominates these autobiographical works. The narrative sequence is determined by their work life: in the majority of memoirs, once the detective has retired, the book comes to an end. Once he has left police service, the rest of his life story is insignificant. Even in memoirs that include a description of his experience as a private detective after retirement from the police, the author's police identity tends to dominate the narrative. Often, his reminiscences of his childhood or youth also anticipate his future engagement with detective work. In such texts, the choice of occupation is portrayed in retrospect almost as preordained, as a product of an inner calling, an uncontrollable drive or destiny (as famous people did). As an adult, his home appears to be conceived as a space dedicated to non-work and therefore not part of his story. The minimal exposure of family life suggests his total and undivided dedication to his work.

Undeniably, the texts can be viewed as success stories and as testimonies of personal triumph. Almost invariably, the self-made authors had managed to transcend class boundaries and climb to positions of command. Although their social background is not highlighted, police detectives did not hide their former lives, and the journey most of them made from poverty or a modest existence to relative comfort cannot be overlooked. As Detective Inspector Robert Fuller asserted proudly in 1912: 'All detectives, at least so far as London is concerned, start from scratch and work their way forward.'[47] This transmitted a powerful message to other low-income sectors that with determination and talent they too could succeed. Still, the memoirs are not tales of individual accomplishment only. The author represents both himself and the organization to which he belongs. Whether speaking for the police as a whole or for the detective constituency specifically, he is a consistent advocate of the work of the police. Detective Inspector Andrew Lansdowne conjures up this sense most succinctly in his book *A Life's Reminiscences of Scotland Yard*: 'Why should I write a book? What is my title to speak for Scotland Yard?', he asks, answering: 'Well, without egotism, I suppose I may say that, having spent twenty years of my life there, and having, for six years prior to that, served in almost all grades of the metropolitan police, I have some claim to talk of the system as it existed during the whole period of my acquaintance with it.'[48] The detective–narrator is the force behind the progression of events, but the police organization is no less of a unifying factor.

Indeed, the narratives do not exactly constitute life histories but rather work histories. The texts are not marked by a confessional mode and are not driven by an urge to disclose inner feelings. They are personal recollections of the occupational life of the authors in the employ of the police, in particular the detective department, and mainly the London CID or Scotland Yard. Spending nearly their entire adult life in this one workplace, detectives looked upon police detection as their lifelong career, even if they set up in private practice as investigators after retirement. Such loyalty is readily discernible in the positive way they depict the CID and in the titles of the memoirs themselves, which often refer either to Scotland Yard or to the authors' occupational identity. Little is told about the jobs they held before they entered the police, and, even when they recount their later work as private detectives in some detail, they interweave references to their police experience and to their identity as police officers. Detective Inspector Lansdowne projected a sense of wanting to bring the readers into his own world and introduce them to the rites of a secret cult.[49]

Many contemporary working-class autobiographies were characterized by a lack of introspection and only minimal accounts of personal life and family, but often the rationale underlying this terseness stemmed primarily from a desire 'to teach the middle and upper classes how members of the working class actually lived in London slums or rural villages' and 'to move the reader...to support the growing demand for social improvements'.[50] The detectives' motivation seems to be different. Becoming authors no doubt underscored their subjectivity and agency. Yet, it was their deep-seated ties to their detective department that ultimately provided the *raison d'être* for their life's work and for the books they wrote about it. The author–detectives function more as representatives of law and order than as individuals with distinct characteristics. This identity allows them to engage in the pursuit of criminals and become all-powerful investigators, legitimizing their activity and decisions even after they have left the police. They owe a great deal to this affiliation. Each detective–author is one of many, and his story is theirs as well. In the early 1930s Detective Chief Inspector James Berrett aptly articulated this feeling by writing: '"I" represents not only myself but the many assistants...who joined with me as part of the organisation to solve the problem before us.'[51]

This intense identification with their vocation constitutes another factor that impelled detectives to author memoirs. Many writers of detective memoirs felt a need to explain this motivation to the public. Often they claimed that they had no literary aspirations, but that other people, notably friends and acquaintances, had pressed them to write about themselves.[52] Others may indeed have fuelled the detectives' initiative and inspired them to embark on a literary journey. Alternatively, this admission may have been simply another literary convention followed by the detectives.[53] Whatever the case, conceivably, it was not only outside pressure and the wish to relive their police experiences through their published memoirs that prompted detectives to set out to publish their recollections. Reading between the lines, another driving force becomes apparent: the detectives' self-perception as organic members of the police who have taken on the task of spokesmen for their vocation. Their books—even those written years after they had retired from the police—are permeated by a sense of mission aimed at eradicating extant misconceptions and illuminating what they insist is the true work of a police detective.[54] The submerged assumption was that knowledge is power and that the written word can influence readers and mould their perceptions.

This motivation—defending the detective police—had been invoked in one of the early pseudo-memoirs, *The Female Detective* (1864). Mrs G of the Metropolitan Police, the central figure in that work, asserts that she writes 'in order to show, in a small way, that the profession to which I belong is so useful that it should not be despised'.[55] She knows well that her 'trade is despised', but she intends to impress upon readers 'that the detective has some demand upon the gratitude of society'.[56] The same theme surfaced in 1889 in 'Revelations by Real Detectives', a pseudo-memoir in which the narrator, police officer George Johnson, undertook to defend 'my much-maligned fellow-defenders of the law' against public intolerance and censorship.[57] He was particularly offended by the widespread reaction when a murderer is not caught—namely, 'there is a terrible cry about the inefficiency of the detective and police forces, and there is a good deal of grumbling about such an amount of the ratepayers' money being wasted in keeping up a body of men who are unable to protect the public from outrage'. Although these defences of the police appeared in fictional works—pseudo-memoirs—they faithfully reflected the desire of real detectives to clear their name, or at least to explain the restraints and pressures under which they worked, as will be seen below.

AUTHOR–DETECTIVES' CRITICISM OF DETECTIVE FICTION

The police-detective memoirists seldom battled against their image in the press. Rather, detective fiction was the target of their attacks, for, although it generally expressed support for the criminal justice system, it did not describe the detectives as they wished to see themselves in print; that is, it frequently portrayed them as incapable. References to the impact of such literature on dominant attitudes towards detectives were made in almost every detective memoir. A dialogue was thus created between fictional texts about detectives and texts by flesh-and-blood detectives, forming an ongoing intertextual exchange that continued after the First World War when memoirs by retired police detectives proliferated.

In this struggle, detectives reiterated the arguments put forward by other defenders of the police. Yet, in attempting to discredit the plausibility of the fictional portrait, they held a trump card that other defenders did not have—first-hand testimony. Implicit in the memoirs was the notion of an objective, 'reliable' version of detective life, as presented in their texts, which was distinct from fictional works.[58] Further, while the fictional detective was entirely imaginary, the authentic detectives offered readers a view of reality, a theme highlighted as well in detectives' memoirs after the First World War.[59]

Notably, the detective–narrators attempted to prove their superiority not only as detectives but also as writers. The tacit competition between fictional and authentic texts was not only about who best represented the occupation, but also about the quality of the texts. The unspoken premiss underlying all the memoirs was that only people who had experienced life as detectives could penetrate beyond appearances and convey the true nature of the occupation to the public. In the same breath, the detectives also seemed to be saying that their texts were more interesting and entertaining than imaginary texts. The rhetoric they used to show the pre-eminence of texts based on facts may be viewed as a continuation of the concerted efforts of the pseudo-memoirs to demonstrate accuracy, and as a response to the public's wish to learn about things as they are (see Chapter 6). It may also be seen as a way of reinforcing an image of credibility. The criminal justice system, after all, was dependent to a large extent on the evidence given by detectives—initially, when determining the culpability of suspects in serious cases, and subsequently when taking evidence and producing it in court. Surely, the detectives' chances of convincing others of the truth of their pronouncements depended, in turn, on the esteem in which their profession was held. Stressing the veracity of their texts could thus serve as a weapon against a potentially unflattering literary image and as a device to enhance their reputation.

Significantly, in the opening words in the introduction to his memoirs, published in 1904, Detective Chief Inspector G. H. Greenham dismissed literary detective stories as 'nearly in every instance... founded entirely on fiction, created by the fertile, imaginative brains of the author', and added that 'to a practical detective they would appear quite impossible, as it would require a person of supernatural instinct and power to unravel the extraordinary mysteries connected with such crimes'.[60] The primacy of factuality was reiterated in many other memoirs. Detective Superintendent Jerome Caminada asserted that the stories he recounted—'unlike so many of the so-called stories of detectives—are founded on facts, and, are, from first to last, and in all their details, truthful histories'.[61] Inspector Maurice Moser, dissociating himself from the realm of pseudo-memoirs, claimed that his stories 'are all founded upon actual experiences and facts' and are 'devoid of sensationalism', unlike those that appealed to the readers by the enticing title of 'Revelations'.[62] Detective Inspector John Sweeney affirmed that he had 'in no way romanced', but only wrote 'facts'.[63] Thus, armed with personal experience, the memoirists posited their version of detective life as a worthy alternative to fiction. In addition, in presenting themselves as experts in sifting fact from fiction in their professional life, they implied that this expertise also carried over to their writing.

Some memoirs include passages aimed specifically at eliminating any confusion between fictional and real sleuths, although, curiously, the memoirists did not refer to the fictional portrait of the official representative of the law. Surely they resented the narratives that pitted police officers against private detectives, with the former depicted as inferior in cerebral ability, and, furthermore, as submitting to the authority of the private detectives. Yet, the prime object of the memoirists' crusade was, rather, the stock figure of the private detective. The portrayal of Sherlock Holmes infuriated them above all. He became the emblem of the distorted image of detectives generally, and evidence of how far removed the persona of the fictional detective was from genuine crime fighters. Detective Sergeant Patrick McIntyre declared in his memoirs in 1895 that his is not a Sherlock Holmes tale, but 'a matter-of-fact description of the real life of a modern detective'.[64] Few were the memoirs written by officers (including those published in the post-war era) that did not mention Holmes. Despite the profusion of other fictional characters of the Holmes variety, he was uppermost in their minds when they challenged these representations, and it was mainly his figure they repudiated, even when they did not refer to him overtly. In their battle against the uncongenial image of the police detective in literature, they simply projected themselves in their memoirs in countervailing terms.

Of the various aspects of the literary detective denigrated by author–detectives, a major focus was on the detection methods he employed. Since detection methods were the criteria by which their own efficiency and professionalism were judged, emphasizing the discrepancies between them and their literary counterparts in this respect was their highest priority. Particular attention was paid to the element of disguise that many private detectives used in fictional narratives. Police detectives also resorted to disguise, but, because of the widespread public suspicion of invisible policing, which had accounted for the initial resistance to the establishment of the police and its detective branch, many memoirists made a point of arguing how little they resorted to this questionable practice—unlike Sherlock Holmes, for example, who often adopted cunning disguises in his attempts to unravel mysteries.[65] The memoirists stressed that role-playing was not a favoured instrument of social control. Imbued with the zeal to set the record straight, Detective Inspector Lansdowne pinpointed 'the popular fallacy that a detective must necessarily be a man of mystery, an astute actor, an accomplished comedian with a wardrobe of an extensive kind, and as difficult to "corner" as a lively eel', attributing 'its continued existence to the exaggerations of sensational writers'.[66] Disabusing his readers of this notion, Lansdowne declared: 'Detectives are neither remarkable for their big feet, nor for their histrionic capabilities and changes of dress.'[67]

Time and again, the real-life detectives contended that, unlike fiction writers, they could not indulge in artistic licence but had to grapple with the real world. Their underlying complaint was that detective fiction, because it was not circumscribed by factual constraints, had created untenable expectations of the real-life detective.

THE GOAL OF IMPROVING THE POLICE DETECTIVES' ADVERSE IMAGE

The most obvious device used by the memoirists in their aim to improve the adverse image of the police detective was unabashed commendation of themselves and of the police organization. These first-person narrators adhered to a rhetorical lexicon that cast them not only as honest and helpful—as, for that matter, in detective fiction—but also as efficient, vigilant, 'patient of endeavour', clever, capable, intelligent, perceptive, 'subtle of instinct' and kind.[68] The narrators seemed to imply that, even if their work did not resemble that of the sophisticated fictional gentleman sleuth, real police detectives were no less professional than imagined detectives. Unlike

Holmes, police agents were ordinary men of lower-class parentage, yet they were no less systematic, cerebral, or courageous, and were endowed with a discerning intellect, street wisdom, and a unique memory. Exceptional powers of observation and shrewd common sense were not second nature to Holmes only, but, according to the memoirs, applied to police detectives as well.[69] Hence they were just as competent in matching their brains against cunning felons, capturing conmen, burglars, and other tricksters, and validating their conclusions rationally both by intuition and imagination. They may not have been as well educated, and were not as well versed in the classics and in sciences as Holmes—although some of them evinced erudite knowledge of the high culture of the time—but, the writers insisted, they could see beneath the surface and they could trace matters to their origin.

The police detectives' talents and occupational skills were sometimes underscored in the memoirs by presenting certain criminals as formidable enemies. Both criminals and detectives were specialists in their own way, but the detectives proved that they could outmanœuvre their prey. Their action restored order in the world and balance to society. Invariably, the objective of their assignments was to achieve moral ends. Equally important was the principle that they operated within the confines of the law and were incorruptible.[70] The memoirists did not hide their relations with criminals, but held that their aim was solely to obtain information and not to pursue shady dealings from which they would profit. They invariably appeared determined, clear about their task, and in control of the situation.[71]

Not only did the memoirs celebrate the qualities of the individual police detective, but their collective work environment appeared no less commendable. In as much as the majority of memoirists were Metropolitan Police CID men, they were singled out for praise as 'cogs in a machine, the workings of which are felt in continents other than ours and across other seas'.[72] Maurice Moser begins his memoir by pointing out that 'the name of "Scotland Yard" has an attraction for most people'.[73] Since many memoir books were written by Yard men, the investigation of offences after they had occurred—considered the more prestigious side of police detection—was overrepresented, thus obscuring the mundane chores of most detectives. Difficulties, however, are not omitted, but, on the contrary, are described in detail. The detective–narrators give the impression consistently that crime investigation is a hard and exacting vocation, demanding all one's energy and time.[74] The life of police detectives, however satisfactory their job, is conveyed as burdensome and altogether a far cry from the comfortable life led by many of the fictional detectives. Their work is in fact depicted as akin to the toil of manual workers, involving a great deal more physical exertion than that expended by the fictional middle-class private detectives, such as Holmes. Their daily tasks demand hours of surveillance or the tracking of suspects, sometimes lying on the ground,[75] sometimes in inclement weather, and often fighting lack of sleep. By contrast, the fictional private detective often got to the bottom of puzzling crimes while sitting in his armchair and using scientific deduction.[76] Some literary figures, such as Sexton Blake, were exposed to serious danger and physical harm, and employed physical might to great effect. Yet, physical confrontations with criminals, and the bodily strength required of genuine detectives, were highlighted more frequently in detective memoirs than in detective fiction.[77] Even if the point was not explicitly made, the impression given was that not only were police detectives similar to fictional detectives in ability, but that their work demanded both mental and physical labour. This combination made them more manly, versatile, and better equipped for the job. Linking police detectives with physical prowess may also have reassured the public that they were in control of the streets and other public spaces.

Still, while showing the sweat on the men's brows, the texts also had the effect of glamorizing police detective work, an aspect infrequently reflected in fiction. With all its hardships, investigative policing was commonly presented as a riveting, deeply satisfying job.[78] In Detective Inspector John Sweeney's view: 'There are to-day few walks of life likely to surpass that of the detective' in terms of intrinsic interest.[79] The routine in the work of detection involved not only physical hardiness but daring exploits. Detailed accounts of the risks faced by detectives heightened this impression.[80] Detective Chief Inspector Littlechild 'shudder[ed] to think of the consequences if these emissaries [the Fenians in the 1880s] had been successful in all their operations', warning that 'the public does not realize the peril in which it was placed'.[81] The stories recounted by the memoirists evoked the thrill of pursuing and capturing law-breakers and the sense of empowerment acquired thereby. Andrew Lansdowne recalled 'incidents and scenes which would appear to me to be fiction, if I did not know them to have been real'.[82] The occasional remark that the covert nature of certain tasks, particularly those performed by the Special Branch, prevented them from revealing details of the entire range of their activities, cloaked the occupation in even greater mystery.[83] The impression conveyed was that there was more than meets the eye in what detectives did, and that they were engaged in adventures that were even more daring than those portrayed in their texts.[84] By aggrandizing the threats facing them, they depicted themselves as saviours of society. Lacking a genteel background, and employed in work that was often rough and violent, the detective–narrator might not have become a hero of Holmes's stature, but he nevertheless projected a worldliness that few working people could hope to acquire.

Time and again, the authors threw the richness and variety of their work into relief.[85] Detective Chief Inspector Littlechild pointed to 'the ever-varying changes in the daily duty, in scene and incident, the uncertainty of movement and lack of monotony that necessarily attaches to the career, and the excitement that must be present with even the coldest and most unimaginative of natures', thereby highlighting the difference between police detection and the routine and repetitive work environments that were available in the labour markets of the time.[86] Moreover, the detective's duties could take him 'from end to end of the United Kingdom', and even abroad.[87] Detective Inspector Robert A. Fuller, writing about the shady as well as the exciting facets of his work, observed that the detective

> sees life at its various angles. Certainly he is oftener in its darkest places than other men are, and, like the rain, he goes among the just and unjust. He is from time to time in close personal contact with the duke and the beggar, the cardinal and the criminal; in fact, every sort and condition of man, woman, and child is encountered.[88]

As a source of shared experience and common identity, the detectives' place of employment seemed to foster team work and a sense of solidarity. Their milieu was not that of a gentleman, but, in contrast to imaginative literature, they were not lone detectives and had the backing of colleagues and the satisfaction of operating in an organization that promoted collective goals. The readers were also made to understand that police detectives were the beneficiaries of adequate material compensation and prospects for promotion.[89] Whether motivated to join the police as a result of a positive encounter with the forces of law and order in childhood, the stimulation of detective fiction, family tradition, the advice of a relative, or an inner drive to fulfil a social goal (see Chapter 2), all the memoirists gave the impression that they had made the right choice. Even if they had experienced moments of frustration and even boredom while fulfilling their duties, their vocation never failed them. Their fascination with crime had been rewarded. Their job, though based partly on physical tasks, was attuned to the norms of respectable society. The notion of the intrinsic advantages of working for the detective police implicitly underlies the great majority of memoirs.

Moreover, their employer was benevolent not only to its employees but also to outsiders and even to its adversaries. As seen in Chapter 3, the police organization, as well as individual detectives, were depicted as helping offenders make an honest living and even assisting them financially, thereby contributing to society by rehabilitating them.[90] It seemed important to detectives—as it was to pseudo-memoirists—to be seen as empathetic, while at the same time presenting themselves as reformers fighting against society's enemies not only by force but also by leading criminals to a path devoid of crime. In sum, detectives were portrayed as servants of the community.[91] Alluding now and then to their human failures, and to the less illustrious sides of police work, only rendered the detectives' accounts more credible.[92]

In essence, the memoirists and their colleagues were ultimately projected as social agents who benefited society as a whole, and not merely select individuals, as did private detectives. Although an undercurrent of belief in individualism pervades detective memoirs—'the central pillar of bourgeois subjectivity'[93]—the memoirists construed themselves as part of a collective entity, driven at once by a sense of inner vocation and public duty. Further, representing state authority and the law, they possessed powers of investigation and arrest denied to private detectives. Pointing to their role in guarding royalty and fighting terrorism underscored their devotion to their rulers and to meeting national needs.[94] The message communicated in the memoirists' stories about national security was that detectives not only looked after the public interest, but also enhanced their country's image. The memoirs thus appealed to the patriotic sentiments of the readers.

Notably, the police memoirists did not set out to represent their class origins or its causes. Neither did they show any identification with it. Class seemed irrelevant to their self-perception. Rather, they used the medium at their disposal to raise the status of their occupation, regardless of social lineage. Not only did the books endeavour to rectify misimpressions, but they also conveyed the deep pride the police detectives took in their work. It may be said that their attacks on detective fiction were an integral part of their efforts to construct an occupational, rather than a social, identity, which accorded with the professional ideal emerging at that time.[95] They demonstrated that police detectives were selected by merit, were highly skilled, could claim expertise, and were autonomous subjects and self-made men. Evincing a determination to be counted as public-sector professionals, and projecting detection not merely as a way of earning a living but as a calling, they clearly aimed at convincing the public that they were worthy of such a status.

Scattered evidence indicates that the sales of the memoirs, if not prodigious, were far from marginal. Some books came out in second editions in Britain, and others in a special American edition. They were read not only by ambitious young men who wanted to become detectives,[96] but even by the objects of detective surveillance.[97] Nevertheless, readers' interpretation of them is hard to measure. The audience may have read these texts without necessarily assimilating the messages inscribed in them. Some readers are known to have been sceptical about the books' content, aware that autobiographical works contained fictive or exaggerated elements, even if they purported to represent reality.[98]

It is plausible to assume, however, that other readers were not conscious of the filtering and sifting of past events, and anyway believed the authors' insistence on the veracity of the printed material. Conceivably, the vast majority of readers were not able to determine where fiction ended and fact began. Yet, even if readers believed only parts of the text, most likely they were led to be positively disposed to regard detectives in a sympathetic light. If so, detectives were instrumental in forging a positive image of their work and in improving their reputation. The fact that these memoirs spoke with authority, and that their narratives corroborated one another, must have strengthened their case. Ultimately, entering print culture in itself conferred social recognition.

If this was indeed the case, the image conveyed in the memoirs worked not only to heighten the professional and social status of detectives but also to reinforce support for the legal system in the country. As both narrator and protagonist, the author was a figure with whom readers could easily identify. Whatever impact the detective memoir had, it transmitted the notion of the indispensability of discipline in society, hand in hand with a recognition of the integrity and fair-mindedness of the police detectives who enforced it.

CONCLUSION

This book has shown how a small group of detectives operating in the headquarters of the Metropolitan Police of London (Scotland Yard), receiving little recognition and initially peripheral to the main thrust of law enforcement, developed into a confident network of specialized police officers whose impact was felt not only in Britain but also across the seas. This network epitomized a decisive shift in crime investigation from mainly private and commercial means in the eighteenth century to a predominantly public responsibility, serving in the name of the general good. Private sleuthing continued throughout the Victorian and Edwardian era, but plain-clothes policing, financed by public funds, was increasingly perceived as the primary apparatus for tackling crime in the country, manifesting the ascendancy of public values at the expense of self-help. Although concepts of laissez-faire were still popular, the governing elite aspired to tighten its control over society and strengthen state institutions. Maintaining effective law enforcement and meeting the security needs of modern society became imperative, and with it the fostering of an official detective community.

As a linchpin in the criminal justice administration, the police detective was charged with selecting his lines of inquiry, producing and evaluating information necessary to lay charges, and building evidence against suspects. This last aspect was particularly important to the British legal system, which prided itself on its uncompromising reliance on corroborative evidence for conviction, a requirement considered by many commentators as yet another indication of the moral superiority of the British nation, especially over France—a common comparative reference.[1] The detective's role was not limited to crime investigation, but extended to the containment of criminality through deterrence, signifying the system's preference for prevention over punishment. In a society experiencing a new lifestyle marked by the accumulation of vast wealth, growing consumption, and an expanding culture of leisure, side by side with endemic poverty, outbursts of political violence, and fears of rampant crime, the police detective fulfilled both functions—detection and prevention—in a concerted police effort to guard state interests, protect private and public property, keep the peace, and instil a sense of safety. The unprecedented growth of cities and towns, and with it the decline of traditional paternalistic power relationships, made the employment of these unseen policemen essential and provided the anonymity vital for their operations.

Confining the recruitment of detectives almost entirely to the uniformed ranks, which consisted mainly of working-class people, meant that detectives by and large shared this particular social and vocational background and, having served for several years in uniform, tended to become long-term police officers. Policy-makers were largely guided by the belief that experience in uniform, and thereafter in plain clothes, provided the most valuable method for the making of good detectives. In any event, vocational training was unavailable outside the police. At its core, albeit unspoken, the policy of internal recruitment of detectives reflected an unequivocal decision regarding the class origins of the official crime fighters in society. Although this policy was criticized both within and outside official circles for not opening the detective ranks—at least in the high-powered unit at Scotland Yard—to a more educated and sophisticated sector, it remained unchanged. Apparently, this was the model the Home Office and police authorities all over the country thought most suitable for the type of English detectives, and law enforcement generally, they had in mind.

Detectives developed vital aptitudes and skills during the long years they spent in service, acquiring a deeper understanding of the tasks at hand, the legal context of their vocation, the confines of the law, and the criminal world. Although initially detectives could draw on the accumulated experience of the Bow Street Runners and other law-enforcement officers who had engaged in detection before 1842, the occupation had lacked a structured body of knowledge, which thereafter evolved by trial and error. With the widening out of the scope of responsibilities, and increased manpower, the occupation was gradually enriched with formal internal rules, investigative practices, specialized knowledge, and expertise in certain fields, the latter most prominently in the central unit at Scotland Yard. No doubt, individual detectives across the hierarchy had significant input in this process.

Altogether, detection underwent a process of professionalization during the period, anchored as well in the policy of controlled entry, merit-based appointments and promotion, the relative autonomy detectives enjoyed in their workplace, and the extensive amount of paperwork they were required to do. The formalization of the training procedures of detectives in the early twentieth century further heightened the professional aura of the vocation, as did the invention of fingerprinting, increasingly identified with skilful observation and precision and the establishment of authoritative methods of criminal investigation acknowledged internationally. While detection was never part of the 'learned professions', and its status was ambiguous, as it was not a typical working-class trade, detectives developed a proficiency that set them apart from amateurs and endowed them with a socially recognized expertise, embellished by an aura of romanticism, which rendered their occupation unique.

In tandem with this process, police detectives forged a strong corporate identity that contributed to the consolidation of the occupation. In addition to the wearing of plain clothes, the distinctive identity of detectives also stemmed from their generally long-term careers and the prestige they commanded as crime investigators within and outside the police. The detectives' feelings of group solidarity are readily discernible in their own discourse. Their published memoirs, which focus almost exclusively on their occupational life, exude self-assurance, self-respect, a strong sense of purpose, and pride in their vocational achievements, reflected as well in biographical sketches that frequently appeared in the press. Reinforcing this trend were special privileges and employment conditions—including higher remuneration—enjoyed by detectives in comparison with uniformed police officers, with whom they worked closely. If this singular status distanced detectives from other police officers, it also strengthened internal cohesion among them.

Basing the modern police force pre-eminently on the preventive principle dictated that detectives constituted only a small portion of the total numerical strength of police officers in England. However, their impact was disproportionate to their numbers. The present study has sought to examine the unique features of the working life of detectives, highlighting not only their role in the enforcement of the law and their special position in the police organization, but also their extensive involvement in administrative work and the active participation of some in print culture, aspects that were unusual for their background. Yet, as shown in the second part of the book, detectives made their greatest mark in the realm of the perceptions of the public. Despite their origins, they garnered mounting attention and cast a captivating image invested with multiple meanings. The governing elite created the detective, but the growth of mass communications made him a household name.

The majority of the population was exposed neither to crime nor to detection, and learnt about the enforcement agents in a mediated way. This was not new. The media of the eighteenth century and even before had consistently shown great curiosity in matters of crime and punishment. Evolving in parallel to the huge expansion of printed matter and readership during the second half of the nineteenth century, the police detective made significant inroads in the various print formats of the time. Evidently, in the rising market economy of the Victorian period, with the media progressively propelled by the profit motive, publishers, editors, novelists, storytellers, journalists, and, towards the end of the century, newspaper magnates discerned that the figure of the detective appealed to all kinds of tastes. In the event, the contemporary print culture also acted as a fertile terrain for the exchange of views regarding this figure. The premiss underlying this volume is that the messages thus conveyed were of paramount importance for the police as a whole and for detectives in particular, since they were pivotal in shaping their standing in society and consequently had wider tangible ramifications.

The material that appeared in the print media about police detectives projected a kaleidoscope of motifs, approaches, and interpretations, integrating both high and popular culture. In an attempt to capture this heterogeneity, the present research has explored the media formats that had the most profound influence on the formation of the detective image—the press, fiction, and the detectives' own memoirs. Despite the varying significance of these materials, a clear conclusion emerges—namely, that the cumulative effect of the media exposure was greatly advantageous to the evolving occupation and its practitioners. To judge by the texts, if the police authorities aimed to dispel fears of undercover policing and to attain acceptance of the legitimacy of such a practice, they surely succeeded. Detectives first emerged in a society that viewed thief-takers as corrupt and self-serving. Yet, police detectives were largely dissociated from this taint, except in the late 1870s, when the complicity between senior police detectives at Scotland Yard and criminals revived it for a brief period. Moreover, if in the first half of the nineteenth century the image of detectives was inextricably bound up with the unsavoury figure of the spy, this link disappeared almost entirely in the latter half. Neither in the press, nor in fiction, and certainly not in their own memoirs did the figure of the detective come across as intrusive, oppressive, or subversively omnipresent. While certain residual fears of the dishonest policeman and his close intimacy with thieves, and of the ramifications of a covert style of policing, lingered on and accompanied detectives into the twentieth century, they were by no means widespread.

For its part, the police leadership, aside from aspiring to banish old prejudices, also sought favourable publicity about the professional performance of detectives. In this respect, however, they were not completely successful. Overall, the implicit intertextual exchange of views portrayed detectives as diligent and loyal to their vocation, but not necessarily as efficient. The fiction of the period persistently and forcefully gave expression to sentiments that police detectives were insufficiently competent and that effectiveness in crime control could be achieved only through close collaboration with the private sector. This literary formula, conveying the notion that the political elite could not adequately protect society against diverse threats, became pervasive in the 1880s and 1890s in the context of an increasingly competitive international economy and the resulting depression in Britain, which created a sense of insecurity in many sectors of society. In the press, while detectives basked in the limelight when successful, botched investigations elicited various levels of condemnation. Even in the detectives' life narratives, with their focus on triumphant closures of cases, the police detective does not manage to sweep clean the locality in which he works or to establish a crime-free society. As in serial detective fiction, his work never stops.

Undoubtedly, the fact of unabating crime in society hampered a more laudatory approach to detectives. No matter how successful detectives were, they were unable to rout crime completely, and therefore could never please the entire social spectrum. Since this book does not concentrate on the specific methods and practices of detectives, no attempt has been made to assess their overall performance, which in any case cannot be measured with any degree of accuracy. Clearly, however, there were built-in obstacles to quelling crime. Although detectives made good use of their plain clothes, this was not always conducive to good results. Catching criminals red-handed was only infrequently feasible, and tackling cases of burglary, thefts committed far from the victim, crimes of low visibility, or where no eyewitness, informer, or suspect was at hand was no simple matter. Producing incriminating evidence was often an uphill struggle or entirely unattainable. Yet, records show that police detectives made many mistakes in pursuing lines of investigation and in pinpointing a suspect. In fact, only a small proportion of reported crimes were resolved through the efforts of detectives. The depiction of police detectives thus reflected both the inherent limitations of law enforcement and the inability of the small number of official crime fighters to catch all the culprits and bring them to justice. Significantly, standards of police behaviour also affected perceived police performance. That allegations of misconduct and abuses of power during investigations or other detection activities were highly publicized from time to time strengthened criticism and cast a shadow on the detectives' professionalism, although with time the press was more troubled by ineffective police efforts than by controversial methods. In fiction, class was another factor in the ambiguous evaluation of police detectives' efficacy. Because of detectives' humble origins, the fiction of the period was not inclined to portray them as towering over other characters in the narrative and becoming the focal point of the story. In contrast to their depiction in the press, they were not portrayed as highly capable—a trope typically associated with the well-born detective; only in a minority of literary texts did they attain the stature of the near perfect gentlemanly private detective.

Still, however circumscribed the detective's reputation, and despite the defects that fiction writers habitually ascribed to him, the evidence at our disposal signifies decisively that the positive image of police detectives coalesced as the century drew to a close. The press—the most effective medium of communication at the time—was mainly responsible for this. Precisely against the growing pessimism about the resilience of British society in the late Victorian years, and in the wake of the Fenian terror as well as the preoccupation with Jack the Ripper in the 1880s, the press gave pride of place to reports about the successful suppression of the anarchist threat during the next decade, highlighting the role of plain-clothes crime fighters and showing a broader acquiescence in the use of secretive means to attain greater effectiveness in this period. With the exception of its radical and socialist margins, the press overwhelmingly conveyed, in both newspapers and periodicals, that, even if police detectives were not infallible, they served the purpose for which they had come into existence; they did their best to confront the pressing need to eliminate danger to their surroundings and to the nation and generally produced good results. In appraising police work during the two decades before the First World War, the press increasingly referred to police detectives as approximating the ideal of professional functionaries. From an object of fear, viewed with reservations, the detective had metamorphosed into a symbol of service and benevolent reform.

Moreover, both the established and the popular press shared a growing fascination with the individual detective, significantly investing him with qualities held up by the middle classes, to which most journalists belonged: determination, quick-wittedness, boldness, an entrepreneurial spirit, and a drive for self-improvement. Added to these qualities were the distinctly masculine values that the police aimed to convey, reflected too in press coverage of both uniformed and plain-clothes officers. This blend of attributes moulded a singularly complex figure, blurring class boundaries. Detectives who were repeatedly assigned to lead highly publicized investigations became celebrities—an order of classless knights. Operating almost exclusively in urban environments, the police detective came to be associated with the imposition of authority on the 'city of dreadful night' and with making the streets safer, and consequently also with city life and modernity itself.

The proliferation of biographical sketches and memoirs of police detectives in the press and in book form in the late nineteenth century amplified this impression. They also delineated the police detective as someone who had managed to overcome the constrictions of background and achieved both economic advancement and a position of authority in society, rendering him a potential role model particularly for the public at the lower end of the social scale. Other distinctive attributes of the police detective underscored in these texts were his embodiment of a strong sense of self side by side with the values of a public servant. This constituted a kind of unwitting response to the emphasis intrinsic in detective fiction on the importance of both components—individuality and a collective consciousness—in law enforcement. Authors spared no effort in stressing the contribution to criminal justice of the detective as an individual: his priorities, decisions, and movements were shown to determine the investigative process. Yet, his institutional affiliation forms the backbone of each portrayal. This was in fact true for many other types of texts. That Scotland Yard, which harboured the most proficient and talented detectives in the country and had acquired international fame, was often posited as the collective face of police detectives, and gained the greatest exposure by far in every form of media, reinforced the heroic aura of all police detectives.

Discourses were no doubt instruments of power, but, as is widely accepted today, one cannot assume audiences' reactions from the information presented to them. Readers were not passive recipients, but had the power to choose what to read and to respond in an independent and even subversive manner. Moreover, various factors influenced effective information-processing, including the origin, education, political orientation, age, gender, experience, and temperament of the reader, and the specific conditions under which the information was received. These variables cannot be extracted in historical research about the Victorian and Edwardian period. Yet, despite these shortcomings, some generalizations can be made about readers' perceptions of detectives and hence about the public as a whole. It is known that some treated the salutary reading material with reservations. After all, alternative interpretations were available to the public. Certainly, audiences were aware of competing accounts of the achievements of detectives. Moreover, evidence other than narratives and discourses confirms the diverse response to them. As noted, segments of the working classes who had personally experienced the heavy hand of detectives (and other police officers) remained hostile to the forces of law and order throughout the period, manifested in the attitude of the policed, commonly inarticulate population in rough areas towards detectives making an arrest, and to certain 'underworld journalists' who were mistaken for police detectives. Similarly, profound suspicions were common among certain political groups and other populations targeted by the police.

Notwithstanding, since armies of readers read the mass-circulation mainstream press and, albeit to a much lesser extent, detective memoirs, and since both formats were widely perceived as recording reality, their repeated supportive presentations must have been treated by many as accurate accounts. As suggested by this study, detectives did not always live up to the ideal behaviour as posited in police manuals and directives, but a fair amount of their activity (including failures, but also preventive action) never reached the media, either because of the detectives' underhanded operations or because the police controlled the information released to the public. The press, for its part, despite dissatisfaction with certain police attitudes, refrained at times from giving unfavourable material any publicity. Its narrative style itself tended to aggrandize the detectives' feats. The resulting selectivity of law-and-order news and commentary meant that readers were exposed to partial and therefore biased coverage. In addition, as indicated in this book, quite a few observers exonerated detectives of responsibility for failures, pointing to constraints imposed by the legal system on detectives' conduct during investigations as limiting their ability to perform their duties to the fullest. Such a standpoint reflected either criticism of the system as too liberal, or support for it as indicating the moral pre-eminence of the British people, who preferred due process and individual rights to incrimination at any cost. Whatever the case, the police detective emerged as a symbol of adherence to legal procedures.

Paradoxically, even the popular portrayal of detectives in fictional tales might have enhanced the reputation of the occupation. Despite the message of ineptitude emanating from detective fiction, it could be said to have advertised the role of detectives in society in sketching the occupation as a whole as necessary and, ideally, requiring exceptional cerebral ability and expertise. Moreover, even though the police detective was often depicted in literary texts as far less clever than his private counterpart, he was nevertheless envisaged not only as indispensable but also as guaranteeing impartial treatment. Notably, the pseudo-memoirs, which flourished in the middle decades of the Victorian era, quite consistently described the police detective in a complimentary way, as did other fictional texts from time to time.

Taken as a whole, the contemporary printed discourse about detectives thus constituted a powerful means for boosting and even idealizing their standing in society, thereby confirming the authority of the police. By implication, it may be said, in support of Foucault's conception, that the print media actually served as a 'discourse of the law', helping to create a 'disciplinary society' without using overt coercion.[2] The image of the detective figure made surveillance and enforcement seem more natural. However, while the corpus of printed texts certainly conveyed the necessity of maintaining the rule of law and the need for inspecting public spaces and regulating behaviour as ways of investigating as well as containing crime, at its heart lay the message that the police should take care not to be too intrusive, and that there was a measure of control beyond which the individual's freedom and privacy might not be invaded.

The importance of print culture in disseminating the favourable image of the detective, while crucial, was not exclusive. The style of police detection as it was moulded by the political elite, combined with the manner in which the non-uniformed policemen interpreted their role in practice, buttressed this image. Social control was a major police goal, and disagreeable means were progressively employed for securing it, but this goal was constrained not only by utilitarian considerations or cost but by the guiding principle of appearing moderate and fair. In addition to impacting on operational conduct, this principle was embodied in the very fact of the small number of detectives throughout the period, and the delayed founding of a political branch. Presumably, the reality that detectives worked closely with uniformed officers, did not try hard to conceal their occupational identity, and were widely known in their locality dispelled residual fears of conspiratorial intentions and conveyed the notion that detectives curbed their own discretionary powers and freedom of action. No doubt the fact that the police were generally unarmed and did not resemble a military police promoted a relaxed attitude towards detectives, whose standing was bound up with that of the entire police force. Moreover, in Clive Emsley's discerning remarks, 'the lack of the occasional mass and murderous politics found elsewhere...together with the stable balance of the two-party system within a generally accepted and revered constitutional monarchy, enabled the perception to emerge and the assertion to be made that England was different' and that 'England enjoyed a unique form of non-political and non-violent police'.[3]

Indeed, whether in texts purporting to depict reality or in fictive texts, the print culture inculcated the theme that the English detective, being English, did things differently. Even if complaints were voiced that the English detective was overexposed and therefore less efficient, these very attributes made him appear much less menacing than his continental counterpart. Moreover, although the restraints imposed by the criminal justice system were viewed by some commentators as hampering his ability to succeed, this was often interpreted as a willingness to sacrifice a measure of crime control for the sake of legal and ethical standards, again in striking contrast to his opposite number across the Channel. Covert behaviour and surveillance were increasingly tolerated, but the accepted opinion was that the English detective resorted to such means to a much lesser extent, and that he did not usually employ deceit unless no other option existed. The notion of the 'English character' was never fixed, cohesive, or unchallenged.[4] However, in the years before the war, the police detective emerged as a sort of national icon, representing much that typified the perceptions of many Englishmen and women about themselves and their institutions—namely, that more than most other nations they were fair-minded and kept a just balance between order and authority, on the one hand, and individual liberty and moral standards of behaviour, on the other.

Conceivably, as was highly desired by police officials, this prevalent detective image encouraged the respectable public (though not the lower end of the social spectrum) to come to the aid of police detectives when the need arose and to provide them with information—so vital for discovering and incriminating culprits. In effect, the strength of the English detective lay to a large extent in his image of restraint and self-control, as it hid the power at his disposal and allowed him more freely to enforce the law in ways he considered desirable. If anything, the discourse about the visibility and ethical preferences of the English detective enabled the public to tolerate reported cases of detectives' misconduct as isolated incidents that did not reflect on the system as a whole.

In addition to raising their morale and self-identity, the growing esteem for police detectives could not but benefit the stature of the state. It helped shape behaviour and hegemonic norms in society and enhanced the political sovereignty of the central as well as local government, which could then more easily manipulate consent. By reinforcing bourgeois precepts and ideals, police detection promoted the agenda of the governing class. Ultimately, the figure of the police detective echoed the tensions, hopes, and concerns of the time. If his rise during the mid-nineteenth century coincided with many of the fundamental changes that heightened Britain's supremacy as an industrial, commercial, and urban society, turning it into a world centre of modernity, the consolidation of his image at the close of the century took place against less sanguine trends. Britannia continued to rule the waves and was an industrial and imperial power; the worst aspects of early industrialization had been eased and living conditions improved. Yet, the economy underwent a deep depression in the late nineteenth century, social problems and poverty still loomed large, and many of the hard-and-fast values of Victorian society were crumbling. Moreover, preceding the outbreak of the First World War, additional ominous changes were in the air and apprehensions about the future of the nation and Empire mounted. Whether the public shared these apprehensions or not, by and large it could draw a measure of comfort and reassurance from the commanding figure of the detective, whose professional standing was then gaining strength, that the authorities were in control and that social problems were being handled. That England had produced a law-enforcer of such high calibre could also serve as a source of pride. While the fictional portrayal of the police detective introduced some doubts about his ability to fulfil the mission entrusted to him, reflecting current cracks in public complacency, these were overridden by a wider belief in his role and his contribution to the well-being of society. The figure of the detective thus satisfied a variety of psychological needs spanning class divisions. All in all, then, the plain-clothes policeman played an integrative role in English society.

NOTES

INTRODUCTION

1. No extant statistics could be found.
2. A notable exception is Stefan Petrow's *Policing Morals* (Oxford: Clarendon Press, 1994), which includes a significant discussion of detective work in London during 1870–1914. For articles and chapters in books, see Paul Lawrence, '"Scoundrels and Scallywags, and Some Honest Men...": Memoirs and the Self-Image of French and English Policemen, *c*.1870–1939', in Barry S. Godfrey, Clive Emsley, and Graeme Dunstall (eds), *Comparative Histories of Crime* (Cullompton: Willan, 2003); R. M. (Bob) Morris, '"Crime Does Not Pay": Thinking again about Detectives in the First Century of the Metropolitan Police', in Clive Emsley and Haia Shpayer-Makov (eds), *Police Detectives in History, 1750–1950* (Aldershot: Ashgate, 2006); R. M. (Bob) Morris, 'History of Criminal Investigation', in Tim Newburn, Tom Williamson, and Alan Wright (eds), *Handbook of Criminal Investigation* (Cullompton: Willan Publishing, 2007).
3. Lucia Zedner, 'Policing before and after the Police', *British Journal of Criminology*, 46/1 (2006), 81.
4. John Beattie's book *The First English Detectives: The Bow Street Runners and the Policing of London, 1750–1840* is forthcoming.
5. 'London Police Duty', *Leisure Hour*, 28 (26 Apr. 1879), 278.
6. 'Our Police System', *Dark Blue*, 2 (Feb. 1872), 697.
7. 'The Police System of London', *Edinburgh Review*, 96 (July 1852), 11.
8. 'The Police System of London', 12.
9. George Dilnot, *Scotland Yard* (London: Percival Marshall & Co., 1915), 62.

CHAPTER 1. POLICE DETECTION IN ENGLAND: EIGHTEENTH CENTURY–FIRST WORLD WAR

1. *General Instruction Book* (London, 1829), 1–2.
2. The City of London held a city status and maintained its own independent police force in an area of just over one square mile.
3. *General Instruction Book*, 20.
4. Edwin Chadwick, 'Preventive Police', *London Review*, 1 (Feb. 1829), 271–3.
5. Chadwick, 'Preventive Police', 273.
6. Historians have emphasized different sets of causes for the rise of the new police. According to orthodox historians, police reform was mainly motivated by the fear of crime and mob disorder (Robert Reiner, *The Politics of the Police* (Brighton: Wheatsheaf Books, 1985), 12).
7. Clive Emsley, 'The History of Crime and Crime Control Institutions', in Mike Maguire, Rod Morgan, and Robert Reiner (eds), *The Oxford Handbook of Criminology* (3rd edn; Oxford: Oxford University Press, 2002), 205.

8. George Robb, *White-Collar Crime in Modern England* (Cambridge: Cambridge University Press, 1992), 1–3.
9. Chadwick, 'Preventive Police', 253.
10. David Philips, 'Three "Moral Enterpreneurs" and the Creation of a "Criminal Class" in England, c.1790–1840s', *Crime, histoire et sociétés/Crime, History & Societies*, 7/1 (2003), 3.
11. In the view of the revisionist school, the main reason for the creation of the new police was the desire for a force that would stabilize class relationships (Reiner, *The Politics of the Police*, 25). Recent historical research suggests a more nuanced interpretation of the causes of reform (see, e.g., Reiner, *The Politics of the Police*, 37–9).
12. Stanley H. Palmer, *Police and Protest in England and Ireland 1780–1850* (Cambridge: Cambridge University Press, 1988), 192; Ewart W. Clay (ed.), *The Leeds Police, 1836–1974* (Leeds: E. J. Arnold & Son, 1975), 27.
13. Pat Thane, 'Government and Society in England and Wales, 1750–1914', in F. M. L. Thompson (ed.), *The Cambridge Social History of Britain 1750–1950* (Cambridge: Cambridge University Press, 1990), iii. 11–12; Allyson May, 'Advocates and Truth-Seeking in the Old Bailey Courtroom', *Journal of Legal History*, 26/1 (2005), 89–90.
14. Mark Neocleous, 'Social Police and the Mechanisms of Prevention', *British Journal of Criminology*, 40/4 (2000), 716. For Liverpool, see Michael Brogden, *The Police: Autonomy and Consent* (London: Academic Press, 1982), 52.
15. David Garland, *Punishment and Modern Society* (Oxford: Clarendon Press, 1991), 145.
16. Francis M. Dodsworth, '"Civic" Police and the Condition of Liberty: The Rationality of Governance in Eighteenth-Century England', *Social History*, 29 (May 2004), 592.
17. John L. McMullan, 'The Arresting Eye: Discourse, Surveillance and Disciplinary Administration in Early English Police Thinking', *Social and Legal Studies*, 7/1 (1998), 99.
18. See, e.g., *Leeds Mercury*, 23 Feb. 1839, p. 7.
19. David J. V. Jones, 'The New Police, Crime and People in England and Wales, 1829–1888', *Transactions of the Royal Historical Society*, 5th ser., 33 (1983), 164–5.
20. Andrew T. Harris, *Policing the City* (Columbus: Ohio State University, 2004), 91.
21. *General Instruction Book*, 41; Police Orders, 3 Oct. 1829. For the Norwich Police, see Maurice Morson, *A Force Remembered* (Derby: Breedon Books, 2000), 12, and, for the Leeds Police, see Clay (ed.), *The Leeds Police*, 13.
22. Police Orders, 3 June 1835.
23. On the evolution of the office of constable, see T. A. Critchley, *A History of Police in England and Wales* (Montclair, NJ: Patterson Smith, 1972; first published 1967), 8–22; On the rural police before mid-century, see Robert D. Storch, 'Policing Rural Southern England before the Police: Opinion and Practice, 1830–1856', in Douglas Hay and Francis Snyder (eds), *Policing and Prosecution in Britain 1750–1850* (Oxford: Clarendon Press, 1989).
24. Clive Emsley, *The English Police* (Hemel Hempstead: Harvester Wheatsheaf, 1991), 11–13; Clive Emsley, *Crime and Society in England, 1750–1900*

(London: Longman, 1987), 172–4; Clive Emsley, *The Great British Bobby* (London: Quercus, 2010; first published 2009), 13–20, 26–38; J. M. Beattie, 'Early Detection: The Bow Street Runners in Late Eighteenth-Century London', in Emsley and Shpayer-Makov(eds), *Police Detectives in History*, 15.
25. David Philips, *Crime and Authority in Victorian England* (London: Croom Helm, 1977), 60–1; Ruth Paley, '"An Imperfect, Inadequate and Wretched System"? Policing London before Peel', *Criminal Justice History*, 10 (1989), 114; Bruce P. Smith, 'The Emergence of Public Prosecution in London, 1790–1850', *Yale Journal of Law & the Humanities*, 18/1 (2006), 41; J. M. Beattie, 'Garrow and the Detectives: Lawyers and Policemen at the Old Bailey in the Late Eighteenth Century', *Crime, histoire et sociétés/Crime, History & Societies*, 11/2 (2007), 8; Harris, *Policing the City*, 13.
26. R. W. England, Jr, 'Investigating Homicides in Northern England, 1800–1824', *Criminal Justice History*, 6 (1985), 115–17.
27. J. M. Beattie, *Policing and Punishment in London, 1660–1750* (Oxford: Oxford University Press, 2001), 131; Peter King, *Crime, Justice, and Discretion in England 1740–1820* (Oxford: Oxford University Press, 2000), 65, 74–5.
28. King, *Crime, Justice, and Discretion*, 62; Leon Radzinowicz, *A History of English Criminal Law and its Administration from 1750* (London: Stevens & Sons, 1956–68), iv. 225.
29. Beattie, *Policing and Punishment*, 131.
30. J. A. Sharpe, *Crime in Early Modern England 1550–1750* (London: Longman, 1984), 21.
31. Douglas Hay, 'Property, Authority and Criminal Law', in Douglas Hay et al., *Albion's Fatal Tree* (New York: Pantheon Books, 1975), 18.
32. Hay, 'Property, Authority and Criminal Law', 22–3, 40–9; John Beattie, *Crime and the Courts in England 1660–1800* (Princeton: Princeton University Press, 1986), ch. 8.
33. David Eastwood, *Governing Rural England* (Oxford: Clarendon Press, 1994), 206–7.
34. Notably, according to common law, every citizen had the right to effect arrests and initiate prosecutions as well as to receive rewards for providing detective services.
35. Smith, 'The Emergence of Public Prosecution in London', 37.
36. Douglas Hay and Francis Snyder, 'Using the Criminal Law, 1750–1850: Policing, Private Prosecution, and the State', in Hay and Snyder (eds), *Policing and Prosecution in Britain*, 21.
37. King, *Crime, Justice, and Discretion*, 17. Malcolm Gaskill, *Crime and Mentalities in Early Modern England* (Cambridge: Cambridge University Press, 2000), 161–73.
38. Philips, *Crime and Authority*, 129; Beattie, *Crime and the Courts*, 42–8, 50–5; John H. Langbein, *The Origins of Adversary Criminal Trial* (Oxford: Oxford University Press, 2003), 148–58.
39. Bruce P. Smith, 'English Criminal Justice Administration, 1650–1850: A Historiographical Essay', *Law and History Review*, 25/3 (Fall 2007), 620–1.
40. Beattie, *Crime and the Courts*, 35.
41. Historian Peter King observes that 'with their extensive rights to search labourers' cottages for game or poaching equipment the gamekeepers represented a powerful form of private policing' (*Crime, Justice, and Discretion*, 64).

42. Beattie, 'Garrow and the Detectives', 8.
43. Ruth Paley, 'Thief-Takers in London in the Age of the McDaniel Gang, c.1745–1754', in Hay and Snyder (eds), *Policing and Prosecution in Britain*, 334.
44. Radzinowicz, *A History of English Criminal Law*, iii. 31–3; Critchley, *A History of Police*, 19; Norma Landau, *The Justices of the Peace, 1679–1760* (Berkeley and Los Angeles: University of California Press, 1984), 185; Emsley, *The English Police*, 18.
45. Paley, 'Thief-Takers in London', 304.
46. J. M. Beattie, 'Sir John Fielding and Public Justice: The Bow Street Magistrates' Court, 1754–1780', *Law and History Review*, 25 (Spring 2007), 64. See also Tim Wales, 'Thief-Takers and their Clients in Later Stuart London', in Paul Griffiths and Mark S. R. Jenner (eds), *Londinopolis* (Manchester: Manchester University Press, 2000), 67, 70.
47. David Bentley, *English Criminal Justice in the Nineteenth Century* (London: Hambledon Press, 1998), 7.
48. Beattie, 'Early Detection', 16.
49. Paley, 'Thief-Takers in London', 305–11.
50. Paley, 'Thief-Takers in London', 326–8.
51. Paley, 'Thief-Takers in London', 323.
52. Beattie, *Policing and Punishment*, 228.
53. David Philips, 'Good Men to Associate and Bad Men to Conspire: Associations for the Prosecution of Felons in England, 1760–1860', in Hay and Snyder (eds), *Policing and Prosecution in Britain*, 115, 120, 122.
54. For further details, see Adrian Shubert, 'Private Initiative in Law Enforcement: Associations for the Prosecution of Felons, 1744–1856', in Victor Bailey (ed.), *Policing and Punishment in Nineteenth-Century Britain* (London: Croom Helm, 1981), 25–41; Peter King, 'Prosecution Associations and their Impact in Eighteenth-Century Essex', in Hay and Snyder (eds), *Policing and Prosecution in Britain*, 71–207; Eastwood, *Governing Rural England*, 230–3.
55. Philips, 'Good Men to Associate', 138.
56. John Styles, 'Sir John Fielding and the Problem of Criminal Investigation in Eighteenth-Century England', *Transactions of the Royal Historical Society*, 5th ser., 33 (1983), 127; John Styles, 'Print and Policing: Crime Advertising in Eighteenth-Century Provincial England', in Hay and Snyder (eds), *Policing and Prosecution in Britain*, 56, 59, 61; King, *Crime, Justice, and Discretion*, 58. See also ch. 5.
57. Styles, 'Print and Policing', 72.
58. Beattie, 'Sir John Fielding and Public Justice', 62; Beattie, 'Garrow and the Detectives', 8.
59. David J. Cox, *A Certain Share of Low Cunning: A History of the Bow Street Runners, 1792–1839* (Cullompton: Willan Publishing, 2010), 241.
60. Beattie, 'Early Detection', 22.
61. Cox, *A Certain Share of Low Cunning*, 28.
62. Anthony Babington, *A House in Bow Street* (Chichester: Barry Rose Law Publishers, 1999), 186–7, 190.
63. Radzinowicz, *A History of English Criminal Law*, iii. 55.
64. Paley, 'Thief-Takers in London', 337.
65. Babington, *A House in Bow Street*, 192–3.

66. Radzinowicz, *A History of English Criminal Law*, iii. 41–54.
67. For further details, see Styles, 'Sir John Fielding and the Problem of Criminal Investigation', 127–49.
68. Beattie, 'Garrow and the Detectives', 5–6, 19.
69. Chadwick, 'Preventive Police', 259.
70. Smith, 'The Emergence of Public Prosecution in London', 32–3, 47–62.
71. *Committee on the State of the Police of the Metropolis*, PP, vol. 5 (1816), 42.
72. Cox, *A Certain Share of Low Cunning*, 38.
73. Peter King, 'Newspaper Reporting and Attitudes to Crime and Justice in Late-Eighteenth- and Early-Nineteenth-Century London', *Continuity and Change*, 22/1 (2007), 78; Beattie, 'Garrow and the Detectives', 5.
74. Philip Thurmond Smith, *Policing Victorian London* (Westport: Greenwood Press, 1985), 64–5; King, *Crime, Justice, and Discretion*, 78–9; Cox, *A Certain Share of Low Cunning*, 43–5.
75. Cox, *A Certain Share of Low Cunning*, 32.
76. Jones, 'The New Police', 154.
77. Elaine A. Reynolds, *Before the Bobbies* (Stanford: Stanford University Press, 1998), 76–7. For an account of the Thames River Police, see Geoffrey Budworth, *The River Beat: The Story of London's River Police since 1798* (London: Historical Publications, 1997).
78. Michael S. Pike, *The Principles of Policing* (Houndmills: Macmillan, 1985), 8.
79. See, e.g., Paley, '"An Imperfect, Inadequate and Wretched System"?'; Beattie, *Policing and Punishment*; Harris, *Policing the City*.
80. Radzinowicz, *A History of English Criminal Law*, iii. 328.
81. Carolyn A. Conley, *The Unwritten Law* (New York: Oxford University Press, 1991), 30; Eastwood, *Governing Rural England*, 237–8; Harris, *Policing the City*, 50.
82. *Select Committee on the Police of the Metropolis*, PP, vol. 4 (1822) (henceforth *1822 Committee*), 101; John Wade, *A Treatise on the Police and Crimes of the Metropolis*, intro. by J. J. Tobias (Montclair, NJ: Patterson Smith, 1972; first published 1829), 2; *Northern Star*, 23 Mar. 1839, p. 4, reporting about a Chartist meeting in which harsh criticism was levelled at proposals to set up police forces in rural England; Radzinowicz, *A History of English Criminal Law*, iii. 344–5; iv. 159.
83. A. A. Clarke, *The Policemen of Hull* (Beverley, East Yorkshire: Hutton Press, 1992), 8.
84. Palmer, *Police and Protest*, 40.
85. Ben Wilson, *What Price Liberty?* (London: Faber and Faber, 2009), 142–3.
86. *1822 Committee*, 101.
87. Wilson, *What Price Liberty?*, 149.
88. Wilson, *What Price Liberty?*, 149.
89. Radzinowicz, *A History of English Criminal Law*, iii. 345.
90. Eastwood, *Governing Rural England*, 192. For the view of the supporters of police reform, see Radzinowicz, *A History of English Criminal Law*, iv. 229.
91. Eastwood, *Governing Rural England*, 199.
92. See, e.g., *Committee on the State of the Police of the Metropolis (Third Report)*, PP, vol. 8 (1818), 32, and the reaction of the *Durham Advertiser* to the County Police Act of 1839, in David Philips, 'A "Weak" State? The English

State, the Magistracy and the Reform of Policing in the 1830s', *English Historical Review*, 119/483 (2004), 876. According to the editor of the paper, 'the police, whatever they may be at the outset, will inevitably degenerate into government spies'.
93. The word 'detector' had, however, a long pedigree, going back to at least the sixteenth century (*OED*). In 1828 *The Times* referred to Vidocq, head of the Paris detective department, as a 'detector' (29 Oct. 1828, p. 2).
94. Philips, 'A "Weak" State?', 876. For other examples, see Storch, 'Policing Rural Southern England', 244; Cox, *A Certain Share of Low Cunning*, 125.
95. Indeed, the 1818 parliamentary committee rejected the concept of preventive police, as it 'would make every servant of every house a spy on the actions of his master, and all classes of society spies on each other' (*Committee on the State of the Police of the Metropolis (Third Report)*, PP, vol. 8 (1818), 32).
96. Cox, *A Certain Share of Low Cunning*, 58.
97. Quoted in Sissela Bok, *Secrets* (New York: Pantheon Books, 1982), 171.
98. Bok, *Secrets*, 25.
99. David Vincent, *The Culture of Secrecy* (Oxford: Oxford University Press, 1998), 5.
100. See the reaction of the home secretary to the use of disguise by a police constable in 1845, in Bernard Porter, *The Origins of the Vigilant State* (London: Weidenfeld and Nicolson, 1987), 5 n. 14.
101. Quoted in Vincent, *The Culture of Secrecy*, 92.
102. *The Times*, 21 Apr. 1842, p. 3, 29 Apr. 1842, p. 4; Cox, *A Certain Share of Low Cunning*, 48–55.
103. Radzinowicz, *A History of English Criminal Law*, iii. 249–51, 470. For an account of the French police at the time, see pp. 539–74. For reasons why the French model was rejected, see Palmer, *Police and Protest*, 71–3.
104. William Cobbett in *Parliamentary Debates*, vol. 20, 7 Aug. 1833, col. 405.
105. Reynolds, *Before the Bobbies*, 5. For an explanation of 'the abrupt acceptance of an idea that for generations had been unthinkable', see Palmer, *Police and Protest*, 286–9. The quotation is on p. 286.
106. Emsley, *The English Police*, 22.
107. A. Wynter, 'The Police and the Thieves', *Quarterly Review*, 99 (June 1856), 163.
108. Wilbur R. Miller, *Cops and Bobbies* (Chicago: University of Chicago Press, 1977; first published 1973), 33.
109. Radzinowicz, *A History of English Criminal Law*, iv. 162.
110. Robert D. Storch, 'The Policeman as Domestic Missionary: Urban Discipline and Popular Culture in Northern England, 1850–1880', *Journal of Social History*, 9 (Summer 1976), 482.
111. *Select Committee on the Petition of Frederick Young and Others*, PP, vol. 13 (1833), 407; Palmer, *Police and Protest*, 312–13.
112. *Select Committee on the Petition of Frederick Young and Others*, PP, vol. 13 (1833), 407.
113. Police Orders, 27 Apr. 1842 and 1 May 1842; Radzinowicz, *A History of English Criminal Law*, iv. 187.
114. *Manchester Times and Gazette*, 15 July 1842, p. 2; Belton Cobb, *The First Detectives and the Early Career of Richard Mayne, Commissioner of Police* (London: Faber and Faber, 1957), 146–8, 153, 172–3.

115. 'Memorandum in Relation to Detective Powers of Police', 14 June 1842, Commissioners of Police of the Metropolis to Home Secretary James Graham, p. 13, HO45/OS/292.
116. Charles Reith, *A New Study of Police History* (Edinburgh: Oliver and Boyd, 1956), 221–2; S. H. Jeyes and F. D. How, *The Life of Sir Howard Vincent* (London: George Allen, 1912), 74.
117. *The Times*, 14 Apr. 1842, p. 3; *Examiner*, 30 Apr. 1842, p. 284; 'Memorandum', 14 June 1842, p. 13, HO45/OS/292.
118. See, e.g., *Morning Chronicle*, 7 May 1840, p. 5; *Ipswich Journal*, 26 Apr. 1842, p. 4; *Examiner*, 30 Apr. 1842, pp. 283–4.
119. *The Times*, 8 May 1840, p. 4. In the event, the identity of the culprit was discovered accidentally by a French woman, whose evidence was instrumental in sending him to the gallows (see ch. 4, p. 168).
120. Radzinowicz, *A History of English Criminal Law*, iv. 173–5. Chief magistrate at Bow Street, Frederick Roe (1832–9), an implacable foe of the Metropolitan Police, believed that the force should restrict its tasks to street duty and not deal with intricate crime (*Select Committee on the Police of the Metropolis*, PP, vol. 16 (1834), 107). The Bow Street Runners did not join the Metropolitan Police. An anonymous contributor to the *Edinburgh Review* explained that they were 'unable to confine their energies within the iron limits of the new discipline, and with conscious superiority unwilling to obey new masters, retired into private life' ('The Police System of London', 12).
121. *Southern Star and London and Brighton Patriot*, 28 June 1840, p. 3.
122. *Examiner*, 30 Apr. 1842, pp. 283–4. For details of the case, see Douglas G. Browne, *The Rise of Scotland Yard* (New York: G. P. Putnam's Sons, 1956), 114–18.
123. See the reaction of the police commissioners to the coverage in the press, 'Memorandum', 14 June 1842, pp. 2, 9, HO45/OS/292.
124. The Home Office regarded the plan 'as an experiment' (S. M. Phillipps to Commissioner of Police, 20 June 1842, HO65/14).
125. The men were constitutionally in the A Division in Whitehall, but, as the headquarters of this division was located in the commissioners' office, they served in practice as detective staff at the Metropolitan Police headquarters, called Scotland Yard as it backed onto a courtyard named Great Scotland Yard (Browne, *The Rise of Scotland Yard*, 80). That is why the term 'Scotland Yard' is commonly used to refer simultaneously to the Metropolitan Police, to its headquarters, to the CID in London, or more specifically to its squad in the head office. In 1890, the headquarters of the Metropolitan Police moved to a new site, on the Victoria Embankment, which James Monro, the commissioner at the time, named New Scotland Yard.
126. Letter by Commissioners, 23 Aug. 1842, HO45/OS/292.
127. Memo by R. Mayne, 23 Jan. 1854, MEPO7/16; *Departmental Committee on the Metropolitan Police*, 1868, HO347/1 (henceforth *1868 Committee*), 313.
128. Memo by R. Mayne, 11 Nov. 1845, MEPO7/11, and Police Orders, 17 Aug. 1862.
129. Since the present volume deals with fully-fledged detectives, all references to plain-clothes officers refer to them exclusively and not to temporary plain-clothes officers, unless otherwise specified.

130. *1868 Committee*, 277–81, 306.
131. *1868 Committee*, 14.
132. See, e.g., Charles Manby Smith, *The Little World of London; or, Pictures in Little of London Life* (London: Arthur Hall, Virtue, & Co., 1857), 145–6; George Augustus Sala, *Twice Round the Clock; or, The Hours of the Day and Night in London* (New York: Leicester University Press, 1971; first published in serial form in 1858; in book form 1859), 65.
133. Christopher Wood, *William Powell Frith: A Painter and his World* (Stroud: Sutton Publishing, 2006), 77.
134. 10 Dec. 1845, MEPO7/11.
135. Samuel Blackstone, 'Paternal Government', *Saint Pauls Magazine*, 12 (June 1873), 725.
136. Memo of 23 Jan. 1854, MEPO7/16.
137. Emsley, *Crime and Society in England*, 228–9.
138. For details, see K. R. M. Short, *The Dynamite War* (Dublin: Gill and Macmillan, 1979), 7–17.
139. *1868 Committee*, 277, 298, 307.
140. *1868 Committee*, 21.
141. *Annual Report of the Commissioner of Police of the Metropolis*, for 1869, PP, vol. 36 (1870), 405.
142. *Annual Report of the Commissioner of Police of the Metropolis*, for 1869, 406.
143. *Departmental Commission on the State, Discipline, and Organisation of the Detective Force of the Metropolitan Police*, 1878, HO45/9442/66692 (henceforth *1878 Commission*), p. v.
144. For a visual illustration of this function during the 1890s, see Alfred Aylmer, 'Detective Day at Holloway', *Windsor Magazine*, 6 (June 1897), 93.
145. *1878 Commission*, pp. v, 71.
146. *1878 Commission*, 54; Clarke, *The Policemen of Hull*, 62.
147. Police Orders, 7 Nov. 1871, 22 Dec. 1879; *1878 Commission*, 253, 259.
148. *1878 Commission*, 186, 207.
149. *1878 Commission*, 141.
150. A Division Superintendent, 31 Aug. 1877, MEPO2/134.
151. *1878 Commission*, pp. v–vi.
152. *1878 Commission*, pp. vi, 141, 206.
153. *1878 Commission*, p. vi.
154. For a detailed discussion of the effects and limitations of the 1869 and 1871 Acts, see Barry S. Godfrey, David J. Cox, and Stephen Farrall, *Serious Offenders: A Historical Study of Habitual Criminals* (Clarendon Criminology Series; Oxford: Oxford University Press, 2011). The need for photographing and recording criminals proved to be an almost impossible task to manage—the Habitual Criminals Registry was underfunded and unwieldy.
155. Petrow, *Policing Morals*, 3–4.
156. *1878 Commission*, pp. vi, 207, 244.
157. *1878 Commission*, p. vi; *Departmental Commission on the State, Discipline, and Organisation of the Metropolitan Police Force (other than the Criminal Investigation Department)* (London: George Edward Eyre & William Spottiswoode, 1879), HO45/9567/74577A (henceforth *1879 Commission*), 220.
158. *1879 Commission*, pp. v, 30, 186.

NOTES

159. *Daily News*, 27 Oct. 1877, p. 3.
160. *Reynolds's News*, 22 July 1877, pp. 5–6.
161. *The Times*, 20 July 1877, p. 12; *Daily News*, 8 Nov. 1877, p. 2. For the full story, see George Dilnot, *The Trial of the Detectives* (New York: Charles Scribner's Sons, 1928).
162. *1878 Commission*, 10. For further discussion, see Stefan Petrow, 'The Rise of the Detective in London, 1869–1914', *Criminal Justice History*, 14 (1993), 94–5.
163. Alfred Aylmer, 'The Detective in Real Life', *Windsor Magazine*, 1 (May 1895), 506.
164. Jeyes and How, *The Life of Sir Howard Vincent*, 57–60.
165. Police Orders, 6 Apr. 1878.
166. So uncomfortable were police officials with the term 'detective' that they were initially planning to call the reorganized police force 'department of crime' and abolish the term 'detective', replacing it with 'officer of the department of crime' (*Graphic*, 3 Nov. 1877, p. 427).
167. *1879 Commission*, 220, 229.
168. *The Times*, 7 Oct. 1878, p. 12.
169. *1878 Commission*, 214, 244.
170. *Report of the Director of Criminal Investigations*, in *Annual Report of the Commissioner of the Police of the Metropolis*, for 1879, PP, vol. 34 (1880), 416.
171. James Monro to Under Secretary of State, 11 Nov. 1889, HO45/10002/A49463/13.
172. *Police Guardian*, 16 Feb. 1889, p. 5. The detective hierarchy in the Metropolitan Police consisted of the following ranks: one chief constable, who assisted the assistant commissioner for the CID (a rank between superintendent and assistant commissioner, introduced in the Metropolitan Police in 1886), two superintendents (one for the CID squad and one for the Special Branch), chief inspectors, first- and second-class inspectors, detective inspectors, first-, second-, and third-class sergeants, and patrol constables. Local inspectors, in charge of the CID in each division, were termed divisional detective inspectors from 1909.
173. Benjamin Leeson, *Lost London* (London: Stanley Paul, 1934), 76; Francis Carlin, *Reminiscences of an Ex-Detective* (London: Hutchinson, 1920), 18; Police Orders, 24 Dec. 1907, p. 1259.
174. 'Our Detective Police', *Saturday Review*, 3 Oct. 1891, p. 383. CID detectives were also stationed in the naval dockyard divisions of the Metropolitan Police to inquire into crime and misappropriation of government stores or on H.M. ships.
175. See, e.g., Leeson, *Lost London*, 43–9.
176. Jenifer Hart, 'Reform of the Borough Police, 1835–1856', *English Historical Review*, 70/276 (July 1955), 422; Jenifer Hart, *The British Police* (London: George Allen & Unwin, 1951), 33; Radzinowicz, *A History of English Criminal Law*, iv. 240; Critchley, *A History of Police*, 116–17.
177. Anthony Brundage, 'Ministers, Magistrates and Reformers: The Genesis of the Rural Constabulary Act of 1839', *Parliamentary History*, 5/1 (1986), 55.
178. Storch, 'Policing Rural Southern England', 213.
179. V. A. C. Gatrell, 'The Decline of Theft and Violence in Victorian and Edwardian England', in V. A. C. Gatrell, Bruce Lenman, and Geoffrey Parker (eds), *Crime and the Law* (London: Europa Publications, 1980), 271–3.

180. Brundage, 'Ministers, Magistrates and Reformers', 56; Jones, 'The New Police', 156–7.
181. Philips, *Crime and Authority*, 60–2. For anti-police riots between 1839 and 1844 and the hostility to the new police, see Palmer, *Police and Protest*, 445–54.
182. For the reasons why the police had become accepted by the mid-1850s, see Palmer, *Police and Protest*, 507–16.
183. In 1871 more than 4,000 parishes in England and Wales were not policed (S. J. Stevenson, 'The "Habitual Criminal" in Nineteenth-Century England: Some Observations on the Figures', *Urban History Yearbook* (1986), 44).
184. Hart, *The British Police*, 35. See this page for the (declining) number of forces during the rest of the period.
185. Hay, 'Property, Authority and Criminal Law', 23–4.
186. Brogden, *The Police*, 65.
187. Government supervision was mainly confined to a team of inspectors who checked annually on whether the police in each locality met certain standards of efficiency, thereby entitling them to a government grant. Each police force was to provide crime and policing statistics for its area.
188. Carolyn Steedman, *Policing the Victorian Community* (London: Routledge & Kegan Paul, 1984), 17–19.
189. James Bent, *Criminal Life: Reminiscences of Forty-Two Years as a Police Officer* (Manchester: John Heywood, 1891), 10; Maureen Scollan, *Sworn to Serve: Police in Essex 1840–1990* (Chichester: Phillimore, 1993), 23, 25. For the City of London Police, see John Stark, 'The City of London Police', in W. Teignmouth Shore (ed.), *Crime and its Detection* (London: Gresham Publishing, 1931), i. 24. A permanent detective department was formed in the City of London Police in 1857 (Donald Rumbelow, *I Spy Blue* (London: Macmillan, 1971), 174–6, 194).
190. *Reports of Inspectors of Constabulary to the Secretary of State. Eastern Counties, Midland, and North Wales District for 1877*, PP, vol. 40 (1878), 7.
191. Richard Jervis, *Chronicles of a Victorian Detective* (Runcorn, Cheshire: P & D Riley, 1995; first published 1907 as *Lancashire's Crime and Criminals*), 19–28.
192. John W. Reilly, *Policing Birmingham* (Birmingham: West Midlands Police, 1989), 16. A sort of detective unit existed in Birmingham in the late 1830s, but it proved to be of short duration.
193. Clay (ed.), *The Leeds Police*, 24.
194. Howard Taylor, 'Rationing Crime: The Political Economy of Criminal Statistics since the 1850s', *Economic History Review*, 51/3 (1998), 572–9.
195. The numbers did not rise significantly in the next few years. From 1877 to 1890 the total number of detectives in the boroughs of the Eastern Counties, Midland, and North Wales District grew only from fifty to sixty-five (*Reports of Inspectors of Constabulary to the Secretary of State. Eastern Counties, Midland, and North Wales District for 1877*, PP, vol. 40 (1878), 7 and for 1890, vol. 42 (1890–1), 7).
196. *1878 Commission*, 183. In 1868, the central detective force of the City of London Police comprised one inspector and twelve detective sergeants and the six divisions had two additional detectives (*1868 Committee*, 407). In the mid-1880s, the force employed thirty-nine full-time detectives (Alex. Innes Shand, 'The City of London Police', *Blackwood's Edinburgh Magazine*, 140 (Nov. 1886), 603).

197. *Instructions for the Liverpool Police Force* (1867), 62; *Regulations and Instructions for the Southport Police Force and Fire Brigade* (1893), 10. I am indebted to Joanne Klein for providing me with provincial police instruction books.
198. *Police Instruction Book* (Manchester, 1908), 86.
199. *Instruction Book for the Government & Guidance of the Bristol Police Force* (1894), 18. See also *Instructions for the Liverpool Constabulary Force* (1856), 7, 18; *Regulations and Instructions for the Southport Police Force and Fire Brigade* (1893), 10–11.
200. *1878 Commission*, 123.
201. *1878 Commission*, 113.
202. *1878 Commission*, 114.
203. *1878 Commission*, 132.
204. *1878 Commission*, 124.
205. *Police Review*, 1 Jan. 1897, p. 22.
206. *1878 Commission*, 125.
207. *1878 Commission*, 26–127, 135; William Henderson, *Clues; or, Leaves from a Detective's Note Book* (New York: White and Allen, 1890; first published Edinburgh, 1889), 61–2; *Committee on the Best Means Available for Identifying Habitual Criminals*, PP, vol. 72 (1893–4), 256.
208. *Jackson's Oxford Journal*, 25 Aug. 1849, p. 1, 7 June 1851, p. 2.
209. *Manchester Times*, 28 May 1851, p. 6.
210. Storch, 'Policing Rural Southern England', 230.
211. Andrew Lansdowne, *A Life's Reminiscences of Scotland Yard* (New York: Garland Publishing, 1984; first published 1890), 7, 82–3.
212. J. W. Stapleton, *The Great Crime of 1860* (London: E. Marlborough & Co., 1861), 73.
213. Kate Summerscale, *The Suspicions of Mr Whicher; or, The Murder at Road Hill House* (London: Bloomsbury, 2009; first published 2008), 126.
214. Whicher belonged to Scotland Yard's first contingent of eight detectives, formed in 1842. For details about the case and its resolution, see Summerscale, *The Suspicions of Mr Whicher*; see also ch. 5.
215. Jervis, *Chronicles of a Victorian Detective*, 21.
216. *1879 Commission*, 222.
217. Steedman, *Policing the Victorian Community*, 131.
218. *1878 Commission*, 206.
219. Charles Tempest Clarkson and J. Hall Richardson, *Police!* (New York: Garland, 1984; first published 1889), 272–3.
220. Jennifer Davis, 'Prosecutions and their Context: The Use of the Criminal Law in Later Nineteenth-Century London', in Hay and Snyder (eds), *Policing and Prosecution in Britain*, 408–19; John P. Locker, '"Quiet Thieves, Quiet Punishment": Private Responses to the "Respectable" Offender, c.1850–1930', *Crime, histoire et sociétés/Crime, History & Societies*, 9/1 (2005), 10; Barry S. Godfrey, Paul Lawrence, and Chris A. Williams, *History and Crime* (Los Angeles: Sage, 2008), 132–6.
221. *Police Guardian*, 8 Feb. 1896, p. 3, quoting an article entitled 'Private Detectives' from *Reynolds's News*. For details about the Pinkerton detectives, see *Police Guardian*, 23 July 1892, p. 7.

NOTES

222. *Police Guardian*, 8 Feb. 1896, p. 3.
223. Philips, 'Good Men to Associate', 123.
224. Taylor, 'Rationing Crime', 576–7; David Garland, *The Culture of Control* (Oxford: Oxford University Press, 2001), 32; Emsley, *Crime and Society in England*, 149–50; Davis, 'Prosecutions and their Context', 400.
225. Philips, *Crime and Authority*, 129; Jennifer Davis, 'A Poor Man's System of Justice: The London Police Courts in the Second Half of the Nineteenth Century', *Historical Journal*, 27 (June 1984), 330–1. For the high costs of investigation and prosecution, see Philips, *Crime and Authority*, 110–16.
226. *Instructions for the Liverpool Police Force* (1867), 57–8, (1878), 95, (1893), 8; *Instruction Book... of the Bristol Police Force* (1894), 19; *Police Instruction Book* (Manchester, 1908), 59; *Daily News*, 25 Aug. 1854, p. 4; *1878 Commission*, 174–5, 180.
227. Chris A. Williams, 'Constables for Hire: The History of Private "Public" Policing in the UK', *Policing and Society*, 18 (June 2008), 201.
228. Jones, 'The New Police', 160; Rob S. Sindall, 'The Criminal Statistics of Nineteenth-Century Cities: A New Approach', *Urban History Yearbook* (1986), 34–5. However, official statistics evinced a rise in the rates of serious property crime at the beginning of the twentieth century.
229. Martin J. Wiener, *Reconstructing the Criminal* (Cambridge: Cambridge University Press, 1990), 217.
230. *1878 Commission*, pp. viii, 36–8, 83.
231. Raymond Fosdick, *European Police Systems* (Montclair, NJ: Patterson Smith, 1969; first published 1915), 275.
232. *1878 Commission*, 123.
233. *Police Guardian*, 2 May 1884, p. 3.
234. *Police Review*, 8 Jan. 1897, p. 19.
235. Joseph F. Broadhurst, *From Vine Street to Jerusalem* (London: Stanley Paul, 1936), 46.
236. *Police Guardian*, 18 Jan. 1896, p. 5.
237. *Daily Mail*, 4 Feb. 1909, p. 6.
238. For a detailed diagram of the organization of the detective branch of the Metropolitan Police, see Fosdick, *European Police Systems*, 276–7.
239. *1878 Commission*, 124; *Committee on the Best Means Available for Identifying Habitual Criminals*, 219–20.
240. For details, see James Monro, *A Report on the History of the Convict Supervision Office* (London, 1886), HO144/184/A45507.
241. 13 June 1889, HO45/10002/A49463/8.
242. For details, see John Moylan, *Scotland Yard and the Metropolitan Police* (London: Putnam, 1929), 237–40.
243. *1878 Commission*, 182.
244. Petrow, *Policing Morals*, 62–3. James Monro served as an assistant commissioner responsible for the CID between 1884 and 1888.
245. For criticism of these methods by detectives, see Lansdowne, *A Life's Reminiscences*, 105; see also *Committee on the Best Means Available for Identifying Habitual Criminals*, 220–7; Moylan, *Scotland Yard and the Metropolitan Police*, 225.
246. Henderson, *Clues*, 241; Petrow, *Policing Morals*, 90.

NOTES

247. Jack Henry, *Detective-Inspector Henry's Famous Cases* (London: Hutchinson, 1949), 10; A. Croxton Smith, 'The Bloodhound as Detective', *Windsor Magazine*, 1 (Apr. 1895), 434, respectively. See also 'Our Detective Police', *Saturday Review*, 26 Sept. 1891, p. 360. Even fictive characters complained at the time that 'criminals and others intent on cunning of any kind, have at their disposal all the wonderful inventions of science, whereas the ordinary detective has to work on the old lines, with nothing more scientific to help him than the album at Scotland Yard and the telephones between the police stations' (Headon Hill, *Clues from a Detective's Camera* (Bristol: J. W. Arrowsmith, 1893), 9). On the search for new means of criminal identification during the 1890s, see Jürgen Thorwald, *The Century of the Detective* (New York: Harcourt, Brace & World, 1964; trans. from the German), 24–48. Scotland Yard also lagged behind the Continent in recognizing the usefulness of forensic medicine for detection (Thorwald, *The Century of the Detective*, 180).
248. For details, see Petrow, *Policing Morals*, 89–96. Bertillon conceived this system in France in the late 1870s, but only from 1883 was it used by the French police to prove the true identity of a habitual criminal, and even then it took another two years before Bertillon gained the respect of the French detective bureau (Colin Beavan, *Fingerprints* (New York: Hyperion, 2001), 87–8, 91–2).
249. The Registry was first established at Scotland Yard in 1869 under the Habitual Criminals Act, but was transferred to the Prisons Department at the Home Office in 1877. In 1913 it was amalgamated with the Convict Supervision Office and Fingerprint Registry to form the Criminal Record Office—a national registry of crimes and criminals.
250. Bentley, *English Criminal Justice*, 205, 298.
251. Simon A. Cole, *Suspect Identities* (Cambridge, MA: Harvard University Press, 2001), 60–6.
252. For Edward Henry's biography, see John Rowland, *The Finger-Print Man* (London: Lutterworth Press, 1959).
253. For an eyewitness account of how the technology was regarded by detectives investigating the Deptford murders, see Broadhurst, *From Vine Street to Jerusalem*, 23–4.
254. *Committee on the Police Service of England, Wales and Scotland* (henceforth *Desborough Committee*), PP, vol. 22 (1920), 612, 618.
255. See the series titled 'The Detection of Crime', in *The Times*, 28, 29, 30 July 1913.
256. Frederick R. Cherrill, *The Finger Print System at Scotland Yard* (London: Her Majesty's Stationery Office, 1954), 8; Mathieu Deflem, *Policing World Society* (Oxford: Oxford University Press, 2002), 94.
257. Porter, *The Origins of the Vigilant State*, 7; *1868 Committee*, 283–4.
258. *1868 Committee*, 304.
259. Edwin T. Woodhall, *Detective and Secret Service Days* (London: Mellifont Press, 1929), 22; *The Times*, 13 Apr. 1883, p. 8.
260. Woodhall, *Detective and Secret Service Days*, 22.
261. *Reynolds's News*, 7 Apr. 1895, p. 5, 28 Apr. 1895, p. 4.
262. *Reynolds's News*, 7 Apr. 1895, p. 5, and Porter, *The Origins of the Vigilant State*, 29, 40–3. For the surveillance of Italian anarchists during this period, see Pietro Di Paola, 'The Spies who Came in from the Heat: The International Surveillance of the Anarchists in London', *European History Quarterly*, 37/2 (2007), 197.

263. See, e.g., *Daily Chronicle*, 2 June 1884, p. 4.
264. 'The Dynamite Inquiries', *Saturday Review*, 19 Apr. 1884, p. 496.
265. *Police Guardian*, 11 Feb. 1881, p. 5, 29 July 1881, p. 2.
266. Porter, *The Origins of the Vigilant State*, 41.
267. *Reynolds's News*, 10 Feb. 1895, p. 5.
268. Clarkson and Richardson, *Police!*, 191.
269. *Reynolds's News*, 10 Feb. 1895, p. 5.
270. *Reynolds's News*, 10 Feb. 1895, p. 5. See also Porter, *The Origins of the Vigilant State*, 57.
271. Porter, *The Origins of the Vigilant State*, 59; Jeyes and How, *The Life of Sir Howard Vincent*, ch. 9. Vincent's successors were no longer called 'Director' but 'Assistant Commissioner'.
272. *Reynolds's News*, 10 Feb. 1895, p. 5.
273. Porter, *The Origins of the Vigilant State*, 60.
274. For Anderson's autobiography, see Robert Anderson, *The Lighter Side of my Official Life* (London: Hodder & Stoughton, 1910).
275. Custom House London to Secretary of the Treasury, 26 Nov. 1885, HO144/133/A34848B/56; see also 14 Mar. 1884.
276. Letter by Secretary of State, 7 Dec. 1886, HO144/133/A34848B/61.
277. *Reynolds's News*, 17 Mar. 1895, p. 5.
278. Porter, *The Origins of the Vigilant State*, 56–7.
279. Lindsay Clutterbuck, 'Countering Irish Republican Terrorism in Britain: Its Origin as a Police Function', *Terrorism and Political Violence*, 18/1 (2006), 114.
280. *Reynolds's News*, 21 Mar. 1895, p. 5.
281. Porter, *The Origins of the Vigilant State*, 85; Andrew Cook, *M: MI5's First Spymaster* (Stroud: Tempus, 2004), 58–9.
282. For further discussion, see Haia Shpayer, 'British Anarchism 1881–1914: Reality and Appearance', Ph.D., University of London, 1981, 114–51.
283. *The Times*, 30 Mar. 1892, p. 14. For the full story of the Walsall affair, see John Quail, *The Slow Burning Fuse* (London: Paladin, 1978), ch. 6.
284. Joseph Conrad based his novel *The Secret Agent* (London: Harper & Brothers Publishers, 1907) on this episode.
285. *Police Review*, 29 May 1893, p. 256.
286. *Freedom* (June 1911), 47.
287. *Freedom* (June 1908), 40, (July 1911), 40.
288. *Freedom* (Aug. 1912), 64.
289. *Evening News*, 12 Sept. 1898, p. 2.
290. CID to Commissioners, 7 July 1909, MEPO2/1297; Harold Brust, *'I Guarded Kings'* (New York: Hillman-Curl, 1936; first published 1935), 85–102.
291. For details, see Browne, *The Rise of Scotland Yard*, 279–90, and ch. 5 in this volume.
292. Brust, *'I Guarded Kings'*, 86.
293. For a failed trailing of the future head of the German secret service, see Woodhall, *Detective and Secret Service Days*, 61–3.
294. For details of the real and imaginary counter-espionage, see Christopher Andrew, *Secret Service* (London: Heinemann, 1985), 37–85. For spy novels in the period, see David A. T. Stafford, 'Spies and Gentlemen: The Birth of the British Spy Novel, 1893–1914', *Victorian Studies*, 24/4 (1981), 489–509.

295. On the assassination and its aftermath, as recounted by a former detective inspector of the Special Branch, Herbert T. Fitch, years later, see Herbert T. Fitch, *Traitors Within* (New York: Doubleday, Doran & Co., 1933), 32–5.
296. CID to Commissioners, 7 July 1909, MEPO2/1297.
297. Porter, *The Origins of the Vigilant State*, 175–6; Clarke, *The Policemen of Hull*, 86.
298. Circular by the Home Office, 11 Sept. 1909, HO144/1043/183461/3.
299. Letter by the Metropolitan Police to the Home Office, 15 Sept. 1909, HO144/1043/183461/1.
300. Report by Superintendent P. Quinn, 10 Nov. 1911, HO144/1119/203651/6; Proceedings of suffragettes' trials on 14 May 1912, 4 Mar. and 1 Apr. 1913, www.oldbaileyonline.org; Woodhall, *Detective and Secret Service Days*, 42; W. H. Thompson, *Guard from the Yard* (London: Jarrolds, 1938), 27.
301. Cecil Bishop, *From Information Received* (London: Hutchinson, 1932), 171.
302. Herbert T. Fitch, *Memoirs of a Royal Detective* (London: Hurst & Blackett, 1936), 19.
303. *Police Review*, 6 July 1900, p. 320; Woodhall, *Detective and Secret Service Days*, 23.
304. Fitch, *Memoirs of a Royal Detective*, 243.
305. Porter, *The Origins of the Vigilant State*, 154, 166.
306. Porter, *The Origins of the Vigilant State*, 179.
307. *Desborough Committee*, 615; Clarke, *The Policemen of Hull*, 62.
308. The proportion of the London CID in the general force increased from 2.4% in 1887 to 3.6% in 1908 (*The Times*, 1 Jan. 1909, p. 37). In 1912 it had 506 men, excluding the Special Branch, the Registry, and the Convict Supervision Office, which comprised 123 men; in 1919 it had 786 men, 45 in the central office and 5 attached to the Royal Dockyards divisions (E. Henry to Under Secretary of State, 13 May 1912, HO45/11000/223532 and *Desborough Committee*, 609). Because of different calculations as to whom to include, figures given by scholars on the size of the London CID diverge greatly. In Middlesbrough, in the immediate pre-war years, the total number of detectives was no more than 6–7 in a force of over 130 men (David Taylor, *Policing the Victorian Town* (Houndmills: Palgrave, 2002), 117).
309. Petrow, *Policing Morals*, 65. Fosdick, *European Police Systems*, 277. London's population at the time approximated seven million.
310. *Royal Commission upon the Duties of the Metropolitan Police*, PP, vols. 50–51 (1908) (henceforth *1908 Commission*), vol. 51, p. 268.
311. Critchley, *A History of Police*, 176.
312. *The Times*, 28 July 1913, p. 3.
313. Home Office to Commissioner, 5 Mar. 1906, HO45/19921. See also letter of 7 Feb. 1906; *The Times*, 10 May 1906, p. 4; Charles Arrow, *Rogues and Others* (London: Duckworth, 1926), 215–16. In 1909, Scotland Yard set up a new network of detectives in the rapidly growing outskirts of London. Until then the local detective inspectors had their headquarters at stations on a smaller circle around the metropolis.
314. E. Henry to Under Secretary of State, 14 Feb. 1906, HO45/19921. See also the letter by Home Office to the chief constables, 2 July 1909, in which reference is made to a case of murder where the victim's body had been washed and the

bloodstains in the house in which the murder occurred obliterated before the arrival of a Yard detective.
315. For the nature and quality of criminal investigation in Britain in this period, see Morris, 'History of Criminal Investigation', 16–27.
316. *Report of the Director of Criminal Investigations*, in *Annual Report of the Commissioner of Police of the Metropolis*, for 1881, PP, vol. 33 (1882), 335; Cook, *M: MI5's First Spymaster*, 133–4.

CHAPTER 2. FROM BOBBY TO DETECTIVE

1. On railway detectives in the nineteenth century, see J. R. Whitbread, *The Railway Policeman* (London: George G. Harrap, 1961), 98–105.
2. For the use of internal labour market mechanisms in such organizations, see Haia Shpayer-Makov, 'Control at the Workplace: Paternalism Reinvented in Victorian Britain', in Clive Emsley, Eric Johnson, and Pieter Spierenburg (eds), *Social Control in Europe*, ii. *1800–2000* (Columbus, OH: Ohio State University Press, 2004).
3. 'Memorandum', 14 June 1842, pp. 14, 17, HO45/OS/292; *1878 Commission*, pp. xv–xvi, 130; Reilly, *Policing Birmingham*, 16.
4. Haia Shpayer-Makov, *The Making of a Policeman: A Social History of a Labour Force in Metropolitan London, 1829–1914* (Aldershot: Ashgate, 2002), 36–7.
5. *1878 Commission*, 126.
6. *1878 Commission*, 4, 15.
7. *1878 Commission*, 14, 16, 23, 167; E. Henry to Under Secretary of State, 13 May 1912, HO45/11000/223532.
8. *1878 Commission*, 15; *1868 Committee*, 282, 291.
9. A study of detectives who were recruited to the Metropolitan Police between 1889 and 1909 shows that more than 80% had engaged in non-manual work before joining the police (Haia Shpayer-Makov, 'Becoming a Police Detective in Victorian and Edwardian London', *Policing and Society*, 14/3 (2004), 9).
10. *1878 Commission*, p. v.
11. *1878 Commission*, 187–8.
12. *1878 Commission*, 75.
13. *1878 Commission*, pp. v, 180.
14. 'Our Police System', 699; *1878 Commission*, 97.
15. *1878 Commission*, 96.
16. George H. Greenham, *Scotland Yard Experiences* (London: George Routledge & Sons, 1904), 3.
17. *1878 Commission*, 96.
18. Leonard Gribble, *Great Manhunters of the Yard* (New York: Roy Publishers, 1966), 19.
19. Greenham, *Scotland Yard Experiences*, 3.
20. *1878 Commission*, 5, 15.
21. *1878 Commission*, 15.
22. *1878 Commission*, 162 (for London); p. 130 (for Liverpool).
23. Thomson was born in Smyrna to an Italian mother and a Scottish father who was a merchant in the East. He spoke Greek, Italian, English, and was taught French when the family lived in Paris (*1868 Committee*, 315).

24. *1868 Committee*, 76.
25. *1868 Committee*, 76.
26. Arrow, *Rogues and Others*, 214–15.
27. *Desborough Committee*, 617.
28. Shpayer-Makov, *The Making of a Policeman*, 56.
29. *1878 Commission*, 2.
30. *1878 Commission*, p. xi.
31. *1878 Commission*, 16, 41.
32. *1878 Commission*, 5, 16.
33. *1878 Commission*, 23. See also Steedman, *Policing the Victorian Community*, 2.
34. *1878 Commission*, 4, 33–4 (for London), p. 130 (for Liverpool).
35. *1878 Commission*, 33.
36. *1878 Commission*, 36.
37. *1878 Commission*, 5.
38. *1878 Commission*, 33.
39. *1878 Commission*, 2. See testimony of the head constable of Leeds (p. 134), and of Williamson to the 1868 committee (*1868 Committee*, 278).
40. *1878 Commission*, 33.
41. *1878 Commission*, 175, 181.
42. *1878 Commission*, 5, 33.
43. *Sporting Gazette*, 18 Jan. 1868, p. 41.
44. *1878 Commission*, 197.
45. *1878 Commission*, 6.
46. *1878 Commission*, 171.
47. *1878 Commission*, 15.
48. *Police Guardian*, 6 Dec. 1878, p. 3.
49. *1878 Commission*, 133. See also *1908 Commission*, vol. 51, p. 382.
50. Greenham, *Scotland Yard Experiences*, 1.
51. Greenham, *Scotland Yard Experiences*, 2.
52. *1878 Commission*, 175.
53. *1878 Commission*, 96.
54. *1878 Commission*, 4.
55. 'Our Police System', 699.
56. *1878 Commission*, 2.
57. *1878 Commission*, 4.
58. See his testimony as head constable of Bristol (*1878 Commission*, 176). Coathupe resumed practical surgery for eighteen months, but, seeing an advertisement in *The Times* for head of the detective department in Manchester, he wrote to Richard Mayne, commissioner of the Metropolitan Police, who had hired him in the first place, and with the commissioner's recommendation he obtained the job. He held the post for eight years before attaining his position in Bristol.
59. *1878 Commission*, 126.
60. While Superintendent Williamson, head of the department in the greatest need of special talents from 1869 onwards, testified to the 1878 commission that he had recruited only three men from the outside, Major C. B. Greig stated that he had never resorted to this measure in all his twenty-five years as head of the force in Liverpool (*1878 Commission*, 2, 5, 121, 126).

61. *1878 Commission*, p. xv.
62. *1878 Commission*, 17.
63. *1908 Commission*, vol. 51, p. 388.
64. Clarkson and Richardson, *Police!*, 262–3.
65. *Departmental Committee of 1889 upon Metropolitan Police Superannuation*, PP, vol. 59 (1890) (henceforth *1890 Committee*), 426, 430.
66. Clarkson and Richardson, *Police!*, 264.
67. Clarkson and Richardson, *Police!*, 263. See also W.L. Melville Lee, *A History of Police in England* (London: Methuen, 1901), 368.
68. *Desborough Committee*, 617.
69. Clarkson and Richardson, *Police!*, 264.
70. *Desborough Committee*, 617.
71. Melville L. Macnaghten, *Days of my Years* (London: Arnold, 1914), 53. An earlier case was that of George Williams (b. in Bolton 1844), who had a good education and worked in Manchester in his uncle's solicitor's office and then in a firm of criminal lawyers (*Police Guardian*, 7 Mar. 1879, p. 2). He was appointed as a superintendent in 1867 in charge of organizing a detective department for the Salford Borough Police, eventually holding managerial posts in both uniformed and plain-clothes branches as he advanced through the ranks. He was appointed chief constable of Hanley in Staffordshire in 1872, chief constable of Wigan in 1875, and chief superintendent of the detective department of the borough of Liverpool in 1879, retiring in 1892.
72. 'Detectives', *Saturday Review*, 9 Feb. 1884, p. 178; P.C., *The Metropolitan Police and its Management: A Reply to Sir Charles Warren's Article in Murray's Magazine* (London: Dyke, 1888), 6.
73. Macnaghten, *Days of my Years*, 65–6.
74. *Pall Mall Gazette*, 8 Oct. 1888, p. 3.
75. *1908 Commission*, vol. 51, p. 388.
76. Memorandum by the Executive Branch, 24 Aug. 1903, MEPO2/697. See also documents in MEPO 2/1570.
77. E. Henry to Under Secretary of State, 13 May 1912, HO45/11000/223532.
78. E. Henry to Under Secretary of State, 13 May 1912, HO45/11000/223532; Shpayer-Makov, *The Making of a Policeman*, 52.
79. G. R. Searle, *The Quest for National Efficiency* (London: Ashfield Press, 1990; first published 1971), 76–7.
80. *Desborough Committee*, 617.
81. New Scotland Yard Proposal, 20 June 1912, HO45/11000/223532.
82. *1878 Commission*, p. viii; *1868 Committee*, 292, 310; Charles Warren, 'The Police of the Metropolis', *Murray's Magazine*, 4 (Nov. 1888), 586.
83. Brust, *'I Guarded Kings'*, 34.
84. *1890 Committee*, 432.
85. [James Fitzjames Stephen], 'Detectives in Fiction and in Real Life', *Saturday Review*, 11 June 1864, p. 713.
86. Bishop, *From Information Received*, 15.
87. Carlin, *Reminiscences of an Ex-Detective*, 17.
88. Percy Savage, *Savage of Scotland Yard* (London: Hutchinson, 1934), 124. See also Brust, *'I Guarded Kings'*, 35.

89. George W. Cornish, *Cornish of Scotland Yard: His Reminiscences and Cases* (New York: Macmillan Co., 1935), 4.
90. Albert Lieck, *Bow Street World* (London: Robert Hale, 1938), 46–7. Albert Lieck served as a chief clerk in the Bow Street Police Court. See also Frederick Porter Wensley, *Forty Years of Scotland Yard* (New York: Doubleday, Doran & Co., 1933; first published 1930), 13.
91. *1908 Commission*, vol. 50, pp. 626–7. For the experience (and portrait) of Detective Inspector John Dart of the Plymouth Borough Force, see *Police Review*, 15 July 1898, p. 330, and of Detective Superintendent F. Knowlson of the Middlesbrough Force, see *Police Review*, 21 Apr. 1899, p. 186.
92. *Desborough Committee*, 609. For descriptions of service on winter patrol, see Leeson, *Lost London*, 76–95; Walter Hambrook, *Hambrook of the Yard* (London: Robert Hale & Co., 1937), 34–8.
93. *1878 Commission*, 75, 99.
94. *1878 Commission*, 139; *1890 Committee*, 426–7.
95. *Police Review*, 14 Sept. 1894, p. 437.
96. *1878 Commission*, 23.
97. Robert A. Fuller, *Recollections of a Detective* (London: John Long, 1912), 18.
98. *1878 Commission*, 34.
99. *1878 Commission*, pp. xvii, 5, 181, 192. See also Clarkson and Richardson, *Police!*, 264, quoting Howard Vincent.
100. For the Metropolitan Police, see *1878 Commission*, 41; for the Liverpool Police, p. 131, and the City of London Police, p. 184.
101. *1878 Commission*, 65.
102. *1878 Commission*, 21; see also testimony of the head constable of Leeds, p. 135.
103. Memo by Frederick Williamson, 22 Oct. 1880, MEPO2/134.
104. James Monro, 'The London Police', *North American Review*, 151 (Nov. 1890), 626; Lee, *A History of Police in England*, 368.
105. *Desborough Committee*, 617.
106. *1878 Commission*, 33, 75, 98.
107. *1878 Commission*, 34.
108. *1878 Commission*, 134; see also the evidence given by Edwin Coathupe, head constable of Bristol in 1877, about the jealousy he encountered when he joined Scotland Yard as a detective, serving there in 1863–6 (p. 176).
109. *1878 Commission*, 134.
110. For details about the promotion system in the Metropolitan Police, see Shpayer-Makov, *The Making of a Policeman*, 191–202; for the provincial forces, see Steedman, *Policing the Victorian Community*, 106–8; W. J. Lowe, 'The Lancashire Constabulary, 1845–1870: The Social and Occupational Function of a Victorian Police Force', *Criminal Justice History*, 4 (1983), 53–4.
111. C. E. Howard Vincent, *A Police Code* (London: Cassell, Petter, Galpin, 1881), 104.
112. *1878 Commission*, 23, 132; see also the testimonies of the head constables of Liverpool and Leeds, pp. 131 and 134, respectively.
113. *Daily Mail*, 2 June 1913, p. 7.
114. James Berrett, *When I was at Scotland Yard* (London: Sampson Low, Marston & Co., 1932), 261.

NOTES

115. *1878 Commission*, 15.
116. *1878 Commission*, 23.
117. *1878 Commission*, 179; Critchley, *A History of Police*, 52.
118. *1878 Commission*, 103.
119. *1878 Commission*, 109.
120. Berrett, *When I was at Scotland Yard*, 261.
121. *Daily Mail*, 2 June 1913, p. 7.
122. Berrett, *When I was at Scotland Yard*, 261.
123. *1878 Commission*, 16.
124. Shpayer-Makov, *The Making of a Policeman*, 77–9, 86–9.
125. Shpayer-Makov, *The Making of a Policeman*, 11.
126. Shpayer-Makov, *The Making of a Policeman*, 156–7. See also ch. 3 in this volume, p. 102.
127. *Daily Mail*, 8 Feb. 1906, p. 6.
128. *1878 Commission*, 7.
129. Dilnot, *Scotland Yard*, 17.
130. See the testimony of the head constable of the Liverpool Police (*1878 Commission*, 123), head constable of Leeds (p. 132), and head constable of Bristol about Manchester detectives (p. 177). For London, see p. 140.
131. *1878 Commission*, 4, 15–16; *1868 Committee*, 292.
132. *1878 Commission*, 16; see also testimony of the head constables of Leeds (p. 137) and Bristol (p. 179).
133. *1878 Commission*, pp. xv, 6, 14, 161–2.
134. In 1840 candidates to the City of London Police had to be at least 5 feet 7 inches tall. Later in the century the height requirement was raised to a minimum of 5 feet 11 inches, the highest requirement in the country.
135. Upon the formation of the Metropolitan Police in 1829, the candidates' age parameters were 18 to 35. In practice, however, candidates were usually not hired if they were over the age of 27, so that 'the police service may not lose the better part of a man's life' (*Pall Mall Gazette*, 1 Oct. 1888, p. 7). For details about the entry regulations in the Metropolitan Police, see Shpayer-Makov, *The Making of a Policeman*, 33–42.
136. Gavin Drewry and Tony Butcher, *The Civil Service Today* (Oxford: Basil Blackwell, 1988), 43–5.
137. David Vincent, *Literacy and Popular Culture* (Cambridge: Cambridge University Press, 1989), 123.
138. *1890 Committee*, 398.
139. Leeson, *Lost London*, 23.
140. Tom Divall, *Scoundrels and Scallywags* (London: Ernest Benn, 1929), 12.
141. Arthur Fowler Neil, *Man-Hunters of Scotland Yard* (New York: Doubleday, Doran & Co., 1933; first published 1932), 264.
142. See, e.g., a draft letter by E. Henry, 10 Aug. 1909, MEPO2/8124.
143. *1890 Committee*, 398.
144. Henry, *Detective-Inspector Henry's Famous Cases*, 10.
145. 'Report of Working of the Scheme for the Examination and Selection of Provincial Recruits with Results Obtained and the Cost of 31 Dec. 1912', 7 Jan. 1913, MEPO2/8124.
146. *1890 Committee*, 396.

147. 'Report of the Recruiting Board on the Results and Costs of the First Three Examinations', 15 Mar. 1910, MEPO 2/8124; 'Report of Working of the Scheme'.
148. *Police Instruction Book* (Manchester, 1908), 87–8; Jalna Hanmer, Jill Radford, and Elizabeth A. Stanko, *Women, Policing, and Male Violence: International Perspectives* (London: Routledge, 1989), 14–17.
149. For details of such cases, see my forthcoming article 'Shedding the Uniform and Acquiring a New Masculine Image: The Case of the Late Victorian and Edwardian English Police Detective', in David G. Barrie and Susan Broomhall (eds), *A History of Police and Masculinities, 1700–2010* (Cullompton: Willan Publishing, forthcoming).
150. Leeson, *Lost London*, 24.
151. *Police Review*, 26 Apr. 1895, p. 200.
152. *Police Review*, 21 Aug. 1893, p. 399, 26 Apr. 1895, p. 200, 1 Sept. 1899, p. 415; *1908 Commission*, vol. 51, pp. 382–3.
153. *1908 Commission*, vol. 51, p. 382.
154. Shpayer-Makov, *The Making of a Policeman*, 52–3.
155. Wynter, 'The Police and the Thieves', 170, 173.
156. Charles E. Leach, *On Top of the Underworld* (London: Sampson Low, Marston & Co., 1933), 16.
157. *1878 Commission*, 131.
158. *1878 Commission*, 4.
159. E. Henry to Under Secretary of State, 13 May 1912, HO45/11000/223532. In the case of Detective Inspector John Conquest of the E Division, it took eight years (*1890 Committee*, 425–6).
160. *1878 Commission*, 140, 161, 184.
161. Police Orders, 16 Nov. 1867.
162. *Police Review*, 14 Sept. 1894, p. 437. Indeed, not all officers started their work in the detective force as constables (*Police Review*, 20 Apr. 1894, p. 187). Some were drafted as sergeants and even from higher ranks (*Police Review*, 1 Oct. 1897, p. 474).
163. *Police Guardian*, 6 Apr. 1895, p. 5, 1 June 1895, p. 5.
164. Berrett, *When I was at Scotland Yard*, 59.
165. *Police Guardian*, 6 Apr. 1895, p. 5, 1 June 1895, p. 5.
166. Bishop, *From Information Received*, 25. See also Lansdowne, *A Life's Reminiscences*, 6; Leeson, *Lost London*, 42–3; *Police Review*, 9 Sept. 1898, p. 426, 19 July 1901, p. 342.
167. *Police Review*, 2 Feb. 1900, p. 79.
168. *1878 Commission*, pp. v, 132 (testimony of the head constable of Leeds).
169. Cornish, *Cornish of Scotland Yard*, 9.
170. *Police Review*, 14 Sept. 1894, p. 437.
171. *1878 Commission*, 183; Savage, *Savage of Scotland Yard*, 123. See also Stark, 'The City of London Police', i. 24.
172. Police Orders, 24 Dec. 1907, p. 1259; Leeson, *Lost London*, 76–7.
173. *1878 Commission*, 75.
174. *1878 Commission*, p. viii.
175. John Sweeney, *At Scotland Yard* (London: Grant Richards, 1904), 4; Arrow, *Rogues and Others*, 26–7; Berrett, *When I was at Scotland Yard*, 68–9; Wensley, *Forty Years of Scotland Yard*, 11.

176. *Reynolds's News*, 10 Feb. 1895, p. 5. Preference for Irishmen was by no means universal. In fact, certain senior officials sought to restrict the number of Irish recruits in the ordinary police, and even in the Special Branch (*Reynolds's News*, 24 Mar. 1895, p. 5; George Dilnot, *The Story of Scotland Yard* (Boston: Houghton Mifflin, 1927), 328 n. 16). The deeply held prejudices against people of Irish extraction impelled the Irish Branchers to prove that they were as 'loyal and faithful servants as either the English, Scotch, or Welsh'.
177. Brust, 'I Guarded Kings', 14–18. A few months thereafter, on 1 Feb. 1908, King Carlos and his heir, Prince Louis, were shot dead by two republican activists in the streets of Lisbon in Brust's presence.
178. Brust, 'I Guarded Kings', 21.
179. Brust, 'I Guarded Kings', 33–4.
180. Brust, 'I Guarded Kings', 14.
181. Brust, 'I Guarded Kings', 34, 36.
182. Macnaghten, *Days of my Years*, 4, 174. See also the memoirs of Edmund Yates, *Edmund Yates: His Recollections and Experiences* (London: Richard Bentley and Son, 1885; first published 1884), 29–30.
183. H. L. Adam, *C.I.D.: Behind the Scenes at Scotland Yard* (London: Sampson Low, Marston & Co., 1931), 186.
184. Henry Smith, *From Constable to Commissioner* (London: Chatto & Windus, 1910), 112–13.
185. *Police Review*, 10 June 1898, p. 270.
186. Cornish, *Cornish of Scotland Yard*, 3. See also the biographical details of Detective Superintendent Walter Hambrook, who 'was born and bred in the small hamlet of Betteshanger' in Kent and left school at the age of 13 (and served in the Metropolitan Police, 1898–1936), in Hambrook, *Hambrook of the Yard*, 19–24.
187. Miners, for example, were skilled workers associated with meagre education (W. B. Stephens, *Education in Britain, 1750–1914* (London: Macmillan, 1998), 86).
188. Thomas Laqueur, 'The Cultural Origins of Popular Literacy in England 1500–1850', *Oxford Review of Education*, 2/3 (1976), 259.
189. Vincent, *Literacy and Popular Culture*, 54.
190. Vincent, *Literacy and Popular Culture*, 54.
191. David Vincent, 'Communication, Community and the State', in Clive Emsley and James Walvin (eds), *Artisans, Peasants & Proletarians, 1760–1860* (London: Croom Helm, 1985), 177.
192. See the memoirs of Lansdowne, Littlechild, Carlin, and Leeson.
193. William C. Gough, *From Kew Observatory to Scotland Yard* (London: Hurst & Blackett, 1927), 11. To name just a few, Francis Carlin, William C. Gough, Charles Leach, Benjamin Leeson, Percy Savage, John Taylor (known as 'Jack the Sleuthhound'), and Frederick Williamson, all of the Metropolitan Police; James Black, detective superintendent of the Birmingham Police; R. Beswick, chief superintendent of the Manchester detective police; Richard Jervis, superintendent in the Lancashire County Constabulary; Thomas, detective inspector of the Birmingham Police; and G. H. Totterdell, detective superintendent of the Essex County Police all had fathers who had served in the police. Black's, Jervis's, Leach's, Thomas's, Totterdell's, and Williamson's fathers had been

superintendents. Ernest Nicholls, who served his entire police career in the City of London Police, had an uncle who was a police superintendent, and Walter Hambrook, who in 1920 organized the famous Flying Squad at Scotland Yard, had a brother who was a policeman. Savage was actually born in the police station where his father served as a station sergeant (*Savage of Scotland Yard*, 17). His father retired in 1893 after serving in the police for twenty-five years—the last eleven as detective inspector in personal attendance to Queen Victoria, the first police officer to hold this appointment. For Savage's father's portrait and further details about his work life, see *Police Review*, 11 Sept. 1893, p. 436.

194. Leeson, *Lost London*, 22.
195. Leach, *On Top of the Underworld*, 10–11. At the time, Charles Leach's father was a local detective inspector in Clerkenwell.
196. Leach, *On Top of the Underworld*, 11–12. Charles's service and that of his father later overlapped for a while.
197. Leach was proud that he 'was born "to the blue"', noting that by the early 1930s, members of his family had been police officers for over 130 years (*On Top of the Underworld*, 10).
198. Leach, *On Top of the Underworld*, 11, 15. See also the experience of Detective Superintendent G. H. Totterdell of the Essex County Police (b. 1892), in G. H. Totterdell, *Country Copper* (London: George G. Harrap, 1956), 29.
199. *Police Review*, 31 Mar. 1904, p. 160, repr. from the *Hour Glass*; Fuller, *Recollections of a Detective*, 19; Percy J. Smith, *Con Man* (London: Herbert Jenkins, 1938), 17.
200. Wensley, *Forty Years of Scotland Yard*, 1. See also Totterdell, *Country Copper*, 9.
201. Carlin, *Reminiscences of an Ex-Detective*, 15.
202. Henry, *Detective-Inspector Henry's Famous Cases*, 9.
203. Frank Leonard Bunn, *No Silver Spoon: The Autobiography of a 'Ranker'* (Stoke-on-Trent: F. L. Bunn, 1970), 5; Frederick R. Cherrill, *Cherrill of the Yard* (London: George G. Harrap, 1954), 5.
204. Walter Dew, *I Caught Crippen* (London: Blackie & Son, 1938), 1. See also Jervis, *Chronicles of a Victorian Detective*, 13.
205. Broadhurst, *From Vine Street to Jerusalem*, 13. The Muswell Hill murderers had broken into the house of an old man, bound him, and battered him to death with a revolver butt, escaping with a safe.
206. Broadhurst, *From Vine Street to Jerusalem*, 14.
207. Broadhurst, *From Vine Street to Jerusalem*, 15.
208. Broadhurst, *From Vine Street to Jerusalem*, 18. Broadhurst served in the London CID until 1924, when he became assistant inspector general of the Palestine Police in charge of the CID.
209. Arrow, *Rogues and Others*, 13–16.
210. Arrow, *Rogues and Others*, 16.
211. Ernest Nicholls, *Crime within the Square Mile* (London: John Long, 1935), 18.
212. *1878 Commission*, 116.
213. Leeson, *Lost London*, 37–8. See also Cornish, *Cornish of Scotland Yard*, 9; Gough, *From Kew Observatory to Scotland Yard*, 19.
214. Divall, *Scoundrels and Scallywags*, 25.
215. Berrett, *When I was at Scotland Yard*, 59.

216. *1878 Commission*, 73; Wensley, *Forty Years of Scotland Yard*, 10.
217. *1879 Commission*, 226.
218. *1879 Commission*. See also Henry, *Detective-Inspector Henry's Famous Cases*, 13.
219. Cornish, *Cornish of Scotland Yard*, 9; Leeson, *Lost London*, 83–4.
220. Cornish, *Cornish of Scotland Yard*, 9.
221. Divall, *Scoundrels and Scallywags*, 25.
222. Woodhall, *Detective and Secret Service Days*, 20.
223. Police Orders, 25 Mar. 1904.
224. Police Orders, 24 Dec. 1907, p. 1256. See this reference for the subjects included in the examination, and 25 Mar. 1904, 2 Aug. 1904, 10 Dec. 1904 for the kind of questions asked.
225. Police Orders, 24 Dec. 1907, p. 1256.
226. Cornish, *Cornish of Scotland Yard*, 9–10.
227. Leeson, *Lost London*, 49.
228. Police Orders, 6 Apr. 1878; *Police Review*, 14 Sept. 1894, p. 437.
229. Police Orders, 27 July 1869.
230. Police Orders, 6 July 1878; *1878 Commission*, 2; *Desborough Committee*, 616.
231. *General Orders* in *Returns Relating to the Old Watch and the New Police*, PP, vol. 8, (1830–1), 284; Douglas J. Elliott, *Policing Shropshire, 1836–1967* (Studley: K. A. F. Brewin Books, 1984), 28.
232. *Annual Report of the Commissioner of Police of the Metropolis*, for 1918 and 1919, pt II, PP, vol. 10 (1920), p. 545.
233. For details, see Shpayer-Makov, *The Making of a Policeman*, 98–109.
234. Woodhall, *Detective and Secret Service Days*, 6.
235. For the training programme of policemen in the Birmingham City Police in 1905, see Reilly, *Policing Birmingham*, 69; in the county of Essex in 1912, see Totterdell, *Country Copper*, 41. The course Totterdell had to take before he was sent out to the streets lasted a month and included drill, police law and procedure, and the by-laws of the county. However, there was no library, and candidates had to purchase their own books. In his words, 'A young copper in the County Police for the greater part had to pick up the work as he went along.... It was all left to the initiative of the individual. If a man wanted to get on it was up to him.'
236. Berrett, *When I was at Scotland Yard*, 59; Savage, *Savage of Scotland Yard*, 22.
237. Cornish, *Cornish of Scotland Yard*, 4.
238. Brust, *'I Guarded Kings'*, 37.
239. *1878 Commission*, 75.
240. *1878 Commission*, 126.
241. *1878 Commission*, 23.
242. *1878 Commission*, pp. iv, 126 (in Liverpool); *1890 Committee*, 424.
243. *1878 Commission*, 65.
244. Leach, *On Top of the Underworld*, 102.
245. *The Times*, 2 Apr. 1878, p. 9; *Chambers's Journal*, 1/22 (31 May 1884), 338.
246. See, e.g., *1908 Commission*, vol. 51, p. 382.

247. Andy Green, 'Technical Education and State Formation in Nineteenth-Century England and France', *History of Education*, 24/2 (1995), 138.
248. E. Henry to Under Secretary of State, 13 May 1912, HO45/11000/223532; New Scotland Yard to Under Secretary of State, 16 Oct. 1913, MEPO2/1570.
249. Dilnot, *Scotland Yard*, 80.
250. Dilnot, *Scotland Yard*, 81–5.
251. Dilnot, *Scotland Yard*, 46.
252. *Annual Report of the Commissioner of Police of the Metropolis*, for 1918 and 1919, pt II, PP, vol. 10 (1920), p. 545.
253. See *The Times*, 1 Jan. 1909, p. 4.
254. For the Metropolitan Police, see *Police Review*, 4 Jan. 1897, p. 22; Lansdowne, *A Life's Reminiscences*, 6, 13. For the system in the City of London Police, see *1878 Commission*, 184.
255. Dew, *I Caught Crippen*, 85.
256. Brust, 'I Guarded Kings', 42.
257. Woodhall, *Detective and Secret Service Days*, 20.
258. Arrow, *Rogues and Others*, 42–3.
259. Broadhurst, *From Vine Street to Jerusalem*, 19.
260. Broadhurst, *From Vine Street to Jerusalem*, 20.
261. Broadhurst, *From Vine Street to Jerusalem*, 20–4.
262. *1878 Commission*, 239; *Instruction Book... of the Bristol Police Force* (1894), 18; *1908 Commission*, vol. 51, p. 202.
263. *1878 Commission*, 23.

CHAPTER 3. THE DETECTIVE AS WAGE-EARNER AND OFFICIAL CRIME FIGHTER

1. For some differences between the police forces in the metropolis, boroughs, and counties, see John Powell Martin and Gail Wilson, *The Police: A Study in Manpower* (London: Heinemann, 1969), 10–12.
2. For details, see Shpayer-Makov, *The Making of a Policeman*, ch. 5.
3. Hart, *The British Police*, 39.
4. Rumbelow, *I Spy Blue*, 220; Steedman, *Policing the Victorian Community*, 116–17.
5. Steedman, *Policing the Victorian Community*, 109–12. For pay to Black Country policemen in 1835–60, see Philips, *Crime and Authority*, 69. For police pay in Lancashire and Middlesbrough (1857–1912), where wages were generally high by contemporary standards, see Lowe, 'The Lancashire Constabulary', 49, and Taylor, *Policing the Victorian Town*, 126–30, respectively. For pay in the City of London Police in 1888, see *1868 Committee*, 397–8; *Police Guardian*, 15 Dec. 1888, p. 6. For an overall view of police wages in the period, see Martin and Wilson, *The Police*, 14–21.
6. For the Metropolitan Police, see Shpayer-Makov, *The Making of a Policeman*, 79; the Black Country, Philips, *Crime and Authority*, 65–8; the City of London Police, Rumbelow, *I Spy Blue*, 154, 207; Lancashire, Lowe, 'The Lancashire Constabulary', 54–9; Middlesbrough, Taylor, *Policing the Victorian Town*, 32–3, 42–5.
7. Steedman, *Policing the Victorian Community*, 161.

NOTES

8. See *Select Committee on Police Superannuation Funds*, PP, vol. 13 (1875), 376–7, 498, 573.
9. Lowe, 'The Lancashire Constabulary', 53. Different forces offered different combinations of these benefits.
10. *1868 Committee*, 403; *Select Committee on Police Superannuation Funds*, PP, vol. 15, (1877), 159; Steedman, *Policing the Victorian Community*, 124–5; Lowe, 'The Lancashire Constabulary', 52–3; Taylor, *Policing the Victorian Town*, 130–1. For a short history of police pensions in our period, see Martin and Wilson, *The Police*, 26–9.
11. Steedman, *Policing the Victorian Community*, 113; Lowe, 'The Lancashire Constabulary', 52.
12. Shpayer-Makov, *The Making of a Policeman*, 181; Joanne Klein, *Invisible Men: The Secret Lives of Police Constables in Liverpool, Manchester, and Birmingham, 1900–1939* (Liverpool: Liverpool University Press, 2010), 8, 285.
13. Morson, *A Force Remembered*, 31, 36; Clay (ed.), *The Leeds Police*, 65.
14. Steedman, *Policing the Victorian Community*, 107; Martin and Wilson, *The Police*, 30.
15. For the disaffection of officers regarding conditions of service in the Metropolitan Police, see Shpayer-Makov, *The Making of a Policeman*, 179–86. For a discussion of organized strikes in provincial Britain, see Steedman, *Policing the Victorian Community*, 132–6. See also Gerald W. Reynolds and Anthony Judge, *The Night the Police Went on Strike* (London: Weidenfeld and Nicolson, 1968).
16. *1879 Commission*, 229.
17. Steedman, *Policing the Victorian Community*, 80–3, 170–1; Martin and Wilson, *The Police*, 13–14; Lowe, 'The Lancashire Constabulary', 55; Taylor, *Policing the Victorian Town*, 50, 113–25.
18. For examples, see the column 'Smart Captures' in the *Police Review*, 16 Feb. 1906, p. 75.
19. Woodhall, *Detective and Secret Service Days*, 18.
20. Sidney Theodore Felstead, *Sir Richard Muir: A Memoir of a Public Prosecutor* (London: John Lane, 1927), 287.
21. *1878 Commission*, 61.
22. For London, see Clarkson and Richardson, *Police!*, 227. For Manchester, see Jerome Caminada, *Twenty-Five Years of Detective Life*, ii (Warrington: Prism Books, 1983; first published 1901), 8. For the City of London Police, see *1878 Commission*, 183.
23. Maurice Moser, *Stories from Scotland Yard* (London: George Routledge and Sons, 1890), 33.
24. Police Orders, 24 Dec. 1907, pp. 1258, 1261.
25. 'The Police of London', *Quarterly Review*, 129 (July 1870), 123.
26. For police leisure activities, see Shpayer-Makov, *The Making of a Policeman*, ch. 7, and 'Relinking Work and Leisure in Late Victorian and Edwardian England', *International Review of Social History*, 47/2 (2002); Klein, *Invisible Men*, 212.
27. *1890 Commission*, 432.
28. Philip John Stead, *The Police of Britain* (London: Macmillan, 1985), 58.
29. *1879 Commission*, 226–7; *Penny Illustrated Paper*, 8 Oct. 1910, p. 463.
30. 'Detectives', *Saturday Review*, 9 Feb. 1884, p. 178. See also above, ch. 1, p. 37.
31. Timothy Cavanagh, *Scotland Yard Past and Present* (London: Chatto & Windus, 1893), 28, 36.

NOTES

32. *1908 Commission*, vol. 50, p. 626, vol. 51, pp. 153, 165; John George Littlechild, *Reminiscences of Chief-Inspector Littlechild* (London: Leadenhall Press, 1894), 3.
33. Leach, *On Top of the Underworld*, 118.
34. James Monro to Under Secretary of State, 11 Nov. 1889, HO45/1002/A49,463/13; E. Henry to Under Secretary of State, 13 May 1912, HO45/11000/223532.
35. 'On Duty in Plain Clothes', *Cassell's Saturday Journal*, 28 May 1892, p. 852.
36. *Police Guardian*, 16 Jan. 1892, p. 6.
37. *1868 Committee*, 287; E. Henry to Under Secretary of State, 13 May 1912, HO45/11000/223532.
38. *1868 Committee*, 299; *Desborough Committee*, 621, 623.
39. Sweeney, *At Scotland Yard*, 19–20.
40. Bishop, *From Information Received*, 169.
41. *1868 Committee*, 300; *Police Review*, 31 July 1893, p. 367; Hambrook, *Hambrook of the Yard*, 75.
42. *Desborough Committee*, 619.
43. 'Detectives and their work', *All the Year Round*, 36 (Apr. 1885), 137.
44. *Police Guardian*, 12 Aug. 1881, p. 3, 13 Mar. 1885, p. 3; *1890 Committee*, 427.
45. Leach, *On Top of the Underworld*, 98. See also Neil, *Man-Hunters of Scotland Yard*, 66.
46. Brust, *'I Guarded Kings'*, 66; Bishop, *From Information Received*, 174.
47. Dew, *I Caught Crippen*, 198.
48. *Police Review*, 29 May 1893, p. 256.
49. Clarke, *The Policemen of Hull*, 82. See also Lansdowne, *A Life's Reminiscences*, 184; Cornish, *Cornish of Scotland Yard*, 31.
50. For a few of the many cases reported in the press, see *Police Guardian*, 2 Sept. 1881, p. 5, 22 Oct. 1886, p. 2, 18 Feb. 1887, p. 2, 20 Jan. 1888, pp. 2–3, 3 Nov. 1888, p. 5, 27 July 1889, p. 4, 16 Jan. 1892, p. 6; *Police Review*, 29 May 1893, p. 256.
51. *Police Guardian*, 30 Apr. 1886, p. 2.
52. *Police Guardian*, 6 Mar. 1885, p. 6, 30 July 1892, p. 5, 19 Oct. 1895, p. 8.
53. Brust, *'I Guarded Kings'*, 114.
54. Brust, *'I Guarded Kings'*, 113.
55. Bishop, *From Information Received*, 174. See also Thompson, *Guard from the Yard*, 29–31.
56. Bishop, *From Information Received*, 175.
57. Leach, *On Top of the Underworld*, 147.
58. Lansdowne, *A Life's Reminiscences*, 127; Caminada, *Twenty-Five Years of Detective Life*, ii. 9.
59. *Daily Chronicle*, 2 June 1884, p. 5.
60. Dew, *I Caught Crippen*, 104. See also Hambrook, *Hambrook of the Yard*, 91.
61. Harold Brust, *In Plain Clothes* (London: Stanley Paul, 1937), 107.
62. Lansdowne, *A Life's Reminiscences*, 39, 167–8.
63. Woodhall, *Detective and Secret Service Days*, 22.
64. Bishop, *From Information Received*, 168, 178.
65. *1868 Committee*, 286, 299.
66. Thomas P. McNaught, *The Recollections of a Glasgow Detective Officer* (London: Simpkin, Marshall & Co., 1887), 7. See also the portrait of George Bates, ex-chief detective of the Leeds police, *Police Review*, 19 July 1907, p. 342.

67. For London, see *1878 Commission*, pp. vii, 65; for Liverpool, p. 122.
68. 'On Duty in Plain Clothes', 852.
69. An example was William Henderson, who became head constable of the Leeds Police. See *1878 Commission*, 133.
70. E. Henry to Under Secretary of State, 13 May 1912, HO45/11000/223532.
71. See *Police Review*, 6 Nov. 1893, p. 530, 13 Mar. 1914, p. 125. See also New Scotland Yard Proposal, 20 June 1912, HO45/11000/223532.
72. E. Henry to Under Secretary of State, 13 May 1912, HO45/11000/223532.
73. *1879 Commission*, 220; *Police Review*, 31 Mar. 1904, p. 160; *Desborough Committee*, 610, 619.
74. *The Times*, 30 May 1840, p. 6.
75. 'Memorandum', 14 June 1842, pp. 15–16, HO45/OS/292.
76. Joan Lock, *Dreadful Deeds and Awful Murders: Scotland Yard's First Detectives, 1829–1878* (Taunton: Barn Owl Books, 1990), 70; *1878 Commission*, p. iii.
77. Memorandum from Mayne to Home Office, 17 Oct. 1844, HO45/OS/724.
78. *1878 Commission*, pp. iii–iv. Pay in the uniformed police in 1868 ranged from £67 12s. per annum for second-class sergeants to £136 11s. for first-class inspectors; for superintendents from £299 17s. 4d. to £424 17s. 8d. (*1868 Committee*, 13).
79. For pay in the Metropolitan Police for all ranks, see *1878 Commission*, appendix B, 265.
80. A. L. Bowley, *Wages and Income* (Cambridge: Cambridge University Press, 1937), 46; Steedman, *Policing the Victorian Community*, 116.
81. *1868 Committee*, 286; *Sporting Gazette*, 18 Jan. 1868, p. 41.
82. *Globe*, 31 July 1878, p. 6; *Morning Post*, 15 Dec. 1877, p. 4. Whether detectives deserved a pay rise was a weighty argument within police circles as well (*1879 Commission*, 220).
83. *Police Guardian*, 14 Sept. 1877, p. 4. For the turf fraud scandal, see above, ch.1, p. 38.
84. *The Times*, 22 Nov. 1877, p. 9.
85. *1878 Commission*, pp. vii–viii, xii, xiv, xvi.
86. *1878 Commission*, p. xvi.
87. *1878 Commission*, 118, 121, 133–4.
88. In Birmingham, even in 1877, while the rate of pay for constables ranged between 23s. and 30s. a week, and that for sergeants from 32s. to 38s., detectives usually earned the highest amount in each rank (*1878 Commission*, 116). In the same year in Liverpool, where a discrepancy existed all along the command structure, the uniformed superintendents' income was £180 a year, while the detective superintendent was paid £280 (*1878 Commission*, 121). The career of Superintendent Lawrence Kehoe, chief of the detective department in the Liverpool Constabulary, illustrates the increase in remuneration with rank (*Police Guardian*, 11 Oct. 1878, p. 2, repr. from the *Globe*). Kehoe joined the force in 1834 and received 16s. a week. With the establishment of the new police in 1835, his wages rose to 18s. and in 1845 to a guinea a week. In 1848 he entered the detective ranks at 25s. a week, and in 1851, upon promotion to detective inspector, he received 30s. In 1853 his pay increased by 3s. a week, and in 1857 he was made a salaried officer at £105. In 1860 he became a head of department and a superintendent with a salary of £200. In 1865 it increased to £235, in 1871 to £250, in 1872 to £260, and in 1873 to £280, with emoluments that brought it

NOTES

to £400 (when the head constable was getting £1,000 a year). Kehoe retired in 1873 at 69 years of age, replaced by 34-year-old George Williams, chief constable of Wigan, who, unlike Kehoe, had had a good education (*Police Guardian*, 7 Mar. 1879, p. 2; see this reference for the age, salary, and length of service of other salaried detectives in Liverpool). For detectives' pay in Hull, see Clarke, *The Policemen of Hull*, 62; in Norwich, Morson, *A Force Remembered*, 30; in the City of London, *1878 Commission*, 184, 191; Rumbelow, *I Spy Blue*, 207.

89. *1878 Commission*, 119.
90. *1868 Committee*, 289; Vincent, *A Police Code*, 279; Police Orders, 14 Jan. 1909.
91. *1878 Commission*, p. iv. For Liverpool and Leeds in the same year, see *1878 Commission*, 130, 133. In Manchester in 1908, superintendents were paid £13 per annum, inspectors £10, sergeants £9, and constables £9 (*Police Instruction Book* (Manchester, 1908), 26). Uniformed officers also received such an allowance when performing duties in plain clothes.
92. Letter from Commissioners to Home Office, 2 Nov. 1844, HO45/OS 724; *1878 Commission*, 7, 234. In 1877, when out of town, the superintendent and the three chief inspectors at Scotland Yard were allotted 15s. a day, the three inspectors 13s., and the twenty-two sergeants 10s. (*1878 Commission*, p. iv; for allowances in the Liverpool police in 1877, see p. 122). In the divisions, sergeants were allocated 4s. 6d., and constables 3s. 6d., with an additional 1s. per night for lodging. In town, if a detective was away from his home for more than eight hours, he was permitted a refreshment allowance—sergeants 2s. and inspectors 3s. (*1878 Commission*, 7, 40; for the City of London Police, see pp. 192–3). For the rates in the London CID in 1912, see Police Orders, 30 Aug. 1912.
93. *1878 Commission*, 176; *Desborough Committee*, 617.
94. *1878 Commission*, 142, 148, 190; Henderson, *Clues*, 187–9, 194, 199.
95. *1878 Commission*, 7, 40.
96. *1878 Commission*, 7, 33, 176.
97. *1878 Commission*, pp. vii, 7, 40. So acute were the detectives' grievances about this matter, that *The Times* was prompted to publish an article about it: see 7 Aug. 1858, p. 11.
98. *1868 Committee*, 307–9; *1878 Commission*, pp. vii, 32, 40, 176; Moser, *Stories from Scotland Yard*, 204.
99. Moser, *Stories from Scotland Yard*, 205.
100. *1878 Commission*, 108.
101. Bishop, *From Information Received*, 269.
102. *1878 Commission*, 32.
103. *1878 Commission*, 8, 210; Klein, *Invisible Men*, 127, 206. For similar charges, see 'Detectives as They Are', *Chambers's Journal*, 7/341 (9 July 1870), 446.
104. For the Metropolitan Police, see *1878 Commission*, 7; *Daily News*, 6 Nov. 1877, p. 2. For Leeds, see *1878 Commission*, 133–4, for Liverpool and Manchester, p. 125; for Birmingham, see *Police Guardian*, 23 Nov. 1877, p. 3.
105. *1878 Commission*, 32.
106. *Police Guardian*, 23 Nov. 1877, p. 3; *1878 Commission*, 85.
107. *1878 Commission*, pp. xii, 8, 33, 85, 189.
108. *1878 Commission*, 7–8.

NOTES

109. *1878 Commission*, pp. xii–xiii, 136–7, 178, 184, 188.
110. Police Orders, 16 May 1878; *Globe*, 5 Aug. 1878, p. 2. For additional instructions, see Police Orders, 18 Feb. 1885, 24 Dec. 1907, p. 1258.
111. *Reynolds's News*, 19 Dec. 1880, p. 4.
112. Leeson, *Lost London*, 187.
113. For details, see Dilnot, *The Story of Scotland Yard*, 260.
114. *1878 Commission*, 47; Littlechild, *Reminiscences of Chief-Inspector Littlechild*, 223; Lansdowne, *A Life's Reminiscences*, 162.
115. *Police Guardian*, 4 Feb. 1881, p. 5, 16 Jan. 1892, p. 6, 17 Aug. 1895, p. 5; *Police Review*, 6 July 1894, p. 320, 28 Jan. 1898, pp. 42–3. For a debate in the House of Commons on the subject of a Home Office reward to provincial officers, see *Police Guardian*, 11 June 1892, p. 5.
116. *Police Guardian*, 5 Jan. 1889, p. 5; Moser, *Stories from Scotland Yard*, 204.
117. *Police Review*, 28 Jan. 1898, p. 42; Savage, *Savage of Scotland Yard*, 18.
118. *Police Review*, 22 Nov. 1895, p. 559.
119. *Police Guardian*, 9 May 1896, p. 4.
120. *Penny Illustrated Paper*, 8 Oct. 1910, p. 463.
121. 'Return of Weekly Rate of Pay and Uniform' (1888), HO45/10002/A49463.
122. The range of earnings of clerks was broad. While very few earned £500 per annum and up, dock clerks earned an average of 24s. per week in the 1890s (Richard N. Price, 'Society, Status and Jingoism: The Social Roots of Lower Middle Class Patriotism, 1870–1900', in Geoffrey Crossick (ed.), *The Lower Middle Class in Britain 1870–1914* (London: Croom Helm, 1977), 98). In 1909, the average annual salary of (male) commercial clerks was £80 and only 23% earned more than £160 (G. L. Anderson, 'The Social Economy of Late-Victorian Clerks', in Crossick (ed.), *The Lower Middle Class in Britain*, 132 n. 56).
123. Cook, *M: MI5's First Spymaster*, 144.
124. For the case of Detective Inspector Ore of the Birmingham Police, see *Police Guardian*, 23 Mar. 1895, p. 1.
125. *Police Review*, 1 Oct. 1897, p. 474.
126. 'Detectives as They Are', 445; Cavanagh, *Scotland Yard Past and Present*, 67; *Reynolds's News*, 14 June 1896, p. 8.
127. *Police Review*, 15 May 1908, p. 204.
128. Caminada, *Twenty-Five Years of Detective Life*, ii. 4.
129. Porter, *The Origins of the Vigilant State*, 129; Cook, *M: MI5's First Spymaster*, 169.
130. Arrow, *Rogues and Others*, 193–6, 209. His arrival in Barcelona caused a great stir. Two thousand people gathered to protest his appointment. A man was killed during the demonstration, inflaming emotions, and an angry crowd attempted to attack him in his office. Placards that were circulated referred to him as 'The Spy, Arrow'.
131. From the unpublished 'Diary of Detective Chief Inspector Frederick George Abberline', courtesy of the Metropolitan Police Museum; Macnaghten, *Days of my Years*, 273–4.
132. Macnaghten, *Days of my Years*, 274; Divall, *Scoundrels and Scallywags*, 183.
133. *Morning Post*, 14 Dec. 1887, p. 1.
134. *Police Review*, 24 Oct. 1902, p. 513.

135. *Illustrated Times*, 2 Feb. 1856, p. 70.
136. 'Abberline Diary', n.p.
137. *Police Review*, 13 July 1894, p. 333, repr. from *Cassell's Saturday Journal*.
138. *Report of the Director of Criminal Investigations*, in *Annual Report of the Commissioner of Police of the Metropolis*, for 1881, PP, vol. 33 (1882), 336; Macnaghten, *Days of my Years*, 128; Smith, *From Constable to Commissioner*, 173.
139. *Penny Illustrated Paper*, 8 Oct. 1910, p. 463.
140. Nicholls, *Crime within the Square Mile*, 121; Leach, *On Top of the Underworld*, 81.
141. For example, Bishop, *From Information Received*, 172–3; Fitch, *Memoirs of a Royal Detective*, p. v; Neil, *Man-Hunters of Scotland Yard*, 2.
142. Fitch, *Traitors Within*, 113; Fitch, *Memoirs of a Royal Detective*, 253.
143. Fitch, *Memoirs of a Royal Detective*, 257, 278.
144. Greenham, *Scotland Yard Experiences*, 3–5. For gifts and awards by foreign sovereigns to other English detectives, see *Police Review*, 4 Oct. 1901, p. 474; *Reynolds's News*, 3 Feb. 1895, p. 5; *The Times*, 7 Dec. 1903, p. 14.
145. *1878 Commission*, 8.
146. *Police Review*, 19 July 1901, p. 342; Leeson, *Lost London*, 7–8; Hambrook, *Hambrook of the Yard*, 90.
147. Dew, *I Caught Crippen*, 82.
148. *Police Guardian*, 29 Apr. 1881, p. 2; *Police Review*, 13 Mar. 1896, p. 127, 28 Jan. 1898, p. 42.
149. *Police Guardian*, 21 July 1888, p. 8, 7 Sept. 1895, p. 2.
150. Moser, *Stories from Scotland Yard*, 224; *Desborough Committee*, 611.
151. *Police Guardian*, 2 Jan. 1892, p. 6, 19 Nov. 1892, p. 6.
152. *Police Guardian*, 14 July 1894, p. 8.
153. *Police and Public*, 6 July 1889, p. 1.
154. *Police Review*, 1 Oct. 1897, p. 474.
155. *Police Review*, 22 Feb. 1902, p. 90; *Police Guardian*, 16 Feb. 1889, p. 5, 16 Mar. 1889, p. 5.
156. Gough, *From Kew Observatory to Scotland Yard*, 207–10.
157. *Police Review*, 22 Feb. 1895, p. 91. See also *Police Guardian*, 13 Oct. 1888, p. 4.
158. Fitch, *Memoirs of a Royal Detective*, 27, 47, 63, 129, 131.
159. 'Our Police System', 698–9. For similar experiences, see Fitch, *Memoirs of a Royal Detective*, 242; Woodhall, *Detective and Secret Service Days*, 21–2. Detective Cecil Bishop, who guarded the Prince of Wales (the future king of England) during his studies at Oxford, used to accompany him everywhere, including riding and hunting (*From Information Received*, 179; see also pp. 171–3, 178).
160. Woodhall, *Detective and Secret Service Days*, 36.
161. Arrow, *Rogues and Others*, 169.
162. *1878 Commission*, 9 (testimony of the superintendent in charge of the detective department at Scotland Yard), p. 123 (testimony of the head constable of the Liverpool force), p. 137 (testimony of the head constable of Leeds), pp. 177, 180 (testimony of the head constable of Bristol).
163. *1878 Commission*, 32.
164. *Police Review*, 13 Mar. 1914, p. 125.
165. Vincent, *A Police Code*, 105; *1878 Commission*, 133.

NOTES

166. *Globe*, 5 Aug. 1878, p. 24.
167. *Desborough Committee*, 616.
168. *1878 Commission*, 211.
169. Memo of 24 Mar. 1845, MEPO7/11.
170. *1878 Commission*, 120; see also Howard Vincent's testimony to the *1879 Commission* (pp. 222–3).
171. Smith, *From Constable to Commissioner*, 95.
172. *Globe*, 5 Aug. 1878, p. 2. For the importance of supervision for the head constable of Birmingham, see *1878 Commission*, 115.
173. Morson, *A Force Remembered*, 56.
174. *Police Review*, 14 Sept. 1894, p. 437.
175. *1878 Commission*, p. v. For the system in Birmingham, see pp. 118–19; in Liverpool, p. 128.
176. *Globe*, 5 Aug. 1878, p. 2.
177. Vincent, *A Police Code*, 106; *The Times*, Jan. 1909, p. 39.
178. *1879 Commission*, 223; Police Orders, 20 Dec. 1904.
179. *Globe*, 5 Aug. 1878, p. 2.
180. *Police Review*, 14 Sept. 1894, p. 437.
181. Police Orders, 5 June 1878; see also 20 Jan. and 12 Feb. 1879; *1879 Commission*, 225.
182. See, e.g., *Instructions for the Liverpool Police Force* (1867), 56, 59; *Police Instruction Book* (Manchester, 1908), 58–9, 86–7.
183. Vincent, *A Police Code*, 106.
184. Police Orders, 20 Dec. 1904. See also *1879 Commission*, 223.
185. Leeson, *Lost London*, 66.
186. 'Detectives', *Saturday Review*, 9 Feb. 1884, p. 178.
187. Vincent, *Literacy and Popular Culture*, 120–1.
188. *Desborough Committee*, 618.
189. Lansdowne, *A Life's Reminiscences*, 1–2; *1878 Commission*, 108; *1890 Committee*, 426, 430. John Littlechild of the Special Branch reported that sometimes, especially when the public was asked to provide information about a case, he and his men had to deal with up to seventy or eighty letters a morning, since 'one never knew which particular letter might contain a particle of information which might be of value' (*1890 Committee*, 436).
190. For details of the many required reports and registers, see, e.g., Police Orders, 24 Dec. 1907, pp. 1261–3.
191. *Report of the Director of Criminal Investigations*, in *Annual Report of the Commissioner of Police of the Metropolis*, for 1879, PP, vol. 34 (1880), 416.
192. Anderson, *The Lighter Side of my Official Life*, 189.
193. *Police Review*, 13 Mar. 1914, p. 125; Klein, *Invisible Men*, 127.
194. 'Our Police System', 697.
195. *Police Review*, 13 Mar. 1893, p. 123; Klein, *Invisible Men*, 127.
196. *1878 Commission*, 187.
197. *Police Review*, 19 Feb. 1897, p. 93.
198. *Police Review*, 13 Mar. 1914, p. 125; Klein, *Invisible Men*, 127.
199. *Police Review*, 12 Feb. 1897, p. 75. See also *Police Review*, 19 Feb. 1897, p. 93. For detectives' responses to such allegations, see *Police Review*, 19 Mar. 1897, p. 147.
200. Monro, 'The London Police', 626.

201. Robert D. Storch, 'Police Control of Street Prostitution in Victorian London', in David H. Bayley, *Police and Society* (Beverly Hills, CA: Sage Publications, 1977), 49; see also pp. 53, 56.
202. Clive Emsley, *Policing and its Context, 1750–1870* (New York: Schocken Books, 1983), 152.
203. William McAdoo, 'The London Police from a New York Point of View', *Century Magazine*, 78 (Sept. 1909), 664.
204. Rob Sindall, 'Middle-Class Crime in Nineteenth-Century England', *Criminal Justice History*, 4 (1983), 23–4.
205. 'Our Police System', 699.
206. Arrow, *Rogues and Others*, 174.
207. In the event, Arrow's action proved to be justified.
208. Caminada, *Twenty-Five Years of Detective Life*, ii. 78, 135.
209. Littlechild, *Reminiscences of Chief-Inspector Littlechild*, 125.
210. For selected parts of this memorandum, see Marie Mulvey Roberts et al. (eds), *The Militants* (London: Routledge, 1994).
211. Judith R. Walkowitz, *Prostitution and Victorian Society* (Cambridge: Cambridge University Press, 1980), 171.
212. Davis, 'Prosecutions and their Context', 398; Godfrey, Lawrence, and Williams, *History and Crime*, 80–90.
213. Jennifer Davis, 'Jennings' Buildings and the Royal Borough', in David Feldman and Gareth Stedman Jones (eds), *Metropolis. London: Histories and Representations since 1800* (London: Routledge, 1989), 11; Jennifer Davis, 'The London Garotting Panic of 1862: A Moral Panic and the Creation of a Criminal Class in Mid-Victorian England', in Gatrell, Lenman, and Parker (eds), *Crime and the Law*, 191–2, 212–13.
214. Wiener, *Reconstructing the Criminal*, 303, 342–5.
215. Raphael Samuel (ed.), *East End Underworld: Chapters in the Life of Arthur Harding* (London: Routledge & Kegan Paul, 1981), 188.
216. Gatrell, 'The Decline of Theft and Violence', 265, 326. Indeed, about half the prisoners in the early 1890s were sentenced to terms of less than six months (p. 330).
217. Gatrell, 'The Decline of Theft and Violence', 265.
218. Jennifer Davis, 'From "Rookeries" to "Communities": Race, Poverty and Policing in London, 1850–1985', *History Workshop*, 28 (Spring 1989), 68; Davis, 'Jennings' Buildings and the Royal Borough', 24–6; Roger Swift, '"Another Stafford Street Row": Law, Order and the Irish Presence in Mid-Victorian Wolverhampton', in Roger Swift and Sheridan Gilley (eds), *The Irish in the Victorian City* (London: Croom Helm, 1985), 179–206.
219. Davis, 'Jennings' Buildings and the Royal Borough', 21, 26.
220. For a fuller picture of police treatment of street-walking prostitutes in Victorian London, see Storch, 'Police Control of Street Prostitution in Victorian London'; Judith R. Walkowitz, *City of Dreadful Delight* (London: Virago, 1992), 127–31; Petrow, *Policing Morals*, 117–46.
221. Benjamin Scott, *A State Iniquity* (New York: Augustus M. Kelley, 1968; first published 1890), 21, 32–3.
222. Samuel (ed.), *East End Underworld*, 189–94. See also 'How the Police Abuse their Power', *Pall Mall Gazette*, 7 July 1887, p. 1. For more details, see Petrow, *Policing Morals*, ch. 3.

223. *Police Guardian*, 7 Nov. 1896, p. 4.
224. Bishop, *From Information Received*, 248–9.
225. *Police Guardian*, 12 July 1878, p. 4. In this case, a London detective beat the suspect with his stick and his fists, but the jury in the trial that followed found him not guilty on the grounds that he had employed necessary force.
226. Bishop, *From Information Received*, 177.
227. Littlechild, *Reminiscences of Chief-Inspector Littlechild*, 75; Leeson, *Lost London*, 102, 123–4; Wensley, *Forty Years of Scotland Yard*, 275–6; Leach, *On Top of the Underworld*, 143–4.
228. *Instructions for the Liverpool Police Force* (1878), 100–1.
229. Jeyes and How, *The Life of Sir Howard Vincent*, 98.
230. *The Times*, 1 Jan. 1909, p. 4.
231. H. L. Adam, *Police Work from Within* (London: Holden and Hardingham, 1913), 133.
232. *Police Guardian*, 12 Oct. 1883, p. 5. For other accounts of assistance to criminals and their families, see Leach, *On Top of the Underworld*, 70–1; Reginald Morrish, *Christ with the C.I.D.* (London: Epworth Press, 1953), 80.
233. Wiener, *Reconstructing the Criminal*, 305.
234. Garland, *The Culture of Control*, 39.
235. Robert Anderson, *Criminals and Crime: Some Facts and Suggestions* (New York: Garland Publishing, 1984; first published 1907), 176.
236. Adam, *Police Work from Within*, 132.
237. Adam, *Police Work from Within*, 132–3.
238. Taylor, 'Rationing Crime', 581, 585–8; Davis, 'Jennings' Buildings and the Royal Borough', 26–8.
239. Davis, 'Jennings' Buildings and the Royal Borough', 28.
240. Samuel (ed.), *East End Underworld*, 200.
241. 'Detectives', *Saturday Review*, 9 Feb. 1884, p. 178; Divall, *Scoundrels and Scallywags*, 72.
242. 'Why Detectives Fail', *London Magazine*, 13 (1904–5), 65.
243. See ch. 1 for a discussion of the innate British aversion to the concept of spying, as personified by the French police.
244. Porter, *The Origins of the Vigilant State*, 69.
245. Porter, *The Origins of the Vigilant State*, 130–48, 185.
246. Shpayer, 'British Anarchism 1881–1914', 337.
247. *The Times*, 7 May 1892, p. 4; *Commonweal*, 9 Jan. 1892, p. 8.
248. *Evening Herald* (Dublin), 25 Apr. 1894, p. 2.
249. Sweeney, *At Scotland Yard*, 72.
250. Sweeney, *At Scotland Yard*, 204–5; *Reynolds's News*, 14 Apr. 1895, p. 5, 28 Apr. 1895, p. 4.
251. *Liberty* (Feb. 1895), p. 109.
252. *The Times*, 10 Feb. 1892, p. 11.
253. For Monro's attitude, see *Reynolds's News*, 5 May 1895. See also Moylan, *Scotland Yard and the Metropolitan Police*, 160; Basil Thomson, *The Story of Scotland Yard* (London: Grayson & Grayson, 1935), 100.
254. *Commonweal*, 5 Mar. 1892, p. 38.
255. *Commonweal*, 5 Mar. 1892, p. 38.

256. David Nicoll, *The Walsall Anarchists* (Sheffield, n.d.), 3; *Commonweal* (Apr. 1891), pp. 28–9.
257. *Commonweal*, 5 Mar. 1892, p. 38; Nicoll, *The Walsall Anarchists*, 9.
258. Cook, *M: MI5's First Spymaster*, 91; *Reynolds's News*, 14 Apr. 1895, p. 5.
259. Cook, *M: MI5's First Spymaster*, 93.
260. For Melville's biography, see Cook, *M: MI5's First Spymaster*.
261. *The Times*, 10 Feb. 1892, p. 11.
262. Cook, *M: MI5's First Spymaster*, 91.
263. *Reynolds's News*, 14 Apr. 1895, p. 5.
264. For details, see Shpayer, 'British Anarchism 1881–1914', 333–8. On one occasion anarchists were arrested for the rare offence of distributing bills without the printers' name and address.
265. See, e.g., Quail, *The Slow Burning Fuse*, 138.
266. *Freedom* (Mar. 1892), p. 1; *Commonweal*, 2 July 1892, p. 2.
267. *Adult*, Oct. 1897, pp. 40–7.
268. Sweeney, *At Scotland Yard*, 181.
269. Sweeney, *At Scotland Yard*, 178–9.
270. Sweeney, *At Scotland Yard*, 189, 186.
271. See Sweeney, *At Scotland Yard*, 190–7, for a similar case.
272. Porter, *The Origins of the Vigilant State*, 189.
273. Porter, *The Origins of the Vigilant State*, 92–3, 145. However, see John Burns's complaints in ch. 5, p. 213.
274. *Daily News*, 6 Nov. 1877, p. 2.
275. The late historian Barbara Weinberger concluded that extra-legal practices of various degrees flourished in urban forces, notably in the Metropolitan Police and among CIDs. This was based on interviews with police officers from different parts of the country regarding police work from the 1930s to the 1960s (Barbara Weinberger, *The Best Police in the World* (Aldershot: Scolar Press, 1995), 185). The evidence for the period covered in this volume suggests this was probably also true in an earlier period.
276. The radical *Penny Illustrated Paper* contended in 1910 that the police made the occasional arrest 'just to keep up appearances, but usually the well-to-do bookie pays a little sum weekly to "be on the right side"' (*Penny Illustrated Paper*, 1 Oct. 1910, p. 429).
277. Samuel (ed.), *East End Underworld*, 200, 203.
278. *Standard*, 18 July 1906, p. 8.
279. *Police Review*, 18 May 1906, p. 231. See also Petrow, *Policing Morals*, 72–5.
280. *Penny Illustrated Paper*, 10 Sept. 1910, p. 330. See also *Police Review*, 13 Mar. 1914, p. 125. For a radical contemporary perspective on why Syme was discharged, see *Penny Illustrated Paper*, 23 July 1910, p. 110, 30 July 1910, p. 143, 13 Aug. 1910, p. 204. For details of his campaign, see Reynolds and Judge, *The Night the Police Went on Strike*, 6–21.
281. *Penny Illustrated Paper*, 10 Sept. 1910, p. 330.
282. *1868 Committee*, 298; Bentley, *English Criminal Justice*, 30, 227, 229.
283. For details, see Angus McLaren, *A Prescription for Murder* (Chicago: Chicago University Press, 1993), 107–10.
284. *1908 Commission*, vol. 51, p. 268.
285. 'Our Police System', 697. See also *1908 Committee*, vol. 51, pp. 250–1.
286. *1868 Committee*, 278, 311; *1878 Commission*, 5, 23, 48.

287. 'Detectives and their Work', 137.
288. 'Detectives and their Work', 137.
289. *Police Service Advertiser*, 17 Feb. 1886, p. 1. For such cases, see *Police Guardian*, 1 Sept. 1888, p. 6; Bishop, *From Information Received*, 30–1.
290. *1878 Commission*, 5.
291. Vincent, *A Police Code*, 105.
292. *1868 Committee*, 278; *1878 Commission*, 5; Littlechild, *Reminiscences of Chief-Inspector Littlechild*, 76; Fuller, *Recollections of a Detective*, 213–14; Leeson, *Lost London*, 142. See also an article in the *Daily News*, repr. in *Police Guardian*, 9 Apr. 1886, pp. 2–3.
293. *1868 Committee*, 278.
294. *1868 Committee*, 294.
295. *Police Review*, 31 July 1893, p. 367.
296. Repr. in *Police Guardian*, 9 Apr. 1886, p. 3.
297. *1868 Committee*, 305; see also pp. 294–5, 297, 305–6.
298. *1868 Committee*, 279, 295.
299. Vincent, *A Police Code*, 105.
300. *1908 Commission*, vol. 51, p. 263; *Police Review*, 8 Jan. 1897, p. 19.
301. For details, see *Police Review*, 28 Dec. 1894, p. 614, repr. from *Answers*.
302. *1868 Committee*, 279, 295.
303. Brust, *In Plain Clothes*, 24; Fitch, *Traitors Within*, 16; Caminada, *Twenty-Five Years of Detective Life*, ii. 9, 115; Divall, *Scoundrels and Scallywags*, 32–3.
304. Carolyn Steedman, *The Radical Soldier's Tale: John Pearman, 1819–1908* (London: Routledge, 1988; written by John Pearman in 1881–2), 190–1.
305. Littlechild, *Reminiscences of Chief-Inspector Littlechild*, 76; *1878 Commission*, 30; Carlin, *Reminiscences of an Ex-Detective*, 220–1; Lansdowne, *A Life's Reminiscences*, 143.
306. Dilnot, *Scotland Yard*, 48.
307. Littlechild, *Reminiscences of Chief-Inspector Littlechild*, 82.
308. *Police Guardian*, 9 Apr. 1886, p. 3, quoting the *Daily News*.
309. Dilnot, *Scotland Yard*, 48; Littlechild, *Reminiscences of Chief-Inspector Littlechild*, 77.
310. Littlechild, *Reminiscences of Chief-Inspector Littlechild*, 70–3.
311. Dilnot, *Scotland Yard*, 48.
312. Arthur Griffiths, *Mysteries of Police and Crime* (London: Cassell, 1899), i. 37. See also *Desborough Committee*, 611.
313. Dew, *I Caught Crippen*, 89.
314. Blanchard Jerrold and Gustave Doré, *London: A Pilgrimage*, intro. by Peter Ackroyd (London: Anthem Press, 2005; first published 1872), 196. See also *1878 Commission*, 5; Leach, *On Top of the Underworld*, 109; *1908 Commission*, vol. 51, pp. 251–2. By contrast, the Paris police, under the Prefect Louis Lépine, made sure that detectives were 'completely nondescript in appearance', refusing to accept men taller than 5 feet 6 inches or having any distinguishing marks (Thorwald, *The Century of the Detective*, 46).
315. *Police Review*, 28 Dec. 1894, p. 614, repr. from *Answers*.
316. *Reynolds's News*, 10 Mar. 1895, p. 5.
317. *Reynolds's News*, 7 Apr. 1895, p. 5.
318. *Globe*, 5 Aug. 1878, p. 1.

NOTES

INTRODUCTION TO PART TWO

1. *1878 Commission*, 192.
2. James Greenwood, *The Seven Curses of London*, intro. by Jeffrey Richards (Oxford: Blackwell, 1981; first published 1869), 123.
3. *Instructions for the Liverpool Constabulary Force* (1856), 27; (1867), 61; (1878), 100.
4. Macnaghten, *Days of my Years*, 124.
5. Superintendent Bent, head of the Manchester Division of the County of Lancaster, admitted that 'were it not for the existence of the pawnbroking trade it would often be an impossibility for the police to find stolen property after the lapse of a few days from the committal of the robbery' (Bent, *Criminal Life*, 216).
6. Neil, *Man-Hunters of Scotland Yard*, 223.
7. For his relations with the police, see Philip John Stead, 'Introduction', in W. L. Melville Lee, *A History of Police in England* (Montclair, NJ: Patterson Smith, 1971; first published London: Methuen, 1901), p. v. (All reference in the notes are to the American edition.)
8. Lee, *A History of Police*, 331. For the City of London Police more specifically, see Shand, 'The City of London Police', 596–7.
9. Lee, *A History of Police*, 329.
10. Lee, *A History of* Police, 330. Lee added another reason why good public relations were necessary for the police as a whole: that they would attract good people to the service.
11. Lee, *A History of* Police, 332.
12. Cavanagh, *Scotland Yard Past and Present*, 100. Boulton and Park were two young men who were arrested in London on 28 Apr. 1870 dressed in female attire, and charged with the intention of committing a felony. Their trial created a sensation and elicited a great deal of commentary.
13. *Daily News*, 21 July 1910, p. 7; Divall, *Scoundrels and Scallywags*, 72–4.
14. Clarkson and Richardson, *Police!*, 277; Leeson, *Lost London*, 158.
15. *The Times*, 27 Mar. 1885, p. 9.
16. E. Henry to Under Secretary of State, 13 May 1912, HO45/11000/223532.
17. George B. Mainwaring, *Observations on the Present State of the Police of the Metropolis* (London: The Pamphleteer, 1822; first published in 1821), 556.
18. *1878 Commission*, 135; *Sun*, 1 Oct. 1897, p. 2; Anderson, *The Lighter Side of my Official Life*, 265. See also Steedman, *Policing the Victorian Community*, 143–4.
19. James Hain Friswell, *Houses with the Fronts Off* (London: James Blackwood, 1854), 78.
20. Cook, *M: MI5's First Spymaster*, 119, 134, 189.
21. Porter, *The Origins of the Vigilant State*, 10–11, 143.
22. Letter by the Metropolitan Police to the Home Office, 15 Sept. 1909, HO144/1043/183461/1.
23. Vincent, *A Police Code*, 105.
24. Police Orders, 20 Aug. 1842; see also 21 Sept. 1842.
25. *Instructions for the Liverpool Constabulary Force* (1856), 27.
26. Report of the Director of Criminal Investigations, in *Annual Report of the Commissioner of Police of the Metropolis*, for 1882, PP, vol. 31 (1883), 368.

346

27. T. O. Hastings Lees, *Snowden's Police Officers' Guide: Tenth Edition* (London: Shaw & Sons, Fetter Lane & Crane Court, 1897), 26.
28. Police Orders, 24 Dec. 1907, p. 1257.
29. The literature on this topic is extensive. A few examples that deal with the period are: Clive Emsley, 'The English Bobby: An Indulgent Tradition', in Roy Porter (ed.), *Myths of the English* (Cambridge: Polity Press, 1992), 115–24; Miller, *Cops and Bobbies*, ch. 5; Reiner, *The Politics of the Police*, ch. 2; Robert D. Storch, 'The Plague of the Blue Locusts: Police Reform and Popular Resistance in Northern England, 1840–57', *International Review of Social History*, 201 (1975), 61–90.
30. Aled Jones, *Powers of the Press: Newspapers, Power and the Public in Nineteenth-Century England* (Aldershot: Scolar Press, 1996), 180. For a similar belief in the eighteenth century, see Hannah Barker, *Newspapers, Politics, and Public Opinion in Late Eighteenth-Century England* (Oxford: Clarendon Press, 1998), 4.
31. Alan J. Lee, *The Origins of the Popular Press in England* (London: Croom Helm, 1976), 78.
32. Joanne Shattock and Michael Wolff (eds), The *Victorian Periodical Press* (Leicester: Leicester University Press, 1982), intro., pp. xiv–xv.

CHAPTER 4. THE UNIQUELY SYMBIOTIC RELATIONSHIP BETWEEN DETECTIVES AND JOURNALISTS

1. See, e.g., Jack London, *The People of the Abyss*, intro. by Jack Lindsay (London: Journeyman Press, 1977; first published 1903), 40.
2. Richard V. Ericson, Patricia M. Baranek, and Janet B. L. Chan, *Negotiating Control: A Study of News Sources* (Toronto: Toronto University Press, 1989), 92. See also the reaction of the liberal *Daily News* (29 Mar. 1900) to the trial of the editor of the *Birmingham Daily Argus* for insulting the Lord Chief Justice of England, declaring that 'the Press has no reason for existence except to represent the public, and any restriction on the right of comment in newspapers upon servants of the State...is in itself bad' (quoted in the *Journalist*, 7 Apr. 1900, p. 109).
3. Philip Elliott, 'Professional Ideology and Organisational Change: The Journalist since 1800', in George Boyce, James Curran, and Pauline Wingate (eds), *Newspaper History* (London: Constable, 1978), 183.
4. On the press as an agency of social control in the nineteenth century, see James Curran, 'The Press as an Agency of Social Control: An Historical Perspective', in Boyce et al. (eds), *Newspaper History*, 51–75.
5. By way of example, the journalist James Greenwood, at the suggestion of his brother, Frederick Greenwood, founding editor of the *Pall Mall Gazette*, spent a night in a workhouse disguised as a 'ruffianly figure, marked with every sign of squalor' in order to be counted as one of the inmates, 'there to learn by actual experience how casual paupers are lodged and fed, and what the "casual" is like' (James Greenwood, *The Seven Curses of London*, p. vi, and *A Night in a Workhouse* (London: Office of the Pall Mall Gazette, 1866; repr. from the *Pall Mall Gazette*), 4–5). He recounted that he had 'mixed with thieves at liberty, an unsuspected spy in their camp, more than once' (*The Seven Curses of London*, 75). The American writer Jack London, too, disguised himself when in 1902 he wandered round the slums of London for

The People of the Abyss. See also George R. Sims, *How the Poor Live, and HorribleLondon* (London: Chatto & Windus, 1889), 30.

6. Rumbelow, *I Spy Blue*, 175.
7. *Reynolds's News*, 17 Feb. 1895, p. 5.
8. Rupert Allason, *The Branch* (London: Secker & Warburg, 1983), 72.
9. J. Hall Richardson, *From the City to Fleet Street* (London: Stanley Paul & Co., 1927), 81, 251. Evidently, impersonating a detective to attain an objective was far from uncommon. On 28 June 1913 *The Times* reported a rape by a man who pretended to be a Scotland Yard detective who came to search a house (p. 3). For other examples, see *Liverpool Mercury*, 8 Feb. 1848, p. 81; *Birmingham Daily Post*, 29 Jan. 1873, p. 6, 9 July 1891, p. 5. This trick was not new. Even before the establishment of modern detective departments, some criminals believed that posing as Bow Street patrols would make it easier for them to get into houses to look for contraband or stolen goods (Clarkson and Richardson, *Police!*, 51).
10. In his wanderings through areas of grinding poverty, which he called 'Povertyopolis', the journalist George R. Sims was suspected of being a detective or policeman (Sims, *How the Poor Live, and Horrible London*, 1, 5, 19). Notably, when his identity was disclosed as 'the poet of the poor, he was welcomed' (Introduction to George R. Sims, *Prepare to Shed Them Now: The Ballads of George R. Sims*, selected and introduced by Arthur Calder-Marshall (London: Hutchinson, 1968), 23). During the search for Jack the Ripper, a journalist who had dressed up as a woman in order to play amateur detective was suspected by patrol officers of being a police detective (Tom A. Cullen, *Autumn of Terror* (London: Collins, 1966; first published 1965), 126–7). See also the experience of the author John Fisher Murray when he entered a lodging house unshaven, with dirty hands and wearing 'a particular old coat, fustian trowsers [sic], and affecting hat, which we don for these select parties', in *The World of London* (London: Richard Bentley, 1853; first published in *Blackwood's Magazine* 1841, as book 1843), 182, and Henry Mayhew, *London Labour and the London Poor* (London: Frank Cass, 1967; first published 1851, 1861–2), i. 58.
11. Richardson, *From the City to Fleet Street*, 3.
12. Charles J. Tibbits, 'Newspapers as Detectives', *London Magazine*, 13 (Oct. 1904).
13. Michael Harris, *London Newspapers in the Age of Walpole* (Cranbury, NJ: Associated University Presses, 1987), 99.
14. Anthony Smith, 'The Long Road to Objectivity and Back Again: The Kinds of Truth We Get in Journalism', in Boyce et al. (eds), *Newspaper History*, 158.
15. Lloyd Davis, 'Journalism and Victorian Fiction', in Barbara Garlick and Margaret Harris (eds), *Victorian Journalism: Exotic and Domestic* (St Lucia, Queensland: University of Queensland Press, 1998), 202.
16. Jones, *Powers of the Press*, 122.
17. For changes introduced in crime reporting during the 1840s, see Steve Chibnall, 'Chronicles of the Gallows: The Social History of Crime Reporting,' in Harry Christian (ed.), *The Sociology of Journalism and the Press* (Sociological Review Monograph 29; Keele: Keele University Press, 1980), 204–5.
18. In his *Industry and Empire* (London: Weidenfeld and Nicolson, 1968), E. J. Hobsbawm quotes the figure of 2,148 'authors, editors, and journalists' for 1871, but probably the number was higher, as journalists who wrote for the quality press were unlikely to have been included (Christopher Kent, 'Higher

Journalism and the Mid-Victorian Clerisy', *Victorian Studies*, 13 (Dec. 1969), 197). The figure of 14,000 is given for the pre-First World War period.

19. King, 'Newspaper Reporting and Attitudes to Crime and Justice', 103; Barker, *Newspapers, Politics, and Public Opinion*, 2.
20. George Boyce, 'The Fourth Estate: The Reappraisal of a Concept', in Boyce et al. (eds), *Newspaper History*, 20. See also A. Aspinall, 'The Social Status of Journalists at the Beginning of the Nineteenth Century', *Review of English Studies*, 21/83 (July 1945), 216. Journalism at its lowest levels was particularly discredited (Kent, 'Higher Journalism and the Mid-Victorian Clerisy', 187). Court reporters were described in mid-century as 'poor despised journalists' who were 'not admitted into "society"' (Friswell, *Houses with the Fronts Off*, 81).
21. See *Modern Journalism: A Guide for Beginners by a London Editor with a Preface by George R. Sims* (London: Sidgwick & Jackson, 1909), p. v; Aspinall, 'The Social Status of Journalists', 230.
22. See, e.g., 'The Status of Working Journalists: How it May be Improved', a paper read in a meeting of the Institute of Journalists of the Manchester District on 21 July 1900 (*Journalist*, 28 June 1900, p. 233), expressing concern that the New Journalism, with its sensational style, threatened the dignity and prestige of the British press (see also *Journalist*, 22 Sept. 1900, p. 293). See also Frederick J. Higginbottom, *The Vivid Life* (London: Simpkin Marshall, 1934), 207.
23. Edward Bulwer-Lytton, *England and the English* (Chicago: University of Chicago Press, 1970; first published 1833), 54.
24. For the men who gathered and reported crime news in the eighteenth century and the manner of their operation, see Chibnall, 'Chronicles of the Gallows', 187–93; for crime reporting in the nineteenth century, see pp. 197–206.
25. Ian A. Bell, *Literature and Crime in Augustan England* (London: Routledge, 1991), 64.
26. King, 'Newspaper Reporting and Attitudes to Crime and Justice', 93–6.
27. On the process by which newspapers replaced the official Sessions Paper as a popular source of information about trials in the Old Bailey, see Simon Devereaux, 'The Fall of the Sessions Paper: The Criminal Trial and the Popular Press in Late Eighteenth-Century London', *Criminal Justice History*, 18 (2003).
28. King, 'Newspaper Reporting and Attitudes to Crime and Justice', 74. See also Esther Snell, 'Discourses of Criminality in the Eighteenth-Century Press: The Presentation of Crime in *The Kentish Post*, 1717–1768', *Continuity and Change*, 22/1 (2007), 15, 36.
29. Richard D. Altick, *The English Common Reader* (Chicago: University of Chicago Press, 1957), 344.
30. Altick, *The English Common Reader*, 87.
31. Lee, *The Origins of the Popular Press in England*, 121.
32. Frederick Greenwood, 'The Newspaper Press', *Nineteenth Century*, 27 (May 1890), 839.
33. See, e.g., Adam, *C.I.D.*, ch. 2, on his close relations with several police heads and senior detectives. According to Adam, it was he who suggested to Assistant Commissioner Macnaghten to write his memoirs (*C.I.D.*, 16).
34. Higginbottom, *The Vivid Life*, 15.
35. Lucy Brown, *Victorian News and Newspapers* (Oxford: Clarendon Press, 1985), 133, 136; Lee, *The Origins of the Popular Press in England*, 101 and 255 n. 120.

36. Christopher Pulling, *Mr Punch and the Police* (London: Butterworths, 1964), 7.
37. George R. Sims, *My Life: Sixty Years' Recollections of Bohemian London* (London: Eveleigh Nash Co., 1917), 138, 322–3. In turn, Detective Sergeant Benjamin Leeson mentions Sims, in his memoirs, as a friend (*Lost London*, 53). See also Fuller, *Recollections of a Detective*, 219, on the 'good many most excellent newspaper men' he had as 'friends'. For other examples of the rewarding contacts between police officers and journalists, see Macnaghten, *Days of my Years*, 20; Richardson, *From the City to Fleet Street*, 186, 190–2, 212; Clarkson and Richardson, *Police!*, p. vii. The book *Police!*, which Richardson wrote together with Charles Tempest Clarkson (a former police officer who had served for thirty-three years), reflects the enterprising collaboration between journalists and police officers.
38. Dickens's impressions of this encounter were published in two articles entitled 'A Detective Police Party', *Household Words*, 1 (27 July and 10 Aug. 1850 respectively).
39. The journalistic habit of spending time with detectives (and uniformed policemen) and later describing 'things as... [they] saw them' proved to be abiding (see, e.g., Peter Laurie, *Scotland Yard* (New York: Holt, Rinehart and Winston, 1970), 9; see also chs 6–7). Laurie spent a great deal of time with officers in the Metropolitan Police in 1967–8, and as a journalist found much in common with detectives (*Scotland Yard*, 127).
40. Clarkson and Richardson, *Police!*, 282.
41. Clarkson and Richardson, *Police!*, 282.
42. Clarkson and Richardson, *Police!*, 282.
43. Nevil Macready, *Annals of an Active Life* (London: Hutchinson, 1924), ii. 416. When the search in 1904 for the body of Camille Holland, who, it turned out, had been murdered four years earlier by her lover, finally ended successfully, two detectives sold the information about the discovery to a London newspaper for 'a nice little sum of money': 'As a consequence that paper was the only one which contained the information that Miss Holland had been shot through the head' (Adam, *Police Work from Within*, 99). Similarly, ex-Detective Inspector Maurice Moser disclosed in *Modern Detective* that 'some detectives give away information—in spite of strict official orders to the contrary—for the sake of a press notice, and customarily for a money payment by journalists' (quoted in *Reynolds's News*, 28 Aug. 1898, p. 8).
44. See, e.g., *Sun*, 29 Sept. 1897, p. 2.
45. *Pall Mall Gazette*, 10 Oct. 1888, p. 1.
46. *Sun*, 28 Sept. 1897, p. 2.
47. Higginbottom, *The Vivid Life*, 208.
48. John Syme, 'Police Witnesses Disgraced by Scotland Yard', *Penny Illustrated Paper*, 22 Oct. 1910, p. 525.
49. Journalistic interest in the routines of detective work was not confined to Britain. British journalists also travelled to other countries, most often to France, to interview detectives and accompany them on their patrols (see, e.g., 'With the French Detectives', *Standard*, 29 Oct. 1881, p. 2).
50. [Charles Dickens], 'On Duty with Inspector Field', *Household Words*, 3 (14 June 1851). For details, see ch. 5.

51. Some early examples of social exploration include William Cobbett, *Rural Rides* (1830), and Frederick Engels, *The Condition of the Working Class in England* (1845) (Peter Keating (ed.), *Into Unknown England, 1866–1913* (London: Fontana, 1976), 9).
52. Elizabeth Wilson, *The Sphinx in the City* (London: Virago Press, 1991), 27.
53. Mayhew, *London Labour and the London Poor*, i, preface.
54. Occasionally, the roles were reversed, and it was journalists who took police officers on a tour. George R. Sims took M. Goron, chief of the Paris detective force, to see London's underside, and was given a reciprocal tour when visiting Paris (Sims, *My Life*, 221).
55. Jerrold wrote for *Household Words* and in 1857 succeeded his father as editor of *Lloyd's Weekly Newspaper*, a post he held for twenty-six years. Doré illustrated several of his books.
56. Jerrold and Doré, *London: A Pilgrimage*, p. xviii.
57. Hyppolite Taine, *Notes on England* (London: Strahan & Co., 1872), 302.
58. Jerrold and Doré, *London: A Pilgrimage*, 166.
59. Jerrold and Doré, *London: A Pilgrimage*, 169.
60. Jerrold and Doré, *London: A Pilgrimage*, 176.
61. Aaron Watson, *A Newspaper Man's Memories* (London: Hutchinson, 1925), 87, 90.
62. Watson, *A Newspaper Man's Memories*, 92.
63. Watson, *A Newspaper Man's Memories*, 87. For another example, see Clarkson and Richardson, *Police!*, 242.
64. Stewart P. Evans and Keith Skinner, *The Ultimate Jack the Ripper Companion* (New York: Carroll & Graf Publishers, 2000), 516–20.
65. J. P. de Oliveira Martins, *The England of Today* (1893, English trans. 1896), quoted in Rick Allen, *The Moving Pageant* (London: Routledge, 1998), 192.
66. Josiah Flynt, 'Police Methods in London', *North American Review*, 176 (Mar. 1903), 437.
67. Flynt, 'Police Methods in London', 437. Before he embarked on his exploration of the London slums in 1902, friends and the Cook travel agency recommended to author Jack London that he 'see the police for a guide' and for advice, but in the event he chose to 'see things for myself' (London, *The People of the Abyss*, 11).
68. Clarkson and Richardson, *Police!*, 237–8, 246.
69. Mayhew, *London Labour and the London Poor*, iv. 298; Jerrold and Doré, *London: A Pilgrimage*, 162.
70. Jerrold and Doré, *London: A Pilgrimage*, 169.
71. Jerrold and Doré, *London: A Pilgrimage*, 172.
72. Jerrold and Doré, *London: A Pilgrimage*, 169–70.
73. Bishop, *From Information Received*, 250. Sims may have been gathering research for his book, *London by Night*, which was published in 1906.
74. Bishop, *From Information Received*, 250–1.
75. Sims, *How the Poor Live, and Horrible London*, 1–2, 11.
76. Sims, *How the Poor Live, and Horrible London*, 1, 5. In his book of memoirs, *My Life*, Sims contended that only once in the entire month during which he explored the poverty and criminal areas of south London for *How the Poor Live* did he and his companion meet with 'a really rough reaction' (p. 137).

77. Mayhew, *London Labour and the London Poor*, iv, p. v; see also iv. 276. The police also provided him with criminal statistics and filled in questionnaires about prostitution.
78. For examples, see Griffiths, *Mysteries of Police and Crime*, and Adam, *Police Work from Within*. Major Arthur Griffiths had an impressive career in the English prison service and was an inspector of prisons and author of several articles and books on the law, crime, and police, as well as detective novels (see ch. 6).
79. Various journalists composed the fourth volume, under the editorial guidance of Mayhew, who wrote the introduction. The quotations are taken from the section 'Thieves and Swindlers' written by John Binny.
80. Mayhew, *London Labour and the London Poor*, iv. 330.
81. Mayhew, *London Labour and the London Poor*, iv. 290.
82. Mayhew, *London Labour and the London Poor*, iv. 341.
83. Mayhew, *London Labour and the London Poor*, iv. 288; see also p. 305.
84. Taine, *Notes on England*, 302. The book was first published as a series of articles in the Parisian paper *Temps*.
85. Jerrold and Doré, *London: A Pilgrimage*, pp. xxvii, 10, 171, 190.
86. Jerrold and Doré, *London: A Pilgrimage*, 174.
87. Jerrold and Doré, *London: A Pilgrimage*, 160.
88. Jerrold and Doré, *London: A Pilgrimage*, 160-1.
89. For other examples of such cases, see Griffiths, *Mysteries of Police and Crime*, i. 11-12.
90. During the investigation of the brutal murder of Leon Beron on Clapham Common in 1911, Superintendent Frank Froest, executive head of the CID, noticed in a photo in one of the newspapers that the culprit was lefthanded, a discovery that supported his culpability (Adam, *Police Work from Within*, 69-70).
91. Beattie, 'Sir John Fielding and Public Justice', 69, 71.
92. Styles, 'Print and Policing', 56, 59.
93. Styles, 'Print and Policing', 88.
94. *Leeds Mercury*, 29 June 1844, p. 1; *Police Guardian*, 13 Aug. 1875, p. 3, 14 Sept. 1877, p. 4, 3 Mar. 1894, p. 4; *The Times*, 20 July 1877, p. 12; Macnaghten, *Days of my Years*, 119.
95. Carlin, *Reminiscences of an Ex-Detective*, 56, 102-3; Divall, *Scoundrels and Scallywags*, 226-7; Neil, *Man-Hunters of Scotland Yard*, 206. See also Macnaghten, *Days of my Years*, 64-5.
96. See, for example, an article about Inspector Field in *The Times*, 17 Sept. 1853, p. 11 (taken from the *Bath Chronicle*) and his portrait in the *Illustrated Times*, 2 Feb. 1856, p. 70; see also p. 93. Charles Dickens had introduced him to the public a few years earlier in his journal *Household Words*, when Field was still a detective at Scotland Yard.
97. See, for example, the heroic story of how Edward Bradford survived a lion attack in India, during which he lost an arm, before he became commissioner of the Metropolitan Police (Flynt, 'Police Methods in London', 436). For less dramatic reports about senior management, see, e.g., Aylmer, 'The Detective in Real Life', 506-8, about Howard Vincent, Robert Anderson, and Melville L. Macnaghten. 'Alfred Aylmer' was the pseudonym for Major Arthur Griffiths (see above, note 78).

98. See, for example, reports about Jerome Caminada's investigations, exploits, and appearances as a key witness in court throughout his career as a detective in the Manchester police force, in *Preston Chronicle*, 7 June 1873, p. 7; *Manchester Times*, 28 Oct. 1876, p. 5; *Birmingham Daily Post*, 9 Dec. 1886, p. 5; *Manchester Times*, 10 Mar. 1888, p. 5, 9 June 1888, p. 6, 12 May 1893, p. 3. The *Birmingham Daily Post*, 22 Feb. 1895, p. 3, reported, with a recommendation, the publication of his memoirs. *Lloyds Weekly Newspaper*, 8 June 1899, p. 15, announced his retirement. See also reports about Detective Inspector Robert Fuller's and Detective Sergeant William C. Gough's appearances in court in the *Daily Telegraph*, 7 Apr. 1906, p. 7.
99. Lansdowne, *A Life's Reminiscences*, 141.
100. *The Times*, 19 Mar. 1861, p. 5, 28 Aug. 1868, p. 10, 9 Aug. 1913, p. 5, 15 Sept. 1913, p. 2; *Birmingham Daily Post*, 9 Dec. 1886, p. 5.
101. See L. Perry Curtis, Jr, *Jack the Ripper and the London Press* (New Haven: Yale University Press, 2001), 91, for the manner in which the morning papers reported felonies and the court proceedings associated with them.
102. Curtis, *Jack the Ripper*, 91–2.
103. Brown, *Victorian News and Newspapers*, 192. See, e.g., *Leeds Mercury*, 16 May 1840, p. 7, and the *Southern Star and London and Brighton Patriot*, 28 June 1840, p. 3.
104. On the formation of the detective force in London, see *Manchester Times and Gazette*, 16 July 1842, p. 4; *Liverpool Mercury*, 22 July 1842, p. 231; *Newcastle Courant*, 22 July 1842, p. 4; *Hampshire Telegraph and Sussex Chronicle*, 25 July 1842, p. 2. On the reorganization of Scotland Yard in 1878, see *Leeds Mercury*, 8 Apr. 1878, p. 3; *Western Mail* (Cardiff), 11 Apr. 1878, p. 3.
105. See, e.g., Aylmer, 'The Detective in Real Life', 504–6, and, about Frederick Williamson and William Melville, pp. 505–6. See also Aylmer, 'Detective Day at Holloway', 91–4.
106. The first three were incarnations of the same journal, which underwent name changes.
107. For the kind of exposure individual detectives attained, see the portrait and illustration of Chief Inspector Conquest in the *Penny Illustrated Paper*, 26 Aug. 1899, p. 126. See also the portrait in the *Sun* of Chief Inspector Frederick Jarvis, after retirement from Scotland Yard, 21 Sept. 1897, p. 2; of Inspector John Walsh on his retirement from the Yard, *The Times*, 15 Apr. 1907, p. 11; and of Detective Sergeant Kemp, *The Times*, 10 Sept. 1913, p. 3. For a list of detectives promoted at Scotland Yard, see the *Sun*, 28 Sept. 1897, p. 2. For a biographical sketch lauding the courage of Detective Sergeant Seal of the Birmingham Police upon his death, see *Police Guardian*, 7 Nov. 1879, p. 4, repr. from the *Birmingham Mail*.
108. Jervis, *Chronicles of a Victorian Detective*, 27, 38, 49. For another case, see *Derby Mercury*, 12 Dec. 1877, p. 2.
109. *East London Observer*, 17 Dec. 1887, p. 6.
110. See the article 'On Duty in Plain Clothes', 852, in which, based on his reminiscences to a reporter, Abberline was portrayed as a knowledgeable, clever, brave, and industrious detective who in each case painstakingly followed every clue until he arrived at the inference that led to the resolution of highly sophisticated crimes.

111. See, for example, a sketch of Detective Superintendent Hallam in the *Spy*, where he is described as 'the man who can tell you right off...how many times you have been convicted of murdering your mother-in-law' (repr. in the *Police Review*, 31 July 1893, p. 367).
112. *Evening News*, 2 May 1892, p. 1; *Daily Argus*, 6, 8, 9, Feb. 1892; *Glasgow Herald*, 15 Sept. 1896, p. 4; letters by E. Bradford, 2 Oct. 1894, HO 45/9744/A56376. See also Aylmer, 'The Detective in Real Life', 505–6; Charles Kingston, *Dramatic Days at the Old Bailey* (London: Stanley Paul & Co., 1923), 261–3.
113. For speculations about McIntyre's dismissal from the Branch, see Porter, *The Origins of the Vigilant State*, 137–8, and Cook, *M: MI5's First Spymaster*, 104–6.
114. *Reynolds's News*, 14 June 1896, p. 8, 20 Sept. 1896, p. 1. The latter article was also published in the *Illustrated Police News*, 26 Sept. 1896, p. 1.
115. *South London Chronicle*, 6 Aug. 1898, p. 5.
116. Lock, *Dreadful Deeds and Awful Murders*, 27; King, 'Newspaper Reporting and Attitudes to Crime and Justice', 95–6.
117. *Police Review*, 10 Aug. 1894, p. 381.
118. Cook, *M: MI5's First Spymaster*, 112, 114, 118.
119. 'The Police of London', *Quarterly Review*, 121, 129.
120. Caminada, *Twenty-Five Years of Detective Life*, ii. 3. Curiously, criminals, too, 'had an almost irresistible weakness for treasuring pictures and pieces of print relating to themselves', according to Nathaniel Druscovich, the detective who was indicted in the famous detective trial of 1877, exposing corruption in Scotland Yard (Tibbits, 'Newspapers as Detectives', 280). See also above, ch. 1.
121. Vincent, *A Police Code*, 104.
122. Flynt, 'Police Methods in London', 443–4.
123. An American journalist working in London summed up this view of policemen generally in an article he wrote for the *Journalist* (8 Mar. 1889, p. 7), by saying: 'When a London newspaper man meets a London policeman there is apt to be trouble.'
124. Adam, *C.I.D.*, 231.
125. *Journalist*, 4 Dec. 1889, p. 3.
126. Clarkson and Richardson, *Police!*, 283, 286. See also the reference by the *Star* to the more obliging attitude of the City of London Police to the representatives of the press, in Martin Fido, *The Crimes, Detection and Death of Jack the Ripper* (New York: Barnes & Noble, 1993), 80.
127. *Journalist*, 16 Nov. 1888, p. 6, 23 Nov. 1888, p. 6.
128. *Reynolds's News*, 24 Mar. 1895, p. 5; Tibbits, 'Newspapers as Detectives', 278.
129. *Journalist*, 16 Nov. 1888, p. 6.
130. See, for example, the admission by a journalist (who actually sued a policeman for assault) that the police 'had frequently given him very valuable assistance' (*Journalist*, 5 Oct. 1888, p. 2).
131. *Star*, 8 Sept. 1888, p. 3, 10 Sept. 1888, p. 3.
132. *Star*, 11 Sept. 1888, p. 1.
133. *Star*, 10 Nov. 1888, p. 1.
134. Clarkson and Richardson, *Police!*, 278.
135. Brown, *Victorian News and Newspapers*, 153–6.
136. Adam, *Police Work from Within*, 79.

137. *Journalist*, 16 Nov. 1888, p. 6.
138. Vincent, *A Police Code*, 253.
139. Quoted in Griffiths, *Mysteries of Police and Crime*, i. 12. This accusation was by no means restricted to police circles. At a conference on criminal anthropology in Geneva in the autumn of 1896, one of the participants, Dr Aubry, argued that detailed press accounts of trials assisted malefactors, teaching them 'all the weak points of the law and all the best methods of avoiding justice' (*Journalist*, 10 Oct. 1896, p. 326). In the same vein, see the *Spectator* (quoted in *Journalist*, 1 Dec. 1900, p. 375); Friswell, *Houses with the Fronts Off*, 81.
140. Anderson, *The Lighter Side of my Official Life*, 199–202.
141. Philip Sugden, *The Complete History of Jack the Ripper* (New York: Carroll & Graf, 2003; first published 1994), 72. The above-mentioned Dr Aubry also recommended vetting criminal reports before publication, because reading about particulars of crimes continually might have negative effects 'on those whose nervous systems are unstable' by prompting them to 'many bad deeds which would otherwise have been unthought of'.
142. *Journalist*, 16 Nov. 1888, p. 6; *Penny Illustrated Paper*, 1 Oct. 1910, p. 428.
143. See, e.g., 'Manchester Police Methods in the "Palatine" Case', *Penny Illustrated Paper*, 1 Oct. 1910, p. 437, recounting how, in order to procure evidence of illicit practices carried out at a certain hotel, a detective went there with a prostitute, took a room and paid for it, and stayed there with her for over an hour. For other articles critical of police methods, see 10 Sept. 1910, p. 340, 22 Oct. 1910, p. 532.
144. *Journalist*, 16 Nov. 1888, p. 6.
145. Clarkson and Richardson, *Police!*, 282; Tibbits, 'Newspapers as Detectives', 278. See also Cullen, *Autumn of Terror*, 126–7; Curtis, *Jack the Ripper*, 100–1. Not only reporters, but members of the community at large, took to sleuthing, especially when the murders of prostitutes by the Ripper continued and the identity of the perpetrator remained unknown.
146. See the description of the journalist Frederick J. Higginbottom, who undertook an independent inquiry into the case of a missing girl when working for the Press Association (*The Vivid Life*, 16–17).
147. For the close surveillance by press agents of all Oscar Wilde's movements on the day of his arrest—from the hotel in which he had stayed, through his journey in a cab to the charge room, to events therein and in his cell, and finally on his way to the police court—see *Illustrated Police Budget*, 13 Apr. 1895, supplement, p. 7. See also Figure 14, p. 221.
148. Curtis, *Jack the Ripper*, 161–2. The police also suspected that the person who had sent the letters signed with the name Jack the Ripper was a journalist (Anderson, *The Lighter Side of my Official Life*, 138).
149. See Adam, *Police Work from Within*, 69, for a case involving a press photographer who overstepped the bounds of his vocation. The presence of reporters at crime scenes, and their practice of publishing details of investigations that they themselves had conducted, continued to infuriate police officials (*Departmental Committee on Detective Work and Procedure* (London: His Majesty's Stationery Office, 1938–9), v. 27), HO45/25052.
150. *Star*, 10 Nov. 1888, p. 1; Tibbits, 'Newspapers as Detectives', 278.
151. See above, n. 12.

152. See, e.g., Fuller, *Recollections of a Detective*, 219; Richardson, *From the City to Fleet Street*, 213.
153. Tibbits, 'Newspapers as Detectives', 278. In *Sun* 29 Sept. 1897, p. 2, one of the paper's reporters, was said to have given a Yard detective 'a long start and a good beating' by locating and interviewing a certain person two hours before the detective found him.
154. Thomas W. Hanshew, *Cleek of Scotland Yard* (New York: McKinley, Stone & Mackenzie, 1912), 3–4. The author was an American who settled in England and published several stories and novels based on the fictional figure Hamilton Cleek.
155. Jones, 'The New Police', 152.
156. Ronald C. Sopenoff, 'The Police of London: The Early History of the Metropolitan Police, 1829–1856', Ph.D., Temple University, 1977, 157–8; Morris, '"Crime Does Not Pay"', 98.
157. Sims, *My Life*, 321. Adolph Beck was charged in 1896 with obtaining articles by fraud on the basis of mistaken identity (by ten women). He was sentenced to seven years' penal servitude. In vain he tried to prove his innocence in court and then in petition after petition from prison. At last (in 1901) he was released on ticket-of-leave, but in 1904 he was again wrongly identified as a swindler, put on trial, and found guilty, though this time the identity of the culprit was revealed before the sentence was passed. This miscarriage of justice, which involved dismissing contradictory evidence by different members of the legal system, drew a vigorous press response (for details, see Eric R. Watson, *Adolf Beck* (Edinburgh: William Hodge & Co., 1924)).
158. Sims closely monitored the progress of the investigations of the Ripper murders in articles in the Sunday newspaper the *Referee* (during which he was identified by a news vendor as a suspect), upbraiding the detective force for 'lacking in the smartness and variety of resource which the most ordinary detective displays in the shilling shocker' (quoted in Stewart P. Evans and Keith Skinner, *Jack the Ripper: Letters from Hell* (Stroud: Sutton Publishing, 2001), 11–13. See also Sims, *My Life*, 141).
159. Sims, *My Life*, 321. Another journalist who knew many high- as well as low-ranking police officers intimately but faced difficulties in his negotiations with police sources was J. Hall Richardson of the *Daily Telegraph* (Richardson, *From the City to Fleet Street*, 13, 186–7, 222).
160. *Penny Illustrated Paper*, 1 Oct. 1910, p. 428. For details of the Crippen case, see ch. 5.
161. *Journalist*, 6 Jan. 1888, p. 3. In this case, the clerk at a provincial police station was instructed not to give the reporter any information without the consent of the superintendent, because he had written a paragraph about a drunken policeman being carried in the streets. The superintendent justified the order on the grounds that the report had brought 'the police into disrepute'. For another case, see *Journalist*, 23 Nov. 1888, p. 6.
162. Watson, *A Newspaper Man's Memories*, 107–8.
163. Ann Rogers, *Secrecy and Power in the British State* (London: Pluto Press, 1997), 13–14.
164. Brown, *Victorian News and Newspapers*, 208–9.
165. *Sun*, 29 Sept. 1897, p. 2.

166. Flynt, 'Police Methods in London', 437.
167. *Daily Mail,* 2 June 1913, p. 7.
168. Jones, *Powers of the Press,* 121–2, 132; Stephen Koss, *The Rise and Fall of the Political Press in Britain* (London: Hamish Hamilton, 1981), i. 187, 216, 254.
169. See, e.g., *Star,* 8 Sept. 1888, p. 3. See also *Journalist,* 6 Jan. 1888, p. 3, 16 Nov. 1888, pp. 6–7, for various critical responses by journalists to their failure to get information.
170. Clarkson and Richardson, *Police!,* 281.
171. Clarkson and Richardson, *Police!,* 285.
172. *Penny Illustrated Paper,* 1 Oct. 1910, p. 428.
173. *Journalist,* 16 Nov. 1888, pp. 6–7.
174. Clarkson and Richardson, *Police!,* 281–5.
175. *Sun,* 29 Sept. 1897, p. 2.
176. Tibbits, 'Newspapers as Detectives', 278.
177. Clarkson and Richardson, *Police!,* 282; quoted in *Journalist,* 4 Dec. 1889, p. 3.
178. See, e.g., Warren, 'The Police of the Metropolis', 589.
179. Macnaghten, *Days of my Years,* 64.
180. *Daily Mail,* 2 June 1913, p. 7.
181. Anderson, *The Lighter Side of my Official Life,* 202.
182. For an example, see Richardson, *From the City to Fleet Street,* 12.
183. *Journalist,* 4 Dec. 1889, p. 3.
184. *Journalist,* 4 Dec. 1889, p. 3.
185. *Penny Illustrated Paper,* 15 Oct. 1910, p. 499. The National Union of Journalists was established in 1907 as an alternative organization to the Institute of Journalists, which, in contrast to the Union, included proprietors as well and was of little use in matters of pay and conditions (Alan Lee, 'The Structure, Ownership and Control of the Press, 1855–1914', in Boyce et al. (eds), *Newspaper History,* 127; Clement J. Bundock, *The National Union of Journalists* (Oxford: Oxford University Press, 1957), 2).
186. *Penny Illustrated Paper,* 1 Oct. 1910, p. 428.
187. McAdoo, 'The London Police from a New York Point of View', 657.
188. McAdoo, 'The London Police from a New York Point of View', 658.
189. For a portrayal, in the same vein, of the differences between Scotland Yard and the New York police in their relations with the media at the end of the twentieth century, see Philip Schlesinger and Howard Tumber, *Reporting Crime* (Oxford: Clarendon Press, 1994), 121–2. Scotland Yard information officers did, however, learn from the American experience better to appreciate the value of publicity, and acted upon it (Steve Chibnall, 'The Metropolitan Police and the News Media', in Simon Holdaway (ed.), *The British Police* (London: Edward Arnold, 1979), 146).
190. See, e.g., *Sun,* 29 Sept. 1897, p. 2.
191. *Punch,* 1 July 1882, p. 306.
192. *Punch,* 22 Sept. 1888, p. 135.
193. *Punch,* 20 Oct. 1888, p. 183.
194. *Punch,* 20 Oct. 1888, p. 189.
195. See, for example, text in the *Spectator* as quoted in *Journalist,* 1 Dec. 1900, p. 375.
196. For an example, see the quotation by Howard Vincent in Clarkson and Richardson, *Police!,* 280.

NOTES

197. Chibnall, 'The Metropolitan Police and the News Media', 136. For the source of this information, see Macready, *Annals of an Active Life*, ii. 417.
198. Tensions between Scotland Yard detectives and journalists were to continue after the First World War. Even in the 1930s, Scotland Yard 'viewed with considerable suspicion journalists who wanted to report crime before it reached the courts' (Jeremy Tunstall, *Journalists at Work* (London: Constable, 1971), 92). In the 1960s, when Scotland Yard had a 'press room' and public-relations officers, journalists continued to complain about Scotland Yard's condescending attitude towards them (Tunstall, *Journalists at Work*, 180). In his book on Scotland Yard, Peter Laurie, a journalist, is told by a detective that right from the outset the notion that 'journalists are bad. Never speak to journalists' was drummed into them (Laurie, *Scotland Yard*, 10).
199. London, *The People of the Abyss*, 11.

CHAPTER 5. THE CHANGING IMAGES OF POLICE DETECTIVES IN THE PRESS

1. Clarkson and Richardson, *Police!*, 71–2.
2. Wynter, 'The Police and the Thieves', 163.
3. George Augustus Sala, *Things I Have Seen and People I Have Known* (London: Cassell & Co., 1894), ii. 109. For the provincial police, see Radzinowicz, *A History of English Criminal Law*, iv. 270.
4. 'The Police of London', *Quarterly Review*, 120. See also Wynter, 'The Police and the Thieves', 163; Ellen L. O'Brien, '"The Most Beautiful Murder": The Transgressive Aesthetics of Murder in Victorian Street Ballads', *Victorian Literature and Culture*, 28/1 (2000), 22. For other responses in the press, see Sopenoff, 'The Police of London', 103–6, 161–4.
5. Miller, *Cops and Bobbies*, 106.
6. Miller, *Cops and Bobbies*, 106.
7. Miller, *Cops and Bobbies*, 106.
8. Robert Reiner, *The Policing of Mass Demonstration in Contemporary Democracies: Policing, Protest, and Disorder in Britain* (San Domenico: European University Institute, 1997), 7–8.
9. Miller, *Cops and Bobbies*, 108. See also Rob S. Sindall, *Street Violence in the Nineteenth Century: Media Panic or Real Danger?* (Leicester: Leicester University Press, 1990), 105–7.
10. Sindall, *Street Violence in the Nineteenth Century*, 95–6.
11. The feeling that London residents now lived in security owing to the 'systematic *surveillance* of the authorities, and the ready submission accorded to the officers of the law' was echoed in John Fisher Murray's detailed depiction of the physiognomy of London in *The World of London*, 44–5.
12. Quoted in *Examiner*, 3 Sept. 1842, p. 570.
13. *Examiner*, 30 Apr. 1842, p. 284.
14. *Examiner*, 3 Sept. 1842, p. 570.
15. *The Times*, 2 Dec. 1845, p. 4.
16. *The Times*, 2 Dec. 1845, p. 4.
17. *Jackson's Oxford Journal*, 13 Aug. 1842, p. 1.

18. Clarkson and Richardson, *Police!*, 71.
19. David Philips, '"A New Engine of Power and Authority": The Institutionalization of Law-Enforcement in England, 1780–1830', in Gatrell, Lenman, and Parker (eds), *Crime and the Law*, 187.
20. See *Punch*'s reactions to the new department, in Pulling, *Mr Punch and the Police*, 43.
21. *Freeman's Journal and Daily Commercial Advertiser*, 5 Sept. 1840, p. 4, quoting the *Morning Advertiser*.
22. 'The Police System of London', 1.
23. Wynter, 'The Police and the Thieves', 164.
24. 'The Sketcher in London: Policeman AE', *Leisure Hour*, 7 (7 Jan. 1858), 14.
25. For details, see Davis, 'The London Garotting Panic of 1862', 191. For press reports about the garotting scares, see Sindall, *Street Violence in the Nineteenth Century*, 38–42.
26. Miller, *Cops and Bobbies*, 111–12.
27. 'The Police of London', *Quarterly Review*, 128.
28. M. Laing Meason, 'The London Police', *Macmillan's Magazine*, 46 (July 1882), 192.
29. Meason, 'The London Police', 193.
30. 'The French and English Police Systems', *Cornhill Magazine*, NS 44 (Oct. 1881), 421. See also 'The Metropolitan Police, and What is Paid for Them', *Chambers's Journal*, 41 (July 1864), 423; 'London Police Duty', 279.
31. Miller, *Cops and Bobbies*, 122, 124. See also *Northern Star*, 23 Mar. 1839, p. 4; *Examiner*, 30 July 1842, p. 481. For the image of the police in the north of the country, see Storch, 'The Policeman as Domestic Missionary', 493.
32. Steedman, *Policing the Victorian Community*, 162; Taylor, *Policing the Victorian Town*, 79–89. For a discussion of the assaults on Metropolitan Police men, see Shpayer-Makov, *The Making of a Policeman*, 139–44. Between 1870 and 1888 an average of fourteen Metropolitan officers a year were invalided out as a result of injury (see Shpayer-Makov, *The Making of a Policeman*, 136, table 4.1).
33. For details about police services to the community, see Sindall, *Street Violence in the Nineteenth Century*, 104–5; Taylor, *Policing the Victorian Town*, 176–7. For the rural areas, see Steedman, *Policing the Victorian Community*, 53–4; Bent, *Criminal Life*, 130–1, 133–5.
34. Miller, *Cops and Bobbies*, 138. For the image of the provincial police, see Steedman, *Policing the Victorian Community*, 31–2, 143–6.
35. 'Our Police System', 700.
36. See 'Police Detectives', *Leisure Hour*, 6 (29 Oct. 1857), 692.
37. *Reynolds's News*, 28 Oct. 1855, p. 11; Blackstone, 'Paternal Government', 725.
38. [James Fitzjames Stephen], 'The Criminal Law and the Detection of Crime', *Cornhill Magazine*, 2 (Dec. 1860), 697.
39. Wynter, 'The Police and the Thieves', 174.
40. 'Police Detectives', 692.
41. [Dickens], 'A Detective Police Party', *Household Words*, 1 (27 July 1850), 409. See 'The London Police', 54, and 'Police', *Chambers's Journal*, 37 (8 Feb. 1862), 86, for a disparaging view of the Bow Street Runners, and 'The Police System of London', 2–3, 11–12, for a complimentary approach, though not one that rated the Runners as superior to the new detective.

42. See 'The Police of London', *Quarterly Review*, 113–15.
43. Caminada, *Twenty-Five Years of Detective Life*, i (Manchester: John Heywood, 1895), 252. The case of Detective Inspector Whicher of Scotland Yard, who investigated the Road Hill House murder of a 3-year-old child, was particularly jarring. His conclusion that the child's older half-sister, Constance Kent (still a schoolgirl), was the perpetrator was rejected by the court. Whicher was humiliated by the defence solicitor during the trial, and was ridiculed by the press, which denounced him as unjust, cruel, frivolous, and incompetent. Overwhelmed by this harsh reaction, he retired from the police (in 1864) before Constance made a full confession upon entering an Anglican sisterhood five years after the murder. She was duly convicted of murder, and a sentence of death was passed but was commuted. (For details about the abusive press reaction, see Bernard Taylor, *Cruelly Murdered* (London: Souvenir Press, 1979), 182–5.) For further details about Jonathan Whicher and the case, see Summerscale, *The Suspicions of Mr Whicher*.
44. *Reynolds's News*, 19 July 1863, p. 3.
45. *Reynolds's News*, 19 July 1863, p. 4.
46. 'Police Detectives', 695. See also 'Our Police System', 700; 'Detectives as They Are', 445–8.
47. 'Police', *Chambers's Journal*, 37 (Feb. 1862), 87. For a fuller explanation of the decline in Victorian-era crime, see Gatrell, 'The Decline of Theft and Violence', 252–66.
48. Peter Haining (ed.), *Hunted Down* (London: Peter Owen, 1996), 10; Philip Collins, *Dickens and Crime* (London: Macmillan, 1964; first published 1962), ch. 1.
49. Sala, *Things I Have Seen*, i. 76.
50. Sala, *Things I Have Seen*, i. 95.
51. Although *Household Words* was intended for a middle-class readership, 'it was cheap enough and popular enough to be read by the literate lower classes'. The circulation figures of this successful journal soon averaged an impressive 36,000–40,000 (Harry Stone (ed.), *The Uncollected Writings of Charles Dickens* (London: Allen Lane, 1969), 21). Altick quotes the figure of 100,000 for the year 1850 (*The English Common Reader*, 347).
52. *Household Words*, 1 (30 Mar. 1850), 1.
53. Stone (ed.), *The Uncollected Writings*, 14.
54. [William H. Wills] 'The Modern Science of Thief-Taking', *Household Words*, 1 (13 July 1850), 368.
55. [Dickens], 'A Detective Police Party', 1 (27 July 1850), 409.
56. Not all the visitors were from the headquarters at Scotland Yard. The group included several divisional plain-clothes men from other parts of the city, as well as Inspector Walker from the Executive Branch, who was not a detective.
57. [Dickens], 'A Detective Police Party', 1 (27 July 1850), 410.
58. Sala, *Things I Have Seen*, i. 96.
59. [Dickens], 'A Detective Police Party', 1 (10 Aug. 1850), 459.
60. [Dickens], 'A Detective Police Party', 1 (10 Aug. 1850), 460.
61. [Charles Dickens], 'Three "Detective" Anecdotes', *Household Words*, 1 (14 Sept. 1850), 577–80.
62. This time Inspector 'Wield' arrived with two detective sergeants.
63. [Charles Dickens], 'Spy Police', *Household Words*, 1 (21 Sept. 1850), 611.

NOTES

64. [Charles Dickens], 'The Metropolitan Protectives', *Household Words*, 3(26 Apr. 1851), 97. The first draft was written by Wills, but Dickens rewrote and amended the piece, adding new portions.
65. Letter to Wills, 3 Apr. 1851, quoted in Stone (ed.), *The Uncollected Writings*, 253.
66. [Dickens], 'The Metropolitan Protectives', 105.
67. [Dickens], 'On Duty with Inspector Field', 265–6.
68. [Dickens], 'On Duty with Inspector Field', 266.
69. [Dickens], 'On Duty with Inspector Field', 267.
70. [Charles Dickens], 'Down with the Tide', *Household Words*, 6 (5 Feb. 1853), 481.
71. Yates, *Edmund Yates: His Recollections and Experiences*, 194.
72. In addition to his journalistic work, Yates was employed by the General Post Office for twenty-three years. While there he was promoted to head the Missing Letter Branch, in which capacity he 'was much mixed up with the leading detectives' in London, including Michael Haydon, 'the celebrated City detective' who was immortalized in William Powell Frith's painting *The Railway Station* (Yates, *Edmund Yates: His Recollections and Experiences*, 369; see also above, ch.1, p. 34, and the cover image of this volume). Yates, too, heaped compliments on the detectives he had met, describing them in his memoirs as brave, shrewd, excellent, and smart.
73. Yates, *Edmund Yates: His Recollections and Experiences*, 194.
74. See, e.g., Wynter, 'The Police and the Thieves', 176; Shand, 'The City of London Police', 594; Griffiths, *Mysteries of Police and Crime*, i. 130.
75. For example, a selection from Hyppolite Taine's *Notes on England* appeared in translation in the *Daily News* between 4 Oct. 1871 and 25 Mar. 1872; see 17 Oct 1871 in particular.
76. Jerrold and Doré, *London: A Pilgrimage*, 172, 176.
77. Jerrold and Doré, *London: A Pilgrimage*, 196.
78. Jerrold and Doré, *London: A Pilgrimage*, 176.
79. 'The Police of London', *Quarterly Review*, 127–8.
80. 'The Police of London', *Quarterly Review*, 100.
81. *Daily News*, 3 Feb. 1858, p. 4.
82. Collins, *Dickens and Crime*, 200.
83. *Daily News*, 21 Nov. 1877, p. 5. For similar phraseology, see *The Times*, 22 Nov. 1877, p. 9; *Morning Post*, 15 Dec. 1877, p. 4.
84. Pulling, *Mr Punch and the Police*, 92.
85. *Globe*, 31 July 1878, p. 1.
86. *Globe*, 5 Aug. 1878, p. 1.
87. *The Times*, 2 Apr. 1878, p. 9, 22 Nov. 1877, p. 9.
88. In the view of *Reynolds's News*, the police mode of operation was a 'cleverly-contrived web for entangling him [Titley] in the meshes of the law' by means of 'lying' and 'deception' (19 Dec. 1881, p. 4). For the reaction of the crusading London evening paper *Pall Mall Gazette*, which under the editorship of John Morley had turned liberal, see 17 Dec. 1880, p. 4. See also *Graphic*, 15 Jan. 1881, p. 50.
89. See, e.g., 'London Detectives', *Police Guardian*, 9 Apr. 1886, pp. 2–3 (repr. from *Daily News*).

90. Laurel Brake, 'Writing, Cultural Production, and the Periodical Press in the Nineteenth Century', in J. B. Bullen (ed.), *Writing and Victorianism* (London: Longman, 1997), 61.
91. Brown, *Victorian News and Newspapers*, 109–10. Brown explains that the publishing cycle of quarterly journals and monthlies was too slow to keep up with the rapidly changing political scene of the late nineteenth century. The political weeklies, operating on a shorter schedule, were therefore more topical.
92. Alvin Sullivan (ed.), *British Literary Magazines* (Westport, CT: Greenwood Press, 1984), iii. 381.
93. 'The Work of the London Police', *Spectator*, 7 Oct. 1882, pp. 1279–80. See also M. Laing Meason, 'Detective Police', *Nineteenth Century*, 13 (May 1883), 765–6; *The Times*, 27 Mar. 1885, p. 9.
94. 'The Dynamite Inquiries', 495. Allegations were made at the time, even by establishment figures, that James Egan, along with John Daly, another Irish revolutionary, who was convicted with him for possession of explosives, were framed by the police. (For details on the plausibility of these allegations, see Porter, *The Origins of the Vigilant State*, 73–7. For a discussion of this possibility and of similar allegations in the House of Commons, see *The Times*, 4 Aug. 1891, p. 4.)
95. 'Detectives', *Saturday Review*, 9 Feb. 1884, p. 178.
96. 'Detectives', *Saturday Review*, 9 Feb. 1884, p. 178.
97. 'The Work of the London Police', 1280. See also Meason, 'Detective Police', 765–6.
98. *Daily Telegraph*, 7 Mar. 1882, p. 2.
99. See, e.g., Aylmer, 'Detective Day at Holloway', 90–1.
100. Meason, 'The London Police', 199, 197. See also 'Our Detective Police', *Chambers's Journal*, 1/22 (31 May 1884), 337.
101. Porter, *The Origins of the Vigilant State*, 51–2.
102. Meason, 'Detective Police', 765.
103. M. Laing Meason, 'The French Detective Police', *Macmillan's Magazine*, 45 (Feb. 1882), 299, 301.
104. Meason, 'Detective Police', 767.
105. Meason, 'Detective Police', 774–5. See also 'Our Detective Police', *Chambers's Journal*, 337.
106. Meason, 'The London Police', 197.
107. Porter, *The Origins of the Vigilant State*, 43–4, 51–2; Short, *The Dynamite War*, 82, 114.
108. See, e.g., Meason, 'The French Detective Police', 175; 'The London and French Police', *Saturday Review*, 8 July 1882, p. 47; 'Detectives', *Saturday Review*, 5 May 1883, pp. 558–9.
109. Meason, 'The French Detective Police', 174.
110. 'The London and French Police', 48; 'Detectives', *Saturday Review*, 5 May 1883, pp. 558–9.
111. Meason, 'The London Police', 199. See also Meason, 'Detective Police', 773.
112. *Daily Telegraph*, 7 Mar. 1882, p. 2.
113. 'The French and English Police Systems', 422–3.
114. 'The French and English Police Systems', 423.
115. 'The French and English Police Systems', 423.

116. Meason, 'The London Police', 194.
117. *The Times*, 24 Nov. 1884, p. 12; 'The French Detective Police', *Saturday Review*, 3 Jan. 1885, pp. 16–17. For this aspect at a later period, see 'Detective Work in England and France Contrasted', *Police Guardian*, 30 Nov. 1895, p. 7 (repr. from *Egyptian Gazette*).
118. Quoted in *Police Guardian*, 9 Apr. 1886, p. 2. More or less at the same time, an anonymous contributor to *Chambers's Journal* described a detective who appeared at his door as 'a tall gentlemanly individual...who spoke with all the tone and manner of a person accustomed to good society' ('My Detective Experiences', *Chambers's Journal*, 3 (3 Apr. 1886), 222).
119. For the reactions of *The Times, Daily Telegraph, Morning Post, Leeds Mercury, Daily News, Standard, Morning Advertiser, Spectator, Statist*, and *Bullionist* to the riots in Feb. 1886, see *Pall Mall Gazette*, 10 Feb. 1886, p. 11, 11 Feb. 1886, pp. 11–12, 13 Feb. 1886, p. 11.
120. *Pall Mall Gazette*, 12 Feb. 1886, pp. 1–3.
121. *Punch*, 26 Feb. 1887, p. 98.
122. One of the five murders took place in the jurisdiction of the City of London.
123. Macnaghten, *Days of my Years*, 55, 59.
124. Curtis, *Jack the Ripper*, 116, 132, 136.
125. 'The Metropolitan Police', *Saturday Review*, 3 Nov. 1888, p. 521. See also 'The Police', *Saturday Review*, 20 Oct. 1888, pp. 455–6.
126. 'The Metropolitan Police', *Saturday Review*, 3 Nov. 1888, pp. 521–2.
127. The *Pall Mall Gazette*, too, insinuated that the CID did not benefit from being exclusively male (8 Oct. 1888, p. 3).
128. Curtis, *Jack the Ripper*, 167.
129. *Pall Mall Gazette*, 8 Oct. 1888, p. 3.
130. *Pall Mall Gazette*, 11 Oct. 1888, p. 3.
131. See, e.g., *Freeman's Journal and Daily Commercial Advertiser*, 3 Jan. 1889, p. 6; *Sun*, 25 Sept. 1897, p. 2, 28 Sept. 1897, p. 2; Griffiths, *Mysteries of Police and Crime*, ii. 2.
132. Carlin, *Reminiscences of an Ex-Detective*, 215. It is now known that many readers' letters were not authentic but were written by editors to promote sales or perpetuate debates. For examples of detective work 'in its least impressive form', see Browne, *The Rise of Scotland Yard*, 238–40, 245–7.
133. Clive Emsley, *Hard Men: The English and Violence since 1750* (London: Hambledon and London, 2005), 32. See also Geoffrey Pearson, *Hooligan: A History of Respectable Fears* (London: Macmillan, 1983), 74–116; Stephen Humphries, *Hooligans or Rebels?* (Oxford: Basil Blackwell, 1984), 174–5.
134. *Sun*, 25, 27 Sept. 1897.
135. *Sun*, 28 Sept. 1897, p. 2.
136. *Penny Illustrated Paper*, 1 Oct. 1910, p. 430; 8 Oct. 1910, p. 463.
137. See, e.g., *Sun*, 27 Sept. 1897, p. 2.
138. See *Reynolds's News*, 3 Feb.–26 May 1895. The *Sun* hailed the publication of McIntyre's memoirs in *Reynolds's News* as casting 'a much-needed light upon the methods of the political informer and the production of political crime' (quoted in *Reynolds's News*, 5 May 1895, p. 3).
139. *Penny Illustrated Paper*, 1 Oct. 1910, p. 430, 8 Oct. 1910, p. 463.

140. *Penny Illustrated Paper*, 15 Oct. 1910, p. 498.
141. Wiener, *Reconstructing the Criminal*, 305–7.
142. See the reports from the *Manchester Courier* in Bent, *Criminal Life*, appendix.
143. *Parliamentary Debates*, vol. 346, 27 June 1890, col. 255.
144. *The Times*, 30 May 1896, p. 11.
145. *St James's Gazette*, 9 July 1894, p. 5. See also press reports in Caminada, *Twenty-Five Years of Detective Life*, i. 330–1.
146. *Daily Chronicle*, 5 Apr. 1892, p. 4; *Reynolds's News*, 10 Apr. 1892, p. 1.
147. For the attitude of the British press to anarchists, see Haia Shpayer-Makov, 'Anarchism in British Public Opinion 1880–1914', *Victorian Studies*, 31 (Summer 1988), 494–504.
148. *Evening News*, 14 Apr. 1892, p. 3.
149. 'The Ethics of Detectives', *Spectator*, 30 Aug. 1890, pp. 271–2.
150. *Daily News*, 19 Feb. 1894, p. 4. See also *Daily Chronicle*, 19 Feb. 1894, p. 5; *Birmingham Daily Post*, 20 Jan. 1893, p. 5; *Bristol Mercury and Daily Post*, 24 Feb. 1894, p. 3, but also *Leeds Mercury*'s criticism of the confiscation of personal anarchist correspondence during the raid on an anarchist club (20 Feb. 1894, p. 5).
151. *Daily News*, 24 Feb. 1894, p. 4.
152. *Reynolds's News*, 14 Apr. 1895, p. 4.
153. See, e.g., *Daily Express*, 17 Sept. 1901, p. 4, 10 Sept. 1901, p. 4.
154. *Spectator*, 18 Feb. 1893, p. 222, in an article entitled 'Espionage as a Profession'.
155. Jane Morgan, *Conflict and Order* (Oxford: Clarendon Press, 1987), 157. On queries in parliament about police behaviour during industrial disputes, see *Police Review*, 21 July 1912, p. 290.
156. Emsley, 'The English Bobby', 118, 124–5.
157. Paul Richard Thompson, *The Edwardians* (London: Weidenfeld and Nicolson, 1984; first published 1975), 133; James Devon, *The Criminal and the Community* (London: John Lane, 1912), 189.
158. Thompson, *The Edwardians*, 133.
159. Woodhall, *Detective and Secret Service Days*, 9–12.
160. Gatrell, 'The Decline of Theft and Violence', 289; see also p. 276, and Taylor, *Policing the Victorian Town*, 172–6.
161. 'What of the Police?', *Westminster Review*, 59 (Mar. 1903), 298.
162. *Daily Chronicle*, 10 Sept. 1901, p. 4. See also *Evening News*, 6 Aug. 1900; *Weekly Times and Echo*, 8 Jan. 1911, p. 1.
163. *The Times*, 1 Jan. 1909, p. 4. This article was part of a series of eleven articles published by *The Times* from 24 Dec. 1908 to 15 Jan. 1909, under the heading 'The Metropolitan Police'. See also 28 Jan. 1913, p. 7.
164. *Evening News*, 29 Dec. 1910, p. 1. The gang managed to escape until most of its members were surrounded and shot in the famous Sidney Street siege on the night of 2–3 Jan. 1911. Detectives were intensely active in the siege and the steps leading up to it (for reminiscences of the affair, see, e.g., Nicholls, *Crime within the Square Mile*, ch. 6, Wensley, *Forty Years of Scotland Yard*, ch. 18, and Leeson, *Lost London*, ch. 15). Detective Sergeant Leeson was shot during the siege and forced to leave police service as a result.

NOTES

165. For details, see Shpayer-Makov, 'Shedding the Uniform and Acquiring a New Masculine Image'.
166. See, e.g., *Illustrated Police Budget*, 11 May 1895, p. 8, on the capture of the embezzler (and Liberal MP) Jabez Balfour, who had fled to South America and was brought back by (then) Detective Inspector Frank Froest of Scotland Yard.
167. *Daily News*, 20 July 1910, p. 7.
168. *Daily News*, 1 Aug. 1910, p. 1; Macnaghten, *Days of my Years*, 189–90. For Dew's version of the case, see Dew, *I Caught Crippen*, 7–82.
169. *The Times*, 27 July 1910, p. 8, 1 Aug. 1910, p. 7.
170. By contrast, readers of the radical *Penny Illustrated Paper* were reminded by its sarcastic comments that Dew did nothing requiring 'any brain effort' and that nonetheless the press, including the liberal dailies, repeatedly made much 'of the worthy inspector's wonderful prowess and skill' (13 Aug. 1910, p. 1; see also 30 July 1910, p. 152, 6 Aug. 1910, p. 167).
171. *The Times*, 1 Aug. 1910, p. 9.
172. For further details of the case, provided by a contemporary, see L. A. Parry, 'Crippen', in Shore, *Crime and its Detection*, ii. 97–119. For the trial, see Filson Young (ed.), *The Trial of Hawley Harvey Crippen* (Edinburgh: William Hodge & Co., 1920). On the tendency of the established press to overlook flaws in the conduct of an investigation, see, for example, the depiction by the Tory *Morning Post* of Scotland Yard detectives as quick and determined during the investigation of the brutal murder of Mrs Emsley of Stepney, London, in 1860, although the detectives had actually missed important evidence in their initial search (10 Sept. 1860, p. 6), and the description by *The Times* of Scotland Yard as a 'hard working force' and the Liverpool Police as 'vigilant' during the Fenian outrages (2 June 1884, p. 6, and 17 Oct. 1884, p. 5, respectively).
173. *Sun*, 27 Sept. 1897, p. 2.
174. *The Times*, 4 Jan. 1909, p. 3.
175. For the replacement of Bertillonage with fingerprinting in France, and Bertillon's embittered attitude to the shift, see Thorwald, *The Century of the Detective*, 83–90. In Thorwald's opinion, if for the British this shift in the system of identification in favour of fingerprinting was mundane, for many French politicians and scientists the retreat from bertillonage was 'an affront to the nation' (p. 83).
176. Interestingly, in the interview he confessed that he was glad of the opportunity to unbosom himself to a reporter, 'after having for several days had no intercourse with any one but detectives'. The interview was summarized in the *Standard*, 22 Mar. 1884, p. 5. Vincent also used the occasion to announce his intention to resign his position in the police and put up his candidacy for a seat in parliament. (For Howard Vincent's parliamentary career, see his obituary in the *Daily Telegraph*, 8 Apr. 1908, pp. 11–12.)
177. Monro, 'The London Police', 628–9.
178. Flynt, 'Police Methods in London', 437.
179. McAdoo, 'The London Police from a New York Point of View', 669.
180. McAdoo, 'The London Police from a New York Point of View', 670. For other foreign visitors who expressed admiration for Scotland Yard, see *The Times*, 16 Jan. 1909, p. 4.

181. For other examples of captions, see *Police and Public*, 13 July 1889, p. 2, referring to a three-month-long pursuit of a forger and embezzler by two Liverpudlian detectives, ending in his capture, and 17 Aug. 1889, p. 11, 5 Oct. 1889, p. 2.
182. Fitch, *Memoirs of a Royal Detective*, 101–2.
183. *Croydon Times*, 2 Apr. 1910.
184. See, e.g., *Penny Illustrated Paper*, 1 Oct. 1910, p. 430, 8 Oct. 1910, p. 463, 15 Oct. 1910, p. 498.
185. Macnaghten revealed that when he was put in charge of the CID he was determined that the first twelve months of his command 'should be unsmirched by anything like an undiscovered murder' (*Days of my Years*, 243).
186. Petrow, *Policing Morals*, 70.
187. Taylor, 'Rationing Crime', 580–1.
188. Clarkson and Richardson, *Police!*, pp. v, vii–viii.
189. Higginbottom, *The Vivid Life*, 12; Curtis, *Jack the Ripper*, 63.
190. [Stephen], 'The Criminal Law and the Detection of Crime', 699–700.
191. The *Yorkshire Post*, responding to allegations by a constable from the Leeds City Police that he could arrange for information not to see print in the press, vouched that, in selecting material, newspaper staffs did not consult the police but used their own trained judgement to decide what was worthy of publication ('The Police and the Press', *Journalist*, 4 Mar. 1893, p. 16).

CHAPTER 6. POLICE DETECTIVES IN FICTION

1. The term 'detective fiction' used here does not refer to a particular narrative structure, but to any fictional texts that feature a detective figure.
2. Lincoln B. Faller, *Turned to Account* (Cambridge: Cambridge University Press, 1987), 8; Hal Gladfelder, *Criminality and Narrative in Eighteenth-Century England* (Baltimore: Johns Hopkins University Press, 2001), 5.
3. See Chibnall, 'Chronicles of the Gallows', 186–7.
4. The Newgate novels were inspired by the highly popular *Newgate Calendar*—collections of criminal biographies published periodically in different versions from the early eighteenth century onwards. For details, see Stephen Knight, *Crime Fiction since 1800* (Houndmills: Palgrave Macmillan, 2010; first published 2004), 5–9, 228–9.
5. Lyn Pykett, 'The Newgate Novel and Sensation Fiction, 1830–1868', in Martin Priestman (ed.), *The Cambridge Companion to Crime Fiction* (Cambridge: Cambridge University Press, 2003), 20.
6. Pykett, 'The Newgate Novel', 20.
7. O'Brien, '"The Most Beautiful Murder"', 20.
8. Greenwood, *The Seven Curses of London*, 112. See also Mayhew, *London Labour and the London Poor*, iv. 221.
9. Wiener, *Reconstructing the Criminal*, 21.
10. For an explanation of the scarcity of detectives in crime fiction and how criminals were caught, as depicted in the *Newgate Calendar*, see Stephen Knight, *Form and Ideology in Crime Fiction* (London: Macmillan, 1980), 9–14.
11. Godwin, considered by many the father of anarchism, recoiled from the practices of spies and informers but recognized the necessity of detection (Caroline

Reitz, *Detecting the Nation* (Columbus, OH: Ohio State University Press, 2004), 8–10). The book also includes a thief-taker figure who hounds Caleb.
12. For more examples of the Bow Street Runners in literary texts, see Cox, *A Certain Share of Low Cunning*, 41 nn. 58, 59.
13. For various views on the authorship of the book, see Ian Ousby, *Bloodhounds of Heaven* (Cambridge, MA: Harvard University Press, 1976), 183 n. 23.
14. *Richmond: Scenes in the Life of a Bow Street Runner, Drawn up from his Private Memoranda*, intro. by E. F. Bleiler (New York: Dover Publications, 1976; first published 1827), 87.
15. A review of the book, which commended the appearance of this new literary form, describing it as 'pseudo-auto-biography', nevertheless called for 'more of the facts and less of the ornaments' (*Literary Gazette*, 24 Mar. 1824, p. 181).
16. James Morton, *The First Detective* (London: Ebury Press, 2004), 197. Vidocq resigned in 1827 at the age of 52, although he continued to work for the Sûreté occasionally and in 1832 again headed it for a period.
17. Morton, *The First Detective*, p. vii.
18. Ousby, *Bloodhounds of Heaven*, 115.
19. Ousby, *Bloodhounds of Heaven*, 115.
20. For details about the detective figures in Dickens's novels, stories, and articles, see Haining (ed.), *Hunted Down*, 7–21; Collins, *Dickens and Crime*, 201–15.
21. For an analysis of the figure of Bucket, see, for example, Ousby, *Bloodhounds of Heaven*, 97–110. *Bleak House* was first published as serialized stories in the weekly *Household Words* in 1852–3. Bucket, not the only detective in the novel (the sinister Tulkinghorn is another), was probably modelled on one of the detectives Dickens had met in real life—the famous Inspector Field (Inspector Wield in Dickens's articles in the press). For the similarities between Bucket and Field, see Julian Symons, *Mortal Consequences* (New York: Harper & Row, 1972), 42.
22. Years before, in the mid-1850s, Collins, still at the beginning of his career, had written two novels, each featuring an amateur detective—a man in *Hide and Seek* (1854) and a woman in *The Dead Secret* (1857). Dickens published sections of *The Moonstone* in his magazine *All the Year Round* in 1867. The figure of Cuff was partly inspired by Inspector Jonathan Whicher, a detective in the group interviewed by Dickens in his office (see above, ch. 5). For the similarities between Whicher and the fictional figure Sergeant Cuff, see Symons, *Mortal Consequences*, 46–7. For a comparison between Bucket and Cuff, see Lock, *Dreadful Deeds and Awful Murders*, 171. *The Moonstone*, and Wilkie Collins's other famous novel, *The Woman in White* (1860), are widely considered to be the first genuine detective narratives in England, though Howard Haycraft maintains that the latter was a mystery rather than a detective novel (*Murder for Pleasure* (New York: D. Appleton-Century, 1941), 18, 38). For other works by Collins that include detective figures, see Robert Ashley, *Wilkie Collins* (New York: Haskell House, 1976; first published 1952), 48, 55, 135.
23. The French literary market was highly enthused over Vidocq, with numerous books about him published there, some written or supervised by him and many more based on his exploits and tales. Only a small proportion was translated into

English. Still, the figure of Vidocq was the subject of more than one play in England. Apart from *VIDOCQ! The French Police Spy*, which was staged immediately after his memoirs had been published in English, another play, entitled *The Thief-Taker of Paris; or, Vidocq*, was staged in the Britannia Theatre in London in 1860 (Philip John Stead, *Vidocq* (London: Staples Press, 1953), 123–4).

24. 'Detective Fiction', *Saturday Review*, 4 Dec. 1886, p. 749; Sita A. Schütt, 'French Crime Fiction', in Priestman (ed.), *The Cambridge Companion to Crime Fiction*, 63; A. E. Murch, *The Development of the Detective Novel* (London: Peter Owen, 1968; first published 1958), 127. Gaboriau wrote detective fiction between 1865 and 1873, and then he died at the age of 38. For French influence on the development of English detective fiction, see Murch, *The Development of the Detective Novel*, 103–10, 127–8, 131–2.
25. 'Detectives', *Saturday Review*, 5 May 1883, p. 558.
26. Murch, *The Development of the Detective Novel*, 138–41, 58–64.
27. Brian W. McCuskey, 'The Kitchen Police: Servant Surveillance and Middle-Class Transgression', *Victorian Literature and Culture*, 28/2 (2000), 359–63.
28. 'A Long Way after Poe', *Nation*, 19 Sept. 1907, p. 251.
29. Haycraft, *Murder for Pleasure*, 18–20; Murch, *The Development of the Detective Novel*, 78, 82, 181.
30. For an example, see 'Secrets of a Private Enquiry Office', *Police and Public*, 6 July–31 Aug. 1889.
31. See, e.g., 'The Detective in America', *Chambers's Journal*, 16 (July–Dec. 1861); 'A Private Detective Story', *Chambers's Journal*, 56 (18 Jan. 1879).
32. In his *XIX Century Fiction: A Bibliographical Record Based on his Own Collection* (London: Constable, 1951), Michael Sadleir lists nearly sixty titles of detective 'reminiscences' published in the period 1850–94 (quoted in Ellery Queen, *Queen's Quorum* (New York: Biblio and Tannen, 1969; first published 1948), 13).
33. Henderson, *Clues*, 7.
34. Ousby, *Bloodhounds of Heaven*, 59.
35. David Reed, *The Popular Magazine in Britain and the United States, 1880–1960* (Toronto: Toronto University Press, 1997), 82.
36. Norman N. Feltes, *Modes of Production of Victorian Novels* (Chicago: University of Chicago Press, 1986), 12–13.
37. Mary Margaret Busk, 'Autobiography', *Blackwood's Edinburgh Magazine*, 159 (Nov. 1829), 738.
38. Rosemary Mitchell, *Picturing the Past* (Oxford: Clarendon Press, 2000), 17–18; Billie Melman, *The Culture of History* (Oxford: Oxford University Press, 2006).
39. Louis James, *Fiction for the Working Man, 1830–50* (London: Oxford University Press, 1963), 39–40.
40. 'Recollections of a Police-Officer', *Chambers's Journal*, NS 12 (July–Dec. 1849), 55. As a detective he sought expiation for the sin of gambling and was forgiven when he saved a youngster from the clutches of a crook who had entrapped her (see the story 'The Widow', *Chambers's Journal*, NS 13 (Jan.–June 1850), 313–18).
41. 'Recollections of a Police-Officer', 58.
42. In the story 'The Revenge', however, he makes a mistake by trusting a woman who has set him up. The moral order is restored, however, when she helps him escape from his captors, and he, in turn, helps her reform (*Chambers's Journal*, NS 14 (July–Dec. 1850), 294–8).

43. However, exceptionally, in 'The Twins', the criminals—who are gentlemen themselves—are allowed by the mother of a kidnapped baby to leave the shores of England (*Chambers's Journal*, NS 13 (Jan.–June 1850), 387–90.
44. Altick, *The English Common Reader*, 246, 332.
45. Altick, *The English Common Reader*, 351.
46. A pirated issue of the book appeared in 1852 (Eric Osborne, introduction to 'Waters', *Recollections of a Detective Police-Officer* (London: Covent Garden Press, 1972)). See the 1972 edition for the publishing history of *Recollections*.
47. The 1859 volume was prompted by the positive reception of the first volume. The advertisement at the end of the 1859 book claimed that 'above 75,000 copies have been sold of these thrilling and exciting "Recollections"'. It was advertised in *The Times* repeatedly before it was due to be published (*The Times*, 22 Dec. 1858, p. 9, 31 Dec. 1858, p. 9, 4 Jan. 1859, p. 9).
48. Apparently, American publishers were even quicker to appreciate the potential marketing value of books containing stories about detectives. As early as 1853, an American edition of Russell's stories was published, entitled *The Recollections of a Policeman*, which also included some of the articles written or inspired by Dickens, thereby providing a broader view of the world of detection and conceivably granting it greater legitimation. The preface to the book pointed out that some of the stories had already been published in American magazines and 'proved exceedingly popular', prompting the decision that 'they deserve a more permanent form' (Thomas Waters, *The Recollections of a Policeman* (New York, 1853), preface). Published only eleven years after the London detective department had been formed, the preface referred to the English detective in glowing terms, dissociating him from 'the informer and spy of the Continent of Europe' and underscoring his dual role as both a preventive and a detective 'protective policeman'. After establishing his credentials as a beneficial and vital public servant, the author went on to portray the occupation of detection as both sober and alluring, a novel combination at that time: 'His occupation is as honorable as it is dangerous. Its difficulties and danger give it an odor of the romantic.' For a similar reception in France, see Murch, *The Development of the Detective Novel*, 88–9.
49. During the next two decades William Russell wrote many other mystery and crime stories, which were published under the pseudonym Waters. In most of them the publishers made a point of affirming his popularity by referring to previously published stories by him, though the single reference repeatedly associated with his name—Waters—is *Recollections*. Evidently, its popularity was the best advertisement for his later books.
50. 'Waters' (ed.), *Experiences of a Real Detective by Inspector F.* (London: Ward & Lock, 1862). The stories were also printed in the *Sixpenny Magazine*, published by Ward & Lock around the same time. In 1870 Russell published *Mrs Waldegrave's Will, and Other Tales by Inspector F.*, edited by 'Waters' (London: Ward, Lock, and Tyler, 1870).
51. 'Waters' (ed.), *Experiences of a Real Detective by Inspector F.*, 1.
52. 'Waters', *Autobiography of an English Detective* (London: John Maxwell, 1863), i. 1–3.
53. Winifred Hughes, *The Maniac in the Cellar* (Princeton: Princeton University Press, 1980), 5.

54. Charles Martel (ed.), *The Detective's Note-Book* (London: Ward & Lock, 1860); Charles Martel (ed.), *Diary of an Ex-Detective* (London: Ward & Lock, 1860).
55. For a discussion of novels and stories featuring female detectives published at the close of the nineteenth century, see Maureen Reddy, 'Women Detectives', in Priestman (ed.), *The Cambridge Companion to Crime Fiction*, 192.
56. *Revelations of a Lady Detective* (London: George Vickers, 1864), 3. The British Library catalogue and various reference books attribute its authorship to William Stephens Hayward (the date of publication is given in different places as 1861 and 1864), author of a long list of other books published by George Vickers. Another popular book at the time was Andrew Forrester, Jr's *The Revelations of a Private Detective* (London: Ward & Lock, 1863). Other books by Forrester were *Secret Service; or, Recollections of a City Detective* (London: Ward & Lock, 1864) and *The Female Detective* (London: Ward & Lock, 1864), the latter appearing in various editions with different titles and stories. The real person behind Forrester is subject to speculation (see Judith Flanders, 'The Hanky-Panky Way', *Times Literary Supplement*, 18 June 2010, pp. 14–15). Interestingly, two famous detectives in the City of London Police, the brothers John and Daniel Forrester, who were (and still are) suspected of being the author, made a point of writing to the *Standard* (16 July 1863, p. 3), dissociating themselves from *The Revelations of a Private Detective*.
57. James McGovan, *Brought to Bay; or, Experiences of a City Detective* (Edinburgh: Edinburgh Publishing Company, 1878); *Hunted Down; or, Recollections of a City Detective* (Edinburgh: Edinburgh Publishing Company, 1879; first published 1878); *Strange Clues: or, Chronicles of a City Detective* (Edinburgh: Edinburgh Publishing Company, 1881); *Traced and Tracked; or, Memoirs of a City Detective* (Edinburgh: John Menzies & Co., 1884); *Solved Mysteries; or, Revelations of a City Detective* (Edinburgh: John Menzies & Co., 1888). From Dec. 1896 to mid-Feb. 1897 the *Sun* published a series of stories by McGovan entitled 'Revelations of a Detective', and from 15 Feb. to 23 Mar. 1897 another series entitled 'Unravelled Crimes'. (The author's name is sometimes referred to as McGovan and sometimes as M'Govan.)
58. McGovan, *Solved Mysteries*, preface. The author in fact derived material from James McLevy's books, which were based on the latter's experience as a detective.
59. See *Academy*, 6 Dec. 1884, p. 374, and advertisements at the end of the books.
60. *Revelations of a Lady Detective*, 3.
61. 'Waters', *Autobiography of an English Detective*, 12; Martel (ed.), *The Detective's Note-Book*, 1.
62. *Tom Fox or The Revelations of a Detective* (2nd edn; London: George Vickers, 1860).
63. *Tom Fox*, p. viii.
64. *Revelations of a Lady Detective* came out under the title *The Lady Detective* (subtitled *A Tale of Female Life and Adventure*) in 1870, and in 1884 as *The Experiences of a Lady Detective*.
65. 'Detectives', *Saturday Review*, 5 May 1883, p. 558.
66. A.C., 'Crime in Current Literature', *Westminster Review*, 147 (Apr. 1897), 437.
67. See Glenn W. Most and William W. Stowe (eds), *The Poetics of Murder* (San Diego: Harcourt, Brace, Jovanovich, 1983).

68. Charles J. Rzepka, *Detective Fiction* (Cambridge: Polity, 2005), 45–7.
69. Joel Black, *The Aesthetics of Murder* (Baltimore: Johns Hopkins University Press, 1991), 42.
70. Howard G. Brown, 'Tips, Traps and Tropes: Catching Thieves in Post-Revolutionary Paris', in Emsley and Shpayer-Makov (eds), *Police Detectives in History*, 40.
71. Beth Kalikoff, *Murder and Moral Decay in Victorian Popular Literature* (Ann Arbor: UMI Research Press, 1986), 91.
72. *Spectator*, 18 Feb. 1893, p. 222.
73. Michel Foucault, *Discipline and Punish* (London: Penguin, 1991; first published in French in 1975), 69.
74. Simon Eliot, 'Some Trends in British Book Production', in John O. Jordan and Robert L. Patten (eds), *Literature in the Marketplace* (Cambridge: Cambridge University Press, 1995), 30.
75. Joseph McAleer, *Popular Reading and Publishing in Britain 1914–1950* (Oxford: Clarendon Press, 1992), 9.
76. McAleer, *Popular Reading and Publishing*, 13, 23.
77. 'Detectives', *Saturday Review*, 5 May 1883, p. 558.
78. Philip Davis, *The Victorians* (Oxford: Oxford University Press, 2002), 222–3
79. Patrick Brantlinger, 'What is "Sensational" about the "Sensation Novel"', *Nineteenth-Century Fiction*, 37/1 (1982), 9–10.
80. For example, in 1888, an unsigned *Scotland Yard Detective Series* of twelve booklets was published in London by The General Publishing Co., each self-contained.
81. Besides the well-known examples of Inspector Bucket and Sergeant Cuff, a character who appeared in ten of Charles Gibbon's novels, Detective Dier, was modelled on the author's long-time friend Detective Reid of the Metropolitan Police (*Police Review*, 12 June 1896, p. 283, from the *Weekly Dispatch*).
82. Shand, 'The City of London Police', 607–8.
83. 'Detectives', *Saturday Review*, 5 May 1883, p. 558.
84. *Standard*, 29 Oct. 1881, p. 2. See also Aylmer, 'The Detective in Real Life', 499. For using Holmes as an example for police detectives to emulate, see *Daily Mail*, 8 Feb. 1906, p. 6.
85. See 'Our Detective Police', *Saturday Review*, 19 Sept. 1891, p. 326.
86. Louis Canler, *Autobiography of a French Detective from 1818 to 1858* (London: Ward and Lock, 1862), p. iii.
87. See, e.g., *Reynolds's News*, 3 Feb. 1895, p. 5.
88. Arthur Griffiths, *Fifty Years of Public Service* (London: Cassell, 1904), 400.
89. See, for example, the description of the literary life of Major Arthur Griffiths (*Fifty Years of Public Service*, 396–7).
90. Bernard Benstock and Thomas F. Staley (eds), *British Mystery Writers, 1860–1919* (Detroit: Bruccoli Clark Layman Book, 1988), 18.
91. 'Detective Fiction', 749.
92. For detective literature in this period, see Symons, *Mortal Consequences*, chs. 6, 7.
93. See, e.g., E.A.B.D. (E. A. Bland), *Constable 42Z* (London: Religious Tract Society, 1887), mentioned in Steedman, *Policing the Victorian Community*, 145, and W. W. Jacobs, 'The Constable's Move', *Strand Magazine*, 30/178 (Oct. 1905), 449–55.

94. For a detailed study of women detectives in English literature from the mid-nineteenth century to the First World War, see Joseph A. Kestner, *Sherlock's Sisters: The British Female Detective, 1864–1913* (Aldershot: Ashgate, 2003). See also Kathleen Gregory Klein, *The Woman Detective: Gender and Genre* (Urbana: University of Chicago Press, 1988), chs 1, 3.
95. Israel Zangwill, *The Big Bow Mystery* (first published 1891), in E. F. Bleiler (ed.), *Three Victorian Detective Novels* (New York: Dover, 1978).
96. Joseph Sheridan Le Fanu, *Checkmate* (Stroud: Sutton Publishing, 1997; first published 1871).
97. H. F. Wood, *The Passenger from Scotland Yard*, intro. by E. F. Bleiler (New York: Dover, 1977; first published 1888), 28.
98. Haycraft, *Murder for Pleasure*, 106.
99. Aylmer, 'The Detective in Real Life', 499.
100. Dennis Porter, *The Pursuit of Crime, Art and Ideology in Detective Fiction* (New Haven: Yale University Press, 1981), 125.
101. Vidocq, though sometimes unsuccessful as a detective, is glorified in texts revolving around him as courageous, intelligent, innovative, ingenious in role playing, and hard working. This portrayal allowed him to attain legendary fame despite his close association with criminal elements.
102. Tom Taylor, *The Ticket-of-Leave Man* (London: Heinemann, 1981; first published 1863).
103. Charles Reade, 'The Knightsbridge Mystery' (first published 1884), in Jack Adrian (ed.), *Twelve Mystery Stories* (Oxford: Oxford University Press, 1988), 61.
104. Edgar Allan Poe, 'The Murders in the Rue Morgue' (first published 1841), in *Tales of Mystery and Imagination* (Ware: Wordsworth Editions, 1993), 74.
105. See 'A French Detective Story', *All the Year Round*, 19 (1877), quoted in Kalikoff, *Murder and Moral Decay*, 134.
106. See, for example, the portrayal of Scotland Yard detective Henry Carter, and of Chief Inspector Faunce, in Mary Elizabeth Braddon's *Henry Dunbar: The Story of an Outcast* (1864) and *Rough Justice* (1898), respectively.
107. Wilkie Collins, *My Lady's Money*, in Bleiler (ed.), *Three Victorian Detective Novels*, 110.
108. An example is Arthur Griffiths's three-volume *Fast and Loose* (London: Chapman and Hall, 1884–5), where an amateur investigator—the highly talented, knowledgeable, and intelligent Sir Richard Daunt—is the one who solves the enigma of the bank fraud, rather than Detective Inspector Faske of Scotland Yard. The publisher also brought out an abridged edition of this book.
109. Wilbur R. Miller, 'From Old Cap Collier to Nick Carter; or, Images of Crime and Criminal Justice in American Dime Novel Detective Stories, 1880–1920', in Amy Gilman Srebnick and René Lévy (eds), *Crime and Culture* (Aldershot: Ashgate, 2005), 202.
110. See, e.g. Joseph A. Kestner, *Sherlock's Men: Masculinity, Conan Doyle, and Cultural History* (Aldershot: Ashgate, 1997); Haycraft, *Murder for Pleasure*, 56–61; Murch, *The Development of the Detective Novel*, 177–91; Symons, *Mortal Consequences*, 64–73; Porter, *The Pursuit of Crime*, 156; Knight, *Form and Ideology in Crime Fiction*, 71–105; Rzepka, *Detective Fiction*, 119–22.
111. Vincent, *The Culture of Secrecy*, 43.

NOTES

112. Robert Louis Stevenson and Fanny van de Grift Stevenson, 'The Dynamiter', in *More New Arabian Nights* (New York: Charles Scribner's Sons, 1901; first published 1885), 7.
113. Arthur Conan Doyle,'The Adventure of the Devil's Foot', in *His Last Bow*, in *The Complete Sherlock Holmes* (London: Penguin Books, 1988), 955.
114. *A Study in Scarlet*, in *Complete Sherlock Holmes*, 20–1. *A Study in Scarlet* was included in 1887 in *Beeton's Christmas Annual*, and was published in book form in 1888.
115. Doyle, 'A Case of Identity', in *The Adventures of Sherlock Holmes* (1892), in *Complete Sherlock Holmes*, 191. *The Adventures of Sherlock Holmes* was originally published as single stories in the *Strand Magazine* from July 1891 to June 1892.
116. Doyle, *A Study in Scarlet*, in *Complete Sherlock Holmes*, 26–7, 36.
117. Doyle, *The Sign of Four*, in *Complete Sherlock Holmes*, 90. The novel first appeared in the Feb. 1890 edition of *Lippincott's Monthly Magazine* as *The Sign of the Four*.
118. Doyle, 'Silver Blaze', in *Complete Sherlock Holmes*, 338–9.
119. Doyle, 'The Adventure of the Six Napoleons', in *The Return of Sherlock Holmes* (1905), in *Complete Sherlock Holmes*, 595. The story was first published in *Collier's Weekly* (Apr. 1904), and *Strand Magazine* (May 1904).
120. Doyle, 'The Adventure of the Dancing Men', in *The Return of Sherlock Holmes*, in *Complete Sherlock Holmes*, 518. The story was first published in the *Strand Magazine* (Dec. 1903). See also the attitude of Inspector Stanley Hopkins to Holmes in the stories 'The Adventure of Black Peter' and 'The Adventure of the Abbey Grange' in the same collection.
121. Doyle, 'The Adventure of the Six Napoleons', in *Complete Sherlock Holmes*, 595.
122. Arthur Morrison, 'The Case of the Lost Foreigner', in *Chronicles of Martin Hewitt* (New York: Books for Libraries Press, 1971; first published 1895), 228.
123. See, e.g., Arthur Morrison, 'The Case of the "Flitterbat Lancers"', in *Adventures of Martin Hewitt* (London: Ward, Lock & Co., 1896), 44.
124. Rzepka, *Detective Fiction*, 137.
125. Arthur Morrison, 'The Case of the Dead Skipper', in *Adventures of Martin Hewitt*, 102.
126. Morrison, 'The Case of the Dead Skipper', in *Adventures of Martin Hewitt*, 83.
127. Arthur Morrison, 'The Affair of Mrs Seton's Child', in *Adventures of Martin Hewitt*, 231.
128. Arthur Morrison, 'The Case of Laker, Absconded', in *Chronicles of Martin Hewitt*, 191–4, 209.
129. Morrison, 'The Case of Laker, Absconded', in *Chronicles of Martin Hewitt*, 15, 39. See also 'The Case of the Dead Skipper' and 'The Case of Mr Geldard's Elopement' in *Adventures of Martin Hewitt*.
130. Headon Hill, *Clues from a Detective's Camera*; and *Zambra the Detective* (London: Chatto & Windus, 1894). Headon Hill was the pseudonym of Francis Edward Grainger.
131. The first Sexton Blake story was featured in 1893 in the penny dreadful *The Halfpenny Marvel*, under the pen-name Harry Blyth, pseudonym of Hal Meredeth. Blake was the hero in numerous publications and other media formats over the next few decades, written by different authors.

132. One example is Gilbert [Edward] Campbell, 'The Mystery of Essex Stairs' (first published by Ward, Lock, Bowden & Co., in 1891), in Michael Cox (ed.), *Victorian Tales of Mystery and Detection* (Oxford: Oxford University Press, 1992).
133. Catherine Louisa Pirkis, *The Experiences of Loveday Brooke, Lady Detective* (London: Hutchinson & Co., 1894), 30, 282.
134. For other examples of a female private detective heroine, see George R. Sims, *Dorcas Dene, Detective* (London: F. V. White & Co., 1897); M. McDonnell Bodkin, *Dora Myrl, The Lady Detective* (London: Chatto & Windus, 1900); Grant Allen, *Miss Caley's Adventures* (London: Grant Richards, 1899) and *Hilda Wade* (London: Grant Richards, 1900).
135. Murch, *The Development of the Detective Novel*, 211.
136. Arnold Bennett, *The Grand Babylon Hotel* ((London: Chatto & Windus, 1902), ch. 11. First published in the *Daily Mail*.
137. R. Austin Freeman, *John Thorndyke's Cases* (London: Chatto & Windus, 1909). For a similar example of early twentieth-century detective literature, see Headon Hill, *Tracked Down* (London: C. Arthur Pearson, 1902).
138. B. Fletcher Robinson and J. Malcolm Fraser, *The Chronicles of Addington Peace and The Trail of the Dead* (Shelburne, Ontario: The Battered Silicon Dispatch Box, 1998), 57. The stories in *The Chronicles of Addington Peace* were first published by *The Lady's Home Magazine of Fiction* in 1904, and in book form in 1905.
139. See also George R. Sims, *Detective Inspector Chance* (London, 1974). The series of nine stories appeared between 9 Aug. and 4 Oct. 1911 in the *Sketch*.
140. Vivian Grey, *Stories of Scotland Yard* (London: Everett & Co., 1906), 3.
141. Grey, *Stories of Scotland Yard*, 118.
142. Grey, *Stories of Scotland Yard*, 68.
143. Grey, *Stories of Scotland Yard*, 118.
144. Christopher Clausen, 'Sherlock Holmes, Order, and the Late-Victorian Mind', *Georgia Review*, 38/1 (Spring 1984), 88. Both these stories, which first appeared in the *Strand Magazine*, were republished in Doyle's *His Last Bow* in 1917.
145. This change continued after 1914. While most fictional detectives in the inter-war period were privately engaged, and the ethos of amateurism persisted, thoughtful and skilful police detective figures, such as Detective Chief Inspector Roderick Alleyn, created by Ngaio Marsh; Inspector Joseph French, created by Freeman Wills Crofts; and Superintendent Henry Wilson, created by G. D. H. Cole, were also popular among readers. However, only in the second half of the twentieth century did fictional police detectives acquire the high status and overwhelming presence in the media associated with them today.
146. Murch, *The Development of the Detective Novel*, 217.
147. See, for example, an article from the *Manchester Evening Mail*, quoted in the *Police Review*, 2 Nov. 1894, p. 524; *The Times*, 22 Apr. 1863, p. 5, 23 Mar. 1868, p. 10, 17 Dec. 1888, p. 9.
148. Francis M. Dodsworth, 'Masculinity as Governance: Police, Public Service and the Embodiment of Authority, c.1700–1850', in Matthew McCormack (ed.), *Public Men: Masculinity and Politics in Modern Britain* (Houndmills: Palgrave Macmillan, 2007), 37; Radzinowicz, *A History of English Criminal Law*, iv. 105.

149. John Carter Wood, 'Self-Policing and the Policing of the Self: Violence, Protection and the Civilizing Bargain in Britain', *Crime, histoire et sociétés/Crime, History & Societies*, 7/1 (2003), 112.
150. Conley, *The Unwritten Law*, 42.
151. *Report of the Director of Criminal Investigations*, in *Annual Report of the Commissioner of the Police of the Metropolis*, for 1881, PP, vol. 33 (1882), 336.
152. Thomas W. Haycraft, *Executive Powers in Relation to Crime and Disorder; or, Powers of Police in England* (London: Butterworth & Co., 1897), 3.
153. Wilkie Collins, *The Fallen Leaves*, bk 8, ch. 3, http://www.gutenberg.org/files/7894/7894-h/7894-h.htm (first published 1879).
154. Anthea Trodd, *Domestic Crime in the Victorian Novel* (New York: St Martin's Press, 1989), 46–7, 161–3.
155. Davis, *The Victorians*, 237.
156. H. F. Wood, *The Night of the 3rd Ult* (New York: George Munro, 1890), 111.
157. Wood, *The Night of the 3rd Ult*, 144.
158. Emmuska Orczy, *Lady Molly of Scotland Yard*, intro. by Alice Thomas Ellis (Pleasantville, NY: Akadine Press, 1999; first published 1910).
159. 'Tale of a Detective', in E. F. Bleiler (ed.), *A Treasury of Victorian Detective Stories* (New York: Charles Scribner's Sons, 1979). The story was published in a collection entitled *A Race for Life and Other Tales*, by The Religious Tract Society, in the early 1870s.
160. Matthew Phipps Shiel, *Prince Zaleski* (London: John Lane, 1895).
161. Stafford, 'Spies and Gentlemen: The Birth of the British Spy Novel, 1893–1914', 490.
162. Allen Grant, 'The Great Ruby Robbery' (first published 1892), in Geraldine Beare (ed.), *Crime Stories from the Strand* (London: Folio Society, 1991).
163. Macnaghten, *Days of my Years*, 277, 288–90.
164. Mrs Henry Wood, 'The Mystery at Number Seven' (first published 1877), in Cox (ed.), *Victorian Tales*; Richard Dowling, 'The Going Out of Alessandro Pozzone' (first published 1878), also in Cox (ed.), *Victorian Tales*.
165. See, e.g., Lillie Thomasina Meade and Robert Eustace, 'The Arrest of Captain Vandaleur', (first published in *Harmsworth Magazine*, July 1894), in Cox (ed.), *Victorian Tales*, and Headon Hill, *Guilty Gold: A Romance of Financial Fraud and City Crime* (London: C. Arthur Pearson, 1896). See also Victor Lorenzo Whitechurch and E. Conway, 'A Warning in Red' (first published in *Harmsworth Magazine*, Sept. 1899), also in Cox (ed.), *Victorian Tales*.
166. For the use of forensic techniques in detective fiction of the period under discussion, see Ronald R. Thomas, *Detective Fiction and the Rise of Forensic Science* (Cambridge: Cambridge University Press, 2001; first published 1999).
167. See, e.g., Fergus Hume, 'The Greenstone God and the Stockbroker' (first published in *The Idler*, Jan. 1894), in Cox (ed.), *Victorian Tales*, 279; Edgar Wallace, *The Four Just Men* (London: Tallis Press, 1905). For amicable relations between a journalist and a detective, see E. C. Bentley's novel *Trent's Last Case* (London: T. Nelson & Sons, 1913).
168. For examples of Marxist critics of detective fiction, see Porter, *The Pursuit of Crime*, and Ernest Mandel, *Delightful Murder* (Minneapolis: University of Minnesota Press, 1984). For Foucauldians, see D. A. Miller, *The Novel and the Police* (Berkeley and Los Angeles: University of California Press, 1988).

NOTES

169. Foucault, *Discipline and Punish*, 209.
170. Miller, *The Novel and the Police*, p. viii, 18–19.
171. Miller, *The Novel and the Police*, pp. viii, 17.
172. Miller, *The Novel and the Police*, 18–23, 52.
173. Miller, *The Novel and the Police*, 3, 7–8.
174. Miller, *The Novel and the Police*,. 14–17.
175. See, e.g., Porter, *The Pursuit of Crime*, 121, 124.
176. Trodd, *Domestic Crime*, 7.
177. See the chapter 'The Policeman and the Lady' in Trodd, *Domestic Crime*, for the many examples in mid-Victorian fiction reflecting anxiety about police intrusion into middle-class homes.
178. Miller, *The Novel and the Police*, 37–8.
179. Miller, *The Novel and the Police*, 38.
180. Allen, 'The Great Ruby Robbery', 53–5. See also Ernest William Hornung, *Dead Men Tell No Tales* (London: Methuen & Co., 1899).
181. Miller, *The Novel and the Police*, 17; Martin A. Kayman, *From Bow Street to Baker Street: Mystery, Detection, and Narrative* (Houndmills: Macmillan, 1992), 118.
182. Wilson, *What Price Liberty?*, 163.
183. Pat Thane, 'Government and Society', 53.
184. Michael Freeden, *The New Liberalism* (Oxford: Clarendon Press, 1978), 14, 32–5, 70.
185. Quoted in Freeden, *The New Liberalism*, 69.
186. Freeden, *The New Liberalism*, 74–5.
187. Freeden, *The New Liberalism*, 60.
188. Gareth Stedman Jones, *Outcast London* (Oxford: Clarendon Press, 1971), 284–314.
189. While not a detective text, the novel juxtaposes Inspector Newcomen of Scotland Yard and Gabriel Utterson, Jekyll's lawyer and friend who acts as an unofficial investigator. The policeman is shown to be very inferior to the amateur in rational thought, although both are repeatedly mistaken in their assumptions and conclusions.

CHAPTER 7. POLICE DETECTIVES AS AUTHORS

1. [Stephen], 'Detectives in Fiction and in Real Life', 713.
2. 'Detectives as They Are', 445.
3. 'Detectives and their Work', 138.
4. 'Detective Fiction', 749. See also the article from the *Daily News*, repr. in the *Police Guardian*, 9 Apr., 1886, p. 3.
5. *The Times*, 1 Jan. 1909, p. 4.
6. Griffiths, *Mysteries of Police and Crime*, ii. 1–2. See, in a similar vein, 'Our Detective Police', *Saturday Review*, 19 Sept. 1891, p. 326, which criticized the publishers of translated French detective fiction for spreading the notion that 'the French criminal police are a much cleverer set of fellows than our own'.
7. Griffiths, *Mysteries of Police and Crime*, ii. 2. See also Macnaghten, *Days of my Years*, 225.
8. Griffiths, *Mysteries of Police and Crime*, ii. 13.

9. Quoted in Clarkson and Richardson, *Police!*, 267.
10. *Police Review*, 2 Jan. 1893, p. 8.
11. *Police Review*, 30 Jan. 1893, p. 49.
12. An exception was Jerome Caminada of the Manchester Police, who published the first volume of his memoirs while still in service. The term 'memoir' is considered to be distinct from autobiography proper in that it emphasizes social and historical data rather than private life (Clinton Machann, *The Genre of Autobiography in Victorian Literature* (Ann Arbor: University of Michigan Press, 1994), 2).
13. The trend among police detectives of writing memoirs continued, and even accelerated, in the inter-war period, faithfully following the conventions inscribed in the pre-war texts. For a bibliography of British police officers' memoirs and biographies, see Martin Stallion, *A Life of Crime* (Leigh-on-Sea: M. R. Stallion, 1998). For a graph describing the number of police memoirs published in England and France between 1861 and 1939, see Lawrence, '"Scoundrels and Scallywags"', 127.
14. Parts of these life stories first appeared in journals and newspapers. By way of example, Detective Chief Inspector John Littlechild first published several of his reminiscences in *Cassell's Saturday Journal* (in 1893) and Detective Chief Inspector Charles Arrow in the *Evening News* (in 1910). See also Moser, *Stories from Scotland Yard*, intro. Some memoirs appeared solely in newspapers and never reached the book market, such as Patrick McIntyre, 'Scotland Yard, its Mysteries and Methods', *Reynolds's News*, (Feb.–May 1895).
15. John Burnett (ed.), *Useful Toil* (London: Allen Lane, 1976), 11–12; David Vincent, *Bread, Knowledge and Freedom* (London: Methuen, 1981), intro.; Jonathan Rose, *The Intellectual Life of the British Working Classes* (New Haven: Yale University Press, 2001), 2. After the First World War, published autobiographies of ordinary people became more common (Mary Evans, *Missing Persons* (London: Routledge, 1999), 8).
16. *Graphic*, 4 Aug. 1894, p. 134.
17. James McLevy, *The Casebook of a Victorian Detective*, ed. and intro. by George Scott-Moncrieff (Edinburgh: Canongate, 1975; first published 1861), p. x.
18. James McLevy, *The Edinburgh Detective*, with foreword by Quintin Jardin (Edinburgh: Mercat Press, 2001; first published 1861), pp. xi–xii. The titles of the books are: *Curiosities of Crime in Edinburgh*, *The Sliding Scale of Life*, and *The Disclosures of a Detective*. For another early memoir of a Scottish police officer, see P. Alexander Clark, *Reminiscences of a Police Officer in the Granite City* (Aberdeen: Lewis Smith, 1873).
19. Canler, *Autobiography*, p. iii.
20. Canler, *Autobiography*, p. iv. Memoirs of foreign private detectives were also published occasionally. Although Allan Pinkerton's records were destroyed in the Chicago fire of 1871, he purportedly recalled enough material to fill eighteen books with different titles (Sigmund A. Lavine, *Allan Pinkerton* (London: Mayflower, 1970; first published 1963), 135).
21. See McNaught, *Recollections* (1887); Henderson, *Clues* (1889); Moser, *Stories from Scotland Yard* (1890); Lansdowne, *A Life's Reminiscences* (1890); Littlechild, *The Reminiscences of Chief-Inspector Littlechild* (1894).

22. Nigel Cross, *The Common Writer: Life in Nineteenth-Century Grub Street* (Cambridge: Cambridge University Press, 1985), 5.
23. A.C., 'Crime in Current Literature', 437.
24. *Graphic*, 4 Aug. 1894, p. 134.
25. *Reynolds's News*, 19 Dec. 1880, p. 2.
26. Aylmer, 'The Detective in Real Life', 499–500.
27. *Morning Post*, 21 Feb. 1895, p. 6.
28. *Birmingham Daily Post*, 22 Feb., 1895, p. 3.
29. Quoted from *Sport, Law, and Police* in *Reynolds's News*, 5 May 1895, p. 5.
30. Christopher Hilliard, *To Exercise our Talents: The Democratization of Writing in Britain* (Cambridge, MA: Harvard University Press, 2006), 15.
31. 'Abberline Diary', 44–5. Similarly, the publication of Detective Chief Inspector Arrow's memoirs in the *Evening News* in 1910 had not been sanctioned (*Penny Illustrated Paper*, 6 Aug. 1910, p. 167).
32. Sweeney, *At Scotland Yard*, p. v; Macnaghten, *Days of my Years*, p. ix. On the post-war period, see Divall, *Scoundrels and Scallywags*, 227. See also references to Detective Superintendent Black of the Birmingham Police, *Police Guardian*, 16 Jan. 1892, p. 6 (repr. from the *Birmingham Daily Mail*), and to Detective Inspector Samuel Lincoln, *Police Review*, 9 Oct. 1893, p. 488.
33. Moser, *Stories from Scotland Yard*, 38; Henderson, *Clues*, 7; Lansdowne, *A Life's Reminiscences*, 2; Sweeney, *At Scotland Yard*, p. v.
34. For editorial services provided to detectives, see Richardson, *From the City to Fleet Street*, 220. See also Sweeney, *At Scotland Yard*.
35. Philip Rawlings, *Drunks, Whores and Idle Apprentices* (London: Routledge, 1992), 8.
36. *Tom Fox*, p. vii.
37. *1908 Commission*, vol. 51, p. 169.
38. *Police Review*, 10 Aug. 1894, p. 381.
39. Adam, *Police Work from Within*, 79.
40. Littlechild, *Reminiscences of Chief-Inspector Littlechild*, 7.
41. Lansdowne, *A Life's Reminiscences*, 5; Greenham, *Scotland Yard Experiences*, 10.
42. Occasionally, the biographical details were given at the end of the book.
43. Memoirs by top officials who did not rise through the ranks but were appointed to their position did not reflect this formula. Assistant Commissioners Robert Anderson and Melville L. Macnaghten, for example, described their lives before they joined the police at length. Still, they too recounted anecdotes and stories about the world of crime and crime investigation, as did their subordinates.
44. Richardson, *From the City to Fleet Street*, 120.
45. Faller, *Turned to Account*, 9, 126.
46. Caminada, *Twenty-Five Years of Detective Life*, i. 5. See also Henderson, *Clues*, 7.
47. Fuller, *Recollections of a Detective*, 18.
48. Lansdowne, *A Life's Reminiscences*, 2.
49. Lansdowne, *A Life's Reminiscences*, 3–4.
50. Nan Hackett, *XIX Century British Working-Class Autobiographies: An Annotated Bibliography* (New York: AMS Press, 1985), 42–3.
51. Berrett, *When I was at Scotland Yard*, p. vi.

NOTES

52. Caminada, *Twenty-Five Years of Detective Life*, i. 5; Lansdowne, *A Life's Reminiscences*, 2; Jervis, *Chronicles of a Victorian Detective*, 11; Anderson, *The Lighter Side of my Official Life*, preface.
53. Memoirists with no connection to law enforcement also used this convention, but it was common in autobiographical narratives about the legal system, whether fictional or not. The theme of writing at the urging of friends appears in some of the pseudo-memoirs (see 'Waters' (ed.), *Experiences of a Real Detective by Inspector F.*, 1). See also the preface to *The Reminiscences of Sir Henry Hawkins*, ed. Richard Harris (London: Thomas Nelson & Sons, 1904). Hawkins was a noted lawyer and judge (1817–1907).
54. McNaught, *Recollections*, 5; Divall, *Scoundrels and Scallywags*, 9.
55. Forrester, *The Female Detective*, 2.
56. Forrester, *The Female Detective*, 2–3.
57. 'Revelations by Real Detectives', *Police and Public*, 3 Aug. 1889, p. 6.
58. Fuller, *Recollections of a Detective*, 196.
59. See, for example, observations by Detective Inspector J. Kenneth Ferrier, who joined the force in 1900 and wrote in a memoir published in 1928 that, unlike the fictional detective, who 'sits in a comfortable chair in a comfortable room smoking a favourite pipe, and creates an imaginary crime, an imaginary criminal, and an imaginary conclusion', the real detective 'has no such pathway of strewn rose petals; he can allow his imagination a free rein and deduce effects from causes, but he cannot sit at home and secure evidence; he has of necessity to face realities and build up his case with hard facts and hard work' (J. Kenneth Ferrier, *Crooks & Crime* (London: Seeley, Service & Co., 1928), 264). Detective Chief Inspector Walter Dew, commenting in his own recollections (published in 1938), pointed out that in detective literature all criminals are caught at the end, and that 'it is easy to unravel a plot which you yourself have created' (*I Caught Crippen*, 148). By contrast, 'the real detective is by no means like the detective of fiction, who is always successful—in the end' (*I Caught Crippen*, 167). Moreover, 'dogged perseverance has brought far more criminals to book than flashes of genius' (*I Caught Crippen*, 167).
60. Greenham, *Scotland Yard Experiences*, 6. His first chapter began with the comment: 'Fiction is often beaten by reality' (p. 9).
61. Caminada, *Twenty-Five Years of Detective Life*, i. 5.
62. Moser, *Stories from Scotland Yard*, 5.
63. Sweeney, *At Scotland Yard*, p. vi. See also Canler, *Autobiography*, p. iii.
64. See *Reynolds's News*, 3 Feb. 1895, p. 5. See also Macnaghten, *Days of my Years*, 225; Anderson, *The Lighter Side of my Official Life*, 137.
65. Littlechild, *Reminiscences of Chief-Inspector Littlechild*, 76; Fuller, *Recollections of a Detective*, 213–14.
66. Lansdowne, *A Life's Reminiscences*, 3.
67. Lansdowne, *A Life's Reminiscences*, 3.
68. See, e.g., Greenham, *Scotland Yard Experiences*, 9; Fuller, *Recollections of a Detective*, 16, and Bent, *Criminal Life*, 129–33, 273–322, about the Manchester police force soup kitchen and other ventures for the relief of the poor.
69. Doyle, *A Study in Scarlet*, in *Complete Sherlock Holmes*, 19–20; Lansdowne, *A Life's Reminiscences*, 66, 122.

70. Moser, *Stories from Scotland Yard*, 59.
71. Fuller, *Recollections of a Detective*, 28.
72. Sweeney, *At Scotland Yard*, 18–19; see also Littlechild, *Reminiscences of Chief-Inspector Littlechild*, 8–10. For similar declarations in the post-war era, see Divall, *Scoundrels and Scallywags*, who asserted in 1929: 'The Metropolitan Police are the admiration of the world, and one constantly reads of high officers of the Police-forces of other nations paying visits to England in order to gain practical hints and information respecting the reason for this wonderful efficiency and discipline' (pp. 9–10); Berrett, *When I was at Scotland Yard*, p. xii; Savage, *Savage of Scotland Yard*, 15; Neil, *Man-Hunters of Scotland Yard*, 2. See also Anderson, *Criminals and Crime*, 80–1.
73. Moser, *Stories from Scotland Yard*, 5.
74. Moser, *Stories from Scotland Yard*, 20; Sweeney, *At Scotland Yard*, 19–20.
75. Bent, *Criminal Life*, 65.
76. Sweeney, *At Scotland Yard*, 18–20; Littlechild, *Reminiscences of Chief-Inspector Littlechild*, 3.
77. Moser, *Stories from Scotland Yard*, 58.
78. Moser, *Stories from Scotland Yard*, 61; Fuller, *Recollections of a Detective*, 16, 18; Sweeney, *At Scotland Yard*, 348.
79. Sweeney, *At Scotland Yard*, 348.
80. Lansdowne, *A Life's Reminiscences*, 184; Sweeney, *At Scotland Yard*, 20–33.
81. Littlechild, *Reminiscences of Chief-Inspector Littlechild*, 12.
82. Lansdowne, *A Life's Reminiscences*, 3.
83. *Reynolds's News*, 3 Feb. 1895, p. 5; Moser, *Stories from Scotland Yard*, 27; Fuller, *Recollections of a Detective*, 51.
84. Addressing the reader, Greenham announced: 'It is scarcely possible... for the general public to picture to their imagination all that an officer has to grapple with in his eventful career' (*Scotland Yard Experiences*, 9–10).
85. Sweeney, *At Scotland Yard*, 19. See also Arrow, *Rogues and Others*, 43.
86. Littlechild, *Reminiscences of Chief-Inspector Littlechild*, 2–3.
87. Sweeney, *At Scotland Yard*, 19. See also Fuller, *Recollections of a Detective*, 186.
88. Fuller, *Recollections of a Detective*, 16.
89. Sweeney, *At Scotland Yard*, 7; Fuller, *Recollections of a Detective*, 18.
90. Littlechild, *Reminiscences of Chief-Inspector Littlechild*, 75.
91. Fuller, *Recollections of a Detective*, 17.
92. Fuller, *Recollections of a Detective*, 196.
93. Ying S. Lee, *Masculinity and the English Working Class* (New York: Routledge, 2007), 12.
94. McNaught, *Recollections*, 1; Littlechild, *Reminiscences of Chief-Inspector Littlechild*, 8, 12; Sweeney, *At Scotland Yard*, 55–113; Fuller, *Recollections of a Detective*, 344–7.
95. For a discussion of the professional ideal, see Harold Perkin, *The Rise of Professional Society* (London: Routledge, 1989), 4.
96. Caminada, *Twenty-Five Years of Detective Life*, ii. 3.
97. See the letter by an ex-Fenian disclosing how interesting and revealing McIntyre's memoirs were to Fenians (*Reynolds's News*, 24 Mar. 1895, p. 5).
98. *Reynolds's News*, 10 Mar. 1895, p. 5.

CONCLUSION

1. [Stephen], 'The Criminal Law and the Detection of Crime', 702–8.
2. Foucault, *Discipline and Punish*, 214–20, 286–92.
3. Emsley, *Hard Men*, 130.
4. Peter Mandler, *The English National Character* (New Haven: Yale University Press, 2006), 4.

SELECT BIBLIOGRAPHY

Primary Sources

The National Archives: Public Record Office

Files consulted

HO44/22
HO44/1043
HO45/292
HO45/724
HO45/9442
HO45/9567
HO45/9744
HO45/10002
HO45/10254
HO45/10566
HO45/11000
HO45/19921
HO65/14
HO144/133
HO144/189
HO144/1043
HO144/1119
MEPO1/53
MEPO2/134
MEPO2/697
MEPO2/741
MEPO2/1148
MEPO2/1297
MEPO2/1570
MEPO2/8124
MEPO3/1760
MEPO4/361–477
MEPO4/487

Specific official documents

HO45/9442/66692. *Departmental Commission on the State, Discipline, and Organisation of the Detective Force of the Metropolitan Police* (1878).

SELECT BIBLIOGRAPHY

HO45/9567/74577 A. *Departmental Commission on the State, Discipline, and Organisation of the Metropolitan Police Force (other than the Criminal Investigation Department)* (London: George Edward Eyre & William Spottiswoode, 1879).

HO45/25052. *Departmental Committee on Detective Work and Procedure* (London: His Majesty's Stationery Office, 1938–9).

HO347/1. *Departmental Committee on the Metropolitan Police* (1868).

HO45/10002/A49463. 'Return of Weekly Rate of Pay and Uniform' (1888).

HO144/184/A45507. James Monro, *A Report on the History of the Convict Supervision Office* (London, 1886).

MEPO2/8124. 'Report of Working of the Scheme for the Examination and Selection of Provincial Recruits with Results Obtained and the Cost of 31 Dec. 1912', 7 Jan. 1913.

MEPO7/1–76. Police Orders.

Parliamentary Debates

Parliamentary Papers (PP)

Annual Reports of the Commissioner of the Police of the Metropolis to the House of Commons.

Committee on the Best Means Available for Identifying Habitual Criminals, vol. 72 (1893–4).

Committee on the Police Service of England, Wales and Scotland (Desborough Committee), vol. 22 (1920).

Committee on the State of the Police of the Metropolis, vol. 5 (1816).

Committee on the State of the Police of the Metropolis (First and Second Reports), vol. 7 (1817).

Committee on the State of the Police of the Metropolis (Third Report), vol. 8 (1818).

Departmental Committee of 1889 upon Metropolitan Police Superannuation, vol. 59 (1890).

Report on the Nightly Watch and Police of the Metropolis, vol. 2 (1812).

Reports of Inspectors of Constabulary to the Secretary of State.

Returns Relating to the Old Watch and the New Police, vol. 8 (1830–1).

Royal Commission upon the Duties of the Metropolitan Police, vols. 50–1 (1908).

Select Committee on Police Superannuation Funds, vol. 13 (1875).

Select Committee on Police Superannuation Funds, vol. 15 (1877).

Select Committee on the Petition of Frederick Young and Others, vol. 13 (1833).

Select Committee on the Police Forces (Weekly-Rest-Day), vol. 9 (1908).

Select Committee on the Police of the Metropolis, vol. 4 (1822).

Select Committee on the Police of the Metropolis, vol. 6 (1828).

Select Committee on the Police of the Metropolis, vol. 16 (1834).

SELECT BIBLIOGRAPHY

Metropolitan Police Museum
'Diary of Detective Chief Inspector Frederick George Abberline', unpublished.
General Instruction Book (London, 1829).
Press cuttings
Scrapbooks and cuttings

Other archives
Instruction Book for the Government & Guidance of the Bristol Police Force (1894).
Instructions for the Liverpool Constabulary Force (1856).
Instructions for the Liverpool Police Force (1867).
Instructions for the Liverpool Police Force (1878).
Police Instruction Book (Manchester, 1908).
Regulations and Instructions for the Southport Police Force and Fire Brigade (1893).

Proceedings of the Old Bailey Online
www.oldbaileyonline.org

Newspapers and journals
Adult
All the Year Round
Birmingham Daily Post
Blackwood's Edinburgh Magazine
Bristol Mercury and Daily Post
Cassell's Saturday Journal
Century Magazine
Chambers's Journal
Commonweal
Cornhill Magazine
Daily Chronicle
Daily News
Daily Telegraph
Derby Mercury
East London Observer
Evening Herald (Dublin)
Evening News
Examiner
Freedom
Freeman's Journal and Daily Commercial Advertiser
Glasgow Herald
Globe

SELECT BIBLIOGRAPHY

Graphic
Hampshire Telegraph and Sussex Chronicle
Household Words
Illustrated Police Budget
Illustrated Times
Ipswich Journal
Jackson's Oxford Journal
Journalist
Leeds Mercury
Leisure Hour
Liberty
Literary Gazette
Liverpool Mercury
Lloyds Weekly Newspaper
London Magazine
Macmillan's Magazine
Manchester Gazette
Manchester Times
Morning Chronicle
Murray's Magazine
Nation
Newcastle Courant
Nineteenth Century
North American Review
Northern Star
Pall Mall Gazette
Penny Illustrated Paper
Police and Public
Police Guardian
Police Review
Police Service Advertiser
Preston Chronicle
Punch
Quarterly Review
Reynolds's News
St James's Gazette
Saturday Review
Southern Star and London and Brighton Patriot
South London Chronicle
Spectator
Sporting Gazette
Standard
Star
Strand Magazine

SELECT BIBLIOGRAPHY

Sun
The Times
Weekly Dispatch
Weekly Times and Echo
Western Mail (Cardiff)
Yorkshire Post

Works of fiction cited in the text

Allen, Grant, 'The Great Ruby Robbery' (first published 1892), in Geraldine Beare (ed.), *Crime Stories from the Strand* (London: Folio Society, 1991).
Allen, Grant, *Hilda Wade* (London: Grant Richards, 1900).
Allen, Grant, *Miss Caley's Adventures* (London: Grant Richards, 1899).
Barr, Robert, *The Triumphs of Eugène Valmont* (London: Hurst & Blackett, 1906).
Bennett, Arnold, *The Grand Babylon Hotel* (London: Chatto & Windus, 1902).
Bennett, Arnold, *The Loot of Cities* (London: Alston Rivers, 1905).
Bentley, E. C., *Trent's Last Case* (London: T. Nelson & Sons, 1913).
Bleiler, E. F. (ed.), *Three Victorian Detective Novels* (New York: Dover, 1978).
Bodkin, M. McDonnell, *Dora Myrl, The Lady Detective* (London: Chatto & Windus, 1900).
Braddon, Mary Elizabeth, *Aurora Floyd* (London: Tinsley Bros., 1863).
Braddon, Mary Elizabeth, *Henry Dunbar: The Story of an Outcast* (London: John Maxwell & Co., 1864).
Braddon, Mary Elizabeth, *Rough Justice* (London: Simpkin, Marshall, Hamilton, Kent, 1898).
Bramah, Ernest, *Max Carrados* (London: Methuen, 1914).
Bulwer-Lytton, Edward, *Paul Clifford* (London: Henry Colburn & Richard Bentley, 1830).
Campbell, Gilbert [Edward], 'The Mystery of Essex Stairs' (first published by Ward, Lock, Bowden & Co., 1891), in Michael Cox (ed.), *Victorian Tales of Mystery and Detection* (Oxford: Oxford University Press, 1992).
Chesterton, G. K., *The Innocence of Father Brown* (London: Cassell & Co., 1911).
Chesterton, G. K., *The Man Who Was Thursday: A Nightmare* (Bristol: Simpkin, Marshall & Co., 1908).
Collins, Wilkie, *The Fallen Leaves* (first published 1879), at http://www.gutenberg.org/files/7894/7894-h/7894-h.htm.
Collins, Wilkie, *My Lady's Money* (first published 1877), in E. F. Bleiler (ed.), *Three Victorian Detective Novels* (New York: Dover, 1978).
Collins, Wilkie, *The Moonstone* (London: Tinsley Bros., 1868).

Collins, Wilkie, *The Woman in White* (London: Sampson Low, Son & Co., 1860).
Conrad, Joseph, *The Secret Agent* (London: Harper & Brothers Publishers, 1907).
Cox, Michael (ed.), *Victorian Tales of Mystery and Detection* (Oxford: Oxford University Press, 1992).
'The Detective in America', *Chambers's Journal*, 16 (July–Dec. 1861).
Dickens, Charles, *Bleak House* (London: Bradbury & Evans, 1853).
Dickens, Charles, *Oliver Twist* (London, 1837).
Dickens, Charles, *Pickwick Papers* (London, 1836–7).
Dowling, Richard, 'The Going Out of Alessandro Pozzone' (first published 1878), in Michael Cox (ed.), *Victorian Tales of Mystery and Detection* (Oxford: Oxford University Press, 1992).
Doyle, Arthur Conan, *The Complete Sherlock Holmes* (London: Penguin Books, 1988).
E.A.B.D (E. A. Bland), *Constable 42Z* (London: Religious Tract Society, 1887).
Forrester, Andrew, Jr, *The Female Detective* (London: Ward & Lock, 1864).
Forrester, Andrew, Jr, *Revelations of a Private Detective* (London: Ward & Lock, 1863).
Forrester, Andrew, Jr, *Secret Service; or, Recollections of a City Detective* (London: Ward & Lock, 1864).
Freeman, R. Austin, *John Thorndyke's Cases* (London: Chatto & Windus, 1909).
Gaskell, Elizabeth, *Mary Barton* (London: Chapman & Hall, 1849; first published 1848).
Gaskell, Elizabeth, *North and South* (London, 1855).
Godwin, William, *Things as They Are; or, The Adventures of Caleb Williams* (London, 1794).
Grey, Vivian, *Stories of Scotland Yard* (London: Everett & Co., 1906).
Griffiths, Arthur, *Fast and Loose* (London: Chapman and Hall, 1884–5).
Griffiths, Arthur, *The Rome Express* (London: Milne [J.] Publisher, 1896).
Hanshew, Thomas W., *Cleek of Scotland Yard* (New York: McKinley, Stone & Mackenzie, 1912).
Hill, Headon, *Clues from a Detective's Camera* (Bristol: J. W. Arrowsmith, 1893).
Hill, Headon, *Guilty Gold: A Romance of Financial Fraud and City Crime* (London: C. Arthur Pearson, 1896).
Hill, Headon, *Tracked Down* (London: C. Arthur Pearson, 1902).
Hill, Headon, *Zambra the Detective* (London: Chatto & Windus, 1894).
Hornung, E. W., *Dead Men Tell No Tales* (London: Methuen & Co., 1899).
Hume, Fergus, 'The Greenstone God and the Stockbrocker' (first published 1894), in Michael Cox (ed.), *Victorian Tales of Mystery and Detection* (Oxford: Oxford University Press, 1992).

Hume, Fergus, *Hagar of the Pawn-Shop* (London: Skeffington & Son, 1898).
Le Fanu, Joseph Sheridan, *Checkmate* (Stroud: Sutton Publishing, 1997; first published 1871).
McGovan, James, *Brought to Bay; or, Experiences of a City Detective* (Edinburgh: Edinburgh Publishing Company, 1878).
McGovan, James, *Hunted Down; or, Recollections of a City Detective* (Edinburgh: Edinburgh Publishing Company, 1879; first published 1878).
McGovan, James, *Solved Mysteries; or, Revelations of a City Detective* (Edinburgh: John Menzies & Co., 1888).
McGovan, James, *Strange Clues; or, Chronicles of a City Detective* (Edinburgh: Edinburgh Publishing Company, 1881).
McGovan, James, *Traced and Tracked; or, Memoirs of a City Detective* (Edinburgh: John Menzies & Co., 1884).
Martel, Charles (ed.), *The Detective's Note-Book* (London: Ward & Lock, 1860).
Martel, Charles (ed.), *Diary of an Ex-Detective* (London: Ward & Lock, 1860).
Mason, A. E. W., *At the Villa Rose* (London: Hodder & Stoughton, 1910).
Meade, Lillie Thomasina, and Robert Eustace, 'The Arrest of Captain Vandaleur' (first published 1894), in Michael Cox (ed.), *Victorian Tales of Mystery and Detection* (Oxford: Oxford University Press, 1992).
Morrison, Arthur, *Adventures of Martin Hewitt* (London: Ward, Lock & Co., 1896).
Morrison, Arthur, *Chronicles of Martin Hewitt* (New York: Books for Libraries Press, 1971; first published 1895).
Morrison, Arthur, *Martin Hewitt, Investigator* (London: Ward & Lock, 1894).
Orczy, Baroness Emmuska, *Lady Molly of Scotland Yard*, intro. by Alice Thomas Ellis (Pleasantville, NY: Akadine Press, 1999; first published 1910).
Orczy, Baroness Emmuska, *The Old Man in the Corner* (first published 1908), at http://www.gutenberg.org/files/10556/10556-8.txt.
Pirkis, Catherine Louisa, *The Experiences of Loveday Brooke, Lady Detective* (London: Hutchinson & Co., 1894).
Poe, Edgar Allan, 'The Murders in the Rue Morgue' (first published 1841), in Edgar Allen Poe, *Tales of Mystery and Imagination* (Ware: Wordsworth Editions, 1993).
Poe, Edgar Allan, 'The Mystery of Marie Rogêt' (first published 1842–3), in Edgar Allen Poe, *Tales of Mystery and Imagination* (Ware: Wordsworth Editions, 1993).
Poe, Edgar Allan, 'The Purloined Letter' (first published 1844), in Sherwin Cody (ed.), *The Best Tales of Edgar Allan Poe* (New York: The Modern Library, 1924).
'A Private Detective Story', *Chambers's Journal*, 56 (18 Jan. 1879).

Reade, Charles, *Hard Cash* (London, 1863).
Reade, Charles, 'The Knightsbridge Mystery' (first published 1884), in Jack Adrian (ed.), *Twelve Mystery Stories* (Oxford: Oxford University Press, 1988).
'Recollections of a Police-Officer', *Chambers's Journal*, NS (July 1849–Sept. 1853).
'Revelations by Real Detectives', *Police and Public*, 6 July–31 Aug. 1889.
Revelations of a Lady Detective (London: George Vickers, 1864).
Richmond: Scenes in the Life of a Bow Street Runner, Drawn up from his Private Memoranda, intro. by E. F. Bleiler (New York: Dover Publications, 1976; first published 1827).
Robinson, B. Fletcher, and J. Malcolm Fraser, *The Chronicles of Addington Peace and The Trail of the Dead* (Shelburne, Ontario: The Battered Silicon Dispatch Box, 1998).
Scotland Yard Detective Series (London: The General Publishing Co., 1888).
'Secrets of a Private Enquiry Office', *Police and Public*, 6 July–31 Aug. 1889.
Shiel, Matthew Phipps, *Prince Zaleski* (London: John Lane, 1895).
Sims, George R., *Detective Inspector Chance* (London, 1974; first published 1911).
Sims, George R., *Dorcas Dene, Detective* (London: F. V. White & Co., 1897).
Stevenson, Robert Louis, *The Strange Case of Dr Jekyll and Mr Hyde* (London, 1886).
Stevenson, Robert Louis, and Fanny van de Grift Stevenson, 'The Dynamiter', in *More New Arabian Nights* (New York: Charles Scribner's Sons, 1901; first published 1885).
'Tale of a Detective', in E. F. Bleiler (ed.), *A Treasury of Victorian Detective Stories* (New York: Charles Scribner's Sons, 1979).
Taylor, Tom, *The Ticket-of-Leave Man* (London: Heinemann, 1981; first published 1863).
Tom Fox or The Revelations of a Detective (2nd edn; London: George Vickers, 1860).
Trollope, Anthony, *The Eustace Diamonds* (London, 1873).
Trollope, Anthony, *He Knew He Was Right* (London, 1869).
Wallace, Edgar, *The Four Just Men* (London: Tallis Press, 1905).
'Waters', *Autobiography of an English Detective* (London: John Maxwell, 1863).
'Waters' (ed.), *Experiences of a Real Detective by Inspector F.* (London: Ward & Lock, 1862).
'Waters', *Mrs Waldegrave's Will, and Other Tales by Inspector F.* (London: Ward, Lock, and Tyler, 1870).
'Waters', *Recollections of a Detective Police-Officer*, intro. by Eric Osborne (London: Covent Garden Press, 1972).
Waters, Thomas, *The Recollections of a Policeman* (New York, 1853).

Whitechurch, Victor Lorenzo, and E. Conway, 'A Warning in Red' (first published 1899), in Michael Cox (ed.), *Victorian Tales of Mystery and Detection* (Oxford: Oxford University Press, 1992).
Wood, Mrs Henry, 'The Mystery at Number Seven' (first published 1877), in Michael Cox (ed.), *Victorian Tales of Mystery and Detection* (Oxford: Oxford University Press, 1992).
Wood, H. F., *The Night of the 3rd Ult* (New York: George Munro, 1890).
Wood, H. F., *The Passenger from Scotland Yard* (first published 1888), intro. by E. F. Bleiler (New York: Dover, 1977).
Zangwill, Israel, 'The Big Bow Mystery', (first published 1891), in E. F. Bleiler (ed.), *Three Victorian Detective Novels* (New York: Dover, 1978).

Memoirs and autobiographies (published)

Anderson, Robert, *The Lighter Side of my Official Life* (London: Hodder & Stoughton, 1910).
Arrow, Charles, *Rogues and Others* (London: Duckworth, 1926).
Bent, James, *Criminal Life: Reminiscences of Forty-Two Years as a Police Officer* (Manchester: John Heywood, 1891).
Berrett, James, *When I was at Scotland Yard* (London: Sampson Low, Marston & Co., 1932).
Bishop, Cecil, *From Information Received* (London: Hutchinson, 1932).
Broadhurst, Joseph F., *From Vine Street to Jerusalem* (London: Stanley Paul, 1936).
Brust Harold, *'I Guarded Kings'* (New York: Hillman-Curl, 1936; first published 1935).
Brust, Harold, *In Plain Clothes* (London: Stanley Paul, 1937).
Bunn, Frank Leonard, *No Silver Spoon: The Autobiography of a 'Ranker'* (Stoke-on-Trent: F. L. Bunn, 1970).
Caminada, Jerome, *Twenty-Five Years of Detective Life*, i (Manchester: John Heywood, 1895); ii (Warrington: Prism Books 1983; first published 1901).
Canler, Louis, *Autobiography of a French Detective from 1818 to 1858* (London: Ward and Lock, 1862).
Carlin, Francis, *Reminiscences of an Ex-Detective* (London: Hutchinson, 1920).
Cavanagh, Timothy, *Scotland Yard Past and Present* (London: Chatto & Windus, 1893).
Cherrill, Frederick R., *Cherrill of the Yard* (London: George G. Harrap, 1954).
Clark, P. Alexander, *Reminiscences of a Police Officer in the Granite City* (Aberdeen: Lewis Smith, 1873).
Cornish, George W., *Cornish of Scotland Yard: His Reminiscences and Cases* (New York: Macmillan Co., 1935).
Dew, Walter, *I Caught Crippen* (London: Blackie & Son, 1938).

SELECT BIBLIOGRAPHY

Divall, Tom, *Scoundrels and Scallywags* (London: Ernest Benn, 1929).
Felstead, Sidney Theodore, *Sir Richard Muir: A Memoir of a Public Prosecutor* (London: John Lane, 1927).
Ferrier, J. Kenneth, *Crooks & Crime* (London: Seeley, Service & Co., 1928).
Fitch, Herbert T., *Memoirs of a Royal Detective* (London: Hurst & Blackett, 1936).
Fitch, Herbert T., *Traitors Within* (New York: Doubleday, Doran & Co., 1933).
Fuller, Robert A., *Recollections of a Detective* (London: John Long, 1912).
Goddard, Henry, *Memoirs of a Bow Street Runner*, intro. by Patrick Pringle (London: Museum Press, 1956).
Gough, William C., *From Kew Observatory to Scotland Yard* (London: Hurst & Blackett, 1927).
Greenham, G. H., *Scotland Yard Experiences* (London: George Routledge & Sons, 1904).
Gribble, Leonard, *Great Manhunters of the Yard* (New York: Roy Publishers, 1966).
Griffiths, Arthur, *Fifty Years of Public Service* (London: Cassell, 1904).
Griffiths, Arthur, *Mysteries of Police and Crime* (London: Cassell, 1899).
Hambrook, Walter, *Hambrook of the Yard* (London: Robert Hale and Co., 1937).
Harris, Richard, *The Reminiscences of Sir Henry Hawkins* (London: Thomas Nelson & Sons, 1904).
Henderson, William, *Clues; or, Leaves from a Detective's Note Book* (New York: White and Allen, 1890; first published Edinburgh, 1889).
Henry, Jack, *Detective-Inspector Henry's Famous Cases* (London: Hutchinson, 1949).
Higginbottom, Frederick J., *The Vivid Life* (London: Simpkin Marshall, 1934).
Jervis, Richard, *Chronicles of a Victorian Detective* (Runcorn, Cheshire: P & D Riley, 1995; first published 1907).
Lansdowne, Andrew, *A Life's Reminiscences of Scotland Yard* (New York: Garland Publishing, 1984; first published 1890).
Leach, Charles E., *On Top of the Underworld* (London: Sampson Low, Marston & Co., 1933).
Leeson, Benjamin, *Lost London* (London: Stanley Paul & Co., 1934).
Lieck, Albert, *Bow Street World* (London: Robert Hale, 1938).
Littlechild, John George, *Reminiscences of Chief-Inspector Littlechild* (London: Leadenhall Press, 1894).
McIntyre, Patrick, 'Scotland Yard, its Mysteries and Methods', *Reynolds's News* (Feb.–May 1895).
McLevy, James, *The Casebook of a Victorian Detective*, ed. and intro. by George Scott-Moncrieff (Edinburgh: Canongate, 1975; first published 1861).

SELECT BIBLIOGRAPHY

McLevy, James, *The Edinburgh Detective*, with foreword by Quintin Jardin (Edinburgh: Mercat Press, 2001; first published 1861).
Macnaghten, Melville L., *Days of my Years* (London: Arnold, 1914).
McNaught, Thomas P., *The Recollections of a Glasgow Detective Officer* (London: Marshall, Hamilton, Kent & Co., 1887).
Macready, Nevil, *Annals of an Active Life* (London: Hutchinson, 1924).
Morrish, Reginald, *Christ with the C.I.D.* (London: Epworth Press, 1953).
Moser, Maurice, *Stories from Scotland Yard* (London: George Routledge and Sons, 1890).
Neil, Arthur Fowler, *Man-Hunters of Scotland Yard* (New York: Doubleday, Doran & Co., 1933; first published 1932).
Nicholls, Ernest, *Crime within the Square Mile* (London: John Long, 1935).
Nott-Bower, John William, *Fifty-Two Years a Policeman* (London: Edward Arnold, 1926).
Richardson, J. Hall, *From the City to Fleet Street* (London: Stanley Paul & Co., 1927).
Sala, George Augustus, *Things I Have Seen and People I Have Known* (London: Cassell & Co., 1894).
Samuel, Raphael (ed.), *East End Underworld: Chapters in the Life of Arthur Harding* (London: Routledge & Kegan Paul, 1981).
Savage, Percy, *Savage of Scotland Yard* (London: Hutchinson, 1934).
Sims, George R., *My Life: Sixty Years' Recollections of Bohemian London* (London: Eveleigh Nash Co., 1917).
Smith, Henry, *From Constable to Commissioner* (London: Chatto and Windus, 1910).
Smith, Percy J., *Con Man* (London: Herbert Jenkins, 1938).
Steedman, Carolyn, *The Radical Soldier's Tale: John Pearman, 1819–1908* (London: Routledge, 1988; written by John Pearman in 1881–2).
Sweeney, John, *At Scotland Yard* (London: Grant Richards, 1904).
Thompson, W. H., *Guard from the Yard* (London: Jarrolds, 1938).
Thomson, Basil, *Queer People* (London: Hodder and Stoughton, 1922).
Thomson, Basil, *The Scene Changes* (London: Collins, 1937).
Totterdell, G. H., *Country Copper* (London: George G. Harrap, 1956).
Vidocq, Eugène-François, *Mémoires* (London: Whittaker, Treacher and Arnot, 1829).
Watson, Aaron, *A Newspaper Man's Memories* (London: Hutchinson, 1925).
Wensley, Frederick Porter, *Forty Years of Scotland Yard* (New York: Doubleday, Doran & Co., 1933; first published 1930).
Woodhall, Edwin T., *Detective and Secret Service Days* (London: Mellifont Press, 1929).
Yates, Edmund, *Edmund Yates: His Recollections and Experiences* (London: Richard Bentley and Son, 1885; first published 1884).

SELECT BIBLIOGRAPHY

Other books

Adam, H. L., *Police Work from Within* (London: Holden and Hardingham, 1913).

Anderson, Robert, *Criminals and Crime: Some Facts and Suggestions* (New York: Garland, 1984; first published 1907).

Buchanan, Walter, *Juvenile Offenders* (London, 1846).

Bulwer-Lytton, Edward, *England and the English* (Chicago: University of Chicago Press, 1970; first published 1833).

Clarkson, Charles Tempest, and J. Hall Richardson, *Police!* (New York: Garland, 1984; first published 1889).

Cobbett, William, *Rural Rides* (1830).

Colquhoun, Patrick, *A Treatise on the Police of the Metropolis* (1795).

Devon, James, *The Criminal and the Community* (London: John Lane, 1912).

Dilnot, George, *Scotland Yard* (London: Percival Marshall & Co., 1915).

Engels, Frederick, *The Condition of the Working Class in England* (1845).

Fosdick, Raymond, *European Police Systems* (Montclair, NJ: Patterson Smith, 1969; first published 1915).

Friswell, James Hain, *Houses with the Fronts Off* (London: James Blackwood, 1854).

Greenwood, James, *A Night in a Workhouse* (London: Office of the Pall Mall Gazette, 1866; repr. from the *Pall Mall Gazette*).

Greenwood, James, *The Seven Curses of London*, intro. by Jeffrey Richards (Oxford: Blackwell, 1981; first published 1869).

Hastings Lees, T. O., *Snowden's Police Officers' Guide: Tenth Edition* (London: Shaw & Sons, Fetter Lane & Crane Court, 1897).

Haycraft, Thomas W., *Executive Powers in Relation to Crime and Disorder; or, Powers of Police in England* (London: Butterworth & Co., 1897).

Jerrold, Blanchard, and Gustave Doré, *London: A Pilgrimage*, intro. by Peter Ackroyd (London: Anthem Press, 2005; first published 1872).

Jeyes, S. H., and F. D. How, *The Life of Sir Howard Vincent* (London: George Allen, 1912).

Le Caron, Henry, *Twenty-Five Years in the Secret Service* (Wakefield: E. P. Publishing, 1974; first published 1893).

Lee, W. L. Melville, *A History of Police in England*, with an intro. by Philip John Stead (Montclair, NJ: Patterson Smith, 1971; first published London: Methuen, 1901).

London, Jack, *The People of the Abyss*, intro. by Jack Lindsay (London: Journeyman Press, 1977; first published 1903).

Mainwaring, George B., *Observations on the Present State of the Police of the Metropolis* (London: The Pamphleteer, 1822; first published 1821).

Mayhew, Henry, *London Labour and the London Poor* (London: Frank Cass, 1967; first published 1851, 1861–2).

Modern Journalism: A Guide for Beginners by a London Editor with a Preface by George R. Sims (London: Sidgwick & Jackson, 1909).
Murray, John Fisher, *The World of London* (London: Richard Bentley, 1853; first published in *Blackwood's Magazine* 1841, as book 1843).
Nicoll, David, *The Walsall Anarchists* (Sheffield, n.d.).
P.C., *The Metropolitan Police and its Management: A Reply to Sir Charles Warren's Article in Murray's Magazine* (London: Dyke, 1888).
Rylands, L. Gordon, *Crime: Its Causes and Remedy* (London: Garland, 1984; first published 1889).
Sala, George Augustus, *Twice Round the Clock; or, The Hours of the Day and Night in London* (New York: Leicester University Press, 1971; first published in serial form 1858; in book form 1859).
Scott, Benjamin, *A State Iniquity* (New York: Augustus M. Kelley, 1968; first published 1890).
Sims, George R., *How the Poor Live, and Horrible London* (London: Chatto & Windus, 1889).
Sims, George R., *Prepare to Shed Them Now: The Ballads of George R. Sims*, selected and introduced by Arthur Calder-Marshall (London: Hutchinson, 1968).
Smith, Charles Manby, *The Little World of London; or, Pictures in Little of London Life* (London: Arthur Hall, Virtue & Co., 1857).
Stapleton, J. W., *The Great Crime of 1860* (London: E. Marlborough & Co., 1861).
Taine, Hyppolite, *Notes on England* (London: Strahan & Co., 1872).
Vincent, C. E. Howard, *A Police Code* (London: Cassell, Petter, Galpin, 1881).
Wade, John, *A Treatise on the Police and Crimes of the Metropolis*, intro. by J. J. Tobias (Montclair, NJ: Patterson Smith, 1972; first published 1829).
Wight, John, *Mornings at Bow Street: A Selection of the Most Humorous and Entertaining Reports which have Appeared in the Morning Herald* (London: Thomas Tegg & Son, 1838; first published 1824).

Articles

A.C., 'Crime in Current Literature', *Westminster Review*, 147 (Apr. 1897).
'A Long Way after Poe', *Nation*, 19 Sept. 1907.
Aylmer, Alfred, 'Detective Day at Holloway', *Windsor Magazine*, 6 (June 1897).
Aylmer, Alfred, 'The Detective in Real Life', *Windsor Magazine*, 1 (May 1895).
Blackstone, Samuel, 'Paternal Government', *Saint Pauls Magazine*, 12 (June 1873).
Busk, Mary Margaret, 'Autobiography', *Blackwood's Edinburgh Magazine*, 159 (Nov. 1829).
Chadwick, Edwin, 'Preventive Police', *London Review*, 1 (Feb. 1829).

'Detective Fiction', *Saturday Review*, 4 Dec. 1886.
'Detectives', *Saturday Review*, 5 May 1883.
'Detectives', *Saturday Review*, 9 Feb. 1884.
'Detectives and their Work', *All the Year Round*, 36 (Apr. 1885).
'Detectives as They Are', *Chambers's Journal*, 341 (9 July 1870).
'Detective Work in England and France Contrasted', *Police Guardian*, 30 Nov. 1895 (repr. from *Egyptian Gazette*).
[Dickens, Charles], 'A Detective Police Party', *Household Words*, 1 (27 July and 10 Aug. 1850).
[Dickens, Charles], 'Down with the Tide', *Household Words*, 6 (5 Feb. 1853).
[Dickens, Charles], 'The Metropolitan Protectives', *Household Words*, 3 (26 Apr. 1851).
[Dickens, Charles], 'On Duty with Inspector Field', *Household Words*, 3 (14 June 1851).
[Dickens, Charles], 'Spy Police', *Household Words*, 1 (21 Sept. 1850).
[Dickens, Charles], 'Three "Detective" Anecdotes', *Household Words*, 1 (14 Sept. 1850).
'The Dynamite Inquiries', *Saturday Review*, 19 Apr. 1884.
'Espionage as a Profession', *Spectator*, 18 Feb. 1893.
'The Ethics of Detectives', *Spectator*, 30 Aug. 1890.
Flynt, Josiah, 'Police Methods in London', *North American Review*, 176 (Mar. 1903).
'The French and English Police Systems', *Cornhill Magazine*, NS 44 (Oct. 1881).
'The French Detective Police', *Saturday Review*, 3 Jan. 1885.
Greenwood, Frederick, 'The Newspaper Press', *Nineteenth Century*, 27 (May 1890).
Jacobs, W. W., 'The Constable's Move', *Strand Magazine*, 30/178 (Oct. 1905).
'London Detectives', *Police Guardian*, 9 Apr. 1886, pp. 2–3 (repr. from *Daily News*).
'The London and French Police', *Saturday Review*, 8 July 1882.
'The London Police', *Chambers's Journal*, 12 (4 March 1843).
'London Police Duty', *Leisure Hour*, 28 (26 Apr. 1879).
McAdoo, William, 'The London Police from a New York Point of View', *Century Magazine*, 78 (Sept. 1909).
'Manchester Police Methods in the "Palatine" Case', *Penny Illustrated Paper*, 1 Oct. 1910.
Meason, M. Laing, 'Detective Police', *Nineteenth Century*, 13 (May 1883).
Meason, M. Laing, 'The French Detective Police', *Macmillan's Magazine*, 45 (Feb. 1882).
Meason, M. Laing, 'The London Police', *Macmillan's Magazine*, 46 (July 1882).

SELECT BIBLIOGRAPHY

'The Metropolitan Police', *Saturday Review*, 3 Nov. 1888.
'The Metropolitan Police, and What is Paid for them', *Chambers's Journal*, 41 (July 1864).
Monro, James, 'The London Police', *North American Review*, 151 (Nov. 1890).
'My Detective Experiences', *Chambers's Journal*, 3 (3 Apr. 1886).
[Oliphant, Margaret], 'Sensation Novels', *Blackwood's Edinburgh Magazine*, 91 (May 1862).
'On Duty in Plain Clothes', *Cassell's Saturday Journal*, 28 May 1892.
'Our Detective Police', *Chambers's Journal*, 1/2 (31 May 1884).
'Our Detective Police', *Saturday Review*, 19, 26 Sept., 3 Oct. 1891.
'Our Police System', *Dark Blue*, 2 (Feb. 1872).
'Police', *Chambers's Journal*, 37 (Feb. 1862).
'The Police', *Saturday Review*, 20 Oct. 1888.
'The Police and the Press', *Journalist*, 4 Mar. 1893.
'Police Detectives', *Leisure Hour*, 6 (29 Oct. 1857).
'The Police of London', *Quarterly Review*, 129 (July 1870).
'The Police System of London', *Edinburgh Review*, 96 (July 1852).
Shand, Alex. Innes, 'The City of London Police', *Blackwood's Edinburgh Magazine*, 140 (Nov. 1886).
'The Sketcher in London: Policeman AE', *Leisure Hour*, 7 (7 Jan. 1858).
Smith, A. Croxton, 'The Bloodhound as Detective', *Windsor Magazine*, 1 (Apr. 1895).
'The Status of Working Journalists: How it May be Improved', a paper read in a meeting of the Institute of Journalists of the Manchester District on 21 July 1900 (*Journalist*, 28 June 1900).
[Stephen, James Fitzjames], 'The Criminal Law and the Detection of Crime', *Cornhill Magazine*, 2 (Dec. 1860).
[Stephen, James Fitzjames], 'Detectives in Fiction and in Real Life', *Saturday Review*, 11 June 1864.
Syme, John, 'Police Witnesses Disgraced by Scotland Yard', *Penny Illustrated Paper*, 22 Oct. 1910.
Tibbits, Charles J., 'Newspapers as Detectives', *London Magazine*, 13 (Oct. 1904).
Warren, Charles, 'The Police of the Metropolis', *Murray's Magazine*, 4 (Nov. 1888).
Watts, W. H., 'Records of an Old Police Court', *St James's Magazine*, 12 (1864).
'What of the Police?', *Westminster Review*, 59 (Mar. 1903).
'Why Detectives Fail', *London Magazine*, 13 (1904–5).
[Wills, William H.], 'The Modern Science of Thief-Taking', *Household Words*, 1 (13 July 1850).
'With the French Detectives', *Standard*, 29 Oct. 1881.
'The Work of the London Police', *Spectator*, 7 Oct. 1882.
Wynter, A. 'The Police and the Thieves', *Quarterly Review*, 99 (June 1856).

SELECT BIBLIOGRAPHY

Secondary Sources

Books

Adam, H. L., *C.I.D.: Behind the Scenes at Scotland Yard* (London: Sampson Low, Marston & Co., 1931).

Allason, Rupert, *The Branch* (London: Secker & Warburg, 1983).

Allen, Rick, *The Moving Pageant* (London: Routledge, 1998).

Altick, Richard D., *The English Common Reader* (Chicago: University of Chicago Press, 1957).

Andrew, Christopher, *Secret Service* (London: Heinemann, 1985).

Armitage, Gilbert, *The History of the Bow Street Runners, 1729–1829* (London: Wishart, 1932).

Ascoli, David, *The Queen's Peace: The Origins and Development of the Metropolitan Police, 1829–1979* (London: Hamish Hamilton, 1979).

Ashley, Robert, *Wilkie Collins* (New York: Haskell House, 1976; first published 1952).

Babington, Anthony, *A House in Bow Street* (Chichester: Barry Rose Law Publishers, 1999).

Bailey, Victor (ed.), *Policing and Punishment in Nineteenth-Century Britain* (London: Croom Helm, 1981).

Barker, Hannah, *Newspapers, Politics, and Public Opinion in Late Eighteenth-Century England* (Oxford: Clarendon Press, 1998).

Bayley, David H. (ed.), *Police and Society* (Beverly Hills, CA: Sage Publications, 1977).

Beattie, J. M., *Crime and the Courts in England 1660–1800* (Princeton: Princeton University Press, 1986).

Beattie, J. M., *Policing and Punishment in London, 1660–1750* (Oxford: Oxford University Press, 2001).

Beavan, Colin, *Fingerprints* (New York: Hyperion, 2001).

Bell, Ian A., *Literature and Crime in Augustan England* (London: Routledge, 1991).

Benstock, Bernard, and Thomas F. Staley (eds), *British Mystery Writers, 1860–1919* (Detroit: Bruccoli Clark Layman Book, 1988).

Bentley, David, *English Criminal Justice in the Nineteenth Century* (London: Hambledon Press, 1998).

Black, Joel, *The Aesthetics of Murder* (Baltimore: Johns Hopkins University Press, 1991).

Bok, Sissela, *Secrets* (New York: Pantheon Books, 1982).

Bowley, A. L., *Wages and Income* (Cambridge: Cambridge University Press, 1937).

Boyce, George, James Curran, and Pauline Wingate (eds), *Newspaper History* (London: Constable, 1978).

Boyle, Thomas, *Black Swine in the Sewers of Hampstead* (New York: Penguin, 1989).
Brake, Laurel, Aled Jones, and Lionel Madden (eds), *Investigating Victorian Journalism* (Houndmills: Macmillan, 1990).
Brewer, John, and John Styles (eds), *An Ungovernable People: The English and their Law in the Seventeenth and Eighteenth Centuries* (London: Hutchinson, 1980).
Brogden, Michael, *The Police: Autonomy and Consent* (London: Academic Press, 1982).
Brown, Lucy, *Victorian News and Newspapers* (Oxford: Clarendon Press, 1985).
Browne, Douglas G., *The Rise of Scotland Yard* (New York: G. P. Putnam's Sons, 1956).
Budworth, Geoffrey, *The River Beat: The Story of London's River Police since 1798* (London: Historical Publications, 1997).
Bundock, Clement J., *The National Union of Journalists* (Oxford: Oxford University Press, 1957).
Bunyan, Tony, *The History and Practice of the Political Police in Britain* (London: Quartet Books, 1977).
Burnett, John (ed.), *Useful Toil* (London: Allen Lane, 1976).
Carter Wood, John, *Violence and Crime in Nineteenth-Century England: The Shadow of our Refinement* (London: Routledge, 2004).
Cawelti, John G., *Adventure, Mystery and Romance* (Chicago: Chicago University Press, 1976).
Cherrill, Frederick R., *The Finger Print System at Scotland Yard* (London: Her Majesty's Stationery Office, 1954).
Chesney, Kellow, *The Victorian Underworld* (London: Temple Smith, 1970).
Clarke, A. A., *The Policemen of Hull* (Beverley, East Yorkshire: Hutton Press, 1992).
Clay, Ewart W. (ed.), *The Leeds Police, 1836–1974* (Leeds: E. J. Arnold & Son, 1975).
Cobb, Belton, *Critical Years at the Yard* (London: Faber and Faber, 1961).
Cobb, Belton, *The First Detectives and the Early Career of Richard Mayne, Commissioner of Police* (London: Faber and Faber, 1957).
Cole, Simon A., *Suspect Identities* (Cambridge, MA: Harvard University Press, 2001).
Collins, Philip, *Dickens and Crime* (London: Macmillan, 1964; first published 1962).
Conley, Carolyn A., *The Unwritten Law* (New York: Oxford University Press, 1991).
Cook, Andrew, *M: MI5's First Spymaster* (Stroud: Tempus, 2004).
Cox, David J., *A Certain Share of Low Cunning: A History of the Bow Street Runners, 1792–1839* (Cullompton: Willan Publishing, 2010).

Critchley, T. A., *A History of Police in England and Wales* (Montclair, NJ: Patterson Smith, 1972; first published 1967).
Cross, Nigel, *The Common Writer: Life in Nineteenth-Century Grub Street* (Cambridge: Cambridge University Press, 1985).
Crossick, Geoffrey (ed.), *The Lower Middle Class in Britain 1870–1914* (London: Croom Helm, 1977).
Cullen, Tom A., *Autumn of Terror* (London: Collins, 1966; first published 1965).
Curtis, L. Perry, Jr, *Jack the Ripper and the London Press* (New Haven: Yale University Press, 2001).
Dandeker, Christopher, *Surveillance, Power and Modernity* (Cambridge: Polity Press, 1990).
Davis, Philip, *The Victorians* (Oxford: Oxford University Press, 2002).
Deflem, Mathieu, *Policing World Society* (Oxford: Oxford University Press, 2002).
Dilnot, George, *The Story of Scotland Yard* (Boston: Houghton Mifflin, 1927).
Dilnot, George, *The Trial of the Detectives* (New York: Charles Scribner's Sons, 1928).
Drewry, Gavin, and Tony Butcher, *The Civil Service Today* (Oxford: Basil Blackwell, 1988).
During, Simon, *Foucault and Literature* (London: Routledge, 1992).
Eastwood, David, *Governing Rural England* (Oxford: Clarendon Press, 1994).
Elliott, Douglas J., *Policing Shropshire, 1836–1967* (Studley: K. A. F. Brewin Books, 1984).
Else, Walter Martyn, and James Main Garrow, *The Detection of Crime* (London: Police Journal, 1934).
Emsley, Clive, *Crime and Society in England, 1750–1900* (London: Longman, 1987).
Emsley, Clive, *The English Police* (Hemel Hempstead: Harvester Wheatsheaf, 1991).
Emsley, Clive, *The Great British Bobby* (London: Quercus, 2010; first published 2009).
Emsley, Clive, *Hard Men: The English and Violence since 1750* (London: Hambledon and London, 2005).
Emsley, Clive, *Policing and its Context, 1750–1870* (New York: Schocken Books, 1983).
Emsley, Clive, and Haia Shpayer-Makov (eds), *Police Detectives in History, 1750–1950* (Aldershot: Ashgate, 2006).
Ericson, Richard V., *Making Crime: A Study of Detective Work* (Toronto: University of Toronto Press, 1993).
Ericson, Richard V., Patricia M. Baranek, and Janet B. L. Chan, *Negotiating Control: A Study of News Sources* (Toronto: Toronto University Press, 1989).

Evans, Mary, *Missing Persons* (London: Routledge, 1999).
Evans, Stewart P., and Keith Skinner, *Jack the Ripper: Letters from Hell* (Stroud: Sutton Publishing, 2001).
Evans, Stewart P., and Keith Skinner, *The Ultimate Jack the Ripper Companion* (New York: Carroll & Graf Publishers, 2000).
Faller, Lincoln B., *Turned to Account* (Cambridge: Cambridge University Press, 1987).
Feather, John, *A History of British Publishing* (London: Routledge, 1998).
Feltes, Norman N., *Modes of Production of Victorian Novels* (Chicago: University of Chicago Press, 1986).
Fido, Martin, *The Crimes, Detection and Death of Jack the Ripper* (New York: Barnes & Noble, 1993).
Fido, Martin, and Keith Skinner, *The Official Encyclopedia of Scotland Yard* (London: Virgin Publishing, 2000; first published 1999).
Foucault, Michel, *Discipline and Punish* (London: Penguin, 1991; first published in French, 1975).
Freeden, Michael, *The New Liberalism* (Oxford: Clarendon Press, 1978).
Garland, David, *The Culture of Control* (Oxford: Oxford University Press, 2001).
Garland, David, *Punishment and Modern Society* (Oxford: Clarendon Press, 1991).
Garlick, Barbara, and Margaret Harris (eds), *Victorian Journalism: Exotic and Domestic* (St Lucia, Queensland: University of Queensland Press, 1998).
Gaskill, Malcolm, *Crime and Mentalities in Early Modern England* (Cambridge: Cambridge University Press, 2000).
Gatrell, V. A. C., Bruce Lenman, and Geoffrey Parker (eds), *Crime and the Law* (London: Europa Publications, 1980).
Giddens, Anthony, *The Nation-State and Violence* (Cambridge: Polity Press, 1985).
Gladfelder, Hal, *Criminality and Narrative in Eighteenth-Century England* (Baltimore: Johns Hopkins University Press, 2001).
Godfrey, Barry S., David J. Cox, and Stephen Farrall, *Serious Offenders: A Historical Study of Habitual Criminals* (Clarendon Criminology Series; Oxford: Oxford University Press, 2011).
Godfrey, Barry S., and Paul Lawrence, *Crime and Justice, 1750–1959* (Cullompton: Willan Publishing, 2005).
Godfrey, Barry S., Paul Lawrence, and Chris A. Williams, *History and Crime* (Los Angeles: Sage, 2008).
Gollomb, Joseph, *Scotland Yard* (London: Hutchinson, 1926).
Hackett, Nan, *XIX Century British Working-Class Autobiographies: An Annotated Bibliography* (New York: AMS Press, 1985).
Haining, Peter (ed.), *Hunted Down* (London: Peter Owen, 1996).

Hanmer, Jalna, Jill Radford, and Elizabeth A. Stanko, *Women, Policing, and Male Violence: International Perspectives* (London: Routledge, 1989).

Harris, Andrew T., *Policing the City* (Columbus: Ohio State University, 2004).

Harris, Michael, *London Newspapers in the Age of Walpole* (Cranbury, NJ: Associated University Presses, 1987).

Hart, Jenifer M., *The British Police* (London: George Allen & Unwin, 1951).

Hay, Douglas, and Francis Snyder (eds), *Policing and Prosecution in Britain 1750–1850* (Oxford: Clarendon Press, 1989).

Haycraft, Howard, *Murder for Pleasure* (New York: D. Appleton-Century, 1941).

Henderson, Tony, *Disorderly Women in Eighteenth-Century London* (London: Longman, 1999).

Hilliard, Christopher, *To Exercise our Talents: The Democratization of Writing in Britain* (Cambridge, MA: Harvard University Press, 2006).

Hobbs, Dick, *Doing the Business* (Oxford: Oxford University Press, 1988).

Hobsbawm, E. H., *Industry and Empire* (London: Weidenfeld and Nicolson, 1968).

Holdaway, Simon (ed.), *The British Police* (London: Edward Arnold, 1979).

Hollingworth, Keith, *The Newgate Novel* (Detroit: Wayne State University Press, 1963).

Hughes, Winifred, *The Maniac in the Cellar* (Princeton: Princeton University Press, 1980).

Humpherys, Anne, *Henry Mayhew* (Boston: Twayne Publishers, 1984).

Humphries, Stephen, *Hooligans or Rebels?* (Oxford: Basil Blackwell, 1984).

Ignatieff, Michael, *A Just Measure of Pain: The Penitentiary in the Industrial Revolution, 1750–1850* (London: Macmillan, 1978).

James, Louis, *Fiction for the Working Man, 1830–50* (London: Oxford University Press, 1963).

Johnston, Les, *The Rebirth of Private Policing* (London: Routledge, 1992).

Jones, Aled, *Powers of the Press: Newspapers, Power and the Public in Nineteenth-Century England* (Aldershot: Scolar Press, 1996).

Jones, David J. V., *Crime, Protest, Community and Police in Nineteenth-Century Britain* (London: Routledge, 1982).

Jones, Gareth Stedman, *Outcast London* (Oxford: Clarendon Press, 1971).

Kalikoff, Beth, *Murder and Moral Decay in Victorian Popular Literature* (Ann Arbor: UMI Research Press, 1986).

Kayman, Martin A., *From Bow Street to Baker Street: Mystery, Detection, and Narrative* (Houndmills: Macmillan, 1992).

Keating, Peter (ed.), *Into Unknown England, 1866–1913* (London: Fontana, 1976).

Kestner, Joseph A., *Sherlock's Men: Masculinity, Conan Doyle, and Cultural History* (Aldershot: Ashgate, 1997).

Kestner, Joseph A., *Sherlock's Sisters: The British Female Detective, 1864–1913* (Aldershot: Ashgate, 2003).

Kilday, Anne-Marie, and David Nash (eds), *Histories of Crime: Britain 1600–2000* (Houndmills: Palgrave Macmillan, 2010).
King, Peter, *Crime and Law in England, 1750–1840* (Cambridge: Cambridge University Press, 2006).
King, Peter, *Crime, Justice, and Discretion in England 1740–1820* (Oxford: Oxford University Press, 2000).
Kingston, Charles, *Dramatic Days at the Old Bailey* (London: Stanley Paul & Co., 1923).
Klein, Joanne, *Invisible Men: The Secret Lives of Police Constables in Liverpool, Manchester, and Birmingham, 1900–1939* (Liverpool: Liverpool University Press, 2010).
Klein, Kathleen Gregory, *The Woman Detective: Gender and Genre* (Urbana: University of Chicago Press, 1988).
Knight, Stephen, *Crime Fiction since 1800* (2nd edn; Houndmills: Palgrave Macmillan, 2010).
Knight, Stephen, *Form and Ideology in Crime Fiction* (London: Macmillan, 1980).
Koss, Stephen, *The Rise and Fall of the Political Press in Britain* (London: Hamish Hamilton, 1981).
Landau, Norma, *The Justices of the Peace, 1679–1760* (Berkeley and Los Angeles: University of California Press, 1984).
Langbein, John H., *The Origins of Adversary Criminal Trial* (Oxford: Oxford University Press, 2003).
Laurie, Peter, *Scotland Yard* (New York: Holt, Rinehart and Winston, 1970).
Lavine, Sigmund A., *Allan Pinkerton* (London: Mayflower, 1970; first published 1963).
Lee, Alan J., *The Origins of the Popular Press in England* (London: Croom Helm, 1976).
Lee, Ying S., *Masculinity and the English Working Class* (New York: Routledge, 2007).
Leps, Marie-Christine, *Apprehending the Criminal* (Durham, NC: Duke University Press, 1992).
Linebaugh, P., *The London Hanged: Crime and Civil Society in the Eighteenth Century* (London: Allen Lane, 1991).
Lock, Joan, *Dreadful Deeds and Awful Murders: Scotland Yard's First Detectives, 1829–1878* (Taunton: Barn Owl Books, 1990).
McAleer, Joseph, *Popular Reading and Publishing in Britain 1914–1950* (Oxford: Clarendon Press, 1992).
Machann, Clinton, *The Genre of Autobiography in Victorian Literature* (Ann Arbor: University of Michigan Press, 1994).
McLaren, Angus, *A Prescription for Murder* (Chicago: Chicago University Press, 1993).
Mandel, Ernest, *Delightful Murder* (Minneapolis: University of Minnesota Press, 1984).

Mandler, Peter, *The English National Character* (New Haven: Yale University Press, 2006).
Mandler, Peter (ed.), *Liberty and Authority in Victorian Britain* (Oxford: Oxford University Press, 2009).
Martin, John Powell, and Gail Wilson, *The Police: A Study in Manpower* (London: Heinemann, 1969).
Melman, Billie, *The Culture of History* (Oxford: Oxford University Press, 2006).
Miller, D.A., *The Novel and the Police* (Berkeley and Los Angeles: University of California Press, 1988).
Miller, Wilbur R., *Cops and Bobbies* (Chicago: University of Chicago Press, 1977; first published 1973).
Mitchell, Rosemary, *Picturing the Past* (Oxford: Clarendon Press, 2000).
Morson, Maurice, *A Force Remembered* (Derby: Breedon Books, 2000).
Morton, James, *The First Detective* (London: Ebury Press, 2004).
Most, Glenn W., and William W. Stowe (eds), *The Poetics of Murder* (San Diego: Harcourt, Brace, Jovanovich, 1983).
Moylan, John, *Scotland Yard and the Metropolitan Police* (London: Putnam, 1929).
Murch, A. E., *The Development of the Detective Novel* (London: Peter Owen, 1968; first published 1958).
Newburn, Tim (ed.), *Handbook of Policing* (Cullompton: Willan Publishing, 2008; first published 2003).
Ousby, Ian, *Bloodhounds of Heaven* (Cambridge, MA: Harvard University Press, 1976).
Palmer, Stanley H., *Police and Protest in England and Ireland 1780–1850* (Cambridge: Cambridge University Press, 1988).
Penn, Roger, *Skilled Workers in the Class Structure* (Cambridge: Cambridge University Press, 1985).
Pearson, Geoffrey, *Hooligan: A History of Respectable Fears* (London: Macmillan, 1983).
Perkin, Harold, *The Rise of Professional Society* (London: Routledge, 1989).
Peterson, Audrey, *Victorian Studies of Mysteries* (New York: Ungar, 1984).
Petrow, Stephen, *Policing Morals* (Oxford: Clarendon Press, 1994).
Philips, David, *Crime and Authority in Victorian England* (London: Croom Helm, 1977).
Philips, David, and Robert D. Storch, *Policing Provincial England, 1829–1856: The Politics of Reform* (London: Leicester University Press, 1999).
Pike, Michael S., *The Principles of Policing* (Houndmills: Macmillan, 1985).
Porter, Bernard, *The Origins of the Vigilant State* (London: Weidenfeld and Nicolson, 1987).

Porter, Bernard, *The Refugee Question* (Cambridge: Cambridge University Press, 1979).
Porter, Dennis, *The Pursuit of Crime, Art and Ideology in Detective Fiction* (New Haven: Yale University Press, 1981).
Priestman, Martin (ed.), *The Cambridge Companion to Crime Fiction* (Cambridge: Cambridge University Press, 2003).
Priestman, Martin, *Detective Fiction and Literature* (Houndmills: Macmillan, 1990).
Prothero, Margaret, *The History of the Criminal Investigation Department at Scotland Yard from Earliest Times until To-Day* (London: H. Jenkins, 1931).
Pulling, Christopher, *Mr Punch and the Police* (London: Butterworths, 1964).
Quail, John, *The Slow Burning Fuse* (London: Paladin, 1978).
Queen, Ellery, *Queen's Quorum* (New York: Biblio and Tannen, 1969; first published 1948).
Rawlings, Philip, *Crime and Power* (London: Longman, 1999).
Rawlings, Philip, *Drunks, Whores and Idle Apprentices* (London: Routledge, 1992).
Radzinowicz, Leon, *A History of English Criminal Law and its Administration from 1750* (London: Stevens & Sons, 1956–68).
Reed, David, *The Popular Magazine in Britain and the United States, 1880–1960* (Toronto: Toronto University Press, 1997).
Reilly, John W., *Policing Birmingham* (Birmingham: West Midlands Police, 1989).
Reiner, Robert (ed.), *Policing* (Aldershot: Dartmouth, 1996).
Reiner, Robert, *The Policing of Mass Demonstration in Contemporary Democracies: Policing, Protest, and Disorder in Britain* (San Domenico: European University Institute, 1997).
Reiner, Robert, *The Politics of the Police* (Brighton: Wheatsheaf Books, 1985).
Reith, Charles, *British Police and the Democratic Ideal* (London: Oxford University Press, 1943).
Reith, Charles, *A New Study of Police History* (Edinburgh: Oliver and Boyd, 1956).
Reitz, Caroline, *Detecting the Nation* (Columbus, OH: Ohio State University Press, 2004).
Reynolds, Elaine A., *Before the Bobbies* (Stanford: Stanford University Press, 1998).
Reynolds, Gerald W., and Anthony Judge, *The Night the Police Went on Strike* (London: Weidenfeld and Nicolson, 1968).
Robb, George, *White-Collar Crime in Modern England* (Cambridge: Cambridge University Press, 1992).

Roberts, Marie Mulvey, et al. (eds), *The Militants* (London: Routledge, 1994).

Rogers, Ann, *Secrecy and Power in the British State* (London: Pluto Press, 1997).

Rose, Jonathan, *The Intellectual Life of the British Working Classes* (New Haven: Yale University Press, 2001).

Rowbotham, Judith, and Kim Stevenson (eds), *Behaving Badly* (Aldershot: Ashgate, 2003).

Rowbotham, Judith, and Kim Stevenson (eds), *Criminal Conversations* (Columbus, OH: Ohio State University Press, 2005).

Rowland, John, *The Finger-Print Man* (London: Lutterworth Press, 1959).

Rumbelow, Donald, *I Spy Blue* (London: Macmillan, 1971).

Rzepka, Charles J., *Detective Fiction* (Cambridge: Polity, 2005).

Sadleir, Michael, *XIX Century Fiction: A Bibliographical Record Based on his Own Collection* (London: Constable, 1951).

Schlesinger, Philip, and Howard Tumber, *Reporting Crime* (Oxford: Clarendon Press, 1994).

Scollan, Maureen, *Sworn to Serve: Police in Essex 1840–1990* (Chichester: Phillimore, 1993).

Searle, G. R., *The Quest for National Efficiency* (London: Ashfield Press, 1990; first published 1971).

Sharpe, J. A., *Crime in Early Modern England, 1550–1750* (London: Longman, 1984).

Shattock, Joanne, and Michael Wolff (eds), *The Victorian Periodical Press* (Leicester: Leicester University Press, 1982).

Short, K. R. M., *The Dynamite War* (Dublin: Gill and Macmillan, 1979).

Shpayer-Makov, Haia, *The Making of a Policeman: A Social History of a Labour Force in Metropolitan London, 1829–1914* (Aldershot: Ashgate, 2002).

Sindall, Rob S., *Street Violence in the Nineteenth Century: Media Panic or Real Danger?* (Leicester: Leicester University Press, 1990).

Smith, K. J. M., *James Fitzjames Stephen* (Cambridge: Cambridge University Press, 1988).

Smith, Philip Thurmond, *Policing Victorian London* (Westport: Greenwood Press, 1985).

Stallion, Martin, *A Life of Crime* (Leigh-on-Sea: M. R. Stallion, 1998).

Stead, Philip John, *The Police of Britain* (London: Macmillan, 1985).

Stead, Philip John, *Vidocq* (London: Staples Press, 1953).

Steedman, Carolyn, *Policing the Victorian Community* (London: Routledge & Kegan Paul, 1984).

Stephens, W. B., *Education in Britain, 1750–1914* (London: Macmillan, 1998).

Stewart, R. F., *And Always a Detective: Chapters on the History of Detective Fiction* (Newton Abbot: David and Charles, 1980).

Stone, Harry (ed.), *The Uncollected Writings of Charles Dickens* (London: Allen Lane, 1969).
Sugden, Philip, *The Complete History of Jack the Ripper* (New York: Carroll & Graf, 2003; first published 1994).
Sullivan, Alvin (ed.), *British Literary Magazines* (Westport, CT: Greenwood Press, 1984).
Summerscale, Kate, *The Suspicions of Mr Whicher; or, The Murder at Road Hill House* (London: Bloomsbury, 2009; first published 2008).
Symons, Julian, *Mortal Consequences* (New York: Harper & Row, 1972).
Taylor, Bernard, *Cruelly Murdered* (London: Souvenir Press, 1979).
Taylor, David, *Crime, Policing and Punishment in England, 1750–1914* (Houndmills: Macmillan Press, 1998).
Taylor, David, *The New Police in Nineteenth-Century England* (Manchester: Manchester University Press, 1997).
Taylor, David, *Policing the Victorian Town* (Houndmills: Palgrave, 2002).
Thomas, Ronald R., *Detective Fiction and the Rise of Forensic Science* (Cambridge: Cambridge University Press, 2001; first published 1999).
Thompson, Jon, *Fiction, Crime, and Empire* (Urbana: University of Illinois Press, 1993).
Thompson, Paul Richard, *The Edwardians* (London: Weidenfeld and Nicolson, 1984; first published 1975).
Thomson, Basil, *The Story of Scotland Yard* (London: Grayson & Grayson, 1935).
Thorwald, Jürgen, *The Century of the Detective* (New York: Harcourt, Brace & World, 1964; trans. from the German).
Tobias, J. J., *Crime and the Police in England 1700–1900* (Dublin: Gill & Macmillan, 1979).
Trodd, Anthea, *Domestic Crime in the Victorian Novel* (New York: St Martin's Press, 1989).
Tunstall, Jeremy, *Journalists at Work* (London: Constable, 1971).
Vincent, David, *Bread, Knowledge and Freedom* (London: Methuen, 1981).
Vincent, David, *The Culture of Secrecy* (Oxford: Oxford University Press, 1998).
Vincent, David, *Literacy and Popular Culture* (Cambridge: Cambridge University Press, 1989).
Walkowitz, Judith R., *City of Dreadful Delight* (London: Virago, 1992).
Walkowitz, Judith R., *Prostitution and Victorian Society* (Cambridge: Cambridge University Press, 1980).
Warwick, Alexandra, and Martin Willis (eds), *Jack the Ripper: Media, Culture, History* (Manchester: Manchester University Press, 2007).
Watson, Eric R., *Adolf Beck* (Edinburgh: William Hodge & Co., 1924).
Weinberger, Barbara, *The Best Police in the World* (Aldershot: Scolar Press, 1995).
Whitbread, J. R., *The Railway Policeman* (London: George G. Harrap, 1961).

White, Jerry, *London in the 19th Century* (London: Vintage Books, 2008; first published 2007).
Wiener, Martin J., *Men of Blood* (Cambridge: Cambridge University Press, 2004).
Wiener, Martin J., *Reconstructing the Criminal* (Cambridge: Cambridge University Press, 1990).
Wilson, Ben, *What Price Liberty?* (London: Faber and Faber, 2009).
Wilson, Elizabeth, *The Sphinx in the City* (London: Virago Press, 1991).
Wood, Christopher, *William Powell Frith: A Painter and his World* (Stroud: Sutton Publishing, 2006).
Worthington, Heather, *The Rise of the Detective in Early Nineteenth-Century Popular Fiction* (Houndmills: Palgrave, 2005).
Wright, Alan, *Policing: An Introduction to Concepts and Practices* (Cullompton: Willan Publishing, 2002).
Young, Filson (ed.), *The Trial of Hawley Harvey Crippen* (Edinburgh: William Hodge & Co., 1920).
Zedner, Lucia, *Women, Crime, and Custody in Victorian England* (Oxford: Clarendon Press, 1991).

Dissertations

Shpayer, Haia, 'British Anarchism 1881–1914: Reality and Appearance', Ph.D., University of London, 1981.
Sopenoff, Ronald, C., 'The Police of London: The Early History of the Metropolitan Police, 1829–1856', Ph.D., Temple University, 1977.

Articles

Anderson, G. L., 'The Social Economy of Late-Victorian Clerks', in Geoffrey Crossick (ed.), *The Lower Middle Class in Britain 1870–1914* (London: Croom Helm, 1977).
Aspinall, A., 'The Social Status of Journalists at the Beginning of the Nineteenth Century', *Review of English Studies*, 21/83 (July 1945).
Beattie, J. M., 'Early Detection: The Bow Street Runners in Late Eighteenth-Century London', in Clive Emsley and Haia Shpayer-Makov (eds), *Police Detectives in History, 1750–1950* (Aldershot: Ashgate, 2006).
Beattie, J. M., 'Garrow and the Detectives: Lawyers and Policemen at the Old Bailey in the Late Eighteenth Century', *Crime, histoire et sociétés/Crime, History & Societies*, 11/2 (2007).
Beattie, J. M., 'Sir John Fielding and Public Justice: The Bow Street Magistrates' Court, 1754–1780', *Law and History Review*, 25 (Spring 2007).
Boyce, George, 'The Fourth Estate: The Reappraisal of a Concept', in George Boyce, James Curran, and Pauline Wingate (eds), *Newspaper History* (London: Constable, 1978).

Brake, Laurel, 'Writing, Cultural Production, and the Periodical Press in the Nineteenth Century', in J. B. Bullen (ed.), *Writing and Victorianism* (London: Longman, 1997).

Brantlinger, Patrick, 'What is "Sensational" about the "Sensation Novel"', *Nineteenth-Century Fiction*, 37/1 (1982).

Brown, Howard G., 'Tips, Traps and Tropes: Catching Thieves in Post-Revolutionary Paris', in Clive Emsley and Haia Shpayer-Makov (eds), *Police Detectives in History, 1750–1950* (Aldershot: Ashgate, 2006).

Brundage, Anthony, 'Ministers, Magistrates and Reformers: The Genesis of the Rural Constabulary Act of 1839', *Parliamentary History*, 5/1 (1986).

Carter Wood, John, 'Self-Policing and the Policing of the Self: Violence, Protection and the Civilizing Bargain in Britain', *Crime, histoire et sociétés/Crime, History & Societies*, 7/1 (2003).

Chibnall, Steve, 'Chronicles of the Gallows: The Social History of Crime Reporting', in Harry Christian (ed.), *The Sociology of Journalism and the Press* (Sociological Review Monograph, 29; Keele: Keele University Press, 1980).

Chibnall, Steve, 'The Metropolitan Police and the News Media', in Simon Holdaway (ed.), *The British Police* (London: Edward Arnold, 1979).

Clausen, Christopher, 'Sherlock Holmes, Order, and the Late-Victorian Mind', *Georgia Review*, 38/1 (Spring 1984).

Clutterbuck, Lindsay, 'Countering Irish Republican Terrorism in Britain: Its Origin as a Police Function', *Terrorism and Political Violence*, 18/1 (2006).

Curran, James, 'The Press as an Agency of Social Control: An Historical Perspective', in George Boyce, James Curran, and Pauline Wingate (eds), *Newspaper History* (London: Constable, 1978).

Davis, Jennifer, 'A Poor Man's System of Justice: The London Police Courts in the Second Half of the Nineteenth Century', *Historical Journal*, 27 (June 1984).

Davis, Jennifer, 'From "Rookeries" to "Communities": Race, Poverty and Policing in London, 1850–1985', *History Workshop*, 28 (Spring 1989).

Davis, Jennifer, 'Jennings' Buildings and the Royal Borough', in David Feldman and Gareth Stedman Jones (eds), *Metropolis. London: Histories and Representations since 1800* (London: Routledge, 1989).

Davis, Jennifer, 'The London Garotting Panic of 1862: A Moral Panic and the Creation of a Criminal Class in Mid-Victorian England', in V. A. C. Gatrell, Bruce Lenman, and Geoffrey Parker (eds), *Crime and the Law* (London: Europa Publications, 1980).

Davis, Jennifer, 'Prosecutions and their Context: The Use of the Criminal Law in Later Nineteenth-Century London', in Douglas Hay and Francis Snyder (eds), *Policing and Prosecution in Britain 1750–1850* (Oxford: Clarendon Press, 1989).

Davis, Lloyd, 'Journalism and Victorian Fiction', in, Barbara Garlick and Margaret Harris (eds), *Victorian Journalism: Exotic and Domestic* (St Lucia, Queensland: University of Queensland Press, 1998).

Devereaux, Simon, 'The Fall of the Sessions Paper: The Criminal Trial and the Popular Press in Late Eighteenth-Century London', *Criminal Justice History*, 18 (2003).

Di Paola, Pietro, 'The Spies who Came in from the Heat: The International Surveillance of the Anarchists in London', *European History Quarterly*, 37/2 (2007).

Dodsworth, Francis M., '"Civic" Police and the Condition of Liberty: The Rationality of Governance in Eighteenth-Century England', *Social History*, 29 (May 2004).

Dodsworth, Francis M., 'Masculinity as Governance: Police, Public Service and the Embodiment of Authority, c.1700–1850', in Matthew McCormack (ed.), *Public Men: Masculinity and Politics in Modern Britain* (Houndmills: Palgrave Macmillan, 2007).

Dodsworth, Francis M., 'Police and the Prevention of Crime: Commerce, Temptation and the Corruption of the Body Politic, from Fielding to Colquhoun', *British Journal of Criminology*, 47/3 (2007).

Eliot, Simon, 'Some Trends in British Book Production', in John O. Jordan and Robert L. Patten (eds), *Literature in the Marketplace* (Cambridge: Cambridge University Press, 1995).

Elliott, Philip, 'Professional Ideology and Organisational Change: The Journalist since 1800', in George Boyce, James Curran, and Pauline Wingate (eds), *Newspaper History* (London: Constable, 1978).

Emsley, Clive, 'The English Bobby: An Indulgent Tradition', in Roy Porter (ed.), *Myths of the English* (Cambridge: Polity Press, 1992).

Emsley, Clive, 'The History of Crime and Crime Control Institutions', in Mike Maguire, Rod Morgan, and Robert Reiner (eds), *The Oxford Handbook of Criminology* (3rd edn; Oxford: Oxford University Press, 2002).

England, R. W., Jr, 'Investigating Homicides in Northern England, 1800–1824', *Criminal Justice History*, 6 (1985).

Feeley, Malcolm M., 'Entrepreneurs of Punishment', *Punishment & Society*, 4/3 (2002).

Flanders, Judith, 'The Hanky-Panky Way', *Times Literary Supplement*, 18 June 2010.

Gatrell, V. A. C., 'Crime, Authority and the Policeman-State', in F. M. L. Thompson (ed.), *The Cambridge Social History of Britain, 1750–1950* (Cambridge: Cambridge University Press, 1990).

Gatrell, V. A. C., 'The Decline of Theft and Violence in Victorian and Edwardian England', in V. A. C. Gatrell, Bruce Lenman, and Geoffrey Parker (eds), *Crime and the Law* (London: Europa Publications, 1980).

Gilling, Daniel, 'Crime Prevention Discourses and the Multi-Agency Approach', *International Journal of the Sociology of Law*, 21/2 (1993).

Godfrey, Barry S., '"Private Policing and the Workplace": The Worsted Committee and the Policing of Labor in Northern England, 1840–1880', *Criminal Justice History*, 16 (2002).

Green, Andy, 'Technical Education and State Formation in Nineteenth-Century England and France', *History of Education*, 24/2 (1995).

Gunn, Simon, 'The Public Sphere, Modernity and Consumption: New Perspectives on the History of the English Middle Class', in Alan Kidd and David Nicholls (eds), *Gender, Civic Culture and Consumerism: Middle-Class Identity in Britain, 1800–1940* (Manchester: Manchester University Press, 1999).

Handler, Phil, 'Forgery and the End of the "Bloody Code" in Early Nineteenth-Century England', *Historical Journal*, 48/3 (2005).

Hart, Jenifer, 'Reform of the Borough Police, 1835–1856', *English Historical Review*, 70/276 (July 1955).

Hay, Douglas, 'Property, Authority and Criminal Law', in Douglas Hay et al., *Albion's Fatal Tree* (New York: Pantheon Books, 1975).

Hay, Douglas, and Francis Snyder, 'Using the Criminal Law, 1750–1850: Policing, Private Prosecution, and the State', in Douglas Hay and Francis Snyder (eds), *Policing and Prosecution in Britain 1750–1850* (Oxford: Clarendon Press, 1989).

Jones, David J. V., 'The New Police, Crime and People in England and Wales, 1829–1888', *Transactions of the Royal Historical Society*, 5th ser., 33 (1983).

Kent, Christopher, 'Higher Journalism and the Mid-Victorian Clerisy', *Victorian Studies*, 13 (Dec. 1969).

King, Peter, 'Newspaper Reporting and Attitudes to Crime and Justice in Late-Eighteenth- and Early-Nineteenth-Century London', *Continuity and Change*, 22/1 (2007).

King, Peter, 'Newspaper Reporting, Prosecution Practice and Perceptions of Urban Crime: The Colchester Crime Wave of 1765', *Continuity and Change*, 2/3 (1987).

King, Peter, 'Prosecution Associations and their Impact in Eighteenth-Century Essex', in Douglas Hay and Francis Snyder (eds), *Policing and Prosecution in Britain 1750–1850* (Oxford: Clarendon Press, 1989).

Laqueur, Thomas, 'The Cultural Origins of Popular Literacy in England 1500–1850', *Oxford Review of Education*, 2/3 (1976).

Lawrence, Paul, 'Images of Poverty and Crime: Police Memoirs in England and France at the End of the Nineteenth Century', *Crime, histoire et sociétés/Crime, History & Societies*, 4/1(2000).

Lawrence, Paul, '"Scoundrels and Scallywags, and Some Honest Men...": Memoirs and the Self-Image of French and English Policemen, c.1870–1939', in Barry S. Godfrey, Clive Emsley, and Graeme Dunstall (eds), *Comparative Histories of Crime* (Cullompton: Willan Publishing, 2003).

Lee, Alan, 'The Structure, Ownership and Control of the Press, 1855–1914', in George Boyce, James Curran, and Pauline Wingate (eds), *Newspaper History* (London: Constable, 1978).

Locker, John P., '"Quiet Thieves, Quiet Punishment": Private Responses to the "Respectable" Offender, c.1850–1930', *Crime, histoire et sociétés/Crime, History & Societies*, 9/1 (2005).
Lowe, W. J., 'The Lancashire Constabulary, 1845–1870: The Social and Occupational Function of a Victorian Police Force', *Criminal Justice History*, 4 (1983).
McCuskey, Brian W., 'The Kitchen Police: Servant Surveillance and Middle-Class Transgression', *Victorian Literature and Culture*, 28/2 (2000).
McMullan, John L., 'The Arresting Eye: Discourse, Surveillance and Disciplinary Administration in Early English Police Thinking', *Social and Legal Studies*, 7/1 (1998).
McMullan, John L., 'The New Improved Monied Police', *British Journal of Criminology*, 36/1 (Winter 1996).
Maidment, B. E., 'Victorian Periodicals and Academic Discourse', in Laurel Brake, Aled Jones, and Lionel Madden (eds), *Investigating Victorian Journalism* (Houndmills: Macmillan, 1990).
May, Allyson N., 'Advocates and Truth-Seeking in the Old Bailey Courtroom', *Journal of Legal History*, 26/1 (2005).
Miller, Wilbur R., 'From Old Cap Collier to Nick Carter; or, Images of Crime and Criminal Justice in American Dime Novel Detective Stories, 1880–1920', in Amy Gilman Srebnick and René Lévy (eds), *Crime and Culture* (Aldershot: Ashgate, 2005).
Miller, Wilbur R., 'London's Police Tradition in a Changing Society', in Simon Holdaway (ed.), *The British Police* (London: Edward Arnold, 1979).
Morgan, Jane, *Conflict and Order* (Oxford: Clarendon Press, 1987).
Morris, R. M. (Bob), '"Crime Does Not Pay": Thinking again about Detectives in the First Century of the Metropolitan Police', in Clive Emsley and Haia Shpayer-Makov (eds), *Police Detectives in History, 1750–1950* (Aldershot: Ashgate, 2006).
Morris, R. M. (Bob), 'History of Criminal Investigation', in Tim Newburn, Tom Williamson, and Alan Wright (eds), *Handbook of Criminal Investigation* (Cullompton: Willan Publishing, 2007).
Neocleous, Mark, 'Social Police and the Mechanisms of Prevention', *British Journal of Criminology*, 40/4 (2000).
O'Brien, Ellen L., '"The Most Beautiful Murder": The Transgressive Aesthetics of Murder in Victorian Street Ballads', *Victorian Literature and Culture*, 28/1 (2000).
Paley, Ruth, '"An Imperfect, Inadequate and Wretched System"? Policing London before Peel', *Criminal Justice History*, 10 (1989).
Paley, Ruth, 'Thief-Takers in London in the Age of the McDaniel Gang, c.1745–1754', in Douglas Hay and Francis Snyder (eds), *Policing and Prosecution in Britain 1750–1850* (Oxford: Clarendon Press, 1989).
Parry, L. A., 'Crippen', in W. Teignmouth Shore (ed.), *Crime and its Detection* (London: Gresham Publishing, 1931).

Petrow, Stefan, 'The Rise of the Detective in London, 1869–1914', *Criminal Justice History*, 14 (1993).

Philips, David, '"A New Engine of Power and Authority": The Institutionalization of Law-Enforcement in England, 1780–1830', in V. A. C. Gatrell, Bruce Lenman, and Geoffrey Parker (eds), *Crime and the Law* (London: Europa Publications, 1980).

Philips, David, 'A "Weak" State? The English State, the Magistracy and the Reform of Policing in the 1830s', *English Historical Review*, 119/483 (2004).

Philips, David, 'Good Men to Associate and Bad Men to Conspire: Associations for the Prosecution of Felons in England, 1760–1860', in Douglas Hay and Francis Snyder (eds), *Policing and Prosecution in Britain 1750–1850* (Oxford: Clarendon Press, 1989).

Philips, David, 'Three "Moral Enterpreneurs" and the Creation of a "Criminal Class" in England, c.1790–1840s', *Crime, histoire et sociétés/ Crime, History & Societies*, 7/1 (2003).

Philips, David, and Robert D. Storch, 'Whigs and Coppers: The Grey Ministry's National Police Scheme, 1832', *Historical Research*, 67/162 (1994), 75–90.

Price, Richard N., 'Society, Status and Jingoism: The Social Roots of Lower Middle Class Patriotism, 1870–1900', in Geoffrey Crossick (ed.), *The Lower Middle Class in Britain 1870–1914* (London: Croom Helm, 1977).

Pykett, Lyn, 'The Newgate Novel and Sensation Fiction, 1830–1868', in Martin Priestman (ed.), *The Cambridge Companion to Crime Fiction* (Cambridge: Cambridge University Press, 2003).

Pykett, Lyn, 'Reading the Periodical Press: Text and Context', in Laurel Brake, Aled Jones, and Lionel Madden (eds), *Investigating Victorian Journalism* (Houndmills: Macmillan, 1990).

Reddy, Maureen, 'Women Detectives', in Martin Priestman (ed.), *The Cambridge Companion to Crime Fiction* (Cambridge: Cambridge University Press, 2003).

Schütt, Sita A., 'French Crime Fiction', in Martin Priestman (ed.), *The Cambridge Companion to Crime Fiction* (Cambridge: Cambridge University Press, 2003).

Shore, Heather, 'Crime, Policing and Punishment', in Chris A. Williams (ed.), *A Companion to Nineteenth-Century Britain* (Oxford: Blackwell, 2004).

Shpayer-Makov, Haia, 'Anarchism in British Public Opinion 1880–1914', *Victorian Studies*, 31 (Summer 1988).

Shpayer-Makov, Haia, 'Becoming a Police Detective in Victorian and Edwardian London', *Policing and Society*, 14/3 (2004).

Shpayer-Makov, Haia, 'Control at the Workplace: Paternalism Reinvented in Victorian Britain', in Clive Emsley, Eric Johnson, and Pieter Spierenburg (eds), *Social Control in Europe*, ii. *1800–2000* (Columbus, OH: Ohio State University Press, 2004).

Shpayer-Makov, Haia, 'Relinking Work and Leisure in Late Victorian and Edwardian England', *International Review of Social History*, 47/2 (2002).

Shpayer-Makov, Haia, 'Shedding the Uniform and Acquiring a New Masculine Image: The Case of the Late Victorian and Edwardian English Police Detective', in David G. Barrie and Susan Broomhall (eds), *A History of Police and Masculinities, 1700–2010* (Cullompton: Willan Publishing, forthcoming).

Shubert, Adrian, 'Private Initiative in Law Enforcement: Associations for the Prosecution of Felons, 1744–1856', in Victor Bailey (ed.), *Policing and Punishment in Nineteenth-Century Britain* (London: Croom Helm, 1981).

Sindall, Rob S., 'The Criminal Statistics of Nineteenth-Century Cities: A New Approach', *Urban History Yearbook* (1986).

Sindall, Rob S., 'Middle-Class Crime in Nineteenth-Century England', *Criminal Justice History*, 4 (1983).

Smith, Anthony, 'The Long Road to Objectivity and Back Again: The Kinds of Truth We Get in Journalism', in George Boyce, James Curran, and Pauline Wingate (eds), *Newspaper History* (London: Constable, 1978).

Smith, Bruce P., 'The Emergence of Public Prosecution in London, 1790–1850', *Yale Journal of Law & the Humanities*, 18/1 (2006).

Smith, Bruce P., 'English Criminal Justice Administration, 1650–1850: A Historiographical Essay', *Law and History Review*, 25/3 (Fall 2007).

Snell, Esther, 'Discourses of Criminality in the Eighteenth-Century Press: The Presentation of Crime in *The Kentish Post*, 1717–1768', *Continuity and Change*, 22/1 (2007).

Stafford, David A. T., 'Spies and Gentlemen: The Birth of the British Spy Novel, 1893–1914', *Victorian Studies*, 24/4 (1981).

Stark, John, 'The City of London Police', in W. Teignmouth Shore (ed.), *Crime and its Detection* (London: Gresham Publishing, 1931).

Stevenson, S. J., 'The "Habitual Criminal" in Nineteenth-Century England: Some Observations on the Figures', *Urban History Yearbook* (1986).

Storch, Robert D., 'The Plague of Blue Locusts: Police Reform and Popular Resistance in Northern England, 1840–57', *International Review of Social History*, 20/1 (1975).

Storch, Robert D., 'Police Control of Street Prostitution in Victorian London', in David H. Bayley, *Police and Society* (Beverly Hills, CA: Sage Publications, 1977).

Storch, Robert D. 'The Policeman as Domestic Missionary: Urban Discipline and Popular Culture in Northern England, 1850–80', *Journal of Social History*, 9 (Summer 1976).

Storch, Robert D., 'Policing Rural Southern England before the Police: Opinion and Practice, 1830–1856', in Douglas Hay and Francis Snyder (eds), *Policing and Prosecution in Britain 1750–1850* (Oxford: Clarendon Press, 1989).

Styles, John, 'Print and Policing: Crime Advertising in Eighteenth-Century Provincial England', in Douglas Hay and Francis Snyder (eds), *Policing and Prosecution in Britain 1750–1850* (Oxford: Clarendon Press, 1989).

Styles, John, 'Sir John Fielding and the Problem of Crime Investigation in Eighteenth Century England', *Transactions of the Royal Historical Society*, 5th ser., 33 (1983).

Swift, Roger, '"Another Stafford Street Row": Law, Order and the Irish Presence in Mid-Victorian Wolverhampton', in Roger Swift and Sheridan Gilley (eds), *The Irish in the Victorian City* (London: Croom Helm, 1985).

Taylor, Howard, 'Rationing Crime: The Political Economy of Criminal Statistics since the 1850s', *Economic History Review*, 51/3 (1998).

Thane, Pat, 'Government and Society in England and Wales, 1750–1914', in F. M. L. Thompson (ed.), *The Cambridge Social History of Britain 1750–1950* (Cambridge: Cambridge University Press, 1990), vol. iii.

Vincent, David, 'Communication, Community and the State', in Clive Emsley and James Walvin (eds), *Artisans, Peasants & Proletarians, 1760–1860* (London: Croom Helm, 1985).

Wales, Tim, 'Thief-Takers and their Clients in Later Stuart London', in Paul Griffiths and Mark S. R. Jenner (eds), *Londinopolis* (Manchester: Manchester University Press, 2000).

Weaver, Michael, 'The New Science of Policing: Crime and the Birmingham Police Force, 1839–1842', *Albion*, 26/2 (1994).

Williams, Chris A., 'Constables for Hire: The History of Private "Public" Policing in the UK', *Policing and Society*, 18 (June 2008).

Zedner, Lucia, 'Policing before and after the Police', *British Journal of Criminology*, 46/1 (2006).

INDEX

Abberline, Frederick G. 107, 119, 171, 281
Acton, Lord 28
Adult, The 135
'Adventure of the Devil's Foot, The' (Conan Doyle) 249
'Adventure of the Red Circle, The' (Conan Doyle) 255
'Adventure of the Six Napoleons, The' (Conan Doyle) 250
'Adventure of Wisteria Lodge, The' (Conan Doyle) 255
Adventures of Martin Hewitt (Morrison) 250–2, 251 Fig.15
agent provocateurs and entrapment 137, 152, 189, 204, 222, 361 n.88
 and Special Branch 133–4, 214
All the Year Round (journal) 200, 367 n.22
 'Detectives and their Work' 274
Allen, Grant 263, 267
amateurism, and the administration of the law 19, 73, 257
anarchists:
 Sidney Street siege (1911) 217–18, 364 n.164
 and Special Branch 56–8, 133–6, 142, 214–15, 216–17, 344 n.264
 spotting detectives 142
 Walsall trial, 1892 134, 214
Anderson, Robert 55, 126, 131, 165, 179, 378 n.43
anthropometric method of identification 50, 51, 51 Fig.2
 see also Bertillon and Bertillonage
Arrow, Charles 91–2, 98–9, 119, 122, 128
Asquith, Herbert Henry 108
associations for the prosecution of felons 22, 47, 256

At the Villa Rose (Mason) 244
Aurora Floyd (Braddon) 247
Autobiography of a French Detective from 1818 to 1858 (Canler) 242, 278
Autobiography of an English Detective (Russell) 236

baby farmers 131
Barr, Robert 244
Bartlett, Ashmead 157
Beck, Adolph 177, 212, 356 n.157
Bennett, Arnold 253
Bentham, Jeremy 14, 28, 201
Beron, Leon, murder 352 n.90
Berrett, James 84, 92–3, 288
Bertillon, Alphonse 50, 322 n.248
Bertillonage 218, 365 n.175
Big Bow Mystery, The (Zangwill) 244
Birkenhead Police force 131
Birmingham Daily Post 280
Birmingham Police force 42, 44, 92, 112, 139–40, 333 n.235, 337 n.88, 341 n.175
 detective branch established 44–5, 319 n.192
 and Irish terrorism 204–5, 362 n.94
Bishop, Cecil 74, 84–5, 108, 109, 130, 165
Black Museum, Scotland Yard 97, 276
Blanc, Louis 192
Bleak House (Dickens) 231, 243, 367 n.21
'Bloody Code' 19–20, 42
Blyth, Harry 252, 373 n.131
Boer War and physical fitness 220, 270
Boisgobey, Fortuné du 243, 275
Bond, Major 92
Bootman, Samuel 87
Boulton and Park affair 150
Bourdin, Martial 57
Bow Street Public Office 22–3, 24, 25, 49, 159

INDEX

Bow Street Runners 23–4, 25, 29, 32, 33, 52, 119, 172, 189, 192, 193, 240, 256, 299, 359 n.41
  abolition of 31–2
  in detective fiction 229, 236, 240, 246
Braddon, Mary Elizabeth 232, 247
Bradford, Sir Edward 165, 178, 352 n.97
Brett, James 34
Broadhurst, Joseph F. 91, 100
Brust, Harold 74, 86–7, 95, 98, 108
Bulwer-Lytton, Edward 158–9, 229
Bunn, Frank 89–90
Burdett-Coutts, William 214
Burke, Thomas Henry 53–4
Burns, John 213
Butcher, Detective Sergeant 69

Café Véry bombing, 1894 57
Caminada, Jerome 118, 280, 281, 286, 291, 353 n.98, 360 n.43, 377 n.12
Canler, Louis 242, 278, 372 n.20
Carlin, Francis 74, 89
Carlos, King of Portugal 86
Carnot, Sadi 57
'Case of the Lost Foreigner, The' (Morrison) 252
Castrillo, Antonio Cánovas del 57
Cavendish, Lord Frederick 53–4
Century Magazine 182
Chadwick, Edwin 14, 15, 42
Chamberlain, William 78, 114
Chambers's Journal 234, 235
  'Detectives as They Are' 273
Chartist movement 41, 44, 157, 187, 189, 192, 314 n.82
Chavette, Eugène 275
Checkmate (Le Fanu) 245
Cherrill, Fred 90
Chester barracks bombing, 1881 53
Chronicles of Addington Peace, The (Robinson) 253
Chulalongkorn, King of Siam 120
Churchill, Winston 73
City of London Police 30, 34, 38, 44, 65, 67, 82, 85, 87, 92, 107, 112, 116, 123, 126, 157
  formation of 2

Houndsditch affair, 1910 216
  travelling abroad on duty 121
City Press 172
civil-service reforms, 1870s 82
Clarke, George 38, 49
Clausen, Christopher 255
Cleek of Scotland Yard (Hanshew) 176
Clerkenwell prison, London 35
Clues from a Detective's Camera (Hill) 252
Coathupe, Edwin 69, 70
Collins, Wilkie 231, 232, 247, 258–9, 275, 367 n.22
Colquhoun, Patrick 29, 30
Common Lodging Houses Act (1851) 163
Conan Doyle, Arthur 238, 243, 248–55, 270, 276
constables, parish 18, 19, 20, 22
Contagious Diseases Acts (1860s) 128
Convict Supervision Office, Metropolitan Police 49, 84
convicts, rehabilitation of 130–1, 296
Cornhill Magazine 191–2, 209
Cornish, George W. 74–5, 85, 87, 95
Coulon, Auguste 133–4
County and Borough Police Act (1856) 41, 42
County Police Acts (1839/1840) 41
courts, role of detectives 74, 85, 125, 240, 341 n.189, 353 n.98
Cozens, William 48
crime:
  attitudes to middle/upper-class criminality 127–8
  early industrial capitalism and 14–17
  rates 1850–1900 47, 127
  and the stability of society 15–16
  unreported 47
  white-collar 15, 80, 96
criminal intelligence 22, 24, 33, 36, 105, 137, 159, 169
Criminal Investigation Department (CID) of the Metropolitan Police:
  formation of 29, 39–40, 69–70, 139, 268

416

see also detectives; Scotland Yard; regional borough forces
criminal justice system, Britain 3, 42, 208, 209
  first director of public prosecutions 47
  modifications to 239
criminal justice system, France 29–30, 218
criminal law 42, 71, 73, 74, 93, 96, 97
Criminal Law Amendment Act (1885) 48
criminal prosecutions by private actions 20, 21
criminals:
  and disguise 165
  as literary heroes 227–8, 230
  newspaper portraits of wanted 169
  as victims of circumstance 239
Crippen case, 1910 177, 217–18, 365 n.170, 365 n.172
Curtis, L. Perry Jr 170, 211
Curzon Wyllie, Sir William Hutt 58

Daily Chronicle 216
Daily Mail 177, 180
Daily News 139, 202, 215
  'London Detectives' 209–10
Daily Telegraph 157, 169, 205, 208, 219
Dark Blue 122, 127, 138, 192
death of suspects in police captivity 130, 343 n.225
Deptford murders, 1904 100
Desborough Committee, 1919 108
detection, growth of in provincial England 41–6
  before the founding of the reformed police 18–26
detective fiction:
  advocating police professionalism 264–5
  advocating public and private initiatives against crime 263–4
  class bias against policeman 257–61
  criticism of, in police memoirs 289–92, 379 n.59
  equilibrium of the individual and the collective 268–9, 271
  Foucauldian analysis of 226, 265–8

French detectives, supposed superiority of 275, 376 n.6
  'gentleman' background of private detectives 248, 258–61
  individualism 271
  Marxist analysis of 265, 266
  origins of 228–32
  police detectives as representing the state 265–71
  and police detectives bureaucracy handicaps 260–1
  police intrusion themes 267
  private detectives, superiority of 7, 248–65, 374 n.145
  private detectives symbolising individualism and bourgeois ideology 261
  realism in literature 259
  role of citizen crime fighters 256–7
  Scotland Yard representations in 242, 253–4, 371 n.80, 371 n.81, 374 n.145
  and social liberalism 269, 271
  women detectives 243–4, 252–3
detectives, police:
  attitudes to middle/upper-class criminality 127–8
  as authors 272–97
  convicts, rehabilitation of 130–1, 296
  corruption and the underworld 38, 123, 136, 149, 202, 203, 213, 222, 255, 344 n.275, 344 n.276
  debate about raising standards of 67–9, 71–2, 79–81, 259, 260
  Dickens's role in elevating image of 194–8, 199–202
  disguise and concealment 29, 31, 34, 138–43, 141 Fig.7, 142 Fig.8, 188–9, 197, 205–7, 206 Fig.12, 292, 345 n.314
  diverging image with private detectives 244–8
  divisional 35–8, 40, 43, 44, 45, 55, 57, 64, 69, 75, 76, 85, 98, 104, 106, 108, 111, 112, 114, 124, 137, 318 n.172, 318 n.174, 324 n.308, 338 n.92

detectives, police: (cont.)
  documentation and report writing 124–5
  ex-convict funds 131
  in fiction 226–71
  French model of detection compared 205–9
  gratuities for service 115–17
  guided tours of lower-class London life by 163–6, 351 n.54
  injuries on duty 108
  internal scrutiny and supervision 123–5
  internal training 94–100
  interrogation methods and confessions 137
  irregular hours 107–8
  low educational level of 64, 68, 69, 71, 72, 73, 79, 83, 88, 112, 205, 259–60, 263, 283, 284, 285, 293, 299
  manner and carriage of officers 138
  memoirs, official opposition to 281–2
  numbers of officers 33, 34, 35, 40, 44, 55, 59, 60, 319 n.195, 319 n.196, 324 n. 308
  as national or local celebrities 171
  occupational culture 107–26
  overlapping duties with uniformed branch 106, 107 Fig.5
  post-retirement opportunities 118–19, 148
  professionalization, process of 32–3, 35, 36, 42, 44, 48–52, 60–1, 62, 97–8, 123, 272, 299–300
  promotion and upward mobility 77, 87, 93, 104, 109–10, 260, 295
  in provincial England, growth of 41–6 *see also* individual borough police forces
  reading, writing and literary skills of 8–9, 64, 69, 72, 78, 81, 82, 88, 93, 124–6, 283–5
  recruitment and selection 4, 73–81, 81–6
    external recruitment 62, 70, 71, 72–3
    length of service before 84
    from middle class 65–6, 70–1, 263
    motivation and background 86–94
    qualities of the recruit 63–4
    role of chief constables and superintendents 84, 85–6
  in retirement 7, 118–19, 148, 162, 171, 263, 272, 276, 281–3, 286–7
  relationship with journalists and the press 7, 156–86, 187–225, 255–6
    benefiting from 167–72
    bribes 161–2, 186
    creating heroic image of 219–20
    creating masculine image of 217
    and crime information 168–9, 172–82, 352 n.90, 355 n.139
    image, consolidation of 221–5
    image, post-1900 212–20
    image, shortly after formation of CID 188–94
    image crisis, late 1880s 209–12
    investigative rivalries 175–6, 355 n.149, 356 n.156
    professional qualities in common with journalists 156–7
    reciprocal advantages 158–72
    selective 'management' of press material 223–4, 366 n.191
    selling stories to 350 n.43
    working alongside 162
  relationship with the public 126–32, 158
  role in policing, early consolidation of 44–5, 46–8
  scientific and technical expertise 50, 96
  semi-autonomous status of 122–3
  school for (1902) 97
  socio-economic class and background of 4, 8, 117–22, 283, 285, 293, 296, 299
  training 99 Fig.4
  training on formal courses 98
  trial and courtroom role 74, 85, 125, 240, 341 n.189, 353 n.98
  violence during arrests 108–9

INDEX

wages and annual increments 81, 110–17, 113 Tab.1, 113 Tab.2, 337 n.88
written and oral examinations 93–4
see also memoirs
detectives, private 47, 61, 148
  in detective fiction 7, 226, 248–62, 262–5, 374 n.145
  diverging image with police detectives 244–8
  'gentleman' backgrounds of fictional 248, 258–61
  press relations 256
  and retired police detectives 119
Detective's Note-Book, The (Martel) 236, 259
'Detectives who Guarded King Edward' (*Penny Illustrated paper*) 120 Fig.6
Dew, Walter 90–1, 98, 109, 119, 121, 217–18, 365 n.170
Diary of an Ex-Detective (Martel) 236
Dickens, Charles 161, 162–3, 168, 229, 234, 243, 275, 352 n.96, 369 n.48
  Charlie Field articles 163, 197, 199
  detection as elevated scientific task 195–6
  detectives in his fiction 229, 230–1, 367 n.21
  role in elevating detective image 194–8, 199–202, 246
  tours of London low-life 199–200, 201–2
Dilnot, Frank 79–80
Dilnot, George 80, 140
dime novels 231, 247
disguise and concealment 29, 31, 34, 132, 138–43, 141 Fig.7, 142, 142 Fig.8, 156, 164, 188–9, 207, 273, 292, 345 n.314
Divall, Tom 82, 93, 119, 282
Domestic Crime in the Victorian Novel (Trodd) 267
Doré, Gustave 163, 164, 166, 201
Dowling, Richard 264
Druscovich, Nathaniel 38, 66–7, 354 n.120

dynamite 54
'Dynamiter, The' (Stevenson and Stevenson) 248–9

East London Observer 171
Edinburgh Review 5
  'The Police System of London' 191
Education Act (1870) 88
Edward, Prince of Wales 220
Egan, James 205, 362 n.94
Elisabeth, Empress of Austria 57
Emsley, Clive 307
entrapment 189
  Thomas Titley, case 137, 204, 214, 361 n.88
  see also agent provocateurs and entrapment
Evening News 164, 214
Examiner 188
Experiences of a Real Detective by Inspector F. (Russell) 236, 242, 369 n.50
Extradition Act (1870) 66
extradition cases 115

fabricated charges 130
Fallen Leaves, The (Collins) 258–9
Fast and Loose (Griffiths) 372 n.108
Female Detective, The (Forrester) 289
Fenian terrorism *see* Irish (Fenian) terrorism
Ferdinand of Bulgaria 120
Ferrier, Kenneth J. 379 n.59
Field, Charlie 119, 197, 199
Fielding, Henry 23–4, 36
Fielding, John 23–4, 36, 169
fingerprinting 61, 72, 97, 218
  bureau establishment 50–2
Fitch, Herbert T. 59, 120, 121
Flynt, Josiah 165, 219
Foucault, Michel 226, 240–1, 265
Fouché, Joseph 188
Fowler, Henry 91
France:
  criminal justice system 29–30, 218
  detective system 30, 39, 50, 188–9, 205–9, 242, 247, 275
  Sûreté 30, 209, 229, 242, 278, 322 n.248
Fraser, Colonel James 65, 126

INDEX

freedom and liberty, and the British police force 26–9, 31, 132, 135, 189, 208, 209, 210, 271, 306, 308
Freeman, R. Austin 253
French Revolution 16
Frith, William Powell 34, 361 n.72
Froest, Frank 96, 181, 182, 352 n.90
Fuller, Robert A. 75, 287, 295

Gaboriau, Émile 231, 242, 243, 275, 368 n.24
gambling clubs 105
Garibaldi, Giuseppe 192
Garrick Club 161
garrotting and violent street robbery, 1862 35
Gaskell, Elizabeth 231
gender:
   and the police forces 82–3
   and police surveillance 129–30
   see also women
German spies 140
Gibbon, Charles 243
Globe 203
Godley, G. 118
Godwin, William 229, 366 n.11
'Going Out of Alessandro Pozzone, The' (Dowling) 264
Good, Daniel 32
Gough, William C. 108–9, 119
Gough, W. C. 119
Graham, James 111
Grand Babylon Hotel, The (Bennett) 253
Great Eastern Railway Company police 119
Great Exhibition (1851) 45, 198
'Great Ruby Robbery, The' (Allen) 263, 267
Green, Anna Katherine 231, 243
Greenham, George Hepburn 65, 66, 68–9, 70, 76–7, 120, 290–1
Greenwood, James 228
Greig, Major C. B. 68
Grey, Vivian 253–4
Griffiths, Major Arthur 243, 244, 275–6, 352 n.78, 352 n.97, 372 n.108

Habitual Criminals Act (1869) 37, 322 n.249
Habitual Criminals Registry 50, 317 n.154, 322 n.249
habitual offenders 49, 128–9, 165
Hallam, John William 139
Hancox, Detective Sergeant 121
hand-bills 22
hanging, public abolition of (1868) 42
Harcourt, Sir William Vernon 52, 56, 276
Hard Cash (Reade) 247
Harding, Arthur 129, 130, 132, 136
Harris, W. 69
Harris, William Henry 117, 213
Havelock Ellis, Henry 135
Haycraft, Thomas W. 257
Haydon, Michael 34, 361 n.72
Henderson, Colonel Edmund 35, 36, 40, 123, 177, 193
Henderson, William 77
Henry, Edward 51, 72–3, 96–7, 110, 172, 178
Henry, Émil 57
Henry, Jack 82, 89
Hesse, Grand Duke of 120
Higginbottom, Frederick J. 162
Hill, Headon 252
History of Police in England, A (Lee) 149, 150
Hobhouse, L. T. 269
Hobson, J. A. 269
Holmes, Sherlock 7, 238, 242, 243, 244, 247–8, 262, 263, 264, 269, 270, 276, 278, 279, 292, 293, 294, 295, 371 n.84
   and the superiority of the private detective 248–55
   viewed by real detectives 291
Home Office 6, 30, 35, 42, 72, 111, 128, 299
   establishment of 25
   financial restraints on policing 79
   policing plan (1906) 60
   and secret agents 55
Home Office, 1868 Committee on the Metropolitan Police 35, 52, 139

INDEX

Home Office, 1878 Commission on the State, Discipline, and Organisation of the Detective Force of the Metropolitan Police (1878), 38–9, 40, 46, 67–9, 70, 75, 76–7, 105, 112, 114, 115, 123, 124
homosexuality 128
Hornung, Ernest William 245
Houndsditch affair, 1910 216
Household Words 161, 195, 197, 199, 200, 360 n.51
  'A Detective Police Party' 196–8
  'Down with the Tide' 199–200
  'The Metropolitan Protectives', 198–9
  'The Modern Science of Thief-Taking' 195, 196
  'On Duty with Inspector Field', 162–3, 199
  'Spy Police' 198
  'Three "Detective" Anecdotes' 198
Hull dockers' strike, 1893 108
Hyde Park riots, 1866 191

Idler Magazine 243
Illustrated Police Budget:
  'The Arrest of Oscar Wilde' 221 Fig.14
  'The Arrest of Hudson for the Yorkshire Murders' 220 Fig.13
Illustrated Police News, 'Uniformed and Non-Uniformed Policemen in Action' 106 Fig.5
Indian nationalism 58
informants ('narks' or 'nosers') 34, 48, 55, 80, 132, 133, 149, 174, 182
  and bribes 114
instruction books 13, 17, 18, 47, 75, 93, 130
interrogation methods and confessions 137
Irish Branch/Brigade and Special Branch 52, 54, 55, 56
Irish nationalist movement 53
Irish Royal Constabulary 55
Irish Special Branch 207

Irish (Fenian) terrorism 49, 52, 53–6, 140, 141–2, 191, 207, 270, 303

Jack the Ripper case 3, 107, 109, 150, 165, 204, 257, 303
  and journalistic investigations 175, 355, n.145, 355 n.148
  negative press reporting 210–12
  and the press 173, 174, 177, 183, 348 n.10, 356 n.158
  and Scotland Yard 49
Jarvis, Frederick 118, 121
Jerrold, Blanchard 163, 164, 166, 168, 201
Jervis, Richard 171
John Thorndyke's Cases (Freeman) 253, 254 Fig.16
Johnson, George 289
journalists:
  benefiting from detectives 160–6
  bribing detectives 161–2, 185
  and disguise 156, 347 n.5
  exploring lower-class life 163–6, 351 n.54
  as foreign visitors 163–5, 167–8, 347 n.5, 351 n.67
  information from the police 172–7, 355 n.139, 356 n.161
  investigative rivalries with detectives 175–6, 355 n.149, 356 n.156
  as investigators 156–7, 175–6, 180, 264
  and police charge-sheets 181
  as police image-moulders 154, 158–9, 167–8, 171–2, 194, 221–4, 303–4
  press passes 181
  pretending to be detectives 157, 348 n.9, 358 n.10
  professional qualities in common with detectives 156–7
  public status of 158, 185
  reciprocal advantages with detectives 158–60
  relationship with detectives and the police 7, 156–86, 194, 200, 216, 223, 224

INDEX

justices of the peace 18–19, 20, 27, 257 *see also* magistrates
trading 21

Kalikoff, Beth 240
Kelly, Mary Jane, murder 173
Kent, Constance, case 360 n.43
see also Road Hill House murder case, 1860
Kent, Samuel 45
King, Peter 159
'Knightsbridge Mystery, The' (Reade) 246, 259

Labalmondrière, Colonel D. W. 40
Lady Molly of Scotland Yard (Orczy) 261
Lambert, James Henry 70
Lansdowne, Andrew 109, 121, 170, 287–8, 292
Le Fanu, Joseph Sheridan 245
Leach, Alfred 88
Leach, Charles 84, 88–9, 96, 108, 109, 137
Leblanc, Maurice 245
Lee, W. L. Melville 149, 150
Leeds Police force 112
detectives 45
establishment of detective branch 44
Leeson, Benjamin 82, 88, 116, 119
Lefroy, Percy 169
Legitimation League 135
Leisure Hour 191, 193
liberty and freedom, and the British police force 26–9, 31, 132, 135, 189, 208, 209, 210, 271, 306, 308
libraries and reading rooms in police stations 93
Life's Reminiscences of Scotland Yard, A (Lansdowne) 287–8
Littlechild, John George 56, 108, 119, 281, 285, 294, 295, 341 n.189, 377 n.14
Liverpool Police force 48, 112, 121, 337 n.88, 365 n.172
detective selection 84
establishment of detective branch 44, 45

Liverpool town hall and police station bombings, 1881 53
London: A Pilgrimage (Jerrold/Doré) 163, 168
London Labour and the London Poor (Mayhew) 165
Lowndes, Marie Belloc 244
Luddite protests 16

Macé, M. Gustave 209
Macnaghten, Melville L. 71, 72, 77–8, 148–9, 161, 178, 180, 211, 366 n.185, 378 n.43
Macready, Nevil 161
magazines *see* press
magistrates 19, 20, 27, 148 *see also* justices of the peace
Maguire, Detective Sergeant 121
Mainwaring, George B. 151
Manchester Police force 44, 118, 167–8, 338 n.91
establishment of detective branch 44–5
Mansion House, London, bombing attempts, 1881/82 53
Martel, Charles (Thomas Delf) 236
Martins, Joaquim Pedro de Oliveira 165
Mary Barton (Gaskell) 231
Mason, A. E. W. 244
Mayhew, Henry 163, 165, 167
Mayne, Richard 31, 34, 111, 165, 176
McAdoo, William 182, 185, 219
McCarthy, John 86, 136, 213
McGovan, James (William Crawford Honeyman) 237, 370 n.57, 370 n.58
McIntyre, Patrick 134, 141, 157, 171–2, 213, 281, 291, 363 n.138
McKinley, President William 57
McLevy, James 237, 277–8, 370 n.58
Meason, M. Laing 205–8, 209
Meiklejohn, John 38, 119, 168
Melville, William 118, 134, 171, 172, 214
memoirs of detectives 154, 276–97, 304–5, 377 n.12, 377 n.13
absence of descriptions of family life 286–7, 288

422

criticism of detective fiction 289–92, 379 n.59
descriptions of Special Branch 294–5
fictional elements 297
and ghost-writers 283
improving image of profession 292–7
officers as 'social agents' 296
official opposition to 281–2
and police culture 281–5
readers' perceptions 305–6
real-life comparisons with detective fiction 289–96
Scotland Yard 276, 277, 285, 287, 293
underlying impulse to write 285–9
as 'work' histories 284, 286–8
see also pseudo-memoirs
Metropolitan Police of London 6, 8, 26, 110, 151, 152, 162, 192, 209, 219
A Division 316 n.125
C Division 122
commendations for officers 120–1
Convict Supervision Office 49, 84, 322 n.249
creation (1829), and early years 2, 13, 16, 30–2, 33, 187
Criminal Investigation Department (CID) established, 1878 2, 9, 39–40, 69–70, 139, 269
and Dickens's *Household Words* 161, 163, 195–200
divisional detectives' clothing allowance (1877) 114
divisional detectives' friction with Scotland Yard 37, 40, 106–7
divisional detectives' pay scales 111
downplaying role of detection 17
drill 30, 95, 97, 138, 139
E Division 150, 153
entrance requirements and examinations 81–2
gratuities for officers 103, 115–17
H Division 171
hire of translators 65
Home Office financial restraints on 79
improving professionalism in CID 97–8
internal instruction classes 93
and Jack the Ripper case 211–12
L Division 78
length of service before selection for CID 84
and Lord Russell murder 32
as model of civilian policing 42
pay, uniformed/CID differentials 112–14
press officers, lack of 184–5
recruiting for foreign language skills 65–7
restructuring of the detective department, 1878 202–3
reward fund 115–16, 117
strikes, 1872/1890 104, 213
system of instruction 94–8
uniformed and detective branch tensions 36, 40, 76, 106–7
uniforms 14, 30
views on CID discipline 123
Middlesex Justices Act (1792) 24, 25
Mill, John Stuart 29
Miller, D. A. 266, 267
Miller, Wilbur R. 187, 192
Milsom, Albert 91
Monro, James 50, 55, 71, 116, 181, 219
Monte Carlo casino 119
Moonstone, The (Collins) 231, 259, 267, 367 n.22
Moore, Henry 119, 165
Morning Post 280
Morrison, Arthur 250–2, 270
Moser, Maurice 114, 119, 291, 293
Municipal Corporation Act (1835) 41
Murch, A. E. 255
'Murders in the Rue Morgue, The' (Poe) 232
Muswell Hill murder case (1896) 91
My Lady's Money (Collins) 247
Mysteries of Police and Crime (Griffiths) 275–6
'Mystery of Marie Rogêt, The' (Poe) 232
'Mystery of Number Seven, The' (Wood) 264

INDEX

Napoleon III 65, 191
National Association of
 Journalists 181
National Political Union 31
National Union of Journalists 181,
 357 n.185
Neil, Arthur Fowler 82
Nelson, Detective Inspector 131
New York Police Department 219
 press coverage 182, 185, 357 n.189
New Zealand Police Force 119
Newgate novels 227, 366 n.4
newspapers *see* press
'Newspapers as Detectives' (*London Magazine*) 176
Nicholls, Ernest 92
Night of the 3d Ult (Wood) 260
night/day watchmen 19
Nobel, Alfred 54
North American Review 219
Notes on England (Taine) 164
Novel and the Police, The (Miller) 266

Observations on the Present State of the Police of the Metropolis (Mainwaring) 151
Official Secrets Act (1889) 174
 and increasing democratization 178
 and information to the press 182
Old Bailey 159
Old Man in the Corner, The (Orczy) 244
Oliver Twist (Dickens) 229
On and Off Duty (police journal) 171
Orczy, Baroness Emmuska 244, 261
Ousby, Ian 230
out of court settlements 20
Outram, Robert 116–17
Oxford debate on the detective force, 1913 220

'Palatine Case', Manchester 355 n.143
Paley, Ruth 21
Pall Mall Gazette 72, 177, 211–12
Palmer, William 38
Parliamentary Committees:
 Conciliation Committee for Woman Suffrage 128
 on extradition (1868) 66
 on the Police of the Metropolis (1822) 27
 on the Sunday Liquor Trade (1868) 34
Passenger from Scotland Yard, The (Wood) 245
Paul Clifford (Bulwer-Lytton) 229
pawnbrokers 114, 149, 346 n.5
Pearce, Nicholas 111
Pearman, John 140
Peel, Robert 30, 42
Penal Servitude Act (1864) 35
'penny bloods' 230
Penny Illustrated Paper 117, 179, 181, 213, 344 n.276, 365 n.170
 'Detectives who Guarded King Edward' 120 Fig.6
Penny Sunday Times and People's Gazette 234
penology, theory of 194
photographs, and policing 37, 49, 317 n.154
Pickwick Papers (Dickens) 234
Pinkerton Agency 47, 119
 contact with Scotland Yard 263
Pirkis, Catherine Louise 253
Poe, Edgar Allen 232, 243, 246–7, 249, 255, 272, 274
Police! (Clarkson and Richardson) 179, 223, 286
Police Act (1890) 103, 118, 282
Police Chronicle (trade journal) 171
Police Code (1881) 138, 139, 172
police forces (uniformed):
 attacks on officers 216
 convalescent homes 103
 corruption and the underworld 136, 344 n.275, 344 n.276
 culture 95, 101–7
 Dickens elevating the image of 198–9
 employee turnover rates (1839–74) 102–3, 104
 examinations for rank of sergeant 93
 formal courses for constables 98
 image abroad 191–2

424

image as benevolent agents
   post-1900 214
image in the press 176–7, 204
injuries on duty 58, 192, 359 n.32
internal recruitment system 63,
   73–81, 113, 138, 299
lodging allowances 103
low pay policy 79, 103–4
overlapping duties with CID 106,
   107 Fig.5
paid sick leave and medical
   care 103
parish constables 18, 19, 20, 22
pay 337 n.78, 337 n.88
pay, compared with other
   sectors 102, 334 n.5
pensions 103, 118, 282
plain-clothes constables 31, 33,
   35, 36
promotions 104
recruitment from the working
   class 77, 83, 113, 257–8, 299
regulation at work 101
rehabilitation of offenders 296
returning lost children 192
selection procedures 81–6
sensitivity to press criticism 174–5
tensions with CID 76
trade union ban 102
training for constables 94–6, 333
   n.235
view of CID discipline 122–3
working-class attitudes to 192,
   215–16
see also Metropolitan Police of
   London; policing
Police Gazette 49
Police Guardian 171, 236
Police Orders 84, 121, 152, 153
Police Review 171, 276
Police Service Advertiser 171
policing:
   advertisements in newspapers
      soliciting information 169
   agents provocateurs and
      entrapment 137, 152, 189,
      204, 222, 361 n.88
   anarchist threat 56–8, 133–6,
      214–15, 216–17, 344 n.264,
      364 n.164

cars on British roads 215
crime viewed as working-class
   phenomenon 128–9
deterrence and pre-emptive strategy
   on crime 13–15, 26, 32,
   132–3, 138, 300
formation of national networks of
   forces 42
gender and surveillance 82–3,
   129–30
habitual offenders 49, 128–9, 165
industrial disputes 215
and non-conformist opinions 135
and the Official Secrets Act
   (1889) 174, 178, 182
poverty, class and crime links
   129–30
and prostitution 19, 37, 48, 75,
   128–9, 210–11, 342 n.220
in provincial England 41–6
and public opinion 151–2, 158–9,
   170, 173, 186, 187–221, 224,
   271, 297, 301–9
reform and personal freedom and
   liberty 26–9, 31
refugee monitoring 152
and social control 307
spying, surveillance and threat to
   liberty and freedom 28–30, 31,
   34, 41, 132, 133, 136, 147,
   152, 188, 189–90, 190 Fig.10,
   193, 202, 210, 267
and the women's suffrage
   movement 59, 108–9, 128,
   130, 152, 157, 180, 270
and the Tory press 211, 222
'wanted lists' 66
Pollock, Walter Herries 204
Poor Law Amendment Act (1834)
   41, 43
Popay, Sergeant William 31
Port Police, amalgamation with
   Special Branch 56
Porter, Bernard 133, 135
Portuguese royal family 86
post office service 63
poverty, class and crime links 129–30
press (newspapers, journals and
   magazines):
   advertisements 22, 47, 169

press (newspapers, journals and
        magazines): (cont.)
    changing image of police
        detectives 187–225
    creation of masculine image for
        detectives 217
    crime information 168–9, 352 n.90
    fascination with detection 304
    heroic image of detectives 219–20
    information leading to arrests 169
    passes 181
    police detectives, relations with 7,
        187–225, 255–6
    portraits of wanted criminals 169
    private detectives, relations
        with 256
    reporting on trials 224
    radical 204, 211, 212, 213–14,
        222, 224
    relaxation of police release of
        information policy 177–82
Prevention of Crimes Act (1871) 37
Prince Zaleski (Shiel) 261–2
Principal Officers, Bow Street 25, 28,
    31 *see also* Bow Street Runners
prison services 63
prostitution and policing 19, 37,
    48, 75, 128–9, 210–11,
    342 n.220
pseudo-memoirs (casebook fiction) of
    detectives 232–8, 242, 246,
    247, 249, 255, 259, 272–3,
    279, 286, 289
Public Offices, London 24–6
publishing developments in
    Britain 159–60, 217, 219,
    227–8, 234, 241, 279–81,
    241–3
Punch 18, 161
    articles attacking Scotland
        Yard 202
    'Bull's Eye on Bobby' 203 Fig.11
    The Detective's Rescue 184
    'The Detective's Triumph' 210
    'How Detectives Are Trained' 99
        Fig.4
    'Is Detection a Failure?' 183, 184
        Fig.9
    'The Police, the Press and the
        Public' 183

'pups of the truncheon' 88–9
'Purloined Letter, The' (Poe) 232

Quarterly Review 191, 193, 202

racecourse prize rings 105
Railway Station, The (Frith) 34, 361
    n.72
Reade, Charles 246, 247
Recollections of a Police-Officer
    (Russell) 234–5, 235–6, 368
    n.40, 368 n.42, 369 n.43, 369
    n.47, 369 n.48,
Record, William 90 Fig 3
recruitment *see under* detectives,
    police
Reform Act (1832) 16, 187
'Revelations by Real Detectives'
    (Johnson) 289
Revelations of a Lady Detective
    236–7, 370 n.56
rewards for thief-taking 21
Reynolds's News 171–2, 193, 213,
    215, 281
Richards, Charles 121
Richardson, J. Hall 157, 161,
    179, 286
*Richmond; or, Scenes in the Life of a
    Bow Street Runner*
    (anon) 229, 230, 233, 240
Road Hill House murder case,
    1860 45–6, 197,
    360 n.43
Robinson, B. Fletcher 253
Rochdale Borough Police Force 87
Rome Express, The (Griffiths) 244
Rowan, Colonel Charles 31, 34, 176
Russell, Lord William, murder
    case 32, 168–9
Russell, William 234–6, 369 n.48,
    369 n.49, 369 n.50

Sagar, Robert 87
Sala, George Augustus 187, 194, 197
Salford Infantry Barracks explosion,
    1881 53
Saturday Review 204, 205, 207, 211,
    238, 272
    'Detective Fiction' 274
Savage, Percy 74

INDEX

Scotland Yard 2, 9, 25, 37, 45, 60, 64, 67, 89, 98, 115, 116, 140, 171, 172, 212, 219, 231, 233, 245, 256, 298, 299, 300, 302, 316 n.125
  agents with linguistic skills 65–6, 86
  Black Museum 97, 276
  and Charles Dickens 161, 196–7, 230–1
  clothing allowance (1877) 114
  and the Crippen case 217–8, 365 n.172
  and the *Daily Mail* 177
  and detective fiction 231, 242, 254, 272–6, 371 n.80, 371 n.81
  and external recruitment 62, 68, 69, 70, 71, 72–3, 74, 78, 79, 80, 86
  fictional representations 253–4, 374 n.145
  friction with divisional detectives 37, 40, 106–7
  'How Detectives Are Trained' 99 Fig.4
  international reputation 2, 52, 61, 219
  Irish terrorist bombing, 1884 54
  memoirs of officers 276, 277, 285, 287, 293
  New York detectives compared 219
  pay scales 111, 113, 338 n.92
  Pinkerton's Agency, contact with 263
  and the press 167, 170–3, 176, 177, 179, 185, 192–3, 202, 209, 210, 215, 216, 218, 353 n.107, 358 n.198
  Punch articles attacking 202
  provincial forces, relationship with 45–6, 49, 56, 60, 97
  reports and documentation 49, 125
  representations in detective fiction 242, 253–4, 371 n.80, 371 n.81, 374 n.145
  reward fund 115–16, 117
  rise of 32–40
  scientific methodology 50, 218, 322 n.247
  and specialist expertise 48–52, 300, 304–5
  Sun attacks on 212–3, 218
  travelling abroad on duty 121, 122
  turf fraud scandal and trial, 1877 38, 39 Fig.1, 49, 66, 112, 119, 123, 124, 136, 137, 168, 202, 255, 302
  see also Special Branch, Scotland Yard
sensation novels 236
serial killings 170 *see also* Jack the Ripper case
Sexual Inversion (Havelock Ellis) 135
Sheppard, Jack 227
Shiel, Matthew Phipps 261–2
'shilling shockers' 230
Shore, John 75, 117, 119
Sidney Street siege, 1911 217–18, 364 n.164
Sign of Four, The (Conan Doyle) 249
'Silver Blaze' (Conan Doyle) 250
Sims, George R. 161, 165, 177, 351 n.54, 351 n.76, 356 n.157
Snowden's Police Officers' Guide (1897) 153
socialism, rise of 270
South London Chronicle 172
Spain, secret services 119
Special Branch, Scotland Yard 52–60, 132, 137, 171, 223
  anarchist threat 56–8, 133–6, 142, 214–15, 216–17, 344 n.264
  anti-terrorist measures 134
  agents provocateurs 133–4, 214
  B section 59
  D section 59
  detective memoirs 294–5
  detectives pretending to be journalists 157
  disguise 214–15
  and foreign travel 121
  gifts and awards to officers 120
  Irish Branch/Brigade 52, 54, 55, 56
  and Irish (Fenian) terrorism 49, 52, 53–6, 140, 191, 207, 270, 303
  and the Legitimation League 135
  post-retirement opportunities 118–19

427

INDEX

Special Branch, Scotland Yard (*cont.*)
  protecting foreign royalty 59
  socio-economic status of
    officers 118
  and the women's suffrage
    movement 59, 108–9, 128,
    130, 152, 157
  Sun attacks on 213
  Walsall anarchists and trial,
    1892 134, 214
  working hours 107–8
Spectator 204, 215, 240
spies 58, 140, 207
spying, surveillance and police threat
  to liberty and freedom 28–30,
  31, 34, 41, 132, 133, 136, 147,
  152, 188, 189–90, 190 Fig.10,
  193, 202, 210, 267
Star 173
state power, growth of 270
Steedman, Carolyn 102
Stephen, James Fitzjames 272–3
Stevenson, Fanny van de Grift 248–9
Stevenson, Robert Louis 248–9, 271
Stock Exchange, London 117
Stories of Scotland Yard (Grey) 253–4
Strand Magazine 243
*Strange Case of Dr Jekyll and Mr
  Hyde, The* (Stevenson) 271
strikes, police 1872/90 104, 213
Stroud, Charles 85
Suckling, William 48, 139–40
Sun 218
  attacks on Scotland Yard
    detectives 212–13
Sûreté, France 30, 209, 229, 242, 278
Sweeney, John 107, 119, 135, 281,
  291, 294
Syme, John 136, 137, 162

Taine, Hyppolite 163–4, 167–8
'Tale of a Detective' (anon) 261, 267
Taylor, John ('Jack the
  Sleuthhound') 49
Taylor, Tom 246, 259
Thames River Police 199–200
  founding of 26
thief-takers 2, 21–2, 23, 29, 115, 147,
  152, 189–90
Thiers, Adolphe 191

*Things as They Are; or, The
  Adventures of Caleb Williams*
  (Godwin) 229
Thomson, Basil 71, 108, 161
Thomson, James 66–7, 150, 153
Thorndyke's strategy 254 Fig.16
Ticket-of Leave Man, The
  (Taylor) 246, 259
ticket-of-leave men (paroled
  prisoners) 35, 130
Times, The 188, 189, 203, 216
  'The Plain-Clothes Man' 216,
  274–5
Titley, Thomas, case 137, 204, 361
  n.88
Todhunter, Joseph 156–7
*Tom Fox or The Revelations of a
  Detective* 237, 283
Tory press, and policing 222
transportation to Australia, abolition
  of 34–5
'Trial of the Detectives' 39 Fig 1
trials, role of detectives 74, 85, 125,
  240, 341 n.189, 353 n.98
'Triumphs of Eugène Valmont, The'
  (Barr) 244
Trodd, Anthea 267
Trollope, Anthony 231
Truro, Lord 203
Tunbridge, John 119
turf fraud scandal and trial, 1877 38,
  39 Fig.1, 49, 66, 112, 119, 123,
  124, 136, 137, 168, 202, 255,
  302
Turner, George 105
Turpin, Dick 227, 228

Ulster problems 59 *see also* Irish
  (Fenian) terrorism
Umberto I of Italy 57
underworld and police corruption 38,
  123, 136, 149, 202, 203, 213,
  222, 255, 344 n.275, 344 n.276
uniforms:
  Metropolitan Police 30
  significance of 14

Veil, Colonel Thomas De 22
Victoria, Queen 33, 66
  assassination attempts 54, 56

INDEX

Vidocq, Eugène-François 30, 229–30, 231, 239–40, 242, 247, 278, 367 n.16, 367–8 n.23, 372 n.101
Vincent, David 82, 88
Vincent, Howard 39–40, 46, 55, 70–1, 73, 83, 110, 112, 125, 131, 138, 152, 174, 177, 205, 219, 365 n.176
Voltaire (French newspaper) 219

Walsall anarchist trial, 1892 134, 214
Warren, Charles 49–50, 181
watchmen 28
Watson, Aaron 164, 177
Wensley, Frederick Porter 75, 89
Westminster Review 238
   'Crime in Current Literature' 279
Whicher, Jonathan 46, 197, 320 n.214, 360 n.43, 367 n.22
Whig Party 16
Whitechapel 74, 164, 200, 201, 210
Whitechapel murders *see* Jack the Ripper case
white-collar crime 15, 80, 96
Wild, Jonathan 227
Wilde, Oscar, arrest of 221 Fig.14
Williams, Charles 164

Williamson, Frederick Adolphus 40, 55, 67, 69, 79, 111, 139
Wills, William H. 195, 196, 198–9
Windsor Magazine 245, 279–80
wireless telegraphy 218
women:
   attitudes in the police force 82–3
   fictional private detectives 243–4, 252–3
   police surveillance of 129–30
women's suffrage movement 59, 108–9, 128, 130, 152, 157, 270
Wood, H. F. 245, 260
Wood, Mrs Henry 264
Woodhall, Edwin T. 93, 95, 98, 109, 122
working class:
   attitudes to the police 188, 192, 215–16
   police recruitment from 77, 83, 113, 257–8, 299
Wraxall, Lascelles 242, 278
Wright, Sampson 24

Yates, Edmund 200, 361 n.72

Zambra the Detective (Hill) 252
Zangwill, Israel 244